PENGUIN BOOKS

## The Penguin Dictionary of Modern Humorous Quotations

Fred Metcalf was born in Yorkshire and educated in Devon. He has worked as a freelance writer in London, Sydney and Los Angeles, writing for Sir Laurence Olivier, Kenny Everett, Jamie Lee Curtis and the Two Ronnies amongst many others. He is also the editor of *The Penguin Dictionary of Jokes*.

W0009891

# The Penguin Dictionary of
# Modern Humorous Quotations

**Second Edition**

Compiled by Fred Metcalf

PENGUIN BOOKS

**For Chris, Lavender, Kate, Laura and Alice**

PENGUIN BOOKS

Published by the Penguin Group
Penguin Books Ltd, 80 Strand, London WC2R 0RL, England
Penguin Putnam Inc., 375 Hudson Street, New York, New York 10014, USA
Penguin Books Australia Ltd, 250 Camberwell Road, Camberwell, Victoria 3124, Australia
Penguin Books Canada Ltd, 10 Alcorn Avenue, Toronto, Ontario, Canada M4V 3B2
Penguin Books India (P) Ltd, 11 Community Centre, Panchsheel Park, New Delhi – 110 017, India
Penguin Books (NZ) Ltd, Cnr Rosedale and Airborne Roads, Albany, Auckland, New Zealand
Penguin Books (South Africa) (Pty) Ltd, 24 Sturdee Avenue, Rosebank 2196, South Africa

Penguin Books Ltd, Registered Offices: 80 Strand, London WC2R 0RL, England

www.penguin.com

First published by Viking 1986
Published in Penguin Books 1987
Second edition published as a Penguin hardback 2001
Published in paperback in Penguin Books 2002
10

Copyright © Fred Metcalf, 1986, 2001
All rights reserved

The moral right of the compiler has been asserted

Typeset in ITC Officina and ITC Stone
Typeset by Rowland Phototypesetting Ltd, Bury St Edmunds, Suffolk
Printed in England by Clays Ltd, St Ives plc

ISBN-13: 978–0–140–24359–8
ISBN-10: 0–140–24359–3

# Contents

# Foreword

Humour, it's said, is the ability to see three sides of the same coin. It can help to emphasize a point, to dispel the gloom, to ridicule the self-important, to lighten the atmosphere or simply to gladden the heart and tickle the funnybone.

As the lone compiler of this book, I have appointed myself the sole and final arbiter of whether a quotation is humorous. The responsibility for describing it as such is all mine. So if a particular quotation leaves you unamused, you've no one to blame but me.

But what makes a quote funny anyway? I wish I could tell you. But nothing strips a joke of its humour faster than trying to work out *why* it's a joke. To paraphrase George Bernard Shaw: He who can, writes humour. He who cannot tries to analyse why it's humorous.

During the revision process since the last edition I have subjected the collection to a modest cull while adding more than 1,300 new quotations. At the same time I've reduced the number of headings in order to limit the number of categories where only one quotation is listed and I've been unable to discover a second – ideally contrasting – quote.

Some pedants might argue that a dictionary of 'modern' quotations is no place to find the work of nineteenth-century authors, still less a handful from the eighteenth century. I argue otherwise. If the language and the sentiment of the quote are not archaic and it retains the potential to amuse then, in my book, it qualifies for inclusion. And this *is* my book.

I have included many quotations for which I have yet to establish a rock-solid provenance. While I continue the search, I believe they're worth including in this collection. They are mostly described here as 'Attrib.' and I've decided to keep them in because they're simply too good to leave out. Friendly readers can get in touch with me via Penguin Books if they happen to have the information which I, at the moment, lack.

I have never had any doubt that the contents of this book – unlike many similar collections – should be arranged thematically. Its main purpose is to provide an apposite quote for writers and speakers wishing to illustrate a point or support an argument. This doesn't mean that the book can't be used by readers looking for quotations by specific writers. By consulting the comprehensive Authors' Index, one can satisfy one's desire to discover and delight in the work of nearly 1,500 writers who have taken on the world with wit as their weapon.

The cross-indexing has been improved to alert the reader to specific single quotes within other, non-related categories as well as to the usual related categories.

For quotations which seem over the decades to have been attributed to more than one source – because humour, like history repeats itself – or which have appeared in slightly different forms, I have generally chosen the earlier or the version most deftly expressed.

The book's secondary purpose is to reward the idle browser who can simply sit back and navigate the broad stream and backwater of wit and wisdom, pausing only to sip sparingly here or quaff ravenously there from this serendipitous source of laughter. Try it yourself and you'll soon agree that browsing is its own reward.

At this point I must thank the heroes of this book: the wits, the comedians and the phrase-makers whose work appears herein. Our debt to them is obvious. These are people who take nothing too seriously – except the job of making the rest of us laugh.

The English biographer Hesketh Pearson believed that the wit 'needs to be pitied, being the only person in the atmosphere of social relaxation who cannot relax. The man who is famous for witty flings', he said, 'is never off duty.' This book then, is my tribute to those humorists and jokewrights who've laboured long and agonized endlessly for our amusement. While all *we've* done is sit back and laugh.

It's been a genuine pleasure to introduce their work to a wider audience. There ought to be a word for someone who accumulates vast amounts of wit and then magnanimously distributes it to the humorously deprived. Perhaps that word is 'philaughropist'.

I must record my thanks to my agent Vivien Greene at Sheil Land Associates, to Will Fanshawe and Judi Brill for their technical assistance and much else. I especially appreciated the patience and professional far-sightedness of my editor,

Martin Toseland, at Penguin Books. His assistant Molly Mackey has a vivacity and resourcefulness which I predict will take her far.

And finally I wish to thank those whose love, loyalty and laughter sustained me through the compiling of this book. They know who they are. But for those who don't, they're Tilly Bagshawe, Sue Howes, Judy Lever and Roger Taylor and Roy Ellsworth. Patricia Ellsworth too, a real writer, gave me valued support before her untimely death.

Thanks are also due to the especially precious Louise Bagshawe, Jessie Lever Taylor and Phoebe Mortimer, and to my very good friends Chris and Julia Allen, the other Bagshawes, John and Jane Birt, Carolyn Brakefield, John and Jan Bridge, Ben Butters, Guy and Lindsay Butters, Tim and Jo Butters, Zeeb and Peter Clarke, Doris and John Cock, the Codringtons, Andrew and Prisca Cox, Alf and Carol Cozens, Bob Dean and Kate Mortimer, Jonathan Dimbleby and Bel Mooney, Kitty Dimbleby, Nick and Gilly Elliott, Jacqueline Fanshawe, John and Gina Florescu, David Frost, Laurence Gorley, Pete and Liz Gorley, Bruce Gowers and Carol Rosenstein, Simon and Tracey Hawkins, the Hughes family, Jane Kalim, Vijay and Daksha Lakhani, Ket Lamb, Billie Lever Taylor, the MacKeiths, Alice Marshment, Margaret Marshment, Andy and Tess Mayer, Xenie Merrix, Bill and Sue Metcalf, Bob and Rae Metcalf, Frances Mortimer, Horatio and Anna Mortimer, Mark Mortimer, Mathew Mortimer, Wiz and Edward Mortimer, Mike and Pat Prout, Norma and Norman Rhodes, Susie Robinson, Emily Rush, Ivan Schutts, Sophia Schutts, Jane Sigaloff, Cathy Simmonds, Jules Slaughter, Anna Warne and Jessica and Paul White.

*Fred Metcalf, Somerset, 2000*

# Introduction

'Brevity is the soul of wit . . . therefore, Penguin Books have asked me to write a 500-word introduction to their dictionary of humorous quotations. How many words is that so far? Only 31? Well, now it's 33 counting 'only 31?' Anyhow, I have read this book from cover to cover (okay, just the page with my quote), and enjoyed it immensely. 61. Only 439 to go.

This wonderful, splendid, terrific, fabulous, uh, thick, tightly bound book contains every humorous word ever said by man, from the classic caveman punchline: 'You're never going to get a girl with that club!' to that astoundingly clever 1999 New Year's Eve joke: 'See you next millennium.' No matter how many time we heard it, it kept getting funnier.

Need a snappy line for the next office meeting? Trying to make a girl think you're wittier than you really are? Want to give one last zinger to the warden before you receive your lethal injection? This is the book for you. Just skimming *The Penguin Dictionary of Modern Humorous Quotations* provided me with a plethora of funny remarks about such classic topics as Lawyers, Marriage, Politics, Taxation, etc. A closer look provided me even more amusing observations on equally hilarious topics such as Cancer, Cannibalism, Poverty and Suicide. Yes, this book has it all.

That's got to be 500 words by now. 230?! Son of a——! 234. Yes, I'm counting the blank space. 240.

Surely there's more I can say about this book . . . I know! I'll give them a quote they'll use in their advertising campaign, so my name might be printed on large cardboard displays in bookstores, or shouted on television late at night by over-enthusiastic announcers. Let's see, how about 'If laughter is the best medicine, then *The Penguin Book of Modern Humorous Quotations* is just what the doctor ordered!' Or 'Toss out your Bible. There's a new Good Book in town!' I know that would make me want to buy it. 331. The end is in sight.

Seriously, *The Penguin Dictionary of Modern Humorous Quotations* is really a lot of fun and highly addictive reading. It is a great honor to not only write the introduction, but also to have dialogue from *The Simpsons* writers included in the book, alongside the words of writers we truly admire, respect and occasionally steal from.

By the way, the fact that a quote of mine happened to be included is purely a coincidence, okay? Do you really think I'm the type of guy who would tell a publisher, 'I'll write the introduction to your book if you use one of my lines in it?' I mean, I'd have to be a pretty pathetic, insecure egomaniac to make a demand like that, wouldn't I? Stop looking at me like that!

And now, with these eleven simple little words, I hit 477. Okay, so I failed. But that shouldn't dampen your enjoyment of this incredibly entertaining book. It's just a silly introduction, right?

Besides, who's counting?

*Mike Scully, Executive Producer,*
The Simpsons

## Abstinence

*See also Chastity; Drink; Moderation; Prohibition.*

**1** Abstinence is a good thing, but it should always be practised in moderation.
**Anon.**

**2** Abstainer, *n.* A weak person who yields to the temptation of denying himself a pleasure.
**Ambrose Bierce**, *The Devil's Dictionary*, 1911

**3** I distrust camels, and anyone else who can go a week without a drink.
**Joe E. Lewis**, 1902–71, American comedian

**4** Sobriety's a real turn-on for me. You can see what you're doing.
**Peter O'Toole**, actor, 1983

## Abuse

*See also Hecklers; Insults; Politics – Insults.*

**1** As to abuse – I thrive on it. Abuse, hearty abuse, is a tonic to all save men of indifferent health.
**Norman Douglas**, *Some Limericks*, 1928

**2** It was commonly said, though I do not vouch for the story, that Sidgwick remarked concerning Jebb, 'All the time that he can spare from the adornment of his person, he devotes to the neglect of his duties.'
**Bertrand Russell**, *Some Cambridge Dons of the Nineties*, 1956

## Accidents

*See also Disasters.*

**1** A snail was crossing the road when he was run over by a tortoise. A policeman came along and asked him how it had happened. 'I don't remember,' said the snail. 'It all happened so fast.'
**Anon.**

**2** SEAGOON: He's been buried alive under a thousand tons of earth.
MINNIE: Thank heavens he's safe.
*The Goon Show*, BBC Radio, 1959

# Accountancy

*See also Money; Professions.*

**1** An accountant is a man hired to explain that you didn't make the money you did.
**Anon.**

**2** . . . in your report here, it says that you are an extremely dull person. Our experts describe you as an appallingly dull fellow, unimaginative, timid, spineless, easily dominated, no sense of humour, tedious company and irrepressibly drab and awful. And whereas in most professions these would be considered drawbacks, in accountancy they are a positive boon.
**John Cleese, Graham Chapman, Terry Jones, Michael Palin and Eric Idle,** *And Now for Something Completely Different,* screenplay, 1971

**3** Never ask of money spent
Where the spender thinks it went.
Nobody was ever meant
To remember or invent
What he did with every cent.
**Robert Frost,** 'The Hardship of Accounting', 1936

# Achievement

*See also Success.*

**1** It is sobering to consider that when Mozart was my age he had already been dead for a year.
**Tom Lehrer,** American songwriter

**2** The world is divided into people who do things – and people who get the credit.
**Dwight Morrow,** 1873–1931, US Senator and Ambassador to Mexico

# Acting

*See also Actors and Actresses; Film; William Shakespeare; Show Business; The Theatre; Theatre – Critics.*

**1** Acting is all about honesty. If you can fake that, you've got it made.
**George Burns** (Attrib.)

**2** A. E. Matthews ambled through *This was a Man* like a charming retriever who has buried a bone and can't quite remember where.
**Noel Coward,** on the Broadway production, 1926

**3** My dear boy, forget about the motivation. Just say the lines and don't trip over the furniture.
**Noel Coward,** to an actor in his *Nude with a Violin* on Broadway, 1957 (Attrib.)

**4** My very first step
Was Shakespearian 'rep'
Where an awful old 'Ham' used to train us.
I'd nothing to do
In *The Dream* and *The Shrew*
But I carried a spear
In *King John* and *King Lear*
And a hatchet in *Coriolanus*.
I ranted for years
In pavilions on piers
Till my spirits were really at zero,
Then I got a small role
Of a Tart with a soul
In a play by Sir Arthur Pinero.
**Noel Coward,** 'Three Theatrical Dames', song from *Night of a Hundred Stars,* London, 1954

**5** Your motivation is your pay packet on Friday. Now get on with it.
**Noel Coward,** to an actor (Attrib.)

**6** I mean, the question actors most often get asked is how they can bear saying the same things over and over again night after night, but God knows the answer to that is, don't we all anyway; might as well get paid for it.
**Elaine Dundy,** *The Dud Avocado,* 1958

**7** Acting is the most minor of gifts and not a very high-class way to earn a living. After all, Shirley Temple could do it at the age of four.
**Katharine Hepburn** (Attrib.)

**8** The important thing in acting is to be able to laugh and cry. If I have to cry, I think of my sex life. If I have to laugh, I think of my sex life.
**Glenda Jackson** (Attrib.)

**9** ERIC: Did you see my Bottom at Stratford-upon-Avon?
ERNIE: I'm afraid not.
ERIC: A pity – many people consider it my best part. But, above all, I consider myself a film actor.
ERNIE: Really?
ERIC: Oh yes. For instance, did you see *Star Wars*?

ERNIE: Yes?
ERIC: So did I. Terrific, wasn't it?
**Eric Morecambe and Ernie Wise**, *The Morecambe and Wise Joke Book*, 1979

**10** ERIC: I'll never forget the first words I spoke in the theatre.
ERNIE: What were they?
ERIC: 'This way please! Programmes! . . .'
**Eric Morecambe and Ernie Wise**, *The Morecambe and Wise Joke Book*, 1979

**11** We used to have actresses trying to become stars; now we have stars trying to become actresses.
**Laurence Olivier** (Attrib.)

**12** Acting is standing up naked and turning around very slowly.
**Rosalind Russell**, *Life is a Banquet*, 1977

**13** Two members of my profession who are not urgently needed by my profession, Mr Ronald Reagan and Mr George Murphy, entered politics, and they've done extremely well. Since there has been no reciprocal tendency in the other direction, it suggests to me that our job is still more difficult than their new one.
**Peter Ustinov**, *Any Questions*, BBC Radio, 1968

**14** I love acting. It is so much more real than life.
**Oscar Wilde**, *The Picture of Dorian Gray*, 1891

**15** He had never acted in his life and couldn't play the pin in *Pinafore*.
**P. G. Wodehouse**, *The Luck of the Bodkins*, 1935

## Action

*See also Behaviour.*

**1** There are two kinds of people: those who don't do what they want to do, so they write down in a diary about what they haven't done, and those who haven't time to write about it because they're out doing it.
**Richard Flournoy and Lewis R. Foster**, *The More the Merrier*, screenplay, 1943

**2** Every normal man must be tempted at times, to spit on his hands, hoist the black flag, and begin slitting throats.
**H. L. Mencken**, *Prejudices*, First Series, 1919

**3** CORIE: . . . there isn't the least bit of

adventure in you. Do you know what you are? You're a Watcher. There are Watchers in this world and there are Do-ers. And the Watchers sit around watching the Do-ers do. Well, tonight you watched and I did.
PAUL: Yeah . . . Well, it was harder to watch what you did than it was for you to do what I was watching.
**Neil Simon**, *Barefoot in the Park*, screenplay, 1964

## Actors and Actresses

*See also Acting; Film; Show Business; The Theatre; Theatre – Critics.*

**1** For an actress to succeed she must have the face of Venus, the brains of Minerva, the grace of Terpsichore, the memory of Macaulay, the figure of Juno and the hide of a rhinoceros.
**Ethel Barrymore**, 1879–1959, actress (Attrib.)

**2** An actor's a guy who, if you ain't talking about him, ain't listening.
**Marlon Brando** (Attrib.)

**3** JOEY: I don't get you. First you hate me, then you sleep with me, then you have nothing to do with me. Now you want me again?
KATE: What's the matter? Haven't you ever dated an actress before?
**Shana Goldberg-Meehan and Scott Silveri**, 'The One with the Screamer', *Friends*, NBC, 1996

**4** I'm now at the age where I've got to prove that I'm just as good as I never was.
**Rex Harrison** (Attrib.)

**5** Actresses will happen in the best regulated families.
**Oliver Herford**, 1864–1935, English-born American writer

**6** I never said all actors are cattle. What I said was all actors should be treated like cattle.
**Alfred Hitchcock**, film director (Attrib.)

**7** Michael Caine can out-act any, well nearly any, telephone kiosk you care to mention.
**Hugh Leonard**, Irish playwright

**8** Some of the greatest love affairs I've known involved one actor, unassisted.
**Wilson Mizner**, 1876–1933, American playwright (Attrib.)

**9** Anyone who works is a fool. I don't work – I merely inflict myself on the public.
**Robert Morley**, English actor (Attrib.)

**10** It is a great help for a man to be in love with himself. For an actor, however, it is absolutely essential.
**Robert Morley**, Playboy, 1979

**11** Scratch an actor – and you'll find an actress.
**Dorothy Parker** (Attrib.)

**12** The physical labor actors have to do wouldn't tax an embryo.
**Neil Simon**, The Sunshine Boys, screenplay, 1975

**13** Every actor in his heart believes everything bad that's printed about him.
**Orson Welles** (Attrib.)

# Adolescence

*See also Children; Teenagers; Young and Old; Youth.*

**1** Adolescence: a stage between infancy and adultery.
**Anon.**

**2** DARIA: How about 'The Bleakness that Lies Ahead'?
JANE: Too sentimental.
DARIA: 'No Life, No Hope, No Future'?
JANE: Too pie-in-the-sky.
DARIA: 'Mommy's Little Hypocrite'?
JANE: Too much like a children's book.
DARIA: I wish I were dead.
JANE: That sounds promising.
**Glenn Eichler**, 'Café Disaffecto' Daria, MTV, 1997

**3** Remember that as a teenager you are at the last stage in your life when you will be happy to hear that the phone is for you.
**Fran Lebowitz**, 'Tips for Teens', Social Studies, 1981

**4** Should you be a teenager blessed with uncommon good looks, document this state of affairs by the taking of photographs. It is the only way anyone will ever believe you in years to come.
**Fran Lebowitz**, 'Tips for Teens', Social Studies, 1981

**5** Think before you speak. Read before you think. This will give you something to think about that you didn't make up yourself – a wise move at any age, but most especially at

seventeen, when you are in the greatest danger of coming to annoying conclusions.
**Fran Lebowitz**, 'Tips for Teens', Social Studies, 1981

**6** You just put on your coat and hat,
And walk yourself to the laundromat.
And when you finish doing that,
Bring in the dog and put out the cat.
*Yakety-yak.*
Don't talk back!
**Jerry Leiber and Mike Stoller**, 'Yakety Yak', song for The Coasters, 1958

**7** I'm always open to new experiences. Just so I don't have to leave my room.
**Peggy Nicoll**, The Daria Database, 1998

**8** Weird clothing is *de rigueur* for teenagers, but today's generation of teens is finding it difficult to be sufficiently weird. This is because the previous generation of teens, who went through adolescence in the sixties and seventies, used up practically all the available weirdness. After what went on in that twenty-year period, almost nothing looks strange to anyone.
**P. J. O'Rourke**, Modern Manners, 1983

**9** Sex is something I really don't understand too hot. You never know where the hell you are. I keep making up these sex rules for myself, and then I break them right away. Last year I made a rule that I was going to stop horsing around with girls that, deep down, gave me a pain in the ass. I broke it, though, the same week I made it – the same night, as a matter of fact. I spent the whole night necking with a terrible phoney named Anne Louise Sherman. Sex is something I just don't understand. I swear to God I don't.
**J. D. Salinger**, The Catcher in the Rye, 1951

**10** That's the thing about girls. Every time they do something pretty, even if they're not much to look at, or even if they're sort of stupid, you fall half in love with them, and then you never know where the hell you are. Girls. Jesus Christ. They can drive you crazy. They really can.
**J. D. Salinger**, The Catcher in the Rye, 1951

**11** My father is a bastard,
My ma's an S.O.B.
My grandpa's always plastered,
My grandma pushes tea.

My sister wears a moustache,
My brother wears a dress.
Goodness gracious, that's why I'm a mess.
**Stephen Sondheim**, 'Gee, Officer Krupke', song from *West Side Story*, 1957

**12** When I was a boy of fourteen, my father was so ignorant I could hardly stand to have the old man around. But when I got to be twenty-one, I was astonished at how much he had learned in seven years.
**Mark Twain** (Attrib.)

## Adulthood
*See also Childhood; Parents; Young and Old.*

**1** When I grow up I want to be a little boy.
**Joseph Heller**, *Something Happened*, 1974

**2** ETH: . . . It's time he was taught you are now an adult.
RON: Exactly what I told him, Eth. I said quite firmly, I said, 'Look, Dad, you got to realize I am now a grown-up adult with all an adult's desires and capabilities.'
ETH: When did you tell him that?
RON: When he was peeling the silver paper off my Easter egg.
**Frank Muir and Denis Norden**, *The Glums*, London Weekend Television, 1978

## Adversity
*See also Misfortune; Sympathy.*

**1** The world is quickly bored by the recital of misfortune and willingly avoids the sight of distress.
**W. Somerset Maugham**, *The Moon and Sixpence*, 1919

**2** By trying we can easily learn to endure adversity. Another man's, I mean.
**Mark Twain**, *Following the Equator*, 1897

## Advertising
*See also Sales and Selling; Television – Commercials.*

**1** In the ad biz, sincerity is a commodity bought and paid for like everything else.
**Newsweek**, 1967

**2** We've upped our standards! Now up yours!
**Radio station jingle**, 1998

**3** The codfish lays ten thousand eggs,
The homely hen lays one.
The codfish never cackles
To tell you what she's done.
And so we scorn the codfish,
While the humble hen we prize,
Which only goes to show you
That it pays to advertise.
**Anon.**, *It Pays to Advertise*

**4** When the client moans and sighs
Make his logo twice the size.
If he still should prove refractory,
Show a picture of his factory.
Only in the gravest cases
Should you show the clients' faces.
**Anon.**

**5** Advertising agency: eighty-five per cent confusion and fifteen per cent commission.
**Fred Allen**

**6** Everybody sat around thinking about Panasonic, the Japanese electronics account. Finally I decided, what the hell, I'll throw a line to loosen them up . . . 'The headline is, the headline is: From Those Wonderful Folks Who Gave You Pearl Harbor.'
Complete silence . . .
**Jerry Della Femina**, *From Those Wonderful Folks Who Gave You Pearl Harbor*, 1970

**7** The longest word in the English language is the one following the phrase: 'And now a word from our sponsor.'
**Hal Eaton**, *Reader's Digest*, 1949

**8** Doing business without advertising is like winking at a girl in the dark: you know what you are doing, but nobody else does.
**Edgar Watson Howe**, 1853–1937, American writer

**9** Advertising may be described as the science of arresting the human intelligence long enough to get money from it.
**Stephen Leacock**, 'The Perfect Salesman', *Garden of Folly*, 1924

**10** I think that I shall never see
A billboard lovely as a tree.
Indeed, unless the billboards fall
I'll never see a tree at all.
**Ogden Nash**, 'Song of the Open Road', *Happy Days*, 1933

**11** Advertising is the rattling of a stick inside a swill bucket.
**George Orwell** (Attrib.)

**12** Advertising that uses superlatives isn't.
**Harry Pesin**, *Sayings to Run an Advertising Agency By*, 1966

**13** Fie on clients who cannot leave copy alone and fie on copywriters who can.
**Harry Pesin**, *Sayings to Run an Advertising Agency By*, 1966

**14** If advertisers spent the same amount of money improving their products as they do on advertising, then they wouldn't have to advertise them.
**Will Rogers**

# Advice
*See also Opinions.*

**1** Nothing's impossible for those who don't have to do it.
**Anon.**

**2** When you go to a restaurant, always choose a table near a waiter.
**Anon.**

**3** Always Remember You're Unique. Just Like Everyone Else.
**T-shirt**, Los Angeles, 1996

**4** Never eat at a place called Mom's. Never play cards with a man named Doc. And never lay down with a woman who's got more troubles than you.
**Nelson Algren**, *What Every Young Man Should Know*

**5** One should try everything once, except incest and folk-dancing.
**Sir Arnold Bax**, *Farewell My Youth*, 1943

**6** Never get into a narrow double bed with a wide single man.
**Quentin Crisp**

**7** I can offer lots of advice. Good advice. Advice that's been passed down from generation to generation and never been used.
**Bob Monkhouse**, *Just Say a Few Words*, 1988

**8** Never floss a stranger.
**Joan Rivers**

**9** Never go to a dentist with blood in his hair. Never holiday in a country where they still point at planes.
**William Rushton**, quoted in *You Won't Believe This But . . .*, by Barry Cryer, 1998

**10** I always pass on good advice. It is the only thing to do with it. It is never any use to oneself.
**Oscar Wilde**, *An Ideal Husband*, 1895

**11** Never put anything on paper, my boy, and never trust a man with a small black moustache.
**P. G. Wodehouse**, *Cocktail Time*, 1958

**12** There are girls, few perhaps but to be found if one searches carefully, who when their advice is ignored and disaster ensues, do not say 'I told you so'. Mavis was not of their number.
**P. G. Wodehouse**, *Pearls, Girls and Monty Bodkin*, 1972

# Aesthetes
*See also Art and Artists; Culture.*

**1** . . . first and foremost, of course, I'm a Cultural Attaché. But don't let that word 'culture' scare the pants off you because I can assure you I'm not one of those long-haired, limp-wristed, head-in-the-clouds, arty-crafty pooftas. No!
**Sir Les Patterson (Barry Humphries)**, *Housewife Superstar*, one-man show, 1976

**2** Dark hair fell in a sweep over his forehead. He looked like a man who would write *vers libre*, as indeed he did.
**P. G. Wodehouse**, *The Girl on the Boat*, 1922

**3** I don't want to wrong anybody, so I won't go so far as to say that she actually wrote poetry, but her conversation, to my mind, was of a nature calculated to excite the liveliest suspicions. Well, I mean to say, when a girl suddenly asks you out of a blue sky if you don't sometimes feel that the stars are God's daisy-chain, you begin to think a bit.
**P. G. Wodehouse**, *Right Ho, Jeeves*, 1934

# Affection
*See also Flirtation; Kissing; Love.*

**1** A mixture of admiration and pity is one of the surest recipes for affection.
**André Maurois**, *Ariel*, 1923

**2** All my life affection has been showered upon me, and every forward step I have made has been taken in spite of it.
**George Bernard Shaw** (Attrib.)

# Africa

**1** When a lion escapes from a circus in Africa, how do they know when they've caught the right one?
**George Carlin**, *Brain Droppings*, 1997

**2** The only thing I know about Africa is that it's far, far away. A thirty-five-hour flight. Imagine the boat ride. The boat ride's so long, there are still slaves on their way here.
**Chris Rock**, American comedian

# Age and Ageing

*See also Adolescence; Adulthood; Middle Age; Old Age; Young and Old; Youth.*

**1** He says he's young at heart – but slightly older in other places.
**Anon.**

**2** Just when I finally got my head together, my body fell apart.
**Anon.**

**3** Growing old is mandatory; growing up is optional.
**Anon.**

**4** A sexagenarian? At his age? I think that's disgusting!
**Gracie Allen**

**5** You're not old until it takes you longer to rest up than it does to get tired.
**Phog Allen**, Kansas basketball coach, at 79, in 1964

**6** I refuse to admit that I am more than fifty-two, even if that does make my sons illegitimate.
**Nancy Astor**, 1879–1964, British politician (Attrib.)

**7** . . . there was a time in my life, decades ago, when I was so full of energy that I was going to not only END WORLD HUNGER but also STOP WAR and ELIMINATE RACISM. Whereas today my life goals, to judge from the notes I leave myself, tend to be along the lines of BUY DETERGENT.
**Dave Barry**, *Comic Relief*, 2000

**8** When I was forty, my doctor advised me that a man in his forties shouldn't play tennis. I heeded his advice carefully and could hardly wait until I reached fifty to start again.
**Hugo Black**, Supreme Court Justice, 1937–71

**9** At my age, I don't even buy green bananas.
**George Burns**

**10** Tonight we honor a man old enough to be his own father . . . a man who embarrassed everyone at the Last Supper by asking for seconds.
**Red Buttons**, of George Burns

**11** I was surprised when I started getting old. I always thought it was one of those things that would happen to someone else.
**George Carlin**, *Brain Droppings*, 1997

**12** My fifty years have shown me that few people know what they are talking about. I don't mean idiots who don't know. I mean everyone.
**John Cleese**, 1990

**13** Old is always fifteen years from now.
**Bill Cosby**

**14** We talked about growing old gracefully
  And Elsie who's seventy-four
  Said, 'A. it's a question of being sincere,
  And B., if you're supple you've nothing
    to fear.'
  Then she swung upside down from a
    glass chandelier,
  I couldn't have liked it more.
**Noel Coward**, 'I've Been to a Marvellous Party', song from *Set to Music*, 1938

**15** I am in the prime of senility.
**Benjamin Franklin**, 1706–90, American writer, philosopher and statesman

**16** Thirty means only going to the pub if there's somewhere to sit down. Thirty means owning at least one classical CD even if it's Now That's What I Call Classical Vol 6.
**Mike Gayle**, *Turning Thirty*, 1999

**17** One day you look in the mirror and you realise that the face you are shaving is your father's.
**Robert Harris**, *Sunday Times*, 1996

**18** The four stages of man are infancy, childhood, adolescence and obsolescence.
**Art Linkletter**, *A Child's Garden of Misinformation*, 1965

**19** Bored? Here's a way the over-fifty can easily kill off a good half-hour:
1. Place your car keys in your right hand.
2. With your left hand, call a friend and confirm a lunch or dinner date.
3. Hang up the phone.
4. Now look for your car keys.
**Steve Martin**, 'Changes in the Memory After Fifty', *Pure Drivel*, 1998

**20** Growing old is no more than a bad habit which a busy man has no time to form.
**André Maurois**, 'The Art of Growing Old', *The Art of Living*, 1940

**21** 75 YEAR OLD (CELEBRATING HIS BIRTHDAY IN A BROTHEL): I haven't had a woman in longer than I care to say. You know, she doesn't have to be beautiful – just patient.
**Polly Platt and Louis Malle**, *Pretty Baby*, screenplay, 1978

**22** As we grow older, our bodies get shorter and our anecdotes longer.
**Robert Quillen**, American author

**23** I was born in 1962. True. And the room next to me was 1963 . . .
**Joan Rivers**, *An Audience with Joan Rivers*, London Weekend Television, 1984

**24** You know you're getting old when you walk into a record store and everything you like has been marked down to $1.99.
**Jack Simmons**, Showtime Comedy Cable

**25** One should never trust a woman who tells one her real age. A woman who would tell one that, would tell one anything.
**Oscar Wilde**, *A Woman of No Importance*, 1893

**26** The old believe everything: the middle-aged suspect everything: the young know everything.
**Oscar Wilde**, 'Phrases and Philosophies for the Use of the Young', 1894

**27** Thirty-five is a very attractive age. London society is full of women of the very highest birth who have, of their own free choice, remained thirty-five for years.
**Oscar Wilde**, *The Importance of Being Earnest*, 1895

**28** First thing I do when I wake up in the morning is breathe on the mirror and hope it fogs.
**Earl Wynn**, Hall of Fame pitcher

# Alcoholism
*See also Abstinence; Drink.*

**1** I've joined Alcoholics Anonymous. I still drink, but under a different name.
**Jerry Dennis**

**2** Alcoholism isn't a spectator sport. Eventually the whole family gets to play.
**Joyce Rebeta-Burditt**, *The Cracker Factory*, 1977

**3** An alcoholic is someone you don't like who drinks as much as you do.
**Dylan Thomas**, 1914–53, Welsh poet (Attrib.)

# Alimony
*See also Divorce; Love – Breaking up.*

**1** The high cost of leaving.
**Anon.**

**2** Alimony is like buying oats for a dead horse.
**Arthur 'Bugs' Baer**

**3** You never realize how short a month is until you pay alimony.
**John Barrymore**, 1882–1942, American actor

**4** I heard from my cat's lawyer today. My cat wants £12,000 a week for Tender Vittles.
**Johnny Carson**, *The Tonight Show*, NBC TV, 1984

**5** Alimony: bounty after the mutiny.
**Max Kauffmann**

**6** Alimony is the curse of the writing classes.
**Norman Mailer**

**7** She cried – and the judge wiped her tears with my checkbook.
**Tommy Manville**, thirteen-times divorced American millionaire

**8** If the income tax is the price we have to pay to keep the government on its feet, alimony is the price we have to pay for sweeping a woman off hers.
**Groucho Marx**, *Newsday*

**9** Alimony – the ransom that the happy pay to the devil.
**H. L. Mencken,** *A Book of Burlesques,* 1920

**10** Zsa Zsa Gabor is an expert housekeeper. Every time she gets divorced, she keeps the house.
**Henny Youngman**

# Amateurs
*See also Sport.*

**1** Professionals built the *Titanic,* amateurs built the ark.
**Anon.**

**2** Amateur: one who plays games for the love of the thing. Unlike the professional, he receives no salary, and is contented with presents of clothes, clubs, rackets, cigarettes, cups, cheques, hotel expenses, fares, and so on.
**Beachcomber ( J. B. Morton),** *Beachcomber: The Works of J. B. Morton,* 1974

# Ambition
*See also Achievement; Success.*

**1** CHANDLER: Hey, you guys in the living room all know what you want to do. You know, you have goals. You have dreams. I don't have a dream.
ROSS: Ah, the lesser known 'I Don't Have a Dream' speech.
**Quoted in Cooking with Friends, 1996**

**2** I want to be what I was when I wanted to be what I am now.
**Graffito,** London, 1980

**3** I Want It All – And I Want It Delivered!
**T-shirt,** Tunbridge Wells, 1998

**4** The vulgar man is always the most distinguished, for the very desire to be distinguished is vulgar.
**G. K. Chesterton,** *All Things Considered,* 1908

**5** He is so ambitious that he squeaks when he walks, and cannot manage to smile at any colleague inferior in rank in case he compromises himself in some way.
**Alan Clark,** of Conservative Education Secretary John Patten, in *Diaries – Into Politics,* 2000

**6** Never keep up with the Joneses. Drag them down to your level; it's cheaper.
**Quentin Crisp,** *Evening Standard,* 1999

**7** ETH: If Ron doesn't mix with better-class people, how's he going to get on in life? In this world it's not what you know, it's who you know, isn't it Ron?
RON: Yes, Eth. And I don't know either of them.
**Frank Muir and Denis Norden,** *The Glums,* BBC Radio

**8** Every morning I get up and look through the *Forbes* list of the Richest People in America. And if I'm not there, I go to work.
**Robert Orben**

**9** People Who Do Things exceed my
  endurance;
  God, for a man that solicits insurance!
**Dorothy Parker,** 'Sunset Gun', 1928

**10** I always wanted to be somebody; but I should have been more specific.
**Lily Tomlin**

**11** Ambition is the last refuge of the failure.
**Oscar Wilde,** 'Phrases and Philosophies for the Use of the Young', 1894

# America and the Americans
*See also America – The South; Boston; California; Chicago; Florida; Los Angeles; New England; New York; Politics – American Presidents; San Francisco; Washington.*

**1** Is the US ready for self-government?
**Graffito,** New York, 1971

**2** Americans like fat books and thin women.
**Russell Baker,** American columnist

**3** He held, too, in his enlightened way, that Americans have a perfect right to exist. But he did often find himself wishing Mr Rhodes had not enabled them to exercise that right in Oxford.
**Max Beerbohm,** *Zuleika Dobson,* 1911

**4** I tell this story about talking to a neighbour in New Hampshire after I'd taken a trip and he asked me who I flew back with. And I said, 'I don't know, they were all complete strangers to me.' And he just looked at me and said, 'No, I meant which airline.'

That's Americans.

**Bill Bryson**, *Independent on Sunday*, 2000

**5** I don't believe there's any problem in this country, no matter how tough it is, that Americans, when they roll up their sleeves, can't completely ignore.

**George Carlin**, *Brain Droppings*, 1997

**6** The Yankee is a dab at electricity and crime,

He tells you how he hustles and it takes him quite a time.

I like his hospitality that's cordial and frank,

I do not mind his money but I do not like his swank.

**G. K. Chesterton**, 'A Song of Self-esteem', *Collected Poems*, 1933

**7** The American language is in a state of flux based on the survival of the unfittest.

**Cyril Connolly**, *Sunday Times*, 1996

**8** I don't know much about Americanism, but it's a damn good word with which to carry an election.

**Warren G. Harding**, American President 1921–3

**9** I can't believe we still have the Miss America pageant. This is America! Where we're not supposed to judge people based on how they look; we're supposed to judge people based on how much money they make.

**Heidi Joyce**, American standup comic

**10** When I first arrived in the States, a shrewd American said to me, 'A European coming to America for the first time, should skip New York and fly directly to Kansas. Start from the Middle. The East will only mislead you.'

**Lord Kinross**, *The Innocents at Home*, 1959

**11** You can always tell the Irish
You can always tell the Dutch
You can always tell a Yankee
But you cannot tell him much.

**Eric Knight**, 1897–1943, British-born American author, 'All Yankees are Liars'

**12** America, where overnight success is both a legend and a major industry.

**John Leggett**, *Ross and Tom*, 1974

**13** From **Top ten things we as Americans can be proud of**

Attendance at Liza Minnelli concerts still optional.

Crumbling landmarks torn down – not made a big fuss over.

Hourly motel rates.

Didn't just give up right away in World War II like some countries we could mention.

Fabulous babes coast to coast.

**David Letterman**, *The Late Show*, CBS

**14** HUSBAND (*to wife*): The egg timer is pinging. The toaster is popping. The coffeepot is perking. Is this it, Alice? Is this the great American dream?

**Henry Martin**, cartoon in the *New Yorker*

**15** The American people, taking one with another, constitute the most timorous, sniveling, poltroonish, ignominious mob of serfs and goosesteppers ever gathered under one flag in Christendom since the end of the Middle Ages.

**H. L. Mencken**, *Prejudices*, Third Series, 1922

**16** America's dissidents are not committed to mental hospitals and sent into exile; they thrive and prosper and buy a house in Nantucket and take flyers in the commodities market.

**Ted Morgan**, *On Becoming American*, 1978

**17** The United States is the greatest single achievement of European civilisation.

**Robert Balmain Mowat**, *The United States of America*, 1938

**18** America – a country that has leapt from barbarism to decadence without touching civilization.

**John O'Hara**, 1905–70, American novelist

**19** The European traveller in America – at least if I may judge by myself – is struck by two peculiarities: first, the extreme similarity of outlook in all parts of the United States (except the Old South), and secondly, the passionate desire of each locality to prove that it is peculiar and different from every other. The second of these is, of course, caused by the first.

**Bertrand Russell**, 'Modern Homogeneity', 1930

**20** Being a great power is no longer much fun.

**David Schoenhaum**, *The New York Times*, 1973

**21** Americans adore me and will go on adoring me until I say something nice about them.
**George Bernard Shaw** (Attrib.)

**22** I like to be in America!
OK by me in America!
Everything free in America
*For a small fee in America!*
**Stephen Sondheim**, 'America', song from *West Side Story*, 1957

**23** [Americans are] better at having a love affair that lasts ten minutes than any other people in the world.
**Stephen Spender**, interviewed in the *New York Post*, 1975

**24** In the United States there is more space where nobody is than where anybody is. That is what makes America what it is.
**Gertrude Stein**, *The Geographical History of America*, 1936

**25** BRITISH CIVIL SERVANT: They don't stand on ceremony . . . They make no distinction about a man's background, his parentage, his education. They say what they mean, and there is a vivid muscularity about the way they say it . . . They are always the first to put their hands in their pockets. They press you to visit them in their own home the moment they meet you, and are irrepressibly good-humoured, ambitious and brimming with self-confidence in any company. Apart from all that I've got nothing against them.
**Tom Stoppard**, *Dirty Linen*, 1976

**26** . . . as American as English muffins and French toast.
**John Russell Taylor**, *The Times*, 1984

**27** America is a large friendly dog in a small room. Every time it wags its tail, it knocks over a chair.
**Arnold Toynbee**, 1889–1975, English historian, 1954

**28** Losing is the great American sin.
**John Tunis**, quoted in *The New York Times*, 1977

**29** America is a vast conspiracy to make you happy.
**John Updike**, *Problems*, 1980

**30** I drive my car to the supermarket,
The way I take is superhigh,
A superlot is where I park it,
And Super Suds are what I buy.
Supersalesmen sell me tonic –
Super-Tone-O for relief.
The planes I ride are supersonic.
In trains, I like the Super Chief.
**John Updike**, 'Superman', *The Carpentered Hen and Other Tame Creatures*, 1958

**31** Every time Europe looks across the Atlantic to see the American eagle, it observes only the rear end of an ostrich.
**H. G. Wells**, *America*, 1908

**32** All Americans lecture . . . I suppose it is something in their climate.
**Oscar Wilde**, *A Woman of No Importance*, 1893

**33** We have really everything in common with America nowadays, except, of course, language.
**Oscar Wilde**, 'The Canterville Ghost', 1887

# America – The South

*See also America and the Americans; Texas.*

**1** My great grandfather . . . was the first Black political candidate in the state of Mississippi. He ran for the border and made it. And the reason he ran for the border, he said, was that the people were very clannish. He didn't mind them having hang-ups, he just didn't want to be one of their hang-ups.
**Redd Foxx**, black comedian, *Esquire*

**2** I happen to know quite a bit about the South. Spent twenty years there one night.
**Dick Gregory**, black comedian

**3** It's high time the rednecks came back to Washington. There are a hell of a lot more rednecks out there than people who eat crepes suzette.
**Mickey Griffin**, campaign organizer for George Wallace, Governor of Alabama 1963–7 and American Independent Party presidential candidate 1968

**4** I really am a fixin'
To go home and start a mixin'
Down below that Mason-Dixon line.
I wanna go back to Alabammy,
Back to the arms of my dear ol' Mammy,
Her cookin's lousy and her hands are clammy,
But what the hell, it's home.

Yes for paradise the Southland is my
  nominee
Just give me a hammock and a grit of
  hominy.
**Tom Lehrer**, 'I Wanna Go Back to Dixie', song, 1959

**5** Southerners can never resist a losing
cause.
**Margaret Mitchell**, Gone with the Wind, 1936

**6** What is the difference between the South
and the rest of America? It was a while
before I figured out there isn't any. The
South *is* America. The South is what we
started out with in this bizarre, slightly
troubling, basically wonderful country –
fun, danger, friendliness, energy,
enthusiasm and brave, crazy, tough people.
After all, America is where the wildest
humans on the planet came to do anything
they damn pleased.
**P. J. O'Rourke**, Rolling Stone, 1982

## Ancestors
*See also The Family; History; The Past; Relatives.*

**1** She's descended from a long line her
mother listened to.
**Gypsy Rose Lee**

**2** ERIC: I come from a very old military
family. One of my ancestors fell at
Waterloo.
ERNIE: Really?
ERIC: Yes, someone pushed him off
Platform Nine.
**Eric Morecambe and Ernie Wise**, The Morecambe and
Wise Joke Book, 1979

## Anger
*See also Abuse; Disgust; Temper.*

**1** *I* am righteously indignant; *you* are
annoyed; *he* is making a fuss about nothing.
**Competition**, New Statesman

**2** He spoke with a certain what-is-it in his
voice, and I could see that, if not actually
disgruntled, he was far from being gruntled.
**P. G. Wodehouse**, The Code of the Woosters, 1938

## Animals
*See also Birds; Cats; Dogs; Fish and Fishing; Pets;
Vets.*

**1** I think animal testing is a terrible idea;
they get all nervous and give the wrong
answers.
**Anon.**

**2** Q: What's the difference between a
buffalo and a bison?
A: You can't wash your hands in a buffalo.
**Anon.**

**3** I shoot the Hippopotamus
  With bullets made of platinum,
  Because if I used leaden ones
  His hide is sure to flatten 'em.
**Hilaire Belloc**, 'The Hippopotamus', Bad Child's Book
of Beasts, 1896

**4** Odd things animals. All dogs look up to
you. All cats look down to you. Only a pig
looks at you as an equal.
**Winston Churchill** (Attrib.)

**5** I find that ducks' opinion of me is greatly
influenced by whether or not I have bread.
**Mitch Hedberg**, American standup comic

**6** I do not like animals. Of any sort. I don't
even like the idea of animals. Animals are
no friends of mine. They are not welcome
in my house. They occupy no space in my
heart. Animals are off my list . . . I might
more accurately state that I do not like
animals, with two exceptions. The first
being in the past tense, at which point I like
them just fine, in the form of nice crispy
spareribs and Bass Weejun penny loafers.
And the second being outside, by which I
mean not merely outside, as in outside the
house, but genuinely outside, as in outside
in the woods, or preferably outside in the
South American jungle. This is, after all,
only fair. I don't go there; why should they
come here?
**Fran Lebowitz**, Social Studies, 1981

**7** O Kangaroo, O Kangaroo,
  Be grateful that you're in the zoo,
  And not transmuted by a boomerang
  To zestful tangy Kangaroo meringue.
**Ogden Nash**, 'The Kangaroo', Good Intentions, 1942

**8** The turtle lives 'twixt plated decks

Which practically conceal its sex.
I think it clever of the turtle
In such a fix to be so fertile.
**Ogden Nash**, 'The Turtle', *Hard Lines*, 1931

**9** Two kangaroos are talking to each other, and one says 'Gee, I hope it doesn't rain today, I just hate it when the children play inside.'
**Henny Youngman**

## Antiques
*See also History; The Past.*

**1** Old? The only thing that kept it standing was the woodworm holding hands.
**Jerry Dennis**

**2** Is anybody looking for a bargain in an Early Pennsylvania washstand in mint condition, circa 1825? It's genuine pumpkin pine, with ball-and-claw feet, the original brasses, and a smear of blood where I tripped over it last night in the dark. I'm holding it at $16, but not so tightly that I wouldn't let it go to the right party for circa ten cents.
**S. J. Perelman**, *Acres and Pains*, 1947

**3** Want to have some fun? Walk into an antique shop and say, 'What's new?'
**Henny Youngman**

## Anxiety
*See also Depression and Despair; Fear; Hypochondria; Paranoia.*

**1** Whenever he thought about global warming he felt terrible. And so at last he came to a fateful decision. He decided not to think about it.
**Anon.**

**2** It's Been Lovely, But I Have to Scream Now.
**Bumper sticker**, Boston, 1999

**3** Caught in the grips of DESPAIR!? Times are tough, huh, Bud? Nobody said it was going to be a bed of roses! So now you've made your bed, so now EAT it! Or, you might say, you've buttered you're bread, now sleep on it! Who do you think YOU are? GOD? What gives YOU the right to think you should have it any better than the NEXT

guy? Forget it? There's NO HOPE! That's right, kids! NO HOPE! Face facts! Look at the world situation! How long can you go on deluding yourself that things will get better? The only thing to do is to resign yourself to the fatal inevitability of it all!
While waiting for death, read *Despair*. It's your kind of comic!
**Robert Crumb**, *Plunge into the Depths of Despair*, comic, 1970

**4** When you don't have any money, the problem is food. When you have money, it's sex. When you have both, it's health. If everything is simply jake, then you're frightened of death.
**J. P. Donleavy**, *The Ginger Man*, 1955

**5** If I knew what I was so anxious about, I wouldn't be so anxious.
**Mignon McLaughlin**, American journalist

**6** I have a new philosophy. I'm only going to dread one day at a time.
**Charles Schulz**, *Peanuts*, cartoon

**7** If you don't relax, I'll break my fingers. Look at this. The only man in the world with clenched hair.
**Neil Simon**, *The Odd Couple*, screenplay, 1966

## Appearance
*See also Beauty; Clothes; Fashion; Looks; Style.*

**1** You look rather rash my dear your colors dont quite match your face.
**Daisy Ashford**, *The Young Visiters*, 1919

**2** I spent seven hours in a beauty shop – and that was just for the estimate.
**Phyllis Diller**

**3** She was a vivacious girl, not pretty by any accepted standards, if anything ugly by any accepted standards, but she could speak Latin and foot a quadrille and sometimes the two simultaneously if the tempo was right.
**Denis Norden**, *Upon My Word*, 1974

**4** . . . an individual whose appearance was so repulsive I had to have my mirrors insured.
**Miss Piggy**, *Miss Piggy's Guide to Life (As Told to Henry Beard)*, 1981

**5** She looked, as far as her clothes went, as

though she had been pulled through brambles and then pushed through a thin tube.
**Gwyn Thomas**, *The Alone to the Alone*, 1947

**6** It is only the shallow people who do not judge by appearances.
**Oscar Wilde**, *The Picture of Dorian Gray*, 1891

**7** She wore far too much rouge last night and not quite enough clothes. That is always a sign of despair in a woman.
**Oscar Wilde**, *An Ideal Husband*, 1895

**8** With an evening coat and a white tie, anybody, even a stockbroker, can gain a reputation for being civilized.
**Oscar Wilde**, *The Picture of Dorian Gray*, 1891

**9** A man who wore a tie that went twice round the neck was sure, sooner or later, to inflict some hideous insult on helpless womanhood. Add tortoiseshell-rimmed glasses, and you had what practically amounted to a fiend in human shape.
**P. G. Wodehouse**, *Mulliner Nights*, 1933

**10** His eyes . . . were set as near together as Nature had been able to manage without actually running them into one another. His under-lip protruded and drooped. Looking at him, one felt instinctively that no judging committee of a beauty contest would hesitate a moment before him.
**P. G. Wodehouse**, *Psmith, Journalist*, 1915

# Archaeology
*See also Antiques; History; The Past.*

**1** An archaeologist is the best husband a woman can have; the older she gets, the more interested he is in her.
**Agatha Christie**, 1890–1976, English novelist

# Architecture
*See also Home; Interior Decorating.*

**1** In my experience, if you have to keep the lavatory door shut by extending your left leg, it's modern architecture.
**Nancy Banks Smith**, *Guardian*, 1969

**2** I'm not sure office buildings are even architecture. They're really a mathematical calculation, just three-dimensional investments.
**Gordon Bunshaft**, 1909–90, American architect, quoted in *Fortune*, 1973

**3** . . . I imagined asking her whether she liked Le Corbusier, and her replying, 'Love some – with a little Benedictine if you've got it.'
**Peter De Vries**, *The Tunnel of Love*, 1954

**4** The village hall was one of those mid-Victorian jobs in glazed red brick which always seem to bob up in these olde-world hamlets and do so much to encourage the drift to towns.
**P. G. Wodehouse**, *The Mating Season*, 1949

**5** The doctor can bury his mistakes, but an architect can only advise his clients to plant vines.
**Frank Lloyd Wright** (Attrib.)

**6** We should learn from the snail: it has devised a home that is both exquisite and functional.
**Frank Lloyd Wright** (Attrib.)

# Arguments
*See also Fighting; Opinions; Protest*

**1** Keep your temper. Do not quarrel with an angry person, but give him a soft answer. It is commanded by the Holy Writ and, furthermore, it makes him madder than anything else you could say.
**Anon.**, *Reader's Digest*, 1949

**2** We started arguing at our wedding. When I said, 'I do,' my wife said, 'Oh, no you don't.'
**Anon.**

**3** You don't have to agree with me, but it's quicker.
**Anon.**

**4** My opinions may have changed but not the fact that I am right.
**Ashleigh Brilliant**

**5** When people are least sure, they are often most dogmatic.
**J. K. Galbraith**, *The Great Crash, 1929*, 1955

**6** Shut up he explained.
**Ring Lardner**, *The Young Immigrants*, 1920

**7** We might as well give up the fiction
That we can argue any view.
For what in me is pure Conviction
Is simple Prejudice in you.
**Phyllis McGinley**, *Times Three: 1932–1960*, 1960

**8** My sad conviction is that people can only agree about what they're not really interested in.
**Bertrand Russell**, *New Statesman*, 1939

**9** Consistency is a paste jewel that only cheap men cherish.
**William Allen White**, *Emporia Gazette*, 1923

**10** He knew the precise psychological moment when to say nothing.
**Oscar Wilde**, *The Picture of Dorian Gray*, 1891

**11** I can stand brute force, but brute reason is quite unreasonable. There is something unfair about its use. It is hitting below the intellect.
**Oscar Wilde**, *The Picture of Dorian Gray*, 1891

**12** I dislike arguments of any kind. They are always vulgar, and often convincing.
**Oscar Wilde**, *The Importance of Being Earnest*, 1895

**13** I like talking to a brick wall, it's the only thing in the world that never contradicts me.
**Oscar Wilde**, *Lady Windermere's Fan*, 1892

# Aristocracy, The

*See also The Establishment; House of Lords; Royalty; Society.*

**1** I'm as drunk as the lord that I am!
**John Betjeman**, quoting inebriated undergraduate peer, *Evening Standard*, 1933

**2** I'm not a social person but I could fall for a duke – they are a great aphrodisiac.
**Tina Brown**, *Tatler*, 1979

**3** Democracy means government by the uneducated, while aristocracy means government by the badly educated.
**G. K. Chesterton**, *The New York Times*, 1931

**4** For the first time I was aware of that layer of blubber which encases an English peer, the sediment of permanent adulation.
**Cyril Connolly**, *Enemies of Promise*, 1938

**5** The Stately Homes of England,
How beautiful they stand,
To prove the upper classes
Have still the upper hand;
Though the fact that they have to be rebuilt
And frequently mortgaged to the hilt
Is inclined to take the gilt
Off the gingerbread,
And certainly damps the fun
Of the eldest son.
**Noel Coward**, 'The Stately Homes of England', song from *Operette*, 1938

**6** The Stately Homes of England
In valley, dale and glen
Produce a race of charming,
Innocuous young men.
Though our mental equipment may be slight
And we barely distinguish left from right,
We are quite prepared to fight
For our principles,
Though none of us know so far
what they really are.
**Noel Coward**, 'The Stately Homes of England', song from *Operette*, 1938

**7** Political toleration is a by-product of the complacency of the ruling class. When that complacency is disturbed there never was a more bloody-minded set of thugs than the British ruling class.
**Michael Foot**, British Labour politician

**8** For she's never heard of Hitler, and she's never thought of war,
She's got twenty-seven servants, and she could get twenty more.
She never sees a paper, and she seldom reads a book,
She is worshipped by her butler, tolerated by her cook.
And her husband treats her nicely, and he's mostly on a horse.
While the children are entirely in the nursery of course.
So no wonder she is happy – she's got nothing else to do.
O, no wonder she is happy, for she hasn't got a clue,
To the future that is waiting, and the funny things she'll do
About . . . thirty-seven years from now.
**Joyce Grenfell**, 'The Countess of Cotely', song from *Stately as a Galleon*, 1978

**9** Life at the Taws moved in the ordinary

routine of a great English household. At 7 a gong sounded for rising, at 8 a horn blew for breakfast, at 8.30 a whistle sounded for prayers, at 1 a flag was run up at half-mast for lunch, at 4 a gun was fired for afternoon tea, at 9 a first bell sounded for dressing, at 9.15 a second bell for going on dressing, while at 9.30 a rocket was sent up to indicate that dinner was ready. At midnight dinner was over, and at 1 a.m. the tolling of a bell summoned the domestics to evening prayers.

**Stephen Leacock**, 'Gertrude the Governess', *Nonsense Novels*, 1911

**10** A fully equipped duke costs as much to keep up as two dreadnoughts; and dukes are just as great a terror and they last longer.

**David Lloyd George**, speech, 1909

**11** An aristocracy in a republic is like a chicken whose head has been cut off; it may run about in a lovely way, but in fact it's dead.

**Nancy Mitford**, *Noblesse Oblige*, 1956

**12** In England, if you are a Duchess, you don't need to be well-dressed – it would be thought quite eccentric.

**Nancy Mitford**, *Noblesse Oblige*, 1956

**13** There is no stronger craving in the world than that of the rich for titles, except that of the titled for riches.

**Hesketh Pearson**, *The Marrying Americans*, 1961

**14** I've been offered titles but I think they get one into disreputable company.

**George Bernard Shaw** (Attrib.)

**15** There is no connection between the political ideas of our educated class and the deep places of the imagination.

**Lionel Trilling**, *The Liberal Imagination*, 1950

**16** LORD ILLINGWORTH: . . . a title is really rather a nuisance in these democratic days. As George Hartford I had everything I wanted. Now I have merely everything that other people want, which isn't nearly so pleasant.

**Oscar Wilde**, *A Woman of No Importance*, 1893

**17** The Peerage is one book a young man about town should know thoroughly and it is the best thing in fiction the English have ever done.

**Oscar Wilde**, *A Woman of No Importance*, 1893

**18** There is always more brass than brains in an aristocracy.

**Oscar Wilde**, *Vera, or The Nihilists*, 1883

**19** Reluctant though one may be to admit it, the entire British aristocracy is seamed and honeycombed with immorality. If you took a pin and jabbed it down anywhere in the pages of *Debrett's Peerage* you would find it piercing the name of someone with a conscience as tender as a sunburned neck.

**P. G. Wodehouse**, *Mulliner Nights*, 1933

**20** . . . those comfortably padded lunatic asylums which are known, euphemistically, as the stately homes of England.

**Virginia Woolf**, *The Common Reader*, 1925

# Army, The

*See also Fighting; The Navy; War.*

**1** If it moves, salute it,
If it doesn't move, pick it up.
If you can't pick it up, paint it.

**Anon.**, *The Sad Sack's Catechism*, 1942

**2** PERCY SUGDEN: When you've made gravy under gunfire, you can do anything.

*Coronation Street*, Granada TV

**3** Colonel Cathcart had courage and never hesitated to volunteer his men for any target available.

**Joseph Heller**, *Catch-22*, 1961

**4** Einstein once said that any man who liked marching had been given his brain for nothing: just the spinal column would have done. But I wasn't Einstein. Since most of one's time in the army is wasted anyway, I preferred to waste it by moving about in a precise manner.

**Clive James**, *Unreliable Memoirs*, 1980

**5** It's Tommy this, an' Tommy that, an'
   'Chuck 'im out, the brute!'
But it's 'Saviour of 'is country' when the
   guns begin to shoot.

**Rudyard Kipling**, 'Tommy', *A Choice of Kipling's Verse*, 1941

**6** When I first went into the active Army you could tell someone to move a chair

across the room – now you have to tell him why.
**Major Robert Lembke,** quoted in *Newsweek*, 1979

**7** I'm still recovering from a shock. I was nearly drafted. It's not that I mind fighting for my country, but they called me at a ridiculous time: in the middle of a war.
**Jackie Mason**

**8** I was almost drafted. Luckily, I was wounded while taking the physical.
**Jackie Mason**

**9** When the military man approaches, the world locks up its spoons and packs off its womankind.
**George Bernard Shaw,** *Man and Superman*, 1903

# Art and Artists

*See also Art – Critics; Modern Art.*

**1** Originality is the art of concealing your sources.
**Anon.**

**2** WOODY ALLEN: That's quite a lovely Jackson Pollock, isn't it?
MUSEUM GIRL: Yes, it is.
WOODY ALLEN: What does it say to you?
MUSEUM GIRL: It restates the negativeness of the universe. The hideous lonely emptiness of existence. The predicament of man forced to live in a barren, godless eternity, like a tiny flame flickering in an immense void with nothing but waste, horror and degradation, forming a useless bleak straitjacket in an absurd cosmos.
WOODY ALLEN: What are you doing Sunday night?
MUSEUM GIRL: Committing suicide.
WOODY ALLEN: What about Friday night?
**Woody Allen,** *Play It Again, Sam*, screenplay, 1972

**3** Life is very nice, but it lacks form. It's the aim of art to give it some.
**Jean Anouilh,** *The Rehearsal*, 1950

**4** What I'm above all primarily concerned with is the substance of life, the pith of reality. If I had to sum up my work, I suppose that's it really: I'm taking the pith out of reality.
**Alan Bennett,** 'The Lonely Pursuit', *On the Margin*, BBC TV, 1966

**5** A woman is fascinated not by art but by the noise made by those in the field.
**Anton Chekhov**

**6** The artistic temperament is a disease that afflicts amateurs.
**G. K. Chesterton,** *Heretics*, 1905

**7** The artist's wife will know that there is no more sombre enemy of good art than the pram in the hall.
**Cyril Connolly,** *Enemies of Promise*, 1938

**8** Anyone can be a cartoonist! It's so simple even a child can do it! 'ART' is just a racket! A HOAX perpetrated on the public by so-called 'Artists' who set themselves up on a pedestal and promoted by pantywaist ivorytower intellectuals and sob-sister 'critics' who think the world owes them a living!
**Robert Crumb,** *Plunge into the Depths of Despair*, comic, 1970

**9** He always did have that 'Touch of Madness' that marks the true artist and breaks the hearts of the young girls from fine homes.
**Robert Crumb,** *Snoid Comics*, 1980

**10** . . . at one point I found myself standing before an oil of a horse that I figured was probably a self-portrait judging from the general execution . . .
**Peter De Vries,** *Let Me Count the Ways*, 1965

**11** To an artist a husband named Bicket
Said, 'Turn your backside, and I'll kick it.
You have painted my wife
In the nude to the life.
Do you think for a moment that's cricket?'
**John Galsworthy,** 1867–1933, English novelist

**12** As my poor father used to say
In 1863,
Once people start on all this Art
Good-bye, moralitee!
And what my father used to say
Is good enough for me.
**A. P. Herbert,** 'Lines for a Worthy Person'

**13** The moment you cheat for the sake of beauty, you know you are an artist.
**Max Jacob,** *Art Poétique*, 1922

**14** The great artists of the world are never

Puritans, and seldom even ordinarily respectable.
**H. L. Mencken**

**15** Treat a work of art like a prince: let it speak to you first.
**Arthur Schopenhauer** (Attrib.)

**16** What sight is sadder than the sight of a lady we admire admiring a nauseating picture.
**Logan Pearsall Smith**, *All Trivia*, 1933

**17** My dear Tristan, to be an artist at all is like living in Switzerland during a world war.
**Tom Stoppard**, *Travesties*, 1975

**18** The artist is a lucky dog . . . In any community of a thousand souls there will be nine hundred doing the work, ninety doing well, nine doing good, and one lucky dog painting or writing about the other nine hundred and ninety-nine.
**Tom Stoppard**, *Artist Descending a Staircase*, BBC Radio, 1972

**19** If Botticelli were alive today, he'd be working for *Vogue*.
**Peter Ustinov**

**20** If you want to know everything about me, just look at the surface of my paintings, it's all there, there's nothing more.
**Andy Warhol**

**21** All art is quite useless.
**Oscar Wilde**, *The Picture of Dorian Gray*, 1891

**22** A true artist takes no notice whatever of the public. The public to him are nonexistent. He leaves that to the popular novelist.
**Oscar Wilde**, 'The Soul of Man under Socialism', 1891

**23** No great artist ever sees things as they really are. If he did he would cease to be an artist.
**Oscar Wilde**, 'The Decay of Lying', 1889

**24** She is like most artists; she has style without any sincerity.
**Oscar Wilde**, 'The Nightingale and the Rose', 1888

**25** I had a private income – the young artist's best friend.
**P. G. Wodehouse**, *Quick Service*, 1940

**26** Like all young artists nowadays, he had always held before him as the goal of his ambition the invention of some new comic animal for the motion pictures. What he burned to do, as Velazquez would have burned to do if he had lived today, was to think of another Mickey Mouse and then give up work and just sit back and watch the money roll in.
**P. G. Wodehouse**, *Lord Emsworth and Others*, 1937

**27** Of all the myriad individuals that went to make up the kaleidoscopic life of New York, Mrs Waddington disliked artists most. They never had any money. They were dissolute and feckless. They attended dances at Webster Hall in strange costumes and frequently played the ukelele.
**P. G. Wodehouse**, *The Small Bachelor*, 1927

# Art – Critics

*See also Art and Artists; Critics.*

**1** Writing about art is like dancing about architecture.
**Anon.**

**2 Museum etiquette**
*Handy phrases* (To Mix'n'Match)
'A poignant melding of Rococo and Neo-Classicism.'
'The delicate blend of texture and color radiates sensuality.'
'The juxtaposition of light and shadow creates a curious tension.'
'The artist's inner turmoil reveals itself through the tortured brushstrokes.'
'Ay caramba!'
**Matt Groening**, *Bart Simpson's Guide to Life*, 1966

# Assassination

*See also Murder; Revolution.*

**1** All these post-Watergate liberals forget that assassination was once a healthy alternative to war. There is only one justification for assassination: to save lives, lots of lives. One life to save many.
**Miles Copeland**, former CIA officer, quoted in *Rolling Stone*, 1986

**2** Assassination is the extreme form of censorship.
**George Bernard Shaw**, 'The Rejected Statement', 1916

## Assertiveness

*See also Decisions; Indecision; Obstinacy.*

**1** Let people push you around. The person who says, believes, and acts on the phrase 'I ain't taking any shit from anybody' is a very busy person indeed. This person must be ever vigilant against news vendors who shortchange him, cab drivers who take him the wrong way around, waiters who serve the other guy first, florists who are charging ten cents more per tulip than the one down the block, pharmacists who make you wait too long and cars that cut you off at the light: they are a veritable miasma of righteous indignation and never have a minute to relax and have a good time.
**Cynthia Heimel**, 'Lower Manhattan Survival Tactics', *Village Voice*, 1983

**2** My mother has gone to a woman's workshop on assertiveness training. Men aren't allowed. I asked my father what 'assertiveness training' is. He said, 'God knows, but whatever it is, it's bad news for me.' . . . then my mother came home and started bossing us around. She said, 'The worm has turned,' and 'Things are going to be different around here,' and things like that. Then she went into the kitchen and started making a chart dividing all the housework into three . . . she put the chart on the wall and said, 'We start tomorrow.'
**Sue Townsend**, *The Secret Diary of Adrian Mole Aged 13³/₄*, 1982

## Astrology

*See also Fate; The Future; The Occult; Superstition.*

**1** RICHARD: What's your sign?
VICTORIA: I'm sorry – it's unlisted.
**Mel Brooks**, *High Anxiety*, screenplay, 1977

**2** There should be three days a week when no one is allowed to say: 'What's your sign?' Violators would have their copies of Kahlil Gibran confiscated.
**Dick Cavett**, *The Dick Cavett Show*, ABC TV, 1978

**3** I don't believe in astrology. The only stars I can blame for my failures are those that walk about the stage.
**Noel Coward** (Attrib.)

**4** You can tell a lot about someone's personality if you know his sign; Jesus: born on 25th December. Fed the 5,000, walked on water – typical Capricorn.
**Harry Hill**, Edinburgh Festival, 1995

**5** The process of balancing the horoscopes of two elevens one against the other was a very delicate and difficult one. A match between the Spurs and the Villa entailed a conflict in the heavens so vast and so complicated that it was not to be wondered at if she sometimes made a mistake about the outcome.
**Aldous Huxley**, *Crome Yellow*, 1921

**6** Astrology proves just one scientific fact: there's one born every minute.
**Patrick Moore**, BBC Radio 4, 2000

## Atheism

*See also Belief; God; Religion.*

**1** Who do atheists talk to during sex?
**Anon.**

**2** Few sailors are atheists, for they are in daily peril.
**Anon.**

**3** Atheism is a non-prophet organization.
**Anon.**

**4** Someone asked [Bertrand] Russell at some meeting: 'Lord Russell, what will you say when you die and are brought face to face with your Maker?' He replied without hesitation: 'God,' I shall say, 'God, why did you make the evidence for your existence so insufficient?'
**A. J. Ayer**, quoted in the *Standard*, 1984

**5** An atheist is a man who has no invisible means of support.
**John Buchan**, *Memory Hold the Door*, 1940

**6** Simon darling, I'm afraid you will have to speak to the children. I caught Tristram believing in God yesterday.
**Marc**, *The Trendy Ape*, cartoon, 1968

**7** . . . the sort of atheist who does not so much disbelieve in God as personally dislike Him.
**George Orwell**, *Down and Out in Paris and London*, 1933

**8** God can stand being told by Professor

Ayer and Marghanita Laski that He doesn't exist.
**J. B. Priestley**, 'The BBC's Duty to Society', *Listener*, 1965

**9** I was told that the Chinese said they would bury me by the Western Lake and build a shrine to my memory. I have some slight regret that this did not happen, as I might have become a god, which would have been very chic for an atheist.
**Bertrand Russell**, *The Autobiography of Bertrand Russell*, vol. 2, 1968

**10** It's an interesting view of atheism, as a sort of crutch for those who can't stand the reality of God . . .
**Tom Stoppard**, *Jumpers*, 1972

**11** She didn't like him being an atheist, and he wouldn't stop being an atheist, and finally he said something about Jonah and the Whale which was impossible for her to overlook. This morning she returned the ring, his letters and china ornament with 'A Present from Blackpool' on it which he had bought her last summer while visiting relatives in the north.
**P. G. Wodehouse**, *The Mating Season*, 1949

# Audiences

*See also Hecklers; Speakers and Speeches; The Theatre.*

**1** The best audience is intelligent, well educated and a little drunk.
**Alben W. Barkley**, American Vice-President, 1949–53 (Attrib.)

**2** Miss Howard let them have it, very slowly and with great feeling, accentuating the melody. She gazed thoughtfully at the ceiling, and all her audience gazed thoughtfully at other inappropriate spots, and Florence gazed at Miss Howard. Mrs Oxney found herself thinking of the late Mr Oxney, and Mrs Bertram thought about coke, and Mrs Holders thought about the enquiry she had sent to the *Sunday Gazette* about their bridge last night, and Mr Kemp with closed eyes thought about his left hip, and Mrs Bliss thought about Mind, and Miss Howard thought about the cost of the frames for her pictures, but all wore precisely the same dreamy and wistful expression.
**E. F. Benson**, *Paying Guests*, 1929

**3** They made me a present of Mornington Crescent,
They threw it a brick at a time.
**Albert Chevalier**, 'The Cockney Trajedian', music-hall song

**4** If they liked you, they didn't applaud – they just let you live.
**Bob Hope**

**5** They were really tough – they used to tie their tomatoes on the end of a yo-yo, so they could hit you twice.
**Bob Hope**

# Aunts

*See also Relatives; Women; Women – the Male View.*

**1** I tell you, Jeeves, behind every poor, innocent, harmless blighter who is going down for the third time in the soup, you will find, if you look carefully enough, the aunt who shoved him into it . . . It is no use telling me there are good aunts and bad aunts. At the core, they are all alike. Sooner or later, out pops the cloven hoof.
**P. G. Wodehouse**, *The Code of the Woosters*, 1938

**2** It has probably occurred to all thinking men that something drastic ought to be done about aunts. If someone were to come to me and say, 'Wooster, would you be interested in joining a society whose aim will be the suppression of aunts, or at least will see to it that they are kept on a short chain and not permitted to roam hither and thither at will, scattering desolation on all sides?' I would reply 'Wilbraham,' if his name was Wilbraham, 'put me down as a foundation member.'
**P. G. Wodehouse**, *A Few Quick Ones*, 1959

# Australia and the Australians

**1** In the world of success and failure,
Have you noticed the genius spark
Seems brightest in folk from Australia?
We all leave an indelible mark.
You just have to go to the opera,
Or an art-show, or glance at your shelves
To see in a trice that Australians

Have done *terribly* well for themselves.
**Dame Edna Everage (Barry Humphries)**, 'Terribly Well', song, 1976

**2** My son Brucie is married to a lovely lass, Joyleen. She's a Sydney girl and he's a Melbourne boy. I warned him about mixed marriages, but he takes no notice.
**Dame Edna Everage (Barry Humphries)**, *Russell Harty Plus*, London Weekend Television, 1973

**3** You may ask with ill-disguised envy
Why we Aussies get all the right breaks.
So here is my recipe for world-wide
    renown:
Mother's love, lots of fun, JUICY STEAKS!
**Dame Edna Everage (Barry Humphries)**, 'Terribly Well', song, 1976

**4 The great Australian adjective**
'___'
He plunged into the —— creek,
The —— horse was ——weak,
The —— stockman's face was a ——
    study!
And though the —— horse was drowned
The —— rider reached the ground
Ejaculating: ——!
——!
**W. T. Goodge**, *The Bulletin Reciter*, 1940

**5** *Armful of chairs*: Something some people would not know whether you were up them with or not.
*Bonzer*: Beaut, extra grouse and fanbloody-tastic.
*Cripes*: jeez.
*Dip around, a*: An activity, usually contemptuous, in which a group of chefs immerse their virile members in a plate of vichyssoise.
*Kookaburra's Khyber, as dry as a*: A condition of the throat prior to the ingurgitation of ice cold lager.
*Spit out the plum, to*: To abandon an English accent.
*Xenophobia*: A love of Australia.
**Barry Humphries**, glossary from *Bazza Pulls It Off*, 1972

**6** *Australian-based*: a person of diminished aspiration who has been successfully bribed with grants and awards to resist the lure of expatriation.
**Barry Humphries**, glossary from *A Nice Night's Entertainment*, 1981

**7** It is Wembley in South-East Asia; a tropical Manchester.
**Barry Humphries**, *Punch Down Under*, 1984

**8** *Koala Triangle*: a mysterious zone in the Southern Hemisphere where persons of talent disappear without trace.
**Barry Humphries**, glossary from *A Nice Night's Entertainment*, 1981

**9** In Australia, not reading poetry is the national pastime.
**Phyllis McGinley**, American poet

**10** *Racial characteristics*: violently loud alcoholic roughnecks whose idea of fun is to throw up on your car. The national sport is breaking furniture and the average daily consumption of beer in Sydney is ten and three quarters Imperial gallons for children under the age of nine.
**P. J. O'Rourke**, 'Foreigners Around the World', *National Lampoon*, 1976

**11** Fair crack of the whip, who reads dictionaries, anyway? You've guessed it sport – old ladies doing the *Women's Weekly* crossword and audio typists who can't spell 'receive'. Correct me if I'm wrong but case in point:
A red-blooded digger puts the hard word on a horny little unit down the local rubbidy . . . she looks like she'll come across so he whips her up to his brick veneer unit and they're both starkers before the froth's gone flat on his Fosters. She's screaming for it, so what does this ratbag do? He sticks his nose (wait for it) in a copy of the *Australian Pocket Oxford Dictionary*! Viewed dispassionately thus, I ask you, readers, what strange minority need does this flaming book meet?
**Sir Les Patterson (Barry Humphries)**, *Sunday Times*, 1977

**12** Now, I would be sticking my neck right out, asking for the chop, if I tried to kid *Sunday Times* readers that the average Australian Joe Blow talks like a limpwristed la-dee-dah Mayfair shirtlifter. Let's face it, you can't demolish two dozen Sydney Rock oysters, a rare T-bone and six chilled tubes with a plum in your flaming mouth!
**Sir Les Patterson (Barry Humphries)**, *Sunday Times*, 1977

**13** Australia!

Land of ravaged desert, shark-infested ocean and thirst-lashed outback.
Australia!
Land of strange, exotic creatures, freaks of evolution, ghastly victims of Mother Nature's vicious whimsy – kangaroo and platypus, potoroo and bandicoot, Richie Benaud and . . .
**Peter Tinniswood**, *The Brigadier Down Under*, 1983

**14** THE DUCHESS OF BERWICK: Do you know, Mr Hopper, dear Agatha and I are so much interested in Australia. It must be so pretty with all the dear little kangaroos flying about.
**Oscar Wilde**, *Lady Windermere's Fan*, 1892

**15** When I look at the map and see what an ugly country Australia is, I feel that I want to go there and see if it cannot be changed into a more beautiful form!
**Oscar Wilde** (Attrib.)

# Autobiography
*See also Diaries; History; Life; Memory.*

**1** Autobiography is now as common as adultery – and hardly less reprehensible.
**Lord Altrincham**

**2** Just as there is nothing between the admirable omelette and the intolerable, so with autobiography.
**Hilaire Belloc**, 1870–1953, French-born English poet, essayist and politician

**3** Interest in autobiography should begin at home . . . my chief interest is to delight and engross myself. A modest or inhibited autobiography is written without entertainment to the writer and read with distrust by the reader.
**Neville Cardus**, introduction to his autobiography, 1947

**4** An autobiography is an obituary in serial form with the last instalment missing.
**Quentin Crisp**, *The Naked Civil Servant*, 1968

**5** Next to the writer of real estate advertisements, the autobiographer is the most suspect of prose artists.
**Donal Henahan**, *The New York Times*, 1977

**6** Nothing I have said is factual except the bits that sound like fiction.
**Clive James**, *Unreliable Memoirs*, 1980

**7** Premature memoirs can only be conceited. I have no excuses against this charge, except to say that self-regard is itself a subject, and that to wait until reminiscence is justified by achievement might mean to wait for ever.
**Clive James**, *Unreliable Memoirs*, 1980

**8** I am being frank about myself in this book. I tell of my first mistake on page 850.
**Henry Kissinger**, of his memoirs *The White House Years*, 1979

**9** Your life story would not make a good book. Don't even try.
**Fran Lebowitz**, *Metropolitan Life*, 1979

**10** When you put down the good things you ought to have done, and leave out the bad things you did do – that's Memoirs.
**Will Rogers**

**11** Only when one has lost all curiosity about the future has one reached the age to write an autobiography.
**Evelyn Waugh** (Attrib.)

# Awards
*See also Achievement; Show Business; Success; Victory and Defeat.*

**1** I don't deserve this, but then, I have arthritis and I don't deserve that either.
**Jack Benny**, on accepting an award

**2** It is with tremendous ill grace that I grudgingly acknowledge the contribution of a few other people.
**Hugh Grant**, accepting a Golden Globe Award for *Four Weddings and a Funeral*, 1995

**3** Hegel said that at the age of 50 no man should speak for longer than he can make love.
**Ian McEwan**, novelist, entire speech at award ceremony, *Mail on Sunday*, 1999

**4** Awards are like piles. Sooner or later, every bum gets one.
**Maureen Lipman**, English actress, *Independent*, 1999

**5** I'd like to thank my mother and father for providing me with the need to seek the love of strangers.
**Betsy Salkind**, American comedy writer, imagining her acceptance speech at the Academy Awards

**6** Nobel Prize money is a lifebelt thrown to a swimmer who has already reached the shore in safety.
**George Bernard Shaw** (Attrib.)

# Babies

*See also Birth; Children; Gynaecology; Mothers; Pregnancy; Twins.*

**1** Except that right side up is best, there is not much to learn about holding a baby. There are 152 distinctly different ways and all are right! At least all will do.
**Heywood Broun**, *Collected Edition*, 1941

**2** It is pretty generally held that all a woman needs to do to know all about children is to have some. This wisdom is attributed to instinct . . . I have seen mothers give beer and spaghetti and Neapolitan ice cream to children in arms, and if they got that from instinct the only conclusion possible is that instinct is not what it used to be.
**Heywood Broun**, *Collected Edition*, 1941

**3** The babe, with a cry brief and dismal,
Fell into the water baptismal;
Ere they'd gathered its plight,
It had sunk out of sight,
For the depth of the font was abysmal.
**Edward Gorey**, 'The babe, with a cry brief and dismal', *The Listing Attic*, 1954

**4** When Baby's cries grew hard to bear
I popped him in the Frigidaire.
I never would have done so if
I'd known that he'd be frozen stiff.
My wife said: 'George, I'm so unhappé!
Our darling's now completely frappé!'
**Harry Graham**, 'L'Enfant Glacé', *Ruthless Rhymes for Heartless Homes*, 1899

**5** Training a child is more or less a matter of pot luck.
**Rod Maclean**, *Reader's Digest*, 1949

**6** A bit of talcum
Is always walcum.
**Ogden Nash**, 'The Baby', *Freewheeling*, 1931

**7** The baby wakes up in the wee wee hours of the morning.
**Robert Robbins**, *Reader's Digest*, 1949

**8** GRANDMOTHER: Let me hold the baby!
BILKO: Let you hold who? What? Who? Who? Who are you?
MOTHER: Oh, this is my mother – the baby's grandma!

BILKO: Oh, all right. But I don't approve of all this armhopping! . . .
UNCLE MAX: Atishoo!
BILKO: Who? Who? Who sneezed?
UNCLE MAX: I sneezed. Why?
BILKO: You'll have to go out! Out!
UNCLE MAX: But I'm Uncle Max!
BILKO: You should have thought of that before you sneezed! Now, out!
**Neil Simon and Terry Ryan**, 'Bilko's Godson', *The Phil Silvers Show*, CBS TV, 1959

# Bachelors
*See also Courtship; Marriage; The Single Life.*

**1** A bachelor never makes the same mistake once.
**Anon.**

**2** She was another one of his near Mrs.
**Alfred McFote**

**3** I belong to Bridegrooms Anonymous. Whenever I feel like getting married, they send over a lady in a housecoat and hair curlers to burn my toast for me.
**Dick Martin**, *Playboy*, 1969

**4** Bachelors know more about women than married men; if they didn't, they'd be married too.
**H. L. Mencken**

**5** A bachelor never quite gets over the idea that he is a thing of beauty and a boy forever.
**Helen Rowland**, 'Bachelors', *A Guide to Men*, 1922

**6** Bachelors are not fashionable any more. They are a damaged lot. Too much is known about them.
**Oscar Wilde**, *An Ideal Husband*, 1895

**7** By persistently remaining single, a man converts himself into a permanent public temptation. Men should be more careful; this very celibacy leads weaker vessels astray.
**Oscar Wilde**, *The Importance of Being Earnest*, 1895

# Baldness
*See also Faces.*

**1** I'm not really bald. I just have a very wide parting.
**Anon.**

**2** The best thing about being bald is when her folks come home, all you have to do is straighten your tie.
**Milton Berle**

# Ballet
*See also Dance; Exercise; The Theatre.*

**1** They were doing the Dying Swan at the ballet. And there was a rumor that some bookmakers had drifted into town from upstate New York and that they had fixed the ballet. There was a lot of money bet on the swan to live.
**Woody Allen**, nightclub act, 1960s

**2** I suppose I'm the only person who remembers one of the most exciting of his ballets – it's the fruit of an unlikely collaboration between Nijinsky on the one hand and Sir Arthur Conan Doyle on the other. I think I'm right in saying that it was the only detective story in ballet and it was called *The Inspector de la Rose*. The choreography was by Fokine. Wasn't up to much. Just the usual Fokine rubbish.
**Alan Bennett**, *The South Bank Show*, London Weekend Television, 1984

# Banking
*See also Borrowing and Lending; Credit; Credit Cards; Money; Professions; Wealth.*

**1** A banker is a man who lends you an umbrella when the weather is fair, and takes it away from you when it rains.
**Anon.**

**2** Banking may well be a career from which no man really recovers.
**J. K. Galbraith**, American economist

**3** From **Top ten tip-offs you've chosen a bad bank**
When you make a deposit, tellers high-five each other.
Your monthly statements are handwritten on cocktail napkins.
They also offer body piercing.
When you try to make a withdrawal, tellers suddenly don't speak English.
Instead of FDIC, it's insured by Skippy's Bank Insurance & Driveway Paving Company.
**David Letterman**, *The Late Show*, CBS

**4** . . . they all observe one rule which woe
  betides the banker who fails to heed it,
  Which is you must never lend any money
  to anybody unless they don't need it.
**Ogden Nash**, 'Bankers are Just Like Anybody Else,
except Richer', *I'm a Stranger Here Myself*, 1938

**5** A lot of people will also urge you to put
some money in a bank, and in fact within
reason – this is very good advice. But don't
go overboard. Remember, what you are
doing is giving your money to somebody
else to hold on to, and I think that it is
worth keeping in mind that the
businessmen who run banks are so worried
about holding on to things that they put
little chains on all their pens.
**Miss Piggy**, *Miss Piggy's Guide to Life (As Told to Henry
Beard)*, 1981

**6** I don't have a savings account because . . .
I don't know my mother's maiden name.
**Paula Poundstone**

**7** There have been three great inventions
since the beginning of time: fire, the wheel
and central banking.
**Will Rogers**

# Baseball

*See also Sport.*

**1** Getting a ball past his bat is like trying to
sneak the sun past a rooster.
**Anonymous pitcher on Hank Aaron**, 1973

**2 Heckle of the Month**
To fielders:
'Does your husband play too?'
'Get that spring out of your glove!'
'Fetch the ball, boy, fetch! *Good* boy!'
'Do you think you'll like this game better
  when you catch on?'

To umpires:
'The optician called . . . they'll be ready in
  30 minutes.'
'I'm gonna break your cane and shoot your
  dog!'
'Punch a hole in that mask. You're missing a
  good game!'
'Do you get any better or is this it?'
'If you're just going to watch the game, buy
  a ticket!'

To pitchers:
'You couldn't hit sand if you fell off a
  camel!'
'If you'd like, we could move the mound
  closer!'
**The Baseball Heckle Depot**, www.heckledepot.com

**3** Some of our hitters are so bad that they
can strike out on two pitches.
**Milton Berle**

**4** If people don't want to come out to the
ball park, nobody's going to stop them.
**Yogi Berra**, New York Yankees Catcher, 1946–63

**5** The tradition of professional baseball
always has been agreeably free of chivalry.
The rule is, 'Do anything you can get away
with.'
**Heywood Broun**, 1888–1939, American journalist

**6** Say this for big league baseball – it is
beyond any question the greatest
conversation piece ever invented in
America.
**Bruce Catton**, 1899–1978, American journalist

**7** Baseball must be a great game to survive
the people who run it.
**Arthur Daley**, sportswriter

**8** I'm throwing twice as hard as I ever did.
The ball's just not getting there as fast.
**'Lefty' Gomez**, pitcher, New York Yankees

**9** Baseball is very big with my people. It
figures. It's the only time we can get to
shake a bat at a white man without starting
a riot.
**Dick Gregory**, *From the Back of the Bus*, 1962

**10** The more we lose, the more he'll fly in.
And the more he flies in, the better the
chance there'll be a plane crash.
**Graig Nettles**, on George Steinbrenner, owner of the
New York Yankees

**11** The most overrated underrated player in
baseball.
**Larry Ritter**, on Tommy Henrich

**12** The secret of managing is to keep the
guys who hate you away from the guys who
are undecided.
**Casey Stengel**, 1890–1975, player and manager

**13** The sneer has gone from Casey's lip, his
  teeth are clenched in hate;

He pounds with cruel violence his bat
  upon the plate.
And now the pitcher holds the ball, and
  now he lets it go,
And now the air is shattered by the force
  of Casey's blow.
Oh, somewhere in this favored land the
  sun is shining bright;
The band is playing somewhere, and
  somewhere hearts are light,
And somewhere men are laughing, and
  somewhere children shout;
But there is no joy in Mudville – mighty
  Casey has struck out.
**Ernest Lawrence Thayer**, 'Casey at the Bat', *San Francisco Examiner*, 1888

**14** Baseball is almost the only orderly thing in a very unorderly world. If you get three strikes, even the best lawyer in the world can't get you off.
**Bill Veeck**, baseball executive

# Baths and Showers
*See also Cleanliness.*

**1** The first law of the shower states that no two shower controls in the universe are the same. The second states that the temperature markings on shower controls bear no relation to the temperature of the water. The third states that, however much a shower control may rotate, the degree of rotation required to change from ice-cold to scalding is never more than one millimetre.
**Joe Bennett**, *Fun Run and Other Oxymorons*, 2000

**2** I believe I will dip my pink-and-white body in yon Roman tub. I feel a bit gritty after the affairs of the day.
**W. C. Fields**, *My Little Chickadee*, screenplay, 1940

**3** Some people shave before bathing,
  And about people who bathe before
    shaving they are scathing,
  While those who bathe before shaving,
  Well, they imply that those who shave
    before bathing are misbehaving.
**Ogden Nash**, 'And Three Hundred and Sixty-six in Leap Year', *Good Intentions*, 1942

**4** I don't like baths. I don't enjoy them in the slightest and, if I could, I'd prefer to go around dirty.
**J. B. Priestley**, *Observer*, 1979

# Beach, The
*See also Holidays; The Sea.*

**1** I have a large seashell collection which I keep scattered along the beaches around the world. Maybe you've seen it.
**Steven Wright**, American comic

# Beatles, The
*See also Music and Musicians; Rock 'n' Roll; The Sixties; Songs and Singers.*

**1** What are the Beatles? I have never been able to understand what one beat singer is saying. Perhaps I shall fare better with four?
**Noel Coward** (Attrib.)

**2** I see the Beatles have arrived from England. They were forty pounds overweight, and that was just their hair.
**Bob Hope**, 1964

**3** Do you remember when everyone began analysing Beatle songs? I don't think *I* understood what some of them were supposed to be about.
**Ringo Starr** (Attrib.)

# Beauty
*See also Appearance; Cosmetics; Faces; Looks; Sexual Attraction.*

**1** A: How do you like bathing beauties?
B: I don't know, I never bathed one.
**Anon.**

**2** *I* am beautiful; *you* have quite good features; *she* isn't bad looking, if you like that type.
**Competition**, *New Statesman*

**3** She walks in beauty, like the night
  Of cloudless climes and starry skies;
  And all that's best of dark and bright
  Meet in her aspect and her eyes:
  And she can do the funky chicken.
***Rolling Stone***

**4** She wore a short skirt and a tight sweater and her figure described a set of parabolas that could cause cardiac arrest in a yak.
**Woody Allen**, *Getting Even*, 1973

**5** It was a blonde. A blonde to make a

bishop kick a hole in a stained-glass window.
**Raymond Chandler,** *Farewell, My Lovely,* 1940

**6** When I go to the beauty parlor, I always use the emergency entrance. Sometimes I just go for an estimate.
**Phyllis Diller**

**7** After a degree of prettiness, one pretty girl is as pretty as another.
**F. Scott Fitzgerald,** *Esquire,* 1936

**8** 'Why is it that beautiful women never seem to have any curiosity?' 'Is it because they know they're classical? With classical things the Lord finished the job. Ordinary ugly people know they're deficient and they go on looking for the pieces.'
**Penelope Gilliatt,** *A State of Change,* 1967

**9** She has eyes that men adore so
And a torso even more so.
**E. Y. Harburg,** 'Lydia, the Tattooed Lady', song for Groucho Marx from *At the Circus,* 1939

**10** The girl in the omnibus had one of those faces of marvellous beauty which are seen casually in the streets but never among one's friends. It was perfect in its softened classicality – a Greek face translated into English. Moreover she was fair, and her hair pale chestnut. Where do these women come from? Who marries them? Who knows them?
**Thomas Hardy,** quoted in *The Early Life of Thomas Hardy, 1840–1891,* 1928

**11** I'm tired of all this nonsense about beauty being only skin-deep. That's deep enough. What do you want – an adorable pancreas?
**Jean Kerr,** *The Snake Has All the Lines,* 1960

**12** Beauty is all very well at first sight; but who ever looks at it when it has been in the house three days.
**George Bernard Shaw,** *Man and Superman,* 1903

# Bed
*See also Breakfast; Dreams; Insomnia; Sleep.*

**1** One good turn gets most of the blanket.
**Anon.**

**2** Lying in bed would be an altogether perfect and supreme experience if only one

had a coloured pencil long enough to draw on the ceiling.
**G. K. Chesterton,** 'On Lying in Bed', *Tremendous Trifles,* 1910

**3** The tone now commonly taken towards the practice of lying in bed is hypocritical and unhealthy . . . Instead of being regarded, as it ought to be, as a matter for personal convenience and adjustment, it has come to be regarded by many as if it were a part of essential morals to get up early in the morning. It is, upon the whole, part of practical wisdom; but there is nothing good about it or bad about its opposite.
**G. K. Chesterton,** 'On Lying in Bed', *Tremendous Trifles,* 1910

**4** It was such a lovely day, I thought it was a pity to get up.
**W. Somerset Maugham,** *Our Betters,* 1923

# Begging
*See also Poverty; Tramps.*

**1** TRAMP: I haven't eaten for three days.
MAN: My dear chap – you must force yourself!
**Anon.**

**2** TRAMP: Would you give me twenty-five pence for a sandwich, lady?
LADY: I don't know – let me see the sandwich.
**Gyles Brandreth,** *1,000 Jokes: The Greatest Joke Book Ever Known,* 1980

**3** I always give homeless people money and my friends yell at me, 'He's only going to buy more alcohol and cigarettes.'
And I'm thinking, 'Oh, and like I *wasn't*.'
**Kathleen Madigan,** American standup comic

**4** Beggars should be abolished entirely! It is annoying to give to them and it is annoying not to give to them.
**Friedrich Wilhelm Nietzsche,** *Thus Spake Zarathustra,* 1883–92

# Behaviour
*See also Action.*

**1** I never observe rules of conduct, and therefore have given up making them.
**George Bernard Shaw** (Attrib.)

**2** Good breeding consists in concealing how much we think of ourselves and how little we think of other persons.
**Mark Twain**, *Notebooks*, 1935

**3** To be natural is such a very difficult pose to keep up.
**Oscar Wilde**, *An Ideal Husband*, 1895

# Belgium
*See also Europe and the EEC.*

**1** Belgium is the most densely populated country in Europe . . . the land is entirely invisible, except in the small hours of the morning, being for the rest of the time completely under foot . . . the sprout was developed by Brussels agronomists, this being the largest cabbage a housewife could possibly carry through the teeming streets.
**Alan Coren**, *The Sanity Inspector*, 1974

**2** Belgium is a country invented by the English to annoy the French.
**Charles de Gaulle**

**3** Belgium is known affectionately to the French as 'the gateway to Germany' and just as affectionately to the Germans as 'the gateway to France'.
**Tony Hendra**, 'EEC! It's the US of E!', *National Lampoon*, 1976

# Belief
*See also Atheism; The Church; Credulity; Cults; God; Heaven; Religion; Spritualism; Truth.*

**1** Did you hear about the insomniac dyslexic agnostic? He stayed awake all night wondering if there really was a dog.
**Anon.**

**2** Science has proof without any certainty. Creationists have certainty without any proof.
**Anon.**

**3** And how can I believe in God when just last week I got my tongue caught in the roller of an electric typewriter?
**Woody Allen**, *Without Feathers*, 1976

**4** In real life, Keaton believes in God. But she also believes that the radio works because there are tiny people inside it.
**Woody Allen**, *Esquire*, 1975

**5** It [the film *Love and Death*] implies that He doesn't exist, or, if He does, He can't really be trusted. (Since coming to this conclusion I have twice been nearly struck by lightning and once forced to engage in a long conversation with a theatrical agent.)
**Woody Allen**, *Esquire*, 1975

**6** Not only is there no God, but try getting a plumber at weekends.
**Woody Allen**, *Getting Even*, 1972

**7** To get into hebben
Don't snap fo' a seben –
Live clean! Don't have no fault!
Oh, I takes dat gospel
Whenever it's pos'ple –
But wid a grain of salt!
**Ira Gershwin and DuBose Heyward**, 'It Ain't Necessarily So', *Porgy and Bess*, 1935

**8** Any stigma is good enough to beat a dogma with.
**Philip Guedalla**, 'Ministers of State', *Masters and Men*, 1923

**9** I'm a man of no convictions – at least I think I am.
**Christopher Hampton**, *The Philanthropist*, 1970

**10** No matter how much I probe and prod
I cannot quite believe in God
But oh! I hope to God that he
Unswervingly believes in me!
**E. Y. Harburg**, *Rhymes for the Irreverent*, 1965

**11** Ever noticed how creationists look really unevolved?
**Bill Hicks**, *Independent on Sunday*, 1994

**12** If there is a God, give me a sign! . . . See, I told you that the knlupt smflrt glpptnrr . . .
**Steve Martin**, 'A Wild and Crazy Guy', album, 1978

**13** I guess I wouldn't believe in anything if it wasn't for my lucky astrology mood watch.
**Steve Martin**

**14** Man is a credulous animal and must believe something. In the absence of good grounds for belief, he will be satisfied with bad ones.
**Bertrand Russell**, *Unpopular Essays*, 1950

**15** 'I've seen the light,' said the policeman, hitherto an atheist, 'and what I wanted to ask you, sir, was do I have to join the

Infants' Bible Class or can I start singing in the choir right away?'
**P. G. Wodehouse**, *The Mating Season*, 1949

# Best-sellers

*See also Books; Publishing; Success; Writers; Writing.*

**1** Best-sellerism is the star system of the book world. A 'best-seller' is a celebrity among books. It is a book known primarily (sometimes exclusively) for its well-knownness.
**Daniel J. Boorstin**, *The Image*, 1962

**2** A best-seller is the gilded tomb of a mediocre talent.
**Logan Pearsall Smith**, *All Trivia*, 1933

# Bible, The

*See also Christianity; The Church; God; Jesus Christ; Religion.*

**1** The first pair ate the first apple.
**Anon.**

**2** And Noah he often said to his wife when he sat down to dine,
'I don't care where the water goes if it doesn't get into the wine.'
**G. K. Chesterton**, 'Wine and Water', *The Flying Inn*, 1914

**3** Chapter one
. . . 26 And God saw everything He had made, and he saw that it was very good; and God said, 'It *just* goes to show Me what the private sector can accomplish. With a lot of fool regulations, this could have taken *billions of years.*'
27 And on the evening of the fifth day, *which had been* the roughest day yet, God said, 'Thank Me it's Friday.' And God made the weekend.
**Tony Hendra and Sean Kelly**, 'The Book of Creation', *Playboy*, 1982

**4** Chapter one
In the beginning, God created dates.
2 And the date WAS Monday, July 4, 4004 BC.
3 And God said, 'Let there be Light'; and there was Light. And *when* there was Light, God *saw* the date, *that* it was an Monday, and He *got* down to work; for, verily He had

an Big Job *to do.* And God made pottery shards and Silurian mollusks and Pre-Cambrian limestone strata; and flints and Jurassic mastodon tusks and Pithecanthropus erectus skulls and Cretaceous Placentalia made He; and those cave paintings at Lascaux. And that was *that* for the first Day.
**Tony Hendra and Sean Kelly**, 'The Book of Creation', *Playboy*, 1982

**5** It is not fair to visit all
The blame on Eve, for Adam's fall;
The most Eve did was to display
Contributory negligé.
**Oliver Herford**, 'Eve: Apropos de Rien'

**6** From **Top ten words used least in the Bible**
Perky
Fudge-a-licious
Rootin'-tootin'
Schweppervescence
Gas-guzzling
**David Letterman**, *The Late Show*, CBS

**7** Say what you will about the Ten Commandments, you always come back to the pleasant fact that there are only ten of them.
**H. L. Mencken** (Attrib.)

**8** NEWSREADER: Good even. Here beginneth the first verse of the news. It has come to pass that the seven elders of the seven tribes have now been abiding in Sodom for seven days and seven nights. There seems little hope of an early settlement. An official spokesman said this afternoon, 'Only a miracle can save us now.'
. . . At the weigh-in for the big fight tomorrow, Goliath tipped the scales this even at 15 stone 3 lbs and David at 14 stone 3 lbs. David's manager said this even, 'The odd stone could make all the difference.'
. . . The news in brief. Lamentations 4: 18–22 and II Kings 14: 2–8.
**Bill Oddie and John Cleese**, *I'm Sorry I'll Read That Again*, BBC Radio

**9** The worst dates are often the result of the fix-up. Why do we fix people up? Because *you* think they'll have a good time. Who the hell are you? It's a little power trip, isn't it? You're playing God. Of course God was the first person to fix people up. Fixed up Adam

and Eve, you know. I'm sure he said to Adam, 'No, she's nice, she's very free about her body, doesn't really wear much. She was going out with a snake – I think that's over though.'
**Jerry Seinfeld**, *SeinLanguage*, 1993

**10** I read the book of Job last night – I don't think God comes well out of it.
**Virginia Woolf**, *The Letters of Virginia Woolf*, vol. ii: *1912–1922*, 1975

# Bigamy
*See also Divorce; Marriage; Monogamy.*

**1** Bigamy is having one wife too many. Monogamy is the same thing.
**Anon.**

**2** Bigamy is one way of avoiding the painful publicity of divorce and the expense of alimony.
**Oliver Herford**, 1864–1935, English-born American writer

**3** There once was an old man of Lyme
Who married three wives at a time.
When asked, 'Why a third?'
He replied, 'One's absurd!
And bigamy, sir, is a crime.'
**William Cosmo Monkhouse**, 1840–1901, poet and critic

**4** CAPTAIN SPAULDING (GROUCHO MARX):
Shall we get married?
MRS RITTENHOUSE: That's bigamy.
CAPTAIN SPAULDING: Of course it's big of me!
**Morrie Ryskind**, *Animal Crackers*, screenplay, 1930

# Big Business
*See also Business; Capitalism; The Office.*

**1** Coca-Cola Co. discovered that it had inadvertently bought Columbia Pictures Inc. Company executives had thought they were buying Columbia, the Central America country. Coca-Cola is asking the movie company for its deposit back.
*Off The Wall Street Journal*, 1982

**2** IBM is making top corporate positions hereditary. The sweeping change is designed to take advantage of new estate tax

laws and stimulate child production among the right people.
*Off The Wall Street Journal*, 1982

**3** Some see private enterprise as a predatory target to be shot, others as a cow to be milked, but few are those who see it as a sturdy horse pulling the wagon.
**Winston Churchill**

**4** We don't care. We don't have to. We're the phone company.
**Ernestine the phone operator (Lily Tomlin)**, *Laugh-In*

**5** The meek may inherit the earth – but not its mineral rights.
**J. Paul Getty**, 1892–1976, American billionaire industrialist

**6** If the government was as afraid of disturbing the consumer as it is of disturbing business, this would be some democracy.
**Kin Hubbard**, 1868–1930, American humorist

**7** Whenever you're sitting across from some important person, always picture him sitting there in a suit of long red underwear. That's the way I always operated in business.
**Joseph P. Kennedy**, quoted in *No Final Victories*, 1974

**8** The business of government is to keep the government out of business – that is, unless business needs government aid.
**Will Rogers**

**9** Nothing is illegal if a hundred businessmen decide to do it, and that's true anywhere in the world.
**Andrew Young**, Congressman and Mayor of Atlanta

# Birds
*See also Animals; Pets.*

**1** Eagles may soar, but weasels don't get sucked into jet engines.
**Anon.**

**2** HE: Every morning, I'd be down in the park and then I'd feed the pigeons.
SHE: What do you feed them? Popcorn?
HE: No. Every morning I'd go down to this park and I'd feed the pigeons. To my cat.
**Tony Hendra and Michael O'Donoghue**, National Lampoon's *Radio Dinner*, album, 1972

**3** Sir,
All thrushes (not only those in this neck of the Glyndebourne woods) sooner or later sing the tune of the first subject of Mozart's G minor Symphony (K.550) – and, what's more, phrase it a sight better than most conductors. The tempo is always dead right and there is no suggestion of an unauthorized accent on the ninth note of the phrase.
Yours &c.,
**Spike Hughes**, letter to *The Times*, 1962

**4** How do you like that bird I sent you home for your birthday? . . . You cooked it? . . . Mama, that was a South American parrot – he spoke five languages! . . . He should have SAID something? . . .
**George Jessel**, 'Phone Call to Mama', 1930s

**5** YOUNG WOMAN IN MUSEUM: What's that bird?
W. P. KER: It's a guillemot.
YOUNG WOMAN: That's not my idea of a guillemot.
W. P. KER: It's *God's* idea of a guillemot.
**W. P. Ker**, dialogue quoted in Geoffrey Madan's *Notebooks*, 1981

**6** Many amateurs still think that when birds sing and hop around, they are being merry and affectionate. They are not, of course; they are being aggressive and demanding the price of a cup of coffee. As, however, human beings are soft at heart and in the head, I suppose we shall go on regarding this thing as a much loved garden bird, even when it beats on the window with its beak and tells you to get that goddam food out on the bird table, or else.
**Miles Kington**, *Nature Made Ridiculously Simple*, 1983

**7** A rare old bird is the pelican;
His bill holds more than his belican.
He can take in his beak
Enough food for a week;
I'm darned if I know how the helican.
**Dixon Merritt**, *Nashville Banner*, 1913

**8** The song of canaries
Never varies
And when they're molting
They're revolting.
**Ogden Nash**, 'The Canary', *The Face is Familiar*, 1940

**9** . . . somewhere in the woods beyond the river a nightingale had begun to sing with all the full-throated zest of a bird conscious of having had a rave notice from the poet Keats and only a couple of nights ago a star spot on the programme of the BBC.
**P. G. Wodehouse**, *Ring for Jeeves*, 1953

# Birth

*See also Babies; Birth Control; Fathers; Gynaecology; Mothers; Pregnancy; Twins.*

**1** When I was born, I was so surprised I couldn't talk for a year and a half.
**Gracie Allen**, *The Robert Burns Panaella Program*, CBS Radio, 1932

**2** People are giving birth underwater now. They say it's less traumatic for the baby because it's in water, then it comes out into water. I guess it probably would be less traumatic for the baby, but certainly more traumatic for the other people in the pool.
**Elayne Boosler**, American comic

**3** Tragically, I was an only twin.
**Peter Cook**, *Sunday Times*, 1995

**4** My wife – God bless her – was in labor for thirty-two hours. And I was faithful to her the entire time.
**Jonathan Katz**, American comic

**5** To my embarrassment, I was born in bed with a lady.
**Wilson Mizner**, 1876–1933, American playwright

**6** Congratulations. We all knew you had it in you.
**Dorothy Parker**, telegram to friend who'd just given birth (Attrib.)

**7** My sister was in labor for 36 hours. Ow! She got wheeled out of delivery, looked at me and said, 'Adopt.'
**Caroline Rhea**, *Comic Relief*, HBO, 1992

**8** If you don't yell during labor, you're a fool. I screamed. Oh, how I screamed. And that was just during the conception.
**Joan Rivers**

**9** . . . I had a Jewish delivery: they knock you out with the first pain; they wake you up when the hairdresser shows.
**Joan Rivers**, *An Audience with Joan Rivers*, London Weekend Television, 1984

**10** My obstetrician was so dumb that when

I gave birth he forgot to cut the cord. For a year that kid followed me everywhere. It was like having a dog on a leash.
**Joan Rivers**, *An Audience with Joan Rivers*, London Weekend Television, 1984

**11** Announcement from the proud parents of a baby daughter. 'We have skirted the issue.'
**Earl Wilson**, 1907–87, American columnist

**12** What they put women through today when they're having a baby! They don't want to medicate them, as compared to previous generations. When my mom had me, she had so much medication, she didn't wake up till I was seven!
**Dennis Wolfberg**, *GQ*, 1999

**13** I was caesarean born. You can't really tell, although whenever I leave a house, I go out through a window.
**Steven Wright**, quoted in *Vanity Fair*, 1984

# Birth Control
*See also Birth; Gynaecology; Pregnancy; Sex.*

**1** Q: What do you call a man who doesn't believe in contraception?
A: Daddy.
**Anon.**

**2** My girlfriend just found out she's been taking aspirins instead of the pill. Well, at least she doesn't have a headache – but I do.
*Laugh-In*, NBC TV, 1969

**3** There's a new birth control pill for women. You put it between your knees and keep it there.
**Bill Barner**

**4** Whenever I hear people discussing birth control, I always remember that I was the fifth.
**Clarence Darrow**, 1857–1938, American lawyer

**5** The Pill came to market and changed the sexual and real-estate habits of millions; motel chains were created to serve them.
**Herbert Gold**, *The New York Times*, 1972

**6** Even though I'm single again, I'm still buying condoms. I don't want the woman at the store to think that I've stopped having sex. I don't really think that's any of her business. Although the condoms are

piling up, so I'm going to have to have a lucky streak or think of a crafts project.
**Jake Johannsen**

**7** He decided to have a vasectomy after a family vote on the matter. His kids voted fifteen to three in favour.
**Max Kauffmann**

**8** In a test program, forty drugstores in Washington State will be dispensing morning-after birth control pills without prescription. In fact, men can buy them in special gift packs with cards that say, 'Thanks, maybe I'll call you sometime.'
**Jay Leno**, *The Tonight Show*, NBC

**9** Contraceptives should be used on every conceivable occasion.
**Spike Milligan**, *The Last Goon Show of All*, BBC Radio, 1972

**10** Skullion had little use for contraceptives at the best of times. Unnatural, he called them, and placed them in the lower social category of things along with elastic-sided boots and made-up bow ties. Not the sort of attire for a gentleman.
**Tom Sharpe**, *Porterhouse Blue*, 1974

# Birthdays
*See also Age and Ageing; Gifts; Greeting Cards.*

**1** The only thing I want for my birthday is not to be reminded of it.
**Anon.**

**2** I always remember my wife's birthday. It's the day after she reminds me of it.
**Jerry Dennis**

**3** I think it's wonderful you could all be here for the forty-third anniversary of my thirty-ninth birthday. We decided not to light the candles this year – we were afraid Pan Am would mistake it for a runway.
**Bob Hope**, on his eighty-second birthday, 1985

# Bisexuality
*See also Homosexuality; Sex.*

**1** I can't understand why more people aren't bisexual. It would double your chances for a date on Saturday night.
**Woody Allen**

**2** Bisexuality is not so much a cop-out as a fearful compromise.
Jill Johnston, *Lesbian Nation*, 1973

## Boasts

*See also Humility; Modesty; Praise; Pride; Vanity.*

**1** When you're as great as I am, it's hard to be humble.
**Muhammad Ali** (Attrib.)

**2** The advantage of doing one's praising for oneself is that one can lay it on so thick and exactly in the right places.
**Samuel Butler**, *The Way of All Flesh*, 1903

**3** If only I had a little humility, I would be perfect.
**Ted Turner**, American broadcasting mogul (Attrib.)

## Body, The

*See also Exercise; Faces; Figures; Hair; Legs; Nudity.*

**1** Your body! After all, what is it? Just a physical covering, that's all – worth chemically thirty-two cents.
**Sidney Buchman and Seton I. Miller**, *Here Comes Mr Jordan*, screenplay, 1941

**2** Skin is like wax paper that holds everything in without dripping.
**Art Linkletter**, *A Child's Garden of Misinformation*, 1965

**3** I see my body as a temple or at least a relatively well-managed Presbyterian youth centre.
**Emo Philips**

## Bomb, The

*See also Nuclear Power; Nuclear War; Pacifism; Peace; War.*

**1** Don't get smart alecksy
With the galaxy
Leave the atom alone.
**E. Y. Harburg**, 'Leave the Atom Alone', 1957

**2** Cogito ergo boom.
**Susan Sontag**, *Styles of Radical Will*, 1969

**3** . . . the French are going the Americans one better with their Michelin bomb: it destroys only restaurants under four stars.
**Robin Williams**, interview in *Playboy*, 1982

## Books

*See also Best-sellers; Books – Critics; Books – Dedications; Dictionaries; Literature; Novels; Publishing; Reading; Writers; Writing.*

**1** Thank you for sending me a copy of your book. I'll waste no time in reading it.
**Anon.**

**2 Book Given as Gift Actually Read**

LONG BEACH, CA – the nation's publishing industry was rocked by Monday's news that a book given as a holiday gift was actually read and enjoyed by its recipient. According to reports, Long Beach schoolteacher Gavin Wallace completed James Gleick's *Genius: The Life and Science of Richard Feynman*, a present from his cousin.
. . . Wallace previously made headlines for his December 1996 consumption of a Hickory Farms gift basket.
*the Onion*, 1999–2000

**3** If I were ever going to read a book, it would be this one.
**Caroline Aherne**, cover quote for *My Canape Hell* by Imogen Edwards-Jones, 2000

**4** Child! do not throw this book about;
Refrain from the unholy pleasure
Of cutting all the pictures out!
Preserve it as your chiefest treasure.
**Hilaire Belloc**, *A Bad Child's Book of Beasts*, 1896

**5** DUFF: We've had a big best-seller . . . I haven't got round to it yet. I suspect the presence of allegory, which is always a slight deterrent.
**Alan Bennett**, *The Old Country*, 1978

**6** MOTHER: Bobby's teacher says he ought to have an encyclopaedia.
FATHER: Let him walk to school like I had to.
**Gyles Brandreth**, *1,000 Jokes: The Greatest Joke Book Ever Known*, 1980

**7** I wonder if what we are publishing now is worth cutting down trees to make paper for the stuff.
**Richard Brautigan**, 1934–84, American novelist and poet (Attrib.)

**8** There is a good saying to the effect that when a new book appears one should read an old one. As an author I would not

recommend too strict an adherence to this saying.
**Winston Churchill**

**9** Never lend books, for no one ever returns them; the only books I have in my library are books that other folk have lent me.
**Anatole France**, 1844–1924, French novelist

**10** Erratum
This slip has been inserted by mistake.
**Alasdair Gray**, erratum slip inserted in *Unlikely Stories, Mostly*, 1983

**11** It is the sort of book I keep meaning to write, very slim, in large type and with lots of illustrations. It must have taken them at least half an hour.
**Angus McGill**, *Standard*, 1983

**12** My favourite writers are Joyce, Tolstoy, Proust and Flaubert, but right now I am reading *The Little Engine That Could*.
**Emo Philips**

**13** Should not the Society of Indexers be known as Indexers, Society of, The?
**Keith Waterhouse**, English humorist

**14** They borrow books they will not buy,
They have no ethics or religions;
I wish some kind Burbankian guy
Could cross my books with homing pigeons.
**Carolyn Wells**, 'Book-borrowers'

**15** *Masterpieces* is a bouquet of pensées, culled, garnered and even untimely ripped from the fertile loins of the Wellsian imagination, time-weathered flotsam plucked from the raging delirium tremens of the creative process.
Here are jewelled insights, lovingly crafted by a veritable Fabergé amongst wordsmiths, hand-polished erections in the global village of contemporary sensibility, perceptions snatched from the outer limits of human experience, great miniatures acid-etched on the tender *film noir* of the mind's membrane . . . *Masterpieces* . . . The paperback!
**John Wells**, *Masterpieces*, 1982

# Books – Critics

*See also Books; Criticism; Critics; Critics – the Artist's View.*

**1** He writes so well, he makes me feel like putting my quill back in my goose.
**Fred Allen**

**2** That trees should have been cut down to provide paper for this book was an ecological affront.
**Anthony Blond**, *Spectator*, 1983

**3** *Sartor Resartus* is simply unreadable, and for me that always sort of spoils a book.
**Will Cuppy**, 1884–1949, American humorist

**4** One always tends to overpraise a long book because one has got through it.
**E. M. Forster**, 'T. E. Lawrence', *Abinger Harvest*, 1935

**5** From the moment I picked it [a book] up until I laid it down, I was convulsed with laughter. Some day I intend reading it.
**Groucho Marx** (Attrib.)

**6** This is not a novel to be tossed aside lightly. It should be thrown with great force.
**Dorothy Parker**, in a book review

**7** I never read a book before reviewing it – it prejudices a man so.
**Sydney Smith**, 1771–1845, clergyman and wit

**8** To see him fumbling with our rich and delicate language is to experience all the horror of seeing a Sèvres vase in the hands of a chimpanzee.
**Evelyn Waugh**, reviewing *World within World* by Stephen Spender, 1951

**9** George Meredith. His style is chaos illuminated by flashes of lightning. As a writer he has mastered everything except language: as a novelist he can do everything except tell a story: as an artist he is everything except articulate.
**Oscar Wilde**, 'The Decay of Lying', 1889

**10** He leads his readers to the latrine and locks them in.
**Oscar Wilde**, of the novelist and playwright George Moore (Attrib.)

**11** Mr Hall Caine, it is true, aims at the grandiose, but then he writes at the top of

his voice. He is so loud that one cannot hear what he says.
**Oscar Wilde**, 'The Decay of Lying', 1889

**12** Mr Henry James writes fiction as if it were a painful duty.
**Oscar Wilde**, 'The Decay of Lying', 1889

**13** M. Zola is determined to show that, if he has not got genius, he can at least be dull.
**Oscar Wilde**, 'The Decay of Lying', 1889

**14** One must have a heart of stone to read the death of Little Nell without laughing.
**Oscar Wilde** (Attrib.)

## Books – Dedications

*See also Books; Gratitude.*

**1** To Herbert Bayard Swope without whose friendly aid and counsel every line in this book was written.
**Franklin P. Adams**, 1881–1960, American journalist

**2** To my daughter Leonora without whose never-failing sympathy and encouragement this book would have been finished in half the time.
**P. G. Wodehouse**, *The Heart of a Goof*, 1926

## Boredom

*See also Bores.*

**1** George Sanders says: 'Here are some of the things that bored me to death.'
Most Boring Tiny Enslaved Country: tiny enslaved Latvia.
Most Boring Satellite: Tiros, the weather satellite.
Most Boring Chaucerian Grammatical Form: petrified dative.
Most Boring Mathematical Concept: tangent bundles.
Most Boring New Force for Social Change: married priests.
Most Boring Telephone Pleasantry: 'Good to hear your voice.'
Most Boring Illiterate Verbalization of Approval or Awe: 'Oh, wow!'
Most Boring Sex: women.
*National Lampoon*, 1972

**2** If you were searching for a word to describe the conversations that go on down the mine, boring would spring to your lips.

Oh, God! They're very boring. If you ever want to hear things like: 'Hello, I've found a bit of coal.' 'Have you really?' 'Yes, no doubt about it, this black substance is coal all right.' 'Jolly good, the very thing we're looking for.' It's not enough to keep the mind alive, is it?
**Peter Cook**, 'Sitting on a Bench', monologue, 1960s

**3** Ennui, felt on the proper occasions, is a sign of intelligence.
**Clifton Fadiman**, *Reading I've Liked*, 1958

**4** Oh don't the days seem lank and long
    When all goes right and nothing goes
        wrong,
    And isn't your life extremely flat
    With nothing whatever to grumble at!
**W. S. Gilbert**, *Princess Ida*, 1884

**5** The capacity of human beings to bore one another seems to be vastly greater than that of any other animals. Some of their most esteemed inventions have no other apparent purpose, for example, the dinner party of more than two, the epic poem, and the science of metaphysics.
**H. L. Mencken** (Attrib.)

**6** Boredom, after all, is a form of criticism.
**William Phillips**, *A Sense of the Present*, 1967

**7** Excuse me, my leg has gone to sleep. Do you mind if I join it?
**Alexander Woollcott**, 1887–1943, American columnist and critic (Attrib.)

## Bores

*See also Boredom; Insults.*

**1** Did you hear about the self-help group for compulsive talkers? It's called On and On Anon.
**Anon.**

**2** Our Billy's talk is just like bottled stout,
    You draw the cork and only froth comes
        out.
**Anon.**, *Truth*, Brisbane, 1916

**3** When there's nothing more to be said, he'll still be saying it.
**Anon.**

**4** VERA DUCKWORTH: One of these days,

someone's going to tie a knot in that flamin' windpipe of hers.
*Coronation Street*, Granada TV, of Hilda Ogden

**5** Doreen was okay, though. There was nothing wrong with her that a vasectomy of the vocal cords wouldn't fix.
**Lisa Alther**, *Kinflicks*, 1976

**6** He hasn't got much to say, but at least he doesn't try to say anything else.
**Robert Benchley** (Attrib.)

**7** He never spares himself in conversation. He gives himself so generously that hardly anybody else is permitted to give anything in his presence.
**Aneurin Bevan**, on Winston Churchill (Attrib.)

**8** You must be careful about giving any drink whatsoever to a bore. A lit-up bore is the worst in the world.
**Lord David Cecil**, 1964

**9** He's a man of few words – which he keeps on repeating.
**Jerry Dennis**

**10** Madam, don't you have any unexpressed thoughts?
**George S. Kaufman**, 1889–1961, American writer

**11** I've just spent an hour talking to Tallulah for a few minutes.
**Fred Keating**, on Tallulah Bankhead (Attrib.)

**12** He is not only a bore, but he bores for England.
**Malcolm Muggeridge**, of Sir Anthony Eden

**13** She has the reputation of being outspoken – by no one!
**Jack Paar**

**14** The only thing that can cheat her out of the last word is an echo.
**Sally Poplin**

**15** [Sen. Joseph] Biden's a good speaker – for the first hour.
**Phil Roeder**, Communications Director, Iowa Democratic Party, quoted in *Newsweek*, 1987

**16** I am one of those unhappy persons who inspire bores to the highest flights of art.
**Edith Sitwell**, 1887–1964, English poet and critic (Attrib.)

**17** Somebody's boring me – I think it's me.
**Dylan Thomas**, 1914–53, Welsh poet

**18** A healthy male adult bore consumes each year one and a half times his own weight in other people's patience.
**John Updike**, *Assorted Prose*, 1965

**19** In modern life nothing produces such an effect as a good platitude. It makes the whole world kin.
**Oscar Wilde**, *An Ideal Husband*, 1895

**20** MRS ALLONBY: . . . you should certainly know Ernest, Lady Stutfield. It is only fair to tell you beforehand he has got no conversation at all.
LADY STUTFIELD: I adore silent men.
MRS ALLONBY: Oh, Ernest isn't silent. He talks the whole time. But he has got no conversation.
**Oscar Wilde**, *A Woman of No Importance*, 1893

# Borrowing and Lending
*See also Banking; Credit; Credit Cards; Debt.*

**1** Don't borrow or lend, but if you must do one, lend.
**Josh Billings**, *The Complete Works of Josh Billings*, 1919

**2** He was an incorrigible borrower of money; he borrowed from all his friends; if he ever repaid a loan the incident failed to pass into history.
**Mark Twain**, *Autobiography*, 1924, of Bret Harte

# Bosses
*See also Big Business; Business; Leadership; The Office; Work.*

**1** You can't help liking the managing director – if you don't, he fires you.
**Anon.**

**2** I don't want any yes-men around me. I want everybody to tell me the truth even if it costs them their jobs.
**Samuel Goldwyn**, 1882–1974, American film producer (Attrib.)

**3** A boss is a person who's early when you're late and late when you're early.
**Sally Poplin**

# Boston

*See also America and the Americans; New England.*

**1** If you hear an owl hoot 'To whom,' instead of 'To who,' you can be certain he was born and educated in Boston.
**Anon.**

**2** Just returned from Boston. It is the only thing to do if you find yourself up there.
**Fred Allen**, letter to Groucho Marx, 1953

**3** I come from the city of Boston,
The home of the bean and the cod,
Where Cabots speak only to Lowells,
And Lowells speak only to God.
**Samuel C. Bushnell**, 'Boston', 1905

**4** Boston is a moral and intellectual nursery, always applying first principles to trifles.
**George Santayana**, 1863–1952, Spanish-born philosopher and critic

# Boxing

*See also Fighting; Self-Defence; Sport.*

**1** It's gonna be a thrilla, a chilla and a killa, when I get the gorilla in Manila.
**Muhammad Ali**, before his fight with Joe Frazier in the Philippines, 1975

**2** If you ever get belted and see three fighters through a haze, go after the one in the middle. That's what ruined me – I went after the two guys on the end.
**Max Baer**, World Heavyweight Champion, 1934–5

**3** It is like someone jammed an electric light bulb in your face and busted it. I thought half my head was blowed off.
**Jim Braddock**, on being hit by Joe Louis, 1937

**4** Nothing is going to stop Tyson that doesn't have a motor attached.
**David Brenner**, *The New York Times*, 1988

**5** [Muhammad Ali] was so quick he would click off the light and be in bed before the room got dark.
**George Foreman**, 1989

**6** He floats like an anchor, stings like a moth.
**Ray Gandolf**, American sports reporter on Muhammad Ali at the age of 39, 1981

**7** I was the only fighter in Cleveland who wore a rear-view mirror.
**Bob Hope**, quoted in *Bob Hope: Portrait of a Superstar*, 1981

**8** The hardest thing about prize fighting is picking up your teeth with a boxing glove on.
**Kin Hubbard**, 1868–1930, American humorist

**9** ERIC: I was a pretty handy fighter in my youth. I could lick any man with one hand . . .
ERNIE: Really?
ERIC: Yes, unfortunately, I could never find anyone with one hand who wanted a fight.
**Eric Morecambe and Ernie Wise**, *The Morecambe and Wise Joke Book*, 1979

**10** ERNIE: How did the fight go?
ERIC: Well, for a minute or two I was in with a great chance. Then it started. The bell went – I raced out of my corner, tried a left, then another left, then a right hook!
ERNIE: Fantastic!
ERIC: Then my opponent came out of his corner. But within a minute, I really had him worried.
ERNIE: Why?
ERIC: He thought he'd killed me.
**Eric Morecambe and Ernie Wise**, *The Morecambe and Wise Joke Book*, 1979

**11** First your legs go. Then you lose your reflexes. Then you lose your friends.
**Willie Pep**, World Featherweight Champion, 1942–8, 1949–50

**12** In boxing the right cross-counter is distinctly one of those things it is more blessed to give than to receive.
**P. G. Wodehouse**, *The Pothunters*, 1902

**13** I'll never forget my first fight . . . all of a sudden I found someone I knew in the fourth row. It was me. He hit me amongst my nose.
**Henny Youngman**, 1940

# Brain, The

*See also Memory; The Mind.*

**1** The brain is a wonderful organ. It starts working the moment you get up in the

morning, and does not stop until you get into the office.
**Robert Frost**, 1874–1963, American poet (Attrib.)

**2** The left hemisphere became the one to have if you were having only one.
**Howard Gardner**, *The Shattered Mind*, 1975

# Breakfast

*See also Bed; Eating; Food; Morning.*

**1** My wife and I tried to breakfast together, but we had to stop or our marriage would have been wrecked.
**Winston Churchill** (Attrib.)

**2** You may brag about your breakfast foods
   you eat at break of day,
   Your crisp, delightful shavings and your
   stack of last year's hay,
   Your toasted flakes of rye and corn that
   fairly swim in cream,
   Or rave about a sawdust mash, an
   epicurean dream.
   But none of these appeals to me, though
   all of them I've tried –
   The breakfast that I liked the best was
   sausage mother fried.
**Edgar A. Guest**, 'Sausage', *Collected Verse*, 1934

**3** The critical period in matrimony is breakfast-time.
**A. P. Herbert**, *Uncommon Law*, 1935

**4** Breakfast cereals that come in the same colors as polyester leisure suits make oversleeping a virtue.
**Fran Lebowitz**, *Metropolitan Life*, 1978

**5** ERIC: I always take my wife morning tea in my pyjamas. But is she grateful? No – she says she'd rather have it in a cup.
**Eric Morecambe and Ernie Wise**, *The Morecambe and Wise Joke Book*, 1979

**6** Continental breakfasts are very sparse, usually just a pot of coffee or tea and a teensy roll that looks like a suitcase handle. My advice is to go right to lunch without pausing.
**Miss Piggy**, *Miss Piggy's Guide to Life (As Told to Henry Beard)*, 1981

**7** In England people actually try to be brilliant at breakfast. That is so dreadful of

them! Only dull people are brilliant at breakfast.
**Oscar Wilde**, *An Ideal Husband*, 1895

# Breaking up

*see Love – Breaking up.*

# Britain and the British

*See also England and the English; Ireland and the Irish; Scotland and the Scots; Wales and the Welsh.*

**1** British Xenophobia takes the form of Insularism, and the Limeys all moved to an island some time ago to 'keep themselves to themselves', which as far as the rest of the world is concerned is a good thing.
*The National Lampoon Encyclopedia of Humor*, 1973

**2** The fact is that this is still the best place in the world for most things – to post a letter, go for a walk, watch television, buy a book, venture out for a drink, go to a museum, use the bank, get lost, seek help, or stand on a hillside and take in the view.
**Bill Bryson**, *Notes from a Small Island*, 1995

**3** I have a feeling that this island is uninhabitable, and therefore people have tried to make it habitable by being reasonable with one another.
**Ralf Dahrendorf**, quoted in *The New York Times*, 1976

**4** In peacetime the British may have many faults; but so far an inferiority complex has not been one of them.
**Lord Gladwyn**, *Observer*, 1967

**5** The British public has always had an unerring taste for ungifted amateurs.
**John Osborne**, 1929–94, English playwright, 1957

**6** You should ask me whether I have any message for the British public. I have. It is this: Might must find a way. Not 'Force', remember, other nations use 'force'; we Britons alone use 'Might'.
**Evelyn Waugh**, *Scoop*, 1938

# Budgets

*See also Accountancy; Economics; Economy; Expenses; Money; Stinginess; Wealth.*

**1** There are several ways in which to

apportion the family income, all of them unsatisfactory.
**Robert Benchley**

**2** Just about the time you think you can make both ends meet, somebody moves the ends.
**Pansy Penner**, *Reader's Digest*

**3** Some couples go over their budgets very carefully every month, others just go over them.
**Sally Poplin**

**4** All decent people live beyond their incomes nowadays, and those who aren't responsible live beyond other people's. A few gifted individuals manage to do both.
**Saki (H. H. Munro)**, 'The Matchmaker', 1911

**5** Solvency is entirely a matter of temperament and not of income.
**Logan Pearsall Smith**, *Afterthoughts*, 1931

**6** Anyone who lives within his means suffers from a lack of imagination.
**Lionel Stander**, American actor, quoted in *Playboy*, 1967

## Bureaucracy
*See also The Civil Service; Government; The Office.*

**1** Some civil servants are neither servants nor civil.
**Winston Churchill**

**2** Dear Mrs, Mr, Miss, or Mr and Mrs Daneeka: Words cannot express the deep personal grief I experienced when your husband, son, father or brother was killed, wounded or reported missing in action.
**Joseph Heller**, *Catch-22*, 1961

**3** If there's anything a public servant hates to do, it's something for the public.
**Kin Hubbard**, 1868–1930, American humorist

**4** The only thing that saves us from the bureaucracy is its inefficiency. An efficient bureaucracy is the greatest threat to liberty.
**Eugene McCarthy**, Senator and Congressman

## Business
*See also Big Business; Bosses; Contracts; The Office; Work.*

**1** There are two essential strategies in business:
1. Never reveal all you know.
**Anon.**

**2** He [the businessman] is the only man who is forever apologizing for his occupation.
**H. L. Mencken** (Attrib.)

# California

*See also America and the Americans; Hollywood; Los Angeles; San Francisco.*

**1** California is a great place – if you happen to be an orange.
**Fred Allen** (Attrib.)

**2** In California everyone goes to a therapist, is a therapist, or is a therapist going to a therapist.
**Truman Capote** (Attrib.)

**3** Mistresses are more common in California – in fact some of them are very common. It's easier for a man to conceal his mistress there because of the smog.
**Groucho Marx** (Attrib.)

# Canada and the Canadians

**1** Canada is a country so square that even the female impersonators are women.
**Richard Benner**, *Outrageous!*, screenplay, 1977

**2** Americans are benevolently ignorant about Canada, while Canadians are malevolently well-informed about the United States.
**John Bartlet Brebner**, Canadian author and scholar

**3** You have to know a man awfully well in Canada to know his surname.
**John Buchan**, 1875–1940, Scottish author and Governor-General of Canada, quoted in the *Observer*, 1950

**4** The beaver is a good national symbol for Canada. He's so busy chewing he can't see what's going on.
**Howard Cable**

**5** Canada could have enjoyed:
English government,
French culture,
and American know-how.
Instead it ended up with:
English know-how,
French government,
and American culture.
**John Robert Colombo**, 'Oh Canada', 1965

**6** Americans like to make money:
Canadians like to audit it. I know of no

country where accountants have a higher social and moral status.
**Northrop Frye**, 1912–91, Canadian critic

**7** In any world menu, Canada must be considered the vichyssoise of nations – it's cold, half-French, and difficult to stir.
**Stuart Keate**, 1913–87, Canadian journalist (Attrib.)

**8** Canadians use English for literature, Scotch for sermons and American for conversation.
**Stephen Leacock**, 1869–1944, Canadian humorist

**9** Canada is the only country in the world that knows how to live without an identity.
**Marshall McLuhan**, 1911–80, Canadian author (Attrib.)

**10** *Racial characteristics*: hard to tell a Canadian from an extremely boring regular white person unless he's dressed to go outdoors. Very little is known of the Canadian country since it is rarely visited by anyone but the Queen and illiterate sport fishermen.
**P. J. O'Rourke**, 'Foreigners Around the World', *National Lampoon*, 1976

# Cancer

*See also Doctors; Health; Hospitals; Illness; Medicine.*

**1** You know, my father died of cancer when I was a teenager. He had it before it became popular.
**Goodman Ace**, quoted in the *New Yorker*, 1977

**2** Cancer is caused by fear of malignant tumors.
**George Carlin**, *Brain Droppings*, 1997

**3** You show me something that doesn't cause cancer, and I'll show you something that isn't on the market yet.
**George Carlin**, *Brain Droppings*, 1997

**4** My final word, before I'm done,
Is 'Cancer can be rather fun.'
Thanks to the nurses and Nye Bevan
The NHS is quite like heaven
Provided one confronts the tumour
With a sufficient sense of humour.
I know that cancer often kills,
But so do cars and sleeping pills;
And it can hurt one till one sweats,

So can bad teeth and unpaid debts.
**J. B. S. Haldane**, 'Cancer's a Funny Thing', *New Statesman*, 1964

**5** DRUMM: I have this . . . tummy trouble. I told a certain person – I don't know why, out of mischief, it isn't like me – I told him cancer was suspected. Quite untrue. Of course he told others, and since then my popularity has soared. I said to one man: 'I know you for a rogue and a blackguard.' Was he offended? 'You're right,' he said, 'come and have a drink.' I did.
CHARLIE: There'll be ructions when you don't die.
DRUMM: There will.
**Hugh Leonard**, *Da*, 1973

# Candour

**1** If you can't be direct, why be?
**Lily Tomlin**

# Cannibalism

*See also Expeditions; Missionaries.*

**1** Cannibals are not vegetarians. They are humanitarians.
**Anon.**

**2** These ferocious cannibals captured a poor missionary – he gave them their first taste of religion.
**Anon.**

**3** A cannibal is a guy who goes into a restaurant and orders the waiter.
**Jack Benny** (Attrib.)

**4** I came across a tribe of cannibals who'd been converted by Roman Catholic missionaries. Now, on Friday, they only eat fishermen.
**Max Kauffmann**

**5** . . . the better sort of Ishmaelites have been Christian for many centuries and will not publicly eat human flesh, uncooked in Lent, without special and costly dispensation from their bishop.
**Evelyn Waugh**, *Scoop*, 1938

# Capitalism

*See also Big Business; Business; Communism; Conservatism; The Conservative Party; Marxism; Socialism.*

**1** The inherent vice of capitalism is the unequal sharing of blessings; the inherent virtue of socialism is the equal sharing of miseries.
**Winston Churchill**

**2** The fundamentals of capitalist ethics require that, 'You shall earn your bread in sweat' – unless you happen to have private means.
**M. Kalecki**, 'Political Aspects of Full Employment'

**3** The trouble with the profit system has always been that it was highly unprofitable to most people.
**E. B. White**, *One Man's Meat*, 1944

# Capital Punishment

*See also Crime; Murder; Prison.*

**1** Why Do We Kill People Who Kill People To Show That Killing People Is Wrong?
**T-shirt**, Florida 2000

**2** When I came back to Dublin, I was court-martialled in my absence and sentenced to death in my absence, so I said they could shoot me in my absence.
**Brendan Behan**, *The Hostage*, 1959

**3** President Bush was *against* abortion, but *for* capital punishment. Spoken like a true fisherman; throw them back, kill them when they're bigger.
**Elayne Boosler**, *Comic Relief*, HBO, 1986

# Cars

*See also Driving; Parking; Travel.*

**1 Trabant jokes**
Q: How do you double the value of a Trabant?
A: Fill the tank with gas.
Q: What information is contained in each new Trabant owner's manual?
A: The bus timetable.
Q: What's the difference between a Trabant and a golf ball?
A: You can drive a golf ball 200 yards.
Q: How do you overtake a Trabant?
A: Just keep walking.
Q: How do you make a Trabant disappear?
A: Apply rust remover.
Q: What are the instructions on the new Trabant airbags?
A: In case of accident, start blowing.
**Anon.**

**2** . . . there are two types of car owners. The first type is those who left school early. Such people crawl under stopped cars, adjust the grommets, strip down the carburettor manifold, suck petrol through the sump gasket, spit it out manfully and make the car go.
The other type is the educated few. We are strong on the ontological insecurity of nineteenth-century novelists. When our cars stop we ring the AA as soon as we have finished crying.
**Joe Bennett**, *Fun Run and Other Oxymorons*, 2000

**3** Brooding upon its unexerted power,
Deep in the gas-tank lay the gasoline
Awaiting the inevitable hour
When from the inward soul of the machine
Would come the Call. Ah, hark! Man's touch awakes
Th'ignition switch! The starting motor hums;
A sound of meshing gears, releasing brakes!
The call of Duty to the gas-tank comes.
**Morris Bishop**, 'Gas and Hot Air', *Spilt Milk*, 1942

**4** It [the Vauxhall 30-98] had great long con-rods that rose majestically and sank again lolloping with easy leisure and dipping into the sump oil.
The old 'Thirty Ninety-eight', when you started her up, used to say, 'Guddugety-Guddugety-Gonk, Guddugety-Guddugety-Gonk' and would speak to no other motor car – unless it was one of W. O. Bentley's majestic green monsters who could civilly reply, 'Berdoobely-Berdoobely-Bonk, Berdoobely-Berdoobely-Bonk'.
**Cassandra (William Connor)**, *Daily Mirror*, 1961

**5** . . . the automotive equivalent of a quail's egg dipped in celery salt and served in Julia Roberts' belly button.
**Jeremy Clarkson**, describing the Ferrari F355

**6** The interior of the V8 may be surprisingly cramped but, despite that, this is not a car for small people. You'd look stupid driving this unless you were at least 6ft. 3in. and 14 stone. Other people who would look stupid in it include Liberal Democrats, Freemasons, folk singers, nancy-boy footballers, vicars, scoutmasters, people who like DIY or Michael Bolton, women, environmentalists and anyone who has ever been to a poetry reading. You can't even think about driving this car if you like salad. Socialists are right out. So are people who use the words 'toilet', 'nourishing' or 'settee' . . . The V8 is for those of us who like our beer brown and our fags to be high on tar and low on lentils.
**Jeremy Clarkson**, *Born to be Riled*, 1999, describing the Aston Martin V8

**7** The automobile changed our dress, manners, social customs, vacation habits, the shape of our cities, consumer purchasing patterns, common tastes and positions in intercourse.
**John Ketas**, *The Insolent Chariots*

**8** Hood ornaments. They were just lovely, and they gave a sense of respect. And they took 'em away because if you can save one human life – that's always the argument – it's worth it, if you can save one human life. Actually, I'd be willing to trade maybe a dozen human lives for a nice hood ornament. I imagine those things really did tend to stick in bicyclists.
**Michael O'Donoghue**, quoted in *Playboy*, 1983

**9** Dear Miss Piggy,
My car engine turns over, but it won't start. I've checked the plugs, the points, the condenser, the coil, the distributor, and I even sprayed carburettor cleaner in the carb, but no dice. What gives?
Stuck.

Dear Stuck,
It sounds to me like your car is broken. If you need it soon, I would get it fixed.
**Miss Piggy**, *Miss Piggy's Guide to Life (As Told to Henry Beard)*, 1981

**10** Take most people, they're crazy about cars . . . I don't even like old cars. I mean they don't even interest me. I'd rather have a goddam horse. A horse is at least human for God's sake.
**J. D. Salinger**, *The Catcher in the Rye*, 1951

**11** Mr Wooster being one of those easy-going young gentlemen who will drive a car but never take the trouble to study its mechanism, I felt justified in becoming technical.
'I think it is the differential gear, sir. Either that, or the exhaust.'
**P. G. Wodehouse**, *Carry on, Jeeves*, 1925

**12** I couldn't repair your brakes so I made your horn louder.
**Steven Wright**, American comic

# Catholicism

*See also Christianity; The Church; Jesus Christ; Religion.*

**1** There's nothing sexier than a lapsed Catholic.
**Woody Allen**, *Alice*, 1990

**2** He was of the faith chiefly in the sense that the church he currently did not attend was Catholic.
**Kingsley Amis**, *One Fat Englishman*, 1963

**3** THE POPE: My brothers, I bring you good news and I bring you bad news. The good news is that I have just received a phone call from Christ, who has returned to earth. The bad news is that he was calling from Salt Lake City.
**Monsignor Geno Baroni**, quoted in the *Wall Street Journal*

**4** Confession, *n.* the acknowledgement made to a priest of a sinful act committed by a friend, neighbor or acquaintance, and to which you reacted with righteous indignation.
**Ambrose Bierce**, *The Devil's Dictionary*, 1911

**5** There's only one difference between Catholics and Jews. Jews are born with guilt and Catholics have to go to school to learn it.
**Elayne Boosler**, American comic

**6** . . . Catholicism is like Howard Johnson, and what they have are these franchises and they give all these people different franchises in the different countries but they have one government, and when you

buy the Howard Johnson franchise you can apply it to the geography – whatever's cool for that area – and then you, you know, pay the bread to the main office.
**Lenny Bruce**, *The Essential Lenny Bruce*, 1972

**7** For what have they not lost, these Latins, with their Catholicism! One limerick is worth all the musty old saints in their Calendar. Saints are dead – they have died out from sheer inability to propagate their species.
**Norman Douglas**, *Some Limericks*, 1928

**8** High Anglo-Catholics are beneath
    contempt –
  All intellectual and moral wrecks.
  They love the frills but hold themselves
    exempt
  From self-denial in the line of sex.
**James Fenton and John Fuller**, 'Poem against Catholics', *New Review*, 1976

**9** They call their horrid children after saints
  And educate them by such dubious
    means
  They eagerly succumb to strange
    complaints
  Or turn psychotic in their early teens.
**James Fenton and John Fuller**, 'Poem against Catholics', *New Review*, 1976

**10** She had once been a Catholic, but discovering that priests were infinitely more attentive when she was in process of losing or regaining faith in Mother Church, she maintained an enchantingly wavering attitude.
**F. Scott Fitzgerald**, *This Side of Paradise*, 1920

**11** As a Roman Catholic I thank God for the heretics. Heresy is only another word for freedom of thought.
**Graham Greene**, 1904–91, British novelist

**12** Give me Catholicism every time. Father Cheeryble with his thurible; Father Chatterjee with his liturgy. What fun they have with all their charades and conundrums. If it weren't for the Christianity they insist on mixing with it, I'd be converted tomorrow.
**Aldous Huxley**, *Time Must Have a Stop*, 1944

**13** It often happens that I wake at night and begin to think about a serious problem and decide I must tell the Pope about it. Then I wake up completely and remember that I *am* the Pope.
**Pope John XXIII**, 1960

**14** It is now quite lawful for a Catholic woman to avoid pregnancy by a resort to mathematics, though she is still forbidden to resort to physics and chemistry.
**H. L. Mencken**, *Minority Report*, 1956

**15** I have nothing against the Jesuits but I wouldn't want my daughter to marry one.
**Patrick Murray**

**16** A Protestant married a devout Catholic
    wife,
  And she led him a catechism and dogma
    life.
**Keith Preston**, quoted in *The Lilt of the Irish*, 1978

# Cats

*See also Animals; Pets; Vets.*

**1** Cat, *n.* a soft, indestructible automaton provided by nature to be kicked when things go wrong in the domestic circle.
**Ambrose Bierce**, *The Devil's Dictionary*, 1911

**2** I don't know what the cat can have eaten. Usually I know exactly what the cat has eaten. Not only have I fed it to the cat, at the cat's keen insistence, but the cat has thrown it up on the rug and someone has tracked it all the way over on to the other rug. I don't know why cats are such habitual vomiters. They don't seem to enjoy it, judging by the sounds they make while doing it. It's in their nature. A dog is going to bark. A cat is going to vomit.
**Roy Blount Jr.**, *Esquire*, 1984

**3** You always ought to have tom cats arranged, you know – it makes 'em more companionable.
**Noel Coward**

**4** I-I-I can't stand it . . . I gotta have a bird . . . I'm weak . . . *I'm weak!* . . . But I don't care! I can't help it! After all, I *am* a pussycat!
**Warren Foster**, *Birds Anonymous*, Warner Bros., cartoon, 1955

**5** Cats are intended to teach us that not everything in nature has a purpose.
**Garrison Keillor**

**6** I saw a commercial for cat food that said, 'All natural food for your cat.' But cat food is made out of horse meat. That's how it works in nature – the cat right above the horse on the food chain. Matter of fact, every time my kitty feels a little cooped up in his environment, I take him down to the racetrack, let him stalk some prey.
**Norm McDonald**

**7** I gave my cat a bath the other day. They love it. He enjoyed it, it was fun for me. The fur would stick to my tongue but other than that . . .
**Steve Martin**

**8** There is something going on now in Mexico that I happen to think is cruelty to animals. What I'm talking about, of course, is cat juggling.
**Steve Martin**

**9** Cats sit in laps because it's warm there. They don't care if it's you or the radiator, so it certainly was a compliment when the owner said the cat liked me. Who had this cat met that it was comparing me to? The maid? Another cat? Here's an animal which can't read, that hasn't been out of the house in God knows when, lives on free milk and garbage, and this bum has an opinion? Two years old, doesn't have a cent. No clothes. Owns one rotten rubber ball. For big entertainment it scratches on the upholstery. And this green-eyed impoverished snob likes me? Thanks a group.
**Henry Morgan**

**10** The trouble with a kitten is
   THAT
   Eventually it becomes a
   CAT.
**Ogden Nash**, 'The Kitten', *The Face is Familiar*, 1940

**11** Cats are to dogs what modern people are to the people we used to have. Cats are slimmer, cleaner, more attractive, disloyal, and lazy. It's easy to understand why the cat has eclipsed the dog as modern America's favorite pet. People like pets to possess the same qualities they do. Cats are irresponsible and recognize no authority, yet are completely dependent on others for their material needs. Cats cannot be made to do anything useful. Cats are mean for the fun of it. In fact, cats possess so many of the same qualities as some people (expensive girlfriends, for instance) that it's often hard to tell the people and the cats apart.
**P. J. O'Rourke**, *Modern Manners*, 1983

**12** Why lefties have such a pronounced affinity for these dislikable, useless, and eminently unendangered knaves of the animal kingdom is no mystery. Cats are disloyal, self-regarding layabouts with nothing but contempt for those who feed and protect them. Left-wingers acknowledge this likeness by giving cats names such as 'Che,' 'Chairman Meow,' and 'Linda Ellerbee.'
**P. J. O'Rourke**, *The Enemies List*, 1996

**13** We've got a cat called Ben Hur. We called it Ben till it had kittens.
**Sally Poplin**

**14** RALPH WIGGUM: My cat's breath smells like cat food.
**Mike Scully**, 'Lisa's Rival', *The Simpsons*, Fox TV, 1994

# Celebrities

*See also Fame.*

**1** I have often thought of forming a Society for the Prevention of Cruelty to Celebrities. Apparently for certain individuals, men and women in the public eye are fair game to be knocked off their balance occasionally and made to look foolish. You know, a central figure at a social function isn't always as happy as he looks.
**Noel Coward** (Attrib.)

**2** To be a celebrity in America is to be forgiven everything.
**Mary McGrory**, quoted in *The New York Times*, 1976

**3** A celebrity is any well-known TV or movie star who looks like he spends more than two hours working on his hair.
**Steve Martin**, *Playboy*, 1984

**4** A celebrity is one who is known to many persons he is glad he doesn't know.
**H. L. Mencken**

**5** You can't shame or humiliate modern celebrities. What used to be called shame and humiliation is now called publicity. And forget traditional character

assassination. If you say a modern celebrity is an adulterer, a pervert, and a drug addict, all it means is that you've read his autobiography.
**P. J. O'Rourke**, *The Enemies List*, 1996

**6 The Five Stages of Stardom**
'First: Who is Tommy Steele?'
'Second: Get me Tommy Steele.'
'Third: Get me a Tommy Steele lookalike.'
'Fourth: Get me a younger Tommy Steele.'
'Fifth: Who is Tommy Steele?'
**Tommy Steele**, Variety Club Showbusiness Awards, 1995

# Celibacy
*See also Abstinence; Chastity; Virginity.*

**1** . . . the worst form of self-abuse.
**Peter De Vries**, quoted in *The New York Times*, 1983

# Censorship
*See also Morality; Obscenity; Pornography; Prudery; Puritanism; Reformers.*

**1** There's so much comedy on television. Does that cause comedy in the streets?
**Dick Cavett**, 1994

**2** When there is official censorship it is a sign that speech is serious. When there is none, it is pretty certain that the official spokesmen have all the loudspeakers.
**Paul Goodman**, *Growing Up Absurd*, 1960

**3** Senator Smoot (Republican, Ut.)
Is planning a ban on smut.
Oh rooti-ti-toot for Smoot of Ut.
And his reverent occiput.
Smite, Smoot, smite for Ut.,
Grit your molars and do your dut.,
Gird up your l——ns,
Smite h——p and th——gh,
We'll all be Kansas
By and by.
**Ogden Nash**, 'Invocation', 1931

**4** A censor is a man who knows more than he thinks you ought to.
**Dr Laurence J. Peter**, *Peter's Quotations*, 1977

**5** If a man is pictured chopping off a woman's breast, it only gets an 'R' rating; but if, God forbid, a man is pictured kissing a woman's breast, it gets an 'X' rating. Why is violence more acceptable than tenderness?
**Sally Struthers**, actress, quoted in *Life*, 1984

**6** If you are a songwriter, did anyone ask you if you wanted to spend the rest of your career modifying your lyric content to suit the spiritual needs of an imaginary eleven-year-old?
**Frank Zappa**, *The Real Frank Zappa Book*, 1989

# Champagne
*See also Drink; Parties; Wine.*

**1** Here's to champagne, the drink divine
That makes us forget our troubles.
It is made of a dollar's worth of wine
And three dollars' worth of bubbles.
**Anon.**

**2** No government could survive without champagne. Champagne in the throat of our diplomatic people is like oil in the wheels of an engine.
**Joseph Dargent**, *New York Herald Tribune*, 1955

**3** I hate champagne more than anything else in the world next to Seven-Up.
**Elaine Dundy**, *The Dud Avocado*, 1958

# Change
*See also Conservatism; Progress.*

**1** Change is inevitable . . . except from a vending machine.
**Anon.**

**2** Constant change is here to stay.
**Anon.**

**3** Most of the change we think we see in life is due to truths being in and out of favor.
**Robert Frost**, 'The Black Cottage', 1914

**4** If you want to make enemies, try to change something.
**Woodrow Wilson**, *Woodrow Wilson Selections for Today*

# Charm
*See also Flirtation; Seduction.*

**1** All charming people have something to conceal, usually their total dependence on the appreciation of others.
**Cyril Connolly**, *Enemies of Promise*, 1938

**2** Charming people live up to the very edge of their charm, and behave just as outrageously as the world will let them.
**Logan Pearsall Smith**, *Afterthoughts*, 1931

**3** A beauty is a woman you notice; a charmer is one who notices you.
**Adlai Stevenson**, speech at Radcliffe College, 1963

**4** All charming people, I fancy, are spoiled. It is the secret of their attraction.
**Oscar Wilde**, 'The Portrait of Mr W.H.', 1901

# Chastity

*See also Abstinence; Celibacy; Prudery; Puritanism; Sex; Virginity.*

**1** Chastity is curable, if detected early.
**Graffito**, Exeter, 1978

**2** The last time I was inside a woman was when I visited the Statue of Liberty.
**Woody Allen**, *Crimes and Misdemeanors*, screenplay, 1989

**3** MRS WICKSTEED: Of course I've known for years our marriage has been a mockery. My body lying there night after night in the wasted moonlight. I know now how the Taj Mahal must feel.
**Alan Bennett**, *Habeas Corpus*, 1973

**4** Of all sexual aberrations, chastity is the strangest.
**Anatole France**, 1844–1924, French novelist

**5** . . . that melancholy sexual perversion known as continence.
**Aldous Huxley**, *Antic Hay*, 1923

**6** The wonderful thing about celibacy is that you don't have to bother reading the manual.
**Sheldon Keller**

**7** I'd the upbringing a nun would envy . . . Until I was fifteen I was more familiar with Africa than my own body.
**Joe Orton**, *Entertaining Mr Sloane*, 1954

**8** As a child of eight Mr Trout had once kissed a girl of six under the mistletoe at a Christmas party, but there his sex life had come to abrupt halt.
**P. G. Wodehouse**, *Bachelors Anonymous*, 1973

# Cheese

*See also Eating; Food; Wine.*

**1** Poets have been mysteriously silent on the subject of cheese.
**G. K. Chesterton**, 1874–1936, English essayist and poet

**2** Claret, dear, not Coca-Cola,
When you're having Gorgonzola –
Be particular to serve the proper wines;
Likewise pick a Beaune, not Coke for
Pointing up a Bleu or Roquefort
Bless the products of the bovines and the vines!
**William Cole**, *What a Friend We Have in Cheeses!*

**3** What a friend we have in cheeses!
For no food more subtly pleases,
Nor plays so grand a gastronomic part;
Cheese imported – not domestic –
For we all get indigestic
From all the pasteurizer's Kraft and sodden art.
**William Cole**, *What a Friend We Have in Cheeses!*

**4** Cheese. The adult form of milk.
**Richard Condon**, *A Talent for Loving*, 1961

**5** Cheese – milk's leap forward to immortality.
**Clifton Fadiman**, *Any Number Can Play*, 1957

# Chicago

*See also America and the Americans.*

**1** Chicago is not the most corrupt American city – it's the most theatrically corrupt.
**Studs Terkel**, *The Dick Cavett Show*, PBS, 1978

# Childhood

*See also Adolescence; Children; Parents; School; Teenagers; Youth.*

**1** I was raised by just my mom. See, my father died when I was eight years old. At least that's what he told us in the letter.
**Drew Carey**

**2** When I played in the sandbox, the cat kept covering me up.
**Rodney Dangerfield**

**3** When I was a kid my parents moved a lot
– but I always found them.
**Rodney Dangerfield**

**4** ERIC: When I was eight I ran away with a
circus.
ERNIE: Really?
ERIC: Yes. Then, when I was nine, they
made me bring it back again.
**Eric Morecambe and Ernie Wise,** *The Morecambe and
Wise Joke Book,* 1979

**5** I was a very unpopular child. I had only
two friends. They were imaginary. And they
would only play with each other.
**Judy Tenuta**

**6** We had a quicksand box in our backyard.
I was an only child. Eventually.
**Steven Wright,** American comic

**7** When I was a kid, I had no watch. I used
to tell the time by my violin. I used to
practice in the middle of the night and the
neighbors would yell, 'Fine time to practice
the violin, three o'clock in the morning!'
**Henny Youngman**

# Children

*See also Adolescence; Babies; Childhood; Orphans;
Parents; School; Teenagers.*

**1 Children's books you *won't* see:**

– Garfield Gets Feline Leukemia
– You Are Different And That's Bad
– Daddy Drinks Because You Cry
– Strangers Have the Best Candy
– Why Can't Mr Fork and Miss Electrical
Outlet Be Friends?
– The Kid's Guide to Hitchhiking
– What Is That Dog Doing to That Other
Dog?
– The Boy Who Died Through Eating All His
Vegetables
– Controlling the Playground – Respect
Through Fear
**Anon.**

**2** Insanity is hereditary. You get it from
your kids.
**Badge,** Brussels, 1984

**3** I wish I'd been a mixed infant.
**Brendan Behan,** *The Hostage,* 1959

**4** A child develops individuality long before
he develops taste. I have seen my kid
struggle into the kitchen in the morning
with outfits that need only one accessory:
an empty gin bottle.
**Erma Bombeck,** *If Life is a Bowl of Cherries – What am I
Doing in the Pits?,* 1978

**5** I read one psychologist's theory that said,
'Never strike a child in anger.' When could I
strike him? When he is kissing me on my
brithday? When he is recuperating from
measles? Do I slap the Bible out of his hand
on a Sunday?
**Erma Bombeck,** *If Life is a Bowl of Cherries – What am I
Doing in the Pits?,* 1978

**6** It puzzles me how a child can see a dairy
bar three miles away, but cannot see a 4 by 6
rug that has scrunched up under his feet
and has been dragged through two rooms.
Maybe you know why a child can reject a
hot dog with mustard served on a soft bun
at home, yet eat six of them two hours later
at fifty cents each.
**Erma Bombeck,** *If Life is a Bowl of Cherries – What am I
Doing in the Pits?,* 1978

**7** I've seen kids ride bicycles, run, play ball,
set up a camp, swing, fight a war, swim and
race for eight hours . . . yet have to be
driven to the garbage can.
**Erma Bombeck,** *If Life is a Bowl of Cherries – What am I
Doing in the Pits?,* 1978

**8** As soon as I stepped out of my mother's
womb on to dry land, I realized that I had
made a mistake – that I shouldn't have
come, but the trouble with children is that
they are not returnable.
**Quentin Crisp,** *The Naked Civil Servant,* 1968

**9** When I was a child, what I wanted to be
when I grew up was an invalid.
**Quentin Crisp,** *The Naked Civil Servant,* 1968

**10** If your parents didn't have any children,
there's a good chance that you won't have
any.
**Clarence Day,** 1874–1935, American writer

**11** I don't believe in smacking children – I
just use a cattle prod.
**Jenny Eclair,** English comedienne

**12** Ah, the patter of little feet around the
house. There's nothing like having a midget
for a butler.
**W. C. Fields** (Attrib.)

**13** Anybody who hates children and dogs can't be all bad.
**W. C. Fields** (Attrib.)

**14** I love children . . . parboiled.
**W. C. Fields** (Attrib.)

**15** I never met a kid I liked.
**W. C. Fields** (Attrib.)

**16** There's not a man in America who at one time or another hasn't had a secret desire to boot a child in the ass.
**W. C. Fields** (Attrib.)

**17** Father, chancing to chastise
His indignant daughter Sue,
Said: 'I hope you realize
That this hurts me more than you.'

Susan straightway ceased to roar;
'If that's really true,' said she,
'I can stand a good deal more;
Pray go on, and don't mind me.'
**Harry Graham**, *Ruthless Rhymes*, 1899

**18** Father heard his Children scream,
So he threw them in the stream,
Saying as he drowned the third,
'Children should be seen, not heard!'
**Harry Graham**, *Ruthless Rhymes*, 1899

**19** STEPHEN: What have you got against having children?
SIMON: Well, Steve, in the first place there isn't enough room. In the second place they seem to start by mucking up their parents' lives, and then go on in the third place to muck up their own. In the fourth place it doesn't seem right to bring them into a world like this in the fifth place and in the sixth place I don't like them very much in the first place. OK.
**Simon Gray**, *Otherwise Engaged*, 1975

**20** All God's children are not beautiful. Most of God's children are, in fact, barely presentable.
**Fran Lebowitz**, *Metropolitan Life*, 1978

**21** Ask your child what he wants for dinner only if he's buying.
**Fran Lebowitz**, *Social Studies*, 1981

**22** Never allow your child to call you by your first name. He hasn't known you long enough.
**Fran Lebowitz**, *Social Studies*, 1981

**23** Notoriously insensitive to subtle shifts in mood, children will persist in discussing the color of a recently sighted cement mixer long after one's own interest in the topic has waned.
**Fran Lebowitz**, *Metropolitan Life*, 1978

**24** By all the published facts in the case,
Children belong to the human race.

Equipped with consciousness, passions, pulse,
They even grow up and become adults.

So why's the resemblance, moral or mental,
Of children to people so coincidental?
**Phyllis McGinley**, 'About Children', *Times Three: 1932–1960*, 1960

**25** Kids. They're not easy. But there has to be some penalty for sex.
**Bill Maher**

**26** If a child shows himself incorrigible, he should be decently and quietly beheaded at the age of twelve.
**Don Marquis**

**27** My mother loved children – she would have given anything if I'd been one.
**Groucho Marx**

**28** I love children. Especially when they cry – for then someone takes them away.
**Nancy Mitford**, 1904–73, English writer

**29** Oh, what a tangled web do parents weave
When they think that their children are naive.
**Ogden Nash**, 'Baby, What Makes the Sky Blue', 1940

**30** THELMA CATES: You're my child!
JESSIE CATES: I'm what became of your child!
**Marsha Norman**, *'Night, Mother*, screenplay, 1986

**31** The quickest way for a parent to get a child's attention is to sit down and look comfortable.
**Lane Olinghouse**, *Wall Street Journal*

**32** Do your kid a favor – don't have any.
**Robert Orben**, *Variety*, 1972

**33** We've begun to long for the pitter-patter of little feet. So we bought a dog. Well, it's cheaper and you get more feet.
**Rita Rudner**

**34** A child hasn't a grown-up person's appetite for affection. A little of it goes a long way with them; and they like a good imitation of it better than the real thing, as every nurse knows.
**George Bernard Shaw**, *Getting Married*, 1911

**35** In my Rogues' Gallery of repulsive small boys I suppose he would come about third.
**P. G. Wodehouse**, *Thank You, Jeeves*, 1934

# Christianity

*See also Belief; The Bible; Catholicism; The Church; God; Jesus Christ; Protestantism; Religion.*

**1** The trouble with born-again Christians is that they are an even bigger pain the second time around.
**Herb Caen**, *San Francisco Chronicle*, 1981

**2** The Christian ideal has not been tried and found wanting, it has been found difficult and left untried.
**G. K. Chesterton**, 'The Unfinished Temple', *What's Wrong with the World*, 1910

**3** Christian endeavor is notoriously hard on female pulchritude.
**H. L. Mencken**, *American Mercury*, 1931

**4** The act of worship, as carried on by Christians, seems to me to be debasing rather than ennobling. It involves groveling before a Being who, if He really exists, deserves to be denounced instead of respected.
**H. L. Mencken** (Attrib.)

**5** If I had been the Virgin Mary, I would have said 'No'.
**Stevie Smith**, 1902–71, English poet

# Christmas

*See also Gifts; Greetings Cards.*

**1** Christmas comes, but once a year is enough.
**Anon.**

**2** It was just before Christmas and I said to my wife, 'Darling, I think we should have your mother round on Christmas Day. She said, 'But we've had her round on Christmas Day for the last thirty years.'

I said, 'I know. But I was thinking that this year we should let her in.'
**Anon.**

**3** In Honor of the Birth of Our Saviour, Try-N-Save is Open All Day Christmas
**Sign outside convenience store**, *The Simpsons*, Fox TV

**4** Santa Claus has the right idea,
Visit people once a year.
**Victor Borge**, Danish pianist

**5** Our children await Christmas presents like politicians getting election returns; there's the Uncle Fred precinct and the Aunt Ruth district still to come in.
**Marcelene Cox**, *Ladies' Home Journal*, 1950

**6** This happened last December when the radio station WHLD called up the British ambassador in Washington and said, if you could have anything for Christmas, what would it be? And he thought 'Oh God, I'd better be careful here. It could be a big scandal – Ambassador Accepts Bribes etc. – I'd better ask for something really small.' So he said he'd like a pair of slippers and some aftershave. Then on Christmas Day the ambassador turned on the radio and heard the announcer say, 'WHLD asked some of the world's leading ambassadors what they would like for Christmas. The French ambassador asked for peace on earth and goodwill to all men. The Chinese representative asked for an end to all wars and the British ambassador asked for a pair of slippers and some aftershave.'
**Kenny Everett**, BBC TV

**7** BART: Aren't we forgetting the true meaning of this day – the birth of Santa?
**Ron Hauge**, 'Miracle on Evergreen Terrace', *The Simpsons*, Fox TV, 1997

**8** The Supreme Court has ruled they cannot have a nativity scene in Washington, D.C. This wasn't for any religious reasons. They couldn't find three wise men and a virgin.
**Jay Leno**, *The Tonight Show*, NBC TV

**9** From **Top ten signs you've hired a bad department-store Santa**
After every toy request says, 'Yeah, *right*'.
Charges $5.95 for the first minute, £2.95 for each additional minute.
Tries unsuccessfully to hide the fact that he's wearing handcuffs.

Keeps sending elves out for more vermouth.
Tells salesgirls, 'Me and Mrs Claus have an
understanding.'
**David Letterman,** *The Late Show,* CBS

**10** ERNIE: Christmas always brings out the
best in people, doesn't it?
ERIC: Well, you tell my wife that.
ERNIE: Why, is she giving you trouble?
ERIC: I'll say. She said to me today, 'You've
done absolutely nothing to help with the
Christmas dinner. Absolutely nothing.'
ERNIE: What did you say to that?
ERIC: I said, 'What! Look at the turkey. I
bought it, I've plucked it and I've stuffed it!'
ERNIE: Good for you!
ERIC: Now, all *she's* got to do is kill it and
put it in the oven.
**Eric Morecambe and Ernie Wise,** *The Morecambe and
Wise Joke Book,* 1979

**11** It's customarily said that Christmas is
done 'for the kids'. Considering how awful
Christmas is and how little our society likes
children, this must be true.
**P. J. O'Rourke,** *Modern Manners,* 1983

**12** I love the Christmas-tide and yet,
   I notice this, each year I live;
   I always like the gifts I get,
   But how I love the gifts I give!
**Carolyn Wells,** 'A Thought'

**13** Still xmas is a good time with all those
presents and good food and i hope it will
never die out or at any rate not until i am
grown up and hav to pay for it all.
**Geoffrey Willans and Ronald Searle,** 'How to be
Topp', *The Compleet Molesworth,* 1958

**14** Xmas all grown ups sa is the season for
the kiddies but this do not prevent them
from taking a tot or 2 from the bot and
having, it may seme, a better time than us.
For children in fact Xmas is often a bit of a
strane wot with pretending that everything
is a surprise. Above all father xmas is a
strane. You canot so much as mention that
there is no father xmas when some
grown-up sa Hush not in front of wee tim.
**Geoffrey Willans and Ronald Searle,** 'How to be
Topp', *The Compleet Molesworth,* 1958

**15** The first rule in buying Christmas
presents is to select something shiny. If the
chosen object is of leather, the leather must
look as if it had been well greased; if of
silver, it must gleam with the light that

never was on sea or land. This is because the
wariest person will often mistake shininess
for expensiveness.
**P. G. Wodehouse,** *Louder and Funnier,* 1963

**16** I love Christmas. I receive a lot of
wonderful presents I can't wait to exchange.
**Henny Youngman**

# Church, The

*See also Catholicism; God; Jesus Christ;
Protestantism; Religion.*

**1** Go to church this Sunday – avoid the
Christmas rush.
**Graffito,** London, 1979

**2** At the Harvest Festival in church the area
behind the pulpit was piled high with tins
of IXL fruit for the old-age pensioners. We
had collected the tinned fruit from door to
door. Most of it came from old-age
pensioners.
**Clive James,** *Unreliable Memoirs,* 1980

**3** People expect the clergy to have the grace
of a swan, the friendliness of a sparrow, the
strength of an eagle and the night-hours of
an owl – and some people expect such a
bird to live on the food of a canary.
**Revd Edward Jeffrey,** 1964

**4** A church is a place in which gentlemen
who have never been to heaven brag about
it to people who will never get there.
**H. L. Mencken** (Attrib.)

**5** Archbishop: a Christian ecclesiastic of a
rank superior to that attained by Christ.
**H. L. Mencken** (Attrib.)

**6** Write me a Book of Common Prayer
   That is not made up of hot air
   With words that are as plain as this
   And, oh boy! that will take the piss
   Out of those who wrote Series 3
   And (I confess it) out of me.
**C. H. Sisson,** reacting against Series 3 Liturgy, 1979

**7** Golly! When you admonish a
congregation, it stays admonished!
**P. G. Wodehouse,** *Eggs, Beans and Crumpets,* 1940

**8** Like so many vicars, he had a poor
opinion of curates.
**P. G. Wodehouse,** *Meet Mr Mulliner,* 1927

**9** The Bishop of Stortford was talking to the local Master of Hounds about the difficulty he had in keeping his vicars off the incense.
**P. G. Wodehouse**, *Mr Mulliner Speaking*, 1929

# CIA, The
*See also Espionage.*

**1** By then, Gold had learned in Washington that the CIA was recruiting mercenaries to fight in Africa. He learned this at breakfast from his morning paper when he read:
CIA DENIES RECRUITING
MERCENARIES TO
FIGHT IN AFRICA
**Joseph Heller**, *Good as Gold*, 1979

# Cinema
*see Film.*

# Circus, The
*See also Show Business.*

**1** He was engaged to a contortionist but she broke it off.
**Anon.**

**2** He was married to an acrobat but she caught him in the act.
**Anon.**

**3** What a life for an Acrobat!
When I watch him loop and loop
I wonder what he's thinking upside down
   on the trapeze
And if he's really happy with his head
   between his knees
And then his face gets crimson
And I know he's going to sneeze!
'Allez-OOp – Allez OOp – Allez OOp!!'
**Noel Coward**, 'The Wife of an Acrobat', *Words and Music*, 1932

# Civil Service, The
*See also Bureaucracy; Government.*

**1** The Civil Service is a self-perpetuating oligarchy, and what better system is there?
**Lord Armstrong**, Head of the Home Civil Service, 1977

**2** The besetting sin of civil servants is to mix too much with each other.
**Sir William Beveridge**, Director of the London School of Economics, 1924

**3** Men who write minutes, who make professional assessments, who are never attacked face to face, who dwell in the Sargasso Sea of the Civil Service and who love the seaweed that conceals them.
**Cassandra (William Connor)**, *Daily Mirror*

**4** I say to myself that I must not let myself be cut off in there, and yet the moment I enter my bag is taken out of my hand, I'm pushed in, shepherded, nursed and above all cut off, alone. Whitehall envelops me.
**Richard Crossman**, *The Diaries of a Cabinet Minister*, 1976

**5** Once it is understood that politicians are public relations officers for their publicity-shy bosses, the Civil Service Permanent Secretaries, Parliament and Politics become intelligible.
**David Frost and Antony Jay**, *To England with Love*, 1967

**6** Members rise from CMG (known sometimes in Whitehall as 'Call me God') to KCMG ('Kindly call me God') to . . . the GCMG ('God calls me God').
**Anthony Sampson**, *The Anatomy of Britain*, 1962

**7** . . . a difficulty for every solution.
**Lord Samuel**, 1870–1963, British Liberal politician

**8** Britain has invented a new missile. It's called the civil servant – it doesn't work and it can't be fired.
**General Sir Walter Walker**, *Observer*, 1981

# Class
*See also The Aristocracy; Etiquette; Rich and Poor; Servants; Status.*

**1** As usual, I have against me the bourgeois, the officers and the diplomatists, and for me only the people who take the Metro.
**Charles de Gaulle**, *Observer*, 1967

**2** I don't believe in class differences, but luckily my butler disagrees with me.
**Marc**, cartoon in *The Times*, 1976

# Cleanliness

*See also Baths and Showers; Squalor.*

**1** I will say this for John: he's fanatically tidy . . . Do you know, after he takes a bath he washes the soap.
**Hugh Leonard**, *Time Was*, 1976

**2** Hygiene is the corruption of medicine by morality.
**H. L. Mencken**, *Prejudices*, Third Series, 1922

**3** ERNIE: Why don't you wash your face – I can see what you had for breakfast this morning!
ERIC: Oh, yeah! What did I have?
ERNIE: Bacon and eggs and tomato sauce.
ERIC: Wrong! That was *yesterday* morning!
**Eric Morecambe and Ernie Wise**, *The Morecambe and Wise Joke Book*, 1979

**4** Have I got a mother-in-law. She's so neat she puts paper under the cuckoo clock.
**Henny Youngman**

# Clichés

*See also Language.*

**1** What does it behove us to proclaim?
Our faith.
In what does it behove us to proclaim our faith?
Democracy.
From what vertiginous eyrie does it behove us to proclaim our faith in democracy?
From the house-tops.
At what time should we proclaim our faith in democracy from the house-tops?
Now, more than ever.
**Myles na Gopaleen**, 'The Myles na Gopaleen Catechism of Cliché', *The Best of Myles*, 1968

# Clothes

*See also Appearance; Fashion; Footwear; Hats; Style.*

**1** MARYANN (*in closet*): Look at his clothes! So this is where the seventies came to die!
**Alan Ball**, *Cybill*, CBS

**2** HILARY: One of the few lessons I have learned in life is that there is invariably something odd about women who wear ankle socks.
**Alan Bennett**, *The Old Country*, 1978

**3** Show me a woman wearing red patent-leather stiletto-heeled shoes and I'll show you a racing certainty.
**Jeffrey Bernard**, *Spectator*, 1986

**4** Give me a wild tie, brother,
One with a cosmic urge!
A tie that will swear and rip and tear
When it sees my old blue serge.
**Stoddard King**, *The Tie that Blinds*

**5** Women's clothes: never wear anything that panics the cat.
**P. J. O'Rourke**, *Modern Manners*, 1983

**6** Brevity is the soul of lingerie.
**Dorothy Parker** (Attrib.)

**7** I got some new underwear the other day. Well, new to me.
**Emo Philips**

**8** A well-tied tie is the first serious step in life.
**Oscar Wilde**, *The Importance of Being Earnest*, 1895

**9** The only way to atone for being occasionally a little over-dressed is by being always absolutely over-educated.
**Oscar Wilde**, 'Phrases and Philosophies for the Use of the Young', 1894

**10** Personally, if anyone had told me that a tie like that suited me, I should have risen and struck them on the mazzard, regardless of their age and sex . . .
**P. G. Wodehouse**, 'Jeeves in the Springtime', 1921

**11** I won't say her bathing suit was skimpy, but I've seen more cotton in the top of an aspirin bottle.
**Henny Youngman**

# Clubs

*See also Drink.*

**1** Any club that would accept me as a member, I wouldn't want to join.
**Groucho Marx** (Attrib.)

**2** . . . mausoleums of inactive masculinity . . . places for men who prefer armchairs to women.
**V. S. Pritchett**, 1900–97, English writer and critic

**3** Most clubs have the atmosphere of a

Duke's house with the Duke lying dead upstairs.

**Douglas Sutherland**, British author

# Coincidence

**1** Would You Believe It? Forty years ago, while sunbathing in her garden, Mrs Betty Lomax of Pugh Street, Ponders End, lost her engagement ring. Yesterday, while digging up the very same garden, her son Wilfred ruptured himself.

**Anon.**

**2** It is only in literature that coincidences seem unnatural.

**Robert Lynd**, 1879–1949, Anglo-Irish journalist

# Collaboration

*See also Work.*

**1** I never could understand how two men can write a book together; to me that's like three people getting together to have a baby.

**Evelyn Waugh** (Attrib.)

# Comedy

*See also Humour; Laughter; Puns; Satire; Wit.*

**1** Unless Cheech and Chong get run over by a truck, the release of these albums is likely to be the two best pieces of news in the comedy field for a while.

*National Lampoon*

**2** Q: Do the Jewish people dominate the field of comedy?
A: Don't be a schmuck.
Q: What is meant when they talk about a 'one-liner'?
A: It all depends what you mean by 'they'. If 'they' are comedians, then a one-liner is a joke that is no longer than one line. If 'they' work for the Matson Steamship Co., then a one-liner probably means some kind of boat.

**Albert Brooks**, 'Albert Brooks' Famous School for Comedians', *Esquire*, 1972

**3** Tragedy is when I cut my finger. Comedy is when *you* walk into an open sewer and die.

**Mel Brooks**, quoted in *The PreHistory of the Far Side* by Gary Larson, 1990

**4** GEORGE: A Charlie Chaplin film! Oh, I love old Chappers, don't you, Cap?
BLACKADDER: Unfortunately, no, I don't. I find his films about as funny as getting an arrow through the neck and then discovering there's a gas bill tied to it.

**Richard Curtis and Ben Elton**, 'Major Star', *Blackadder Goes Forth*, BBC TV, 1989

**5** Comedy, like sodomy, is an unnatural act.

**Marty Feldman**, *The Times*, 1969

**6** An amateur thinks it's funny if you dress a man up as an old lady, put him in a wheelchair, and give the wheelchair a push that sends it spinning down a slope towards a stone wall. For a pro, it's got to be a real old lady.

**Groucho Marx**

**7** The first rule of comedy is not to perform in a town where they still point at aeroplanes.

**Bobby Mills**

**8** They laughed when I said I was going to be a comedian . . . They're not laughing now.

**Bob Monkhouse**, English comedian, 1999

**9** Stand-up comedy hasn't changed. It's still the last refuge of the bitter alcoholic.

**Bob Odenkirk**

**10** It's whirly, it's whacky, it's slick, it's savvy; it's the madcap, daffy, fractured, ding-a-ling, ring-a-ding, loony, zany, side-splitting, rib-tickling, slap-happy, scuzzy dreary, irksome, tedious, banal, pointless, smutty world of Phono Phunnies!

**Michael O'Donoghue and Tony Hendra**, *National Lampoon's Radio Dinner*, album, 1972

**11** Comedy is the blues for people who can't sing.

**Chris Rock**, *Los Angeles Times*, 1991

**12** I love comedy. It's the only art form that's also a social grace. You meet a sculptor at a party, you can't say, 'He's terrific, look what he can do with the potato salad.'

**Paul Reiser**, Los Angeles stand-up comic, quoted in *GQ*, 1984

# Committees

*See also Conferences; Decisions; Meetings.*

**1** A group that takes minutes and wastes hours.
**Anon.**

**2** A group of the unfit appointed by the unwilling to do the unnecessary.
**Carl C. Byers**

**3** We always carry out by committee anything in which any of us alone would be too reasonable to persist.
**Frank Moore Colby**, 1865–1925, American writer and editor

**4** To get something done a committee should consist of no more than three men, two of whom are absent.
**Robert Copeland**

**5** Committee work is like a soft chair – easy to get into but hard to get out of.
**Kenneth J. Shively**

# Communication

*See also Letters; Mail; Telephones.*

**1** HELEN: What were you lecturing on in India?
PATTERSON: Harold Pinter and the failure of communication.
HELEN: How did it go?
PATTERSON: I don't know. They didn't seem to understand a word I said.
**Malcolm Bradbury and Christopher Bigsby**, *The After Dinner Game*, BBC TV, 1975

# Communism

*See also Equality; Marxism; Russia and the Russians; Socialism.*

**1** A communist is one who has nothing and wishes to share it with the world.
**Anon.**

**2** A communist is a socialist without a sense of humour.
**George Cutton**

**3** What is a communist? One who hath yearnings
For equal division of unequal earnings,
Idler or bungler, or both, he is willing

To fork out his copper and pocket your shilling.
**Ebenezer Elliott**, 'Epigram', 1850

**4** The Marxist law of distribution of wealth is that shortages will be divided equally among the peasants.
**John Guftason**

**5** Send your son to Moscow and he will return an anti-Communist; send him to the Sorbonne and he will return a Communist.
**Félix Houphouët-Boigny**, 1905–93, President of the Ivory Coast, 1963

**6** Communism might be likened to a race in which all competitors come in first with no prizes.
**Lord Inchcape**, quoted in the *Observer*, 1924

**7** Can you imagine lying in bed on a Sunday morning with the love of your life a cup of tea and a bacon sandwich, and all you had to read was the *Socialist Worker*?
**Derek Jameson**, Editor, *Daily Express*, 1979

**8** No member of our generation who wasn't a communist or a dropout in the thirties is worth a damn.
**Lyndon B. Johnson** (Attrib.)

**9** Communism requires of its adherents that they arise early and participate in a strenuous round of calisthenics. To someone who wishes that cigarettes came already lit the thought of such exertion at an hour when decent people are just nodding off is thoroughly abhorrent.
**Fran Lebowitz**, *Metropolitan Life*, 1978

**10** Communists all seem to wear small caps, a look I consider better suited to tubes of toothpaste than to people.
**Fran Lebowitz**, *Metropolitan Life*, 1978

**11** 'From each according to his ability, to each according to his needs' is not a decision I care to leave to politicians, for I do not believe that an ability to remark humorously on the passing scene would carry much weight with one's comrades or that one could convince them of the need for a really reliable answering service.
**Fran Lebowitz**, *Metropolitan Life*, 1978

**12** Communism is the opiate of the intellectuals.
**Clare Boothe Luce,** 1903–87, American Congresswoman and ambassador

**13** The objection to a Communist always resolves itself into the fact that he is not a gentleman.
**H. L. Mencken,** *Minority Report,* 1956

**14** . . . there's one delightful and entertaining feature of the Eisenhower years which is wholly absent from the contemporary scene – old-fashioned red-baiting. Where's our McCarthyism? . . . God knows the problem is not lack of Commies. There are more fuzzy-minded one-worlders, pasty-faced peace creeps and bleeding-heart bed wetters in America now than there ever were in 1954. The redskis have infiltrated the all-important exercise-video industry, not to mention movies and TV. Academia, too, is a veritable compost heap of Bolshie brainmulch. Beardo the Weirdo may have been laughed out of real life during the 1970s, but he found a home in our nation's colleges, where he whiles away the wait for the next Woodstock Nation by pestering undergraduates with collectivist twaddle when they should be thinking about better car stereos.
**P. J. O'Rourke,** *The Enemies List,* 1996

**15** Communism is the exploitation of the strong by the weak. In communism, inequality springs from placing mediocrity on a level with excellence.
**Pierre-Joseph Proudhon,** 1809–65, French political theorist

**16** How do you tell a communist? Well, it's someone who reads Marx and Lenin. And how do you tell an anti-communist? It's someone who understands Marx and Lenin.
**Ronald Reagan,** Republican President, 1981–9

**17** Communism is like Prohibition, it's a good idea but it won't work.
**Will Rogers,** *The Autobiography of Will Rogers,* 1949

**18** DOONESBURY: . . . That's complete nonsense. China and Russia are deadly enemies. China invaded Vietnam. Vietnam invaded Cambodia. Russia invaded Afghanistan. The only countries communists have been invading lately are communist!
B.D.: Of *course,* dummy! They invade each other to stay in shape!
**Garry Trudeau,** *Doonesbury,* cartoon, 1983

# Competitions
*See also Victory and Defeat.*

**1** Bloke at work, went in for a competition and won a trip to China. He's out there now trying to win a trip back!
**Jerry Dennis**

# Compliments
*See also Flattery; Praise.*

**1** FAN: You were superb in *Romeo and Juliet.*
ACTOR: I'll bet you say that to everyone who's superb.
**Anon.**

# Composers
*See also Music and Musicians; Opera; Songs and Singers.*

**1** It may be that when the angels go about their task of praising God, they play only Bach. I am sure, however, that when they are together *en famille*, they play Mozart.
**Karl Barth,** Swiss theologian, *Wolfgang Amadeus Mozart,* 1956

**2** Wagner is the Puccini of music.
**Beachcomber ( J. B. Morton),** English comic writer (Attrib.)

**3** Too much counterpoint; what is worse, Protestant counterpoint.
**Thomas Beecham,** *Guardian,* 1971, on Bach

**4** Ah Mozart! He was happily married but his wife wasn't.
**Victor Borge,** Danish pianist

**5** Beethoven was so hard of hearing he thought he was a painter.
**George Carlin**

**6** The public doesn't want new music; the main thing it demands of a composer is that he be dead.
**Arthur Honegger,** 1892–1955, Swiss composer

# Computers

*See also Internet; Modern Life; Technology.*

**1** Eye halve a spelling checker
It came with my Pea Sea,
It plane lee marks four my revue
Miss steaks aye dew knot sea.

Eye ran this poem threw it,
Your sure reel glad two no.
Its vary polished in it's weigh
My checker tolled me sew . . .
**Anon.**, 'An Owed Two The Spelling Checker'

**2** Fifteen oxymorons:

Pretty ugly
Act naturally
Advanced BASIC
Genuine imitation
Good grief
Working holiday
Almost exactly
Government organization
Alone together
Business ethics
Military intelligence
Peace force
Charm offensive
Fun run
Microsoft Works
**Anon.**

**3** Q: How many Bill Gateses does it take to change a light bulb?
A: None. He calls a meeting and makes darkness the standard.
**Anon.**

**4** Q: How many Microsoft tech-support people does it take to change a light bulb?
A: Please continue to hold. Your call is very important to us.
**Anon.**

**5** Six rules of the computer:

There's never time to do it right, but always time to do it again.
Inside every large program is a small program trying to get out.
It's morally wrong to allow naïve end-users to keep their money.
Abandon all hope, you who press Enter here.
Never test for errors you can't handle.

If you think the problem is bad now, just wait until we've solved it.
**Anon.**

**6** To err is human, but to really foul things up requires a computer.
**Anon.**

**7** Announcing the new Built-in Orderly Organised Knowledge device: BOOK.
The BOOK is a revolutionary breakthrough in technology: no wires, no batteries, nothing to be connected or switched on. It's so easy to use even a child can operate it. Just lift its cover. Compact and portable, it can be used anywhere, yet it is powerful enough to hold as much information as a CD-ROM disc. Each BOOK is constructed of sequentially numbered sheets of paper, each capable of holding thousands of bits of information. Each sheet is scanned optically, registering information directly into your brain. A flick of the finger takes you to the next sheet. The BOOK never crashes and never needs re-booting. The 'browse' feature allows you to move instantly to any sheet. Many come with an 'index' feature, which pinpoints the exact location of any selected information for instant retrieval. An optional 'BOOKmark' accessory allows you to open the BOOK to the exact place you left it in a previous session. The BOOK is ideal for long-term archive use. Several field trials have proved that the medium will still be readable in several centuries' time.

You can also make personal notes next to BOOK text entries with an optional programming tool, the Portable Erasable Nib Cryptic Intercommunication Language Stylus (PENCILS). The BOOK's appeal seems so certain that thousands of content creators have committed to the platform.
**Internet**

**8** It's Not a Bug, It's a Feature!
**T-shirt**, Los Angeles, 1993

**9** Smash Forehead on Keyboard to Continue
**T-shirt**, Los Angeles, 1996

**10** SOFTWARE: These are the PROGRAMS that you put on the HARD DRIVE by sticking them through the little SLOT. The function

of the software is to give instructions to the CPU, which is a set of three initials inside the computer that rapidly processes billions of tiny facts, called BYTES, and within a fraction of a second sends you an ERROR MESSAGE that requires you to call the CUSTOMER SUPPORT HOTLINE and be placed on HOLD for approximately the life span of a CARIBOU.
**Dave Barry,** *Dave Barry in Cyberspace,* 1996

**11** Incompatible operating systems have taken over where religious differences left off.
**Cathy Guisewite,** quoted in *Whole Earth Software Catalog,* 1986

**12** My computer dating bureau came up with a perfect gentleman. Still, I've got another three goes.
**Sally Poplin**

**13** DOONESBURY: Excuse me, sir. Do you have any user-friendly sales reps?
STORE MANAGER: You mean, consumer compatible liveware? No, he's off today.
**Garry Trudeau,** *Doonesbury,* cartoon, 1983

**14** We used to have lots of questions to which there were no answers. Now, with the computer there are lots of answers to which we haven't thought up the questions.
**Peter Ustinov,** *Illustrated London News*

**15** When I'm around hard-core computer geeks, I wanna say, 'Come outside, the graphics are great!'
**Matt Weinhold**

## Conciliation
*See also Peace.*

**1** The one sure way to conciliate a tiger is to allow oneself to be devoured.
**Konrad Adenauer,** first West German Chancellor

**2** An appeaser is one who feeds a crocodile hoping it will eat him last.
**Winston Churchill**

## Conferences
*See also Committees; Meetings.*

**1** A conference is a meeting held to decide when the next meeting will take place.
**Anon.**

**2** A conference is a gathering of important people who singly can do nothing, but together can decide that nothing can be done.
**Fred Allen**

**3** Those that can, do. Those that can't, call a conference.
**Freddie Oliver,** English writer

## Conformity
*See also Etiquette; Manners.*

**1** When people are free to do as they please, they usually imitate each other.
**Eric Hoffer,** *Passionate State of Mind,* 1955

**2** Consistency is the last refuge of the unimaginative.
**Oscar Wilde** (Attrib.)

## Congress
*See also Politics and Politicians; Politics – The American Presidency; The Senate; Washington.*

**1** You can't use tact with a congressman! A congressman is a hog! You must take a stick and hit him on the snout!
**Henry Adams,** 1838–1918, American writer and scholar

**2** Congress, *n.* A body of men who meet to repeal laws.
**Ambrose Bierce,** *The Devil's Dictionary,* 1911

**3** Talk is cheap – except when Congress does it.
**Cullen Hightower,** American commentator

**4** Congress is so strange. A man gets up to speak and says nothing. Nobody listens – and then everybody disagrees.
**Boris Marshalov,** *Reader's Digest,* 1941

**5** This country has come to feel the same when Congress is in session as we do when the baby gets hold of the hammer. It's just a question of how much damage he can do

with it before we can take it away from him.
**Will Rogers**, quoted in *Will Rogers: His Life and Times*, 1973

**6** With Congress, every time they make a joke it's a law, and every time they make a law it's a joke.
**Will Rogers**

**7** Congress does from a third to half of what I think is the minimum that it ought to do, and I am profoundly grateful that I get as much.
**Theodore Roosevelt**, American President, 1901–9

**8** Reader, suppose you were an idiot. And suppose you were a member of Congress. But I repeat myself.
**Mark Twain**

# Conscience
*See also Duty; Guilt.*

**1** Conscience gets a lot of credit that belongs to cold feet.
**Anon.**

**2** Conscience: something that feels terrible when everything else feels swell.
**Anon.**, *Reader's Digest*, 1949

**3** The Nonconformist Conscience makes cowards of us all.
**Max Beerbohm**, 'King George the Fourth', *Yellow Book*, 1894

**4** Conscience is thoroughly well-bred and soon leaves off talking to those who do not wish to hear it.
**Samuel Butler**, *Further Extracts from Notebooks*, 1934

**5** Conscience is the inner voice that warns us that someone may be looking.
**H. L. Mencken**, *Sententiae*, 1920

**6** Conscience: the still small voice that makes you feel still smaller.
**James A. Sanaker**, *Reader's Digest*

**7** Conscience and cowardice are really the same things. Conscience is the trade name of the firm.
**Oscar Wilde**, *The Picture of Dorian Gray*, 1891

**8** A clear conscience is usually the sign of a bad memory.
**Steven Wright**, American comic

# Conservatism
*See also Capitalism; Change; The Conservative Party; The Labour Party; The Liberal Party; Politics – British Prime Ministers; Politics and Politicians; The Republican Party.*

**1** A conservative is someone who admires radicals a century after they're dead.
**Anon.**

**2** 'What do you want?'
'Gradual change!'
'When do we want it?'
'In due course!'
**Anon.**, battle cry of the *Really* Conservative Party

**3** When a nation's young men are conservative, its funeral bell is already rung.
**Henry Ward Beecher**, *Proverbs from Plymouth Pulpit*, 1887

**4** POLLY: He's a socialist but he doesn't like people.
BRIAN: Nor do I, much.
POLLY: You're a Conservative. You don't have to.
**Alan Bennett**, *Getting On*, 1971

**5** A conservative is someone who demands a square deal for the rich.
**David Frost**, TVam, 1983

**6** I never dared be radical when young
For fear it would make me conservative
when old.
**Robert Frost**, 'Precaution', 1936

**7** The modern conservative is engaged in one of man's oldest exercises in moral philosophy, that is the search for a superior moral justification for selfishness.
**J. K. Galbraith**, American economist

**8** . . . contemporary Conservatism . . . is, like contemporary art, seldom much admired at the time; it only achieves acceptance and admiration in retrospect.
**Sir Ian Gilmour**, *Inside Right*, 1977

**9** It is perhaps foolish to expect the Conservatives to be anything other than Conservative.
**Jo Grimond**, Liberal politician, 1967

**10** A conservative is a man who is too cowardly to fight and too fat to run.
**Elbert Hubbard**, *The Notebook*, 1927

**11** Some fellows get credit for being conservative when they are only stupid.
**Kin Hubbard**, 1868–1930, American humorist

**12** A conservative is a man who will not look at the new moon, out of respect for that ancient institution, the old one.
**Douglas Jerrold**, 1803–57, English playwright and journalist

**13** If you want things to stay the same, things are going to have to change.
**Giuseppe Tomasi di Lampedusa**, *The Leopard*, 1957

**14** Men who are orthodox when they are young are in danger of being middle aged all their lives.
**Walter Lippmann**, 1889–1974, American political commentator

**15** Dying and letting die, they call 'living and letting live';
They do not even make mistakes for live ones to forgive;
Wouldst thou be Nothing? Then, my son, be a conservative!
**Edwin Meade Robinson**, 'Conservatives'

**16** A conservative is a man with two perfectly good legs who, however, has never learned to walk forward.
**Franklin D. Roosevelt** (Attrib.)

**17** There was the Don who, whenever any reform was proposed, made exactly the same speech. He would say: 'Whenever a measure of this kind is suggested, I ask myself two questions: "Has the old system worked badly?" "Is the new system likely to work better?" I see no reason to answer either question in the affirmative, and I shall therefore vote against the proposal.'
**Bertrand Russell**, *Portraits from Memory*, 1956

**18** A conservative is someone who believes in reform. But not now.
**Mort Sahl**, American comedian

**19** The radical invents the views. When he has worn them out, the conservative adopts them.
**Mark Twain**, *Notebook*, 1935

**20** . . . a businessman's candidate, hovering around the status quo like a sick kitten around a hot brick.
**William Evans White**, newspaper editor, of Charles Evans Hughes, unsuccessful Republican presidential candidate, 1916

**21** He thinks like a Tory and talks like a Radical, and that's so important nowadays.
**Oscar Wilde**, *Lady Windermere's Fan*, 1892

**22** Sir,
Dr Roget included the following entry in his Thesaurus: 'Inaction, passiveness, abstinence from action; non-interference; conservative policy.'
  Can there be a moral somewhere in this?
                                        Yours, &c.
**A. J. Woodman**, letter to *The Times*, 1967

# Conservative Party, The
*See also Conservatism; Politics and Politicians.*

**1** It is a bizarre fact that the Conservative Party can be directed along a sensible left-wing path only by a leader with impeccable aristocratic connections.
**Humphrey Berkeley**, of Harold Macmillan

**2** Tories are not always wrong, but they are always wrong at the right moment.
**Lady Violet Bonham-Carter**, 1887–1969, British Liberal politician

**3** The Conservative Party is an organized hypocrisy.
**Benjamin Disraeli**, speech in the House of Commons, 1845

**4** They are nothing else but a load of kippers – two-faced, with no guts.
**Eric Heffer**, Labour MP (Attrib.)

**5** The trouble with the Conservative Party is that it has not turned the clock back a single second.
**Evelyn Waugh** (Attrib.)

# Consultants
*See also Business; Experts; Work.*

**1** A consultant is a man sent in after the battle to bayonet the wounded.
**Anon.**

**2** Anyone who makes a business decision to hire a consultant, needs a consultant to help with their business decisions.
**Anon.**

**3** Those that do, do. Those that did but now don't, consult.
**Anon.**

**4** Consult, *v.* To seek another's approval of a course already decided upon.
**Ambrose Bierce**, *The Devil's Dictionary*, 1911

**5** A consultant is a man who knows 129 ways to make love, but doesn't know any women.
**Jerry Dennis**

**6** It used to be when all else failed, you went into the army; now you become a consultant.
**Jerry Dennis**

# Consumerism
*See also Consumers; Shopping.*

**1** Dear Ned,
Soon after I received my Acme pencil (11 cents), it rolled off the desk and on to the floor. Upon retrieving it, I hit my head on the desk. Can I hold Acme responsible?
[Boiling Mad]

Dear Boiling,
This is what's known as an open-and-shut case. If you don't sue them, I will.
[Ned]
**R. Chast**, 'Ned's Consumer Hot Line', cartoon, *New Yorker*, 1984

**2** When Ralph Nader tells me he wants my car to be cheap, ugly and slow, he's imposing a way of life on me that I'm going to resist to the bitter end.
**Timothy Leary** (Attrib.)

# Consumers
*See also Consumerism; Shopping.*

**1** The One Who Has The Most Toys When They Die, Wins!
**Licence-plate holder**, Los Angeles, 1984

**2** The customer's always right, my boys,
The customer's always right.
The son-of-a-bitch
Is probably rich
So smile with all your might.
**Noel Coward**, 'The Customer's Always Right', *Sail Away*, 1962

**3** I like to walk down Bond Street, thinking of all the things I don't want.
**Logan Pearsall Smith**, *Afterthoughts*, 1931

**4** The grocer sells me addled eggs; the tailor
      sells me shoddy,
I'm only a consumer, and I am not
      anybody.
The cobbler pegs me paper soles, the
      dairyman short-weights me,
I'm only a consumer, and most everybody
      hates me.
There's turnip in my pumpkin pie and
      ashes in my pepper,
The world's my lazaretto, and I'm
      nothing but a leper;
So lay me in my lonely grave and tread
      the turf down flatter,
I'm only a consumer and it doesn't really
      matter.
**Nixon Waterman**, 'Cheer for the Consumer', *The Oxford Book of American Light Verse*, 1979

# Contracts
*See also Big Business; Business; The Law.*

**1** A verbal agreement isn't worth the paper it's written on.
**Louis B. Mayer** (Attrib.)

**2** Contract: an agreement that is binding only on the weaker party.
**Frederick Sawyer**

# Conversation
*See also Gossip; Telephone.*

**1** A gossip talks about others, a bore talks about himself – and a brilliant conversationalist talks about you.
**Anon.**

**2** 'Hello! How are you? How's your wife?'
'Didn't you know? She's dead.'
'Oh, um, right – but she's still in the same cemetery?'
**Anon.**

**3** The trouble with telling a good story is that it invariably reminds the other fellow of a bad one.
**Sid Caesar**

**4 Surefire conversation stoppers**
'Can I ask you a personal question?'
'I don't care WHAT they say about you – you're OK in my book.'
'I literally have hornets flying around inside my brain.'

'I'm writing a screenplay.'
'I had a dream I was being chased by giant salamis. I wonder what that meant?'
'See this gun?'
**Matt Groening**, *Life in Hell*, 1992

**5** No man would listen to you talk if he didn't know it was his turn next.
**Edgar Watson Howe**, 1853–1937, American writer

**6** A good listener is usually thinking about something else.
**Kin Hubbard**, 1868–1930, American humorist

**7** The opposite of talking isn't listening. The opposite of talking is waiting.
**Fran Lebowitz**, *Social Studies*, 1981

**8** Buffet, ball, banquet, quilting bee,
  Wherever conversation's flowing,
  Why must I feel it falls on me
  To keep things going?
**Phyllis McGinley**, *Times Three: 1932–1960*, 1960

**9** We've had our clichés framed
  and hung up on the wall
  so now for conversation
  we don't have to talk at all.
**Roger McGough**, 'Mute Consent', *Worse Verse*, 1969

**10** There is only one rule for being a good talker. Learn to listen.
**Christopher Morley**, 1890–1957, American writer

**11** Practically anything you say will seem amusing if you're on all fours.
**P. J. O'Rourke**, *Modern Manners*, 1983

**12** He has occasional flashes of silence that make his conversation perfectly delightful.
**Sydney Smith**, 1771–1845, clergyman and wit, on statesman and historian Thomas Babington Macaulay (Attrib.)

**13** Mr Salter's side of the conversation was limited to expressions of assent. When Lord Copper was right he said, 'Definitely, Lord Copper'; when he was wrong, 'Up to a point.'
  'Let me see, what's the name of the place I mean? Capital of Japan? Yokohama, isn't it?'
  'Up to a point, Lord Copper.'
  'And Hong Kong belongs to us, doesn't it?'
  'Definitely, Lord Copper.'
**Evelyn Waugh**, *Scoop*, 1938

**14** I like to do all the talking myself. It saves time and prevents arguments.
**Oscar Wilde**, 'The Remarkable Rocket'

**15** Learned conversation is either the affectation of the ignorant or the profession of the mentally unemployed.
**Oscar Wilde**, 'The Critic as Artist', 1891

**16** '. . . you wouldn't find me grousing if I were a male newt.'
  'But if you were a male newt, Madeline Bassett wouldn't look at you. Not with the eye of love, I mean.'
  'She would, if she were a female newt.'
  'But she isn't a female newt.'
  'No, but suppose she was.'
  'Well, if she was, you wouldn't be in love with her.'
  'Yes, I would, if I were a male newt.'
  A slight throbbing about the temples told me that this discussion had reached saturation point.
**P. G. Wodehouse**, *Right Ho, Jeeves*, 1934

**17** 'What Ho!' I said, 'What Ho!' said Motty.
  'What Ho! What Ho!'
  'What Ho! What Ho! What Ho!'
  After that it seemed rather difficult to go on with the conversation.
**P. G. Wodehouse**, *Carry On, Jeeves*, 1925

# Cooks and Cookery

*See also Breakfast; Eating; Food; Restaurants.*

**1** Sir,
The hymn 'Onward Christian Soldiers', sung to the right tune and in a not-too-brisk tempo, makes a very good egg timer. If you put the egg into boiling water and sing all five verses and chorus, the egg will be just right when you come to Amen.
**Letter** in the *Daily Telegraph*, 1983

**2** The proper way to cook a cockatoo is to put the bird and an axehead into a billy. Boil them until the axehead is soft. The cockatoo is then ready to eat.
**Anon.**, traditional, quoted in the *Australian*, 1954

**3** Where there's smoke, there's toast.
**Anon.**

**4** [Chefs are] . . . wacked-out moral degenerates, dope fiends, refugees, a

thuggish assortment of drunks, sneak thieves, sluts and psychopaths.
**Anthony Bourdain**, *Kitchen Confidential*, 2000

**5** Life is too short to stuff a mushroom.
**Shirley Conran**, *Superwoman*, 1975

**6** . . . nobody really likes capers no matter what you do with them. Some people *pretend* to like capers, but the truth is that any dish that tastes good with capers in it, tastes even better with capers not in it.
**Nora Ephron**, *Heartburn*, 1983

**7** What I love about cooking is that after a hard day, there is something comforting about the fact that if you melt butter and add flour and then hot stock, IT WILL GET THICK! It's a sure thing! It's a sure thing in a world where nothing is sure; it has a mathematical certainty in a world where those of us who long for some kind of certainty are forced to settle for crossword puzzles.
**Nora Ephron**, *Heartburn*, 1983

**8** Couples who cook together stay together. (Maybe because they can't decide who'll get the Cuisinart.)
**Erica Jong**

**9** Dear Miss Piggy,
Whenever I cook spaghetti, it always gets all tangled up into clumps. What am I doing wrong?
[Frustrated]

Dear Frustrated,
I am not sure, but you might try a light cream rinse, followed by a quick once-over with a blow-dryer.
**Miss Piggy**, *Miss Piggy's Guide to Life (As Told to Henry Beard)*, 1981

**10** Do not make a stingy sandwich;
Pile the cold-cuts high;
Customers should see salami
Coming through the rye.
**Allan Sherman**, 'Coming Through the Rye', song, 1963

**11** My wife does wonderful things with leftovers – she throws them out.
**Herb Shriner**, *Reader's Digest*, 1956

**12** This week I'm going to tell you some of the many interesting things you can do with yak. There's yak à l'orange, yak

pastries, yak kebab, yak fingers, yak on a spit – and yak in its jacket. But my family's favourite is a simply scrumptious dessert – coupe yak. Take your yak, pluck it and bone it – take an ordinary saucepan, the type you use for broiling hippopotamus, when it's tender, cool it and smother it in raspberry ice cream, sprinkle on a little ground coconut – three tons should be enough – and serve with a hip bath of custard. Some people claim that the coconut and ice cream disguise the natural flavour of the yak meat – but when I served my husband with it his immediate reaction on tasting it was –
Yak!
**Barry Took and Marty Feldman**, *Round the Horne*, BBC Radio, 1967

**13** To make a good salad is to be a brilliant diplomatist – the problem is entirely the same in both cases. To know exactly how much oil one must put with one's vinegar.
**Oscar Wilde**, *Vera, or The Nihilists*, 1883

# Cosmetics
*See also Appearance; Beauty; Faces; Perfume*

**1** Most women are not so young as they are painted.
**Max Beerbohm**, *A Defence of Cosmetics*, 1894

**2** A girl whose cheeks are covered with paint
Has an advantage with me over one whose ain't.
**Ogden Nash**, 'Biological Reflection', *Hard Lines*, 1931

# Countries
*See also Foreigners.*

**1** . . . King Quasi of Quasiland. His country was five feet wide and eleven miles long, and its main exports were rope and pasta.
**Jonathan Winters**, quoted by Robin Williams, *Playboy*, 1982

# Country, The
*See also Farms and Farming; Nature.*

**1** I have never understood why anybody agreed to go on being a rustic after about 1400.
**Kingsley Amis**, *The Green Man*, 1969

**2** Now, nature, as I am only too well aware, has her enthusiasts, but on the whole, I am not to be counted among them. To put it rather bluntly, I am not the type who wants to go back to the land; I am the type who wants to go back to the hotel.

**Fran Lebowitz**, *Social Studies*, 1981

**3** . . . to me the outdoors is what you must pass through in order to get from your apartment into a taxicab.

**Fran Lebowitz**, *Metropolitan Life*, 1978

**4** No country home is complete without a surly figure seated in the kitchen like Rodin's thinker, wishing she was back in a hot little room under the Third Avenue Elevated.

**S. J. Perelman**, *Acres and Pains*, 1947

**5** Lovers of the town have been content, for the most part, to say they loved it. They do not brag about its uplifting qualities. They have none of the infernal smugness which makes the lover of the country insupportable.

**Agnes Repplier**, *Times and Tendencies*, 1931

**6** My living in Yorkshire was so far out of the way, that it was actually twelve miles from a lemon.

**Sydney Smith**, 1771–1845, clergyman and wit

**7** It is pure unadulterated country life. They get up early because they have so much to do and go to bed early because they have so little to think about.

**Oscar Wilde**, *The Picture of Dorian Gray*, 1891

# Couples

*See also Courtship; Engagements; Marriage; Proposals; Relationships; Sexual Attraction.*

**1** Told her I had always lived alone
And I probably always would,
And all I wanted was my freedom,
And she told me that she understood.
But I let her do some of my laundry
And she slipped a few meals in between,
The next time I remember she was all moved in
And I was buying her a washing machine.

**Jackson Browne**, 'Ready or Not', song, 1974

**2** RICK: I mean, what AM I supposed to call you? My 'Girl Friend'? My 'Companion'?

My 'Roommate'? Nothing sounds quite right!
JOANIE: How about your 'Reason for Living'?
RICK: No, no, I need something I can use around the office.

**Garry Trudeau**, *Doonesbury*, cartoon

# Courage

*See also Cowardice: Fear; Heroes; War.*

**1** What makes every Englishman
A fighter through and through?
It isn't roast beef or ale or home or mother;
It's just a little thing they sing to one another:
(*Refrain*)
Stiff upper lip! Stout fella!
When you're in a stew –
Sober or blotto,
This is your motto:
Keep muddling through!

**Ira Gershwin**, 'Stiff Upper Lip', song from *A Damsel in Distress*, 1937

**2** The important thing when you are going to do something brave is to have someone on hand to witness it.

**Michael Howard, MC**, Professor of the History of War, Oxford, 1980

**3** If you can keep your head when all about you are losing theirs, it's just possible you haven't grasped the situation.

**Jean Kerr**, *Please Don't Eat the Daisies*, 1957

# Courtship

*See also Couples; Dating; Flirtation; Love; Love – Breaking Up; Rejection; Seduction; Sexual Attraction.*

**1** SHE: I've heard plenty about your lovemaking.
HE: Oh, it's nothing.
SHE: That's what I heard.

*Laugh-In*, NBC TV, 1969

**2** From **9 secret love techniques women find well-nigh irresistible**

BE MASCULINE! That's right! Move yer arms around. Flex yer muscles. Puff out yer chest. Stand up straight. Swagger down the street. Squint. Snarl. Sneer. Mutter angry gibberish to no one in particular. Don't take no guff.

LISTEN AT HER! Uh huh! Nothing – but nothing – puts a woman off guard like if she thinks yer paying attention to her ceaseless prattle. Meanwhiles, you got some important thinking of your own to get done – so you gotta learn the subtle gestures and murmurs that'll keep you out of hot water! 'My my.' 'Hmmm.' 'Is that so?' 'Well ain't that a corker.'

SHOW HER WHO'S BOSS! Watch out! This one's a doozy, what with all the ding-dang fuss over 'equality,' 'freedom,' and 'justice.' But if you stick to yer guns, jut out yer chin like a tough guy, and bellow 'Ahh, shuddup' enough times, she'll get the message. Remember: some women are easier to fool than others.

    HE: I said getcher ass in here!
    SHE: WHAT?
    HE: Oh . . . nothing.
**Matt Groening**, *Life in Hell*, 1982

**3** From **9 secret love techniques that could possibly turn men into putty in your hands**

FEIGN INTEREST IN THEIR TEDIOUS JABBER. Men dig it when they can babble on endlessly year after year about guns, blimps and cigars without being challenged to change the subject. All you have to do is learn a few simple words and develop a capacity for lengthy monologues on carburetors, home computers and Curly of the Three Stooges. 'Rilly?' 'My goodness.' 'Rilly?'

ACCEDE TO THEIR SICKO EROTIC REQUESTS. Men can be likened to rutting grizzly bears, snurfling wolverines, or sex-crazed white rabbits with just one thing on their disgusting minds. Actually, you can play it two ways: Either fuck their brains out, for which you will be rewarded with doglike devotion, or withhold all sexual favors for which you will be rewarded with doglike devotion.

DEFLATE 'EM. It's surprisingly easy to puncture the egos of slow-witted male behemoths with a quick verbal jab or an unyielding moral/political exhortation. Curiously, men feel a tremendous amount of guilt that is held in check only by an equally hefty load of unfocused rage – and you can work this to your advantage.

    HE: Hey, look at this silly cartoon.

    SHE: Why, in this time of changing values and female liberation, do men persist in laughing at women?
    HE: I . . . am filled with shame.
**Matt Groening**, *Life in Hell*, 1982

**4** A: You've been seeing my daughter Nellie for nearly a year now. What are your intentions – honorable or dishonorable?
B: You mean I've got a choice?
**Harry Hershfield**

**5** She was a lovely girl. Our courtship was fast and furious – I was fast and she was furious.
**Max Kauffmann**

**6** To differentiate between girls who put out and girls who don't. Girls who put out are tramps. Girls who don't are ladies. This is, however, a rather archaic usage of the word. Should one of you boys happen upon a girl who doesn't put out, do not jump to the conclusion that you have found a lady. What you have probably found is a lesbian.
**Fran Lebowitz**, *Metropolitan Life*, 1978

**7** Not for her potatoes
   and puddings made of rice
   she takes carbohydrates
   like God takes advice
   a surfeit of ambition
   is her particular vice
   Valerie fondles lovers
   like a mousetrap fondles mice
**Roger McGough**, 'Discretion', *The Mersey Sound*, 1967

**8** ERIC: Who was that lady I seen you with last night?
ERNIE: You mean, '*I saw*'.
ERIC: Sorry. Who was that eyesore I seen you with last night?
**Eric Morecambe and Ernie Wise**, *The Morecambe and Wise Joke Book*, 1979

**9** The hardest task in a girl's life is to prove to a man that his intentions are serious.
**Helen Rowland**, *Reflections of a Bachelor Girl*, 1903

**10** It is assumed that the woman must wait, motionless, until she is wooed. That is how the spider waits for the fly.
**George Bernard Shaw** (Attrib.)

**11** FIREFLY (GROUCHO MARX): Oh, er, I suppose you'll think me a sentimental old fluff, but, er, would you mind giving me a lock of your hair?

MRS TEASDALE: A lock of my hair? Why, I had no idea . . .

FIREFLY: I'm letting you off easy. I was going to ask for the whole wig.

**Arthur Sheekman and Nat Perrin**, *Duck Soup*, screenplay, 1933

**12** When he dances he's all feet and when he stops he's all hands.

**Arthur Sheekman**, *Welcome Stranger*, screenplay, 1947

**13** GIRL: I saw you the other day at the corner of Hollywood and Vine winking at the girls.

RUDY VALLEE: I wasn't winking. That's a windy corner. Something got in my eye.

GIRL: She got in your car too.

**Rudy Vallee**, *The Rudy Vallee Show*, American radio, 1930s

# Cowardice

*See also Courage; Fear.*

**1** Coward, *n.* One who, in a perilous emergency, thinks with his legs.

**Ambrose Bierce**, *The Devil's Dictionary*, 1911

**2** Retreat, retreat,
  Drop your swords and run;
  Our foe is near,
  Our choice is clear,
  Get outa here,
  Hurray for fear,
  We're done.
  Run away, run away,
  If you run away
  You live to run away another day.

**Mel Brooks**, 'Retreat', song from *To Be or Not to Be*, 1984

# Cowboys

*See also America and the Americans.*

**1** BOY: You seem mighty thirsty. Have a long, dry ride?

COWBOY: No – I had a herring for breakfast.

BOY: What's your name stranger?

COWBOY: Folks call me . . . Strange.

BOY: Strange? What's your first name?

COWBOY: Very. But you can call me Strange.

*Your Show of Shows*, NBC TV, 1950s, parody of *Shane*

**2** These people are simple farmers, people

of the land, the common clay of the New West. You know – morons.

**Mel Brooks**, *Blazing Saddles*, screenplay, 1974

**3** ELLER: I'd like to say a word for the cowboy

The road he treads is difficult and lonely.
He rides for days on end
With jist a pony fer a friend.

ADO ANNIE: I shore am feeling sorry fer the pony.

**Richard Rodgers and Oscar Hammerstein II**, 'The Farmer and the Cowman', song from *Oklahoma*, 1943

# Creativity

*See also Art and Artists; Ideas; Writers; Writing.*

**1** Creativity is great but plagiarism is faster.

**Anon.**

**2** When in doubt, make a fool of yourself. There is a microscopically thin line between being brilliantly creative and acting like the most gigantic idiot on earth. So what the hell, leap.

**Cynthia Heimel**, 'Lower Manhattan Survival Tactics', *Village Voice*, 1983

**3** Very few people possess true artistic ability. It is therefore both unseemly and unproductive to irritate the situation by making an effort. If you have a burning, restless urge to write or paint, simply eat something sweet and the feeling will pass.

**Fran Lebowitz**, *Metropolitan Life*, 1978

**4** My sole inspiration is a telephone call from a producer.

**Cole Porter**, interview, 1955

# Credit

*See also Banking; Borrowing and Lending; Credit Cards; Debt; Money; Shopping.*

**1** IN GOD WE TRUST. All others pay cash.

**Anon.**

**2** Do I live within my income? No way! It's all I can do to live within my credit!

**Jerry Dennis**

**3** No man's credit is as good as his money.

**Edgar Watson Howe**, 1853–1937, American writer

## Credit Cards

*See also Credit; Debt; Money; Shopping.*

**1** A credit card is a convenient device that saves you the trouble of counting your change.
**Anon.**

**2** My motto is 'Veni, vidi, Visa' – We came, we saw, we went shopping.
**Sally Poplin**

**3** FRIEND: My wife had her credit card stolen.
DAGWOOD: That's terrible!
FRIEND: It's not so terrible – the thief's been spending less than she did!
**Dean Young and Jim Raymond**, *Blondie*, cartoon

## Credulity

*See also Belief; Truth.*

**1** He had been kicked in the head when young and believed everything he read in the Sunday papers.
**George Ade**, *The America of George Ade*, 1962

**2** Some people will believe anything if you whisper it to them.
**Louis B. Nizer**, *Thinking on Your Feet*, 1940

## Cremation

*See also Death; Funerals.*

**1** We're all cremated equal.
**Goodman Ace**, quoted in the *New Yorker*, 1977

**2** SHE: Arthur.
HE: Yes, love?
SHE: I think I'd like to be cremated.
HE: OK love – get your coat on.
**Jerry Dennis**

**3** A: It's no good – I've got one foot in the grate.
B: You mean '*grave*'.
A: No, I mean '*grate*'. I want to be cremated.
**Max Kauffmann**

## Cricket

*See also Sport.*

**1 Cricket explained – 1:**
You have two sides, one out in the field and one in. Each man in the side that's in, goes out and when he's out, he comes in and the next man goes in until he's out.

When they're all out, the side that's out comes in and the side that's been in goes out and tries to get those coming in out.

Sometimes you get men still in and not out. When both sides have been in and out, including not outs, that's the end of the game.

**Cricket explained – 2**
Two old men in white coats walk together to the middle of a large green field, each carrying three long sticks and two little ones.

Each plants his three sticks in the ground, 22 yards apart and puts the little sticks on top.

They then turn around and look towards 22 younger men at the edge of the field – and it starts to rain.
**Anon.**

**2** RAQUEL: I'm beginning to think life's too short for cricket.
*Coronation Street*, Granada TV

**3** The score piles up – somebody's slammed
    a one
  And run it out: Rodmell is going gay.
  Hugh with a zest that's rather overdone
  Has stumped the umpire, and his loud
    hooray
  Recalls the slumbering Major to the fray.
  And now begins a kind of jamboree
  Of overthrows. You think we're still at
    bay
  Give me the village bat and you shall see.
**Beachcomber (J. B. Morton)**, 'Ballade of the Rodmell Cricket Match'

**4** I thought they were only allowed two bouncers in one over.
**Bill Frindall**, BBC Radio 4's *Test Match Special* scorer, on the appearance of a streaker, 1995

**5** Oh God, if there be cricket in heaven, let there also be rain.
**Sir Alec Douglas Home** (Attrib.)

**6** My wife had an uncle who could never walk down the nave of his abbey without wondering whether it would take spin.
**Sir Alec Douglas Home**, *The Twentieth Century Revisited*, BBC TV, 1982

**7** Cricket is a game which the British, not being a spiritual people, had to invent in order to have some concept of eternity.
**Lord Mancroft**, *Bees in Some Bonnets*, 1979

**8** Many continentals think life is a game, the English think cricket is a game.
**George Mikes**, *How to be an Alien*, 1946

**9** It's a funny kind of month, October. For the really keen cricket fan it's when you discover that your wife left you in May.
**Denis Norden**, *She*, 1977

**10** Everyone knows which comes first when it's a question of cricket or sex – all discerning people recognize that.
**Harold Pinter** (Attrib.)

**11** You can have sex either before cricket or after cricket – the fundamental fact is that cricket must be there at the centre of things.
**Harold Pinter**, 1980

**12** Personally, I have always looked upon cricket as organized loafing.
**William Temple**, Archbishop of Canterbury, 1925

**13** There is only one thing in criket and that is the *strate bat*. Keep yore bat strate boy and all will be all right in life as in criket. So headmasters sa, but when my bat is strate i still get bowled is that an omen chiz. Aktually i usually prefer to hav a slosh: i get bowled just the same but it is more satisfactory.
**Geoffrey Willans and Ronald Searle**, 'How to be Topp', *The Compleet Molesworth*, 1958

**14** I do not play cricket because it requires me to assume such indecent positions.
**Oscar Wilde**

**15** 'The last time I played in a village cricket match,' said Psmith, 'I was caught at point by a man in braces. It would have been madness to risk another such shock to the system.'
**P. G. Wodehouse**, *Mike*, 1909

**16** The sun in heavens was beaming;
The breeze bore an odour of hay,
My flannels were spotless and gleaming,
My heart was unclouded and gay;
The ladies, all gaily apparelled,
Sat round looking on at the match,
In the tree-tops the dicky-birds carolled,
All was peace till I bungled that catch.
**P. G. Wodehouse**, 'Missed!'

# Crime

*See also Capital Punishment; Dishonesty; Guns; Kidnapping; The Law; The Mafia; Police; Prison.*

**1** After an incident in Croydon involving a prison van and a concrete mixer, police are looking for eighteen hardened criminals.
*The Two Ronnies*, BBC TV

**2** A kleptomaniac is a person who helps himself because he can't help himself.
**Anon.**

**3** I think crime pays. The hours are good, you travel a lot.
**Woody Allen**, *Take the Money and Run*, screenplay, 1969

**4** Al Capone, in mood benign,
Sent a massive Valentine,
Those who got his commendation
Shot up in his estimation.
**Will Bellenger**, *New Statesman*, 1984

**5** Thieves respect property; they merely wish the property to become their property that they may more perfectly respect it.
**G. K. Chesterton**, *The Man Who Was Thursday*, 1908

**6** A broad definition of crime in England is that it is any lower-class activity which is displeasing to the upper class. Crime is committed by the lower class and punished by the upper class.
**David Frost and Antony Jay**, *To England with Love*, 1967

**7** From **Top ten signs the guy mugging you has never mugged before**
Announces, 'This is a nugging.'
Asks you to hold his gun while he puts on some Chap Stick.
Wears a paper hat that says 'Trainee.'
Warns, 'Don't make me use this realistic-looking squirt gun!'
During police line-up, he waves to you and shouts, 'Remember me?'
**David Letterman**, *The Late Show*, CBS

**8** Obviously crime pays or there would be no crime.
**G. Gordon Liddy**, Watergate conspirator and radio host

**9** ERNIE: Is there a price on your head?
ERIC: Yes, but I won't sell. They've offered one thousand pounds if I'm captured dead.
ERNIE: Yes?
ERIC: Two thousand pounds if I'm captured alive.
ERNIE: Yes?
ERIC: And three thousand pounds if I'm captured dead and alive. And all for one lousy overdue library book!
ERNIE: What's the charge?
ERIC: Tuppence a day. Oh, I see what you mean – Borrowing with Intent!
**Eric Morecambe and Ernie Wise**, *The Morecambe and Wise Joke Book*, 1979

**10** ETH: A professional burglar! Mr Glum, you told me Ron's Uncle Charlie was a biologist.
MR GLUM: All I said was, he studies cell structures.
**Frank Muir and Denis Norden**, *The Glums*, London Weekend Television, 1978

**11** Next thing you know, they'll be letting jaywalkers off with life.
**Peggy Nicoll**, *The Daria Database*, 1998

**12** I was walking through the park. I had a very bad asthmatic attack. These three asthmatics attacked me. I know . . . I should have heard them hiding.
**Emo Philips**

**13** One way to make sure crime doesn't pay would be to let the government run it.
**Ronald Reagan**, Republican President, 1981–9

**14** I'm all for bringing back the birch. But only between consenting adults.
**Gore Vidal**, interviewed on *The Frost Programme*, 1966

# Criticism

*See also Abuse; Art – Critics; Critics; Critics – The Artist's View; Insults.*

**1** A thick skin is a gift from God.
**Konrad Adenauer**, German Chancellor 1949–63

**2** I can take any amount of criticism, so long as it is unqualified praise.
**Noel Coward** (Attrib.)

**3** Honest criticism is hard to take, particularly from a relative, a friend, an acquaintance or a stranger.
**Franklin P. Jones**, American comic writer

**4** I have never found in a long experience of politics that criticism is ever inhibited by ignorance.
**Harold Macmillan**, British Conservative Prime Minister, 1957–63

**5** People ask you for criticism, but they only want praise.
**W. Somerset Maugham**, *Of Human Bondage*, 1915

# Critics

*See also Art – Critics; Books – Critics; Criticism; Critics – The Artist's View; Film – Critics; Rock 'n' Roll – Critics; Theatre – Critics.*

**1** A good writer is not, per se, a good critic. No more than a good drunk is automatically a good bartender.
**Jim Bishop**

**2** Either criticism is no good at all (a very defensible position) or else criticism means saying about an author the very things that would have made him jump out of his boots.
**G. K. Chesterton**, *Charles Dickens*, 1906

**3** So many people want me to be apologetic, I'm beginning to refer to myself as Mayor Culpa.
**Ed Koch**, New York Mayor

**4** I could see by the way she sniffed that she was about to become critical. There had always been a strong strain of book-reviewer blood in her.
**P. G. Wodehouse**, *Aunts Aren't Gentlemen*, 1974

# Critics – The Artist's View

*See also Art – Critics; Books – Critics; Criticism; Critics; Film – Critics; Rock 'n' Roll – Critics; Theatre – Critics.*

**1** A critic is a bunch of biases held loosely together by a sense of taste.
**Witney Balliett**, *Dinosaurs in the Morning*, 1962

**2** . . . drooling, drivelling, doleful, depressing, dropsical drips.
**Sir Thomas Beecham**, British conductor, 1955

**3** Critics are like eunuchs in a harem: they know how it's done, they've seen it done every day, but they're unable to do it themselves.
**Brendan Behan**, Irish writer (Attrib.)

**4** Critics can't even make music by rubbing their back legs together.
**Mel Brooks**, quoted in *The New York Times*, 1975

**5** If the critics unanimously take exception to one particular scene it is advisable to move that scene to a more conspicuous place in the programme.
**Noel Coward** (Attrib.)

**6** The day when I shall begin to worry is when the critics declare: 'This is Noel Coward's greatest play.' But I know they bloody well won't.
**Noel Coward** (Attrib.)

**7** You know who the critics are? The men who have failed in literature and art.
**Benjamin Disraeli**, *Lothair*, 1870

**8** Taking to pieces is the trade of those who cannot construct.
**Ralph Waldo Emerson** (Attrib.)

**9** He takes the long review of things;
He asks and gives no quarter.
And you can sail with him on wings
Or read the book. It's shorter.
**David McCord**, *To a Certain Most Certainly Certain Critic*

**10** A drama critic is a person who surprises the playwright by informing him what he meant.
**Wilson Mizner**, 1876–1933, American playwright

**11** Asking a working writer what he feels about critics is like asking a lamp-post what it feels about dogs.
**John Osborne**, 1929–94, English playwright (Attrib.)

**12** A critic is a legless man who teaches running.
**Channing Pollock**, 1880–1946, American humorist (Attrib.)

**13** I had another dream the other day about music critics. They were small and rodent-like with padlocked ears, as if they had stepped out of a painting by Goya.
**Igor Stravinsky**, 1882–1971, Russian-born composer quoted in the *Evening Standard*, 1969

**14** A critic is a man who knows the way but can't drive the car.
**Kenneth Tynan**, *The New York Times*, 1966

**15** They search for ages for the wrong word which, to give them credit, they eventually find.
**Peter Ustinov**, *On Critics*, BBC Radio, 1952

**16** It is exactly because a man cannot do a thing that he is the proper judge of it.
**Oscar Wilde**, 'The Critic as Artist', 1890

**17** Has anyone ever seen a dramatic critic in the daytime? Of course not. They come out after dark, up to no good.
**P. G. Wodehouse**

**18** It is the nature of the artist to mind excessively what is said about him. Literature is strewn with the wreckage of men who have minded beyond reason the opinions of others.
**Virginia Woolf**, *A Room of One's Own*, 1929

**19** . . . inkstained wretches.
**Alexander Woollcott**, 1887–1943, American columnist and critic

**20** Rock journalism is people who can't write interviewing people who can't talk for people who can't read.
**Frank Zappa**, 1940–93, musician and songwriter (Attrib.)

# Cults

*See also Religion.*

**1** What's a cult? It just means not enough people to make a minority.
**Robert Altman**, 1981

**2** My son has taken up meditation – at least it's better than sitting doing nothing.
**Max Kauffmann**

**3** The Amish are a surly sect.
They paint their bulging barns with hex
Designs, pronounce a dialect
Of Deutsch, inbreed, and wink at sex.
They have no use for buttons, tea,
Life insurance, cigarettes,
Churches, liquor, Sea & Ski,
Public power, or regrets.
**John Updike**, 'The Amish', *Telegraph Poles and Other Poems*, 1969

# Culture

*See also Aesthetes; Art and Artists; The Theatre.*

**1** Botticelli isn't a wine, you Juggins!
Botticelli's a *cheese*!
*Punch*, 1894

**2** One of the basic freedoms of the
Englishman is freedom from culture.
**Lord Goodman**, Chairman of the Arts Council, 1967

**3** Culture is roughly anything we do and
the monkeys don't.
**Lord Raglan** (Attrib.)

**4** Mrs Ballinger is one of the ladies who
pursue Culture in bands, as though it were
dangerous to meet it alone.
**Edith Wharton**, *Xingu*, 1916

# Cynicism

**1** Your Vigor for Life Appalls Me
**Robert Crumb**, title, *Your Vigor for Life Appalls Me:
Robert Crumb Letters 1958–1977*, 1998

**2** The idiot who praises with enthusiastic
    tone,
    All centuries but this, and every country
    but his own.
**W. S. Gilbert**, *The Mikado*, 1885

**3** Cynicism – the intellectual cripple's
substitute for intelligence.
**Russell Lynes**, American writer and critic

**4** A cynic is a man who, when he smells
flowers, looks around for a coffin.
**H. L. Mencken** (Attrib.)

**5** It is a sin to believe evil of others, but it is
seldom a mistake.
**H. L. Mencken** (Attrib.)

**6** I was going to buy a copy of *The Power of
Positive Thinking* and then I thought: What
the hell good would that do?
**Ronnie Shakes**

**7** No matter how cynical you get, it's
impossible to keep up.
**Lily Tomlin**

**8** CECIL GRAHAM: What is a cynic?
LORD DARLINGTON: A man who knows the
price of everything and the value of
nothing.
**Oscar Wilde**, *Lady Windermere's Fan*, 1892

# Dance

*See also Ballet; Exercise; The Theatre.*

**1** Dancing is the perpendicular expression of a horizontal desire.
**Anon.**

**2** Down with the modern dance!
   That craze we'll quickly smother.
   It looks all right
   If your coat's on tight
   And you really love each other.
   Down with the Shimmie Shake
   That makes poor Auntie hot!
   We'll see that every dance club fails,
   And slap Pavlova till she wails.
   What about Salome and her seven veils?
   Down with the whole damn lot!
**Noel Coward**, 'Down with the Whole Damn Lot!', *Co-optimists*, 1928

**3** Senorita Nina
   From Argentina
   Despised the Tango
   And though she never was a girl to let a
      man go
   She wouldn't sacrifice her principles for
      sex.
   She looked with scorn on the gyrations
   Of her relations
   Who danced the Conga
   And swore that if she had to stand it any
      longer
   She'd lose all dignity and wring their silly
      necks!
**Noel Coward**, 'Nina', *Sigh No More*, 1945

**4** Though no one ever could be keener
   Than little Nina
   On quite a number
   Of very eligible men who did the Rhumba
   When they proposed to her she simply
      left them flat.
   She said that love should be impulsive
   But not convulsive
   And syncopation
   Has a discouraging effect on procreation
   And that she'd rather read a book – and
      that was that!
**Noel Coward**, 'Nina', *Sigh No More*, 1945

**5** May I have the pleasure of the next sadly outdated courting ritual.
**Michael Leunig**, *The Bedtime Leunig*, cartoon, 1981

**6** Teenagers and old people may know how to dance, but real people who go to real parties haven't the slightest. The only dances they even half remember how to do are the ones they learned twenty years ago. This is what the old Supremes tape is for: stiff and overweight versions of the Jerk, the Mashed Potato, the Pony, the Swim, and the Watusi. And after six drinks everyone will revert to the Twist.

**P. J. O'Rourke**, *Modern Manners*, 1983

**7** He makes you feel more danced against than with.

**Sally Poplin**

**8** I was a ballerina when I started. I had to quit the ballet though after I injured a groin muscle. It wasn't mine. He's doing very well though, really. He's a soprano with the Vienna Boys Choir.

**Rita Rudner**, *A Gala Comedy Hour*, ITV, 1996

**9** My father originated the limbo dance – trying to get into a pay toilet.

**Slappy White**

**10** 'Can you dance?' said the girl. Lancelot gave a short, amused laugh. He was a man who never let his left hip know what his right hip was doing.

**P. G. Wodehouse**, 'Came the Dawn', *Meet Mr Mulliner*, 1927

# Dating

*See also Couples; Courtship; Flirtation; Petting.*

**1** I don't believe we've met. I'm Mr Right.

If national security were at stake, would you spend the night with a man whose name you don't even know?

I'm glad you don't recognize me. I'd rather have you like me for myself.

I don't dance. But I'd love to hold you while you do.

**'Four Tested Opening Lines'**, advertisement, *Playboy*, 1969

**2 Chat-up lines and comebacks:**

HE: So what do you do for a living?
SHE: I'm a female impersonator.

HE: Is this seat empty?
SHE: Yes – and this one will be too, if you sit down.

HE: How do you like your eggs in the morning?
SHE: Unfertilised!
**Anon.**

**3 Responses to chat-up lines:**

Sorry, I don't date outside my species.
Sorry, I'm looking for someone a bit higher up the food chain.
**Anon.**

**4** MONICA: Okay, everybody. Relax. This is not a date. It's just two people going out to dinner and not having sex.
CHANDLER: Sounds like a date to me.
*Cooking with Friends*, 1996

**5** JOEY: Monica, I'm telling you this guy is perfect for you!
MONICA: Forget it. Not after your cousin who could belch the alphabet.
*Cooking with Friends*, 1996

**6** BOBBY BIGHEAD: So, where you girls been all our lives?
DARIA: Waiting here for you. We were born in this room, we grew up in this room, and we thought we would die here, alone. But now you've arrived and our lives can truly begin.
BOBBY BIGHEAD: (To his friend) She likes you!
**Anne D. Bernstein**, 'The Invitation', *Daria*, MTV, 1997

**7** One woman I was dating said, 'Come on over, there's nobody home.' I went over – nobody was home.
**Rodney Dangerfield**

**8** 7.30 p.m. Complete panic stations. Mark Darcy is coming round to pick me up in half an hour. Just got home from work with mad hair and unfortunate laundry crisis outfit on. Help oh help. Was planning to wear white 501s but suddenly occurs to me he may be the type who will take me to a posh scary restaurant. Oh God, do not have anything posh to wear. Do you think he will expect me to put bunny tail on? Not that I'm interested in him or anything.
**Helen Fielding**, *Bridget Jones's Diary*, 1996

**9 What is a date?**

A date, at this juncture in history, is any prearranged meeting with a member of the opposite sex toward whom you have indecent intentions . . . One does not have to sleep with, or even touch, someone who has paid for your meal. All those obligations are hereby rendered null and void, and any man who doesn't think so needs a quick jab in the kidney.

**Cynthia Heimel,** *Sex Tips for Girls,* 1983

**10** JERRY: So what're you doing now?
ELAINE: Oh, I'm going to take a little stroll through the park.
JERRY: With a gentleman caller?
ELAINE: Yes. His name is Hal.
JERRY: The walking date's a good date. You don't have to look right at the person.
ELAINE: Hey, it's the next best thing to being alone!

**Gregg Kavet and Andy Robin,** *Seinfeld,* NBC TV, 1997

**11** From **Top ten tip-offs to guys: you're on a bad date**

Doesn't laugh when you give yourself ketchup sideburns.
It's been four hours since she left for the ladies' room.
You catch her giving her phone number to the guy squeegeeing your windshield.
Lunges at you several times with a steak knife.
'Whoa! Is it 8:15 already?'

**David Letterman,** *The Late Show,* CBS

**12** From **Top ten tip-offs to women: you're on a bad date**

You order a Double Whopper and he says, 'Hey, my name ain't Rockefeller, honey.'
You have never heard anyone speak at such length and with such intensity about an ant farm.
He gets really angry when you tell him you like his Siamese twin brother better.
He's proud of how long he can sustain a burp.
You check a dozen encyclopedias and almanacs, but his story about being a Beatle just doesn't pan out.

**David Letterman,** *The Late Show,* CBS

**13** I've been on so many blind dates I should get a free dog.

**Wendy Liebman**

**14** GEORGE: You're doomed. You're gonna have to have all your sex at women's

apartments. It'll be like a permanent road trip. Forget about the home bed advantage.
JERRY: But I need the home bed advantage.
GEORGE: Of course, we all do.

**Peter Mehlman,** 'The Apartment', *Seinfeld,* NBC TV, 1991

**15** Dates used to be made days or even weeks in advance. Now dates tend to be made the day after. That is, you get a phone call from someone who says, 'If anyone asks, I was out to dinner with you last night, okay?'

**P. J. O'Rourke,** *Modern Manners,* 1983

**16** . . . men generally pay for all expenses on a date . . . Either sex, however, may bring a little gift, its value to be determined by the bizarreness of the sexual request to be made later that evening.

**P. J. O'Rourke,** *Modern Manners,* 1983

**17** Lots of women go out with me just to further their careers – damn anthropologists!

**Emo Philips**

**18** *What should a woman do if a man stands her up on a date?*
If the man is genuinely apologetic, I would let him off with a large bunch of flowers, an expensive present, and a lavish make-up dinner. On the other hand, if he treats it in an offhand manner, he is obviously the kind of person who is not going to knock himself out for you, and you should do it for him.

**Miss Piggy,** *Miss Piggy's Guide to Life (As Told to Henry Beard),* 1981

**19** I was always meeting men who didn't want to get involved. I dated my last boyfriend for about two years and finally I just gave him an ultimatum. I said, 'Listen, either you tell me your name or it's over.'

**Rita Rudner,** *A Gala Comedy Hour,* ITV, 1996

**20** What is a date really, but a job interview that lasts all night?

**Jerry Seinfeld,** *SeinLanguage,* 1993

**21** I wouldn't mind being the last man on earth – just to see if all those girls were telling me the truth.

**Ronnie Shakes**

**22** I met a new girl at a barbecue. A very

pretty blond girl, I think. I don't know for sure. Her hair was on fire. And all she talked about was herself. 'I'm on fire!' You know the type. 'Jesus Christ, help me! Put me out!' Come on, can we talk about *me* a little bit?
**Garry Shandling**

**23** I'm dating a homeless woman. It's easier to talk her into staying over.
**Garry Shandling**

**24** How many of you ever started dating someone 'cause you were too lazy to commit suicide?
**Judy Tenuta**

**25** You sleep with a guy once and, before you know it, he wants to take you to dinner.
**Myers Yori**

# Deafness

*See also Ears; Noise; Silence.*

**1** My grandfather is hard-of-hearing. He needs to read lips. I don't mind him reading lips, but he uses one of those yellow highlighters.
**Brian Kiley**, *G Q*, 1999

# Death

*See also Cremation; Epitaphs; Funerals; Immortality; Last Words; Martyrdom; Reincarnation; Suicide.*

**1** Death is nature's way of telling you to slow down.
**Graffito**, London, 1978

**2** Death is the greatest kick of all – that's why they save it till last.
**Graffito**, Los Angeles, 1981

**3** A lawyer phoned his client overseas.
   He said, 'I'm afraid your mother-in-law has just passed away in her sleep. Shall we order burial, embalming or cremation?'
   'Take no chances – go for all three.'
**Anon.**

**4** I don't believe in an afterlife, although I am bringing a change of underwear.
**Woody Allen**

**5** It is impossible to experience one's own death objectively and still carry a tune.
**Woody Allen**

**6** It's not that I'm afraid to die, I just don't want to be there when it happens.
**Woody Allen**, *Without Feathers*, 1976

**7** On the plus side, death is one of the few things that can be done as easily lying down.
**Woody Allen**, *Getting Even*, 1972

**8** If my doctor told me I only had six minutes to live, I wouldn't brood. I'd type a little faster.
**Isaac Asimov**, *Life*, 1984

**9** As the poets have mournfully sung,
   Death takes the innocent young,
   The rolling-in-money,
   The screamingly-funny,
   And those who are very well hung.
**W. H. Auden**, 'The Aesthetic Point of View', *Collected Poems*, 1977

**10** Dr Ramsden cannot read
   *The Times* obituary today
   He's dead.
   Let monographs on silk worms
   By other people be
   Thrown away
   Unread.
   For he who best could understand and
      criticize them, he
   Lies clay. In bed.
**John Betjeman**, obituary poem for Dr Walter Ramsden, 1947

**11** Death comes along like a gas bill one can't pay – and that's all one can say about it.
**Anthony Burgess**, interview, *Playboy*, 1974

**12** While other people's deaths are deeply sad, one's own is surely a bit of a joke.
**James Cameron**, *Observer*, 1982

**13** Seems to me it wasn't all that long ago that when an OLD PERSON DIED the UNDERTAKER put him in a COFFIN, and then you sent FLOWERS to the FUNERAL HOME where the MORTICIAN held the WAKE. Then, after the FUNERAL, they put him in a HEARSE and DROVE him to the CEMETERY, where they BURIED his BODY in a GRAVE.
   Now when a SENIOR CITIZEN PASSES AWAY, he is placed in a BURIAL CONTAINER and you send FLORAL TRIBUTES to the SLUMBER ROOM where the GRIEF THERAPIST supervises the VIEWING. After the

MEMORIAL SERVICE, the FUNERAL COACH
TRANSPORTS THE DEPARTED to the GARDEN
OF REMEMBRANCE, where his EARTHLY
REMAINS are INTERRED in their FINAL
RESTING PLACE.

**George Carlin**, 'DEATH IS ALMOST FUN THESE DAYS',
*Brain Droppings*, 1997

**14** For three days after death, hair and
fingernails continue to grow but phone calls
taper off.

**Johnny Carson**, *The Tonight Show*, NBC TV

**15** Few men by their death can have given
such deep satisfaction to so many.

**Cassandra (William Connor)**, 'Farewell to Joseph
Stalin', *Daily Mirror*, 1953

**16** I am ready to meet my Maker. Whether
my Maker is prepared for the ordeal of
meeting me is another matter.

**Winston Churchill**, on his seventy-fifth birthday, 1949

**17** Mrs McFadden has gone from this life;
    She has left all its sorrows and cares;
    She caught the rheumatics in both of
        her legs
    While scrubbing the cellar and stairs.
    They put mustard-plasters upon her in
        vain;
    They bathed her in whisky and rum;
    But Thursday her spirit departed, and
        left
    Her body entirely numb.

**Charles Heber Clark ('Max Adeler')**, 'Mrs McFadden',
*Mr Slimmer's Funeral Verses for the Morning Argus*

**18** We have lost our little Hanner in a very
        painful manner,
    And we often asked, how can her harsh
        sufferings be borne?
    When her death was first reported, her
        aunt got up and snorted
    With the grief that she supported, for it
        made her feel forlorn.
    She was such a little seraph that her
        father, who is sheriff,
    Really doesn't seem to care if he ne'er
        smiles in life again.
    She has gone, we hope, to heaven, at the
        early age of seven
    (Funeral starts off at eleven), where she'll
        never more have pain.

**Charles Heber Clark ('Max Adeler')**, 'Hanner', *Mr
Slimmer's Funeral Verses for the Morning Argus*

**19** It's passed on. This parrot is no more. It
has ceased to be. It's expired and gone to see
its maker. This is a late parrot. It's a stiff.
Bereft of life. It rests in peace. If you hadn't
nailed it to the perch, it would be pushing
up the daisies. It's rung down the curtain
and joined the choir invisible. THIS is an ex-
parrot.

**John Cleese and Graham Chapman**, *And Now for
Something Completely Different*, 1971

**20** PETE: Have you ever thought about
death? Do you realize that we each must
die?
DUD: Of course we must die, but not yet. It's
only half past four of a Wednesday
afternoon.
PETE: No one knows when God in His
Almighty Wisdom will choose to vouchsafe
His precious gift of Death.
DUD: Granted. But chances are He won't be
making a pounce at this time of day.

**Peter Cook and Dudley Moore**, *The Dagenham
Dialogues*, 1971

**21** Immortality is a long shot, I admit. But
somebody has to be first.

**Bill Cosby**

**22** Everyone is afraid of dying alone. I don't
understand. Who wants to die and have to
be polite at the same time?

**Quentin Crisp**

**23** I know he's dead because I sat with him
while he died, but on the other hand he is
*not*. I think it most likely that our dead
aren't nearly as far away as Scotland.

**Alice Thomas Ellis**, *Spectator*, 1986

**24** It's a funny old world – a man's lucky if
he can get out of it alive.

**W. C. Fields**, *You're Telling Me*, screenplay, 1934

**25** 'Hallelujah!' was the only observation
    That escaped Lieutenant-Colonel Mary
        Jane,
    When she tumbled off the platform in
        the station,
    And was cut in little pieces by the train.
    Mary Jane, the train is through yer!
    Hallelujah, Hallelujah!
    We shall gather up the fragments that
        remain.

**A. E. Housman**, 'On the Death of a Female Officer of
the Salvation Army', *Complete Poems*, 1956

**26** My father passed away very quietly in his sleep . . . between the bar and the gents.
**Barry Humphries**, *Les Patterson Has a Stand-Up*, 1996

**27** Hardly a man is now alive
  Who recalls that in 1795
  Occurred the death of a Mr James
    Boswell;
  A joke on his doctor, who'd thought
    that he was well.
**Ring Lardner**, 'Hardly a man is now alive'

**28** Dying is a very dull, dreary affair. And my advice to you is to have nothing whatever to do with it.
**W. Somerset Maugham** (Attrib.)

**29** Public display of mourning is no longer made by people of fashion, although some flashier kinds of widows may insist on sleeping with only black men during the first year after the death. Normal social life, however, may not be resumed by a widow because there has been no normal social life in the United States since 1966.
**P. J. O'Rourke**, *Modern Manners*, 1983

**30** The purpose of a funeral service is to comfort the living. It is important at a funeral to display excessive grief. This will show others how kind-hearted and loving you are and their improved opinion of you will be very comforting.
   As anyone familiar with modern fiction and motion pictures knows, excessive grief cannot be expressed by means of tears or a mournful face. It is necessary to break things, hit people, and throw yourself on to the top of the coffin, at least.
**P. J. O'Rourke**, *Modern Manners*, 1983

**31** He lies below, correct in cypress wood,
  And entertains the most exclusive
    worms.
**Dorothy Parker**, *The Very Rich Man*

**32** It costs me never a stab nor squirm
  To tread by chance upon a worm.
  'Aha, my little dear,' I say,
  'your clan will pay me back one day.'
**Dorothy Parker**, 'Sunset Gun', 1928

**33** GROUCHO MARX: Either this man is dead or my watch has stopped.
**Robert Pirosh and George Seaton**, *A Day at the Races*, screenplay, 1937

**34** The late F. W. H. Myers used to tell how he asked a man at a dinner table what he thought would happen to him when he died. The man tried to ignore the question, but, on being pressed, replied: 'Oh well, I suppose I shall inherit eternal bliss, but I wish you wouldn't talk about such unpleasant subjects.'
**Bertrand Russell**, *Stoicism and Mental Health*, 1928

**35** You haven't lived until you've died in California.
**Mort Sahl**, American comedian

**36** Boy, when you're dead, they really fix you up. I hope to hell when I *do* die somebody has sense enough to just dump me in the river or something. Anything except sticking me in a goddam cemetery. People coming and putting a bunch of flowers on your stomach on Sunday, and all that crap. Who wants flowers when you're dead? Nobody.
**J. D. Salinger**, *The Catcher in the Rye*, 1951

**37** HOMER: I'm gonna die! Jesus, Allah, Buddha – I love you all!
**David M. Stern**, 'Marge Simpson in: "Screaming Yellow Honkers" ', *The Simpsons*, Fox TV, 1999

**38** Eternity is a terrible thought. I mean, where's it going to end?
**Tom Stoppard**, *Rosencrantz and Guildenstern are Dead*, 1967

**39** I did not attend his funeral; but I wrote a nice letter saying I approved of it.
**Mark Twain**, of a deceased politician (Attrib.)

**40** The reports of my death are greatly exaggerated.
**Mark Twain**, cable from Europe to the Associated Press, 1897

**41** Her capacity for family affection is extraordinary. When her third husband died, her hair turned quite gold from grief.
**Oscar Wilde**, *The Picture of Dorian Gray*, 1891

**42** I'm not afraid of death. It's the make-over at the undertaker's that scares me . . . They try to make you look as lifelike as possible, which defeats the whole purpose. It's hard to feel bad for somebody who looks better than you do.
**Anita Wise**

# Debt

*See also Banking; Budgets; Credit; Credit Cards; Extravagance; Money.*

**1** If it isn't the sheriff it's the finance company. I've got more attachments on me than a vacuum cleaner.
**John Barrymore**, 1882–1942, American actor

**2** Never run into debt, not if you can find anything else to run into.
**Josh Billings**, *The Complete Works of Josh Billings*, 1919

**3** I need just enough to tide me over until I need more.
**Jerry Dennis**

**4** If there's anyone listening to whom I owe money, I'm prepared to forget if you are.
**Errol Flynn**, on Australian radio

**5** If you owe the bank $100, that's your problem. If you owe the bank $100 million, that's the bank's problem.
**J. Paul Getty**, 1892–1976, American billionaire industrialist

# Decisions

*See also Assertiveness; Committees; Indecision.*

**1** It must be remembered that the real purpose of any attempt to find a preparatory basis for agreement is to establish a position from which the whole question can be surveyed with a view to subsequent discussion of the points at issue.

It is only by examining the whole question that its various complications can be understood, and only by being understood that they can be dealt with. It can never be repeated too often that the more often it is repeated that if nothing is done soon it will be too late to do anything. Wind variable on high ground.
**Beachcomber ( J. B. Morton)**, *Daily Express*

**2** You may be sure that when a man begins to call himself a realist he is preparing to do something that he is secretly ashamed of doing.
**Sydney J. Harris**, 1917–86, English-born American columnist

**3** A decision is what a man makes when he can't get anyone to serve on a committee.
**Fletcher Knebel**, American columnist

**4** When a person tells you, 'I'll think it over and let you know' – you know.
**Olin Miller**, American writer

**5** All our final decisions are made in a state of mind that is not going to last.
**Marcel Proust**

# Democracy

*See also Equality; Government; Politics and Politicians.*

**1** Democracy is like sex. When it's good, it's very, very good. And when it's bad, it's still pretty good.
**Anon.**

**2** Democracy means government by discussion but it is only effective if you can stop people talking.
**Clement Attlee**, British Labour politician, speech at Oxford, 1957

**3** It has been said that Democracy is the worst form of government except all those other forms that have been tried from time to time.
**Winston Churchill**, speech in the House of Commons, November 1947

**4** Democracy consists of choosing your dictators, after they've told you what you think it is you want to hear.
**Alan Coren**, *Daily Mail*, 1975

**5** Two cheers for Democracy: one because it admits variety and two because it permits criticism. Two cheers are quite enough: there is no occasion to give three.
**E. M. Forster**, 'What I Believe', *Two Cheers for Democracy*, 1951

**6** In an autocracy, one person has his way; in an aristocracy a few people have their way; in a democracy no one has his way.
**Celia Green**, *The Decline and Fall of Science*

**7** One fifth of the people are against everything all the time.
**Robert Kennedy**, quoted in the *Observer*, 1964

**8** Democracy is an interesting, even laudable, notion and there is no question but that when compared to Communism, which is too dull, or Fascism, which is too exciting, it emerges as the most palatable

form of government. This is not to say that
it is without its drawbacks – chief among
them being its regrettable tendency to
encourage people in the belief that all men
are created equal. And although the vast
majority need only take a quick look
around the room to see that this is hardly
the case, a great many remain utterly
convinced.
**Fran Lebowitz**, *Metropolitan Life*, 1978

**9** Democracy is . . . a form of religion; it is
the worship of jackals by jackasses.
**H. L. Mencken**, *Sententiae*, 1920

**10** Democracy is that system of
government under which the people,
having 35,717,342 native-born adult whites
to choose from, including thousands who
are handsome and many who are wise, pick
out a Coolidge to be head of the State.
**H. L. Mencken**, *Prejudices*, Fifth Series, 1926

**11** Democracy is the art of running the
circus from the monkey cage.
**H. L. Mencken** (Attrib.)

**12** Democracy is the theory that the
common people know what they want, and
deserve to get it good and hard.
**H. L. Mencken**, *A Book of Burlesques*, 1916

**13** Under democracy, one party always
devotes its chief energies to trying to prove
that the other party is unfit to rule – and
both commonly succeed, and are right.
**H. L. Mencken**, *Minority Report*, 1956

**14** In a democracy everybody has the right
to be represented, including the jerks.
**Christ Patten**, *Evening Standard*, 1991

**15** Democracy is too good to share with
just anybody.
**Nigel Rees**, *A Year of Graffiti*, 1983

**16** Democracy is a device that ensures we
shall be governed no better than we
deserve.
**George Bernard Shaw** (Attrib.)

**17** Democracy substitutes election by the
incompetent many for appointment by the
corrupt few.
**George Bernard Shaw**, *Maxims For Revolutionists*, 1903

**18** I have great faith in the people; as for

their wisdom – well, Coca-Cola still outsells
champagne.
**Adlai Stevenson**

**19** It is by the goodness of God that in our
country we have those three unspeakably
precious things: freedom of speech, freedom
of conscience, and the prudence never to
practice either of them.
**Mark Twain**, *Following the Equator*, 1897

**20** High hopes were once formed of
democracy; but democracy means simply
the bludgeoning of the people by the
people for the people.
**Oscar Wilde**, 'The Soul of Man under Socialism', 1891

# Democratic Party, The

*See also Democrats and Republicans; Liberals;
Political Parties; Politics and Politicians; The
Republican Party; Washington.*

**1** The Democratic Party is like a man riding
backward in a carriage. It never sees a thing
until it has gone by.
**Benjamin F. Butler**, 1818–93, Republican Congressman
and Governor

**2** I never said all Democrats were saloon-
keepers; what I said was all saloon-keepers
were Democrats.
**Horace Greeley**, 1811–72, American newspaper editor

**3** The Democratic Party at its worst is better
for the country than the Republican Party at
its best.
**Lyndon B. Johnson**

**4** The [Democratic] Government's view of
the economy could be summed up in a few
short phrases: If it moves, tax it. If it keeps
moving, regulate it. And if it stops moving,
subsidize it.
**Ronald Reagan**, Republican President, 1981–9

**5** I belong to no organized party – I am a
Democrat.
**Will Rogers** (Attrib.)

**6** The Democratic Party is like a mule
without pride of ancestry or hope of
posterity.
**Emory Speer**, Republican, Georgia (Attrib.)

# Democrats and Republicans

*See also The Democratic Party; Political Parties; The Republican Party.*

**1** It seems to be a law of nature that Republicans are more boring than Democrats.
**Stewart Alsop**, 1914–74, American journalist

**2** A Democrat sees the glass of water as half full. A Republican looks at the same glass and wonders who the hell drank half his glass of water.
**Jeff Cesario**

**3** Democrats give away their old clothes; Republicans wear theirs. Republicans employ exterminators; Democrats step on the bugs. Democrats eat the fish they catch; Republicans stuff 'em and hang 'em on the wall.
**Sean Donlon**, Irish Ambassador to the United States, quoted in the *Washington Post*, 1981

**4** Democrats make up plans and then do something else. Republicans follow the plans their grandfathers made . . . Republican boys date Democratic girls. They plan to marry Republican girls, but feel they're entitled to a little fun first.
**Andrew Jacobs, Jr.**, Democratic Congressman, House debate, 1983

**5** We need Democrats. They are on this world to distribute wealth. But we first need a party that can create the wealth to distribute.
**Jack F. Kemp**, Republican Congressman, 'Firing Line', *PBS*, 1988

**6** I relate to both parties. I eat like an elephant and act like a jackass.
**Rich Little**, *Sunday Morning*, CBS TV, 1988

**7** . . . while the Republicans are smart enough to make money, the Democrats are smart enough to get in office every two or three times a century and take it away from 'em.
**Will Rogers**, radio talk, 1934

**8** Republicans raise dahlias, Dalmatians, and eyebrows. Democrats raise Airedales, kids and taxes.
**Will Stanton**, 'How to Tell a Democrat from a Republican', *Ladies' Home Journal*, 1962

**9** Republicans sleep in twin beds – some even in separate rooms. That is why there are more Democrats.
**Will Stanton**, 'How to Tell a Democrat from a Republican', *Ladies' Home Journal*, 1962

**10** Republicans study the financial pages of the newspaper. Democrats put them in the bottom of the bird cage.
**Will Stanton**, 'How to Tell a Democrat from a Republican', *Ladies' Home Journal*, 1962

# Denmark and the Danes

**1** From Hamlet to Kierkegaard, the word 'Danish' has been synonymous with fun, fun, fun . . . Who else would have the sense of humor to stuff prunes and toecheese into lumps of wet dough and *serve it to you for breakfast*? . . . Let's hear it for those very wonderful kooky, very crazy, very whacky, very witty Danes! They're the *living end*! And vice versa.
**Tony Hendra**, 'EEC! It's the US of E!', *National Lampoon*, 1965

# Dentists
*see Teeth.*

# Depression and Despair
*See also Anxiety; Psychiatry; Psychoanalysis; Suicide.*

**1** Sometimes you wake up in the morning and wish your parents had never met.
**Bill Fitch**, basketball coach, during a losing run

**2** He's turned his life around. He used to be depressed and miserable. Now he's miserable and depressed.
**David Frost**, TVam, 1984

**3** The secret of being miserable is to have leisure to bother about whether you are happy or not. The cure for it is occupation.
**George Bernard Shaw**, *Parents and Children*, 1914

**4** Noble deeds and hot baths are the best cures for depression.
**Dodie Smith**, *I Capture the Castle*, 1948

**5** Bingo uttered a stricken woofle like a bull-dog that has been refused cake.
**P. G. Wodehouse**, *Very Good, Jeeves*, 1930

**6** Depression is merely anger without enthusiasm.
**Steven Wright**, American comic

# Desires

**1** In this world there are only two tragedies. One is not getting what one wants and the other is getting it.
**Oscar Wilde**, *Lady Windermere's Fan*, 1892

**2** All the things I really like to do are either immoral, illegal or fattening.
**Alexander Woollcott**, 1887–1943, American columnist and critic

# Diaries

*See also Autobiography.*

**1** Keep a diary and one day it'll keep you.
**Mae West**

**2** I never travel without my diary. One should always have something sensational to read in the train.
**Oscar Wilde**, *The Importance of Being Earnest*, 1895

# Dictionaries

**1** Circular Definition: see Definition, Circular.
**Anon.**

# Diets and Dieting

*See also Eating; Exercise; Figures; Food.*

**1** Can it be a coincidence that 'STRESSED' is 'DESSERTS' spelled backwards?
**Anon.**

**2** Diets are for those who are thick and tired of it.
**Anon.**

**3** Eat drink and be merry, for tomorrow we diet!
**Anon.**

**4** I have a great diet. You're allowed to eat anything you want, but you must eat it with naked fat people.
**Ed Bluestone**, American comic

**5** I've been on a constant diet for the last two decades. I've lost a total of 789 pounds. By all accounts, I should be hanging from a charm bracelet.
**Erma Bombeck**

**6** Those magazine dieting stories always have the testimonial of a woman who wore a dress that could slipcover New Jersey in one photo and thirty days later looked like a well-dressed thermometer.
**Erma Bombeck**, quoted in *Time*, 1984

**7** A man trying to diet is in fact dying to try it.
**Jerry Dennis**

**8** Health nuts are going to feel stupid someday, lying in hospital dying of nothing.
**Redd Foxx**, black comedian

**9** The second day of a diet is always easier than the first. By the second day, you're off it.
**Jackie Gleason**

**10** If you eat something but no one else sees you eat it, it has no calories.
If you fatten up everyone else around you, then you look thinner.
**Lewis Grizzard**

**11** A really busy person never knows how much he weighs.
**Edgar Watson Howe**, *Country Town Sayings*, 1911

**12** I feel about airplanes the way I feel about diets. It seems to me they are wonderful things for other people to go on.
**Jean Kerr**, *The Snake Has All the Lines*, 1960

**13** Take, O take the cream away,
Take away the sugar, too;
Let the morning coffee stay
As a black and bitter brew.
I have gained since yesternight –
Shoot the calories on sight!
**Stoddard King**, *Breakfast Song in Time of Diet*

**14** The best way to lose weight is to close

your mouth – something very difficult for a politician.
**Ed Koch**, Mayor of New York

**15** I went on a diet, swore off drinking and heavy eating, and in fourteen days I lost two weeks.
**Joe E. Lewis**, 1902–71, American comedian

**16** So I think it is very nice for ladies to be lithe and lissome,
But not so much that you cut yourself if you happen to embrace or kissome.
**Ogden Nash**, 'Curl Up and Diet', *I'm a Stranger Here Myself*, 1938

**17** Diet Tips
Never eat anything at one sitting that you can't lift.
Always use one of the new – and far more reliable – elastic measuring tapes to check on your waistline.
**Miss Piggy**, *Miss Piggy's Guide to Life (As Told to Henry Beard)*, 1981

**18** HOLLY (12 YEARS OLD): I don't like sweets!
ELLEN: All right. But don't come crying to me when you're 75 with a mouthful of teeth!
**David Walpert**, *Ellen*, ABC TV, 1998

**19** I never worry about diets. The only carrots that interest me are the number you get in a diamond.
**Mae West**

**20** My wife is on a diet. Coconuts and bananas. She hasn't lost any weight, but can she climb a tree!
**Henny Youngman**

## Dignity

**1** It is only people of small moral stature who have to stand on their dignity.
**Arnold Bennett**, 1867–1931, English novelist

**2** I know of no case where a man added to his dignity by standing on it.
**Winston Churchill**

## Diplomacy
*See also Government; Politics and Politicians.*

**1** Diplomacy, *n.* the patriotic art of lying for one's country.
**Ambrose Bierce**, *The Devil's Dictionary*, 1911

**2** Diplomacy is the art of saying 'Nice Doggie!' till you can find a rock.
**Wynn Catlin**

**3** Diplomacy is the art of letting somebody else have your way.
**David Frost**, TVam, 1983

**4** Diplomacy: lying in state.
**Oliver Herford**, 1864–1935, English-born American writer

**5** I got a call from Haig [US Secretary of State], who offered me the job of explaining the Administration's foreign policy to the Chinese – one by one.
**Henry Kissinger**

**6** There cannot be a crisis next week. My schedule is already full.
**Henry Kissinger**, quoted in *The New York Times Magazine*, 1969

**7** The chief distinction of a diplomat is that he can say no in such a way that it sounds like yes.
**Lester Bowles Pearson**, Canadian Prime Minister 1963–8

**8** A diplomat is a man who thinks twice before he says nothing.
**Frederick Sawyer**

**9** A diplomat is a person who can tell you to go to hell in such a way that you actually look forward to the trip.
**Caskie Stinnett**, *Out of the Red*, 1960

**10** It was 95% ego and 5% patriotism. I think.
**Robert Strauss**, on accepting the position of Ambassador to Moscow under the Bush administration

**11** . . . babies in silk hats playing with dynamite.
**Alexander Woollcott**, 1887–1943, American columnist and critic (Attrib.)

# Disasters

*See also Accidents.*

**1** I realized the car wasn't having problems; the *ground* was having problems.
**Driver** on the San Francisco–Oakland Bay bridge during the 1989 earthquake

**2** SANDI: Let's get out of here while there's time to walk. Running for your life looks so *geeky*.
**Glenn Eichler and Peter Elwell**, 'Daria! – The Musical', *Daria*, MTV, 1999

# Disc Jockeys

*See also Music and Musicians; News; Rock 'n' Roll; Songs and Singers.*

**1** If you are a disc jockey, kindly remember that your job is to play records that people will enjoy dancing to and not to impress possible visiting disc jockeys with your esoteric taste. People generally enjoy dancing to songs that have words and are of reasonable length.
**Fran Lebowitz**, *Metropolitan Life*, 1978

**2** Radio news is bearable. This is due to the fact that while the news is being broadcast the disc jockey is not allowed to talk.
**Fran Lebowitz**, *Metropolitan Life*, 1978

# Disgust

*See also Anger; Nausea.*

**1** Gold was not altogether certain what, anatomically, a gorge was, but he knew that his was rising.
**Joseph Heller**, *Good as Gold*, 1979

# Dishonesty

*See also Crime; Guilt; Lies; Truth.*

**1** He's the only man I ever knew who had rubber pockets so he could steal soup.
**Wilson Mizner**, 1876–1933, American playwright, of a Hollywood studio chief

**2** It is almost always worth while to be cheated; people's little frauds have an interest which more than repays what they cost us.
**Logan Pearsall Smith**, *Afterthoughts*, 1931

**3** Many a time in the past, when an active

operator in the Street, he had done things to the Small Investor which would have caused raised eyebrows on the fo'c's'le of a pirate sloop – and done them without a blush.
**P. G. Wodehouse**, *The Heart of a Goof*, 1926

# Divorce

*See also Alimony; Love – Breaking up; Marriage; Rejection.*

**1** JUDGE: You want a divorce on the grounds that your husband is careless about his appearance?
WIFE: Yes, your honour – he hasn't made one for three years.
**Anon.**

**2** I miss my ex . . . but my aim is getting better.
**Bumper sticker**, California, 1999

**3** For a while we pondered whether to take a vacation or get a divorce. We decided that a trip to Bermuda is over in two weeks, but a divorce is something you always have.
**Woody Allen**, nightclub act, 1960s

**4** Many a man owes his success to his first wife and his second wife to his success.
**Jim Backus**

**5** The difference between divorce and legal separation is that a legal separation gives a husband time to hide his money.
**Johnny Carson**, *The Tonight Show*, NBC TV

**6** The happiest time of anyone's life is just after the first divorce.
**J. K. Galbraith**, American economist

**7** I don't think I'll get married again . . . I'll just find a woman I don't like and give her a house.
**Lewis Grizzard**

**8** It's a sad fact that 50 per cent of marriages in this country end in divorce. But hey, the other half end in death. You could be one of the lucky ones!
**Richard Jeni**

**9** A divorce costs so much more than a wedding – but it's worth it.
**Max Kauffmann**

**10** . . . being divorced is like being hit by a

Mack truck. If you live through it, you start looking very carefully to the right and to the left.

**Jean Kerr**, *Mary, Mary*, 1960

**11** WOMAN STANDING WITH PACKED SUITCASES: I'm leaving you, Frank, because you're a shiftless, low-down, good-for-nothing imbecile . . . and, might I finally add, you have the head of a chicken.

**Gary Larson**, *The Far Side*, cartoon, 1985

**12** You don't know a woman till you've met her in court.

**Norman Mailer**

**13** ERIC: My father was very disappointed when I was born.
ERNIE: Why? Did he want a girl?
ERIC: No, he wanted a divorce.

**Eric Morecambe and Ernie Wise**, *The Morecambe and Wise Joke Book*, 1979

**14** When a couple decide to divorce, they should inform both sets of parents before having a party and telling all their friends. This is not only courteous but practical. Parents may be very willing to pitch in with comments, criticism and malicious gossip of their own to help the divorce along.

**P. J. O'Rourke**, *Modern Manners*, 1983

**15** Relationships don't last anymore. When I meet a guy, the first question I ask myself is, 'Is this the man I want my children to spend their weekends with?'

**Rita Rudner**

**16** God made men. God made women. And when God found that men could not get along with women, God invented Mexico.

**Larry Storch**

**17** My mother and father are both speaking to solicitors. I expect they are fighting over who gets custody of me. I will be a tug-of-love child, and my picture will be in the newspapers. I hope my spots clear up before then.

**Sue Townsend**, *The Secret Diary of Adrian Mole Aged 13³/₄*, 1982

**18** My wife and I were considering a divorce, but after pricing lawyers we decided to buy a new car instead.

**Henny Youngman**

# Doctors

*See also Gynaecology; Health; Hospitals; Illness; Medicine.*

**1** The chief defect of Henry King
Was chewing little bits of string.
At last he swallowed some which tied
Itself in ugly Knots inside.
Physicians of the Utmost Fame
Were called at once; but when they came
They answered, as they took their Fees,
'There is no cure for this disease.'

**Hilaire Belloc**, 'Henry King', *Cautionary Tales for Children*, 1907

**2** WICKSTEED: The longer I practise medicine, the more convinced I am there are only two types of cases: those that involve taking the trousers off and those that don't.

**Alan Bennett**, *Habeas Corpus*, 1973

**3** My doctor is wonderful. Once, in 1955, when I couldn't afford an operation, he touched up the X-rays.

**Joey Bishop**

**4** Keep away from physicians. It is all probing and guessing and pretending with them. They leave it to Nature to cure in her own time, but they take the credit. As well as very fat fees.

**Anthony Burgess**, *Nothing Like the Sun*, 1964

**5** Doctors think a lot of patients are cured who have simply quit in disgust.

**Don Herold**, 1889–1966, American writer and cartoonist

**6** ERNIE: Doctor, I don't know what's wrong with me. Do you think I'll ever get better?
ERIC: I don't know – let me feel your purse.
ERNIE: But Doctor . . .
ERIC: Sit down and tell me about it . . .
ERNIE: Doctor, I'm not a private patient. I'm on the National Health.
ERIC: . . . in less than two minutes.

**Eric Morecambe and Ernie Wise**, *The Morecambe and Wise Joke Book*, 1979

**7** ERNIE: Stick your tongue out and say, 'Ah.'
ERIC: Ah.
ERNIE: Well, your tongue looks all right – but why the postage stamp?

ERIC: So that's where I left it.
**Eric Morecambe and Ernie Wise**, *The Morecambe and Wise Joke Book*, 1979

**8** Optimistic lies have such immense therapeutic value that a doctor who cannot tell them convincingly has mistaken his profession.
**George Bernard Shaw**, *Misalliance*, 1914

**9** PATIENT: And I've got rheumatism on the back of my neck. It's a bad place to have rheumatism – on the back of my neck.
DOCTOR: No, no – where would you want a better place than on the back of your neck?
PATIENT: On the back of your neck!
**Smith and Dale**, 'Dr Kronkheit and His Only Living Patient', American vaudeville act

# Dogs
*See also Animals; Pets; Vets.*

**1** He knew what people thought of his kind: 'High Strung.' 'Spoiled Rotten.' 'French.'
But in the next twenty-four hours, he's going to change all that . . .
He's SMALL.
He's BLACK.
He's MAD AS HELL.
He's POODLE with a MOHAWK.
'You'll never call him Fifi again!'
**Lynda Barry**, 'Poodle with a Mohawk', *Big Ideas*, cartoon, 1983

**2** You will find that the woman who is really kind to dogs is always one who has failed to inspire sympathy in men.
**Max Beerbohm**, *Zuleika Dobson*, 1911

**3** A dog teaches a boy fidelity, perseverance and to turn round three times before lying down.
**Robert Benchley**

**4** A dog is the only thing on earth that loves you more than you love yourself.
**Josh Billings**, *The Complete Work of Josh Billings*, 1919

**5** Every day, the dog and I, we go for a tramp in the woods. And he loves it! Mind you, the tramp is getting a bit fed up!
**Jerry Dennis**

**6** They had a . . . dog called Bluey. A known psychopath, Bluey would attack himself if nothing else was available. He used to chase himself in circles trying to bite his own balls off.
**Clive James**, *Unreliable Memoirs*, 1980

**7** WHAT WE SAY TO DOGS: Okay, Ginger! I've had it! You stay out of the garbage! Understand, Ginger? Stay out of the garbage, or else!
WHAT THEY HEAR: blah blah GINGER blah blah blah blah blah blah blah blah GINGER blah blah blah blah blah . . .
**Gary Larson**, *The Far Side*, cartoon, 1983

**8** A Canadian psychologist is selling a video that teaches you how to test your dog's IQ. Here's how it works: if you spend $12.99 for the video, your dog is smarter than you.
**Jay Leno**, *The Tonight Show*, NBC

**9** ERIC: He's a lovely dog . . . Last Saturday he took first prize at the cat show.
ERNIE: How was that?
ERIC: He took the cat.
ERNIE: Didn't you punish him?
ERIC: I should have done. Trouble is, I spoil him. It works, though. Most of the time I've got him eating out of my leg . . . Last night . . . he gave my leg quite a nasty bite.
ERNIE: Did you put anything on it?
ERIC: No, he liked it just as it was.
**Eric Morecambe and Ernie Wise**, *The Morecambe and Wise Joke Book*, 1979

**10** A door is what a dog is perpetually on the wrong side of.
**Ogden Nash**, 'A Dog's Best Friend is his Illiteracy', 1953

**11** They say the dog is man's best friend. I don't believe that. How many of your friends have you neutered?
**Larry Reeb**

**12** I have a dog that's half pitbull, half poodle. Not much of a guard dog, but a vicious gossip.
**Craig Shoemaker**

**13** . . . that indefatigable and unsavoury engine of pollution, the dog.
**John Sparrow**, 1906–92, English academic, letter to *The Times*, 1975

**14** My friend George walked his dog all at once. Walked him from Boston to Fort Lauderdale and back.
  He said, 'Now you're *done*!'
**Steven Wright**, *Just for Laughs*, 1987

# Do-it-yourself

*See also Home; Interior Decorating.*

**1** Put a hammer in my husband's hand and you've put together two things with roughly the same IQ.
**Anon.**

**2** The quickest way to make your own anti-freeze is to hide her nightie.
**Anon.**

# Dreams

*See also Bed; Sleep.*

**1** He dreamed he was eating shredded wheat and woke up to find the mattress half gone.
**Fred Allen**

**2** People who insist on telling their dreams are among the terrors of the breakfast table.
**Max Beerbohm**

**3** From **Your dreams and what they're trying to tell you.**

IF YOU SEE YOURSELF IN A DREAM: *Floating in a vat of pancake batter.*
IT MEANS: The cards are stacked in your favor.
*Selling beets to talking pigs?* You will be sent to the principal's office.
*Having your hair cut by a dancing policeman?* You will get a free backstage concert pass.
*Worshipping rabbits?* You will found a media empire.
*Gargling creamed corn?* You will join the circus.
*Where your parents have become bowling pins?* You will be granted a wish.
*Dreaming you are in a dream?* You watch too much TV.
**Matt Groening**, *Bart Simpson's Guide to Life*, 1996

# Drink

*See also Alcoholism; Champagne; Hangovers; Prohibition; Restaurants; Thirst; Wine.*

**1** After four martinis, my husband turns into a disgusting beast. And after the fifth, I pass out altogether.
**Anon.**

**2** A skeleton walks into a bar and says, 'Give me a beer and a mop.'
**Anon.**

**3** It was early last December,
  As near as I remember,
  I was walking down the street in tipsy pride;
No one was I disturbing
As I lay down by the curbing,
And a pig came up and lay down by my side.

As I lay there in the gutter
Thinking thoughts I shall not utter,
A lady passing by was heard to say:
'You can tell a man who boozes
By the company he chooses';
And the pig got up and slowly walked away.
**Anon., 'The Drunkard and the Pig'**, *The Oxford Book of American Light Verse*, 1979

**4** On the chest of a barmaid in Sale
  Were tattooed the prices of ale,
  And on her behind,
  For the sake of the blind,
  Was the same information in Braille.
**Anon.**

**5** *I* am sparkling; *you* are unusually talkative; *he* is drunk.
**Competition**, *New Statesman*

**6** STAN OGDEN: Drinking's a serious business. You gotta keep at it – like training for a football match.
*Coronation Street*, Granada TV

**7** One reason I don't drink is that I want to know when I'm having a good time.
**Nancy Astor**, 1879–1964, British politician

**8** Actually, it only takes one drink to get me loaded. Trouble is, I can't remember if it's the thirteenth or fourteenth.
**George Burns**

**9** By all means, let's breath-test pedestrians involved in road accidents – if they're still breathing.
**The Bishop of Ely**, *Observer*, 1967

**10** A woman drove me to drink and I never even had the courtesy to thank her.
**W. C. Fields** (Attrib.)

**11** Either you're drunk or your braces are lopsided.
**W. C. Fields** (Attrib.)

**12** I always keep a stimulant handy in case I see a snake – which I also keep handy.
**W. C. Fields** (Attrib.)

**13** What contemptible scoundrel stole the cork from my lunch?
**W. C. Fields** (Attrib.)

**14** Don't drink and drive. Instead, the next time you get too drunk to drive, walk into a local Dominos and order a pizza.
Then when they go to deliver it, ask for a ride home.
**Todd Glass**

**15** I didn't realize he was a teetotaller until he went off to fix himself a stiff drink and came back with an ice lolly.
**Max Kauffmann**

**16** My favorite drink is the next one.
**Max Kauffmann**

**17** I can't think of anything worse after a night of drinking than waking up next to someone and not being able to remember their name or how you met or why they're dead.
**Laura Kightlinger,** *GQ*, 1999

**18** I don't drink. I don't like it. It makes me feel good.
**Oscar Levant,** 1906–72, American composer and wit

**19** I envy people who drink. At least they know what to blame everything on.
**Oscar Levant**

**20** A man is never drunk if he can lay on the floor without holding on.
**Joe E. Lewis,** 1902–71, American comedian

**21** I always wake up at the crack of ice.
**Joe E. Lewis**

**22** I drink to forget I drink.
**Joe E. Lewis**

**23** WOODY: Can I pour you a draft, Mr Peterson?
NORM: A little early, isn't it Woody?
WOODY: For a beer?
NORM: No, for stupid questions!
**David Lloyd,** 'Let Sleeping Drakes Lie', *Cheers,* NBC TV, 1988

**24** I haven't touched a drop of alcohol since the invention of the funnel.
**Malachy McCourt**

**25** There was a young fellow named Sydney
Who drank till he ruined his kidney.
It shriveled and shrank
As he sat there and drank,
But he had a good time at it, didn't he.
**Don Marquis**

**26** He's not an ordinary drunk. He donated his body to science and he's preserving it in alcohol until they need it.
**Bob Monkhouse,** English comedian

**27** If you don't drink, when you wake up in the morning, that's the best you're going to feel all day.
**Martin Mull**

**28** Candy
Is dandy
But liquor
Is quicker.
**Ogden Nash,** 'Reflections on Ice-breaking', *Hard Lines,* 1931

**29** I meant to address important questions such as: When is it appropriate to get drunk? (When you're sober.) When is it appropriate to sober up? (When you come to and find your dog is wearing a negligée.) Are there things you shouldn't say after letting go of the water wagons with both hands? ('I do.')
**P. J. O'Rourke,** *Men's Journal,* 2000

**30** One more drink and I'll be under the host.
**Dorothy Parker,** at a cocktail party (Attrib.)

**31** COACH: How's a beer sound, Norm?
NORM: I dunno. I usually finish them before they get a word in.
**Heide Perlman,** 'Fortune and Men's Weights', *Cheers,* NBC TV, 1984

**32** SAM: What will you have, Norm?
NORM: Well, I'm in a gambling mood, Sammy. I'll take a glass of whatever comes out of that tap.
SAM: Oh, looks like beer, Norm.
NORM: Call me Mister Lucky!
**Heide Perlman,** 'The Executive's Executioner', *Cheers,* NBC TV, 1985

**33** HOMER: To alcohol! The cause of – and solution to – all of life's problems!
John Swartzwelder, 'Homer vs. The Eighteenth Amendment', *The Simpsons*, Fox TV, 1997

**34** Water taken in moderation cannot hurt anybody.
Mark Twain, *Notebook*, 1935

**35** After a particularly lively trip to Amsterdam, one wag invented the . . . cocktail: Take one hotel washbasin and insert plug; take one minibar and empty contents into washbasin. Drink with straw.
Martin Vander Weyer, *Falling Eagle, the Decline of Barclays Bank*, 2000

**36** I have made an important discovery . . . that alcohol, taken in sufficient quantities, produces all the effects of intoxication.
Oscar Wilde (Attrib.)

**37** He died of cirrhosis of the liver. It costs money to die of cirrhosis of the liver.
P. G. Wodehouse, 'Success Story', *Nothing Serious*, 1950

**38** I must get out of these wet clothes and into a dry martini.
Alexander Woollcott, 1887–1943, American columnist and critic (Attrib.)

**39** Twenty-four hours in a day . . . twenty-four beers in a case. Coincidence?
Steven Wright, American comic

**40** My dad was the town drunk. A lot of times that's not so bad – but New York City?
Henny Youngman, *Henny Youngman's Greatest One Liners*, 1970

# Driving

*See also Cars; Motorcycling; Parking.*

**1** He who hesitates is not only lost, but miles from the next exit.
Anon.

**2** The traffic was so bad driving home that I changed a flat tire without losing my place in line.
Anon.

**3** Driving in London's my pleasure
I prize it above any other,
One hand on the wheel
The fingers like steel
And the A–Z clenched

In the other.
Pam Ayres, 'A–Z', *Thoughts of a Late-night Knitter*, 1978

**4** There are no liberals behind steering wheels.
Russell Baker, *Poor Russell's Almanac*, 1972

**5** It's worse with women. I once found myself at the side of the M40 watching my wife drive off into the distance. And all I'd done was point out, quite gently, that the children would be less car sick if she could maintain a constant speed. 'Accelerating to 100 then coasting down to 40 before repeating the process isn't smooth,' I said. 'Get out,' she replied.
Jeremy Clarkson, *Sunday Times*, 2000

**6** KERMIT: Fozzie, where did you learn to drive?
FOZZIE: I took a correspondence course.
Jerry Juhl and Jack Burns, *The Muppet Movie*, screenplay, 1979

**7** The rush-hour traffic I'd just as soon miss
When car
aftercarismovinglikethis.
Robert Lauher, *Reader's Digest*, 1964

**8** . . . er, how fast were you going when Mr Adams jumped from the car? . . . Seventy-five? . . . And where was that? . . . In your driveway? . . . How far had Mr Adams gotten in the lesson? . . . Backing out?!
Bob Newhart, 'The Driving Instructor', *The Button-down Mind of Bob Newhart*, album, 1960

**9** I was stopped once for going fifty-three in a thirty-five-mile zone, but I told 'em I had dyslexia.
Spanky

**10** I bought my wife a new car. She called me and said there was water in the carburetor. I said where's the car? She said in the lake.
Henny Youngman

# Drugs

*See also Drink; Smoking.*

**1** Very little has been discovered by Weekend Update scientists to show that the smoking of marijuana is harmful in any way. White rabbits, forced to smoke eighty-seven joints a day, are encouraged not to operate heavy machinery or drive on the freeways.

**'Weekend Update'**, *Saturday Night Live*, NBC TV

**2** I smoked pot at a drive-in movie theater. But the screen was this tiny. It was itsy-bitsy thumb and forefinger tiny. Till I realized I was so stoned I'd backed in and was watching it from my rearview mirror.

**Sandy Baron**

**3** Here's what another of my friends had to say, someone who used to put on earphones and get high every night, just to unwind: 'If I get high with other people, I become convinced that they think, and have always thought, that I'm pathetic. So I start saying things to prove I'm not pathetic, and then I think about the things I've just said and realize I'm much more pathetic than they even think I am.'

**Marcelle Clements**, 'Why the Sixties Generation Has Quit Smoking Pot', *Rolling Stone*, 1982

**4** Says a former activist, 'Once marijuana was a sociopolitical and philosophical gesture. Now it just means spending hours in my room by myself looking for objects I keep misplacing.'

**Marcelle Clements**, 'Why the Sixties Generation Has Quit Smoking Pot', *Rolling Stone*, 1982

**5** It's not called cocaine anymore. It's now referred to as 'Crack Classic.'

**Billiam Coronel**, American comic

**6** Avoid all needle drugs – the only dope worth shooting is Richard Nixon.

**Abbie Hoffman**, *Steal This Book*, 1971

**7** SON: Have you ever smoked opium? FATHER: Certainly not! Gives you constipation. Dreadful binding effect. Ever seen those pictures of the wretched poet Coleridge? Green around the gills. And a stranger to the lavatory. Avoid opium.

**John Mortimer**, *A Voyage Round My Father*, screenplay, 1970

**8** Drugs have taught an entire generation of American kids the metric system.

**P. J. O'Rourke**, *Modern Manners*, 1983

**9** Marijuana . . . makes you sensitive. Courtesy has a great deal to do with being sensitive. Unfortunately marijuana makes you the kind of sensitive where you insist on everyone listening to the drum solo in Iron Butterfly's 'In-a-Gadda-Da-Vida' fifty or sixty times at 78 rpm, and that's quite rude.

**P. J. O'Rourke**, *Modern Manners*, 1983

**10** Now they're calling taking drugs an epidemic – that's 'cos white folks are doing it.

**Richard Pryor**, *Richard Pryor Here and Now*, 1984

**11** Pot is like a gang of Mexican bandits in your brain. They wait for thoughts to come down the road, then tie them up and trash them.

**Kevin Rooney**, quoted in *G Q*, 1984

**12** I was so stoned in college that when my mom would call I would still keep smoking out of my bong.

She'd hear the bubbles and say, 'What's going on over there – are you sinking?'

**Scott Silverman**

**13** I'm one of those people who can't operate a screwdriver, but I could roll a joint in a twister.

**Scott Thompson**

**14** Reality is just a crutch for people who can't cope with drugs.

**Lily Tomlin**

**15** Cocaine is God's way of saying you're making too much money.

**Robin Williams**

# Duty

*See also Conscience; Ethics.*

**1** When a stupid man is doing something he is ashamed of, he always declares that it is his duty.

**George Bernard Shaw**, *Caesar and Cleopatra*, 1898

**2** . . . duty is what one expects from others, it is not what one does oneself.

**Oscar Wilde**, *A Woman of No Importance*, 1893

**3** . . . my duty is a thing I never do, on principle.

**Oscar Wilde**, *An Ideal Husband*, 1895

# Dyslexia

*See also Reading.*

**1** Dyslexia means never having to say your
syrro.
**Anon.**

**2** BOSS: This typing is terrible! Are you
dyslexic?
TYPIST: On!
**Anon.**

**3** It's not easy having dyslexia. Last week I
went to a toga party as a goat.
**Anon.**

# Ears

*See also Deafness; Faces; Noise; Silence.*

**1** The ear may be a dust trap, but when it comes to keeping your sunglasses on, it has clear advantages over a drawing-pin pressed into the side of your head.
**Alan Coren**, *Punch*, 1975

**2** His ears make him look like a taxicab with both doors open.
**Howard Hughes**, on Clark Gable (Attrib.)

# Eating

*See also Breakfast; Cooks and Cookery; Diets and Dieting; Food; Fruit; Indigestion; Picnics; Restaurants; Vegetables; Vegetarianism.*

**1** *I* am an epicure; *you* are a gourmand; *he* has both feet in the trough.
**Competition**, *New Statesman*

**2** Never drink black coffee at lunch; it will keep you awake in the afternoon.
**Jilly Cooper**, *How to Survive from Nine to Five*, 1970

**3** How to eat like a child.
Spinach: divide into little piles. Rearrange again into new piles. After five or six maneuvers, sit back and say you are full. Chocolate-chip cookies: half-sit, half-lie on the bed, propped up by a pillow. Read a book. Place cookies next to you on the sheet so that crumbs get in the bed. As you eat the cookies, remove each chocolate chip and place it on your stomach. When all the cookies are consumed, eat the chips one by one, allowing two per page.
**Delia Ephron**, *The New York Times*, 1983

**4** The best number for a dinner party is two – myself and a damn good head waiter.
**Nubar Gulbenkian**, quoted in the *Observer*, 1965

**5** Dinner at the Huntercombes' possessed 'only two dramatic features – the wine was a farce and the food a tragedy'.
**Anthony Powell**, *The Acceptance World*, 1955

**6** Seeing is deceiving. It's eating that's believing.
**James Thurber**, *Further Fables for Our Time*, 1956

**7** 'Have you ever seen Spode eat asparagus?' 'No.'

'Revolting. It alters one's whole conception of Man as Nature's last word.'
**P. G. Wodehouse**, *The Code of the Woosters*, 1938

# Ecology

*See also The Environment; Pollution.*

**1** Ecology became a household word. My husband became a nut on recycling. Until a few years ago he thought recycling was an extra setting on the washer that tore the buttons off his shirts and shredded his underwear. Now, he sits around making towel racks out of over-sexed coat hangers.
**Erma Bombeck**, *If Life is a Bowl of Cherries – What am I Doing in the Pits?*, 1978

**2** We must realize that we can no longer throw our wastes away because there is no 'away'.
**William T. Cahill**, Republican Governor of New Jersey, 1971

**3** The other day I bought a wastepaper basket and carried it home in a paper bag. And when I got home, I put the paper bag in the basket.
**Lily Tomlin**

# Economics

*See also Budgets; Economy; Inflation; Money; Stock Market.*

**1** If you're not confused, you're not paying attention.
**Anon.**, *Wall Street Week*

**2** Price, *n.* value, plus a reasonable sum for the wear and tear of conscience in demanding it.
**Ambrose Bierce**, *The Devil's Dictionary*, 1911

**3** Everybody is always in favour of general economy and particular expenditure.
**Sir Anthony Eden**, 1897–1977, Conservative Prime Minister of Great Britain

**4** Economics is extremely useful as a form of employment for economists.
**J. K. Galbraith**, American economist

**5** We can safely abandon the basic doctrine of the Eighties: namely that the rich were not working because they had too little

money, the poor because they had too much.
**J. K. Galbraith**, *Observer*, 1991

**6** There are three things not worth running for – a bus, a woman or a new economic panacea; if you wait a bit another one will come along.
**Derick Heathcoat-Amory**, British Chancellor of the Exchequer, 1958–60

**7** Blessed are the young, for they shall inherit the national debt.
**Herbert Hoover**, 1874–1964, Republican President

**8** I learned more about economics from one South Dakota dust storm than I did in all my years in college.
**Hubert Humphrey**, 1911–78, Democratic Vice-President, 1965

**9** Saying we're in a slow recovery, not a recession, is like saying we don't have any unemployed – we just have a lot of people who are really, really late for work.
**Jay Leno**, *The Tonight Show*

**10** Economics is an entire scientific discipline of not knowing what you're talking about.
**P. J. O'Rourke**, *Eat the Rich*, 1998

**11** An economist is someone who sees something that works in practice and wonders if it would work in theory.
**Ronald Reagan**, Republican President, 1981–9

**12** A friend of mine was asked to a costume ball a short time ago. He slapped some egg on his face and went as a liberal economist.
**Ronald Reagan**

**13** A recession is when a neighbour loses his job. A depression is when you lose yours. And a recovery is when Jimmy Carter loses his job.
**Ronald Reagan**, during the 1980 presidential campaign

**14** If all economists were laid end to end, they would not reach a conclusion.
**George Bernard Shaw** (Attrib.)

**15** It is not possible for this nation to be at once politically internationalist and economically isolationist. This is just as insane as asking one Siamese twin to high dive while the other plays the piano.
**Adlai Stevenson**, speech in New Orleans, 1952

**16** Nobody who has wealth to distribute ever omits himself.
**Leon Trotsky**, 1879–1940, Russian revolutionary

**17** The way to stop financial joy-riding is to arrest the chauffeur, not the automobile.
**Woodrow Wilson**, 1856–1924, Democratic President, 1913–21

# Economy
*See also Budgets; Economics; Stinginess.*

**1** Save Water, Shower with a Friend.
**Badge**, 1970s

**2** I would rather have my people laugh at my economies than weep for my extravagance.
**Oscar II**, King of Sweden, 1872–1907

# Education
*See also Examinations; School; Teachers and Teaching; University.*

**1** I had the worst study habits in the history of college, until I found out what I was doing wrong – highlighting with a black magic marker.
**Jeff Altman**

**2** My education was severely disrupted by the outbreak of World War II. It had actually taken place sixteen years previously, but I was still very upset about it.
**Barry Cryer**, at the Cambridge Union, quoted in *The Times*, 1984

**3** Educational television should be absolutely forbidden. It can only lead to unreasonable expectations and eventual disappointment when your child discovers that the letters of the alphabet do not leap up out of books and dance around the room with royal-blue chickens.
**Fran Lebowitz**, *Social Studies*, 1981

**4** Education! I was always led to suppose that no educated person ever spoke of notepaper, and yet I hear poor Fanny asking Sadie for notepaper. What is this education? Fanny talks about mirrors and mantelpieces, handbags and perfume, she takes sugar in her coffee, has a tassel on her umbrella, and I have no doubt that if she is ever fortunate enough to catch a husband she will call his father and mother Father and Mother. Will the wonderful education she is getting make up to the unhappy brute for all these endless pinpricks? Fancy hearing one's wife talk about notepaper – the irritation!
**Nancy Mitford**, *The Pursuit of Love*, 1945

**5** ERIC: When it came to education, my father wanted me to have all the opportunities he never had.
ERNIE: So what did he do?
ERIC: He sent me to a girls' school.
**Eric Morecambe and Ernie Wise**, *The Morecambe and Wise Joke Book*, 1979

**6** The idea [Francis Fukuyama's *The End of History*] has today's young people filled with hope. If we've experienced the end of history, the end of algebra cannot be far behind.
**P. J. O'Rourke**, 1989

**7** Education . . . has produced a vast population able to read but unable to distinguish what is worth reading.
**G. M. Trevelyan**, *English Social History*, 1944

**8** Education: the path from cocky ignorance to miserable uncertainty.
**Mark Twain**

**9** Education is an admirable thing, but it is well to remember from time to time that nothing that is worth knowing can be taught.
**Oscar Wilde**, 'The Critic as Artist', 1890

**10** . . . in England, at any rate, education produces no effect whatsoever. If it did, it would prove a serious danger to the upper classes, and would probably lead to acts of violence in Grosvenor Square.
**Oscar Wilde**, *The Importance of Being Earnest*, 1895

# Egotism
*See also Narcissism; Selfishness; Vanity.*

**1** The missus says that if someone in the street doesn't recognise me, I go back and tell them who I am.
**Ron Atkinson**, English football manager

**2** If egotism means a terrific interest in one's self, egotism is absolutely essential to efficient living.
**Arnold Bennett**, 1867–1931, English novelist

**3** Egotist, *n*. a person . . . more interested in himself than in me.

**Ambrose Bierce**, *The Devil's Dictionary*, 1911

**4** CC BLOOM: Well, enough about me. Let's talk about you. What do you think about me?

**Mary Agnes Donoghue**, *Beaches*, screenplay, 1988

**5** When we make love, she calls out her own name.

**Steven Kampmann, Peter Torokvei and Harold Ramis**, *Back to School*, screenplay, 1986

**6** The capacity to admire others is not my most fully developed trait.

**Henry Kissinger**

**7** Egotism – usually just a case of mistaken nonentity.

**Barbara Stanwyck**, American actress

# Elections

*See also Government; Parliament; Politics and Politicians.*

**1** If Voting Changed Anything, They'd Make It Illegal

**Badge**, London, 1983

**2** Be Thankful Only One Of Them Can Win

**Bumper sticker**, Nixon/Kennedy presidential election, 1960

**3** Vote for the man who promises least; he'll be the least disappointing.

**Bernard M. Baruch**, American businessman and statesman

**4** Have you ever seen a candidate talking to a rich person on television?

**Art Buchwald**

**5** We don't have to do what the candidates do – talk about huge issues in 30 seconds in a field somewhere, trying to make sure cows don't urinate on our shoes.

**Mario Cuomo**, New York Governor on the Presidential campaign, 1988

**6** If God had wanted us to vote, he would have given us candidates.

**Jay Leno**, *The Tonight Show*, NBC TV

**7** People on whom I do not bother to dote
 Are people who do not bother to vote.

**Ogden Nash**, 'Election Day is a Holiday', *Happy Days*, 1933

**8** They have such refined and delicate palates
 That they can discover no one worthy of their ballots,
 And then when someone terrible gets elected
 They say, There, that's just what I expected!

**Ogden Nash**, 'Election Day is a Holiday', *Happy Days*, 1933

**9** QUIMBY. If you were running for mayor, he'd vote for you.

**Bill Oakley and Josh Weinstein**, election campaign slogan in 'Sideshow Bob Roberts', *The Simpsons*, Fox TV, 1994

**10** The devil appears before the candidate and tempts him, saying, 'I can grant you victory in the Iowa caucuses. I can give you the New Hampshire primary, the South, New York, California and all the rest . . . But in return you must sell me your soul. You must betray all decent principles. You must pander, trivialize and deceive. You must gain victory by exploiting bigotry, fear, envy and greed. And you must conduct a campaign based on lies, sham, hype and distortion.'

'So,' the presidential candidate replied, 'What's the catch?'

**Roger Simon**, quoted in *Road Show*, 1990

**11** A candidate has a hard life – he has to shave twice a day.

**Adlai Stevenson**

**12** It is not enough to have every intelligent person in the country voting for me – I need a majority.

**Adlai Stevenson**

# Electricity

*See also Energy; Inventions; Technology.*

**1** . . . what with having perforce to change a light bulb here and tune in a transistor radio there, I have picked up a pretty sound working knowledge of electrical matters. It is not comprehensive, God knows – I still can't fully understand why you can't boil an egg on an electric guitar . . .

**Keith Waterhouse**, *The Passing of the Third-floor Buck*, 1974

**2** Benjamin Franklin may have discovered

electricity, but it was the man who invented the meter who made the money.
**Earl Wilson**, 1907–87, American columnist

# Embarrassment

**1** I won't tell you what he did but even my shock-proof watch was embarrassed.
**Anon.**

**2** Man is the only animal that blushes. Or needs to.
**Mark Twain**, *Following the Equator*, 1897

**3** There is a good deal to be said for blushing, if one can do it at the proper moment.
**Oscar Wilde**, *A Woman of No Importance*, 1893

# Enemies

*See also Friends; Hate; Mothers-in-Law; Revenge; War.*

**1** Love your enemy – it'll drive him nuts.
**Anon.**

**2** He hasn't an enemy in the world – but all his friends hate him.
**Eddie Cantor**, *The Chase and Sanborn Hour*, NBC Radio, 1933

**3** I do not brake for Jeff Lundberg. If I were walking along a cliff and saw him hanging by one hand from the edge, I would get out a nail file and do his nails for him. If I saw him choking on a piece of meat, I would give him a reverse Heimlich.
**Garrison Keillor**, *Me*, 1999

**4** We have met the enemy, and he is us.
**Walt Kelly**, Pogo poster for Earth Day, 1971

**5** Forgive your enemies, but never forget their names.
**John F. Kennedy**

**6** I make enemies deliberately. They are the *sauce piquante* to my dish of life.
**Elsa Maxwell**, 1883–1963, American actress and socialite

**7** Nancy and Don tried to patch things up. They met privately over lunch. Just the two of them – and their food tasters.
**Ronald Reagan**, on his wife and former White House Chief of Staff Donald Regan

# Energy

*See also Electricity; The Environment; Nuclear Power.*

**1** Whenever there's one of these bogus shortages, the oil companies give you those stupid brochures, *Fifty Ways to Save Energy*. They spill eighty million gallons in Alaska and they want you to go to the bathroom in the dark and save three cents a year.
**Jay Leno**, *The Tonight Show*

# Engagements

*See also Couples; Courtship; Proposals; Weddings.*

**1** I hear you're engaged. So who's the lucky woman?
  Her mother.
**Anon.**

**2** She was just a passing fiancée.
**Alfred McFote**

**3** Some engagements end happily, but in most cases the parties get married.
**Sally Poplin**

# England and the English

*See also Britain and the British; Cricket; The English Language; London.*

**1** The English instinctively admire any man who has no talent and is modest about it.
**James Agee**, 1909–55, American poet and novelist

**2** The English may not like music but they absolutely love the noise it makes.
**Sir Thomas Beecham**, *A Mingled Chime*, 1944

**3** So little, England. Little music. Little art. Timid. Tasteful. Nice.
**Alan Bennett**, *An Englishman Abroad*, BBC TV, 1983

**4** His face was rosy from the cold bath, which was one of the reasons why Englishmen were stronger than anybody else, and he stronger than any other Englishman, and his whistle betokened his distinguished approval of the dealings of Providence.
**E. F. Benson**, *Paying Guests*, 1929

**5** Think of what our nation stands for
  Books from Boots and country lanes

Free speech, free passes, class distinction,
Democracy and proper drains.
**John Betjeman**, 'In Westminster Abbey', 1940

**6** The Englishman fox-trots as he fox-
hunts, with all his being, through thickets,
through ditches, over hedges, through
chiffons, through waiters, over saxophones,
to the victorious finish: and who goes home
depends on how many the ambulance will
accommodate.
**Nancy Boyd** (pseudonym of Edna St Vincent Millay)

**7** The most dangerous thing in the world is
to make a friend of an Englishman, because
he'll come sleep in your closet rather than
spend ten shillings on a hotel.
**Truman Capote**, 1966

**8** The English never draw a line without
blurring it.
**Winston Churchill**, speech, House of Commons, 1948

**9** When I warned them [the French
Government] that Britain would fight on
alone whatever they did, their Generals told
their PM and his divided Cabinet: 'In three
weeks England will have her neck wrung
like a chicken.' Some chicken! Some neck!
**Winston Churchill**, speech, Canadian Parliament,
1941

**10** Mad dogs and Englishmen
  Go out in the midday sun,
  The Japanese don't care to.
  The Chinese wouldn't dare to,
  Hindoos and Argentines sleep firmly
    from twelve to one.
  But Englishmen detest a siesta.
**Noel Coward**, 'Mad Dogs and Englishmen', *Words
and Music*, 1932

**11** In England, failure is all the rage.
**Quentin Crisp**, *The Naked Civil Servant*, 1968

**12** The English think incompetence is the
same thing as sincerity.
**Quentin Crisp**, quoted in *The New York Times*, 1977

**13** Q: dwo
  Q: dwo
  we know of anything which can
  be as dull as one englishman
  A: to
**e.e. cummings**, *Complete Poems*, 1968

**14** Lisa, hello! How are you doing in
England? Remember, an elevator is called a
'lift,' a mile is called a 'kilometer,' and
botulism is called 'steak and kidney pie.'
**Greg Daniels**, 'Lisa's Wedding', *The Simpsons*, Fox TV,
1995

**15** It is said, I believe, that to behold the
Englishman at his *best* one should watch
him play tip-and-run.
**Ronald Firbank**, *The Flower Beneath the Foot*, 1923

**16** The English find ill-health not only
interesting but respectable and often
experience death in the effort to avoid a
fuss.
**Pamela Frankau**, *Pen to Paper*, 1961

**17** But after all, what would the English be
without their sweet unreasonableness?
**John Galsworthy**, 'The Roof', 1929

**18** Contrary to popular belief, English
women do not wear tweed nightgowns.
**Hermione Gingold**, *Saturday Review*, 1955

**19** The climate of England has been the
world's most powerful colonizing impulse.
**Russell Green**

**20** An Englishman is a man who lives on
an island in the North Sea governed by
Scotsmen.
**Philip Guedalla**, *Supers and Supermen*, 1920

**21** From time immemorial, the English,
saddled with a climate that produced
nothing tastier than mangelwurzels and
suet, have been forced to import anything
that would stay down for more than ten
seconds.
**Tony Hendra**, 'EEC! It's the US of E!', *National
Lampoon*, 1976

**22** If it is good to have one foot in England,
it is still better, or at least as good, to have
the other out of it.
**Henry James** (Attrib.)

**23** The Englishman's way of speaking
    absolutely classifies him,
  The moment he talks he makes some
    other Englishman despise him.
**Alan Jay Lerner and Frederick Loewe**, 'Why Can't the
English?', song from *My Fair Lady*, 1956

**24** Nothing, I am sure, equals my

thankfulness when I meet an Englishman who is not like every other.

**James Russell Lowell**, American poet and essayist, 'On a Certain Condescension to Foreigners', 1869

**25** If you want to eat well in England, eat three breakfasts.

**W. Somerset Maugham**

**26** It is good to be on your guard against an Englishman who speaks French perfectly; he is very likely to be a card-sharper or an attaché in the diplomatic service.

**W. Somerset Maugham**, *The Summing Up*, 1938

**27** An Englishman, even if he is alone, forms an orderly queue of one.

**George Mikes**, *How to be an Alien*, 1946

**28** The world still consists of two clearly divided groups: the English and the foreigners. One group consists of less than 50 million people; the other of 3,950 million. The latter group does not really count.

**George Mikes**, *How to Be Decadent*, 1977

**29** It has to be admitted that we English have sex on the brain, which is a very unsatisfactory place to have it.

**Malcolm Muggeridge**, 1964

**30** Let us pause to consider the English,
   Who when they pause to consider
      themselves they get all reticently
      thrilled and tinglish,
   Because every Englishman is convinced
      of one thing, viz.:
   That to be an Englishman is to belong to
      the most exclusive club there is.

**Ogden Nash**, 'England Expects', *I'm a Stranger Here Myself*, 1938

**31** *Racial characteristics*: cold-blooded queers with nasty complexions and terrible teeth who once conquered half the world but still haven't figured out central heating. They warm their beers and chill their baths and boil all their food, including bread.

**P. J. O'Rourke**, 'Foreigners Around the World', *National Lampoon*, 1976

**32** England is the most class-ridden country under the sun. It is a land of snobbery and privilege, ruled largely by the old and silly.

**George Orwell**, *The Lion and the Unicorn*, 1941

**33** Deploring change is the unchangeable habit of all Englishmen.

**Raymond Postgate**

**34** The sheer inertia of Englishmen for whom the past was always sacred and inviolable and who prided themselves on their obstinacy. 'We didn't win the war,' thought Sir Godber, 'we just refused to lose it.'

**Tom Sharpe**, *Porterhouse Blue*, 1974

**35** An Englishman thinks he is moral when he is only uncomfortable.

**George Bernard Shaw**, *Man and Superman*, 1903

**36** Go anywhere in England where there are natural, wholesome, contented, and really nice English people; and what do you always find? That the stables are the real centre of the household . . .

**George Bernard Shaw**, *Heartbreak House*, 1919

**37** If you eliminate smoking and gambling, you will be amazed to find that almost all an Englishman's pleasures can be, and mostly are, shared by his dog.

**George Bernard Shaw** (Attrib.)

**38** No Englishman is ever fairly beaten.

**George Bernard Shaw**, *Saint Joan*, 1924

**39** English cuisine is generally so threadbare that for years there has been a gentlemen's agreement in the civilized world to allow the Brits pre-eminence in the matter of tea – which, after all, comes down to little more than the ability to boil water.

**Wilfrid Sheed**, 'Taking Pride in Prejudice', *GQ*, 1984

**40** In England we have come to rely on a comfortable time-lag of fifty years or a century intervening between the perception that something ought to be done and a serious attempt to do it.

**H. G. Wells**, *The Work, Wealth and Happiness of Mankind*, 1931

**41** . . . a typical Englishman, always dull and usually violent.

**Oscar Wilde**, *An Ideal Husband*, 1895

**42** I don't desire to change anything in England except the weather.

**Oscar Wilde**, *The Picture of Dorian Gray*, 1891

**43** I did a picture in England one winter and it was so cold I almost got married.
**Shelley Winters**, American actress

**44** The English have an extraordinary ability for flying into a great calm.
**Alexander Woollcott**, 1887–1943, American columnist and critic

# English Language, The

*See also Grammar; Idioms; Language; Pronunciation; Speakers and Speeches; Words; Writers; Writing.*

**1** A spelling reformer indicted
For fudge was before the court cicted.
The judge said: 'Enough –
His candle we'll snough,
And his sepulcher shall not be whicted.
**Anon.**, quoted in *The Devil's Dictionary* by Ambrose Bierce, 1911

**2** When the American people get through with the English language, it will look as if it had been run over by a musical comedy.
**Finley Peter Dunne**, *Mr Dooley at His Best*, 1938

# Enjoyment

*See also Happiness.*

**1** I don't think we enjoy other people's suffering; it isn't actually enjoyment, but we feel better for it.
**Finley Peter Dunne**, American journalist

**2** Are We Having Fun Yet?
**Bill Griffith**, Zippy the Pinhead book title, 1985

# Entrances and Exits

**1** I wish I could stay longer, but my girlfriend's getting pregnant tonight and I'd like to be there when it happens.
**Teddy Bergeron**

**2** I got a wonderful tribute at the airport. They fired 21 shots in the air in my honour. Of course, it would have been nicer if they'd waited for the plane to land.
**Bob Hope**

**3** Lord Ronald said nothing; he flung himself from the room, flung himself upon his horse and rode madly off in all directions.
**Stephen Leacock**, 'Gertrude the Governess', *Nonsense Novels*, 1914

**4** The whistle shrilled, and in a moment I was chugging out of Grand Central's dreaming spires . . . I had chugged only a few feet when I realized that I had left without the train, so I had to run back and wait for it to start.
**S. J. Perelman**, *Strictly from Hunger*, 1937

**5** I have nothing to declare except my genius.
**Oscar Wilde**, arriving at Customs in New York, 1882 (Attrib.)

**6** And, closing the door with the delicate caution of one brushing flies off a sleeping Venus, he passed out of my life.
**P. G. Wodehouse**, *Very Good, Jeeves*, 1930

**7** In this matter of shimmering into rooms the chappie is rummy to a degree.
**P. G. Wodehouse**, *My Man Jeeves*, 1919

**8** There came from without the hoof-beats of a galloping relative, and Aunt Dahlia whizzed in.
**P. G. Wodehouse**, *The Code of the Woosters*, 1938

**9** There was a flash of blonde hair and a whiff of Chanel No. 5 and a girl came sailing in, a girl whom I was able to classify at a single glance as a pipterino of the first water.
**P. G. Wodehouse**, *Jeeves and the Feudal Spirit*, 1954

# Environment, The

*See also Ecology; Pollution.*

**1** Save the Whales. Collect the Whole Set!
**Bumper sticker**, Boston, 1999

**2** Now there is one outstandingly important fact regarding Spaceship Earth, and that is that no instruction book came with it.
**R. Buckminster Fuller**, *Operating Manual for Spaceship Earth*, 1969

**3** If sunbeams were weapons of war, we would have had solar energy long ago.
**George Porter**, British chemist, 1973

# Epigrams

*See also Proverbs; Quotations; Sayings; Wit.*

**1** Epigram and truth are rarely commensurate. Truth has to be somewhat chiselled, as it were, before it will fit into an epigram.
**Joseph Farrell**, *Lectures of a Certain Professor*

**2** An epigram is only a wisecrack that's played Carnegie Hall.
**Oscar Levant**, 1906–72, American composer and wit

# Epitaphs

*See also Death.*

**1** When I am dead, I hope it may be said, 'His sins were scarlet, but his books were read.'
**Hilaire Belloc**, 'On His Books', 1923

**2** ERNIE: What would you like them to put on your tombstone?
ERIC: Something short and simple.
ERNIE: What?
ERIC: 'Back in Five Minutes.'
**Eddie Braben**, *The Best of Morecambe and Wise*, 1974

**3** I Would Rather Be Living in Philadelphia
**W. C. Fields**, suggested epitaph for himself, *Vanity Fair*, 1925

**4** Over my dead body!
**George S. Kaufman**, suggested epitaph for himself, *Vanity Fair*, 1925

**5** Excuse My Dust
**Dorothy Parker**, suggested epitaph for herself, *Vanity Fair*, 1925

# Equality

*See also Class; Communism; Democracy; Feminism; Marxism; Sexual Equality; Socialism.*

**1** His Lordship may compel us to be equal upstairs, but there will never be equality in the servants' hall.
**J. M. Barrie**, *The Admirable Crichton*, 1902

**2** Women run everything. The only thing that I have done within my house in the last 20 years is to recognise Angola as an independent state.
**Brian Clough**, football manager

**3** I treat women as my equal. Of course, most women don't like to be treated like a paranoid balding Jew with contact lenses.
**David Feldman**

**4** Now that's the kind of King for me –
He wished all men as rich as he,
So to the top of every tree
Promoted everybody!
Lord Chancellors were cheap as sprats,
And Bishops in their shovel hats
Were plentiful as tabby cats –
In point of fact, too many.
Ambassadors cropped up like hay,
Prime Ministers and such as they
Grew like asparagus in May,
And Dukes were three a penny.
**W. S. Gilbert**, *The Gondoliers*, 1889

**5** Inequality is as dear to the American heart as liberty itself.
**William Dean Howells**, *Impressions and Experiences*

**6** That all men are equal is a proposition to which, in ordinary times, no sane individual has ever given his assent.
**Aldous Huxley**, *Proper Studies*, 1927

**7** All men are born equal, but quite a few eventually get over it.
**Lord Mancroft**, *Observer*, 1967

**8** ONE BUSINESSMAN (*to another*): Treat people as equals and the first thing you know they believe they are.
**James Mulligan**, cartoon in the *New Yorker*, 1982

**9** . . . I'd like to talk about a bad idea: closing the global wealth gap. That is a very bad idea. I mean, do we want to close the beauty gap and make everybody look like Dick Morris? Do we want to close the virtue gap and encourage Mother Teresa to have a deathbed affair, or appoint that Kennedy kid, Michael, to run the Save the Children Foundation? Do we want to close the talent gap and have an NBA full of players who have the height and talent of, for instance, me? If we had a world without gaps, where everyone was the same color, size, social class and sex, who would get pregnant? If everyone had the same information, what would we talk about?
**P. J. O'Rourke**, speech to the Cato Institute, 1997

**10** All animals are equal, but some animals are more equal than others.
**George Orwell**, *Animal Farm*, 1946

**11** Democracy demands that all of its citizens begin the race even. Egalitarianism insists that they all *finish* even.
**Roger Price**, *The Great Roob Revolution*, 1970

**12** Idiots are always in favour of inequality of income (their only chance of eminence), and the really great in favour of equality.
**George Bernard Shaw**, *The Intelligent Woman's Guide to Socialism and Capitalism*, 1928

# Espionage
*See also The CIA.*

**1** Variety is the life of spies.
**Anon.**

**2** FIRST SPY: When you arrive you will meet a man in a black trench coat. He will ask you for the diamonds.
SECOND SPY: And I give him the diamonds?
FIRST SPY: No. Don't. He asks everyone for the diamonds. You will then meet a lovely redhead. Give her the diamonds.
SECOND SPY: Who is she?
FIRST SPY: That will be me.
SECOND SPY: Oh, you'll be in disguise.
FIRST SPY: No, I'm in disguise now.
**Neil Simon**, *Your Show of Shows*, NBC TV, 1950s

**3** COLONEL HAVERSTRAP: Alright Horne – here's your equipment. These are your small arms, these are your puny hairy legs and this is your tiny bald head – you know how to use them I take it. Here's a plastic Japanese junior spy kit, comprising a small plastic dagger, the egg in bag trick, a revolving bow tie, nail through finger trick, an exploding banjo – and this . . .
HORNE: Good heavens – what is it?
COLONEL HAVERSTRAP: Ah well, the trade name is – *Naughty Doggie – Fido Gets The Blame*. Only use it if you're in a tight corner.
HORNE: How does it help me escape?
COLONEL HAVERSTRAP: While they're beating the daylights out of the dog, you can slip out unnoticed.
**Barry Took and Marty Feldman**, *Round the Horne*, BBC Radio, 1965

# Establishment, The
*See also The Aristocracy; Government; Royalty; Society.*

**1** After a long life I have come to the conclusion that when all the Establishment is united it is always wrong.
**Harold Macmillan**, British Conservative Prime Minister, 1957–63

# Ethics
*See also Duty; Morality.*

**1** FRANKLIN: Have you ever thought, Headmaster, that your standards might perhaps be a little out of date?
HEADMASTER: Of course they're out of date. Standards always are out of date. That is what makes them standards.
**Alan Bennett**, *Forty Years On*, 1968

**2** An ethical man is a Christian holding four aces.
**Mark Twain** (Attrib.)

**3** Any preoccupation with ideas of what is right or wrong in conduct shows an arrested intellectual development.
**Oscar Wilde**, 'Phrases and Philosophies for the Use of the Young', 1894

# Etiquette
*See also Class; Conformity; Manners.*

**1** Social tact is making your company feel at home, even though you wish they were.
**Anon.**

**2** Though she lacked imagination, Brenda would go to any lengths rather than cause herself embarrassment. It was her upbringing. As a child she had been taught it was rude to say no unless she didn't mean it. If she was offered another piece of cake and she wanted it she was obliged to refuse out of politeness. And if she didn't want it she had to say yes, even if it choked her.
**Beryl Bainbridge**, *The Bottle Factory Outing*, 1974

**3** No matter if your food is dry or it's oily, it's sure to look better when placed on a doily. Thank you!
**Ron Barrett**, 'Politenessman', cartoon, *National Lampoon*, 1983

**4** No matter what their religion or race, never sneeze in a person's face. Thank you!
**Ron Barrett**, 'Politenessman', cartoon, *National Lampoon*, 1982

**5** Tact consists in knowing how far to go too far.
**Jean Cocteau**, *Le Rappel à L'ordre*, 1926

**6** No longer are her invitations sought and
  fought for eagerly,
 Her parties once so popular are now
  attended meagerly.
 A blunder unforgivable made life no
  longer livable,
 For she served the sparkling burgundy in
  glasses made for port.
**Newman Levey**, 'The Glass of Fashion'

**7** Dear Miss Manners,
What am I supposed to say when I am introduced to a homosexual couple?

Gentle Reader,
'How do you do?' 'How do you do?'
**Judith Martin**, *Miss Manners' Guide to Excruciatingly Correct Behaviour*, 1982

**8** There was a brave girl of Connecticut
 Who flagged the express with her
  pecticut.
 Which her elders defined
 As presence of mind,
 But deplorable absence of ecticut.
**Ogden Nash**, 'Benjamin', *The Primrose Path*, 1935

**9** At the end of dinner it used to be that the men would retire to the billiard room and the women would go into the parlor. Men and women no longer separate after dinner, however. They now separate after twenty years of apparently happy marriage.
**P. J. O'Rourke**, *Modern Manners*, 1983

**10** . . . manners . . . have nothing to do with what you do, only how you do it. For example, Karl Marx was always polite in the British Museum. He was courteous to the staff, never read with his hat on, and didn't make lip-farts when he came across passages in Hegel with which he disagreed. Despite the fact that his political exhortations have caused the deaths of millions, he is today more revered than not. On the other hand, John W. Hinckley, Jr. was rude only once, to a retired Hollywood movie actor, and

Hinckley will be in a mental institution for the rest of his life.
**P. J. O'Rourke**, *Modern Manners*, 1983

**11** When the Chinese Ambassador's wife
   unfurls
  After three drinks of anisette,
  Don't ask if it's true about Chinese girls,
  It ain't etiquette.
**Cole Porter**, 'It Ain't Etiquette', song from *Du Barry was a Lady*, 1939

**12** Gentlemen do not throw wine at ladies. They pour it over them.
**Auberon Waugh**, *Spectator*, 1983

**13** 'I suppose it would be a breach of hospitality if I socked my hostess's sister in the eye?'
 'The County would purse its lips.'
**P. G. Wodehouse**, *Spring Fever*, 1948

# Europe and the EEC

*See also Belgium; Denmark and the Danes; Foreigners; France and the French; Germany and the Germans; Government; Greece and the Greeks; Holland and the Dutch; Ireland and the Irish; Italy and the Italians; Spain and the Spaniards; Sweden and the Swedes; Travel; Xenophobia.*

**1** The last time Britain went into Europe with any degree of success was on 6 June 1944.
*Daily Express*, 1980

**2** Up yours, Delors.
*Sun* headline, 1990, addressed to Jacques Delors, President of the European Commission, accused by the paper of seeking to increase his powers

**3** Protestant fears have been aroused by the theory that this is a treaty with Rome, but this is not so.
**R. A. Butler**, British Foreign Secretary, 1963

**4** What Caesar couldn't do, what Charlemagne couldn't do, what Innocent III and Hitler couldn't do, it looks like the dough-faced burgher wimps of Brussels might finally be able to pull off – the unification of that portion of the earth's surface known . . . as Europe. What it took a country ten times its size less than a hundred years to accomplish, armed with only machine guns and a few trillion dollars, it has taken the squabbling, babbling tribes of Europe almost three millennia of wars, migrations, crusades,

plague, pillage, partition, diets, dumas, duels, vendettas, incursions, invasions, intrusions, regicides, switching sides and genocide to accomplish.
**Tony Hendra**, 'EEC! It's the US of E!', *National Lampoon*, 1976

**5** I do not find Northern Europe an ideal zone for human habitation. It is a fine place for industrial productivity, but its climate breeds puritans and the terrible dictates of the Protestant Work Ethic. The Romans were right to pull out when they did.
**Kenneth Tynan**, *The Sound of Two Hands Clapping*, 1975

**6** I do not see the EEC as a great love affair. It is more like nine middle-aged couples with failing marriages meeting at a Brussels hotel for a group grope.
**Kenneth Tynan**, 1975

**7** European Community institutions have produced European beets, butter, cheese, wine, veal and even pigs. But they have not produced Europeans.
**Louise Weiss**, MEP, *Observer*, 1980

**8** Gloria, gloria, Europhoria!
   Common faith and common goal!
   Meat and milk and wine and butter
   Make a smashing casserole!
   Let the end of all our striving
   Be the peace that love promotes,
   With our hands in perfect friendship
   Firmly round each other's throats!
**Roger Woddis**, *Spectator*, 1984

# Evil

*See also Goodness; Sin; Vice and Virtue.*

**1** Between two evils, I always pick the one I never tried before.
**Mae West**, *Klondike Annie*, screenplay, 1936

**2** Wickedness is a myth invented by good people to account for the curious attractiveness of others.
**Oscar Wilde**, 'Phrases and Philosophies for the Use of the Young', 1894

# Evolution

*See also Progress.*

**1** A hen is only an egg's way of making another egg.
**Samuel Butler**, *Life and Habit*, 1878

**2** All modern men are descended from a wormlike creature, but it shows more on some people.
**Will Cuppy**, 1884–1949, American humorist

**3** Some folks seem to have descended from the chimpanzees much later than others.
**Kin Hubbard**, 1868–1930, American humorist

# Examinations

*See also Education; School; Teachers and Teaching; University.*

**1** Yes, I could have been a judge but I never had the Latin, never had the Latin for the judging, I just never had sufficient of it to get through the rigorous judging exams. They're noted for their rigour. People come staggering out saying, 'My God, what a rigorous exam.' And so I became a miner instead. A coal miner. I managed to get through the mining exams – they're not very rigorous, they only ask you one question, they say 'Who are you?' and I got seventy-five per cent on that.
**Peter Cook**, 'Sitting on a Bench', nightclub act, 1960s

**2** Do not on any account attempt to write on both sides of the paper at once.
**W. C. Sellar and R. J. Yeatman**, *1066 and All That*, 1930

# Excess

*See also Extravagance; Moderation.*

**1** I have not been afraid of excess: excess on occasion is exhilarating. It prevents moderation from acquiring the deadening effect of a habit.
**W. Somerset Maugham**, *The Summing Up*, 1938

**2** Drink and dance and laugh and lie,
   Love, the reeling midnight through,
   For tomorrow we may die!
   (But, alas, we never do.)
**Dorothy Parker**, 'The Flaw in Paganism', *Death and Taxes*, 1931

**3** I hate to advocate drugs, alcohol, violence, or insanity to anyone, but they've always worked for me.
**Hunter S. Thompson**

**4** Moderation is a fatal thing, Lady Hunstanton. Nothing succeeds like excess.
**Oscar Wilde**, *A Woman of No Importance*, 1893

# Excuses

*See also Guilt.*

**1** One icy winter morning, an employee was explaining to his boss why he had turned up for work 45 minutes late. He said, 'It was so slippery out there that for every step I took forward, I slipped back two.'

The boss eyed him suspiciously and said, 'Oh yeah? So how did you ever get here?'

And the man said, 'Well, I finally gave up and headed for home.'
**Anon.**

**2** . . . several excuses are always less convincing than one.
**Aldous Huxley,** *Point Counter Point*, 1928

**3** . . . I am prevented from coming in consequence of a subsequent engagement. I think that would be a rather nice excuse: it would have all the surprise of candour.
**Oscar Wilde,** *The Picture of Dorian Gray*, 1891

# Exercise

*See also The Body; Diets and Dieting; Sport.*

**1** I like long walks, especially when they are taken by people who annoy me.
**Fred Allen**

**2** The only reason I would take up jogging is so that I could hear heavy breathing again.
**Erma Bombeck**

**3** MR UNIVERSE: Don't forget, Mr Carson, your body is the only home you'll ever have.
CARSON: Yes, my home *is* pretty messy. But I have a woman who comes in once a week.
**Johnny Carson,** *The Tonight Show*, NBC TV

**4** My grandmother started walking five miles a day when she was sixty. She's ninety-three today and we don't know where the hell she is.
**Ellen DeGeneres**

**5** Contrary to popular cable TV-induced opinion, aerobics have absolutely nothing to do with squeezing our body into hideous shiny Spandex, grinning like a deranged orangutan, and doing cretinous dance steps to debauched disco music.
**Cynthia Heimel,** *Sex Tips for Girls*, 1983

**6** I'm trying to get in shape. I'm doing 20 sit-ups every morning. That may not sound like a lot, but you can only hit that snooze alarm so many times.
**J. Scott Homan,** American comic

**7** Married people don't have to exercise, because our attitude is 'They've seen us naked already – and they like it.'
**Carol Montgomery**

**8** Try This Exercise – It'll Make You Feel *Great.*
From a seated position, get up and walk to the bar. Mix one jigger of dry vermouth with seven jiggers of gin. Pour over three quarters of a cup of cracked ice and stir well. Strain and pour into a glass. Twist one lemon peel over the top.
Sit down and drink.
Repeat.
Build your stamina slowly and soon you'll be able to do ten or twelve of these!
**P. J. O'Rourke,** *National Lampoon*, 1979

**9** Violent exercise is like a cold shower; you think it does you good because you feel better when you stop.
**Robert Quillen,** American author

**10** I don't exercise. If God wanted me to bend over, he would have put diamonds on the floor.
**Joan Rivers**

**11** I can't work out in front of women. I don't want them to see me when I'm on my way to my goal – which is them.
**Craig Shoemaker**

**12** Jogging is for people who aren't intelligent enough to watch breakfast television.
**Victoria Wood,** *Mens Sana in Thingummy Doodah*, 1990

# Expeditions

*See also Travel.*

**1** The equipment for this camp had to be carried from the railhead at Chaikhosi, a distance of 500 miles. Five porters would be needed for this. Two porters would be needed to carry the food for these five, and another would carry the food for these two. His food would be carried by a boy. The boy would carry his own food. The first supporting party would be established at 38,000 feet, also with a fortnight's supplies which necessitated another eight porters and a boy. In all, to transport tents and equipment, food, radio, scientific and photographic gear, personal effects, and so on, 3,000 porters and 375 boys would be required.

**W. E. Bowman**, *The Ascent of Rum Doodle*, 1956

## Expenses

*See also Credit Cards; Money.*

**1** In Brighton she was Brenda,
She was Patsy up in Perth,
In Cambridge she was Candida
The sweetest girl on earth.
In Stafford she was Stella,
The pick of all the bunch,
But down on his expenses,
She was *Petrol, Oil and Lunch.*

**Anon.**

## Experience

**1** We learn from experience that we never learn from experience.
**George Bernard Shaw**

**2** Experience is the name everyone gives to their mistakes.
**Oscar Wilde**, *Lady Windermere's Fan*, 1892

**3** Experience is something you don't get until just after you need it.
**Steven Wright**, American comic

## Experts

*See also Consultants; Opinions.*

**1** An expert is a person who avoids the small errors while sweeping on to the grand fallacy.
**Arthur Bloch**, *Murphy's Law and Other Reasons Why Things Go Wrong*, 1977

**2** An expert is somebody who is more than

fifty miles from home, has no responsibility for implementing the advice he gives, and shows slides.
**Ed Meese**, US Attorney General, 1985–8

## Extravagance

*See also Credit; Debt; Expenses; Money.*

**1** It seems he wholly lacked a sense
Of limiting the day's expense,
And money ran between his hands
Like water through the Ocean Sands.
Such conduct could not but affect
His parent's fortune, which was wrecked
Like many and many another one
By folly in a spendthrift son:
By that most tragical mischance,
An Only Child's Extravagance.
**Hilaire Belloc**, 'Peter Goole', *New Cautionary Tales*, 1930

**2** All decent people live beyond their incomes; those who aren't respectable live beyond other people's; a few gifted individuals manage to do both.
**Saki (H. H. Munro)**, *Chronicles of Clovis*, 1911

## Eyes

*See also Faces; Spectacles.*

**1** A: Have your eyes ever been checked?
B: No, Doctor, they've always been blue.
**Anon.**

**2** His eyes are so bad, he has to wear contact lenses to see his glasses.
**Anon.**

**3** Met a guy this morning with a glass eye. He didn't tell me – it just came out in the conversation.
**Jerry Dennis**

**4** He had but one eye and the popular prejudice runs in favour of two.
**Charles Dickens**, *Nicholas Nickleby*, 1839

**5** This woman is so cross-eyed, she can go to a tennis match and never move her head.
**Phyllis Diller**

**6** I've got such poor vision, I could date anyone.
**Garry Shandling**

# Faces

*See also Appearance; Baldness; Beauty; Cosmetics; Hair; Looks.*

**1** . . . a face like a wedding cake left out in the rain.
**Anon.**, of W. H. Auden

**2** A: Her face looks like a million.
B: Yes, all green and wrinkled.
**Anon.**

**3** Your mother is so ugly, she looks like she sleeps on a bed of nails, face down.
*Snaps* 4, 1998

**4** Nature played a cruel trick upon her by giving her a waxed moustache.
**Alan Bennett**, *Forty Years On*, 1968

**5** I have a face that is a cross between two pounds of halibut and an explosion in an old-clothes closet. If it isn't mobile, it's dead.
**David Niven**, actor

**6** You look at Ernest Borgnine and you think to yourself: was there anybody else hurt in the accident?
**Don Rickles**

**7** . . . his hostess's daughter, a dowdy dull girl, with one of those characteristic British faces that, once seen, are never remembered.
**Oscar Wilde**, *The Picture of Dorian Gray*, 1891

# Facts

*See also Knowledge; Truth.*

**1** The trouble with facts is that there are so many of them.
**Samuel McChord Crothers**, *The Gentle Reader*

**2** Facts are ventriloquists' dummies. Sitting on a wise man's knee they may be made to utter words of wisdom; elsewhere, they say nothing, or talk nonsense, or indulge in sheer diabolism.
**Aldous Huxley**, *Time Must Have a Stop*, 1944

**3** Oh, don't tell me of facts – I never believe facts; you know Canning said nothing was so fallacious as facts, except figures.
**Sydney Smith**, 1771–1845, clergyman and wit

**4** It is the spirit of the age to believe that any fact, no matter how suspect, is superior to any imaginative exercise, no matter how true.

**Gore Vidal**, *Encounter*, 1967

# Failure

*See also Success.*

**1** I started out with nothing and I've still got most of it left.

**Anon.**

**2** There is much to be said for failure. It is more interesting than success.

**Max Beerbohm**, *Mainly on the Air*, 1947

**3** . . . I've always been after the trappings of great luxury you see, I really, really have. But all I've got hold of are the trappings of great poverty. I've got hold of the wrong load of trappings, and a rotten load of trappings they are too, ones I could have very well done without.

**Peter Cook**, 'Sitting on a Bench', nightclub act, 1960s

**4** That poor man. He's completely unspoiled by failure.

**Noel Coward**, of a fellow playwright (Attrib.)

**5** A man may fail many times but he isn't a failure until he begins to blame somebody else.

**J. Paul Getty**, 1892–1976, American billionaire industrialist

**6** There is the greatest practical benefit in making a few failures early in life.

**T. H. Huxley**, *On Medical Education*, 1870

**7** Failure has gone to his head.

**Wilson Mizner**, 1876–1933, American playwright, of a still-buoyant bankrupt (Attrib.)

**8** If I were not a gloriously successful person, in England they would have dismissed me as an Irishman and in America as a Socialist.

**George Bernard Shaw** (Attrib.)

**9** To avoid criticism, say nothing, do nothing, be nothing.

**Fred Shero**, hockey coach, Philadelphia Flyers, 1925–90

**10** We women adore failures. They lean on us.

**Oscar Wilde**, *A Woman of No Importance*, 1893

# Faith

*See also Atheism; Belief; God; Heaven; Religion; Trust.*

**1** If there was no faith there would be no living in this world. We couldn't even eat hash with any safety.

**Josh Billings**, *The Complete Works of Josh Billings*, 1919

**2** Faith, to my mind, is a stiffening process, a sort of mental starch, which ought to be applied as sparingly as possible.

**E. M. Forster**, *Two Cheers for Democracy*, 1951

**3** Faith is much better than belief. Belief is when someone *else* does the thinking.

**R. Buckminster Fuller**, 1895–1983, American architect

**4** i once heard the survivors
of a colony of ants
that had been partially
obliterated by a cow's foot
seriously debating
the intention of the gods
towards their civilization

**Don Marquis**, 'certain maxims of archy', *archy and mehitabel*, 1927

**5** Faith may be defined briefly as an illogical belief in the occurrence of the improbable.

**H. L. Mencken**, *Prejudices*, Third Series, 1922

**6** I respect faith, but doubt is what gets you an education.

**Wilson Mizner**, 1876–1933, American playwright

**7** We have not lost faith, but we have transferred it from God to the medical profession.

**George Bernard Shaw** (Attrib.)

**8** Scepticism is the beginning of Faith.

**Oscar Wilde**, *The Picture of Dorian Gray*, 1891

# Falklands, The

*See also The Army; The Navy; Politics – British Prime Ministers: Margaret Thatcher; War.*

**1** From Michael Foot's statements, one would draw the conclusion that Labour is in favour of warmongering, provided there is no war.

*Labour Herald*, 1982

**2** Sir: Your coverage of the Falklands episode has cleared up one small point:

whether you run a fairly responsible journal of the libertarian Right or a fairly entertaining magazine. You run a fairly entertaining magazine. However, there are so few of these about nowadays that I am probably justified in keeping up my subscription, though I suppose it is a bit frivolous of me.
**Kingsley Amis,** letter to the *Spectator*, 28 August 1982

**3** Sir: Kingsley Amis's letter about your coverage of the Falklands episode has cleared up one small point: whether he is a fairly serious commentator on current events or a fairly entertaining writer of light fiction with strong political prejudices. He is a fairly entertaining writer of light fiction with strong political prejudices. However, there are so few of these about nowadays that we are probably justified in continuing to read him, though he is less entertaining and more prejudiced than he used to be.
**Arthur Freeman,** letter to the *Spectator*, 4 September 1982

**4** The Falklands Incident was a quarrel between two bald men over a comb.
**Jorge Luis Borges,** 1983

**5** This has been a pimple on the ass of progress festering for 200 years, and I guess someone decided to lance it.
**Alexander Haig,** US Secretary of State, quoted in the *Sunday Times*, 1982

**6** The conflict over the Falklands is a moment dislodged from its natural home in the late nineteenth century.
**Lance Morrow,** *Observer*, 1982

**7** Saturday 3 April
8 a.m. Britain is at war with Argentina!!! Radio Four has just announced it. I am overcome with excitement. Half of me thinks it is tragic and the other half of me thinks it is dead exciting.
10 a.m. Woke my father up to tell him Argentina has invaded the Falklands. He shot out of bed because he thought the Falklands lay off the coast of Scotland. When I pointed out that they were eight thousand miles away he got back into bed and pulled the covers over his head.
**Sue Townsend,** *The Secret Diary of Adrian Mole Aged 13³/₄*, 1982

# Fame

*See also Celebrities; Reputation.*

**1** The final test of fame is to have a crazy person imagine he is you.
**Anon.**

**2** A celebrity is a person who works hard all his life to become well known, then wears dark glasses to avoid being recognized.
**Fred Allen**

**3** It took me fifteen years to discover I had no talent for writing, but I couldn't give it up because by that time I was too famous.
**Robert Benchley,** quoted in *Robert Benchley*, by Nat Benchley, 1955

**4** Some are born great, some achieve greatness, and some hire public relations officers.
**Daniel Boorstin,** *The Image*, 1962

**5** You're always a little disappointing in person because you can't be the edited essence of yourself.
**Mel Brooks,** interview in the *New York Post*, 1975

**6** In the march up to the heights of fame there comes a spot close to the summit in which a man reads nothing but detective stories.
**Heywood Broun,** 1888–1939, American journalist

**7** There is a lot to be said for not being known to the readers of the *Daily Mirror*.
**Anthony Burgess,** *Inside Mr Enderby*, 1966

**8** Fame is being asked to sign your autograph on the back of a cigarette packet.
**Billy Connolly,** Scottish comedian

**9** He's very, very well known. I'd say he's world-famous in Melbourne.
**Dame Edna Everage (Barry Humphries),** *Russell Harty Plus*, London Weekend Television, 1973

**10** MAÎTRE D': Sorry old man. Because of the weak imagery, scanty plot and pedestrian language in your latest, we've turned your table over to Joyce Carol Oates.
**William Hamilton,** *William Hamilton's Anti-Social Register*, cartoon, 1974

**11** Being stared at is not fun . . . There are times when someone on the street says, 'Are

you William Hurt?' and I will say, 'No, not at the moment.'
**William Hurt**, *Sunday Telegraph*, 2000

**12** The nice thing about being a celebrity is that when you bore people they think it's their fault.
**Henry Kissinger**, quoted in *Reader's Digest*, 1985

**13** I'm never going to be famous. My name will never be writ large on the roster of Those Who Do Things. I don't do anything. Not one single thing. I used to bite my nails, but I don't even do that anymore.
**Dorothy Parker**, 'The Little Hours', *The Portable Dorothy Parker*, 1944

**14** I was the toast of two continents: Greenland and Australia.
**Dorothy Parker** (Attrib.)

**15** I'm famous. That's my job.
**Jerry Rubin**, *Growing (Up) at 37*, 1976

**16** In the future, everyone will be famous for fifteen minutes.
**Andy Warhol**, 1960s

# Family, The

*See also Children; Fathers; Mothers; Nepotism; Parents; Relatives.*

**1** To my way of thinking, the American family started to decline when parents began to communicate with their children. When we began to 'rap', 'feed into one another', 'let things hang out' that mother didn't know about and would rather not.
**Erma Bombeck**, *If Life is a Bowl of Cherries – What am I Doing in the Pits?*, 1978

**2** Happiness is having a large, loving, caring, close-knit family in another city.
**George Burns**

**3** Where does the family start? It starts with a young man falling in love with a girl – no superior alternative has yet been found.
**Winston Churchill** (Attrib.)

**4** Human beings are the only creatures on earth that allow their children to come back home.
**Bill Cosby**

**5** The families of one's friends are always a disappointment.
**Norman Douglas**

**6** Your basic extended family today includes your ex-husband or -wife, your ex's new mate, your new mate, possibly your new mate's ex and any new mate that your new mate's ex has acquired.
**Delia Ephron**, *Funny Sauce*, 1986

**7** A man's womenfolk, whatever their outward show of respect for his merit and authority, always regard him secretly as an ass, and with something akin to pity.
**H. L. Mencken**, *In Defense of Women*, 1922

**8** DAPHNE: Oh, Dr. Crane, why is it so easy to love our family, but so hard to like them?
FRASIER: Daphne, that's one of those questions that makes life so rich and psychiatrists richer.
**Linda Morris and Vic Rauseo**, 'You Can Go Home Again', *Frasier*, NBC, 1996

**9** A family is a unit composed not only of children, but of men, women, an occasional animal, and the common cold.
**Ogden Nash**

**10** One would be in less danger
From the wiles of the stranger
If one's own kin and kith
Were more fun to be with.
**Ogden Nash**, 'Family Court', *Hard Lines*, 1931

**11** The Family! Home of all social evils, a charitable institution for indolent women, a prison workshop for the slaving breadwinner, and a hell for children.
**August Strindberg**, *The Son of a Servant*, 1886

**12** Whether family life is physically harmful is still in dispute. The incidence of men who go down with a coronary upon learning that their teenage daughters are in the pudding club is indisputably higher among family men than among those who have never indulged; so is indigestion, backache, alcoholism, and going purple in the face when the bath is full of tights and knickers.
**Keith Waterhouse**, *The Passing of the Third-floor Buck*, 1974

# Farms and Farming

*See also The Country.*

**1** He [Major Major's father] was a long-limbed farmer, a God-fearing, freedom-

loving, law-abiding rugged individualist who held that federal aid to anyone but farmers was creeping socialism.
**Joseph Heller**, Catch-22, 1961

**2** A farm is an irregular patch of nettles bounded by short-term notes, containing a fool and his wife who didn't know enough to stay in the city.
**S. J. Perelman**

**3** A good farmer is nothing more nor less than a handy man with a sense of humus.
**E. B. White**, One Man's Meat, 1944

# Fashion

*See also Appearance; Beauty; Clothes; Looks; Style; Taste.*

**1** *I* have the New Look; *you* have let down your hem; *she* has had that dress since 1934.
**Competition**, New Statesman

**2** There'll be little change in men's pockets this year.
**Anon.**, Wall Street Journal, 1948

**3** Her hat is a creation that will never go out of style. It will look just as ridiculous year after year.
**Fred Allen**

**4** By actual count, there are only six women in the country who looked well in a jumpsuit. Five of them were terminal and the other was sired by a Xerox machine.
**Erma Bombeck**, If Life is a Bowl of Cherries – What am I Doing in the Pits?, 1978

**5** While clothes with pictures and/or writing on them are not entirely an invention of the modern age, they are an unpleasant indication of the general state of things . . . I mean, be realistic. If people don't want to listen to you what makes you think they want to hear from your sweater?
**Fran Lebowitz**, Metropolitan Life, 1978

**6** Fashion is what one wears oneself. What is unfashionable is what other people wear.
**Oscar Wilde**, An Ideal Husband, 1895

# Fastidiousness

*See also Cleanliness.*

**1** *I* am fastidious; *you* are fussy; *he* is an old woman.
**Competition**, New Statesman

# Fate

*See also Astrology.*

**1** See how the Fates their gifts allot,
For A is happy – B is not.
Yet B is worthy, I dare say,
Of more prosperity than A!
**W. S. Gilbert**, The Mikado, 1885

**2** Lots of folks confuse bad management with destiny.
**Kin Hubbard**

**3** Unseen, in the background, Fate was quietly slipping the lead into the boxing gloves.
**P. G. Wodehouse**, Very Good, Jeeves, 1930

# Fathers

*See also Children; The Family; Mothers; Parents.*

**1** Providing for one's family as a good husband and father is a watertight excuse for making money hand over fist. Greed may be a sin, exploitation of other people might, on the face of it, look rather nasty, but who can blame a man for 'doing the best' for his children?
**Eva Figes**, Nova, 1973

**2** To be a successful father there's one absolute rule: when you have a kid, don't look at it for the first two years.
**Ernest Hemingway**, quoted in Papa Hemingway, 1966

**3** I never got along with my dad. Kids used to come up to me and say, 'My dad can beat up your dad.'
I'd say, 'Yeah? When?'
**Bill Hicks**, American comedian

**4** The fundamental defect of fathers is that they want their children to be a credit to them.
**Bertrand Russell**, The New York Times, 1963

**5** Fathers should neither be seen nor heard. That is the only proper basis for family life.
**Oscar Wilde**, *An Ideal Husband*, 1895

**6** 'Jeeves, I wish I had a daughter. I wonder what the procedure is?'

'Marriage is, I believe, considered the preliminary step, sir.'
**P. G. Wodehouse**, *Carry on Jeeves*, 1925

# Fear
*See also Anxiety; Courage; Cowardice.*

**1** From **Honest-to-God phobias**

Blennophobia – fear of slime
Pteronophobia – fear of being tickled by feathers
Papaphobia – fear of the Pope
Soceraphobia – fear of parents-in-law
Bolshephobia – fear of Bolshevism
Cherophobia – fear of gaiety
Metrophobia – fear of poetry
Phobophobia – fear of fear itself
**Matt Groening**, *Bart Simpson's Guide to Life*, 1996

**2** He cowered before Aunt Dahlia like a wet sock.
**P. G. Wodehouse**, *The Code of the Woosters*, 1938

**3** The good old persp. was bedewing my forehead by this time in a pretty lavish manner. I don't know when I've been so rattled.

'Do you find the room a trifle warm?'

'Oh no, no, rather not. Just right.'
**P. G. Wodehouse**, 'Jeeves in the Springtime', 1921

**4** A lot of people are afraid of heights. Not me – I'm afraid of widths.
**Steven Wright**, American comic

# Feminism
*See also Equality; Sexism; Sexual Equality; Women; Women – The Male View.*

**1** A woman who strives to be like a man lacks ambition.
**Graffito**, New York, 1982

**2** A woman's work is never done by men.
**Graffito**, London, 1980

**3** Equality is a myth – women are better.
**Graffito**, London, 1980

**4** My father is liberated – he gave my mother permission to vote Labour.
**Graffito**, London, 1980

**5** Q: What happened when women stood up for their rights?
A: They lost their seats on the bus.
*The Big Book of Jokes and Riddles*, 1978

**6** If men could get pregnant, abortion would be a sacrament.
**Postcard** produced by the Center for Constitutional Rights

**7** These are very confusing times. For the first time in history a woman is expected to combine: intelligence with a sharp hairdo, a raised consciousness with high heels, and an open, non-sexist relationship with a tan guy who has a great bod.
**Lynda Barry**, *Why are Women Crazy?*, cartoon, *Esquire*, 1984

**8** WIFE: Cooking! Cleaning! Why should women do it?
HUSBAND: You're right – let's get an au pair girl.
**Mel Calman**, *Couples*, cartoon, 1972

**9** A feminist man is like a jumbo shrimp. Neither makes any sense.
**Cassandra Davis**

**10** Of course I'm a feminist. You have to be these days – it's the only way to pull the chicks.
**Ben Elton, Rick Mayall and Lise Meyer**, *The Young Ones*, BBC TV, 1988

**11** . . . the major concrete achievement of the women's movement in the 1970s was the Dutch treat.
**Nora Ephron**, *Heartburn*, 1983

**12** We have lived through the era when happiness was a warm puppy, and the era when happiness was a dry martini, and now we have come to the era when happiness is 'knowing what your uterus looks like'.
**Nora Ephron**, *Crazy Salad*, 1975

**13** . . . the women's movement hasn't changed my sex life at all. It wouldn't dare.
**Zsa Zsa Gabor**, quoted in *Playboy*, 1979

**14** Anyone can have the key to the

executive washroom, but once a woman gets inside, what is there? A lavatory.
**Germaine Greer**, quoted in *Time*, 1984

**15** Is it too much to ask that women be spared the daily struggle for superhuman beauty in order to offer it to the caresses of a subhumanly ugly mate?
**Germaine Greer**, *The Female Eunuch*, 1970

**16** Emeralds! Aren't they divine? Jack gave them to me to shut up about Women's Lib.
**William Hamilton**, *William Hamilton's Anti-Social Register*, cartoon, 1974

**17** During the feminist revolution, the battle lines were again simple. It was easy to tell the enemy, he was the one with the penis. This is no longer strictly true. Some men are okay now. We're allowed to like them again. We still have to keep them in line, of course, but we no longer have to shoot them on sight.
**Cynthia Heimel**, *Sex Tips for Girls*, 1983

**18** Feminism is far, far from dead, but it is true that the movement has lost some of its zip. It was breezing along fine there for a while, with everyone all optimistic and fervent and charging around opening daycare centers, but things have undoubtedly slackened. Women seem scared and don't know where to look for guidance, since it seems as if all the leaders of the feminist movement have retreated into their individual lairs, emerging only at infrequent intervals to snarl. Very upsetting, but we mustn't blame our erstwhile leaders. They're tired. They've been slogging away for years and are sick of being called strident bull-dykes. Who can blame them for being out of sorts?
**Cynthia Heimel**, *Sex Tips for Girls*, 1983

**19** I'm lost when it comes to the status of the backlash. There was feminism and a male backlash against feminism then a feminist backlash against the male backlash and now there seems to be, correct me if I'm wrong, a male backlash against the feminist backlash.
**Cynthia Heimel**, 'The Shame of Male-Bashing', *Playboy*, 1994

**20** Nobody can argue any longer about the rights of women. It's like arguing about earthquakes.
**Lillian Hellman**, 1905–84, American playwright (Attrib.)

**21** *Feminist*: a woman, usually ill-favoured . . . in whom the film-making instinct has displaced the maternal.
**Barry Humphries**, glossary from *A Nice Night's Entertainment*, 1981

**22** It is hard to fight an enemy who has outposts in your head.
**Sally Kempton**, *Esquire*, 1970

**23** *Ms*: the wise avoid this word entirely but (a) it may be used in public by harried members of the publishing world who find it necessary to abbreviate the word 'manuscript'; (b) or by native residents of the south and south-eastern portions of United States as follows: 'I sho do ms that purty little gal.'
**Fran Lebowitz**, *Metropolitan Life*, 1978

**24** I'm furious about the Women's Liberationists. They keep getting up on soapboxes and proclaiming that women are brighter than men. That's true, but it should be kept very quiet or it ruins the whole racket.
**Anita Loos**, *Observer*, 1973

**25** If you were on a sinking ship and yelled, 'Women and children first!' how much feminist opposition do you think you'd get? . . . Women want to fight men for equal pay, but how often do they fight a man for the check?
. . . And any man who questions a woman's physical capabilities gets branded a sexist – but who do they call when there's a spider to be killed?
Convenient feminism – crackpot theory or dangerous lunacy?
**Bill Maher**, *Politically Incorrect*, 1993

**26** It took women's liberation to make me realise that women can be just as rotten and lousy as men.
**Norman Mailer**, *Daily Telegraph*, 1991

**27** No one is going to take Women's Liberation seriously until women recognize that they will not be thought of as equals in

the secret privacy of men's most private
mental parts until they eschew alimony.
**Norman Mailer** (Attrib.)

**28** Dear Miss Manners,
As a businessman, how do I allow a
businesswoman to pay for my lunch?

Gentle Reader,
With credit card or cash, as she prefers.
**Judith Martin**, *Miss Manners' Guide to Excruciatingly
Correct Behaviour*, 1983

**29** Let it all hang out; let it seem bitchy,
catty, dykey, frustrated, crazy, Solanesque,
nutty, frigid, ridiculous, bitter,
embarrassing, man-hating, libelous, pure,
unfair, envious, intuitive, lowdown, stupid,
petty, liberating; we are the women that
men have warned us about.
**Robin Morgan**, *Rat*, 1970

**30** LISA: It's not funny, Bart! Millions of
girls will grow up thinking that this is the
right way to act – that they can never be
more than vacuous ninnies whose only goal
is to look pretty, land a rich husband, and
spend all day on the phone with their
equally vacuous friends talking about how
damn terrific it is to look pretty and have a
rich husband!!
BART: Just what I was gonna say.
**Bill Oakley and Josh Weinstein**, 'Lisa vs. Malibu
Stacy', *The Simpsons*, Fox TV, 1994

**31** . . . feminism is the result of a few
ignorant and literal-minded women letting
the cat out of the bag about which is the
superior sex. Once women made it public
that they could do things better than men,
they were, of course, forced to do them.
Now women have to be elected to political
office, get jobs as officers of major
corporations, and so on, instead of ruling
the earth by batting their eyelashes the way
they used to.
**P. J. O'Rourke**, *Modern Manners*, 1983

**32** How much fame, money, and power
does a woman have to achieve on her own
before you can punch her in the face?
**P. J. O'Rourke**, *Modern Manners*, 1983

**33** Men have always been expected to be
helpful to women. The same is true now but
the mode of helpfulness has changed with
changing sex roles. One example will

suffice. In the past a man was expected to
give his seat on a bus to a woman. Today it
would be much more courteous for that
man to give her his job.
**P. J. O'Rourke**, *Modern Manners*, 1983

**34** . . . there's still a place in the world for
men. Women want to be a lot of things
traditionally considered masculine: doctors,
rock stars, body builders, presidents of the
United States. But there are plenty of
masculine things women have, so far,
shown no desire to be: pipe smokers, first-
rate spin-casters, wise old drunks, quiet.
And there is one thing women can never
take away from men. We die sooner.
**P. J. O'Rourke**, *Modern Manners*, 1983

**35** Boys don't make passes at female smart-
asses.
**Letty Cottin Pogrebin**, *The First Ms Reader*, 1972

**36** Ginger Rogers did everything Fred
Astaire did. She just did it backwards and in
high heels.
**Ann Richards**, Governor of Texas, keynote address,
Democratic National Convention, 1988

**37** We're living in an age where you have
to call a chick and ask her if she'll wear a
dress tonight. And they say 'You're weird'.
**Tim Rose**

**38** . . . during your innermost and private
. . . quest for THE TRUTH, libbywise, you
might consider the following suggestion:
namely, that it is naïve in the extreme for
women to expect to be regarded as equals
by men . . . so long as they persist in a
subhuman (I.E., animal-like) behavior
during sexual intercourse. I'm referring, as
you doubtless know, to the outlandish
PANTING, GASPING, MOANING, SOBBING,
WRITHING, SCRATCHING, BITING,
SCREAMING conniptions, and the seemingly
invariable 'OH MY GOD . . . OH MY GOD . . .
OH MY GOD' all so predictably integral to
the pre-, post-, AND orgasmic stages of
intercourse.
**Terry Southern**, 'Letter to the Editor of *Ms*', *National
Lampoon Encyclopedia of Humor*, 1972

**39** Some of us are becoming the men we
wanted to marry.
**Gloria Steinem**, *Ms*, 1982

**40** I sometimes wish I lived in pre-feminist

times when if a man washed a teaspoon he was regarded as 'a big Jessie'. It must have been great when women did all the work, and men just lolled about reading the paper.

I asked my father about those days when we were preparing the Brussels sprouts, the carrots and the potatoes, etc, etc. His eyes took on a faraway misty look. 'It was a golden age,' he said, almost choking with emotion. 'I'm only sorry that you never lived to see it as an adult man, I'd come home from work, my dinner would be on the table, my shirts ironed, my socks in balls. I didn't know how to turn the stove *on*, let alone cook on the bleeding thing.' His eyes then narrowed, his voice became a hiss as he said, 'That bloody Germaine Greer ruined my life. Your mother was never the same after reading that bleeding book.'

**Sue Townsend**, *Adrian Mole: The Cappuccino Years*, 1999

**41** Whatever women do, they must do twice as well as men to be thought half as good. Luckily, this is not difficult.
**Charlotte Whitton**, former Mayor of Ottawa

**42** Sexual harassment at work – is it a problem for the self-employed?
**Victoria Wood**, one-woman show, 1984

# Fidelity

*See also Chastity; Infidelity; Marriage; Monogamy; Vice and Virtue.*

**1** While tearing off
A game of golf
I may make a play for the caddy.
But when I do
I don't follow through
'Cause my heart belongs to Daddy.
**Cole Porter**, 'My Heart Belongs to Daddy', song, 1938

# Fifties, The

**1** The fifties were ten years of foreplay.
**Germaine Greer**, *The Late Clive James*, Channel Four, 1984

# Fighting

*See also The Army; Boxing; Self-Defence; Violence; War.*

**1** ERNIE: Did he put up a fight?
ERIC: You bet – we went at it hammer and tongs!
ERNIE: Hammer and tongs?
ERIC: Yes. I won in the end though. I had the hammer.
**Eric Morecambe and Ernie Wise**, *The Morecambe and Wise Joke Book*, 1979

# Figures

*See also The Body; Diets and Dieting; Exercise; Height.*

**1** Her husband is so bow-legged, she has to iron his underpants on a boomerang.
**Anon.**

**2** This guy was so fat he had back-up lights.
**Anon.**

**3** Your mother is so fat, when she sings, it's over.
*Snaps 4*, 1998

**4** Your mother is so fat, she has her own area code.
*Snaps*, 1994

**5** How Dare You Presume I'd Rather Be Thin?
**American badge**, 1980s

**6** I went to the beach the other day. I held my stomach in so much, I threw out my back.
**Milton Berle**

**7** I had no intention of giving her my vital statistics. 'Let me put it this way,' I said. 'According to my girth, I should be a ninety-food redwood.'
**Erma Bombeck**, *If Life is a Bowl of Cherries – What am I Doing in the Pits?*, 1978

**8** When I was a child, I was so fat I was the one chosen to play Bethlehem in the school Nativity play.
**Jo Brand**, English comedienne

**9** It is a point of pride for the American

male to keep the same size Jockey shorts for his entire life.
**Bill Cosby**

**10** Every so often I lose weight, and, to my utter horror and indignation, I find in the quiet of the night somebody has put it back on.
**Lord Goodman**, English lawyer, 1973

**11** This guy has muscles in places where I don't even have places.
**Bob Hope**

**12** Is she fat? Her favorite food is seconds.
**Joan Rivers**, of Elizabeth Taylor, 1983

**13** ... she's so fat, she's my two best friends. She wears stretch kaftans. She's got more chins than the Chinese telephone directory.
**Joan Rivers**

**14** You guys – you gain thirty pounds and we call you cuddly. We gain an ounce and you call us taxis. Then you don't call us at all.
**Carol Siskind**, American comic

**15** How dare he tell me what to do when he has a circumference to rival the equator.
**Ann Widdecombe**, former Conservative minister on healthy eating advice from Health Minister Frank Dobson, 1998

**16** Country butter and the easy life these curates lead had added a pound or two to an always impressive figure. To find the lean, finely trained Stinker of my nonage, I felt that one would have to catch him in Lent.
**P. G. Wodehouse**, *The Code of the Woosters*, 1938

**17** The lunches of fifty-seven years had caused his chest to slip down to the mezzanine floor.
**P. G. Wodehouse**, *The Heart of a Goof*, 1926

**18** The Right Hon. was a tubby little chap who looked as if he had been poured into his clothes and had forgotten to say 'When!'
**P. G. Wodehouse**, *Very Good, Jeeves*, 1930

# Film

*See also Acting; Actors and Actresses; Film – Critics; Hollywood.*

**1 Seven things you'd never know without the movies**

When they're alone, all foreigners prefer to speak English to each other.
Any lock can be picked by a credit card or a paper clip in seconds – unless it's the door to a burning building with a child trapped inside.
It is not necessary to speak German to pass yourself off as a German officer. Something approximating a German accent will do.
When in love, it is customary to burst into song.
One man shooting at 20 men has a better chance of killing all of them than 20 men have of shooting one man.
Police departments give their officers personality tests to ensure they assign partners who are total opposites.
A man will show no pain while taking the most ferocious beating, but he will wince when a woman tries to clean his wounds.
**Anon.**

**2** Imagine their delighted surprise when I read them the script of *Love and Death*, with its plot that went from war to political assassination, ending with the death of its hero caused by a cruel trick of God. Never having witnessed eight film executives go into cardiac arrest simultaneously, I was quite amused.
**Woody Allen**, *Esquire*, 1975

**3** Making a funny film provides all the enjoyment of getting your leg caught in the blades of a threshing machine. As a matter of fact, it's not even that pleasurable; with the threshing machine the end comes much quicker.
**Woody Allen**, *Esquire*, 1975

**4** Though they [United Artists executives] were agreed that death and atheism were indeed provocative subjects for farce, they said they would call the police if I didn't leave their office and never come back. Invoking the artistic-prerogative clause in my contract, a clause that gives me total control over what necktie I can wear while

rewriting, I insisted that I go forward with the project.
**Woody Allen**, *Esquire*, 1975

**5** An adult Western is where the hero still kisses his horse at the end, only now he worries about it.
**Milton Berle**, *Variety*, 1978

**6** Makes *Jaws* look like a toothpaste commercial.
Makes *King Kong* look like *Lassie Come Home*.
Makes *Towering Inferno* look like a bonfire in a bungalow.
**David Frost**, horror film synopsis, 1978

**7** It's the kissiest business in the world. You *have* to keep kissing people.
**Ava Gardner**

**8** It might be a fight like you see on the screen;
A swain getting slain for the love of a queen,
Some great Shakespearian scene
Where the Ghost and the Prince meet
And everyone ends in mincemeat.
**Arthur Schwartz and Howard Dietz**, 'That's Entertainment', song from *The Band Wagon*, 1953

**9** Mickey Mouse, the veteran American comic, is back in London. He is here to launch the forthcoming series of his best comedies, soon to be shown here by the BBC.
Still wearing the big-buttoned Bermuda shorts, round-topped shoes and stitch-back gloves that made him famous, he greeted me in the foyer at Claridges with a sprightly grace that belied his eighty-one years. A simple 'Hi Pal!', a gentle wave of introduction to his wife Minnie, seventy-nine, . . . and we were sunk deep in the generous sofas, sipping martinis and talking nostalgically about the Good Old Days with Pluto, Donald, Goofy and the Twins.
**John Wells**, *Masterpieces*, 1982

**10** An actor entering through the door, you've got nothing. But if he enters through the window, you've got a situation.
**Billy Wilder**

**11** Shoot a few scenes out of focus. I want you to win the foreign film award.
**Billy Wilder**, to a cameraman (Attrib.)

# Film – Critics
*See also Critics – The Artist's View; Film.*

**1** Me No Leica.
**Anon.**, reviewing *I am a Camera*, 1955 (possibly apocryphal)

**2** A mishmash: of Stalinism with New Dealism with Hollywoodism with opportunism with shaky experimentalism with mesmerism with onanism, all mosaicked into a remarkable portrait of what the makers of the film think the Soviet Union is like – a great glad two-million-dollar bowl of canned borscht, eminently approvable by the Institute of Good Housekeeping.
**James Agee**, reviewing *Mission to Moscow*, 1943

**3** A variety show including everyone at Paramount who was not overseas, in hiding or out to lunch.
**James Agee**, reviewing *Star Spangled Rhythm*, 1942

**4** I have nothing in the world against this picture except that at least half of it seemed to me enormously tiresome.
**James Agee**, reviewing *The Jolson Story*, 1946

**5** I would like to recommend this film to those who can stay interested in Ronald Colman's amnesia for two hours and who could with pleasure eat a bowl of Yardley's shaving soap for breakfast.
**James Agee**, reviewing *Random Harvest*, 1942

**6** Several tons of dynamite are set off in this picture – none of it under the right people.
**James Agee**, reviewing *Tycoon*, 1947

**7** The money spent on this production might easily have kept Mozart and Schubert alive and busy to the age of sixty, with enough left over to finance five of the best movies ever made. It might even have been invested in a good movie musical.
**James Agee**, reviewing *This Time for Keeps*, 1947

**8** . . . a pair of million dollar babies in a five and ten cent flick.
**Charles Champlin**, reviewing *The Missouri Breaks* (starring Marlon Brando and Jack Nicholson), *Los Angeles Times*, 1976

**9** . . . so mediocre you can't get mad at it.
**Judith Crist**, reviewing *Five Card Stud*, 1968

**10** You think we watch any of your movies, Harry? I've seen better film on teeth.
**Scott Frank**, *Get Shorty*, screenplay, 1996 (based on the novel by Elmore Leonard)

**11** This long but tiny film . . .
**Stanley Kauffmann**, reviewing *Isadora*, 1969

**12** This film needs a certain something. Possibly burial.
**David Lardner**, reviewing *Panama Hattie*, 1942

# Fish and Fishing

*See also Oysters; The Sea; Sport.*

**1** Oh, give me grace to catch a fish
   So big that even I
   When talking of it afterwards
   May have no need to lie.
**Anon.**, 'A Fisherman's Prayer'

**2** There's a fine line between fishing and standing on the riverside looking like an idiot.
**Anon.**

**3** Work Is For People Who Don't Know How to Fish
**Bumper sticker**, Key Biscayne, 1997

**4** ANDY: You don't know nothing about music. What is a scale?
AMOS: A scale is a feather on a fish.
ANDY: Fishes don't have feathers.
AMOS: How about flying fishes?
**Amos 'n' Andy**, 1929

**5** A shark could never harm you. The shark is a benign creature of the sea. Of course, if you thrash about in the water or if you wear shiny bracelets, the shark will be attracted to you. On occasion, the shark has followed people out of the water and has gone to their blanket and eaten their beach ball. One time, the shark followed my brother Irving home on the Brighton local, and, upon being admitted to the apartment house, the shark entered his apartment – Apartment 4B – and ate his entire family and a brand new hat. Apart from that, the shark is a pussycat.
**Mel Brooks**, TV interview with David Susskind, 1970

**6** In literature, fishing is indeed an exhilarating sport; but, so far as my experience goes, it does not pan out when you carry the idea further.
**Irvin S. Cobb**, 1876–1944, American journalist

**7** Oh, the slimy, squirmy, slithery eel!
   He swallows your hook with malignant zeal,
   He tangles your line and he gums your reel,
   The slimy, squirmy, slithery eel.
   Oh, the slimy, squirmy, slithery eel!
   He cannot be held in a grip of steel,
   And when he is dead he is hard to peel,
   The slimy, squirmy, slithery eel.'
**Arthur Guiterman**, 'Song of Hate for Eels'

**8** Fishing is a delusion entirely surrounded by liars in old clothes.
**Don Marquis**, American journalist

**9** the octopus's secret wish
   is not to be a formal fish
   he dreams that some time he may grow
   another set of legs or so
   and be a broadway music show
**Don Marquis**, 'archy at the zoo', *archy and mehitabel*, 1927

**10** We're fishing and my wife had a problem with killing the fish. I wasn't crazy with that part either, but I figured if we just wait for them to die naturally, it could take forever. Certainly till after supper.
**Paul Reiser**

**11** All you need to be a fisherman is patience and a worm.
**Herb Shriner**

**12** The curious thing about fishing is you never want to go home. If you catch anything, you can't stop. If you don't catch anything, you hate to leave in case something might bite.
**Gladys Taber**, *Ladies' Home Journal*, 1941

**13** Oh, no doubt the cod is a splendid swimmer – admirable for swimming purposes but not for eating.
**Oscar Wilde** (Attrib.)

# Flattery

*See also Compliments; Praise.*

**1** You're the top!
You're Miss Pinkham's tonic
You're the top!
You're a high colonic.
You're the burning heat of a bridal suite
    in use,
You're the breasts of Venus,
You're King Kong's penis,
You're self-abuse.
You're an arch
In the Rome collection.
You're the starch
In a groom's erection.
I'm a eunuch who
Has just been through an op,
But if, Baby, I'm the bottom
You're the top.
**Anon.** (parody attributed – probably erroneously – to
Cole Porter), *Anything Goes*, 1934, *The Complete Lyrics
of Cole Porter*

**2** Flattery must be pretty thick before
anybody objects to it.
**William Feather**, *The Business of Life*

**3** You're the top!
You're an Arrow collar.
You're the top!
You're a Coolidge dollar.
You're the nimble tread of the feet of Fred
    Astaire.
You're an O'Neill drama.
You're Whistler's mama,
You're Camembert.
You're a rose,
You're Inferno's Dante
You're the nose
On the great Durante.
I'm just in the way, as the French would
    say 'De trop',
But if, Baby, I'm the bottom
You're the top.
**Cole Porter**, 'You're the Top', song, 1934

**4** What really flatters a man is that you
think him worth flattering.
**George Bernard Shaw**, *John Bull's Other Island*, 1904

**5** Baloney is flattery so thick it cannot be
true; blarney is flattery so thin we like it.
**Fulton J. Sheen**, American Roman Catholic
Archbishop

**6** Flattery is like a cigarette – it's all right so
long as you don't inhale.
**Adlai Stevenson**, speech, 1961

**7** The only man who wasn't spoiled by
being lionized was Daniel.
**Sir H. Beerbohm Tree**

# Flirtation

*See also Charm; Couples; Courtship; Love;
Seduction; Sexual Attraction.*

**1** Flirt: a woman who thinks it's every man
for herself.
**Anon.**

**2** George Moore unexpectedly pinched my
behind. I felt rather honoured that my
behind should have drawn the attention of
the great master of English prose.
**Ilka Chase**

**3** My heart is a bargain today. Will you take
it?
**W. C. Fields** (Attrib.)

**4** She plucked from my lapel the invisible
strand of lint (the universal act of women to
proclaim ownership).
**O. Henry**, 'Strictly Business', 1910

**5** STEVE GUTTENBERG: I'd give anything to
see your thighs. I don't suppose you'd
describe them for me?
KIM CATTRALL: Well, they're tan, of course.
Very supple, well rounded and luxuriant to
the touch.
**Neal Israel, Pat Profit and Hugh Wilson**, *Police
Academy*, screenplay, 1984

**6** She's been on more laps than a napkin.
**Walter Winchell**, American newspaper columnist

# Florida

*See also America and the Americans.*

**1** I like Florida; everything is in the eighties.
The temperatures, the ages and the IQs.
**George Carlin**, *Brain Droppings*, 1997

**2** In winter when the days get horrider,
    We long for Florider.
**Bill Vaughan**

# Flying

*See also Flying – Fear of; Holidays; Travel.*

**1** Q: What's a sure sign you're flying with the wrong airline?
A: The pilot has a heart attack and air traffic control talks a flight attendant through takeoff.
**Anon.**

**2** If the Lord had wanted people to fly, He would have made it simpler for people to get to the airport.
**Milton Berle**

**3** Dr Rudolf Von Rudder explains how aircraft fly:
It's a simple theory. Matter is lighter than air. You see, the motors, they pull the plane forward and they cause a draft, and then it taxis faster down the field and the motors go faster and the whole plane vibrates, and then, when there's enough of a draft and a vacuum created, the plane rises off the runway into the air. From then on, it's a miracle. I don't know what keeps it up.
**Mel Brooks**, *Your Show of Shows*, NBC TV, 1950s

**4** Beware of men on airplanes.
The minute a man reaches 30,000 feet, he immediately becomes consumed by distasteful sexual fantasies which involve doing uncomfortable things in those tiny toilets. These men should not be encouraged, their fantasies are sadly low-rent and unimaginative. Affect an aloof, cool demeanor as soon as any man tries to draw you out. Unless, of course, he's the pilot.
**Cynthia Heimel**, *Sex Tips for Girls*, 1983

**5** Flying? I've been to almost as many places as my luggage!
**Bob Hope**

**6** From **Top ten signs you have a bad airline pilot**
When you take off he yells, 'Wheeeeeeeee!'
For the past two hours, you've been going straight up.
Rolls down cockpit window so his dog can stick his head out.
Mentions engine trouble and warns, 'We might have to rest on a big cloud for a while.'

You're deep in the Andes Mountains eating human flesh right this minute.
**David Letterman**, *The Late Show*, CBS

**7** ERNIE: Hey, look at all those people down there – they look like ants.
ERIC: They *are* ants – we haven't taken off yet.
**Eric Morecambe and Ernie Wise**, *The Morecambe and Wise Joke Book*, 1979

**8** **Miss Piggy's Rules to Leave by**
*Tickets and travelling documents*: these should be kept in a handy place where you can check them several hundred times.
*Travel arrangements*: whenever possible, avoid airlines which have anyone's first name in their titles, like Bob's International Airline or Air Fred.
*Companions*: if you're travelling alone, beware of seatmates who by way of starting a conversation make remarks like, 'I just have to talk to someone – my teeth are spying on me' or 'Did you know that squirrels are the devil's oven mitts?'
**Miss Piggy**, *Miss Piggy's Guide to Life (As Told to Henry Beard)*, 1981

**9** I flew here on one of those dinky commuter airlines. My plane was delayed 'cause it got caught in some kid's kite.
**Keith Robinson**

**10** The flight attendant will always tell you the name of your pilot. Like anyone goes, 'Oh, he's good. I like his work.'
**David Spade**

**11** KENNETH HORNE: I relaxed in the luxury first-class compartment of the Super Constellation Pan World Airways Swept Wing Sopwith Camel that was to take me to my rendezvous with fate. The hostess bent over me.
AIR HOSTESS: You're about to take off, sir. Would you like boiled sweets or cotton wool?
KENNETH HORNE: I won't have the boiled sweets. They just fall out of my ears. I'll just have some cotton wool.
AIR HOSTESS: Here you are, sir.
KENNETH HORNE: Thank you . . . Delicious.
**Barry Took and Marty Feldman**, *Round the Horne*, BBC Radio, 1966

# Flying – Fear of

*See also Fear; Flying; Travel.*

**1** . . . I say to myself, 'Well, I'm strapping myself into the seat. Because if I wasn't strapped into this seat, there's a very good chance that I will fall *out* of this seat. If the plane came to a sudden stop. Like against a mountain.
**Shelley Berman**, airline routine, 1960s

**2** I'll take three hours in the dentist's waiting room, with four cavities and an impacted wisdom tooth, in preference to fifteen minutes at any airport waiting for an aeroplane.
**Patrick Campbell**, *Daily Mail*, 1947

**3** If God had intended us to fly, he would never have given us railways.
**Michael Flanders** (Attrib.)

**4** Doc Daneeka hated to fly. He felt imprisoned in an airplane. In an airplane there was absolutely no place in the world to go except to another part of the airplane.
**Joseph Heller**, *Catch-22*, 1961

**5** I never worry about the plane crashing. Remember – in the case of an accident, the pilot is always first on the scene.
**Max Kauffmann**

**6** CAPTAIN: If we should have to ditch, you'll receive plenty of warning because our co-pilot becomes hysterical. And he'll start running up and down the aisles yelling 'We're going to crash!' or something like that . . .
**Bob Newhart**, *The Grace L. Ferguson Air Line*, album

# Folk Music

*See also Music and Musicians; Songs and Singers.*

**1** A folksinger is someone who sings through his nose by ear.
**Anon.**

**2** A folk song is a song that nobody ever wrote.
**Anon.**

**3** For Wigan men are hearty
And Bolton men are bold,
There's something coy in a Blackpool boy
And the Bedford lads have hearts of gold,
But the chaps that live on Dartmoor
Are breezy bright and gay,
Singing Hey ha ha with a fa la la and a
hey nonny no and whack folly o,
Ha ha ha ha ha ha ha ha ha ha ha ha HA
HA HA HA!
**Noel Coward**, 'Devon', song, 1950s

**4** I was involved in the Great Folk Music Scare back in the sixties. When it *almost* caught on. It was close for a time, but fortunately . . .
**Martin Mull**, BBC TV, 1985

**5** . . . I've come up with a very tender and furtive madrigal, which has been passed down from father to son, until the handle dropped off. 'Tis an old Sussex courting song and tells the story of a young swain who stands beneath his loved one's bower – he's a very small swain, but then she's got a very low bower . . . and he tells her of his love as follows:

Will you love me Mary-oh
When my grussets be bended low
When my orbs grow dim and my splod
grows white
And my cordwangle makes an ugly sight
And my grussets be bended low-oh!
My grussets be bended low.
**Barry Took and Marty Feldman**, *Round the Horne*,
BBC Radio, 1966

**6** 'Tis a hoary old folk song that I picked up from a home for hoary old folks. 'Tis a courting song or air which tells of the coming of Spring to Clapham Junction and 'tis about this young swain of they parts who every Spring feels the sap rising and gets a kind of March Madness which is common to the young men of they parts and is known as swain fever. He wanders about the bosky haunts and verdant pasture-lands of Clapham High Street and as he hears the little hedge sparrow coughing and sees the young lambs hanging up in the butcher's shop, he feels a primeval urge. And he goes forth to seek his true love.
**Barry Took and Marty Feldman**, *Round the Horne*,
BBC Radio, 1966

# Food

*See also Cheese; Cooks and Cookery; Diets and Dieting; Eating; Fruit; Greed; Oysters; Picnics; Restaurants; Vegetables; Wine.*

**1** Tomato Ketchup.
  If you do not shake the bottle
  None'll come and then a lot'll.
**Anon.**

**2** Just Give Me Chocolate And Nobody Gets Hurt
**T-shirt, New York, 1999**

**3** When Marilyn Monroe was married to Arthur Miller, his mother always made matzo ball soup. After the tenth time, Marilyn said, 'Gee Arthur, these matzo balls are pretty nice, but isn't there any other part of the matzo you can eat?'
**Ann Barr and Paul Levy,** *The Foodie Handbook,* 1984

**4** INTERVIEWER: Sir, how do you survive in New York City? . . . What do you eat?
JUNGLE BOY: Pigeon.
INTERVIEWER: Don't the pigeons object?
JUNGLE BOY: Only for a minute.
**Mel Brooks,** *Your Show of Shows,* NBC TV, 1950

**5** Sometimes on television they tell you to buy a frozen Mexican dinner. Well, it sounds like a good idea, but actually, before you take him out to dinner, I should think it might be a good idea to bring him in the house and let him warm up a little. A frozen Mexican probably wouldn't be thinking mainly about food.
**George Carlin,** *Brain Droppings,* 1997

**6** I have eaten octopus – or squid, I can never quite tell the difference – but never with wholehearted enjoyment on account of not caring for the taste of hot india rubber.
**Noel Coward** (Attrib.)

**7** If there's an end
  On which I'd spend
  My last remaining cash,
  It's sausage, friend,
  It's sausage, friend,
  It's sausage, friend, and mash.

  . . . When Love is dead
  Ambition fled,
  And Pleasure, lad, and Pash,

You'll still enjoy
  A sausage, boy,
  A sausage, boy, and mash.
**A. P. Herbert,** 'Sausage and Mash'

**8** Bread that must be sliced with an axe is bread that is too nourishing.
**Fran Lebowitz,** *Metropolitan Life,* 1978

**9** Food is an important part of a balanced diet.
**Fran Lebowitz,** *Metropolitan Life,* 1978

**10** Watercress? I'd just as soon eat my way across a front lawn.
**Anita Loos and Jane Murfin,** *The Women,* screenplay, 1939

**11** I was standing at a bar the other day and there was a fellow there eating olives on a string. Eating olives on a string! I said, 'What are you eating them like that for?' He said, 'I may not like 'em.'
**Max Miller,** *The Max Miller Blue Book,* 1975

**12** Parsley
  Is gharsley.
**Ogden Nash,** 'Further Reflections on Parsley', *Good Intentions,* 1942

**13** The pig, if I am not mistaken,
  Supplies us sausage, ham, and bacon.
  Let others say his heart is big –
  I call it stupid of the pig.
**Ogden Nash,** 'The Pig', *Happy Days,* 1933

**14** *Artichokes.* These things are just plain annoying . . . after all the trouble you go to, you get about as much actual 'food' out of eating an artichoke as you would from licking thirty or forty postage stamps. Have the shrimp cocktail instead.
**Miss Piggy,** *Miss Piggy's Guide to Life (As Told to Henry Beard),* 1981

**15** *Clams.* I simply cannot imagine why anyone would eat something slimy served in an ashtray.
**Miss Piggy,** *Miss Piggy's Guide to Life (As Told to Henry Beard),* 1981

**16** *Lobsters.* Although these are delicious, getting them out of their shells involves giving them quite a brutal going-over. The way I look at it, they never did anything to me (although they are quite nasty-looking, and I do not like the way they stare at you from those fish tanks when you come into the restaurant – it is quite rude). On the other hand, if they serve you just the good parts already removed from the shell, that is quite a different matter, since the element of personal participation in the massacre is eliminated.

**Miss Piggy,** *Miss Piggy's Guide to Life (As Told to Henry Beard)*, 1981

**17** *Snails.* I find this a somewhat disturbing dish, but the sauce is divine. What I do is order escargots, and tell them to 'hold' the snails.

**Miss Piggy,** *Miss Piggy's Guide to Life (As Told to Henry Beard)*, 1981

**18** The two biggest sellers in any bookstore are the cookbooks and the diet books. The cookbooks tell you how to prepare the food, and the diet books tell you how not to eat any of it.

**Andy Rooney**

**19** Madam, I have been looking for a person who disliked gravy all my life; let us swear eternal friendship.

**Sydney Smith,** *Lady Holland's Memoir*, 1855

**20** Bananas are a waste of time. After you skin them and throw the bone away, there's nothing left to eat.

**Charley Weaver**

**21** It is very poor consolation to be told that a man who has given one a bad dinner, or poor wine, is irreproachable in private life. Even the cardinal virtues cannot atone for half-cold entrées.

**Oscar Wilde,** *The Picture of Dorian Gray*, 1891

**22** For a long time I thought coq au vin meant love in a lorry.

**Victoria Wood,** English comedienne

**23** I bought some powdered water, but I didn't know what to add.

**Steven Wright,** American comic

# Football – American

*See also America and the Americans; Sport; Victory and Defeat.*

**1** Secant, cosine, tangent, sine
Logarithm, logarithm,
Hyperbolic sine
3 point 1 4 1 5 9
Slipstick, sliderule

TECH TECH TECH!

**Anon.,** cheer of the California Institute of Technology 'Beavers'

**2** If the FBI went back far enough, I was always suspect: I never liked football.

**Father Daniel Berrigan,** on his release from jail, 1972

**3** Football is, after all, a wonderful way to get rid of aggressions without going to jail for it.

**Heywood Hale Broun,** *Tumultuous Merriment*, 1979

**4** Football is not a contact sport. It's a collision sport. Dancing is a good example of a contact sport.

**Duffy Daugherty,** Michigan State University coach, 1967

**5** Pro football is like nuclear warfare. There are no winners, only survivors.

**Frank Gifford,** quoted in *Sports Illustrated*, 1960

**6** To see some of our best-educated boys spending the afternoon knocking each other down, while thousands cheer them on, hardly gives a picture of a peace-loving nation.

**Lyndon B. Johnson,** quoted in *The New York Times*, 1967

**7** Football is a game of clichés and I believe in every one of them.

**Vince Lombardi,** 1913–70, American football coach

**8** It is committee meetings, called huddles, separated by outbursts of violence.

**George Will,** *Newsweek*, 1976

# Footwear

*See also Clothes; Legs.*

**1** And what about Gladiator boots. Remember them? They were the polished leather boots that hit just above the knee. You could look stylish in them or sit down. You couldn't do both.

**Erma Bombeck,** *If Life is a Bowl of Cherries – What am I Doing in the Pits?*, 1978

**2** There was a young lady of Twickenham
Whose shoes were too tight to walk quick in 'em.
She came back from a walk
Looking whiter than chalk

And took 'em both off and was sick in
'em.

**Oliver Herford**, 1864–1935, English-born American
writer

**3** Come, galoshers, be assertive,
Drop that air discreet and furtive!
Let galosh shops' stocks be lavish
With designs and hues that ravish –
Men's galoshes black and British, but for
    ladies colours skittish
(And galoshes could make rings
Round those silly plastic things
Which tie up with clumsy strings)
Let us all have this *rapprochement* with
    galoshes
And see what health and happiness it
    brings!

**Paul Jennings**, 'Galoshes', *Model Oddlies*, 1956

**4** I am having a *rapprochement* with galoshes
And some would say this heralds middle
    age;
Yes, sneering they would say
'Does he always wear *pince-nez*?
Old jossers wore galoshes when ladies'
    hats were cloches,
Ha! Woolen combinations are this
    dodderer's next stage!'

**Paul Jennings**, 'Galoshes', *Model Oddlies*, 1956

## Foreigners

*See also Immigration; Travel; Xenophobia.*

**1** I don't hold with abroad and think that
foreigners speak English when our backs are
turned.

**Quentin Crisp**, *The Naked Civil Servant*, 1968

**2** Abroad is unutterably bloody and
foreigners are fiends.

**Nancy Mitford**, *The Pursuit of Love*, 1945

**3** Foreigners have a very roundabout and
confused way of saying things. Here's how I
cope. I am in a restaurant, and I want a
piece of the delicious chocolate cake I see
displayed on a shelf, 'Personality who
bringulates les munchables,' I call,
summoning the waiter. When he arrives, I
give my order. 'If it does you please,
transportez (trans-por-TAY) to moi's tablette
one gigantical smithereeni de that
chocolate cakefication avec as immense a

velocité (vee-luss-ee-TAY) as possible.' And
there you are!

**Miss Piggy**, *Miss Piggy's Guide to Life (As Told to Henry
Beard)*, 1981

**4** They spell it Vinci and pronounce it
Vinchy; foreigners always spell better than
they pronounce.

**Mark Twain**, *The Innocents Abroad*, 1869

## Forgiveness

**1** To err is human; to forgive, unusual.
**Anon.**

**2** To err is human,
To forgive takes restraint;
To forget you forgave
Is the mark of a saint.

**Suzanne Douglass**, *Reader's Digest*, 1966

**3** Always forgive your enemies – nothing
annoys them so much.

**Oscar Wilde** (Attrib.)

## France and the French

*See also Europe and the EEC.*

**1** *Pas de deux*: father of twins.
*Coup de grace*: lawnmower.
**Anon.**

**2** The French elections: the defeated
Gaullists are accused of staying in Toulon
and deserving Toulouse.
**Anon.**

**3** . . . xenophobia is a consequence, for the
most part, of reading newspapers, although
tourism is responsible to a great extent.
Probably the worst xenophobes on earth are
the French, a nation protected by a cloud of
garlic breath which still built the Maginot
line to keep foreigners out. Chauvinism is a
French word which cannot even be
translated, so Froggie is the emotion it
describes.

*The National Lampoon Encyclopedia of Humor*, 1973

**4** We traveled in a big truck through the
nation of France on our way to Belgium,
and every time we passed through a little
town, we'd see these signs – 'Boulangerie',
'Patisserie', and 'Rue' this, and 'Rue' that,
and rue the day you came here, young man.
When we got to our hundred and eightieth

French village, I screamed at the top of my lungs, 'The joke is over! English, PLEASE!' I couldn't believe that a whole country couldn't speak English. One third of a nation, all right, but not a whole country.
**Mel Brooks,** quoted by Kenneth Tynan in *Show People*, 1980

**5** The simple thing is to consider the French as an erratic and brilliant people . . . who have all the gifts except that of running their country.
**James Cameron,** *News Chronicle*, 1954

**6** Oh, how I love Humanity,
    With love so pure and pringlish,
    And how I hate the horrid French,
    Who never will be English!
**G. K. Chesterton,** 'The World State', *Collected Poems*, 1933

**7** France is the largest country in Europe, a great boon for drunks, who need room to fall . . .
**Alan Coren,** *The Sanity Inspector*, 1974

**8** But there's always something fishy about the French!
    Whether Prince or Politician
    We've a sinister suspicion
    That behind their *savoir-faire*
    They share
    A common contempt
    For every mother's son of us.
**Noel Coward,** 'There's Always Something Fishy about the French', song from *Conversation Piece*, 1934

**9** The French will only be united under the threat of danger. Nobody can simply bring together a country that has 265 kinds of cheese.
**Charles de Gaulle,** speech, 1951

**10** It is unthinkable for a Frenchman to arrive at middle age without having syphilis and the Croix de la Légion d'Honneur.
**André Gide** (Attrib.)

**11** The French drink to get loosened up for an event, to celebrate an event, and even to recover from an event.
**Geneviève Guérin,** French Commission on Alcoholism, 1980

**12** Bonjour.
    Parlez-vous Franglais?
    C'est un doddle.
    Si vous etes un fluent English-speaker, et si vous avez un 'O' Level français, Franglais est un morceau de gâteau.
    Un 'O' Level de French est normalement inutile. Un nothing. Un wash-out. Les habitants de la France ne parlent pas 'O' Level French. Ils ne comprennent pas 'O' Level French. Un 'O' Level en français est un passeport à nowhere.
**Miles Kington,** *Let's Parler Franglais*, 1979

**13** *Les crudités*: genitals.
**Andy Kirby,** competition, *New Statesman*, 1985

**14** Paris is a great beauty. As such it possesses all the qualities that one finds in any other great beauty: chic, sexiness, grandeur, arrogance, and the absolute inability and refusal to listen to reason. So if you are going there you would do well to remember this: no matter how politely and distinctly you ask a Parisian a question, he will persist in answering you in French.
**Fran Lebowitz,** *Metropolitan Life*, 1978

**15** *Fin de siècle*: tail light of a bicycle.
**Russell Lucas,** competition, *New Statesman*, 1985

**16** When Frenchmen are talking, never lift the needle off the gramophone; it only goes back to the beginning.
**Oliver Lyttleton,** 1893–1972, British statesman and industrialist

**17** *Esprit de corps*: embalming fluid.
**R. S. MacLeod,** competition, *New Statesman*, 1985

**18** Boy, those French, they have a different word for everything.
**Steve Martin**

**19** There's something Vichy about the French.
**Ivor Novello** (Attrib.), 1941

**20** *Racial characteristics*: sawed-off cissies who eat snails and slugs and cheese that smells like people's feet . . . Utter cowards who force their own children to drink wine, they gibber like baboons even when you try to speak to them in their own wimpy language.
**P. J. O'Rourke,** 'Foreigners Around the World', *National Lampoon*, 1976

**21** France is a place where the money falls apart in your hands but you can't tear the toilet paper.
**Billy Wilder**

**22** I have not always in my dealings with General de Gaulle found quotations from Trafalgar and Waterloo necessarily productive, and he has been very tactful about the Battle of Hastings.
**Harold Wilson**, 1967

**Charles de Gaulle (President, 1958–1969)**

**1** . . . is one of the biggest sons of bitches who ever straddled a pot.
**Charles E. Bohlen**, US Ambassador to the USSR, *Witness to History, 1929–1969*, 1973

**2** Of all the crosses I have to bear, the heaviest is the Cross of Lorraine.
**Winston Churchill** (Attrib.), 1943

**3** When I want to know what France thinks, I ask myself.
**Charles de Gaulle**, quoted in *Sons of France*, 1966

**4** . . . an artlessly sincere megalomaniac.
**H. G. Wells**, 1866–1946, English novelist (Attrib.), 1943

# Friends

*See also Enemies; Love; Popularity; Relationships.*

**1** Your friend is the man who knows all about you, and still likes you.
**Elbert Hubbard**, *The Notebook*, 1927

**2** A friend is one who has the same enemies you have.
**Abraham Lincoln**

**3** A man of active and resilient mind outwears his friendships just as certainly as he outwears his love affairs, his politics and his epistemology.
**H. L. Mencken**, *Prejudices*, Third Series, 1922

**4** A friend in need is a friend to be avoided.
**Lord Samuel**, 1870–1963, British Liberal politician

**5** Whenever a friend succeeds, a little something in me dies.
**Gore Vidal**, quoted in the *Sunday Times Magazine*, 1973

**6** I have lost friends, some by death . . . others by sheer inability to cross the street.
**Virginia Woolf**, *The Waves*, 1931

# Fruit

*See also Eating; Food; Vegetables.*

**1** A: There's a lot of juice in this grapefruit.
B: Yes – more than meets the eye!
**Anon.**

**2** Gripe: a ripe grape.
**Anon.**, 'Dizzy Daffinitions', *The Big Book of Jokes and Riddles*, 1978

# Funerals

*See also Cremation; Deaths; Epitaphs.*

**1** If you don't go to people's funerals, they won't come to yours.
**Anon.**

**2** In the city a funeral is just an interruption of traffic; in the country it is a form of popular entertainment.
**George Ade**, 1866–1944, American playwright

**3** My grandfather had a wonderful funeral. My grandfather was a very insignificant man, actually. At his funeral his hearse *followed* the other cars. It was a nice funeral, though, you would have liked it – it was a catered funeral. It was held in a big hall with accordion players. On the buffet table there was a replica of the deceased in potato salad.
**Woody Allen**, *The Nightclub Years, 1964–1968*, album, 1972

**4** A funeral eulogy is a belated plea for the defense delivered after the evidence is all in.
**Irvin S. Cobb**, 1876–1944, American journalist

**5** They say such nice things about people at their funerals that it makes me sad to realise I'm going to miss mine by just a few days.
**Garrison Keillor**, 'Lecture in San Francisco', *Lake Wobegon Days*, 1984

**6** SON: Do you want to be buried, mum? Or shall we have you cremated?
MOTHER: Oh, I don't know love. Surprise me!
**Deric Longden**, *Lost for Words*, screenplay, Yorkshire Television, 1999

**7** There is nothing like a morning funeral for sharpening the appetite for lunch.
**Arthur Marshall**, *Life's Rich Pageant*, 1984

**8** A damn good funeral is still one of our best and cheapest acts of theatre.
**Gwyn Thomas**, *SAP*, 1974

**9** In India when a man dies, his widow throws herself on the funeral pyre. Over here, she says, 'Fifty ham baps, Beryl – you slice, I'll butter.'
**Victoria Wood**, English comedienne

# Future, The

*See also Astrology; Fate; The Past.*

**1** An optimist is someone who thinks the future is uncertain.
**Anon.**

**2** The future ain't what it used to be.
**Yogi Berra**, New York Yankees Catcher, 1946–63 (Attrib.)

**3** Future, *n.* that period of time in which our affairs prosper, our friends are true and our happiness is assured.
**Ambrose Bierce**, *The Devil's Dictionary*, 1911

**4 In the Year 2000 . . .**
Robots will do 80% of our housework. But we will do 90% of theirs.
Women will admit the whole 'different from men' thing was a big hoax to get free meals and drinks.
The Miss America Pageant will once again be criticised when the public votes to keep the 'faking an orgasm' competition.
Time travel will be so commonplace that Domino's will change its guarantee to 'thirty minutes ago or it's free.'
The world food shortage will be so severe that midgets will be known as 'appetisers'.
The product '2000 Flushes' will be renamed 'A Flush a Year Since Christ Was Born.'
The entertainment world will be shocked to learn that more than half the characters in the beloved Peanuts comic strip are flamboyant homosexuals.
Mike Tyson's record will drop to 40 wins and 500 losses, after opponents realise he's extremely vulnerable to the 'your shoelaces are untied' trick.
**Conan O'Brien**, *Late Night with Conan O'Brien*, NBC TV

# Gambling

*See also Debt; Horses and Horse Racing; Money; Victory and Defeat.*

**1** This guy runs in the front door and yells at his wife, 'Pack your bags, honey! I've just won the lottery!'

She says, 'Fantastic! Shall I pack for the beach or the mountains?'

And he says, 'I don't care! Just get the hell out!'
**Anon.**

**2** . . . one of my most precious treasures . . . is an exquisite pair of loaded dice, bearing the date of my graduation from high school.
**W. C. Fields**, *Let's Look at the Record*, 1939

**3** If there was no action around, he would play solitaire – and bet against himself.
**Groucho Marx**, of his brother Chico (Attrib.)

**4** The way his horses ran could be summed up in a word.

Last.

He once had a horse who finished ahead of the winner of the 1942 Kentucky Derby.

Unfortunately, the horse started running in the 1941 Kentucky Derby.
**Groucho Marx**, *Esquire*, 1972

**5** The sure way of getting nothing for something.
**Wilson Mizner**, 1876–1933, American playwright

**6** There are two times in a man's life when he should not speculate: when he can't afford it, and when he can.
**Mark Twain**

# Games

**1** Life's too short for chess.
**Henry James Byron**, 1834–84, British dramatist, *Our Boys*

**2** . . . as elaborate a waste of human intelligence as you can find outside an advertising agency.
**Raymond Chandler**, on chess

**3** A Smith and Wesson beats four aces.
**Michael Enright**

**4** It is impossible to win gracefully at chess.

No man has yet said 'Mate!' in a voice which failed to sound to his opponent bitter, boastful and malicious.
**A. A. Milne,** *Not That It Matters,* 1919

**5** It was a little all-too-devouring, just gobble, gobble. No social content.
**Ralph Nader,** on 'Pac-Man'

**6** A computer once beat me at chess. But it was no match for me at kick boxing.
**Emo Philips**

# Gardening

*See also Fruit; Home; Vegetables.*

**1** I've had enough of gardening – I'm just about ready to throw in the trowel.
**Anon.**

**2** Airborne filth settling on aphis honeydew would asphyxiate all those plants which survive the sucking, biting, chewing, riddling activities of the insects, if it were not for the fact that they are generally pecked to death by sparrows, dug up, trodden on, sat on or stolen, or simply annihilated by a blast of animal urine or overwhelmed by a cloaking turd, long before that.
**Rose Blight (Germaine Greer),** *The Revolting Garden,* 1979

**3** Laws of Gardening:
1. Other people's tools work only in other people's gardens.
2. Fancy gizmos don't work.
3. If nobody uses it, there's a reason.
4. You get the most of what you need the least.
**Arthur Bloch,** *Murphy's Law and Other Reasons Why Things Go Wrong,* 1977

**4** What is a weed? A plant whose virtues have not been discovered.
**Ralph Waldo Emerson,** *Fortune of the Republic,* 1878

**5** If you want to be happy for a short time, get drunk; happy for a long time, fall in love; happy for ever, take up gardening.
**Arthur Smith,** comedian and playwright, quoted in the *Sunday Times,* 2000

**6** What a man needs in gardening is a cast-iron back, with a hinge in it.
**Charles Dudley Warner,** *My Summer in a Garden,* 1871

**7** I don't believe the half I hear,
  Nor the quarter of what I see!
But I have one faith, sublime and true,
  That nothing can shake or slay;
Each spring I firmly believe anew
  All the seed catalogues say!
**Carolyn Wells,** *One Firm Faith*

# Gaucheness

*See also Adolescence; Culture.*

**1** . . . I glanced at the totally incomprehensible menu and replied, in the well-rounded, thoughtful tones of the *Michelin Guide* man doing the final check on a restaurant to which he is considering awarding three stars: 'I think I'll have the lyonnaise.' 'The lyonnaise is the potatoes, sir,' replied the waiter, contemptuously scratching his leg. 'That's what I want,' I lied, with a miserable attempt at haughtiness. 'With chips.'
**Michael Frayn,** *The Day of the Dog,* 1962

# Genius

*See also Intellectuals; Talent.*

**1** Geniuses are like ocean liners: they should never meet.
**Louis Aragon,** French poet and novelist, 1897–1982

**2** Genius is one per cent inspiration and ninety-nine per cent perspiration.
**Thomas Alva Edison,** newspaper interview, 1931

**3** The public is wonderfully tolerant. It forgives everything except genius.
**Oscar Wilde,** 'The Critic as Artist', 1890

# Gentlemen

*See also Etiquette; Men; Men – The Female View; Society.*

**1** A gentleman is one who never swears at his wife while ladies are present.
**Anon.**

**2** A gentleman is one who, when he invites a girl up to show her his etchings, shows her his etchings.
**Anon.**

**3** A true gentleman is a man who knows how to play the bagpipes – but doesn't.
**Anon.**

**4** I do hope I shall enjoy myself with you . . . I am parshial to ladies if they are nice I suppose it is my nature. I am not quite a gentleman but you would hardly notice it.
**Daisy Ashford**, *The Young Visiters*, 1919

**5** A gentleman is one who never strikes a woman without provocation.
**H. L. Mencken**

**6** . . . one of Nature's gentlemen, the worst type of gentleman I know.
**Oscar Wilde**, *Lady Windermere's Fan*, 1892

# Germany and the Germans

*See also Europe and the EEC.*

**1** . . . German – a language . . . which was developed solely to afford the speaker the opportunity to spit at strangers under the guise of polite conversation.
*The National Lampoon Encyclopedia of Humor*, 1973

**2** GERMAN: Will you please stop talking about the war?
BASIL FAWLTY: Me? You started it!
GERMAN: We did not start it.
BASIL FAWLTY: Yes you did, you invaded Poland . . .
**John Cleese and Connie Booth**, *Fawlty Towers*, BBC TV, 1975

**3** They are a fine people but quick to catch the disease of anti-humanity. I think it's because of their poor elimination. Germany is a headquarters for constipation.
**George Grosz**, 1893–1959, German artist

**4** From **Top ten names for the reunited Germany**
Just plain Volks
Aryan Acres
Argentina East
Nazichusetts
Switzerland's Bad-Ass Neighbour
**David Letterman**, *The Late Show*, CBS

**5** The Germans are like women, you can scarcely ever fathom their depths – they haven't any.
**Friedrich Wilhelm Nietzsche**, *The Antichrist*, 1888

**6** Waiting for the German verb is surely the ultimate thrill.
**Flann O'Brien**, 1911–66, Irish novelist and journalist

**7** *Racial characteristics*: piggish-looking sadomasochistic automatons whose only known forms of relaxation are swilling watery beer from vast tubs and singing the idiotically repetitive verses of their porcine folk tunes . . . Their language lacks any semblance of civilized speech. Their usual diet consists almost wholly of old cabbage and sections of animal intestines filled with blood and gore.
**P. J. O'Rourke**, 'Foreigners Around the World', *National Lampoon*, 1976

**8** German is the most extravagantly ugly language. It sounds like someone using a sick-bag on a 747.
**William Rushton**, *Holiday Inn, Ghent*, 1984

**9** A verb has a hard time enough of it in this world when it's all together. It's downright inhuman to split it up. But that's just what those Germans do. They take part of a verb and put it down here, like a stake, and they take the other part of it and put it away over yonder like another stake, and between those two limits they just shovel in German.
**Mark Twain**, speech, New York, 1900

**10** Whenever the literary German dives into a sentence, that is the last you are going to see of him till he emerges on the other side of his Atlantic with his verb in his mouth.
**Mark Twain**, *A Connecticut Yankee in King Arthur's Court*, 1889

**11** The German people are an orderly, vain, deeply sentimental and rather insensitive people. They seem to feel at their best when they are singing in chorus, saluting or obeying orders.
**H. G. Wells**, *Travels of a Republican Radical in Search of Hot Water*, 1939

# Gifts

*See also Birthdays; Christmas; Gratitude; Philanthropy.*

**1** The worst gift is a fruitcake. There is only one fruitcake in the entire world, and people keep sending it to each other.
**Johnny Carson**, *The Tonight Show*, NBC TV

**2** You know men's problem? They're hunters. We're gatherers. We browse, they

run in and buy the first thing they see. What they really want to do is walk in with a big bloody buck on their shoulders, plop it at our feet and say, 'Merry Christmas.'
**Cynthia Heimel**, *If You Leave Me, Can I Come Too?*, 1995

**3** You never want to give a man a present when he's feeling good. You want to do it when he's down.
**Lyndon B. Johnson** (Attrib.)

**4** Why is it no one ever sent me yet
One perfect limousine, do you suppose?
Ah no, it's always just my luck to get
One perfect rose.
**Dorothy Parker**, 'One Perfect Rose', *The Portable Dorothy Parker*, 1944

**5** One should never give a woman anything she can't wear in the evening.
**Oscar Wilde**, *An Ideal Husband*, 1895

# God

*See also Belief; The Bible; Christianity; The Church; Faith; Jesus Christ; Religion.*

**1** God is alive – he just doesn't want to get involved.
**Graffito**, 1975

**2** God is dead. But don't worry – the Virgin Mary is pregnant again.
**Graffito**, Los Angeles, 1981

**3** God is not dead. He is alive and autographing Bibles today at Brentano's.
**Graffito**, New York, 1979

**4** God's plan made a hopeful beginning,
But man spoiled his chances by sinning.
We trust that the story
Will end in God's glory,
But, at present, the other side's winning.
**Anon.**, *The New York Times Magazine*, 1946

**5** Between projects I go into the park and bite the grass and wail, 'Why do You make me aware of the fact that I have to die one day?' God says, 'Please, I have Chinese people yelling at me, I haven't time for this.' I say all right. God is like a Jewish waiter, he has too many tables.
**Mel Brooks**, quoted in the *Guardian*, 1984

**6** It is the final proof of God's omnipotence that he need not exist in order to save us.
**Peter De Vries**, *The Mackerel Plaza*, 1958

**7** Good God, how much reverence can you have for a Supreme Being who finds it necessary to include such phenomena as phlegm and tooth decay in His divine system of Creation?
**Joseph Heller**, *Catch-22*, 1961

**8** God is the immemorial refuge of the incompetent, the helpless, the miserable. They find not only sanctuary in His arms, but also a kind of superiority, soothing to their macerated egos; He will set them above their betters.
**H. L. Mencken**, *Minority Report*, 1956

**9** It takes a long while for a naturally trustful person to reconcile himself to the idea that after all God will not help him.
**H. L. Mencken**, *Minority Report*, 1956

**10** Is man one of God's blunders or is God one of man's blunders?
**Friedrich Wilhelm Nietzsche**

**11** There was an Old Man with a Beard,
Who said: 'I demand to be feared.
Address Me as God,
And love Me, you sod!'
And Man did just that, which was weird.
**Roger Woddis**, English poet

# Gold Diggers

*See also Greed.*

**1** A 70-year-old millionaire had just married a beautiful blonde 20 year old.
'You crafty old codger,' said an envious friend. 'How on earth did you get such a lovely young woman to marry you?'
'Easy,' said the millionaire, 'I told her I was 95.'
**Anon.**

**2** What first, Debbie, attracted you to the millionaire Paul Daniels?
**Caroline Aherne**, *The Mrs Merton Show*, BBC 2

# Golf

*See also Sport.*

**1** If you want to take long walks, take long walks. If you want to hit things with a stick,

hit things with a stick. But there's no excuse for combining the two and putting the results on TV. Golf is not so much a sport as an insult to lawns.
*National Lampoon*, 1979

**2** Oh the dirty little pill
Went rolling down the hill
And rolled right into the bunker
From there to the green
I took thirteen
And then by God I sunk her!
**Traditional**

**3** Give me my golf clubs, fresh air and a beautiful partner, and you can keep my golf clubs and the fresh air.
**Jack Benny**

**4** Golf is a game in which a ball (one and a half inches in diameter) is placed on a ball (eight thousand miles in diameter). The object being to hit the small ball but not the larger.
**John Cunningham**

**5** I know I'm getting better at golf because I'm hitting fewer spectators.
**Gerald Ford**, Republican President, 1974–7

**6** The Coarse Golfer: one who has to shout 'Fore' when he putts.
**Michael Green**, *The Art of Coarse Golf*, 1967

**7** You know why they call it golf, don't you? Because all the good four-letter words were already taken.
**Lewis Grizzard**

**8** Golf may be played on Sunday, not being a game within view of the law, but being a form of moral effort.
**Stephen Leacock**, 'Why I Refuse to Play Golf', *Over the Footlights*, 1923

**9** ERIC: My wife says if I don't give up golf, she'll leave me.
ERNIE: That's terrible.
ERIC: I know – I'm really going to miss her.
**Eric Morecambe and Ernie Wise**, *The Morecambe and Wise Joke Book*, 1979

**10** ERIC: You know what your main trouble is?
ERNIE: What?
ERIC: You stand too close to the ball after you've hit it.
ERNIE: I still think I'm improving.

ERIC: Oh, you are. Why, only yesterday you hit the ball in one.
ERNIE: Absolutely! And anyway, this is a terrible golf course. Just look at the state of it!
ERIC: This isn't the course, you know. We left that half an hour ago.
ERNIE: Really? Is that why you keep looking at your watch?
ERIC: This isn't a watch – this is a compass!
**Eric Morecambe and Ernie Wise**, *The Morecambe and Wise Joke Book*, 1979

**11** A: Why aren't you playing golf with the colonel any more?
B: What! Would *you* play with a man who swears and curses with every shot, who cheats in the bunkers and who enters false scores on his cards?
A: Certainly not!
B: Well neither will the colonel.
**Freddie Oliver**, English writer

**12** It's still embarrassing. I asked my caddie for a sand wedge and ten minutes later he came back with a ham on rye.
**Chi Chi Rodrigues**, Puerto Rican golfer

**13** You don't know what pressure is in golf until you play for five bucks with only two in your pocket.
**Lee Trevino**

**14** Golf is a good walk spoiled.
**Mark Twain** (Attrib.)

**15** The uglier a man's legs are, the better he plays golf. It's almost a law.
**H. G. Wells**, *Bealby*, 1915

**16** 'After all, golf is only a game,' said Millicent.
Women say these things without thinking. It does not mean that there is any kink in their character. They simply don't realize what they are saying.
**P. G. Wodehouse**, *The Clicking of Cuthbert*, 1922

**17** 'Mortimer, you must choose between golf and me.'
'But, darling, I went round in a hundred and one yesterday. You can't expect a fellow to give up golf when he is at the top of his game.'
**P. G. Wodehouse**, *The Clicking of Cuthbert*, 1922

**18** The least thing upsets him on the links.

He misses short putts because of the uproar of the butterflies in the adjoining meadows.
**P. G. Wodehouse**, *The Clicking of Cuthbert*, 1922

# Goodness

*See also Evil; Tolerance.*

**1** Nice guys finish last.
**Leo Durocher**, baseball coach

**2** What, after all,
Is a halo? It's only one more thing to keep
clean.
**Christopher Fry**, *The Lady's not for Burning*, 1949

**3** How sick one gets of being 'good', how much I should respect myself if I could burst out and make everyone wretched for twenty-four hours . . .
**Alice James**, letter to her brother, 1889

**4** The greatest pleasure I know is to do a good action by stealth, and to have it found out by accident.
**Charles Lamb**, 'Table Talk by the Late Elia', *Athenaeum*, 1834

**5** Few things are harder to put up with than the annoyance of a good example.
**Mark Twain**, *Pudd'nhead Wilson*, 1894

**6** 'Goodness, what beautiful diamonds!'
'*Goodness had nothing to do with it!*'
**Mae West**, *Night after Night*, screenplay, 1932

**7** To be good, according to the vulgar standard of goodness, is obviously quite easy. It merely requires a certain amount of sordid terror, a certain lack of imaginative thought, and a certain low passion for middle-class respectability.
**Oscar Wilde**, 'The Critic as Artist', 1891

**8** If all the good people were clever,
And all clever people were good,
The world would be nicer than ever
We thought that it possibly could.
But somehow, 'tis seldom or never
The two hit it off as they should;
The good are so harsh to the clever,
The clever so rude to the good!
**Elizabeth Wordsworth**, 'Good and Clever'

# Gossip

*See also Conversation; Scandals.*

**1** Absolute knowledge have I none.
But my aunt's washerwoman's sister's son
Heard a policeman on his beat
Say to a labourer on the street
That he had a letter just last week –
A letter that he did not seek –
From a Chinese merchant in Timbuctoo,
Who said that his brother in Cuba knew
Of an Indian chief in a Texan town,
Who got the dope from a circus clown,
That a man in Klondike had it straight
From a guy in a South American state,
That a wild man over in Borneo
Was told by a woman who claimed to
know . . . etc. etc.
**Anon.**

**2** At last the secret is out, as it always must
come in the end,
The delicious story is ripe to tell to the
intimate friend;
Over the tea-cups and in the square the
tongue has its desire;
Still waters run deep, my friend, there's
never smoke without fire.
**W. H. Auden**, song from *The Ascent of F6*, 1936

**3** GIRL: Of course I wouldn't say anything about her unless I could say something good. And, oh boy, is this good . . .
**Bill King**, *Collier's*, cartoon

**4** If You Can't Say Something Good About Someone, Sit Right Here By Me.
**Alice Roosevelt Longworth**, allegedly embroidered on a cushion in her sitting-room

**5** Never gossip about people you don't know. This deprives simple artisans like Truman Capote of work. The best subject of gossip is someone you and your audience love dearly. The enjoyment of gossip is thus doubled: to the delight of disapprobation is added the additional delight of pity.
**P. J. O'Rourke**, *Modern Manners*, 1983

**6** She always tells stories in the present vindictive.
**Tom Peace**, *Reader's Digest*, 1957

**7** The things most people want to know about are usually none of their business.
**George Bernard Shaw**

**8** I don't at all like knowing what people say of me behind my back. It makes one far too conceited.

Oscar Wilde, *An Ideal Husband*, 1895

**9** It is perfectly monstrous the way people go about nowadays saying things against one behind one's back that are absolutely and entirely true.

Oscar Wilde, *A Woman of No Importance*, 1893

**10** There is only one thing in the world worse than being talked about, and that is not being talked about.

Oscar Wilde, *The Picture of Dorian Gray*, 1891

**11** Gossip is when you hear something you like about someone you don't.

Earl Wilson, 1907–87, American columnist

# Government

*See also Bureaucracy; The Civil Service; Congress; Parliament; Politics and Politicians; The Senate; Washington.*

**1** This island is almost made of coal and surrounded by fish. Only an organizing genius could produce a shortage of coal and fish in Great Britain at the same time.

Aneurin Bevan, speech, 1945

**2** The only good government . . . is a bad one in a hell of a fright.

Joyce Cary, *The Horse's Mouth*, 1944

**3** As far as I am concerned, dirty tricks are part and parcel of effective government.

Alan Clark, former Conservative Defence Minister, quoted in the *Sunday Times*, 1993

**4** The government solution to a problem is usually as bad as the problem.

Milton Friedman, American economist (Attrib.)

**5** CIVIL SERVANT: What I mean is that I'm fully seized of your aims and, of course, I will do my utmost to see that they're put into practice. To that end, I recommend that we set up an interdepartmental committee with fairly broad terms of reference so that at the end of the day we'll be in a position to think through the various implications and arrive at a decision based on long-term considerations rather than rush prematurely into precipitate and possibly ill-conceived action which might well have unforeseen repercussions.

MINISTER: You mean, no?

Antony Jay and Jonathan Lynn, *Yes, Minister*, BBC TV, 1981

**6** I think it will be a clash between the political will and the administrative won't.

Antony Jay and Jonathan Lynn, *Yes, Prime Minister*, BBC TV

**7** 'Opposition's about asking awkward questions.'

'Yes . . . and government's about not answering them.'

Antony Jay and Jonathan Lynn, *Yes, Minister*, BBC TV

**8** It is inaccurate to say I hate everything. I am strongly in favor of common sense, common honesty and common decency. This makes me forever ineligible for any public office.

H. L. Mencken

**9** We're getting a lot of government these days, but we'd probably be worse off if we were getting as much as we're paying for.

Olin Miller, American writer

**10** The single most exciting thing you encounter in government is competence, because it's so rare.

Daniel Patrick Moynihan, Democratic senator

**11** Put a federal agency in charge of the Sahara Desert and it would run out of sand.

Peggy Noonan, Presidential speechwriter

**12** Giving money and power to the government is like giving whisky and car keys to teenage boys.

P. J. O'Rourke, *Parliament of Whores*, 1991

**13** You know, if government were a product, selling it would be illegal.

P. J. O'Rourke, speech to the Cato Institute, 1993

**14** The nine most terrifying words in the English language are, 'I'm from the government and I'm here to help.'

Ronald Reagan, Republican President, 1981–9

**15** How come there's only one Monopolies Commission?

Nigel Rees, *Graffiti 4*, 1982

**16** I don't make jokes. I just watch the government and report the facts.
**Will Rogers**

**17** There's no trick to being a humorist when you have the whole government working for you.
**Will Rogers**

**18** MRS PARADOCK: There's somebody at the door wanting you to form a government.
MR PARADOCK: What does he look like?
MRS PARADOCK: He says he's working through the street directory.
**N. F. Simpson**, *A Resounding Tinkle*, 1958

**19** You can fool too many of the people too much of the time.
**James Thurber**, *The Thurber Carnival*, 1945

**20** Whenever you have an efficient government you have a dictatorship.
**Harry S. Truman**, lecture at Columbia University, 1959

**21** I see no need for a Royal Commission [on trades unions] which will take minutes and waste years.
**Harold Wilson**, 1964

# Graffiti

**1** I hate graffiti.
*I hate ALL Italian food!*
**Graffito**, London, 1981

**2** Alas, poor yorlik, I knew him backwards.
**Graffito**, Exeter, 1984

**3** If you feel strongly about graffiti, sign a partition.
**Graffito**, Manchester, 1978

# Grammar

*See also The English Language; Pronunciation; Writers; Writing.*

**1** The grammar has a rule absurd
Which I would call an outworn myth:
'A proposition is a word
You mustn't end a sentence with!'
**Berton Braley**, No Rule to be Afraid of

**2** I don't split 'em. When I go to work on an infinitive, I break it up in little pieces.
**Jimmy Durante** (Attrib.)

**3** I adore adverbs; they are the only qualifications I really much respect.
**Henry James**

**4** As far as I'm concerned, 'whom' is a word that was invented to make everyone sound like a butler.
**Calvin Trillin**, 'Whom Says So?', *Nation*, 1985

# Gratitude

*See also Gifts.*

**1** Gratitude, like love, is never a dependable international emotion.
**Joseph Alsop**, American political columnist, 1952

**2** Next to ingratitude, the most painful thing to bear is gratitude.
**Henry Ward Beecher**, *Proverbs from Plymouth Pulpit*, 1870

**3** Blessed is he who expects no gratitude, for he shall not be disappointed.
**W. C. Bennett**, American clergyman

# Greece and the Greeks

*See also Europe and the EEC.*

**1** *Racial characteristics*: degenerate, dirty, and impoverished descendants of a bunch of la-de-da fruit salads who invented democracy and then forgot how to use it while walking around dressed up like girls.
**P. J. O'Rourke**, 'Foreigners Around the World', *National Lampoon*, 1976

# Greed

*See also Eating; Food; Gold Diggers; Rich and Poor; Wealth.*

**1** My wife is very particular about her food. There has to be lots of it.
**Anon.**

**2** He's so greedy, when he goes to a buffet, they have to install speed bumps.
**Anon.**

**3** To be clever enough to get all that money, one must be stupid enough to want it.
**G. K. Chesterton**, *The Wisdom of Father Brown*, 1914

**4** Wealth is like sea-water; the more we

drink, the thirstier we become; and the same is true of fame.

**Arthur Schopenhauer**, German philosopher, 1788–1860

# Greetings

**1** Don't Tell Me What Kind of Day To Have!
**Bumper sticker**, Los Angeles, 1995

**2** That's the trouble with 'Have a nice day!' It puts all the pressure on you.
**George Carlin**

**3** FLANDERS: Hi diddly ho, neighbour!
HOMER: Get lost Flanders!
FLANDERS: Okl-ee dokl-ee!

**David Richardson**, 'Homer Loves Flanders', *The Simpsons*, Fox TV, 1994

## Greetings Cards

*See also Birthdays; Christmas.*

**1** VALENTINE, I'M NOT SURE HOW I FEEL ABOUT YOU.
**Christine Barber**

CONGRATULATIONS AND HAPPY BIRTHDAY ON YOUR ANNIVERSARY THIS VALENTINE'S DAY, BAR MITZVAH BOY, HOPE YOU FEEL BETTER SOON
**Ed Brodsky**

GOOD LUCK ON YOUR SUBWAY RIDE
**Sissy Cargill**

SO YOU'VE JUST FOUND OUT YOU WERE ADOPTED!
**Jeff Monasch**

THANK YOU FOR THE ONE-NIGHT STAND
**Les Powell**

BEST WISHES FOR A HAPPY AND SUCCESSFUL FIRST MARRIAGE
**Marc Rosen**

DEEPEST SYMPATHY AND BELATED BIRTHDAY WISHES
**Stephen Sadowsky**

IN APPRECIATION OF YOUR THANKS FOR MY RESPONSE TO YOUR BEST WISHES AFTER MY EXPRESSION OF GOOD LUCK FOLLOWING YOUR CONGRATULATIONS ON MY ANNOUNCEMENT
**Joel Schechter**

SO YOU BOYCOTTED YOUR FIRST OLYMPIC GAMES!
**Ronald Weinger**

'Unconventional Greeting Card Competition', *New York Magazine*, 1976

**2** From **Top ten rejected Hallmark cards:**
'Nobody Knows Exactly When Your Birthday Is, But I Hope It's a Good One, Boy-Raised-By-Wolves!'
'The Screaming Voices in My Head Have Ordered Me to Send You This Valentine.'
'With Heartfelt Wishes As Big As Your Ass.'
'Sorry You Freaked Out on the Eggnogg, My Lactose-Intolerant Friend.'
**David Letterman**, *The Late Show*, CBS TV

**3** . . . Hallmark will prove that with their 'Get Laid Soon' card in May, and their 'Congratulations, You Finally Did Her' in July.
**Bill Maher**, *Politically Incorrect*, ABC, 1994

**4** Don't send funny greeting cards on birthdays or at Christmas. Save them for funerals, when their cheery effect is needed.
**P. J. O'Rourke**, *Modern Manners*, 1983

# Guilt

*See also Conscience; Crime; Sin.*

**1** To be honest, what I feel really bad about is that I don't feel worse. That is the intellectual's problem in a nutshell.
**Michael Frayn**, *Observer*, 1963

**2** A guilty conscience is the mother of invention.
**Carolyn Wells**

**3** Jill had that direct, honest gaze which many nice girls have, and as a rule Bill liked it. But at the moment he could have done with something that did not pierce quite so like a red-hot gimlet to his inmost soul. A sense of guilt makes a man allergic to direct, honest gazes.
**P. G. Wodehouse**, *Ring for Jeeves*, 1953

# Guns

*See also Crime; Hunting; Murder.*

**1** They're right. Guns don't kill people. Bullets do.
**Anon.**

**2** Why do I need a gun license? It's only for use around the house.
**Charles Addams**, cartoon, *New Yorker*

**3** You can get a lot more done with a kind word and a gun than with a kind word alone.
**Al Capone**, 1889–1947, American gangster (Attrib.)

**4** . . . remember, guns don't kill people – unless you practice real hard.
**Bill Maher**, *Politically Incorrect*, ABC

**5** The NRA is attempting to lift the ban on machine-gun sales. Well, as an avid hunting enthusiast, I've been hoping to buy a fully automatic Uzi. One thing about a machine gun, it really takes the guesswork out of duck hunting.
**Mark Russell**, American political comedian

**6** (Homer grabs for his gun but the cashier holds on to it.)
CASHIER: Sorry, the law requires a five-day waiting period. We've got to run a background check.
HOMER: Five days? But I'm mad now!
(The cashier pulls the gun away from Homer.)
HOMER: I'd kill you if I had my gun.
CASHIER: Yeah, well, you don't.
**John Swartzwelder**, 'The Cartridge Family', *The Simpsons*, Fox TV, 1997

# Gynaecology

*See also Babies; Birth; Birth Control; Doctors; Mothers; Pregnancy.*

**1** PATIENT: Are you the gynaecologist?
GYNAECOLOGIST: At your cervix, madam!
PATIENT: Dilated to meet you!
**Anon.**

**2** In what other business could a guy tell a girl to get undressed – and send the bill to her husband?
**Jackie Mason**

# Hair

*See also Appearance; Baldness; Beauty; Faces; Hats; Looks.*

**1** It looked as if she'd combed her hair with an electric toothbrush.
**Anon.**

**2** If you see someone with a stunning haircut, grab her by the wrist and demand fiercely to know the name, address and home phone number of her hairdresser. If she refuses to tell you, burst into tears.
**Cynthia Heimel**, *Sex Tips for Girls*, 1983

**3** . . . keep away from hairdos altogether. A hairdo, by definition, always makes you look like someone else. Or think you do.
**Cynthia Heimel**, *Sex Tips for Girls*, 1983

**4** Violet will be a good color for hair at just about the same time that brunette becomes a good color for flowers.
**Fran Lebowitz**, *Social Studies*, 1981

**5** Blondes have more fun, don't they? They must. How many brunettes do you see walking down the street with blonde roots?
**Rita Rudner**, *Comic Relief*, HBO, 1991

**6** Why don't you get a haircut? You look like a chrysanthemum.
**P. G. Wodehouse**

# Hallowe'en

**1** You know you're not much on looks when you can go trick-or-treating dressed as is!
**Milton Berle**

**2** Ducking for apples – change one letter and it's the story of my life.
**Dorothy Parker**, at a Hallowe'en party (Attrib.)

# Hangovers

*See also Drink; Nausea.*

**1** The cocktail is a pleasant drink;
It's mild and harmless – I don't think.
When you've had one, you call for two,
And then you don't care what you do.
Last night I hoisted twenty-three
Of these arrangements into me.
My wealth increased, I swelled with pride,

I was pickled, primed, and ossified;
But R - E - M - O - R - S - E!
The water wagon is the place for me.
**George Ade**, 'R - E - M - O - R - S - E', *The Sultan of Sulu*, 1903

**2** For a bad hangover, take the juice of two quarts of whiskey.
**Eddie Condon** (Attrib.)

**3** I'd take a bromo, but I can't stand the noise.
**Joe E. Lewis**, 1902–71, American comedian

# Happiness
*See also Enjoyment; Smiles; Unhappiness.*

**1** Happiness is bumping into Raquel Welch . . . very slowly.
*Laugh-In*, NBC TV, 1969

**2** VERONICA: Are you happy?
HILARY: Why does everybody keep asking me that? No. I'm not happy. But I'm not unhappy about it.
**Alan Bennett**, *The Old Country*, 1978

**3** Happiness makes up in height for what it lacks in length.
**Robert Frost**, 1874–1963, title of poem

**4** Happiness is the sublime moment when you get out of your corsets at night.
**Joyce Grenfell** (Attrib.)

**5** A good bed, good food, the freshest milk and butter, flowers before my window and a few fine trees before my door; and if God wants to make my happiness complete, he will grant me the joy of seeing some six or seven of my enemies hanging from those trees.
**Heinrich Heine**, 1797–1856, German poet

**6** The search for happiness is one of the chief sources of unhappiness.
**Eric Hoffer**, *The Passionate State of Mind*, 1955

**7** It's pretty hard to tell what does bring happiness; poverty and wealth have both failed.
**Kin Hubbard**

**8** Happiness isn't something you experience. It's something you remember.
**Oscar Levant**, 1906–72, American composer and wit

**9** Most of us believe in trying to make other people happy only if they can be happy in ways which we approve.
**Robert Lynd**, *Life's Little Oddities*

**10** Happy is the man with a wife to tell him what to do and a secretary to do it.
**Lord Mancroft**, 1914–87, politician

**11** I have to tell you something. I cannot help being happy. I've struggled against it but no good. Apart from an odd five minutes here and there, I have been happy all my life. There is, I am well aware, no virtue whatever in this. It results from a combination of heredity, health, good fortune and shallow intellect.
**Arthur Marshall**, *Taking Liberties*, 1977

**12** The only really happy folk are married women and single men.
**H. L. Mencken**

**13** Gilbert White discovered the formula for complete happiness but he died before making the announcement, leaving it for me to do so. It is to be very busy with the unimportant.
**A. Edward Newton**, *This Book-Collecting Game*

**14** I was at my happiest during my six-month rabies quarantine at Heathrow.
**Emo Philips**

**15** Happiness is not a goal; it is a by-product.
**Eleanor Roosevelt**

**16** Happiness is a Warm Puppy.
**Charles Schulz**, title of Peanuts book, 1962

**17** A lifetime of happiness! No man alive could bear it: it would be hell on earth.
**George Bernard Shaw**, *Man and Superman*, 1903

**18** If only we'd stop trying to be happy we could have a pretty good time.
**Edith Wharton**, 1862–1937, American author

**19** When I was young, I used to think that wealth and power would bring me happiness . . . I was right.
**Gahan Wilson**, *The Weird World of Gahan Wilson*, cartoon, 1975

# Hate

*See also Enemies; Xenophobia.*

**1** I am free of all prejudice. I hate everyone equally.
**W. C. Fields**

**2** Passionate hatred can give meaning and purpose to an empty life.
**Eric Hoffer**, American philosopher

**3** Hatred is the coward's revenge for being intimidated.
**George Bernard Shaw**, *Major Barbara*, 1905

# Hats

*See also Appearance; Clothes; Hair.*

**1** FIRST WOMAN: Whenever I'm down in the dumps, I get myself another hat.
SECOND WOMAN: I always wondered where you found them.
**Anon.**

**2** I began wearing hats as a young lawyer because it helped me to establish my professional identity. Before that, whenever I was at a meeting, someone would ask me to get coffee – they assumed I was a secretary.
**Bella Abzug**, American Democratic Congresswoman and feminist

**3** A hat should be taken off when you greet a lady and left off for the rest of your life. Nothing looks more stupid than a hat. When you put on a hat you are surrendering to the same urge that makes children wear mouse ears at Disney World or drunks wear lampshades at parties. Wearing a hat implies that you are bald if you are a man and that your hair is dirty if you are a woman. Every style of hat is identified with some form of undesirable (derby = corrupt ward heeler; fedora = Italian gangster; top hat = rich bum; pillbox = Kennedy wife, et cetera).
**P. J. O'Rourke**, *Modern Manners*, 1983

**4** One's chapeau provides the perfect opportunity for a profound fashion statement. Your hat should not merely say, 'here is my head' but rather it should convey a sense of allure, mystery, even intrigue. Here moi's chapeau is saying, 'Oui,

I have time for one quick chocolate malted in that café with the umbrellas that have tables on their handles, but then I must board the Oriental Express for a rendezvous with the Duke of Candelabra in the lovely, yet sinister, Kingdom of Rutabagia.'
**Miss Piggy**, *Miss Piggy's Guide to Life (As Told to Henry Beard)*, 1981

**5 Sticky situations**

Someone you like is wearing an ugly hat, and she asks you to give her your honest opinion of it:

'What a lovely chapeau! But if I may make one teensy suggestion? If it blows off, don't chase it.'
**Miss Piggy**, *Miss Piggy's Guide to Life (As Told to Henry Beard)*, 1981

**6** Hats divide generally into three classes: offensive hats, defensive hats, and shrapnel. Shrapnel hats look as if they have dropped on to the wearer's head by accident . . .

I have recently acquired a new hat of such ferocity that it has been running my whole life for me, I wake up in the morning thinking 'who shall I wear my hat at today?'
**Katharine Whitehorn**, 'How to Wear a Hat', *Shouts and Murmurs*, 1963

**7** My dear, you're the only woman who'd have known the right hat to wear on an occasion like this.
**Oscar Wilde**, to Mrs Leverson, on his leaving prison, 1897 (Attrib.)

**8** 'Don't you like this hat?'
'No, sir.'
'Well, I do,' I replied rather cleverly, and went out with it tilted just that merest shade over the left eye which makes all the difference.
**P. G. Wodehouse**, *Stiff Upper Lip, Jeeves*, 1963

# Haughtiness

*See also Snobbery; Status.*

**1** I am, in point of fact, a particularly haughty and exclusive person, of pre-Adamite ancestral descent. You will understand this when I tell you that I can trace my ancestry back to a protoplasmal primordial atomic globule. Consequently, my family pride is something

inconceivable. I can't help it. I was born sneering.
**W. S. Gilbert**, *The Mikado*, 1885

**2** Aunt Dahlia can turn in a flash into a carbon copy of a Duchess of the old school reducing an underling to a spot of grease, and what is so remarkable is that she doesn't have to use a lorgnette; just does it all with the power of the human eye.
**P. G. Wodehouse**, *Much Obliged, Jeeves*, 1971

**3** Ice formed on the butler's upper slopes.
**P. G. Wodehouse**, *Pigs Have Wings*, 1952

**4** It was the look which caused her to be known in native bearer and halfcaste circles as 'Mgobi-Mgumbi', which may be loosely translated as She On Whom It is Unsafe To Try Any Oompus Boompus.
**P. G. Wodehouse**, *Money in the Bank*, 1946

# Health

*See also Cancer; Diets; Exercise; Food; Illness.*

**1** If you want to clear your system out, sit on a piece of cheese and swallow a mouse.
**Johnny Carson**, *The Tonight Show*, NBC TV

**2** Did you ever see the customers in health-food stores? They are pale, skinny people who look half dead. In a steak house, you see robust, ruddy people. They're dying, of course, but they look terrific.
**Bill Cosby**

**3** Early to rise and early to bed
   Makes a male healthy and wealthy and dead.
**James Thurber**, *Fables for Our Time*, 1940

# Heaven

*See also Belief; God; Heaven and Hell; Hell; Reincarnation; Religion.*

**1** Heaven is the place where the donkey at last catches up with the carrot.
**Anon.**

**2** My life I squandered waiting
   Then let my chance go by.
   One day we'll meet in Heaven.
   That Matlock in the sky.
**Alan Bennett**, *Habeas Corpus*, 1973

**3** What! You been keeping records on me? I

wasn't so bad! How many times did I take the Lord's name in vain? One million and six? Jesus Ch . . . !
**Steve Martin**, *A Wild and Crazy Guy*, album, 1978

**4** Heaven, as conventionally conceived, is a place so inane, so dull, so useless, so miserable, that nobody has ever ventured to describe a whole day in heaven, though plenty of people have described a day at the seaside.
**George Bernard Shaw**, *Misalliance*, 1914

**5** If you go to heaven without being naturally qualified for it, you will not enjoy yourself there.
**George Bernard Shaw**, *Man and Superman*, 1903

**6** My idea of heaven is eating *paté de foie gras* to the sound of trumpets.
**Sydney Smith**, 1771–1845, clergyman and wit, quoted in H. Pearson's *The Smith of Smiths*, 1934

# Heaven and Hell

*See also Heaven; Hell.*

**1** Heaven is where the police are British, the chefs are French, the mechanics are German, the lovers are Italian and it's all organised by the Swiss.
   Hell is where the chefs are British, the mechanics are French, the lovers are Swiss, the police are German and it's all organised by the Italians.
**Anon.**

**2** Hell is Heaven enjoying itself.
**Anon.**

**3** *My* idea of Hell is to be stuck in *his* idea of Heaven.
**Alfred McFote**

**4** I don't like to commit myself about heaven and hell – you see, I have friends in both places.
**Mark Twain**

**5** . . . the minister told him that each place had its advantages – heaven for climate, and hell for society.
**Mark Twain**, speech to the Acorn Club, New York, 1901

# Hecklers

*See also Abuse; Audiences; Insults.*

**1** If I throw a stick, will you leave?
**Anon.**

**2** If you had half a brain, you'd be dangerous.
**Anon.**

**3** Isn't it a shame when cousins marry?
**Anon.**

**4** I thought alcoholics were supposed to be anonymous.
**Anon.**

**5** *Responses to . . .*
Wait – I'm trying to imagine you with a personality!
**Anon.**

**6** Save your breath! You'll need it to inflate your girlfriend!
**Anon.**

**7** Twelve Heckler Retorts:
If there's ever a price on your head take it!
Why don't you go down to the morgue and tell them you're ready!
Tell me, is that your lower lip or are you wearing a turtle-neck sweater?
You've got a fine personality, sir – but not for a human being!
When he was born, his father came into the room and gave him a funny look. And as you can see, he's still got it!
You're the sort of person Dr Spooner would have called a shining wit!
Will you please follow the example of your head and come to the point!
That reminds me of a very funny story – will you take it from there, Sir?
Why don't you move closer to the wall – that's plastered already!
I'd like to help you out – tell me, which way did you come in?
What exactly is on your mind? If you'll excuse the exaggeration?
You've got a wonderful head on your shoulders. Tell me: whose is it?
**Anon.**

**8** When your IQ gets to 80, sell!
**Anon.**

**9** Why don't you just pull your lower lip over your head and swallow?
**Anon.**

**10** Yes, I remember MY first pint!
**Anon.**

**11** You know what they say – every village has one.
**Anon.**

**12** Sir, I have a mike and you have a beer . . . God has a plan and you're not in it.
**Richard Belzer**

**13** What do you use for birth control? Your personality?
**Richard Belzer**

**14** If you ever become a mother, can I have one of the puppies?
**Charles Pierce**

**15** You remind me of my brother Bosco. Only he had a human head.
**Judy Tenuta**

# Height

*See also The Body; Figures.*

**1** Your father is so short you can see his feet on his driver's license.
*Snaps, 1994*

**2** Your brother is so tall, he has to bend over so planes can pass.
*Snaps, 1994*

**3** Your father is so short, he has a job cleaning ankles.
*Snaps 4, 1998*

**4** Short? He's the only man I know who can milk a cow standing up.
**Fred Allen**

**5** LADY RUMPERS: Rumpers was a little man too. He made no secret of his height.
**Alan Bennett,** *Habeas Corpus,* 1973

**6** He's so small, he's the only man I know who has turn-ups on his underpants.
**Jerry Dennis**

**7** He's very superstitious – he thinks it's unlucky to walk under a black cat.
**Max Kauffmann**

# Hell

*See also Heaven; Heaven and Hell.*

**1** . . . Hell is other people.
**Jean-Paul Sartre,** *Huis Clos,* 1944

**2** Hell is full of musical amateurs: music is the brandy of the damned.
**George Bernard Shaw,** *Man and Superman,* 1903

# Heroes

*See also Courage; War.*

**1** We can't all be heroes because somebody has to sit on the curb and clap as they go by.
**Will Rogers**

**2** This thing of being a hero, about the main thing to do is to know when to die. Prolonged life has ruined more men than it ever made.
**Will Rogers,** *The Autobiography of Will Rogers,* 1949

**3** Formerly we used to canonize our heroes. The modern method is to vulgarize them. Cheap editions of great books may be delightful, but cheap editions of great men are absolutely detestable.
**Oscar Wilde,** 'The True Function and Value of Criticism', 1890

# History

*See also Ancestors; Antiques; Autobiography; The Past.*

**1** History is a hard core of interpretation surrounded by a pulp of disputable facts.
**Anon.**

**2** History is a set of lies agreed upon by the victor.
**Anon.**

**3** History is the sum total of the things that could have been avoided.
**Konrad Adenauer,** Chancellor of West Germany, 1949–63

**4** History, *n.* an account, mostly false, of events, mostly unimportant, which are brought about by rulers, mostly knaves, and soldiers, mostly fools.
**Ambrose Bierce,** *The Devil's Dictionary,* 1911

**5** History teaches us that men and nations behave wisely once they have exhausted all other alternatives.
**Abba Eban,** speech in London, 1970

**6** History is bunk.
**Henry Ford,** giving evidence in a libel action, 1919

**7** History never looks like history when you are living through it. It always looks confusing and messy, and it always feels uncomfortable.
**John W. Gardner,** *No Easy Victories,* 1968

**8** History repeats itself; historians repeat each other.
**Philip Guedalla,** *Supers and Supermen,* 1920

**9** History was a trash bag of random coincidences torn open in a wind. Surely, Watt with his steam engine, Faraday with his electric motor, and Edison with his incandescent light bulb did not have it as their goal to contribute to a fuel shortage some day that would place their countries at the mercy of Arab oil.
**Joseph Heller,** *Good as Gold,* 1979

**10** History is too serious to be left to historians.
**Iain Macleod,** Leader of the House of Commons, quoted in the *Observer,* 1961

**11** HISTORY TEACHER: Who was Joan of Arc?
TED: Uhhh . . . Noah's wife?
**Chris Matheson and Ed Solomon,** *Bill and Ted's Excellent Adventure,* screenplay, 1988

**12** . . . broadly speaking, anything done against kings was to be applauded – unless, indeed, it were done by priests, like Becket, in which case one sided with the king.
**Bertrand Russell,** *Portraits from Memory,* 1956

**13 Bluff King Hal.**
Henry VIII was a strong king with a very strong sense of humour and VIII wives, memorable amongst whom are Katherine the Arrogant, Anne of Cloves, Lady Jane Austin and Anne Hathaway. His beard was, however, red.
In his youth Henry was fond of playing tennis and after his accession is believed never to have lost a set. He also invented a game called 'Bluff King Hal', which he invited ministers to play with him. The players were blindfolded and knelt down

with their heads on a block of wood; they then guessed who the King would marry next.

**W. C. Sellar and R. J. Yeatman**, *1066 and All That*, 1930

**14 Rufus. A ruddy king.**

This monarch was always very angry and red in the face and was therefore unpopular, so that his death was a Good Thing: it occurred in the following memorable way. Rufus was hunting one day in the New Forest, when William Tell (the memorable crackshot, inventor of Crossbow puzzles) took unerring aim at a reddish apple, which had fallen on to the King's head, and shot him through the heart. Sir Isaac Walton, who happened to be present at the time, thereupon invented the Law of Gravity. Thus was the reign of Rufus brought to a Good End.

**W. C. Sellar and R. J. Yeatman**, *1066 and All That*, 1930

**15** Hegel was right when he said that we learn from history that men never learn anything from history.

**George Bernard Shaw**, *Heartbreak House*, 1919

**16** Any event, once it has occurred, can be made to appear inevitable by a competent historian.

**Lee Simonson**, American designer and critic, 1888–1967

**17** History would be a wonderful thing – if it were only true.

**Leo Tolstoy**

**18** 'History repeats itself' and 'History never repeats itself' are about equally true.

**G. M. Trevelyan**, English historian

**19** The one duty we owe to history is to rewrite it.

**Oscar Wilde**, 'The Critic as Artist', 1890

**20** Hindsight is always twenty-twenty.

**Billy Wilder** (Attrib.)

# Hitler, Adolf

*See also War.*

**1** The moustache of Hitler
Could hardly be littler
Was the thought that kept recurring
To Field Marshal Goering.

**E. C. Bentley**, 'Clerihews', *Punch*, 1939

**2** HITLER: I don't want war! All I want is Peace! Peace! Peace!
(*Sings*) A little piece of Poland,
A little piece of France,
A little piece of Portugal
And Austria perchance.
A little slice of Turkey
And all that that entails,
And then a piece of England, Scotland,
Ireland and Wales.

**Mel Brooks**, *To Be Or Not To Be*, screenplay, 1983

**3** Hitler was better-looking than Churchill, a better dresser than Churchill, he had more hair, he told funnier jokes and he could dance the pants off Churchill.

**Mel Brooks**, *The Producers*, screenplay, 1968

**4** Springtime for Hitler and Germany,
Deutschland is happy and gay.
We're moving to a faster pace,
Look out, here comes the Master Race!
Springtime for Hitler and Germany,
Winter for Poland and France.
Springtime for Hitler and Germany,
Come on Germans, go into your dance!

**Mel Brooks**, 'Springtime for Hitler', song from *The Producers*, 1968

**5** If Hitler invaded Hell I would make at least a favourable reference to the Devil in the House of Commons.

**Winston Churchill**, 1941, quoted in *The Grand Alliance*, 1950

**6** This man is dangerous; he believes what he says.

**Joseph Goebbels** (Attrib.)

**7** Do you think Der Fuhrer could keep on being Der Fuhrer
If he saw what everybody else sees every time he looks in the muhrer?

**Ogden Nash**

# Holidays

*See also Expeditions; The Sea; Travel.*

**1** *I* am a traveller
*You* are a sightseer
*He* is a tourist.

*Our* children enjoyed pommes frites
*Your* children ate french fries
*Their* children stuffed themselves with chips.

*Our* children are in high spirits
*Your* children are letting off steam
*Their* children are an utter nuisance.

*I* barter
*You* haggle
*He* argues.
**Craig Brown**, 'The Holiday Primer – Lesson 1: Conjugation', *Daily Telegraph*, 2000

**2** Honolulu – it's got everything. Sand for the children, sun for the wife, sharks for the wife's mother.
**Ken Dodd**, English comedian

**3** ERIC: Did you know I used to be a lifeguard?
ERNIE: Really? When?
ERIC: Last summer.
ERNIE: What did you do?
ERIC: I saved women.
ERNIE: What for?
ERIC: The winter.
ERNIE: Didn't you help any men?
ERIC: Yes – I gave them the occasional woman.
**Eric Morecambe and Ernie Wise**, *The Morecambe and Wise Joke Book*, 1979

**4** ERIC: Excuse me, are you the manager of this holiday camp?
ERNIE: I certainly am, sir – Bobkins' Holiday Camps at your service! You're one of our earliest holiday-makers this year. The camp has only been open a week.
ERIC: I know – I like to get in early while the sheets are still clean.
ERNIE: Anyway, sir, can I help you?
ERIC: Yes, it's about the roof of my chalet.
ERNIE: What about it?
ERIC: I'd like one.
**Eric Morecambe and Ernie Wise**, *The Morecambe and Wise Joke Book*, 1979

**5** A good holiday is one spent among people whose notions of time are vaguer than yours.
**J. B. Priestley**

## Holland and the Dutch

*See also Europe and the EEC.*

**1** Apart from cheese and tulips, the main product of the country is advocaat, a drink made from lawyers.
**Alan Coren**, *The Sanity Inspector*, 1974

**2** Like the Germans, the Dutch fall into two quite distinct physical types: the small, corpulent, red-faced Edams, and the thinner, paler, larger Goudas.
**Alan Coren**, *The Sanity Inspector*, 1974

**3** All hail the Dutch, long-suffering neutrons in the endless movement against oppression and exploitation. Let us hear it for the Dutch, bland and obliging victims of innumerable wars which have rendered their lands as flat as their treats . . . Every one of them is an uncle, not a one can muster real courage . . . All hail the Dutch, nonpeople in the people's war!
**Tony Hendra**, 'EEC! It's the US of E!', *National Lampoon*, 1976

## Hollywood

*See also Acting; Actors and Actresses; California; Film; Los Angeles.*

**1** Hollywood – where people from Iowa mistake each other for movie stars.
**Fred Allen**

**2** You can take all the sincerity in Hollywood, place it in the navel of a fruit fly and still have room enough for three caraway seeds and a producer's heart.
**Fred Allen**

**3** What I like about Hollywood is that one can get along by knowing two words of English – swell and lousy.
**Vicki Baum** (Attrib.)

**4** Hollywood – an emotional Detroit.
**Lillian Gish**

**5** Deep below the glitter, it's all solid tinsel.
**Samuel Goldwyn**, 1882–1974, American film producer (Attrib.)

**6** With a mental equipment which allows me to tell the difference between hot and cold, I stand out in this community like a modern-day Cicero. Dropped into any other city of the world, I'd rate as a possibly adequate night-watchman.
**Anita Loos**, *No Mother to Guide Her*, 1961

**7** No one ever went broke in Hollywood underestimating the intelligence of the public.
**Elsa Maxwell**, 1883–1963, American actress and socialite

**8** Just outside pious Los Angeles is Hollywood, a colony of moving picture actors. Its morals are those of Port Said.
**H. L. Mencken**, *Americana*, 1925

**9** . . . a delightful trip through a sewer in a glass-bottomed boat.
**Wilson Mizner**, 1876–1933, American playwright

**10** Hollywood is a sewer – with service from the Ritz-Carlton.
**Wilson Mizner**

**11** I've had several years in Hollywood and I still think the movie heroes are in the audience.
**Wilson Mizner**

**12** *Gandhi* was everything the voting members of the Academy would like to be: moral, tan and thin.
**Joe Morgenstern**, *Los Angeles Herald Examiner*, April 1983

**13** Ten million dollars' worth of intricate and highly ingenious machinery functioning elaborately to put skin on baloney.
**George Jean Nathan**, 1882–1958, critic

**14** When Gertrude Stein returned to New York after a short sojourn in Hollywood somebody asked her . . . 'What is it like out there?' To which, with little delay, and the minimum of careful thought the sage replied . . . 'There *is* no "There" there.'
**David Niven**, *Bring on the Empty Horses*, 1975

**15** Hollywood money isn't money. It's congealed snow, melts in your hand, and there you are.
**Dorothy Parker**, interviewed in *Writers at Work*, 1958

**16** Hollywood is where, if you don't have happiness, you send out for it.
**Rex Reed**

**17** In Hollywood, marriage is a success if it outlives milk.
**Rita Rudner**

**18** Beverly Hills is very exclusive. For instance, their fire department won't make house calls.
**Mort Sahl**, American comedian (Attrib.)

**19** They know only one word of more than one syllable here, and that is *fillum*.
**Louis Sherwin**

**20** There are only two types of exercise in Hollywood: jogging and helping a divorced friend move.
**Robert Wagner**

**21** A place where they shoot too many pictures and not enough actors.
**Walter Winchell**, American newspaper columnist

**22** Everybody liked Bill Shannon, even in Hollywood, where nobody likes anybody.
**P. G. Wodehouse**, *The Old Reliable*, 1951

# Home
*See also Gardening; Interior Decorating; Real Estate.*

**1** They live in a beautiful little apartment overlooking the rent.
**Anon.**

**2** ALEC GILROY: Burglars? Your house? Anything worth pinching they'd have to bring with 'em!
*Coronation Street*, Granada TV

**3** Home life as we understand it is no more natural to us than a cage is natural to a cockatoo.
**George Bernard Shaw**, 'Preface', *Getting Married*, 1908

**4** Home, nowadays, is a place where part of the family waits till the rest of the family brings the car back.
**Earl Wilson**, 1907–87, American columnist

# Homosexuality
*See also Bisexuality; Sex.*

**1** My mother made me a homosexual. *If I gave her the wool, would she make me one too?*
**Graffito**, London, 1978

**2** The world dictates that heteros make love while gays have sex.
**Boy George**

**3** My lesbianism is an act of Christian charity. All those women out there are praying for a man, and I'm giving them my share.
**Rita Mae Brown**, 1978

**4** If God had meant us to have

homosexuals, he would have created Adam and Bruce.

**Anita Bryant**, American singer and anti-gay activist

**5** Homosexuality is a sickness, just as are baby-rape or wanting to become head of General Motors.

**Eldridge Cleaver**, *Soul on Ice*, 1968

**6** I became one of the stately homos of England.

**Quentin Crisp**, *The Naked Civil Servant*, 1968

**7** The worst part of being gay in the twentieth century is all that damn disco music to which one has to listen.

**Quentin Crisp**, *Manners From Heaven*, 1984

**8** I discarded a whole book because the leading character wasn't on my wavelength. She was a lesbian with doubts about her masculinity.

**Peter De Vries**, quoted in *The New York Times*, 1967

**9** Lesbianism has always seemed to me an extremely inventive response to the shortage of men, but otherwise not worth the trouble.

**Nora Ephron**, *Heartburn*, 1983

**10** JOE: Ellen's a very private person whose sexuality is on a need-to-know basis.
ELLEN: Thank you, Joe, 'preciate it. And while you're at it, can you erase that chalkboard. I don't think there's such a thing as *'Lesbo-licious coffee . . .'* . . . Mmmm this *'gaypuccino'* is *'homo-riffic.'* But let's just call it *'Cinnamon Coffee,'* OK?

**David Flebotte and Alex Herschlag**, *Ellen*, ABC TV, 1998

**11** Using the word 'gay' as a euphemism for homosexuality is fine, I guess. But I've always thought a word like 'fabulous' might have been better. Sure would be a lot easier to tell your parents, 'Mom, Dad – I'm *fabulous*! And my friends are fabulous too!'

**Michael Greer**

**12** TEXAN WOMAN: Are you a homo? We don't have homos in Texas – live ones, anyway.

**Susan Harris**, *Soap*, ABC TV, 1978

**13** What do you call a man who marries another man?

A vicar!

**Benny Hill**

**14** In New York now they have Harvey Milk High School for gay students. They don't have much of a football team, but the half-time show . . .

**Bill Maher**, *Politically Incorrect*, ABC, 1993

**15** It was out of the closet and into the streets for the nation's homosexuals in the seventies. This didn't do much for the streets, but on the other hand your average closet was improved immeasurably.

**Rick Meyerowitz and John Weidman**, *National Lampoon*, 1980

**16** Oprah Winfrey issued a statement saying that even though she appeared on the 'Ellen' coming-out episode, she's not gay.
   Meanwhile, Ellen DeGeneres issued a statement saying that even though she appeared on 'Oprah,' she's not black.

**Conan O'Brien**, *Late Night with Conan O'Brien*, NBC TV, 1998

**17** It is the height of fashion to think, dress, and act like a homosexual. But, suddenly, it has become very unfashionable to be one. This may be the result of the immense fatigue everyone is feeling with the concept of equality. With blacks, Hispanics, dolphins, and so on all demanding to be treated as equals, homosexuals are just one more voice of complaint in a complaint-ridden world. And since homosexuals are often wealthy and famous, treating them as equals is not only difficult but can actually be construed as rudeness. The whole thing is a social mess.

**P. J. O'Rourke**, *Modern Manners*, 1983

**18** I'd rather be black than gay because when you're black you don't have to tell your mother.

**Charles Pierce**, American female impersonator

**19** Straight people are fine – I have one of them fix my car. They do great work.

**Michael Rasky**

**20** I am not gay. I am however, thin, single and neat. Sometimes when someone is thin, single and neat, people assume they are gay because that is the stereotype. You normally

don't think of gay people as fat, sloppy and married. Although I'm sure some are – I don't want to perpetuate a stereotype – but they're probably in the minority within the gay community. They're probably discriminated against because of that. People say to them, 'You know Joe, I enjoy being gay with you, but I think it's about time you got in shape, tucked your shirt in and lost the wife.'
**Jerry Seinfeld**, *SeinLanguage*, 1993

**21** It wasn't easy telling my family that I'm gay. I made my carefully worded announcement at Thanksgiving. It was very Norman Rockwell. I said, 'Mom, would you please pass the gravy to a homosexual?' She passed it to my father. A terrible scene followed. Just kidding, Dad.
**Bob Smith**

**22** My Aunt Lorraine said, 'Bob, you're gay. Are you seeing a psychiatrist?' I said, 'No, I'm seeing a lieutenant in the Navy.'
**Bob Smith**

## Honesty
*See also Dishonesty; Hypocrisy; Morality; Sincerity; Trust; Truth; Vice and Virtue.*

**1** The louder he talked of his honor, the faster we counted the spoons.
**Ralph Waldo Emerson**, *The Conduct of Life*, 1860

**2** Cross my heart and hope to eat my weight in goslings.
**W. C. Fields**

**3** Some persons are likable in spite of their unswerving integrity.
**Don Marquis**, 1878–1937, American journalist

## Honeymoons
*See also Couples; Hotels; Sex; Weddings.*

**1** Honeymoon – the morning after the knot before.
**Anon.**

**2** Honeymooning is a very overrated occupation.
**Noel Coward**, *Private Lives*, 1930

**3** JASON CORD: What would you like to see on your honeymoon?

MONICA WINTHROP: Lots of lovely ceilings.
**John Michael Hayes**, *The Carpetbaggers*, screenplay, 1964

**4** The honeymoon is over when she starts wondering what happened to the man she married and he starts wondering what happened to the girl he didn't.
**Sally Poplin**

**5** People take shorter honeymoons nowadays, but they take them more often.
**Sally Poplin**

## Honours
*See also Achievement; Awards.*

**1** ERNIE: My name is Colonel Napoleon Davenport, DSO, MC, OBE.
ERIC: That's a funny way to spell 'Davenport'.
**Eric Morecambe and Ernie Wise**, *The Morecambe and Wise Joke Book*, 1979

## Horses and Horse Racing
*See also Animals; Cowboys; Gambling.*

**1** It's awf'lly bad luck on Diana
Her ponies have swallowed their bits;
She fished down their throats with a spanner
And frightened them all into fits.
**John Betjeman**, *A Few Late Chrysanthemums*, 1954

**2** EDMUND: You ride a horse rather less well than another horse would.
**Richard Curtis and Rowan Atkinson**, 'The Black Seal', *The Black Adder*, BBC TV, 1983

**3** I follow the horses. And the horses I follow, follow horses.
**Joe E. Lewis**, 1902–71, American comedian

**4** There is nothing better for the inside of a man than the outside of a horse.
**Ronald Reagan**, Republican President, 1981–9

**5** If you could call the thing a horse. If it hadn't shown a flash of speed in the straight, it would have got mixed up with the next race.
**P. G. Wodehouse**, *Very Good, Jeeves*, 1930

**6** I just played a horse yesterday so slow the jockey kept a diary of the trip.
**Henny Youngman**, 1940

# Hospitals

*See also Accidents; Doctors; Health; Illness; Medicine.*

**1** There was a young man with a hernia
Who said to his doctor, 'Goldernia
When improving my middle
Be sure you don't fiddle
With matters that do not concernia.'
**Heywood Broun**, 1888–1939, American journalist

**2** I had a chest X-ray last month and they found a spot on my lung. Fortunately, it was barbecue sauce.
**George Carlin**, *Brain Droppings*, 1997

**3** After two days in hospital, I took a turn for the nurse.
**W. C. Fields**

**4** A hospital bed is a parked taxi with the meter running.
**Groucho Marx**

**5** KENT BROCKMAN (READING THE NEWS): At 3 p.m. Friday, local autocrat C. Montgomery Burns was shot following a tense confrontation at Town Hall. Burns was rushed to a nearby hospital where he was pronounced dead. He was then transferred to a better hospital where doctors upgraded his condition to 'alive.'
**Bill Oakley and Josh Weinstein**, 'Who Shot Mr Burns? Part Two', *The Simpsons*, Fox TV, 1995

# Hotels

*See also Holidays; Restaurants; Travel.*

**1** Twenty-four-hour room service generally refers to the length of time that it takes for the club sandwich to arrive. This is indeed disheartening, particularly when you've ordered scrambled eggs.
**Fran Lebowitz**, *Social Studies*, 1981

**2** ERIC: The manager said, 'You won't find a single flea in any of my beds.' He was right – they were all married with families.
ERNIE: What sort of room did you have?
ERIC: It was quite nice actually. We had a double room with bath – pity about them being in separate buildings.
**Eric Morecambe and Ernie Wise**, *The Morecambe and Wise Joke Book*, 1979

**3** Generally speaking, the length and grandness of a hotel's name are an exact opposite reflection of its quality. Thus the Hotel Central will prove to be a clean, pleasant place in a good part of town, and the Hotel Royal Majestic-Fantastic will be a fleabag next to a topless-bowling alley.
**Miss Piggy**, *Miss Piggy's Guide to Life (As Told to Henry Beard)*, 1981

**4** I stayed at one of the better hotels . . . I was at a place called The Fractured Arms. I paid my rent in advance – they put the window back in my room . . . You can imagine how big my room was when I closed the door, the doorknob got in bed with me. It was so small, even the mice were hunchback. I had a headache, the guy next door had to take the aspirin.
**Henny Youngman**, 1940

# House of Commons

*See also Congress; Elections; House of Lords; Parliament; Politics and Politicians.*

**1** What have you done? cried Christine
You've wrecked the whole party machine!
To lie in the nude may be rude,
But to lie in the House is obscene!
**Anon.**, of John Profumo who lied to the House of Commons concerning his relationship with Christine Keeler, 1963

**2** I do not know what the Right Hon. Lady the Minister for Education [Miss Florence Horsbrugh] is grinning at. I was told by one of my Hon. friends this afternoon that this is a face which has sunk a thousand scholarships.
**Aneurin Bevan**, speech on cuts in the Education budget, House of Commons, 1953

**3** If, from any speech in the House, one begins to see any results within five to ten years after it has been delivered, one will have done very well indeed.
**Robert Boothby**, Member of Parliament, 1936

**4** I slept for two hours this afternoon in the Library of the House of Commons! A deep House of Commons sleep. There is no sleep to compare with it – rich, deep and guilty.
**Henry 'Chips' Channon**, 1939

**5** As we had great interests there and also on general grounds, I thought that it would be a good thing to have diplomatic representation. But if you recognize anyone, it does not mean that you like him. We all, for instance, recognize the Right Hon Gentleman the Member of Ebbw Vale [Aneurin Bevan].

**Winston Churchill**, speech on the recognition of Communist China, House of Commons, 1952

**6** BESSIE BRADDOCK: Winston, you're drunk!

CHURCHILL: Bessie, you're ugly. But tomorrow I shall be sober.

**Winston Churchill**, probably apocryphal

**7** LADY ASTOR: If you were my husband, I'd poison your coffee.

CHURCHILL: If you were my wife, I'd drink it.

**Winston Churchill**, at Blenheim Palace, 1912, probably apocryphal

**8** . . . a Bill to make attendance at the House of Commons compulsory has been passed by three votes to two.

**David Frost and Antony Jay**, *To England with Love*, 1967

**9** When in that House MPs divide,
   If they've a brain and cerebellum, too,
   They've got to leave that brain outside,
   And vote just as their leaders tell 'em to.
   But then the prospect of a lot
   Of dull MPs in close proximity,
   All thinking for themselves, is what
   No man can face with equanimity.

**W. S. Gilbert**, 'Private Willis', *Iolanthe*, 1882

**10** It is a truth not sufficiently appreciated that any political proposal which commends itself to both front benches of the House of Commons is at best useless and at worst against the public interest; one which also appeals to both main parties' back benches is likely to be a constitutional outrage and certain to be seriously damaging to the people's liberty, prosperity or both.

**Bernard Levin**, *The Times*, 1984

**11** I have nothing against Hampstead. I used to live there myself when I was an intellectual. I gave that up when I became Leader of the House.

**Norman St John-Stevas**, *Observer*, 1980

**12** Parliament is the longest running farce in the West End.

**Cyril Smith**, Liberal MP, 1973

**13** Only people who look dull ever get into the House of Commons, and only people who are dull ever succeed there.

**Oscar Wilde**, *An Ideal Husband*, 1895

# House of Lords

*See also The Aristocracy; House of Commons; Parliament; Politics and Politicians.*

**1** The cure for admiring the House of Lords is to go and look at it.

**Walter Bagehot**

**2** It was but a few weeks since he had taken his seat in the Lords; and this afternoon, for want of anything better to do, he strayed in.

**Max Beerbohm**, *Zuleika Dobson*, 1911

**3** The House of Lords is the British Outer Mongolia for retired politicians.

**Tony Benn**, speech, 1962

**4** Like many other anachronisms in British public life, the House of Lords has one supreme merit. It works.

**Lord Boothby** (Attrib.)

**5** . . . dead, but in the Elysian fields.

**Benjamin Disraeli**

**6** The House of Lords is a model of how to care for the elderly.

**Frank Field**, Labour MP, 1981

**7** . . . on great matters of State it does have the vital constitutional right to say 'Yes' or 'Yes, but not for a few weeks.'

**David Frost and Antony Jay**, *To England with Love*, 1967

**8** When Wellington thrashed Bonaparte,
   As every child can tell,
   The House of Peers, throughout the war,
   Did nothing in particular,
   And did it very well:
   Yet Britain set the world ablaze
   In good King George's glorious days!

**W. S. Gilbert**, 'Lord Mountararat', *Iolanthe*, 1882

**9** The House of Lords is not the watchdog of the constitution: it is Mr Balfour's poodle. It fetches and carries for him. It

barks for him. It bites anybody that he sets it on to!
**David Lloyd George**, speech, House of Commons, 1908

**10** You can't say: 'The noble and gallant Lord is a silly old fool.' It just wouldn't sound right.
**Lady Phillips**, *Observer*, 1967

**11** The House of Lords has a value . . . it is good evidence of life after death.
**Lord Soper** (Attrib.)

**12** The House of Lords is a perfect eventide home.
**Lady Stocks** (Attrib.), 1970

**13** LORD ILLINGWORTH: We in the House of Lords are never in touch with public opinion. That makes us a civilized body.
**Oscar Wilde**, *A Woman of No Importance*, 1893

# Housewives
*See also Home; Husbands; Mothers; Women.*

**1** When my husband comes home, if the kids are still alive, I figure I've done my job.
**Roseanne Barr**

**2** No one knows what her life expectancy is, but I have a horror of leaving this world and not having anyone in the entire family know how to replace a toilet tissue spindle.
**Erma Bombeck**, *If Life is a Bowl of Cherries – What am I Doing in the Pits?*, 1978

**3** There was no need to do any housework at all. After the first four years the dirt doesn't get any worse.
**Quentin Crisp**, *The Naked Civil Servant*, 1968

**4** Cleaning your house while your kids are still growing
Is like shoveling the walk before it stops snowing.
**Phyllis Diller**, *Phyllis Diller's Housekeeping Hints*, 1966

**5** I'll be there,
Waiting until his mind is clear
While he looks through me – right through me.
Waiting to say, 'Good evening, dear, I'm pregnant –
What's new with you from downtown?'
Oh, to be loved by a man I respect,

To bask in the glow of his perfectly understandable neglect.
Oh to belong in the aura of his frown,
Darling-busy frown,
Such heaven!
**Frank Loesser**, 'Happy to Keep His Dinner Warm', *How to Succeed in Business without Really Trying*, 1961

**6** I hate housework! You make the beds, you do the dishes – and six months later you have to start all over again.
**Joan Rivers**

# Humility
*See also Modesty; Pride.*

**1** Humility is not renunciation of pride but the substitution of one pride for another.
**Eric Hoffer**, American philosopher

**2** It is going to be fun to watch and see how long the meek can keep the earth after they inherit it.
**Kin Hubbard**, *Abe Martin's Sayings*, 1915

**3** It is God, not man, who should be humble when he reflects upon the indifferent job he has made of a human being.
**W. Somerset Maugham**

**4** Don't be humble. You're not that great.
**Golda Meir**, Israeli Prime Minister (1969–74), to Moshe Dayan, general and statesman

**5** Christian humility is preached by the clergy, but practised only by the lower classes.
**Bertrand Russell**, *Autobiography*, 1967

# Humour
*See also Comedy; Laughter; Puns; Riddles; Satire; Wit.*

**1** *Caustic*: adjective applied to the wit of magistrates and judges, as in the sentence, 'The judge then asked who was this gentleman, Mussolini, who appeared to be an Italian?'
**Beachcomber (J. B. Morton)**, *Beachcomber: The Works of J. B. Morton*, 1974

**2** Mark my words, when a society has to resort to the lavatory for its humour, the writing is on the wall.
**Alan Bennett**, *Forty Years On*, 1968

**3** Humor is falling downstairs, if you do it in the act of warning your wife not to.
**Kenneth Bird**, British cartoonist, 1887–1965

**4** There are best-selling humorists who do get my goat. Andy Rooney springs to mind. Wry. Who needs wry? I haven't got time for wry.
**Roy Blount, Jr.**, *Esquire*, 1984

**5** A difference of taste in jokes is a great strain on the affections.
**George Eliot**, *Daniel Deronda*, 1876

**6** There is no reason why a joke should not be appreciated more than once. Imagine how little good music there would be if, for example, a conductor refused to play Beethoven's Fifth Symphony on the ground that his audience might have heard it before.
**A. P. Herbert**, 1890–1971, English writer and humorist

**7** FISH: That would be funny if it wasn't so humorous.
**David E. Kelley**, *Ally McBeal*, Fox TV

**8** Humor has been analysed with great success by any number of people who haven't written any.
**Henry Morgan**

**9** It is better in the long run to possess an
    abscess or a tumor
Than to possess a sense of humor.
People who have senses of humor have a
    very good time,
But they never accomplish anything of
    note, either despicable or sublime,
Because how can anybody accomplish
    anything immortal
When they realize they look pretty funny
    doing it and have to stop to chortle?
**Ogden Nash**, 'Don't Grin, or You'll Have to Bear It', *I'm a Stranger Here Myself*, 1938

**10** Wit has truth in it; wisecracking is simply calisthenics with words.
**Dorothy Parker**, interviewed in *Writers at Work*, 1958

**11** People without a sense of humour shouldn't be put in charge of anything.
**Robert Runcie**, Archbishop of Canterbury 1980–91, *Loose Ends*, BBC Radio 4, 2000

**12** Humor is emotional chaos remembered in tranquility.
**James Thurber**

**13** Humor can be dissected, as a frog can, but the thing dies in the process and the innards are discouraging to any but the pure scientific mind.
**E. B. White**, 1899–1985, American author and editor

**14** Nothing spoils a romance so much as a sense of humour in the woman – or the want of it in a man.
**Oscar Wilde**, *A Woman of No Importance*, 1893

# Hunting
*See also The Country; Guns; Sport.*

**1** We'll be talking to a gunsmith who's invented a sage-and-onion bullet that shoots the goose and stuffs it at the same time.
**The Two Ronnies**, BBC TV

**2** If God didn't want man to hunt, he wouldn't have given us plaid shirts.
**Johnny Carson**, *The Tonight Show*, NBC TV

**3** I only kill in self-defense. What would *you* do if a rabbit pulled a knife on you?
**Johnny Carson**, *The Tonight Show*, NBC TV

**4** ERIC: One day we suddenly came face to face with a ferocious lion.
ERNIE: Did it give you a start?
ERIC: I didn't need one. But I'd read a book about lions, so I knew exactly what steps to take . . . long ones.
**Eric Morecambe and Ernie Wise**, *The Morecambe and Wise Joke Book*, 1979

**5** LADY UTTERWORLD: . . . everybody can see that the people who hunt are the right people and the people who don't are the wrong ones.
**George Bernard Shaw**, *Heartbreak House*, 1919

**6** No sportsman wants to kill the fox or the pheasant as I want to kill him when I see him doing it.
**George Bernard Shaw**

**7** The English country gentleman galloping after a fox – the unspeakable in full pursuit of the uneatable.
**Oscar Wilde**, *A Woman of No Importance*, 1893

# Husbands

*See also Fathers; Housewives; Men; Men – The Female View.*

**1** Small band of men, armed only with wallets, besieged by a horde of wives and children.
*National Lampoon*, 1979

**2** I've been asked to say a couple of words about my husband, Fang. How about 'short' and 'cheap'.
**Phyllis Diller**

**3** Husbands are like fires. They go out if unattended.
**Zsa Zsa Gabor**

**4** He tells you when you've got on too much lipstick,
And helps you with your girdle when your hips stick.
**Ogden Nash**, 'The Perfect Husband', *Versus*, 1949

**5** A husband is what is left of the lover after the nerve has been extracted.
**Helen Rowland**, 'Prelude', *A Guide to Men*, 1922

**6** Men are horribly tedious when they are good husbands, and abominably conceited when they are not.
**Oscar Wilde**, *A Woman of No Importance*, 1893

# Hypochondria

*See also Health; Illness.*

**1** Hypochondria is the only disease I haven't got.
**Graffito**, New York, 1978

**2** Hypochondriac: someone who enjoys bad health.
**Anon.**

**3** MAN (*in bed*): Even hypochondriacs get ill . . .
**Mel Calman**, cartoon in *Dr Calman's Dictionary of Psychoanalysis*, 1979

**4** Hungry Joe collected lists of fatal diseases and arranged them in alphabetical order so that he could put his finger without delay on any one he wanted to worry about.
**Joseph Heller**, *Catch-22*, 1961

**5** Contentment preserves one even from catching cold. Has a woman who knew that she was well dressed ever caught a cold? –
No, not even when she had scarcely a rag to her back.
**Friedrich Wilhelm Nietzsche**, *The Twilight of the Idols*, 1889

**6** All sorts of bodily diseases are produced by half-used minds.
**George Bernard Shaw**

**7** So I went to the doctor's and he said, 'You've got hypochondria.' I said, 'Not that as well!'
**Tim Vine**, *Loose Ends*, BBC Radio, 2000

# Hypocrisy

*See also Flattery; Honesty; Lies.*

**1** A hypocrite always practises what he preaches – against.
**Anon.**

**2** Most people have seen worse things in private than they pretend to be shocked at in public.
**Edgar Watson Howe**, *Country Town Sayings*, 1911

**3** Hypocrisy is the most difficult and nerve-racking vice that any man can pursue; it needs an unceasing vigilance and a rare detachment of spirit. It cannot, like adultery or gluttony, be practised at spare moments; it is a wholetime job.
**W. Somerset Maugham**, *Cakes and Ale*, 1930

**4** All Reformers, however strict their social conscience, live in houses just as big as they can pay for.
**Logan Pearsall Smith**, 'Other People', *Afterthoughts*, 1931

# Idealism
*See also Belief; Opinions.*

**1** Idealism increases in direct proportion to one's distance from the problem.
**John Galsworthy**, 1867–1933, English novelist

**2** An idealist is one who, on noticing that a rose smells better than a cabbage, concludes that it will also make better soup.
**H. L. Mencken**, *Sententiae*, 1920

# Ideas
*See also Creativity.*

**1** An idea isn't responsible for the people who believe in it.
**Don Marquis**, *New York Sun*

**2** An idea that is not dangerous is unworthy of being called an idea at all.
**Oscar Wilde**, 'The Critic as Artist', 1890

# Idioms
*See also The English Language; Language.*

**1** It's like the bitchenest, like neatest way to talk, I'm sure, totally. It's so awesome, I mean, fer shurr, toadly, toe-dully! To the max! Come onnnnn – bag your face you geek, you grody totally shanky spaz, if you can't talk like a total Valley Girl, rilly, I'm shurrr. Gag me with a spoooooon! Ohhhhmigawwwd! OK: Valspeak is, I meannnn, wow!, the funniest, most totally radical language, I guess, like in the whole mega gnarly city of Los Angeles? Fer shur-r-r-r!
**Bart Mills**, 'A Glossary of Valspeak', *Guardian*, 1982

# Ignorance
*See also Knowledge; Stupidity.*

**1** What he doesn't know would make a library anybody would be proud of.
**Anon.**

**2** Every now and then you meet a man whose ignorance is encyclopaedic.
**Stanislaw J. Lec**, Polish writer, 1909–66

**3** You know everybody is ignorant, only on different subjects.
**Will Rogers**, quoted in *The New York Times*, 1924

**4** The less I know about a subject, the more confidence I have, and the more new light I throw on it.
**Mark Twain**

## Illness

*See also Cancer; Doctors; Health; Hospitals; Hypochondria; Indigestion; Medicine; Nausea.*

**1** I've got Parkinson's disease. And he's got mine.
**Anon.**

**2** DOCTOR: I don't like the looks of your husband.
WIFE: I don't either, but he's good to the children.
**Joke inside Sainsbury's Christmas cracker, 1984**

**3** To Bary Jade
The bood is beabig brighdly, love;
The sdars are shidig too;
While I ab gazig dreabily,
Add thigkig, love, of you.
You caddot, oh! you caddot kdow,
By darlig, how I biss you –
(Oh, whadt a fearful cold I've got! –
Ck-TISH-u! Ck-ck-TISH-u!)
**Charles Follen Adams,** *Yawcob Strauss and Other Poems,* 1910

**4** LEE-ANN: Anyway, it must be wonderfully healthy, out here in the country. Fewer coronaries.
GAYNOR: Don't knock coronaries. They're all we women have got to guarantee us a prosperous and exciting middle age.
**Malcolm Bradbury and Christopher Bigsby,** *The After Dinner Game,* BBC TV, 1975

**5** I asked him if he had the results of the x-rays. He took me into his surgery . . . He gave me one of those looks of his, redolent of the cemetery, and said that I should buy day-returns from now on instead of season tickets.
**Hugh Leonard,** *A Life,* 1979

**6** One of the minor pleasures of life is to be slightly ill.
**Harold Nicolson,** quoted in the *Observer,* 1950

**7** Illness of any kind is hardly a thing to be encouraged in others. Health is the primary duty of life.
**Oscar Wilde,** *Lady Windermere's Fan,* 1892

## Immigration

*See also Foreigners; Xenophobia.*

**1** Immigration is the sincerest form of flattery.
**Anon.**

**2** RAY LANGTON: You've got to hand it to these foreigners. They come over here with two bob in their pockets and before you can turn around, they've got a chain of hotels and they've nicked all 'us birds.
*Coronation Street,* Granada TV

**3** All the problems we face in the United States today can be traced to an unenlightened immigration policy on the part of the American Indian.
**Pat Paulsen**

**4** Remember always that all of us . . . are descended from immigrants.
**Franklin D. Roosevelt,** quoted in *The New York Times,* 1938

**5** I'm in favor of liberalized immigration because of the effect it would have on restaurants. I'd let just about everybody in except the English.
**Calvin Trillin,** American journalist

## Immortality

*See also Death; Fame.*

**1** If man were immortal, do you realize what his meat bills would be?
**Woody Allen**

**2** I intend to live forever.
So far, so good.
**Steven Wright,** American comic

## Incompatibility

*See also Arguments; Love – Breaking up.*

**1** Temperamentally they go together like port and . . . something that doesn't go with port.
**Nancy Banks Smith,** *Guardian,* 1995

## Indecision

*See also Decisions.*

**1** His indecision is final.
**Anon.**

**2** They call him 'Jigsaw' because every time he's faced with a problem, he goes to pieces.
**Anon.**

**3** . . . decided only to be undecided, resolved to be irresolute, adamant for drift, solid for fluidity, all-powerful to be impotent.
**Winston Churchill**, speech to the House of Commons, attacking the Baldwin government, 1936

**4** Nothing is so exhausting as indecision, and nothing is so futile.
**Bertrand Russell**, *The Conquest of Happiness*, 1930

# India

**1** India is no more a political personality than Europe. India is a geographical term. It is no more a united nation than the equator.
**Winston Churchill**, speech, 1931

**2** 'Sub-' is no idle prefix in its application to this continent.
**P. J. O'Rourke**, 'Foreigners Around the World', *National Lampoon*, 1976

# Indigestion
*See also Eating; Food; Illness.*

**1** I would like to find a stew that will give me heartburn immediately, instead of at three o'clock in the morning.
**John Barrymore**, 1882–1942, American actor

**2** No country can touch us when it comes to heartburn and upset stomachs. This nation, under God, with liberty and justice for all, neutralizes more stomach acid in one day than the Soviet Union does in a year. We give more relief from discomfort of the intestinal tract than China and Japan combined.

They can say what they will about us, but we Americans know what to do with our excess gas.
**Art Buchwald**, 'Acid Indigestion', *Esquire*, 1975

**3** To eat is human, to digest, divine.
**Mark Twain**

# Infatuation
*See also Courtship; Flirtation; Love; Romance; Sexual Attraction.*

**1** There's nothing to be ashamed of. Under this thin veneer of civilisation, we're all savages – man, woman, hopelessly enmeshed. We're on a great toboggan. We can't stop it. We can't steer it. It's too late to run. The beguine has begun.
**George Axelrod and Billy Wilder**, *The Seven Year Itch*, screenplay, 1955

**2** SECRETARY (*to boss*): I do think it was terribly sweet of you to have our initials strip-mined in the Nevada desert, but Mr Hargrave, I already have a boyfriend.
**T. Haggerty**, cartoon in *National Lampoon*, 1984

**3** NILES: I can't get her out of my mind. You probably haven't noticed, but sometimes, just to be near her, I make up silly excuses to come over to your house.
FRASIER: Yes, I began to suspect that when you dropped by yesterday to remind us to always buckle our seat belts.
**Chuck Ranberg and Anne Flett-Giordano**, 'A Mid-Winter Night's Dream', *Frasier*, NBC, 1994

**4** Doris, I think I'm in love with you. I mean, it's crazy. Really crazy! I mean I don't even know if you've read *The Catcher in the Rye*.
**Bernard Slade**, *Same Time, Next Year*, 1978

**5** Infatuation is when you think that he's as sexy as Robert Redford, as smart as Henry Kissinger, as noble as Ralph Nader, as funny as Woody Allen and as athletic as Jimmy Connors. Love is when you realize that he's as sexy as Woody Allen, as smart as Jimmy Connors, as funny as Ralph Nader, as athletic as Henry Kissinger and nothing like Robert Redford – but you'll take him anyway.
**Judith Viorst**, *Redbook*, 1975

**6** I'd be crazy to propose to her, but when I see that profile of hers I feel the only thing worth doing in the world is to grab her and start shouting for clergymen and bridesmaids to come running.
**P. G. Wodehouse**, *Plum Pie*, 1966

# Inferiority

*See also Snobbery.*

**1** I don't know if you'd call it an inferiority complex but I've an exaggerated idea of my own unimportance.
**Anon.**

**2** I have low self-esteem. When we were in bed together, I would fantasize that *I* was someone else.
**Richard Lewis**

**3** No one can make you feel inferior without your consent.
**Eleanor Roosevelt**, *This Is My Story*, 1937

# Infidelity

*See also Bigamy; Divorce; Fidelity; Promiscuity; Sex.*

**1** A man has to do something to relieve the monogamy.
**Anon.**

**2** Executive Mistresses' Influence Mounting in US Boardrooms.
. . . Who is she? The executive mistress, that important figure found standing behind so many top executives and kneeling in front of still more.
   A nationwide survey conducted by *Off The Wall Street Journal* shows that 86 per cent of the senior officers in 65 per cent of the Fortune 500 companies keep a mistress currently, have kept a mistress in the past or intend to find one as soon as they finish reading this article.
*Off The Wall Street Journal*, 1982

**3** 'My executive often arrives at the apartment exhausted and emotionally detached after a hard day of corporate manipulation and chicanery,' says Karen C. (not her real initial). 'He depends on me to raise his lowered interest rate and stimulate his private sector.'
*Off The Wall Street Journal*, 1982

**4** *Off The Wall Street Journal*'s incredibly exhaustive survey of 18,845 exhausted mistresses showed that fully 75 per cent are subject to the same kind of stress, tension and high vulnerability to heart attacks, cancer and suicide suffered by the high-level executives who keep them – as well as amexophobia, the fear of abrupt credit cancellation . . . Surprisingly, more than three quarters of the mistresses surveyed say they find the mistress–executive relationship to be stimulating, honest, emotionally gratifying, financially rewarding and in all ways preferable to marriage, although if the executive offered to marry them they'd grab it in a second.
*Off The Wall Street Journal*, 1982

**5** Once, in a simpler time, mistresses were considered mere playthings, trinkets that a busy executive could enjoy at his leisure, then toss aside like a crumpled Kleenex or generic tissue. Today's mistress is a far different breed. She is better educated, better trained, more assertive and more skilled at her demanding task. Many mistresses have mastered speech, adding an entirely new facet to what was once a one-dimensional relationship.
*Off The Wall Street Journal*, 1982

**6** WENDLE: I'm not a suspicious woman but I don't think my husband 'as been entirely faithful to me.
PELLET: Whatever makes you think that?
WENDLE: My last child doesn't resemble him in the least.
**Noel Coward**, 'Law and Order', *This Year of Grace*, 1928

**7** I told my wife the truth. I told her I was seeing a psychiatrist. Then she told *me* the truth: that she was seeing a psychiatrist, two plumbers and a bartender.
**Rodney Dangerfield**

**8** Stan Waltz has decided to take unto himself a wife but he hasn't decided yet whose . . .
**Peter De Vries**, *Let Me Count the Ways*, 1965

**9** You mustn't think too harshly of my secretaries. They were kind and understanding when I came to the office after a hard day at home.
**Julius J. and Philip G. Epstein**, *Mr Skeffington*, screenplay, 1944

**10** Few things in life are more embarrassing than the necessity of having to inform an old friend that you have just got engaged to his fiancée.
**W. C. Fields**, *Big Money*, 1931

**11** Thou shalt not commit adultery . . .
unless in the mood.
**W. C. Fields**

**12** *A Code of Honor*: never approach a
friend's girlfriend or wife with mischief as
your goal. There are just too many women
in the world to justify that sort of
dishonorable behavior. Unless she's *really*
attractive.
**Bruce Jay Friedman**, 'Sex and the Lonely Guy',
*Esquire*, 1977

**13** The Deacon's wife was a bit desirish
  And liked her sex relations wild,
So she lay with one of the shanty Irish
  And he begot the Deacon's child.
The Deacon himself was a man of
    money
  And upright life and a bosom shirt;
Which made her infidelity funny
  And gave her pleasure in doing him dirt.
And yet for all her romantic sneakin'
  Out the back door and over the wall
How was she sure the child of the
    Deacon
  Wasn't the Deacon's after all?
**Robert Frost**, 'Pride of Ancestry'

**14** The most depressing thing, you know,
*the* most depressing thing is that I used to
feel a certain amount of post-coital tristesse.
Well, guilt. But these days I can scarcely be
bothered to feel shifty when I get home.
Extra-marital sex is as overrated as
premarital sex. And marital sex, come to
think of it.
**Simon Gray**, *Two Sundays*, BBC TV, 1975

**15** I Could Never Have Sex With Any Man
Who Has So Little Regard For My Husband
**Dan Greenburg**, film title

**16** I said to the wife, 'Guess what I heard in
the pub? They reckon the milkman has
made love to every woman in this road
except one.' And she said, 'I'll bet it's that
stuck-up Phyllis at number 23.'
**Max Kauffmann**

**17** Adultery is the application of democracy
to love.
**H. L. Mencken**, *Sententiae*, 1920

**18** An old man of ninety got married,
  The bride was so young and so bold,
In his car they both went
    honeymooning –
  She married the old man for gold.
A year later he was a daddy,
  At ninety he still had the knack;
He took one look at the baby –
  And then gave the chauffeur the sack.
**Max Miller**, 'The Hiking Song', *The Max Miller Blue
Book*, 1975

**19** I discovered my wife in bed with
another man and I was crushed. So I said,
'Get off me, you two!'
**Emo Philips**

**20** Even in civilized mankind faint traces of
monogamous instinct can be perceived.
**Bertrand Russell**, 1872–1970, British philosopher

**21** There was a couple drinking doubles in
a bar. And the waitress goes over and says,
'Miss, your husband just slipped under the
table.'
  And the woman said, 'No, my husband
just walked in the door.'
**Slappy White**

**22** Those who are faithful know only the
trivial side of love: it is the faithless who
know love's tragedies.
**Oscar Wilde**, *The Picture of Dorian Gray*, 1891

**23** Young men want to be faithful, and are
not; old men want to be faithless, and
cannot.
**Oscar Wilde**, *The Picture of Dorian Gray*, 1891

**24** SHELDRAKE: Come on, Fran – don't be
like that. You just going to sit there and
keep bawling? . . .
FRAN: How could I be so stupid? You'd
think I would have learned by now when
you're in love with a married man, you
shouldn't wear mascara.
**Billy Wilder and I. A. L. Diamond**, *The Apartment*,
screenplay, 1960

**25** I've been in love with the same woman
for forty-one years. If my wife finds out,
she'll kill me.
**Henny Youngman**, *Henny Youngman's Greatest One
Liners*, 1970

# Inflation

*See also Economics; Money.*

**1** Among the things that money can't buy is what it used to.
**Max Kauffmann**

**2** Time for belt tightening. You can't live on a million a year anymore.
**Randy Newman**, 1983

**3** Americans are getting stronger. Twenty years ago, it took two people to carry ten dollars' worth of groceries. Today, a five-year-old can do it.
**Henny Youngman**

# Inheritance

*See also Death; Money.*

**1** It is a gorgeous gold pocket watch. I'm proud of it. My grandfather, on his deathbed, sold me this watch.
**Woody Allen**, *The Nightclub Years, 1965–1968*, album, 1972

**2** 'This is the last and solemn Will
Of Uncle William – known as Bill.
I do bequeath, devise and give
By Executive Mandative
The whole amount of what I've got
(It comes to a tremendous lot!)
In seizin to devote upon
My well-beloved nephew John.
(And here the witnesses will sign
Their names upon the dotted line.)'
**Hilaire Belloc**, 'About John', *More Cautionary Tales*, 1930

# Injustice

*See also Crime; Dishonesty; The Law.*

**1** To have a grievance is to have a purpose in life.
**Eric Hoffer**, *The Passionate State of Mind*, 1954

# Insanity

*See also Illness; Paranoia; Psychiatry; Psychoanalysis; Schizophrenia.*

**1** She used to eat chops in the small hours and sleep in a hat. Once she arrived home at seven a.m. carrying a gate. Who am I to say there was anything wrong with her?
**Alan Coren**, *The Sanity Inspector*, 1974

**2** That's the truest sign of insanity – insane people are always sure they're just fine. It's only the sane people who are willing to admit they're crazy.
**Nora Ephron**, *Heartburn*, 1983

**3** There was only one catch and that was *Catch-22*, which specified that a concern for one's own safety in the face of dangers that were real and immediate was the process of a rational mind. Orr was crazy and could be grounded. All he had to do was ask; and as soon as he did, he would no longer be crazy and would have to fly more missions. Orr would be crazy to fly more missions and sane if he didn't, but if he was sane he had to fly them. If he flew them he was crazy and didn't have to; but if he didn't want to he was sane and had to. Yossarian was moved very deeply by the absolute simplicity of this clause of *Catch-22*, and let out a respectful whistle.
**Joseph Heller**, *Catch-22*, 1961

**4** An international team of psychiatrists has flown to Uganda in an attempt to discover exactly what makes General Amin tick. And, more especially, what makes him go cuckoo every half hour.
**Fred Metcalf** for David Frost, *David Frost Revue*, NBC TV, 1972

**5** There's such a fine line between lunacy and insanity.
**Peggy Nicoll**, *The Daria Database*, 1998

**6** PSYCHIATRIST: The idea that all the people locked up in mental hospitals are sane while the people walking about outside are all mad is merely a literary cliché, put about by people who should be locked up. I assure you there's not much in it. Taken as a whole, the sane are out there and the sick are in here. For example, YOU are in here because you have delusions that sane people are put in mental hospitals.
ALEXANDER: But I *am* in a mental hospital.
PSYCHIATRIST: That's what I said.
**Tom Stoppard**, *Every Good Boy Deserves Favour*, 1977

# Insects

*See also Pests.*

**1** I am . . . perfectly willing to share the room with a fly, as long as he is patrolling that portion of the room that I don't occupy. But if he starts that smart-ass fly shit, buzzing my head and repeatedly landing on my arm, he is engaging in high-risk behaviour. That's when I roll up the sports section and become Bwana, the great white fly hunter.
**George Carlin**, *Brain Droppings*, 1997

**2** Ants can carry twenty times their own body weight. Which is useful information if you're moving out and you need help getting a potato chip across town.
**Ron Darian**

**3** It's only when you look at an ant through a magnifying glass on a sunny day that you realize how often they burst into flames.
**Harry Hill**, English comedian

**4** When the insects take over the world, we hope they will remember with gratitude how we took them along on all our picnics.
**Bill Vaughan**

# Insomnia

*See also Bed; Sleep.*

**1** A: How's your insomnia?
B: Worse. I can't even sleep when it's time to get up.
**Anon.**

**2** A good cure for insomnia is to get plenty of sleep.
**W. C. Fields**

**3** When you're lying awake with a dismal headache, and repose is taboo'd by anxiety,
  I conceive you may use any language you choose to indulge in, without impropriety;
  For your brain is on fire – the bedclothes conspire of usual slumber to plunder you:
  First your counterpane goes, and uncovers your toes, and your sheet slips demurely from under you;
  Then the blanketing tickles – you feel like

mixed pickles – so terribly sharp is the pricking,
  And you're hot and you're cross, and you tumble and toss till there's nothing 'twixt you and the ticking.
  Then the bedclothes all creep to the ground in a heap, and you pick 'em all up in a tangle;
  Then your pillow resigns and politely declines to remain at its usual angle!
**W. S. Gilbert**, 'Lord Chancellor', *Iolanthe*, 1882

**4** CHICO MARX: Don't wake him up. He's got insomnia. He's trying to sleep it off.
**George S. Kaufman and Morrie Ryskind**, *A Night at the Opera*, screenplay, 1935

# Insults

*See also Abuse; Bores; Hecklers; Ignorance; Politics – American Presidents; Politics – British Prime Ministers; Politics – Insults; Rogues; Stupidity.*

**1** Excerpts from employee evaluations:
'I would not breed from this employee.'
'He would be out of his depth in a car-park puddle.'
'This man is depriving a village somewhere of an idiot.'
'He has the wisdom of youth and the energy of old age.'
'This young lady has delusions of adequacy.'
'She sets low personal standards and then consistently fails to achieve them.'
'He's a prime candidate for natural deselection.'
'This man must have entered the gene pool while the lifeguard wasn't watching.'
**Anon.**

**2** He's a few peas short of a pod.
He's a sandwich short of a picnic.
She's a couplet short of a sonnet.
He couldn't pour water out of a boot even if the instructions were written on the heel.
His mouth is in gear but his brain is in neutral.
She's knitting with only one needle.
If his IQ were two points higher, he'd be a rock.
Somebody's blown out his pilot light.
He's suffering from Clue Deficit Disorder.
**Anon.**

**3** He's so clumsy, he could trip over a cordless phone.
Anon.

**4** He's so dumb . . .

He thought a quarterback was a refund.
It takes him two hours to watch Sixty Minutes.
At the bottom of the form, where it says, 'Sign Here,' he wrote 'Capricorn.'
He arranged to meet at the corner of 'WALK' and 'DON'T WALK.'
Anon.

**5** If idiots could fly, this place would be an airport.
Anon.

**6** My mother-in-law used to make yoghurt. She would take a bottle of milk and stare at it.
Anon.

**7** My mother-in-law works at Heathrow airport – sniffing luggage.
Anon.

**8** What he lacks in intelligence, he makes up for in stupidity.
Anon.

**9** DES BARNES: The Duckworths are primitive life forms. If you're talking evolution, they're one step above fungus.
*Coronation Street*, Granada TV

**10** ELSIE TANNER: There you go again, Hilda. Lowering the rateable value wherever you go.
*Coronation Street*, Granada TV

**11** Your mother is so dumb, she went cordless bungee-jumping.
*Snaps*, 1994

**12** Your brother is so dumb, he tries to do wheelies on a unicycle.
*Double Snaps*, 1995

**13** Your father is so stupid, he thought fruit punch was a gay boxer.
*Triple Snaps*, 1996

**14** Your mother was so stupid, she thought an IOU was a college.
*Triple Snaps*, 1996

**15** Your father is so dumb, he turned himself in to collect the reward money.
*Snaps 4*, 1998

**16** You're so stupid, when you graduated kindergarten you got so excited you cut yourself shaving.
*Snaps 4*, 1998

**17** Your sister is so dumb, she thinks Chernobyl is Cher's full name.
*Snaps 4*, 1998

**18** If I say that he's extremely stupid, I don't mean that in any derogatory sense. I simply mean that he's not very intelligent. If he were more intelligent, he'd be very clever. But he isn't and there we are.
Alan Bennett, 'The Critics', *On the Margin*, BBC TV, 1966

**19** I said I didn't think Chevy Chase could ad-lib a fart after a baked-bean dinner. I think he took umbrage at that a little bit.
Johnny Carson (Attrib.)

**20** EDMUND: Your brain would make a grain of sand look large and ungainly . . .
Richard Curtis and Rowan Atkinson, 'The Black Seal', *The Black Adder*, BBC TV, 1983

**21** BLACKADDER: . . . 'Look, there's thick George, he's got a brain the size of a weasel's wedding tackle.'
Richard Curtis and Ben Elton, 'Ink and Incapability', *Blackadder the Third*, BBC TV, 1987

**22** BLACKADDER: Your brain's so minute, Baldrick, that if a hungry cannibal cracked your head open, there wouldn't be enough to cover a small water biscuit . . .
Richard Curtis and Ben Elton, 'Captain Cook', *Blackadder Goes Forth*, BBC TV, 1989

**23** A day away from Tallulah is like a month in the country.
Howard Dietz

**24** I won't eat anything that has intelligent life but I would gladly eat a network executive or a politician.
Marty Feldman

**25** He has left his body to science – and science is contesting the will.
David Frost, *Live from London*, 1983

**26** I hope you won't take this amiss, Charles, but I don't think I've ever met a man who reminded me less of Jeremy Irons.
J. B. Handelsman, cartoon in the *New Yorker*, 1984

**27** . . . like being savaged by a dead sheep.
**Denis Healey**, on Geoffrey Howe's attack on his budget, House of Commons, 1978

**28** If his IQ slips any lower, we'll have to water him twice a day.
**Molly Ivins**, of a local Congressman, *Dallas Time-Herald*

**29** I treasure every moment that I do not see her.
**Oscar Levant**, 1906–72, American composer and wit, on Phyllis Diller (Attrib.)

**30** The only gracious way to accept an insult is to ignore it; if you can't ignore it, top it; if you can't top it, laugh at it; if you can't laugh at it, it's probably deserved.
**Russell Lynes**, American writer and critic

**31** He's been called cold, rude, self-centred, arrogant and egotistical. But that's just his family's opinion.
**Bob Monkhouse**, *Just Say a Few Words*, 1988

**32** Make yourself at home, Frank. Hit somebody.
**Don Rickles**, to Frank Sinatra (Attrib.)

**33** Deserves to be preached to death by wild curates.
**Sydney Smith**, *Lady Holland's Memoirs*, 1855

**34** You take the lies out of him, and he'll shrink to the size of your hat; you take the malice out of him and he'll disappear.
**Mark Twain**, *Life on the Mississippi*, 1883

**35** Why do you sit there looking like an envelope without any address on it?
**Mark Twain**

**36** RAM: Didn't you know there's no faggots allowed in this cafeteria?
JASON DEAN: No, but I guess there's an open-door policy on assholes!
**Daniel Waters**, *Heathers*, screenplay, 1989

**37** Ricky turned on the Duke of Dunstable. 'You are without exception the worst tick and bounder that ever got fatty degeneration of the heart through half a century of gorging food and swilling wine wrenched from the lips of a starving proletariat. You make me sick. You poison the air. Good-bye, Uncle Alaric,' said Ricky, drawing himself away rather ostentatiously.

'I think we had better terminate this interview, or I may become brusque.'
**P. G. Wodehouse**, *Uncle Fred in the Springtime*, 1939

**38** The nicest thing I can say about Frances Farmer is that she is unbearable.
**William Wyler** (Attrib.)

# Insurance
*See also Professions.*

**1** I don't want to tell you how much insurance I carry with the Prudential, but all I can say is: when I go, *they* go.
**Jack Benny** (Attrib.)

**2** Insurance, *n.* an ingenious modern game of chance in which the player is permitted to enjoy the comfortable conviction that he is beating the man who keeps the table.
**Ambrose Bierce**, *The Devil's Dictionary*, 1911

**3** . . . the Act of God designation on all insurance policies; which means roughly, that you cannot be insured for the accidents that are most likely to happen to you. If your ox kicks a hole in your neighbour's Maserati, however, indemnity is instantaneous.
**Alan Coren**, *The Lady from Stalingrad Mansions*, 1977

**4** I detest life-insurance agents. They always argue that I shall some day die, which is not so.
**Stephen Leacock**, *Literary Lapses*, 1910

**5** About 10 years ago, the insurance companies discovered that they didn't have all the money in the world and they wanted the rest of it.
**Joe Tuley**, independent pharmacist, on his insurance costs

**6** I took a physical for some life insurance. All they would give me was fire and theft.
**Henny Youngman**

# Intellectuals
*See also Genius; Knowledge; The Mind.*

**1** Lord Birkenhead is very clever, but sometimes his brains go to his head.
**Margot Asquith**

**2** To the man-in-the-street, who, I'm sorry to say,

Is a keen observer of life,
The word 'Intellectual' suggests straight
     away
A man who's untrue to his wife.
**W. H. Auden**, *Collected Shorter Poems, 1927–1957*, 1966

**3** Everyone agreed that Clevinger was
certain to go far in the academic world. In
short, Clevinger was one of those people
with lots of intelligence and no brains, and
everyone knew it except those who soon
found it out.
     In short, he was a dope.
**Joseph Heller**, *Catch-22*, 1961

**4** The learned are seldom pretty fellows,
and in many cases their appearance tends to
discourage a love of study in the young.
**H. L. Mencken**

**5** What is a highbrow? He is a man who has
found something more interesting than
women.
**Edgar Wallace**, *The New York Times*, 1932

**6** People who refer to themselves as
intellectuals are automatically committing a
social crime and, also, usually an error.
**Tracy Young**, *Vanity Fair*, 1984

# Interior Decorating

*See also Do-it-yourself; Home; Style.*

**1** You mean you can actually spend 70,000
dollars at Woolworth's?
**Bob Krasnow**, after seeing Ike and Tina Turner's house

**2** I wanted to buy some carpeting. You
know how much they want for carpeting?
Fifteen dollars a square yard! And I'm sorry,
I'm not going to pay that for carpeting. So
what I did, I bought two square yards, and
when I go home I strap them to my feet.
**Steve Martin**

# Internet

*See also Computers; Modern Life; Technology.*

**1** Give a man a fish and you feed him for a
day. Teach him to use the Net and he won't
bother you for weeks.
**Anon.**

**2** EDUCATION. Picture this scenario: It's
8 p.m. on a weekday night, and your 12-
year-old child suddenly remembers that he
has a major school report on the Spanish-
American War due tomorrow. He needs to
do some research, but the library is closed.
No problem! Your cyber-savvy youngster
simply turns on your computer, activates
your modem, logs on to the Internet – the
revolutionary 'Information Superhighway' –
and, in a matter of minutes, is exchanging
pictures of naked women with other
youngsters all over North America.
**Dave Barry**, *Dave Barry in Cyberspace*, 1996

**3 Dave's FAQ on the Internet**
Q: What, exactly, is the Internet?
A: The Internet is a world-wide network of
university, government, business, and
private computer systems.
Q: Who runs it?
A: A 13-year-old named Jason.
**Dave Barry**, *Dave Barry in Cyberspace*, 1996

**4** . . . Q: What happens on these forums?
A: Well, on the Barry Manilow forum, for
example, fans post messages about how
much they love Barry Manilow, and other
fans respond by posting messages about
how much *they* love Barry Manilow, too.
And then sometimes the forum is invaded
by people posting messages about how
much they *hate* Barry Manilow, which in
turn leads to angry counter-messages and
vicious name-calling that can go on for
*months*.
Q: Just like junior high school!
A: But even more pointless.
**Dave Barry**, *Dave Barry in Cyberspace*, 1996

**5** This Ken Starr report is now posted on
the Internet. I'll bet Clinton's glad he put a
computer in every classroom now.
**Jay Leno**, *The Tonight Show*, NBC TV, 1998

**6** MIKE: You know, I still can't believe we
got away with it . . . Companies never used
to go public until they had established
sound fundamentals – like demonstrated
markets and actual profits. But now, thanks
to an insane new economic order I deplore,
we've overnight acquired wealth that can
only be described as obscene!
KIM: You knew the risks.
MIKE: Spare me the Gen-Y irony, OK? I'm in
pain here!
**Garry Trudeau**, *Doonesbury*, 1999

# Intuition

**1** DIANE: Do you believe in intuition?
WOODIE: No, but I have this strange feeling that someday I will.
*Cheers*, NBC TV

**2** Intuition: that strange instinct that tells a woman she is right, whether she is or not.
*Methodist Recorder*

# Inventions

*See also Modern Life; Technology.*

**1** Who invented the brush they put next to the toilet? That thing hurts!
**Andy Andrews**

**2** We owe a lot to Thomas Edison – if it wasn't for him, we'd be watching television by candlelight.
**Milton Berle**, *Variety*

**3** The guy who invented the first wheel was an idiot. The guy who invented the other three, he was a genius.
**Sid Caesar**

**4** You know, there's a new cloth you can wear in the rain? It gets soaking wet, but you can wear it in the rain!
**Henny Youngman**

# Ireland and the Irish

*See also Britain and the British; Europe and the EEC.*

**1** Other people have a nationality. The Irish and the Jews have a psychosis.
**Brendan Behan**, *Richard's Cork Leg*, 1973

**2** PAT: He was an Anglo-Irishman.
MEG: In the blessed name of God, what's that?
PAT: A Protestant with a horse.
**Brendan Behan**, *The Hostage*, 1959

**3** The English and Americans dislike only *some* Irish – the same Irish that the Irish themselves detest, Irish writers – the ones that *think*.
**Brendan Behan**, *Richard's Cork Leg*, 1973

**4** And if ever ye ride in Ireland,
  The jest may yet be said:
  There is the land of broken hearts,
  And the land of broken heads.
**G K. Chesterton**, *Notes to a Tourist*

**5** We have always found the Irish a bit odd. They refuse to be English.
**Winston Churchill** (Attrib.)

**6** Down with the bold Sinn Fein!
  We'll rout them willy-nilly.
  They flaunt their crimes
  In the *Belfast Times*,
  Which makes us look so silly.
  Down with the Ulster men!
  They don't know which from what.
  If Ireland sunk beneath the sea
  How peaceful everyone would be!
  You haven't said a word about the RUC?
  Down with the whole damn lot!
**Noel Coward**, 'Down with the Whole Damn Lot!', song from *Co-optimists*, 1920s

**7** . . . the Irish behave exactly as they have been portrayed as behaving for years. Charming, soft-voiced, quarrelsome, priest-ridden, feckless and happily devoid of the slightest integrity in our stodgy English sense of the word.
**Noel Coward**, *Diary*, 1960

**8** I never met anyone in Ireland who understood the Irish question, except one Englishman who had only been there a week.
**Major Sir Keith Fraser**, MP, 1919

**9** Order is an exotic in Ireland. It has been imported from England but it will not grow. It suits neither soil nor climate.
**J. A. Froude**, *The Two Chiefs of Dunboy*, 1889

**10** Politics is the chloroform of the Irish people, or, rather, the hashish.
**Oliver St John Gogarty**, *As I Was Going Down Sackville Street*, 1937

**11** The Irish people do not gladly suffer common sense.
**Oliver St John Gogarty**, 1935

**12** Ireland is the old sow that eats her farrow.
**James Joyce**, *A Portrait of the Artist as a Young Man*, 1914

**13** This lovely land that has always sent
  Her writers and artists to banishment
  And in a spirit of Irish fun
  Betrayed her own leaders, one by one . . .

Oh Ireland my first and only love
Where Christ and Caesar are hand in
    glove!
O lovely land where the shamrock
    grows!
(Allow me, ladies, to blow my nose).

**James Joyce**, 'Gas from a Burner', 1912

**14** The problem with Ireland is that it's a country full of genius, but with absolutely no talent.

**Hugh Leonard**, Irish playwright, interview in *The Times*, 1977

**15** Every St Patrick's Day every Irishman goes out to find another Irishman to make a speech to.

**Shane Leslie**, *American Wonderland*, 1936

**16** If, in the eyes of an Irishman, there is anyone being more ridiculous than an Englishman, it is an Englishman who loves Ireland.

**André Maurois**, *Ariel*, 1923

**17** My one claim to originality among Irishmen is that I never made a speech.

**George Moore**, *Ave*, 1911

**18** An Irishman is a guy who:
  Believes everything he can't see, and nothing he can.
  Has such great respect for the truth, he only uses it in emergencies.
  Can lick any man in the house he is sole occupant of.
  Believes salvation can be achieved by means of a weekly envelope.
  . . . we are a very perverse, complex people. It's what makes us lovable. We're banking heavily that God has a sense of humor.

**Jim Murray**, *Los Angeles Times*, 1976

**19** When anyone asks me about the Irish character, I say – look at the trees. Maimed, stark and misshapen, but ferociously tenacious. The Irish have got gab but are too touchy to be humorous. Me too.

**Edna O'Brien**

**20** An Englishman thinks seated; a Frenchman, standing; an American, pacing; an Irishman, afterward.

**Austin O'Malley**, 1898–1932, American writer

**21** The English should give Ireland home rule – and reserve the motion picture rights.

**Will Rogers**, *The Autobiography of Will Rogers*, 1949

**22** [Gladstone] spent his declining years trying to guess the answer to the Irish Question; unfortunately, whenever he was getting warm, the Irish secretly changed the Question . . .

**W. C. Sellar and R. J. Yeatman**, *1066 and All That*, 1930

**23** At last I went to Ireland,
  'Twas raining cats and dogs:
  I found no music in the glens,
  Nor purple in the bogs,
  And as far as angels' laughter in the
      smelly Liffy's tide –
  Well, my Irish daddy said it, but the dear
      old humbug lied.

**George Bernard Shaw**, envoi added to the song 'My Irish Daddy' by Maisie Hurl

**24** The moment the very name of Ireland is mentioned, the English seem to bid adieu to common feeling, common prudence, and common sense, and to act with the barbarity of tyrants, and the fatuity of idiots.

**Sydney Smith**, *Peter Plymley's Letters*, 1929

**25** The Irish are difficult for us to deal with. For one thing the English do not understand their innate love of fighting and blows. If on either side of an Irishman's road to Paradise shillelahs grew, which automatically hit him on the head, yet he would not be satisfied.

**Alfred, Lord Tennyson**, quoted in *Alfred, Lord Tennyson: A Memoir*, 1897

**26** 'Irishmen don't talk like that,' said Gussie. 'Have you read J. M. Synge's *Riders to the Sea*? If you can show me a single character in it who says "faith and begob" I'll give you a shilling. Irishmen are poets. They talk about their souls and mists and so on. They say things like, "An evening like this, it makes me wish I was back in the County Clare, watching the cows in the tall grass."'

**P. G. Wodehouse**, *The Mating Season*, 1949

**27** 'You disapprove of the Swedes?'
  'Yes, sir.'
  'Why?'
  'Their heads are too square, sir.'

'And you disapprove of the Irish?'
'Yes, sir.'
'Why?'
'Because they are Irish, sir.'
**P. G. Wodehouse**, *The Small Bachelor*, 1927

# Israel
*See also Jews.*

**1** If we lose this war, I'll start another in my wife's name.
**Moshe Dayan**, during the Six-day War, 1967

**2** I will tell you that this nation of four million citizens is really an uneasy coalition of four million prime ministers, if not four million self-appointed prophets and messiahs.
**Amos Oz**, 'Israel', *Granta 17*, 1985

# Italy and the Italians
*See also Europe and the EEC; Venice.*

**1** The median Italian . . . is a cowardly baritone who consumes 78.3 kilometres of carbohydrates a month and drives about in a car slightly smaller than he is, looking for a divorce.
**Alan Coren**, *The Sanity Inspector*, 1974

**2** Nobody in Rome works and if it rains in Rome *and* they happen to notice it they blame it on Milan. In Rome people spend most of their time having lunch. And they do it very well – Rome is unquestionably the lunch capital of the world.
**Fran Lebowitz**, *Metropolitan Life*, 1978

**3** She said that all the sights in Rome were called after London cinemas.
**Nancy Mitford**, *Pigeon Pie*, 1940

**4** Very little counts for less in Italy than the state.
**Peter Nichols**, *Italia, Italia*, 1973

**5** By 1948 the Italians had begun to pull themselves together, demonstrating once more their astonishing ability to cope with disaster which is so perfectly balanced by their absolute inability to deal with success.
**Gore Vidal**, *Matters of Fact and Fiction*, 1977

# Japan

**1** Japanese food is very pretty and undoubtedly a suitable cuisine in Japan, which is largely populated by people of below average size. Hostesses hell-bent on serving such food to occidentals would be well advised to supplement it with something more substantial and to keep in mind that almost everybody likes French fries.
**Fran Lebowitz**, *Metropolitan Life*, 1978

**2** Japanese Prime Minister Tomiichi Murayama apologized for Japan's part in World War II. However, he still hasn't mentioned anything about karaoke.
**David Letterman**, *The Late Show*, CBS

# Jazz

*See also Music and Musicians; Rock 'n' Roll; Songs and Singers.*

**1** If you have to ask what jazz, is, you'll never know.
**Louis Armstrong**

**2** Jazz . . . was illiterate, instinctual, impulsive, aleatoric, unscorable, unpredictable – therein lay its charm.
**Anthony Burgess**, 'The Weasels of Pop', *Punch*, 1967

**3** Thus it came to pass that jazz multiplied all over the face of the earth and the wriggling of bottoms was tremendous.
**Peter Clayton and Peter Gammond**, *14 Miles on a Clear Night*, 1966

**4** Playing 'bop' is like playing scrabble with all the vowels missing.
**Duke Ellington**, *Look*, 1954

**5** If you're in jazz and more than ten people like you, you're labelled 'commercial'.
**Wally Stott**, English musician

# Jealousy

**1** The dullard's envy of brilliant men is always assuaged by the suspicion that they will come to a bad end.
**Max Beerbohm**, *Zuleika Dobson*, 1911

**2** Calamities are of two kinds: misfortune to ourselves and good fortune to others.
**Ambrose Bierce**, *The Devil's Dictionary*, 1911

**3** Never be possessive. If a female friend lets on that she is going out with another man, be kind and understanding. If she says she would like to go out with all the Dallas Cowboys, including the coaching staff, the same rule applies. Tell her: 'Kath, you just go right ahead and do what you feel is right.' Unless you actually care for her, in which case you must see to it that she has no male contact whatsoever.
**Bruce Jay Friedman**, 'Sex and the Lonely Guy', *Esquire*, 1977

**4** . . . he made the even more serious mistake of welcoming envy into his heart, instead of going on pretending, as is sensible and usual, that he hadn't noticed it was there. It was a demanding and time-consuming guest . . . He envied television announcers, disc-jockeys, sprinters and politicians. He envied Mick Jagger and Herbert von Karajan and Andrew Lloyd Webber and Stockhausen and the panel of *Any Questions* . . . He didn't have a clue who Barry Sheene was, but he envied him. His envy was rapacious and did not discriminate on the grounds of race, colour, creed, age or sex. It simply hurt more if the object were his age, male and Jewish. If he also knew him personally it was agony.
**Howard Jacobson**, *Coming from Behind*, 1983

**5** Few of us can stand prosperity – another man's, I mean.
**Mark Twain**

**6** Anybody can sympathize with the sufferings of a friend, but it requires a very fine nature to sympathize with a friend's success.
**Oscar Wilde**, 'The Soul of Man under Socialism', 1891

**7** He was a man of strong passions, and the green-eyed monster ran up his leg and bit him to the bone.
**P. G. Wodehouse**, *Full Moon*, 1947

# Jesus Christ
*See also Belief; The Bible; Christianity; The Church; God; Heaven; Religion.*

**1** Jesus Is Coming! Everybody look busy!
**Anon.**

**2** Jesus Loves Me But He Can't Stand You.
**Song**, Texas Lounge Lizards

**3** No one ever made more trouble than the 'gentle Jesus meek and mild'.
**James M. Gillis**, *This Our Day*

**4** Prove to me that you're no fool.
Walk across my swimming pool.
**Tim Rice**, *Jesus Christ Superstar*, 1971

# Jews
*See also Israel.*

**1** How odd
of God
To choose
the Jews.
**Anon.**

**2** Not odd
of God.
Goyim
Annoy'im.
**Leo Rosten**

**3** Q: Why do Jews answer a question with a question?
A: Why shouldn't Jews answer a question with a question?
**Anon.**

**4 How to explain the three main groups within the Jewish faith:**
If you go to an orthodox wedding, the mother of the bride is pregnant.
If you go to a conservative wedding, the bride is pregnant.
And if you go to a reform wedding? The rabbi is pregnant.
**Anon.**

**5** . . . I landed at Orly airport and discovered my luggage wasn't on the same plane. My bags were finally traced to Israel where they were opened and all my trousers were altered.
**Woody Allen**, *Esquire*, 1975

**6** I was raised in the Jewish tradition, taught never to marry a Gentile woman, shave on Saturday and, most especially, never to shave a Gentile woman on Saturday.
**Woody Allen,** *Esquire,* 1975

**7** We were married by a reformed rabbi in Long Island. A *very* reformed rabbi. A Nazi.
**Woody Allen,** *The Nightclub Years, 1964–1968,* album, 1972

**8** A Jewish grandmother is watching her grandchild playing on the beach when a huge wave comes and takes him out to sea. She pleads, 'Please, God, save my only grandson! Bring him back!' And a big wave comes and washes the boy back onto the beach, good as new.

She looks up to Heaven and says, 'He had a hat!'
**Myron Cohen**

**9** Mr Deasy halted, breathing hard and swallowing his breath.

– I just wanted to say, he said. Ireland, they say, has the honour of being the only country which never persecuted the jews. Do you know that? No. And do you know why?

He frowned sternly on the bright air.

– Why sir? Stephen asked, beginning to smile.

– Because she never let them in, Mr Deasy said solemnly.
**James Joyce,** *Ulysses,* 1922

**10** If you ever forget you're a Jew, a gentile will remind you.
**Bernard Malamud**

**11** Q: What is a Jewish grandmother's favourite nine-letter word?
A: 'Eateateat!'
**Bob Monkhouse,** *Just Say a Few Words,* 1988

**12** The Jewish man with parents alive is a fifteen-year-old boy and will remain a fifteen-year-old boy till they die.
**Philip Roth,** *Portnoy's Complaint,* 1969

**13** I belong to a Reform congregation – we're called Jews R Us.
**Dennis Wolfberg**

**14** My father is a German Jew and my mother is a French Jew. So that makes me – just really lucky to be here.
**Jackie Wollner**

**15** Why do Jewish divorces cost so much? They're worth it.
**Henny Youngmann**

# Jingoism

*See also Patriotism; Xenophobia.*

**1** He majored in English history, which was a mistake.

'*English* history!' roared the silver-maned senior Senator from his state indignantly. 'What's the matter with American history? American history is as good as any history in the world!'
**Joseph Heller,** *Catch-22,* 1961

# Journalism

*See also News; Newspapers; Writing.*

**1** Anyone Here Been Raped and Speaks English?
**Edward Behr,** book title, 1978; inspired by an incident at an airport in the Congo, when a British TV reporter allegedly approached groups of Belgian refugees fleeing from rebel troops with this question

**2** Journalism largely consists in saying 'Lord Jones Dead' to people who never knew Lord Jones was alive.
**G. K. Chesterton,** *The Wisdom of Father Brown,* 1914

**3** . . . adjectives do most of the work, smuggling in actual information under the guise of normal journalism. Thus the use of soft-spoken (mousy), loyal (dumb), high-minded (inept), hardworking (plodding), self-made (crooked), and pragmatic (totally immoral).
**John Leo,** 'Journalese for the Lay Reader', *Time,* 1985

**4** Cronyism is the curse of journalism. After many years I have reached the firm conclusion that it is impossible for any objective newspaperman to be a friend of a President.
**Walter Lippmann,** 1889–1974, American political commentator

**5** The art of newspaper paragraphing is to

stroke a platitude until it purrs like an
epigram.
**Don Marquis**, quoted in *O Rare Don Marquis*, by
E. Anthony, 1962

**6** I once thought of becoming a political
cartoonist because they only have to come
up with one idea a day. Then I thought I'd
become a sportswriter instead, because they
don't have to come up with any.
**Sam Snead**, golfer

**7** A foreign correspondent is someone who
lives in foreign parts and corresponds,
usually in the form of essays containing no
new facts. Otherwise he's someone who flies
around from hotel to hotel and thinks that
the most interesting thing about any story
is the fact that he has arrived to cover it.
**Tom Stoppard**, *Night and Day*, 1978

**8** RUTH: Perhaps I'll get him a reporter doll
for Christmas. Wind it up and it gets it
wrong. What does it say when you press its
stomach? Come on, Dick!
DICK: I name the guilty man.
**Tom Stoppard**, *Night and Day*, 1978

**9** There are only two forces that can carry
light to all corners of the globe – the sun in
the heavens and the Associated Press.
**Mark Twain**, speech to the Annual Dinner of the
Associated Press, New York, 1906

**10** The public have an insatiable curiosity
to know everything. Except what is worth
knowing. Journalism, conscious of this, and
having tradesman-like habits, supplies their
demands.
**Oscar Wilde**, 'The Soul of Man under Socialism', 1891

**11** With regard to modern journalists, they
always apologize to one in private for what
they have written against one in public.
**Oscar Wilde**, 'The Soul of Man under Socialism', 1891

**12** You cannot hope
    to bribe or twist,
    thank God! the
    British journalist.
    But, seeing what
    the man will do
    unbribed, there's
    no occasion to.
**Humbert Wolfe**, 'Over the Fire', *The Uncelestial City*

# Kidnapping

*See also Crime; The Law.*

**1** When I was kidnapped, my parents snapped into action. They rented out my room.
**Woody Allen**

# Kissing

*See also Courtship; Flirtation; Love; Petting; Sex.*

**1** She frowned and called him Mr.
Because in sport he kr.
And so in spite
That very nite
This Mr. kr. sr.
**Anon.**

**2** Her kisses left something to be desired – the rest of her.
**Anon.**

**3** It takes a lot of experience for a girl to kiss like a beginner.
*Ladies' Home Journal*, 1948

**4** A delectable gal from Augusta
vowed that nobody ever had bussed her.
But an expert from France
took a bilingual chance
and the mixture of tongues quite
nonplussed her.
**Conrad Aiken**, *A Seizure of Limericks*, 1965

**5** If you want to kiss me any time during the evening, Nick, just let me know and I'll be glad to arrange it for you. Just mention my name.
**F. Scott Ftizgerald**, *The Great Gatsby*, 1925

**6** It's even better when you help.
**Ernest Hemingway, Jules Furthman and William Faulkner**, *To Have and Have Not*, Lauren Bacall to Humphrey Bogart, 1944

**7** I don't know how to kiss or I would kiss you. Where do the noses go?
**Ernest Hemingway and Dudley Nichols**, *For Whom the Bell Tolls*, Ingrid Bergman to Gary Cooper, 1943

**8** Frankly, my child, I had a sudden, powerful and very ignoble desire to kiss you till your lips were somewhat bruised.
**F. Hugh Herbert**, *The Moon is Blue*, David Niven to Maggie McNamara, 1953

**9** . . . we did one of those quick, awkward

kisses where each of you gets a nose in the eye.
**Clive James**, *Unreliable Memoirs*, 1980

# Knowledge

*See also Facts; Ignorance.*

**1** Strange how much you've got to know,
Before you know how little you know.
**Anon.**

**2** I'm not young enough to know everything.
**J. M. Barrie**, *The Admirable Crichton*, 1902

**3** It ain't what a man don't know that makes him a fool, but what he does know that ain't so.
**Josh Billings**, *The Complete Works of Josh Billings*, 1919

**4** It is not generally known (ie, I have just found out) that . . .
**Alan Coren**, *A Bit on the Side*, 1995

**5** We are here and it is now. Further than that, all human knowledge is moonshine.
**H. L. Mencken**

**6** I am sufficiently proud of my knowing something to be modest about my not knowing everything.
**Vladimir Nabokov**, *Lolita*, 1955

**7** He not only overflowed with learning, but stood in the slop.
**Sidney Smith**, 1771–1845, clergyman and wit

**8** There are only two kinds of people who are really fascinating – people who know absolutely everything, and people who know absolutely nothing.
**Oscar Wilde**, *The Picture of Dorian Gray*, 1891

# Labour Party, The

*See also The Conservative Party; The Liberal Party; Socialism; Trade Unions.*

**1** The Labour Party Marxists see the consequences of their own folly all around them and call it the collapse of capitalism.
**Jon Akass**, *Sun*, 1976

**2** . . . that bunch of rootless intellectuals, alien Jews and international pederasts who call themselves the Labour Party.
**Alan Bennett**, *Forty Years On*, 1968

**3** They are not fit to manage a whelk stall.
**Winston Churchill** (Attrib.)

**4** I do not often attack the Labour Party. They do it so well themselves.
**Edward Heath**, speech, 1973

**5** It must never be forgotten that, whatever they say, the things that divide the [Labour] party are much greater than the things that unite it.
**Frank Johnson**, *The Times*, 1981

**6** . . . reminding us . . . of the Labour Party's enduring commitment to resentment and the general, surly feeling that we are always being done by anyone in the remotest position of authority.
**Frank Johnson**, *The Times*, 1984

**7** [Minister of Technology, Anthony Wedgwood] Benn flung himself into the Sixties technology with the enthusiasm (not to say language) of a newly enrolled Boy Scout demonstrating knot-tying to his indulgent parents.
**Bernard Levin**, *The Pendulum Years*, 1970

**8** The 1984 Labour Party conference last night exceeded its wildest expectations of its traditionally wild behaviour. In a pent-up frenzy of balloting . . . it managed to vote against everything in sight. This has long been the position of many of the comrades where real life is concerned. But it has never been official party policy up to now, the preferred compromise being to vote in favour of conflicting things.
**Michael White**, *Guardian*, 1984

**9** The Labour Party is like a stage-coach. If you rattle along at great speed, everybody inside is too exhilarated or too seasick to cause any trouble. But if you stop, everybody gets out and argues about where to go next.

**Harold Wilson**, quoted in *Harold Wilson, The Authentic Portrait*

### Aneurin (Nye) Bevan (Minister of Health, 1945–1951)

**1** If thy Nye offend thee, pluck it out.
**Clement Attlee**, speech to the Labour NEC, 1955

**2** He will be as great a curse to this country in peace as he was a squalid nuisance in time of war.
**Winston Churchill**, speech in the House of Commons, 1945

**3** He enjoys prophesying the imminent end of the capitalist system and is prepared to play a part, any part, in its burial except that of a mute.
**Harold Macmillan** (Attrib.)

### Stafford Cripps (President of the Board of Trade and Chancellor of the Exchequer, 1945–1950)

**1** Sir Stafford has a brilliant mind until it is made up.
**Margot Asquith** (Attrib.)

**2** Neither of his colleagues can compare with him in that acuteness and energy of mind with which he devotes himself to so many topics injurious to the strength and welfare of the state.
**Winston Churchill**, speech in the House of Commons, 1946

### Hugh Gaitskill (Party Leader, 1955–1963)

**1** . . . a desiccated calculating machine.
**Aneurin Bevan** (Attrib.)

## Language

*See also Clichés; The English Language; Grammar; Idioms; Pronunciation.*

**1** Remember, double negatives are a complete no-no.
**Anon.**

**2** TEACHER: Although a double negative is taken to mean an affirmative, a double affirmative is never taken to mean a negative.
STUDENT: Yeah, right!
**Anon.**

**3** BROOKS (*as 2,000-year-old man*): We spoke Rock. Basic Rock . . . Two hundred years before Hebrew, there was the Rock Language. Or Rock talk.
REINER (*as interviewer*): Could you give us an example of that?
BROOKS: Yes. 'Hey, don't throw that rock at me! What are you doing with that rock? Put down that rock!'
**Mel Brooks and Carl Reiner**, *The 2,000-year-old Man*

**4** Everybody has a right to pronounce foreign names as he chooses.
**Winston Churchill** (Attrib.)

**5** *Watt* is the lightest of colors: 'Yew look watt as a sheet.'
*Pour* is having little or no means of support: 'Them folks is downriot pour.'
*Ward* is a unit of language: 'Pardon me, could ah have a ward with yawl?'
*Owe* is an overwhelming feeling of reverence: 'There's one thing I stand in owe of.'
And *Thank*: 'Ah hope yawl enjoyed raidin' this book. But just thank of what yew must sound lack to a Texan.'
**Jim Everhart**, *The Illustrated Texas Dictionary*

**6** The word 'meaningful' when used today is nearly always meaningless.
**Paul Johnson**, *Observer*, 1982

**7** SON: Mother, I've got something to tell you. I've just met the most wonderful girl. We love each other and we're going to get married.
MOTHER: Mama mia! What you saying? Ain't I been a gudda mudder to you, my leedle bambino? Doan I givva you lasagna, manicotti, spaghetti, ricotto, antipasto? Why you wanna doa dis to me? You no luvva me?
SON: Mother, you can't speak to me like this.
MOTHER: Why canna I speaka dissa way to you? Ain't I youa mudda?
SON: Mother, you can't speak to me like this because you're not Italian.
**Max Kauffmann**

**8** Listen, someone's screaming in agony – fortunately I speak it fluently.
**Spike Milligan**, *The Goon Show*, BBC Radio, 1959

**9** Man invented language to satisfy his deep need to complain.
**Lily Tomlin**

## Last Words

*See also Death.*

**1** Die, my dear doctor? That's the last thing I shall do.
**Lord Palmerston** (Attrib.), 1865

**2** If this is dying, I don't think much of it.
**Lytton Strachey** (Attrib.), 1932

**3** Either they go, or I do.
**Oscar Wilde**, of his new bedroom curtains (Attrib.), 1900

## Laughter

*See also Comedy; Humour; Smiles.*

**1** Laughter is the sensation of feeling good all over, and showing it principally in one spot.
**Josh Billings**, *The Complete Works of Josh Billings*, 1919

**2** I suppose one of the reasons why I grew up feeling the need to cause laughter was perpetual fear of being its unwitting object.
**Clive James**, *Unreliable Memoirs*, 1980

**3** . . . no victims dare complain lest they be accused of having no sense of humor, the worst charge that can be levelled against an American citizen.
   . . . the funniest line in English is 'Get it?' When you say that, everyone chortles.
**Garrison Keillor**, 'Introduction', *We Are Still Married*, 1989

**4** One horse-laugh is worth ten thousand syllogisms. It is not only more effective; it is also vastly more intelligent.
**H. L. Mencken**, *Prejudices*, Fourth Series, 1924

**5** He who laughs, lasts.
**Mary Pettibone Poole**, 'A Glass Eye at the Keyhole'

**6** Aunt Dahlia guffawed more liberally than I had ever heard a woman guffaw. If there had been an aisle, she would have rolled in it . . . She was giving the impression of a hyena which had just heard a good one from another hyena.
**P. G. Wodehouse**, *Much Obliged, Jeeves*, 1971

**7** Madeline Bassett laughed the tinkling, silvery laugh which was one of the things that had got her so disliked by the better element.
**P. G. Wodehouse**, *The Code of the Woosters*, 1938

**8** She had a penetrating sort of laugh. Rather like a train going into a tunnel.
**P. G. Wodehouse**, *The Inimitable Jeeves*, 1923

## Law, The

*See also Crime; Injustice; Law and Order; Lawyers and the Law; Police.*

**1** COUNSEL: Have you any idea what your defence is going to be?
DEFENDANT: Well, I didn't do it, sir.
COUNSEL: Yes, well, er, I think we can afford to fill that out a little. It's not in itself a cast-iron defence.
DEFENDANT: Well I didn't do it, sir! I didn't do it! And if I did it, may God strike me dead on the spot, sir!
COUNSEL: Well, we'll just give him a moment shall we . . .
**Alan Bennett**, 'The Defending Counsel', *On the Margin*, BBC TV, 1966

**2** COUNSEL: I shall of course try to discredit the character of widow Coddington. I notice she's got a Polish lodger which, in the eyes of the law, is synonymous with moral laxity. It hasn't yet been made statutory.
**Alan Bennett**, 'The Defending Counsel', *On the Margin*, BBC TV, 1966

**3** It is illegal to make liquor privately or water publicly.
**Lord Birkett** (Attrib.)

**4** . . . all in all I'd rather have been a judge than a miner. And what is more, being a miner, as soon as you are too old and tired and sick and stupid to do the job properly, you have to go. Well, the very opposite applies with the judges.
**Peter Cook**, 'Sitting on a Bench', nightclub act, 1960s

**5** LAWYER (*to judge*): And as a precedent,

your honor, I offer a Perry Mason case first televised four years ago in which . . .
**Chon Day**, *DAC News*, cartoon, 1969

**6** A jury consists of twelve persons chosen to decide who has the better lawyer.
**Robert Frost**, 1874–1963, American poet (Attrib.)

**7** DEFENDANT: I don't recognize this court!
JUDGE: Why not?
DEFENDANT: You've had it decorated!
**Eric Morecambe and Ernie Wise**, *The Morecambe and Wise Joke Book*, 1979

**8** I don't want a lawyer to tell me what I cannot do; I hired him to tell me how to do what I want to do.
**J. Pierpont Morgan**, 1837–1913, American financier and philanthropist

**9** MORGENHALL: . . . if they ever give you a brief, old fellow, attack the medical evidence. Remember, the jury's full of rheumatism and arthritis and shocking gastric troubles. They love to see a medical man put through it.
**John Mortimer**, *The Dock Brief*, 1958

**10** No brilliance is needed in the law. Nothing but common sense, and relatively clean fingernails.
**John Mortimer**, *A Voyage Round My Father*, screenplay, 1972

**11** . . . I don't think you can make a lawyer honest by an act of legislature. You've got to work on his conscience. And his lack of conscience is what makes him a lawyer.
**Will Rogers**, 1927

**12** For certain people, after fifty, litigation takes the place of sex.
**Gore Vidal**, *Evening Standard*, 1981

**13** JUDGE: Don't take that 'judge not, lest ye be judged' line with *me*, young man.
**Gahan Wilson**, *The Weird World of Gahan Wilson*, cartoon, 1975

**14** That's what comes of being a solicitor, it saps the vital juices. Johnny doesn't even embezzle his clients' money, which I should have thought was about the only fun a solicitor can get out of life.
**P. G. Wodehouse**, *Ice in the Bedroom*, 1961

# Law and Order

*See also Crime; The Law; Lawyers and the Law; Police.*

**1** Law and Order is like patriotism – anyone who comes on strong about patriotism has got something to hide; it never fails. They always turn out to be a crook or an asshole or a traitor or something.
**Bill Mauldin**

**2** Distrust all in whom the impulse to punish is powerful.
**Friedrich Wilhelm Nietzsche**, *Thus Spoke Zarathustra*, 1883–92

# Laws

*See also Truth.*

**1** *Murphy's Law*: If anything can go wrong, it will.
*O'Toole's Commentary on Murphy's Law*: Murphy was an optimist.
*Harper's Magazine Law*: You never find an article until you replace it.
*Law of Selective Gravity*: An object will fall so as to do the most damage.
*Jenning's Corollary*: The chance of bread falling with the buttered side up is directly proportional to the cost of the carpet.
*Klipstein's Corollary*: The most delicate component will be the one to drop.
**Arthur Bloch**, *Murphy's Law and Other Reasons Why Things Go Wrong*, 1977

**2** The Peter Principle: In a hierarchy every employee tends to rise to his level of incompetence.
**Dr Laurence J. Peter**, *The Peter Principle*, 1969

# Lawyers and the Law

*See also Crime; The Law.*

**1** Did you hear about the terrorist who hijacked a 747 full of lawyers? He threatened to release one every hour until his demands were met.
**Anon.**

**2** Pride comes before a fall – compensation comes after.
**Anon.**

**3** Q: What do you have when a lawyer is buried up to his neck in wet cement?

A: Not enough cement.
**Anon.**

**4** Why Experiment on Animals With So Many Lawyers Out There?
**Bumper sticker,** Key West, 1997

**5** LAWYER: To save the state the expense of a trial, Your Honor, my client has escaped.
**Chon Day,** cartoon

**6** One of the things I like most about lawyers is the big shock absorber they have strapped to their brains. Put it this way, if a lawyer's ego was hit by lightning, the lightning would be hospitalised.
**Kathy Lette,** Altar Ego, 1998

**7** Juries scare me. I don't want to put my faith in twelve people who weren't smart enough to get out of jury duty.
**Monica Piper**

**8** 99% of lawyers give the rest a bad name.
**Steven Wright,** American comic

## Laziness
*See also Work.*

**1** As a boy, he swallowed a teaspoon. And he hasn't stirred since.
**Anon.**

**2** His idea of roughing it is to turn his electric blanket down to Medium.
**Anon.**

**3** I've found a great way to start the day – I go straight back to bed!
**Anon.**

**4** He works 8 hours a day and sleeps 8 hours a day – the same 8 hours.
**Milton Berle**

**5** Lazy? He used to ride his bike over cobblestones to knock the ash off his ciggie.
**Les Dawson,** The Les Dawson Joke Book, 1979

**6** My husband has always felt that marriage and a career don't mix; that's why he's never worked.
**Phyllis Diller**

**7** The laziest man I ever met put popcorn in his pancakes so they would turn over by themselves.
**W. C. Fields** (Attrib.)

**8** It is impossible to enjoy idling thoroughly unless one has plenty of work to do.
**Jerome K. Jerome,** Idle Thoughts of an Idle Fellow, 1886

**9** Well, we can't stand around here doing nothing, people will think we're workmen.
**Spike Milligan,** The Goon Show, BBC Radio, 1959

**10** It is better to have loafed and lost than never to have loafed at all.
**James Thurber,** Fables for Our Time, 1943

**11** Hard work pays off in the future. Laziness pays off now.
**Steven Wright,** American comic

## Leadership
*See also Bosses; Politics – The American Presidency; Victory and Defeat.*

**1** A political leader must keep looking over his shoulder all the time to see if the boys are still there. If they aren't still there, he's no longer a political leader.
**Bernard Baruch,** 1870–1965, American businessman and statesman

**2** In enterprise of martial kind
  When there was any fighting,
  He led his regiment from behind –
  He found it less exciting.
  But when away his regiment ran,
  His place was at the fore, O –
  That celebrated,
  Cultivated,
  Underrated
  Nobleman, The Duke of Plaza-Toro!
**W. S. Gilbert,** 'The Duke of Plaza-Toro', The Gondoliers, 1889

**3** I must follow them. I am their leader.
**Andrew Bonar Law,** Conservative Prime Minister, 1922–3 (Attrib.)

## Legs
*See also The Body; Footwear.*

**1** – Her legs are without equal.
– You mean they know no parallel.
**Anon.**

**2** He told her her stockings were wrinkled. Trouble was, she wasn't wearing any.
**Anon.**

**3** GERALD: I have heard it said that her legs leave something to be desired.
LADY D: All legs leave something to be desired, do they not. That is part of their functions and all of their charm.
**Alan Bennett**, *Forty Years On*, 1968

# Letters

*See also Communication; Greetings Cards; Mail; Writers; Writing.*

**1** The great secret in life . . . not to open your letters for a fortnight. At the expiration of that period you will find that nearly all of them have answered themselves.
**Arthur Binstead**, *Pitcher's Proverbs*, 1909

**2** I found a letter to my sister the other day that I had forgotten to mail.
It just needed a little updating to send. After 'the baby is . . .' I crossed out 'toilet trained' and wrote in 'graduating from high school this month'.
**Erma Bombeck**, *If Life is a Bowl of Cherries – What am I Doing in the Pits?*, 1978

**3** He's a distinguished man of letters. He works for the Post Office.
**Max Kauffmann**

**4** Such a sweet gift – a piece of handmade writing, in an envelope that is not a bill, sitting in our friend's path when she trudges home from a long day spent among wahoos and savages, a day our words will help repair. They don't need to be immortal, just sincere. She can read them twice and again tomorrow.
**Garrison Keillor**, 'How To Write a Letter', *We Are Still Married*, 1989

**5** To the Editor of *The Times*
Sir,
I have just written you a long letter.
On reading it over, I have thrown it into the wastepaper basket.
Hoping this will meet with your approval.
I am
Sir
Your obedient servant
**Lt. Col. A. D. Wintle**, unpublished letter to *The Times*, 1946

**6** What a girl! He had never in his life before met a woman who could write a letter without a postscript, and this was but the smallest of her unusual gifts.
**P. G. Wodehouse**, *A Damsel in Distress*, 1919

# Liberal Party, The

*See also The Conservative Party; The Labour Party; Liberals; Liberals and Conservatives; Parliament; Politics and Politicians.*

**1** Basically the Liberal Party is divided between wispy beards and others. Wispy beards . . . wear T-shirts with slogans on, usually faintly dated, e.g. 'The Only Safe Fast Breeder is a Rabbit'. They tend to have ill-fitting jeans, and those heavy shoes which look like Cornish pasties. They have briefcases stuffed with documents, chiefly about community politics, nuclear power and ecology. They drink real ale.
**Simon Hoggart**, *On The House*, 1981

**2** As usual the Liberals offer a mixture of sound and original ideas. Unfortunately, none of the sound ideas is original and none of the original ideas is sound.
**Harold Macmillan**, British Conservative Prime Minister, 1957–63 speech, 1961

**3** . . . the small troupe of exhibitionists, failed vaudeville artists, juicy young Boy Scouts and degenerate old voluptuaries which is the Liberal Party.
**Auberon Waugh**, *Private Eye*

# Liberals

*See also The Liberal Party; Liberals and Conservatives; Politics and Politicians.*

**1** A liberal is a conservative who's been mugged by reality.
**Anon.**

**2** The liberals can understand everything but people who don't understand them.
**Anon.**

**3** GOOD: You know what they say; if God had been a liberal, we wouldn't have had the ten commandments. We'd have the ten suggestions.
**Malcolm Bradbury and Christopher Bigsby**, *The After Dinner Game*, BBC TV, 1975

**4** You liberals think that goats are just sheep from broken homes.
**Malcolm Bradbury and Christopher Bigsby**, *The After Dinner Game*, BBC TV, 1975

**5** A liberal is a man who leaves the room when a fight begins.
**Heywood Broun**, 1888–1939, American journalist

**6** What the liberal really wants is to bring about change which will not in any way endanger his position.
**Stokely Carmichael**, American Black Power leader, 1941–98

**7** A liberal is a man too broadminded to take his own side in a quarrel.
**Robert Frost**, 1874–1963, American poet

**8** A rich man told me recently that a liberal is a man who tells other people what to do with their money.
**LeRoi Jones**, *Home*, 1966

**9** So much of left-wing thought is a kind of playing with fire by people who don't even know that fire is hot.
**George Orwell**

**10** I can remember way back when a liberal was one who was generous with his own money.
**Will Rogers**

**11** Liberals are variously described as limousine, double-domed, screaming, knee-jerk, professional and 'bleeding heart'.
**William Safire**, *The New Language of Politics*, 1968

**12** It is easy for the Liberals to say that something should be done on a bigger scale. They never have to do these things.
**Patrick Gordon Walker**, Labour Minister, 1967

## Liberals and Conservatives

*See also Conservatives; Democrats and Republicans; Political Parties.*

**1** A conservative believes in the present what liberals forced on the world in the past.
**Anon.**

**2** I said to my Liberal friend that we are fundamentally the same. I spend money like it's my money and you spend money like it's my money.
**Richard K. Armey**, Republican Congressman, 'Firing Line', *PBS*, 1990

**3** Conservative, *n.* a statesman who is enamoured of existing evils, as distinguished from the Liberal, who wishes to replace them with others.
**Ambrose Bierce**, *The Devil's Dictionary*, 1911

**4** If you're not a liberal at twenty you have no heart, and if you're not a conservative at forty, you have no head.
**Winston Churchill**

**5** A radical is a man with both feet firmly planted – in the air. A conservative is a man with two perfectly good legs who, however, has never learned to walk forward.
**Franklin D. Roosevelt**, radio address, 1939

**6** The radical invents the views. When he has worn them out, the conservative adopts them.
**Mark Twain** (Attrib.)

## Liberty

*See also Democracy.*

**1** Oh Liberty! What liberties are taken in thy name!
**Anon.**

**2** It's not the liberties we have but the liberties we take that cause all the trouble.
**Anon.**

**3** Liberty means responsibility. That is why most men dread it.
**George Bernard Shaw**, *Maxims for Revolutionists*, 1903

**4** My definition of a free society is a society where it is safe to be unpopular.
**Adlai Stevenson**, speech in Detroit, 1952

## Lies

*See also Dishonesty; Truth.*

**1** Matilda told such Dreadful Lies,
It made one Gasp and Stretch one's Eyes;
Her Aunt, who, from her Earliest Youth,
Had kept a Strict Regard for Truth,
Attempted to Believe Matilda:

The effort very nearly killed her.
**Hilaire Belloc,** 'Matilda', *Cautionary Tales for Children,* 1907

**2** A lie can be half-way round the world before the truth has got its boots on.
**James Callaghan,** quoted in *The Times,* 1976

**3** There is a great deal of hard lying in the world; especially among people whose characters are above suspicion.
**Benjamin Jowett,** 1817–93, English classicist (Attrib.)

**4** Women have a hard enough time in this world; telling them the truth would be too cruel.
**H. L. Mencken**

**5** They say that George Washington could never tell a lie. My wife can. As soon as she hears it.
**Bob Monkhouse,** *Just Say a Few Words,* 1988

**6** How does a person get to be a capable
　　liar?
　That is something that I respectfully
　　inquiar,
　Because I don't believe a person will ever
　　set the world on fire
　Unless they are a capable lire.
**Ogden Nash,** 'Golly, How Truth Will Out!', *The Face is Familiar,* 1940

**7** A little inaccuracy sometimes saves tons of explanation.
**Saki (H. H. Munro),** *The Square Egg,* 1924

**8** A lie is an abomination unto the Lord and a very present help in trouble.
**Adlai Stevenson,** 1951

**9** I offer my opponents a bargain: if they will stop telling falsehoods about us, I will stop telling the truth about them.
**Adlai Stevenson,** during the Presidential campaign, 1952

**10** I was brought up in a clergyman's household so I am a first-class liar.
**Dame Sybil Thorndike**

# Life
*See also Autobiography; Death; Mankind.*

**1** You spend your whole life believing that you're on the right track, only to discover that you're on the wrong train.
**Anon.**

**2** Life is a hereditary disease.
**Graffito,** London, 1984

**3** CLIFF: How's life in the fast lane?
NORM: I dunno. I can't get on the on-ramp.
*Cheers,* NBC TV

**4** There are, of course, many problems connected with life, of which some of the most popular are 'Why are people born?' 'Why do they die?' 'Why do they spend so much of the intervening time wearing digital watches?'
**Douglas Adams,** *The Hitch Hiker's Guide to the Galaxy,* 1979

**5** Life is a wonderful thing to talk about, or to read about in history books – but it is terrible when one has to live it.
**Jean Anouilh,** *Time Remembered,* 1939

**6** VICAR: You know, Life – Life, is rather like opening a tin of sardines. We are all of us looking for the key. Some of us think we've found the key, don't we? We roll back the lid of the sardine tin of Life, we reveal the sardines, the riches of Life, therein and we get them out, we enjoy them. But, you know, there's always a little piece in the corner you can't get out. I wonder – I wonder, is there a little piece in the corner of your life? I know there is in mine.
**Alan Bennett,** *Beyond the Fringe,* 1959

**7** Human life is mainly a process of filling in time until the arrival of death or Santa Claus . . .
**Eric Berne,** *Games People Play,* 1964

**8** All animals, except man, know that the principal business of life is to enjoy it.
**Samuel Butler,** *The Way of all Flesh,* 1903

**9** Life is one long process of getting tired.
**Samuel Butler,** *The Notebooks of Samuel Butler,* 1912

**10** There are two great rules of life, the one general and the other particular. The first is that everyone can, in the end, get what he wants if he only tries. This is the general rule. The particular rule is that every individual is more or less an exception to the general rule.
**Samuel Butler,** *The Notebooks of Samuel Butler,* 1912

**11** Life is a moderately good play with a badly written third act.
**Truman Capote**

**12** Life is a near-death experience.
**George Carlin**, *Brain Droppings*, 1997

**13** If life was fair, Elvis would be alive and all the impersonators would be dead.
**Johnny Carson**, *The Tonight Show*, NBC TV

**14** Life is a maze in which we take the wrong turning before we have learned to walk.
**Cyril Connolly**, *The Unquiet Grave*, 1944

**15** PAUL: Hey, Norm, how's the world been treating you?
NORM: Like a baby treats a diaper . . .
**Andy Cowan and David S. Williger**, 'The Bar Stoolie', *Cheers*, NBC TV, 1985

**16** Is not the whole world a vast house of assignation to which the filing system has been lost?
**Quentin Crisp**, *The Naked Civil Servant*, 1968

**17** Life was a funny thing that occurred on the way to the grave.
**Quentin Crisp**, *The Naked Civil Servant*, 1968

**18** If you want my final opinion on the mystery of life and all that, I can give it to you in a nutshell. The universe is like a safe to which there is a combination. But the combination is locked up in the safe.
**Peter De Vries**, *Let Me Count the Ways*, 1965

**19** It's a funny old world – a man's lucky if he gets out of it alive.
**W. C. Fields**, *You're Telling Me*, 1934

**20** When I hear somebody sigh, 'Life is hard,' I am always tempted to ask, 'Compared to what?'
**Sydney J. Harris**, *Majority of One*

**21** Life is a fatal complaint and an eminently contagious one.
**Oliver Wendell Holmes**, *The Poet at the Breakfast Table*, 1872

**22** . . . life is something to do when you can't get to sleep.
**Fran Lebowitz**, *Metropolitan Life*, 1978

**23** . . . we must first deal with the . . . question of *what is life*. Here we discover that others have preceded us and provided quite a range of answers. We consider each answer individually but we are invariably disappointed. A bowl of cherries? Too pat. A cabaret? Not in this neighbourhood. Real? Hardly. Earnest? Please.
**Fran Lebowitz**, *Metropolitan Life*, 1978

**24** Life is like a sewer. What you get out of it depends on what you put into it.
**Tom Lehrer**, 'We Will All Go Together When We Go', song from *An Evening Wasted with Tom Lehrer*, 1959

**25** Life is what happens to you while you're busy making other plans.
**John Lennon**, 'Beautiful Boy'

**26** The basic fact about human existence is not that it is a tragedy, but that it is a bore. It is not so much a war as an endless standing in line.
**H. L. Mencken**, *Prejudices*, Sixth Series, 1927

**27** Life's a tough proposition, and the first hundred years are the hardest.
**Wilson Mizner**, 1876–1933, American playwright

**28** Life is not for everyone.
**Michael O'Donoghue**, quoted in *Playboy*, 1983

**29** My life has a superb cast – I just can't figure out the plot.
**Freddie Oliver**, English writer, probably apocryphal

**30** All life is six to five against.
**Damon Runyan** (Attrib.)

**31** My whole life is a movie. It's just that there are no dissolves. I have to live every agonizing moment of it. My life needs editing.
**Mort Sahl**, American comedian

**32** Life is too short for men to take it seriously.
**George Bernard Shaw**, *Back to Methuselah*, 1921

**33** Life is a gamble at terrible odds – if it was a bet, you wouldn't take it.
**Tom Stoppard**, *Rosencrantz and Guildenstern are Dead*, 1967

**34** Oh, isn't life a terrible thing, thank God?
**Dylan Thomas**, *Under Milk Wood*, 1954

**35** Life is like an overlong drama through which we sit being nagged by the vague memories of having read the reviews.
**John Updike**, *The Coup*, 1979

**36** Life is much too important a thing ever to talk seriously about it.
**Oscar Wilde**, *Vera, or The Nihilists*, 1883

# Limericks

*See also Poets and Poetry.*

**1** The limerick packs laughs anatomical
Into space that is quite economical.
But the good ones I've seen
So seldom are clean
And the clean ones so seldom are comical.
**Anon.**

**2** The limerick's an art-form complex
Whose contents run chiefly to sex.
It's famous for virgins
And masculine urgin's
And vulgar erotic effects.
**Anon.**, quoted in W. S. Baring-Gould, *The Lure of the Limerick*, 1968

**3** There was an old man of St Bees
Who was stung on the arm by a wasp.
When asked, 'Does it hurt?'
He said, 'No, it doesn't,
I'm so glad it wasn't a hornet.'
**Anon.**

**4** Well, it's partly the shape of the thing
That gives the old limerick wing;
These accordion pleats
Full of airy conceits
Take it up like a kite on a string.
**Anon.**, quoted in W. S. Baring-Gould, *The Lure of the Limerick*, 1968

**5** The limerick's, admitted, a verse form:
a terse form: a curse form; a hearse form.
It may not be lyric,
and at best it's Satyric,
and a whale of a tail in perverse form.
**Conrad Aiken**, *A Seizure of Limericks*, 1965

**6** Most women loathe limericks, for the same reason that calves hate cookbooks.
**Gershon Legman**

**7** There are three kinds of limericks: limericks when ladies are present, limericks when ladies are absent but clergymen are present, and limericks.
**Don Marquis**

**8** The limerick, peculiar to English,
Is a verse form that's hard to extinguish.
Once Congress in session
Decreed its suppression
But people got around it by writing the
last line without any rhyme or meter.
**Professor T. J. Spencer**

# Literature

*See also Books; Novels; Poets and Poetry; Quotations; Reading; William Shakespeare; Writers; Writing.*

**1** Literature exists so that where one man has lived finely, ten thousand may afterwards live finely.
**Arnold Bennett**, 1867–1931, English novelist

**2** He [Clevinger] knew everything about literature except how to enjoy it.
**Joseph Heller**, *Catch-22*, 1961

**3** A man with his belly full of the classics is an enemy of the human race.
**Henry Miller**, *Tropic of Cancer*, 1930

**4** If F. Scott and Zelda are Class
Cellini made things out of brass,
And Dacron is fur,
Air-Wick smells like myrrh,
And plastic's as good as stained glass!
**Michael O'Donoghue**, *The National Lampoon Encyclopedia of Humor*, 1973

**5** A classic is something that everybody wants to have read and nobody wants to read.
**Mark Twain**, *The Disappearance of Literature*, 1900

**6** I hate vulgar realism in literature. The man who would call a spade a spade should be compelled to use one. It is the only thing he is fit for.
**Oscar Wilde**, *The Picture of Dorian Gray*, 1891

# London

*See also Britain and the British; England and the English.*

**1** London is a splendid place to live for those who can get out of it.
**Lord Balfour of Burleigh**, quoted in the *Observer*, 1944

**2** I don't know what London's coming to – the higher the buildings the lower the morals.
**Noel Coward**, 'Law and Order', *This Year of Grace*, 1928

**3** London is a university with ten million graduates qualified to live and let live.
**Oliver St John Gogarty**, *As I Was Going Down Sackville Street*, 1937

**4** When it's three o'clock in New York, it's still 1938 in London.
**Bette Midler**, quoted in *The Times*, 1978

**5** London is too full of fogs – and serious people. Whether the fogs produce the serious people or whether the serious people produce the fogs, I don't know, but the whole thing rather gets on my nerves.
**Oscar Wilde**, *Lady Windermere's Fan*, 1892

# Loneliness

**1** I Feel So Miserable Without You, It's Almost Like Having You Here.
**Stephen Bishop**, song title

**2** There are no books like a dame
And nothin' looks like a dame.
There are no drinks like a dame
And nothin' thinks like a dame,
Nothin' acts like a dame
Or attracts like a dame.
There ain't a thing that's wrong with any man here
That can't be cured by putting him near
A girly, womanly, female, feminine dame!
**Oscar Hammerstein II**, 'There is Nothin' Like a Dame', song from *South Pacific*, 1949

**3** If there's anything worse than a woman living alone, it's a woman saying she likes it.
**Stanley Shapiro and Maurice Richlin**, *Pillow Talk*, screenplay, 1959

**4** Remember, we're all in this alone.
**Lily Tomlin**

**5** When so many are lonely as seem to be lonely, it would be inexcusably selfish to be lonely alone.
**Tennessee Williams**, *Camino Real*, 1953

# Looks

*See also Appearance; Beauty; Clothes; Faces; Fashion; Style.*

**1** As a beauty I'm not a great star,
There are others more handsome by far,
But my face I don't mind it,
Because I'm behind it –

'Tis the folks in the front that I jar.
**Anthony Euwer**, 'The Face', *The Oxford Book of American Light Verse*, 1979

**2** Phyllis Diller's had so many face lifts, there's nothing left in her shoes.
**Bob Hope**

**3** My last girlfriend looked like Claudia Schiffer – only shorter and Korean.
**Max Kauffmann**

**4** Circumstances alter faces.
**Carolyn Wells**

**5** As long as a woman can look ten years younger than her own daughter, she is perfectly satisfied.
**Oscar Wilde**, *The Picture of Dorian Gray*, 1891

**6** Good looks are a snare that every sensible man would like to be caught in.
**Oscar Wilde**, *The Importance of Being Earnest*, 1895

# Los Angeles

*See also America and the Americans; California; Hollywood.*

**1** I don't want to live in a city where the only cultural advantage is that you can make a right turn on a red light.
**Woody Allen and Marshall Brickman**, *Annie Hall*, screenplay, 1977

**2** They don't throw their garbage away. They make it into television shows.
**Woody Allen and Marshall Brickman**, *Annie Hall*, screenplay, 1977

**3** 'I went to Los Angeles once,' goes a favorite line, 'but I couldn't find it.'
**Herb Caen**, *Vanity Fair*, 1984

**4** A big hard-boiled city with no more personality than a paper cup.
**Raymond Chandler**, *The Little Sister*, 1949

**5** . . . is a large citylike area surrounding the Beverly Hills Hotel . . . In 1956 the population of Los Angeles was 2,243,901. By 1970 it had risen to 2,811,801, 1,650,917 of whom are currently up for a series.
**Fran Lebowitz**, *Social Studies*, 1981

**6** The chief products of Los Angeles are novelizations, salad, game-show hosts, points, muscle tone, mini-series and rewrites. They export all of these items with

the twin exceptions of muscle tone and points, neither of which seem to travel well.
**Fran Lebowitz**, *Social Studies*, 1981

**7** . . . a circus without a tent.
**Carey McWilliams**, *Southern California Country*, 1946

**8** Is it true what they say about Los Angeles,
 that Los Angeles is erratic,
That in the sweet national symphony of
 common sense Los Angeles is the static?
Yes it is true, Los Angeles is not only
 erratic, not only erotic,
Los Angeles is crotchety, centrifugal,
 vertiginous, esoteric and exotic.
**Ogden Nash**, 'Don't Shoot Los Angeles', *Good Intentions*, 1942

**9** I have a theory about L.A. architecture. I think all the houses had a costume party and they all came as other countries.
**Michael O'Donoghue**, quoted in *Playboy*, 1983

**10** Seventy-two suburbs in search of a city.
**Dorothy Parker** (Attrib.)

**11** The violet hush of twilight was descending over Los Angeles as my hostess, Violet Hush, and I left its suburbs headed towards Hollywood. In the distance a glow of huge piles of burning motion-picture scripts lit up the sky. The crisp tang of frying writers and directors whetted my appetite. How good it was to be alive, I thought, inhaling deep lungfuls of carbon monoxide.
**S. J. Perelman**, *Strictly from Hunger*, 1937

**12** The difference between Los Angeles and yogurt is that yogurt has real culture.
**Tom Taussik**, *Legless in Gaza*, 1982

# Love

*See also Affection; Courtship; Flirtation; Infatuation; Love – Breaking up; Romance; Seduction; Sex; Sexual Attraction.*

**1** People in love, it is well known, suffer extreme conceptual delusions; the most common of these being that other people find your condition as thrilling and eye-watering as you do yourselves.
**Julian Barnes**, *Observer*, 1984

**2** If it is your time love will track you down like a cruise missile. If you say 'No! I don't want it right now.' That's when you'll get it

for sure. Love will make a way out of no way. Love is an exploding cigar which we willingly smoke.
**Lynda Barry**, *Big Ideas*, cartoon, 1983

**3** Love . . . the delightful interval between meeting a beautiful girl and discovering that she looks like a haddock.
**John Barrymore**, 1882–1942, American actor (Attrib.)

**4** Just say you love me. You don't have to mean it.
**Paddy Chayefsky**, *The Bachelor Party*, screenplay, 1957

**5** CHARLES: I really feel, um, uh, in short, to recap in a slightly clearer version, uh, in the words of David Cassidy in fact, um, while he was still with *The Partridge Family*, uh, I think I love you.
**Richard Curtis**, *Four Weddings and a Funeral*, screenplay, 1994

**6** Love is the irresistible desire to be irresistibly desired.
**Robert Frost**, 1874–1963, American poet

**7** Love is like the measles – all the worse when it comes late in life.
**Douglas Jerrold**, 1803–57, English playwright and journalist

**8** He gave her a look you could have poured on a waffle.
**Ring Lardner**

**9** Pride – that's a luxury a woman in love can't afford.
**Clare Boothe Luce**, 1903–87, American Congresswoman and ambassador

**10** Love is only the dirty trick played on us to achieve continuation of the species.
**W. Somerset Maugham**, *A Writer's Notebook*, 1949

**11** The love that lasts longest is the love that is never returned.
**W. Somerset Maugham**, quoted in his obituaries, 1965

**12** Love is based on a view of women that is impossible to those who have had any experience with them.
**H. L. Mencken**, *Prejudices*, Fourth Series, 1924

**13** Love is like war: easy to begin but very hard to stop.
**H. L. Mencken**

**14** Love is the delusion that one woman differs from another.
**H. L. Mencken,** *A Mencken Chrestomathy,* 1949

**15** To fall in love you have to be in the state of mind for it to take, like a disease.
**Nancy Mitford,** 1904–73, English writer

**16** ETH: Oh, Ron . . .
RON: Yes, Eth?
ETH: You did *mean* those three little words you whispered to me in the cinema, didn't you?
RON: 'Course I did, Eth . . . I *had* seen it.
**Frank Muir and Denis Norden,** 'The Glums', *Take It from Here,* BBC Radio

**17** More than a catbird hates a cat,
    Or a criminal hates a clue,
    Or the Axis hates the United States,
    That's how much I love you.
**Ogden Nash,** 'To My Valentine', *Good Intentions,* 1942

**18** Every love's the love before
    In a duller dress.
**Dorothy Parker,** 'Summary', *Death and Taxes,* 1931

**19** Love is like quicksilver in the hand. Leave the fingers open and it stays. Clutch it, and it darts away.
**Dorothy Parker** (Attrib.)

**20** Oh, life is a glorious cycle of song,
    A medley of extemporanea;
    And love is a thing that can never go
        wrong;
    And I am Marie of Roumania.
**Dorothy Parker,** 'Comment', *Enough Rope,* 1926

**21** Scratch a lover and find a foe.
**Dorothy Parker**

**22** Love is not the dying moan of a distant violin – it is the triumphant twang of a bedspring.
**S. J. Perelman** (Attrib.)

**23** Electric eels, I might add, do it,
    Though it shocks 'em, I know,
    Why ask if shad do it?
    Waiter, bring me shad roe.
    In shallow shoals, English soles do it,
    Gold-fish in the privacy of bowls, do it,
    Let's do it, let's fall in love.
**Cole Porter,** 'Let's Do It', song, 1930

**24** Old sloths who hang down from twigs
        do it,

Though the effort is great,
    Sweet guinea-pigs do it,
    Buy a couple and wait.
    The world admits bears in pits do it,
    Even pekineses in the Ritz, do it,
    Let's do it, let's fall in love.
**Cole Porter,** 'Let's Do It', song, 1930

**25** I can see from your utter misery, from your eagerness to misunderstand each other, and from your thoroughly bad temper, that this is the real thing.
**Peter Ustinov,** *Romanoff and Juliet,* 1957

**26** I can understand companionship. I can understand bought sex in the afternoon. I cannot understand the love affair.
**Gore Vidal,** *Sunday Times,* 1973

**27** Love is much nicer to be in than an automobile accident, a tight girdle, a higher tax bracket or a holding pattern over Philadelphia.
**Judith Viorst,** *Redbook,* 1975

**28** Love is the same as like except you feel sexier. And more romantic. And also more annoyed when he talks with his mouth full. And you also resent it more when he interrupts you. And you also respect him less when he shows any weakness. And furthermore, when you ask him to pick you up at the airport and he tells you he can't do it because he's busy, it's only when you love him that you hate him.
**Judith Viorst,** *Redbook,* 1975

**29** Love conquers all things except poverty and toothache.
**Mae West**

**30** . . . a really *grand passion* is comparatively rare nowadays. It is the privilege of people who have nothing to do. That is the one use of the idle classes in a country.
**Oscar Wilde,** *A Woman of No Importance,* 1893

**31** It's curious how, when you're in love, you yearn to go about doing acts of kindness to everybody. I am bursting with a sort of yeasty benevolence these days, like one of those chaps in Dickens. I very nearly bought you a tie in London, Bertie.
**P. G. Wodehouse,** *The Mating Season,* 1949

**32** 'Love,' she said, 'seems to pump me full

of vitamins. It makes me feel as if the sun were shining and my hat was right and my shoes were right and my frock was right and my stockings were right, and somebody had just left me ten thousand a year.'

**P. G. Wodehouse**, *Spring Fever*, 1948

# Love – Breaking up

*See also Alimony; Divorce; Incompatibility; Infidelity; Love; Rejection.*

**1** How Can I Miss You If You Won't Go Away?

**T-shirt**, Pasadena, 1996

**2** *What to do with your time*
DO: *Drink black coffee and smoke numerous cigs. You NEED to eat and this will do, *Find out who 'she' is and introduce yourself. Scrutinize her appearance and comfort yourself with thoughts of her large pores or taste in clothes. *Drink mass quantities of alcohol and watch TV all you can. *Abandon personal hygiene and cleaning your house. *Kick his car.
DON'T: *Take up a new hobby. When the most hellish period has passed you will be unable to do this activity ever again in your life. *Try to meet a new lovemate through church organizations or night classes in ballroom dancing. *Try to feel happy or good for thirty days. *Go anywhere or do anything. *Go near high bridges, open windows, trucks that are moving fast or couples holding hands.

**Lynda Barry**, *Big Ideas*, cartoon, 1983

**3** When people say, 'You're breaking my heart', they do in fact mean that you're breaking their genitals.

**Jeffrey Bernard**, 1985

**4** MONICA: It's weird, but I don't want to throw this away. It's like all I have left of him . . . gross drain hair.

**Michael Curtis & Gregory Malins**, 'The One with the Princess Leia Fantasy', *Friends*, NBC, 1995

**5** Love is just a simple-minded little euphemism for a grab-bag of primitive sexual impulses, unrelenting neediness, neurotic anxiety, and brain-squeezing social pressure. You're pushed to couple with your so-called soulmate with all the poetry and rapture of two sea-slugs encountering each other on the bottom of the ocean. And I'm not just saying this because my girlfriend dumped me three weeks ago.

**Matt Groening**, *Life in Hell*, 1992

**6 Warning signs your lover is getting bored**
1. Passionless kisses.
2. Frequent sighing.
3. Moved; left no forwarding address.

**Matt Groening**, *Life in Hell*, 1992

**7** If You Leave Me, Can I Come Too?

**Cynthia Heimel**, book title, 1995

**8** How Can I Dump Him When He Hasn't Called Me?

**Cynthia Heimel**, *If You Leave Me, Can I Come Too?*, 1995

**9** Get Your Tongue Out of My Mouth, I'm Kissing You Goodbye!

**Cynthia Heimel**, 1994

**10** If You Can't Live Without Me, Why Aren't You Dead Yet?

**Cynthia Heimel**, 1992

**11** She always believed in the old adage leave them while you're looking good.

**Anita Loos**, *Gentlemen Prefer Blondes*, 1925

**12** I only miss you on days that end in 'Y.'

**Jim Malloy and Even Stevens**, 'Days That End in ''Y'' ', song, 1975

**13** There is one thing I would break up over, and that is if she caught me with another woman. I won't stand for that.

**Steven Martin**

**14** I just broke up with someone and the last thing she said to me was: 'You'll never find anyone like me again!' I'm thinking, 'I should hope not! If I don't want you, why would I want someone *like* you?'

**Larry Miller**

**15** *Is there a 'cure' for a broken heart?*
Only time can heal your broken heart, just as only time can heal his broken arms and legs.

**Miss Peggy**, *Miss Piggy's Guide to Life (As Told to Henry Beard)*, 1981

**16** My boyfriend and I broke up. He wanted to get married, and I didn't want him to.

**Rita Rudner**, quoted in *Ms*, 1984

**17** When I want to end relationships, I just say, 'I want to marry you so we can live together forever.' Sometimes they leave skid marks.
**Rita Rudner**

**18** I broke up with my girlfriend. She moved in with another guy and I draw the line at that.
**Garry Shandling**

**19** My tears have washed 'I Love You' from the blackboard of my heart.
**Hank Tompson and Lyle Gaston**, 'Blackboard of My Heart', song, 1956

**20** There is always something ridiculous about the emotions of people whom one has ceased to love.
**Oscar Wilde**, *The Picture of Dorian Gray*, 1891

**21** I was in rare fettle and the heart had touched a new high. I don't know anything that braces one up like finding you haven't got to get married after all.
**P. G. Wodehouse**, *Jeeves in the Offing*, 1960

## Luck
*See also Gambling.*

**1** I'm very lucky. The only time I was ever up shit creek, I just happened to have a paddle with me.
**George Carlin**, *Brain Droppings*, 1997

**2** I believe in luck: how else can you explain the success of those you dislike?
**Jean Cocteau**, 1889–1963, French playwright and film director

**3** I am a great believer in luck and I find the harder I work the more I have of it.
**Stephen Leacock**, *Literary Lapses*, 1910

**4** I broke a mirror in my house, which is supposed to be seven years' bad luck. My lawyer thinks he can get me five.
**Steven Wright**, American comic

## Luxembourg
*See also Europe and the EEC.*

**1** On a clear day, from the terrace . . . you can't see Luxembourg at all. This is because a tree is in the way.
**Alan Coren**, *The Sanity Inspector*, 1974

# MacArthur, Douglas
**(American Army General)**
*See also The Army; War.*

**1** MacArthur is the type of man who thinks that when he gets to heaven, God will step down from the great white throne and bow him into His vacated seat.
**Harold Ickes,** *Diary*, 1933

**2** I fired him because he wouldn't respect the authority of the President. That's the answer to that. I didn't fire him because he was a dumb son of a bitch, although he was, but that's not against the law for generals. If it was, half to three quarters of them would be in jail.
**Harry S. Truman,** on his sacking of General MacArthur from the post of Commander-in-Chief of the US forces in Korea, 1951, quoted in *Plain Speaking: An Oral Biography of Harry S. Truman* by Merle Miller

# Mafia, The
*See also Crime.*

**1** Death is one of the worst things that can happen to a Cosa Nostra member, and many prefer simply to pay a fine.
**Woody Allen,** 'A Look at Organized Crime', *New Yorker*

**2** LOUIE: Hey! It's Krusty all right. Should I shoot him gangland-style or execution-style?
FAT TONY: Listen to your heart.
**John Swartzwelder,** 'Homie the Clown', *The Simpsons*, Fox TV, 1995

# Mail
*See also Communications; Letters.*

**1** Bills travel through the mail at twice the speed of checks.
**Anon.**

**2** Now I know why the Post Office has raised postage rates. The extra four cents is for storage.
**Anon.**

# Mankind

*See also Life; The Public.*

**1** Man is Nature's sole mistake.
**W. S. Gilbert**, *Princess Ida*, 1884

**2** Man is a beautiful machine that works very badly. He is like a watch of which the most that can be said is that its cosmetic effect is good.
**H. L. Mencken**, *Minority Report*, 1956

**3** Human beings were invented by water as a device for transporting itself from one place to another.
**Tom Robbins**, *Another Roadside Attraction*, 1973

**4** Man is the only animal that blushes. Or needs to.
**Mark Twain**, *Following the Equator*, 1897

**5** The noblest work of God? Man. Who found it out? Man.
**Mark Twain**, *Autobiography*, 1924

# Manners

*See also Conformity; Etiquette.*

**1** Politenessman says: THANK YOU FOR LOOKING AT THIS BUTTON!
**Ron Barrett**, 'Politenessman', *National Lampoon* 1980s

**2** The man with the manners gals all adore is the man who never spits on the floor. Thank you!
**Ron Barrett**, 'Politenessman', *National Lampoon*, 1982

**3** He is the very pineapple of politeness!
**Richard Brinsley Sheridan**, *The Rivals*, 1775

**4** Good breeding consists in concealing how much we think of ourselves and how little we think of the other person.
**Mark Twain**, *Notebooks*, 1935

**5** Manners are especially the need of the plain. The pretty can get away with anything.
**Evelyn Waugh**, quoted in the *Observer*, 1962

# Marriage

*See also Bigamy; Divorce; The Family; Weddings.*

**1** Advice to persons about to marry – 'Don't.'
**Anon.**, *Punch*, 1845

**2** Marriage is not a word but a sentence.
**Anon.**

**3** Marriage is the price men pay for sex, sex is the price women pay for marriage.
**Anon.**

**4** My wife tells me I'm not passionate enough. That's ridiculous! I've a good mind to send her a memo!
**Anon.**

**5** For the first year of marriage I had a basically bad attitude. I tended to place my wife underneath a pedestal.
**Woody Allen**, nightclub act, 1960s

**6** You must come to our house next time. Absolute peace. Neither of us ever says a word to each other. That's the secret of a successful union.
**Alan Ayckbourn**, *Absent Friends*, 1975

**7** They think it's your destiny to clean and I guess it's their destiny to have a couch surgically implanted on their behind. You may marry the man of your dreams, ladies, but years later you're married to a couch that burps.
**Roseanne Barr**

**8** The other night I said to my wife Ruth, 'Do you feel that the sex and excitement has gone out of our marriage?' Ruth said, 'I'll discuss it with you during the next commercial.'
**Milton Berle**, *Variety*

**9** HORNCASTLE: The whole point of marriage is to stop you getting anywhere near real life. You think it's a great struggle with the mystery of being. It's more like . . . being smothered in warm cocoa. There's sex, but it's not what you think. Marvellous, for the first fortnight. Then every Wednesday. If there isn't a good late-night concert on the Third. Meanwhile you become a biological functionary. An agent of the great female womb, spawning away, dumping its goods in your lap for succour. Daddy, daddy, we're here and we're expensive.

**Malcolm Bradbury**, *Love on a Gunboat*, BBC TV, 1977

**10** Dr Heinrich von Heartburn's advice on keeping one's marriage alive: Make it interesting . . . I showed a friend of mine once how to keep his marriage exciting . . . One day he'd come home from work, his wife would open the door, he's a French soldier . . . The next day he's a policeman, he comes in, he starts to run around with the handcuffs and the badges, and the next day he don't come through the door, he jumps through the window, he's a clown. He somersaults all over the living room and throws his wife all around the place. [*Pause*] She left him. He was a maniac.

**Mel Brooks**, *Your Show of Shows*, NBC TV

**11** I married the first man I ever kissed. When I tell that to my children, they just about throw up.

**Barbara Bush**, on husband George

**12** It was very good of God to let Carlyle and Mrs Carlyle marry one another and so make only two people miserable instead of four.

**Samuel Butler**, letter to Miss E. M. A. Savage, 1884

**13** Wedlock: the deep, deep peace of the double bed after the hurly-burly of the *chaise longue*.

**Mrs Patrick Campbell**

**14** A man's friends like him but leave him as he is: his wife loves him and is always trying to turn him into somebody else.

**G. K. Chesterton**, *Orthodoxy*, 1908

**15** I think of my wife, and I think of Lot,
    And I think of the lucky break he got.

**William Cole**, 'Marriage Couplet', *The Oxford Book of American Light Verse*, 1979

**16** Marriage is like a bank account. You put it in, you take it out, you lose interest.

**Professor Irwin Corey**

**17** For a marriage to have any chance, every day at least six things should go unsaid.

**Jill Craigie**, British writer

**18** We sleep in separate rooms, we have

dinner apart, we take separate vacations – we're doing everything we can to keep our marriage together.

**Rodney Dangerfield**

**19** It is true that I never should have married, but I didn't want to live without a man. Brought up to respect the conventions, love had to end in marriage. I'm afraid it did.

**Bette Davis**, *The Lonely Life*, 1962

**20** Never go to bed mad. Stay up and fight.

**Phyllis Diller**, *Phyllis Diller's Housekeeping Hints*, 1966

**21** Every woman should marry – and no man.

**Benjamin Disraeli**, *Lothair*, 1870

**22** The reasons husbands and wives do not understand each other is because they belong to different sexes.

**Dorothy Dix**, 1861–1951, American columnist

**23 A Lexicon for Fighting Marital Fights, Arranged According to Subject**

*Amnesia*: 'Who do you think you ARE?'
*Apology*: 'PARdon me for LIVing!'
*Family Tree*: 'She's YOUR mother, not mine.'
*Hearing impairments*: 'Could you speak up a little? They can't hear you in Europe.'
*Language barrier*: 'What's the matter, don't you understand English?'
*Mining*: 'I hadn't realized we'd descended to that level.'
*Wildlife*: 'That's right, use physical violence. That's all an animal like you knows anyway.'

**Dan Greenburg and Suzanne O'Malley**, *How to Avoid Love and Marriage*, 1983

**24 Fighting: Style and Syntax**

Anything you say in a marital fight will have more bounce if you utilize a melodramatic style and an archaic syntax. A statement like 'I'm sorry I ever met you' is effective enough, but how much more piquant is the same communication expressed as: '*I rue the day* I met you' . . . Asking whether your mate has time for a discussion is tapioca pudding compared with asking whether your mate *would deign to favor you* with his or her attention.

**Dan Greenburg and Suzanne O'Malley**, *How to Avoid Love and Marriage*, 1983

## 25 Wallpaper Design for the Marital Bedroom

EXCUSE ME COULD YOU PLEASE SAY THAT AGAIN I DON'T BELIEVE I HEARD YOU CORRECTLY LISTEN JUST WHO THE HELL DO YOU THINK YOU ARE FOR GOD'S SAKE WHAT AM I SUPPOSED TO BE YOUR SERVANT DON'T YOU DARE TALK TO ME IN THAT TONE OF VOICE I GUESS WE JUST AREN'T MEANT TO BE TOGETHER THAT'S ALL I'VE HAD IT UP TO HERE WITH YOU THAT'S RIGHT YOU HEARD ME THAT'S NOT MEANT TO BE A THREAT WE'RE JUST IN DIFFERENT TIMES IN OUR LIFE O.K. GO AHEAD THEN LEAVE I'LL HELP YOU PACK YOUR BAGS I GUESS WE DON'T NEED TO BE TOGETHER OH THAT'S CUTE REAL CUTE I DON'T HAVE TO STAND

**Dan Greenburg and Suzanne O'Malley**, *How to Avoid Love and Marriage*, 1983

**26** Marriage is a great institution – no family should be without it.
**Bob Hope**

**27** Zsa Zsa Gabor got married as a one-off and it was so successful she turned it into a series.
**Bob Hope**

**28** I never knew what real happiness was until I got married. And by then it was too late.
**Max Kauffmann**

**29** The trouble was, I went into marriage with both eyes closed – her father closed one and her brother closed the other.
**Max Kauffmann**

**30** Marrying a man is like buying something you've been admiring for a long time in a shop window. You may love it when you get it home, but it doesn't always go with everything else in the house.
**Jean Kerr**, *The Snake Has All the Lines*, 1960

**31** I love being married. I was single for a long time and I just got so sick of finishing my own sentences.
**Brian Kiley**

**32** Marriage is nature's way of keeping people from fighting with strangers.
**Alan King**

**33** We do not squabble, fight or have rows. We collect grudges. We're in an arms race, storing up warheads for the domestic Armageddon.
**Hugh Leonard**, *Time Was*, 1976

**34** WIFE: Mr Watt next door blows his wife a kiss every morning as he leaves the house. I wish you'd do that.
HUSBAND: But I hardly know the woman!
**Alfred McFote**

**35** When a man brings his wife flowers for no reason – there's a reason.
**Molly McGee**

**36** The fundamental trouble with marriage is that it shakes a man's confidence in himself, and so greatly diminishes his general competence and effectiveness. His habit of mind becomes that of a commander who has lost a decisive and calamitous battle. He never quite trusts himself thereafter.
**H. L. Mencken**, *Prejudices*, Second Series, 1920

**37** . . . just as I am unsure of the difference between flora and fauna and flotsam and jetsam.
I am quite sure that marriage is the alliance of two people one of whom never remembers birthdays and the other never forgetsam.
**Ogden Nash**, 'I Do, I Will, I Have', *Versus*, 1949

**38** To keep your marriage brimming
With love in the marriage cup,
Whenever you're wrong, admit it;
Whenever you're right, shut up.
**Ogden Nash**, 'A Word to Husbands', *Everyone but Thee and Me*, 1962

**39** Marriage is really tough because you have to deal with feelings . . . and lawyers.
**Richard Pryor**

**40** Our oldest friends, the Purgavies . . . have been to stay this week. Over dinner we counted up and realised that they have been happily married longer than most. Jane says she has no particular handy hints to pass on, except she's found it helps to start each new day by arriving down at breakfast, throwing her arms in the air and announcing apologetically, 'It's all my fault.'
**Anne Robinson**, *The Times*, 1999

**41** Marriage is popular because it combines

the maximum of temptation with the maximum of opportunity.
**George Bernard Shaw**, *Maxims for Revolutionists*, 1903

**42** Marriage is not a man's idea. A woman must have thought of it. Years ago some guy said, 'Let me get this straight, honey. I can't sleep with anyone else for the rest of my life, and if things don't work out, you get to keep half my stuff? What a great idea.'
**Bobby Slayton**

**43** Once you get married, you understand how wars start.
**Fay Weldon**, English novelist

**44** Marriage is a great institution, but I'm not ready for an institution yet.
**Mae West** (Attrib.)

**45** How marriage ruins a man. It's as demoralizing as cigarettes, and far more expensive.
**Oscar Wilde**, *Lady Windermere's Fan*, 1892

**46** I am not in favour of long engagements. They give people the opportunity of finding out each other's character before marriage, which I think is never advisable.
**Oscar Wilde**, *The Importance of Being Earnest*, 1895

**47** It's most dangerous nowadays for a husband to pay any attention to his wife in public. It always makes people think that he beats her when they're alone.
**Oscar Wilde**, *Lady Windermere's Fan*, 1892

**48** Men marry because they are tired; women because they are curious. Both are disappointed.
**Oscar Wilde**, *A Woman of No Importance*, 1893

**49** The amount of women in London who flirt with their own husbands is perfectly scandalous. It looks so bad. It is simply washing one's clean linen in public.
**Oscar Wilde**, *The Importance of Being Earnest*, 1895

**50** The one charm of marriage is that it makes a life of deception absolutely necessary for both parties.
**Oscar Wilde**, *The Picture of Dorian Gray*, 1891

**51** There's nothing in the world like the devotion of a married woman. It's a thing no married man knows anything about.
**Oscar Wilde**, *Lady Windermere's Fan*, 1892

**52** Marriage is a bribe to make a housekeeper think she's a householder.
**Thornton Wilder**, *The Merchant of Yonkers*, 1939

**53** In Hollywood all marriages are happy. It's trying to live together afterwards that causes all the problems.
**Shelley Winters**, American actress (Attrib.)

**54** Do you know what it means to come home at night to a woman who'll give you a little love, a little affection, a little tenderness? It means you're in the wrong house, that's what it means.
**Henny Youngman**, *Henny Youngman's Greatest One Liners*, 1970

**55** Some people ask the secret of our long marriage. We take time to go to a restaurant two times a week. A little candlelight, dinner, soft music and dancing. She goes Tuesdays, I go Fridays.
**Henny Youngman**

**56** Take my wife . . . please!
**Henny Youngman**

**57** The first part of our marriage was very happy. But then, on the way back from the ceremony . . .
**Henny Youngman**

# Martyrdom
*See also Death; Faith; Religion.*

**1** Martyrdom is the only way in which a man can become famous without ability.
**George Bernard Shaw**, *Essays in Fabian Socialism*, 1908

**2** . . . a thing is not necessarily true because a man dies for it.
**Oscar Wilde**, 'The Portrait of Mr W.H.', 1889

# Marxism
*See also Communism; Russia and the Russians; Socialism.*

**1** I could go for Marxism as long as it meant overthrowing a junta, but I don't want to live under it.
**Roy Blount, Jr.**, *Playboy*, 1983

**2** M is for Marx
And Movement of Masses
And Massing of Arses.

And Clashing of Classes.

**Cyril Connolly,** 'Where Engels Fear to Tread', 1945

# Mathematics

*See also Computers; Metrication; Statistics.*

**1** Five out of four people have trouble with fractions.

**Anon.**

**2** There are three kinds of people: those who can count and those who can't.

**Anon.**

**3** 'Tis a favorite project of mine
  A new value of pi to assign.
  I would fix it at 3
  For it's simpler, you see,
  Than 3 point 14159.

**Professor Harvey L. Carter**

# Maxims

*See also Epigrams; Politics – Axioms; Proverbs; Sayings.*

**1** Nothing is so useless as a general maxim.

**Thomas Macaulay,** 1800–59, English historian and politician

**2** I forgot who it was that recommended men for their soul's good to do each day two things they disliked; it was a wise man, and it is a precept that I have followed scrupulously, for every day I have got up and I have gone to bed.

**W. Somerset Maugham,** *The Moon and Sixpence*, 1919

# Medicine

*See also Cancer; Doctors; Health; Hospitals; Illness.*

**1** A minor operation: one performed on somebody else.

**Anon.**

**2** And in our new series, *Medical Hints by Well-known Actresses*, tonight, your very own Googie Withers – and what to do if it does.

*The Two Ronnies*, BBC TV

**3** Medicine: The Nation's Number One Killer.

*National Lampoon*, 1975

**4** TB or not TB, that is the congestion.

**Woody Allen,** *Everything You Always Wanted to Know about Sex*, screenplay, 1972

**5** DOCTOR: A pint is a perfectly normal quantity to take!
BLOOD DONOR: You don't seriously expect me to believe that! I mean, I came here in all good faith to help my country. I don't mind giving a reasonable amount, but a pint – that's very nearly an armful!

**Ray Galton and Alan Simpson** for Tony Hancock in *The Blood Donor*, BBC TV, 1961

**6** ERIC: I went to see the specialist about my slipped disc.
ERNIE: What happened?
ERIC: He said he'd have me back on my feet in a fortnight.
ERNIE: And did he?
ERIC: Yes – I had to sell the car to pay him.

**Eric Morecambe and Ernie Wise,** *The Morecambe and Wise Joke Book*, 1979

**7** Let no one suppose that the words doctor and patient can disguise from the parties the fact that they are employer and employee.

**George Bernard Shaw,** *The Doctor's Dilemma*, 1913

**8** DR KRUGMAN: So we open the kid up, and what do you think we find? Three buttons, a thumb tack, and twenty-seven cents in change . . . The parents couldn't afford to pay for the operation, so I kept the twenty-seven cents.

**Billy Wilder and I. A. L. Diamond,** *The Fortune Cookie*, screenplay, 1966

# Mediocrity

**1** Some men are born mediocre, some men achieve mediocrity, and some men have mediocrity thrust upon them. With Major Major it had been all three.

**Joseph Heller,** *Catch-22*, 1961

**2** Women want mediocre men, and men are working hard to be as mediocre as possible.

**Margaret Mead,** American anthropologist, 1901–78

# Mediterranean, The

*See also Holidays; Travel.*

**1** VERONICA: The Mediterranean? Not any more, dear. It's the Elsan of Europe.
**Alan Bennett**, *The Old Country*, 1978

# Meetings

*See also Bosses; Committees; Conferences; Negotiations; The Office; Parties.*

**1** I met Curzon in Downing Street from whom I got the sort of greeting a corpse would give to an undertaker.
**Stanley Baldwin**, 1867–1947, British Conservative Prime Minister

**2** Meetings . . . are rather like cocktail parties. You don't want to go, but you're cross not to be asked.
**Jilly Cooper**, *How to Survive from Nine to Five*, 1970

**3** Meetings are indispensable when you don't want to do anything.
**J. K. Galbraith**, *Ambassador's Journal*, 1969

**4** *The Law of Triviality.* Briefly stated, it means that the time spent on any item of the agenda will be in inverse proportion to the sum involved.
**C. Northcote Parkinson**, 'High Finance', *Parkinson's Law*, 1957

# Memory

*See also The Brain; The Mind; Nostalgia.*

**1 Tip Of Area Man's Tongue Refuses To Relinquish Richard Crenna's Name**

MINNEAPOLIS, MN – Despite the best efforts of area resident Guy Reid, the tip of Reid's tongue remained steadfast Tuesday in its refusal to relinquish the name of veteran film and television actor Richard Crenna . . . the tongue has previously withheld the names of Hector Elizondo, Mark Linn-Baker and Ben Gazzara.
*the Onion*, 1998

**2** Our memories are card indexes consulted, and then put back in disorder by authorities whom we do not control.
**Cyril Connolly**, *The Unquiet Grave*, 1945

**3** I have a memory like an elephant. In fact, elephants often consult me.
**Noel Coward** (Attrib.)

**4** A retentive memory may be a good thing, but the ability to forget is the true token of greatness.
**Elbert Hubbard**, *The Notebook*, 1927

**5** HARRY SECOMBE: Good morning – my name is Neddy Seagoon.
SPIKE MILLIGAN: What a memory you have!
**Spike Milligan**, *The Goon Show*, BBC Radio, 1955

**6** ERIC: My wife's got a terrible memory.
ERNIE: Really?
ERIC: Yes, she never forgets a thing.
**Eric Morecambe and Ernie Wise**, *The Morecambe and Wise Joke Book*, 1979

**7** RITA: Do you ever have déjà vu?
PHIL: Didn't you just ask me that?
**Danny Rubin and Harold Ramis**, *Groundhog Day*, screenplay, 1993

**8** No woman should have a memory. Memory in a woman is the beginning of dowdiness.
**Oscar Wilde**, *A Woman of No Importance*, 1893

**9** Right now I'm having amnesia and déjà vu at the same time. I think I've forgotten this before.
**Steven Wright**, American comic

# Men

*See also Fathers; Gentlemen; Husbands; Men – The Female View; Men and Women; Parents.*

**1** Q: What kind of cakes do boys hate?
A: Cakes of soap!
**Basil Brush**, *Basil's Joke Machine*, Border Television, 1986

**2** *Meet the Snoid*
Now here's a dude with absolute self-confidence! Never had a self-doubt in his entire life! And no qualms of conscience have ever stood in his way! The result: this ugly little creep has more cute girls chasing after him than a 747 jet-plane can haul! There's no law to prevent the landscape from being littered with the women this nasty little fellow has used up and thrown away!
**Robert Crumb**, *Snoid Comics*, 1980

**3** American men are all mixed up today . . . There was a time when this was a nation of Ernest Hemingways. REAL MEN. The kind of men who could defoliate an entire forest to make a breakfast fire – and then wipe out an endangered species while hunting for lunch. But not anymore. We've become a nation of wimps. Pansies. Alan Alda types who cook and clean and 'relate' to their wives. Phil Donahue clones who are 'sensitive' and 'vulnerable' and 'understanding' of their children. And where's it gotten us? I'll tell you where. The Japanese make better cars. The Israelis, better soldiers . . . And the rest of the world is using our embassies for target practice.
**Bruce Feirstein**, 'Real Men Don't Eat Quiche', *Playboy*, 1982

**4** Is there a way to accept the concept of the female orgasm and still command the respect of your foreign-auto mechanic?
**Bruce Feirstein**, 'Real Men Don't Eat Quiche', *Playboy*, 1982

**5** Men have a much better time of it than women; for one thing they marry later; for another thing they die earlier.
**H. L. Mencken**

**6** It's rough being a man. See, men have to have money, have to try to look good, have to have the right job, the right prestige. Women can be working in McDonald's, we'll still try to get your phone number.
**Sinbad**

# Men – The Female View
*See also Men; Women – The Male View.*

**1** My husband is as strong as a horse. I only wish he had the IQ of one.
**Anon.**

**2** Q: What's a man's idea of a romantic evening?
A: A candlelit football stadium.

Q: How can you tell when a man's had an orgasm?
A: You can hear him snoring.

Q: Why did God put men on earth?
A: Because vibrators can't mow the lawn.

Q: What's the difference between a man and a chimpanzee?

A: One is hairy and smelly and is always scratching his rear. And the other's a chimpanzee.
**Anon.**

**3** Women have their faults
Men have only two:
Everything they say,
Everything they do.
**Anon.**

**4** Don't argue with your mate in the kitchen. Because we know where everything is and you don't.
**Diane Amos**

**5** There isn't any New Man. The New Man is the old man, only he whines more.
**Roseanne Barr**, *New Yorker*, 1996

**6** I don't think women want to be equal to men. I think we'd have to have lobotomies to do that.
**Roseanne Barr**, *Politically Incorrect*, ABC, 1993

**7** Every man who is high up loves to think he has done it all himself, and the wife smiles, and lets it go at that. It's our only joke. Every woman knows that.
**J. M. Barrie**, *What Every Woman Knows*, 1908

**8** It's no news to anyone that nice guys finish last. Almost every female I know has had the uncomfortable experience of going out with a 'nice man'. Spelled 'N-E-R-D'. How many times has your girlfriend said, 'He's SO sweet and so cute so why don't I like him?' Let's face it, when an attractive but ALOOF ('cool') man comes along, there are some of us who offer to shine his shoes with our underpants. If he has a mean streak, somehow this is 'attractive'. There are thousands of scientific concepts as to why this is so, and yes, yes, it's very sick – but none of this helps.
**Lynda Barry**, *Big Ideas*, cartoon, 1983

**9** The useless piece of flesh at the end of a penis is called a man.
**Jo Brand**, English comedienne

**10** I refuse to consign the whole male sex to the nursery. I insist on believing that some men are my equals.
**Brigid Brophy**

**11** I'd never seen men hold each other. I

thought the only thing they were allowed to do was shake hands or fight.
**Rita Mae Brown**

**12** Women are putting off marriage for as long as they can – because every wedding has to have a bridegroom.
**Julie Burchill**, quoted in the *Daily Mail*, 2000

**13** The male is a domestic animal which, if treated with firmness and kindness, can be trained to do most things.
**Jilly Cooper**, *Cosmopolitan*, 1972

**14** What makes men so tedious
Is the need to show off and compete.
They'll bore you to death for hours and hours,
Before they'll admit defeat.
**Wendy Cope**, 'Men and their boring arguments', 1988

**15** I never married because there was no need. I have three pets at home which answer the same purpose as a husband. I have a dog which growls every morning, a parrot which swears every afternoon and a cat that comes home late at night.
**Marie Corelli**

**16** PELLET: Men are all alike.
WENDLE: Only some more than others.
**Noel Coward**, 'Law and Order', *This Year of Grace*, 1928

**17** . . . beware of men who cry. It's true that men who cry are sensitive to and in touch with feelings, but the only feelings they tend to be sensitive to and in touch with are their own.
**Nora Ephron**, *Heartburn*, 1983

**18** Macho does not prove mucho.
**Zsa Zsa Gabor**

**19** The only place men want depth in a woman is in her *décolletage*.
**Zsa Zsa Gabor** (Attrib.)

**20** Probably the only place where a man can feel really secure is in a maximum security prison, except for the imminent threat of release.
**Germaine Greer**, *The Female Eunuch*, 1970

**21** None of you [men] ask for anything – except everything, but just for so long as you need it.
**Doris Lessing**, *The Golden Notebook*, 1962

**22** I require only three things of a man. He must be handsome, ruthless and stupid.
**Dorothy Parker**, quoted in *You Might As Well Live*, 1971

**23** Some men break your heart in two,
Some men fawn and flatter,
Some men never look at you;
And that cleans up the matter.
**Dorothy Parker**, 'Experience', *Enough Rope*, 1926

**24** Women find men who have a sense of humor EXTREMELY SEXY! You don't have to look like Robert Redford. All you have to do is tickle her funny bone, and she'll follow you anywhere! If you can make her laugh, you've got it made!
MAN: One to call her Dad and the other to open the Diet Pepsi!
WOMAN: Oh stop! You're KILLING me! Take off all your clothes quick!
**Mimi Pond**, *Mimi Pond's Secrets of the Powder Room*, cartoon, 1983

**25** When I eventually met Mr Right, I had no idea that his first name was 'Always.'
**Rita Rudner**

**26** In politics, if you want anything said, ask a man; if you want anything done, ask a woman.
**Margaret Thatcher**, 1975

**27** A hard man is good to find.
**Mae West**

**28** I like two kinds of men: domestic and foreign.
**Mae West**

**29** It's not the men in my life that count; it's the life in my men.
**Mae West**, *I'm No Angel*, screenplay, 1933

**30** When women go wrong, men go right after them.
**Mae West**

**31** No nice men are good at getting taxis.
**Katharine Whitehorn**, *Observer*, 1977

# Men and Women

*See also Couples; Men; Men – The Female View; Relationships; Women; Women – The Male View.*

**1** **Five things you'll never hear a man say:**
Sex isn't that important. Sometimes I just want to be held.

You know, I'd like to see her again, but the problem is her breasts are just too big.

While I'm up, darling, may I get you anything?

Here, honey, YOU use the remote.

Isn't it time to do the Christmas cards?

### Five things you'll never hear a woman say:

Can't our relationship get a little more physical? I'm so tired of being 'just good friends.'

Does my bum look too small in this?

No, darling, don't stop to ask directions. I'm sure you'll be able to figure out how to get there.

No! This diamond is way too big!

Today's our anniversary? You're kidding!

**Anon.**

### 2 Twelve reasons why it's great to be a guy

Your last name stays put.

One mood, all the time.

The occasional well-executed belch is practically expected.

Flowers fix everything.

You get extra credit for the slightest act of thoughtfulness.

People never glance at your chest when you're talking to them.

Phone conversations are over in 30 seconds flat.

You can open all your own jars.

Foreplay is optional.

You can wear a white shirt to a water park.

You can eat a banana in a hardware store.

You can drop by to see a friend without taking a little gift.

**Anon.**

**3** How to impress a woman: wine her, dine her, call her, hug her, hold her, surprise her, compliment her, smile at her, laugh with her, cry with her, cuddle her, shop with her, give her jewellery, buy her flowers, hold her hand, write love letters to her, write poetry for her, go to the ends of the earth and back for her.

How to impress a man: show up naked, bring beer.

**Anon., 1999**

**4** Give a woman an inch and she thinks she's a ruler.

*Stars and Stripes*

**5** Meaningful relationships between men and women don't last. There's a chemical in our bodies that makes it so we get on each other's nerves sooner or later.

**Woody Allen,** *Sleeper,* screenplay, 1973

**6** I married beneath me. All women do.

**Nancy Astor,** 1879–1964, British politician

**7** The first time Adam had a chance, he laid the blame on women.

**Nancy Astor**

**8** 'If you men are so good at cooking, then,' said Cynthia, 'why didn't you cook dinner?'

'I thought paying for it was sufficient.'

I made that forty-thirty to him.

**Jeffrey Bernard,** *Punch,* 1985

**9** . . . all women dress like their mothers, that is their tragedy. No man ever does. That is his.

**Alan Bennett,** *Forty Years On,* 1968

**10** Guys are like dogs. They keep comin' back. Ladies are like cats. Yell at a cat one time, they're gone.

**Lenny Bruce**

**11** The sad lesson of life is that you treat a girl like that with respect, and the next guy comes along and he's banging the hell out of her.

**Art Buchwald,** *Herald Tribune,* 1975

**12** In the sex-war, thoughtlessness is the weapon of the male, vindictiveness of the female.

**Cyril Connolly,** *The Unquiet Grave,* 1945

**13** Most women set out to try to change a man, and when they have changed him they do not like him.

**Marlene Dietrich** (Attrib.)

**14** Men and women do not have the faintest idea of what to do with one another. Each sex looks at the other with suspicion. The slightest gesture (scratching an ear), the most casual remark ('How are your tomatoes?') are seen as hostile acts. Now that women are equal, they feel awful about it and wonder if they should have pushed so hard. Men would like to reach out and help but are afraid they will be smashed in the head.

**Bruce Jay Friedman,** 'Sex and the Lonely Guy', *Esquire,* 1977

**15** 'They eat him, same as a hen-spider eats a cock-spider. That's what women do – if a man lets 'em.'

'Indeed,' commented Flora.

'Ay – but I said "if" a man lets 'em. Now I – I don't let no woman eat me – I eats them instead.'

Flora thought an appreciative silence was the best policy to pursue at this point . . .

'That shocks you, eh?' said Seth, misinterpreting her silence . . .

'I'm afraid I wasn't listening to all of it,' she replied, 'but I am sure it was very interesting. You must tell me all about your work sometime. What do you do now, on the evenings when you aren't – er – eating people.'
**Stella Gibbons**, *Cold Comfort Farm*, 1932

**16** My mother said it was simple to keep a man; you must be a maid in the living room, a cook in the kitchen and a whore in the bedroom. I said I'd hire the other two and take care of the bedroom bit myself.
**Jerry Hall**, 1985

**17** . . . we can call each other girls, chicks, broads, birds and dames with equanimity. Many of us prefer to do so since the word 'woman', being two syllables, is long, unwieldy, and earnest.

But a man must watch his ass. Never may a man be permitted to call any female a 'chick'. He may call you a broad or a dame only if he is a close friend and fond of John Garfield movies. The term 'bird', generally used by fatuous Englishmen, is always frowned upon.
**Cynthia Heimel**, *Sex Tips for Girls*, 1983

**18** You're not too smart, are you? I like that in a man.
**Lawrence Kasdan**, *Body Heat*, screenplay, 1981

**19** Women complain about sex more often than men. Their gripes fall into two major categories: (1) Not enough. (2) Too much.
**Ann Landers**, *Ann Landers Says Truth is Stranger . . .*, 1968

**20** I think men talk to women so they can sleep with them and women sleep with men so they can talk to them.
**Jay McInerny**, *Brightness Falls*, 1992

**21** A woman can forgive a man for the harm he does her, but she can never forgive him for the sacrifices he makes on her account.
**W. Somerset Maugham**, *The Moon and Sixpence*, 1919

**22** A man's womenfolk, whatever their outward show of respect for his merit and authority, always regard him secretly as an ass, and with something akin to pity.
**H. L. Mencken**, *In Defense of Women*, 1922

**23** On one issue at least, men and women agree: they both distrust women.
**H. L. Mencken** (Attrib.)

**24** If you women knew what we were thinking, you'd never stop slapping us.
**Larry Miller**

**25** Society is now influenced, shaped, and even to a large extent controlled by women. This is a far cry from the world of our childhood, when society was controlled by . . . Well, as the author recalls, society was controlled by Mom. Christmas dinner for all the relatives, square dancing, the PTA, split-level ranch houses with two and a half baths – surely no man thought these up. Feminism seems to be a case of women having won a leg-wrestling match with their own other leg. There is only one thing for men to do in response to this confusing situation, which is the same thing men have always done, which is anything women want.
**P. J. O'Rourke**, *Modern Manners*, 1983

**26** Boys don't make passes at female smart-asses.
**Letty Cottin Pogrebin**, *The First Ms Reader*, 1972

**27** I have to talk to my girlfriend every day on the phone. My husband says, 'Why do you have to talk to her today? You just talked to her yesterday. What could you possibly have to tell her?' 'Well, for one thing, I have to tell her you just said that.'
**Rita Rudner**

**28** God created man, and finding him not sufficiently alone, gave him a companion to make him feel his solitude more.
**Paul Valéry**, *Tel Quel*, 1943

**29** A man can be happy with any woman as long as he does not love her.
**Oscar Wilde**, *The Picture of Dorian Gray*, 1891

**30** Between men and women there is no friendship possible. There is passion, enmity, worship, love, but no friendship.
**Oscar Wilde**, *Lady Windermere's Fan*, 1892

**31** Women are never disarmed by compliments. Men always are. That is the difference between the sexes.
**Oscar Wilde**, *An Ideal Husband*, 1895

**32** Men play the game; women know the score.
**Roger Woddis**, *Spectator*

# Metrication

*See also Mathematics.*

**1** On 1 July 1977 all US humor will be converted to the metric system, bringing American humor into conformity with the humor of the rest of the world. On that date, the decimal metric system of risibles, mimics, mockers, grims, and merdes will replace such US Customary humor units as jokes, jibes, jests, railleries, satires, burlesques, and clowning around as the proper measure of comic activity.
**P. J. O'Rourke**, *National Lampoon*, 1977

**2** I adore
a Viennese waltz in 3/4
but my love would not survive
a change to 0.75.
**Fritz Spiegl**, 'Decimal Waltz', *Worse Verse*, 1969

# Middle Age

*See also Age and Ageing; Old Age; Young and Old.*

**1** Middle age is when we can do just as much as ever – but would rather not.
**Anon.**

**2** Years ago we discovered the exact point, the dead centre of middle age. It occurs when you are too young to take up golf and too old to rush up to the net.
**Franklin P. Adams**, *Nods and Becks*, 1944

**3** Middle is a dispiritingly practical age. There is a tendency to sift through unfulfilled dreams and begin chucking out the wilder ones, because they are never going to be any use to you, and to be sensible about making room in the dwindling attic of possibility for just a few

of the tamer numbers. I no longer, for example, expect to be asked to make up a four for the north face of the Eiger, or to have the dividing door of my Inverness sleeper burst open, precipitating a sloe-eyed heiress into my bunk.
**Alan Coren**, *The Times*, 1991

**4** I have everything now I had twenty years ago – except now it's all lower.
**Gypsy Rose Lee**, quoted in *Newsweek*, 1968

**5** Middle age is when, whenever you go on holiday, you pack a sweater.
**Denis Norden**, *My Word*, BBC Radio, 1976

**6** At 50, everyone has the face he deserves.
**George Orwell**, last words in his notebook, 1949

**7** But it's hard to be hip over thirty
When everyone else is nineteen,
When the last dance we learned was the Lindy,
And the last we heard, girls who looked like Barbra Streisand
Were trying to do something about it.
**Judith Viorst**, *It's Hard to be Hip Over Thirty . . .* , 1968

# Mind, The

*See also The Brain.*

**1** All those who believe in telekinesis, raise my hand.
**Steven Wright**, American comic

# Missionaries

*See also Cannibalism; Christianity; The Church; Religion.*

**1** A missionary is a person who teaches cannibals to say grace before they eat him.
**Anon.**

**2** Poor Uncle Harry
Having become a missionary
Found the natives' morals rather crude.
He and Aunt Mary
Swiftly imposed an arbitrary
Ban upon them shopping in the nude.
They all considered this silly and decided to rebel,
They burnt his boots and several suits which made a horrible smell,
The subtle implication was that Uncle could go to hell,

Uncle Harry's not a missionary now . . .
**Noel Coward**, 'Uncle Harry', song from *Pacific 1860*, 1946

**3** Missionaries, my dear! Don't you realize that missionaries are the divinely provided food for destitute and underfed cannibals? Whenever they are on the brink of starvation, Heaven in its infinite mercy sends them a nice plump missionary.
**Oscar Wilde** (Attrib.)

## Mistakes

*See also Misfortune.*

**1** All wrong-doing is done in the sincere belief that it is the best thing to do.
**Arnold Bennett**, 1867–1931, English novelist

**2** Foolproof systems do not take into account the ingenuity of fools.
**Gene Brown**

**3** If only one could have two lives: the first in which to make one's mistakes, which seem as if they have to be made; and the second in which to profit by them.
**D. H. Lawrence**, *The Collected Letters of D. H. Lawrence*, 1962

**4** I don't make mistakes. I make prophecies which immediately turn out to be wrong.
**Murray Walker**, motor racing commentator

**5** Nowadays most people die of a sort of creeping common sense, and discover when it is too late that the only things one never regrets are one's mistakes.
**Oscar Wilde**, *The Picture of Dorian Gray*, 1891

**6** Whenever a man does a thoroughly stupid thing, it is always from the noblest of motives.
**Oscar Wilde**, *The Picture of Dorian Gray*, 1891

## Moderation

*See also Abstinence; Excess; Neutrality.*

**1** Moderation is a virtue only in those who are thought to have an alternative.
**Henry Kissinger**, *Observer*, 1982

**2** Thou shalt not carry moderation into excess.
**Arthur Koestler**, writer and journalist, 1905–1983

## Modern Art

*See also Art and Artists; Modern Life.*

**1** GALLERY OWNER: Now this, Mr Kingsley, is Paul Klee. In Klee you see everything one looks for in modern art: rapid capital growth, sound long-term prospects, and excellent relative liquidity.
**William Hamilton**, *William Hamilton's Anti-Social Register*, cartoon, 1974

**2** Skill without imagination is craftsmanship and gives us many useful objects such as wickerwork picnic baskets. Imagination without skill gives us modern art.
**Tom Stoppard**, *Artist Descending a Staircase*, BBC Radio, 1972

**3** Another unsettling element in modern art is that common symptom of immaturity, the dread of doing what has been done before.
**Edith Wharton**, *The Writing of Fiction*, 1925

**4** . . . collecting contemporary art, the leading edge, the latest thing, warm and wet from the Loft, appeals specifically to those who feel most uneasy about their own commercial wealth . . . See? I'm not like THEM – those Jaycees, those United Fund chairmen, those Young Presidents, those mindless New York A.C. GOYISHEH hog-jowled, stripe-tied goddamn-good-to-see-you-you-old-bastard-you oyster-bar trenchermen . . . Avant-garde art, more than any other, takes the Mammon and the Moloch out of money, puts Levi's, turtlenecks, muttonchops, and other mantles and laurels of bohemian grace upon it.
**Tom Wolfe**, *The Painted Word*, 1975

**5** It was the thaw! It was spring again! The press embraced Pop Art with priapic delight. That goddamned Abstract Expressionism had been so solemn, so grim . . . 'Shards of interpenetrated sensibility make their way, tentatively, through a not always compromisable field of cobalt blue –' How could you write about the freaking stuff? Pop Art you could have fun with.
**Tom Wolfe**, *The Painted Word*, 1975

# Modern Life

*See also Inventions; Modern Art; Progress; Space; Technology; Video Games.*

**1** Yesterday I got my tie stuck in the fax machine. Next thing I knew, I was in Los Angeles.
**Anon.**

**2** I can only please one person per day. Today is not your day. Tomorrow isn't looking good either.
**Scott Adams**, *Dilbert*

**3** VERONICA: I saw somebody peeing in Jermyn Street the other day. I thought, Is this the end of civilization as we know it. Or is it simply somebody peeing in Jermyn Street?
**Alan Bennett**, *The Old Country*, 1978

**4** And where's the roof of golden thatch?
The chimney-stack of stone?
The crown-glass panes that used to match
Each sunset with their own?
Oh now the walls are red and smart
The roof has emerald tiles.
The neon sign's a work of art
And visible for miles.
**John Betjeman**, 'The Village Inn', *A Few Late Chrysanthemums*, 1954

**5** It's hard for me to get used to these changing times. I can remember when the air was clean and sex was dirty.
**George Burns**

**6** I have tried at various times in my life to grasp the rudiments of such inventions as the telephone, the camera, wireless telegraphy and even the ordinary motorcar, but without success. Television, of course, and radar and atomic energy are so far beyond my comprehension that my brain shudders at the thought of them and scurries for cover like a primitive tribesman confronted for the first time with a Dunhill cigarette lighter.
**Noel Coward** (Attrib.)

**7** There is something wrong when you wait in line thirty minutes to get a hamburger that was cooked for ninety seconds an hour ago.
**Lewis Grizzard**

**8** The marvels of modern technology include the development of a soda can which, when discarded, will last forever and a $7,000 car, which, when properly cared for, will rust out in two or three years.
**Paul Harwitz**, *Wall Street Journal*

**9** The past few years have seen a steady increase in the number of people playing music in the streets. The past few years have also seen a steady increase in the number of malignant diseases. Are these two facts related?
**Fran Lebowitz**, *Metropolitan Life*, 1978

**10** Every New Yorker knows the indignity of waiting at a red light, trying to avoid some guy with a sponge and a bucket, and then getting squeegeed against your will. Of course, it's not quite so bad if you're in a car . . .
**Bill Maher**, *Politically Incorrect*, ABC, 1994

**11** There is one fault that I must find with the twentieth century,
And I'll put it in a couple of words: Too adventury.
What I'd like would be some nice dull monotony
If anyone's gotny.
**Ogden Nash**, 'Put Back those Whiskers, I Know You', *Good Intentions*, 1942

**12** Why does the cell phone always ring while you're having sex? This would be OK if the ringer were set on 'vibrate' and the cell phone were properly located. But it isn't. The cell phone is located in the pocket of your pants, which are hanging over the back of a chair next to the bed, with your neighbor's wife in it, that you are hiding under because your neighbor has just returned, unexpectedly, from a business trip.
**P. J. O'Rourke**, *Rolling Stone*, 2000

**13** Ev'rythin's up to date in Kansas City.
They've gone about as fur as they c'n go!
They went and built a skyscraper seven stories high –
About as high as a buildin' orta grow.
Ev'rythin's like a dream in Kansas City.
It's better than a magic-lantern show.
Y' c'n turn the radiator on whenever you want some heat,

· With ev'ry kind o' comfort ev'ry house is
all complete,
You c'n walk to privies in the rain an'
never wet yer feet –
They've gone about as fur as they c'n go!
Yes, sir!
They've gone about as far as they c'n go!

**Richard Rodgers and Oscar Hammerstein II**, 'Kansas
City', song from *Oklahoma*, 1943

**14** No man . . . who has wrestled with a
self-adjusting card table can ever quite be
the man he once was.

**James Thurber**, 'Sex ex Machina', *Let Your Mind Alone*,
1937

# Modesty

*See also Humility; Morality; Virginity.*

**1** Modesty is the art of encouraging people
to find out for themselves how wonderful
you are.
**Anon.**

**2** Modesty is a vastly overrated virtue.
**J. K. Galbraith**, American economist (Attrib.)

**3** Modesty: the gentle art of enhancing
your charm by pretending not to be aware
of it.
**Oliver Herford**, 1864–1935, English-born American
writer

**4** A modest man is usually admired – if
people ever hear of him.
**Edgar Watson Howe**, *Ventures in Common Sense*, 1919

# Money

*See also Banking; Budgets; Credit; Credit Cards;
Debt; Economics; Economy; Greed; Rich and Poor;
Saving; Stock Market; Taxation; Wealth.*

**1** Money isn't everything: usually it isn't
even enough.
**Anon.**

**2** Money is better than poverty, if only for
financial reasons.
**Woody Allen**, *Without Feathers*, 1972

**3** Money can't buy you love – but it
certainly puts you in a wonderful
bargaining position.
**Harrison Baker**

**4** Money isn't everything, but it sure keeps
you in touch with your children.
**J. Paul Getty**, 1892–1976, American billionaire
industrialist

**5** Can money make your hands get rough,
As washing dishes does?
Can money make you smell the way
That cooking fishes does?
It may buy you gems and fancy clothes
And juicy steaks to carve,
But it cannot build your character
Or teach you how to starve!
. . . Money *isn't* everything
As long as you have dough!
**Oscar Hammerstein II**, 'Money isn't Everything', song
from *Allegro*, 1947

**6** All right, so I like spending money! But
name one other extravagance!
**Max Kauffmann**

**7** Money is something you've gotta make
in case you don't die.
**Max Kauffmann**

**8** Money is like a sixth sense without which
you cannot make a complete use of the
other five.
**W. Somerset Maugham**, *Of Human Bondage*, 1915

**9** Money can't buy friends but you can get
a better class of enemy.
**Spike Milligan**, *Puckoon*, 1963

**10** Money is the great equalizer. Money
takes away all your faults. Money will turn a
bald spot into a part!
**Chris Rock**, *Politically Incorrect*, ABC, 1994

**11** The great rule is not to talk about
money with people who have much more
or much less than you.
**Katharine Whitehorn**, English columnist

**12** I don't want money. It is only people
who pay their bills who want that, and I
never pay mine.
**Oscar Wilde**, *The Picture of Dorian Gray*, 1891

# Monogamy

*See also Bigamy; Fidelity; Marriage.*

**1** Monogamy is a custom established to
protect men who are incapable of
protecting themselves.
**Anon.**

**2** Monogamy leaves a lot to be desired.
**Graffito**, London, 1982

## Morality

*See also Conscience; Puritanism; Reformers;
Rogues; Vice and Virtue.*

**1** We know of no spectacle so ridiculous as
the British public in one of its periodical fits
of morality.
**Thomas Macaulay**, *Edinburgh Review*, 1831

**2** Morality consists in suspecting other
people of not being legally married.
**George Bernard Shaw**, *The Doctor's Dilemma*, 1906

**3** PICKERING: Have you no morals, man?
DOOLITTLE: Can't afford them, Governor.
**George Bernard Shaw**, *Pygmalion*, 1912

**4** Moral indignation is jealousy with a halo.
**H. G. Wells**, *The Wife of Sir Isaac Harman*, 1914

**5** A man who moralizes is usually a
hypocrite, and a woman who moralizes is
invariably plain.
**Oscar Wilde**, *Lady Windermere's Fan*, 1892

**6** Morality is simply the attitude we adopt
to people whom we personally dislike.
**Oscar Wilde**, *An Ideal Husband*, 1895

## Morning

*See also Breakfast.*

**1** The average, healthy, well-adjusted adult
gets up at seven thirty in the morning
feeling just plain terrible.
**Jean Kerr**, *Please Don't Eat the Daisies*, 1957

**2** Don't forget I was up early this morning.
I was up at the crack of 6, took a brisk walk
to the window, was back in bed by 6.05. I
stood under that cold shower for ten
minutes. Tomorrow I'm going to turn the
water on.
**Henny Youngman**, 1940

## Mothers

*See also Children; Fathers; Housewives; Women.*

**1** Never marry a man who hates his mother
because he'll end up hating you.
**Jill Bennett**, English actress (Attrib.)

**2** The parting injunctions

Of mothers and wives
Are one of those functions
That poison their lives.
**Clarence Day**, *Scenes from Mesozoic*

**3** Before I became a mother I was such a
free spirit. I used to say, 'No man will ever
dominate me.'
   Now I have a six-year-old master.
**Sally Diaz**

**4** Nobody can misunderstand a boy like his
own mother.
**Norman Douglas** (Attrib.)

**5** I get those maternal feelings. Like when
I'm lying on the couch and can't reach the
remote. 'Boy, a kid would be nice, right
now.'
**Kathleen Madigan**, American standup comic

**6** Few misfortunes can befall a boy which
bring worse consequences than to have a
really affectionate mother.
**W. Somerset Maugham**, *A Writer's Notebook*, 1949

**7** My daughter thinks I'm nosy. At least
that's what she says in her diary.
**Sally Poplin**

**8** No woman can shake off her mother.
There should be no mothers, only women.
**George Bernard Shaw**, *Too True to be Good*, 1934

**9** MOTHER: Do you love me, Albert?
ALBERT: Yes.
MOTHER: Yes – what?
ALBERT: Yes, please.
**Tom Stoppard**, *Albert's Bridge*, BBC Radio, 1967

**10** On her face was the look of a mother
whose daughter had seen the light and will
shortly be marrying a deserving young
clergyman with a bachelor uncle high up in
the shipping business.
**P. G. Wodehouse**, *Blandings Castle and Elsewhere*, 1935

## Mothers-in-Law

*See also Husbands; Marriage; Women.*

**1** My mother-in-law broke up my marriage.
My wife came home from work one day and
found me in bed with her.
**Lenny Bruce**

**2** The mother-in-law thinks I'm effeminate:

not that I mind that because, beside her, I am!

**Les Dawson**, *The Les Dawson Joke Book*, 1979

**3** I haven't spoken to my mother-in-law for eighteen months – I don't like to interrupt her.

**Ken Dodd**, English comedian

**4** Behind every successful man stands a surprised mother-in-law.

**Hubert Humphrey**, 1911–78, Democratic Vice-President, speech, 1964

**5** ERIC: But I will say this for her: there was one time in my life when I think I would have cut my throat if it wasn't for my mother-in-law.
ERNIE: How d'you mean?
ERIC: She was using my razor.

**Eric Morecambe and Ernie Wise**, *The Morecambe and Wise Joke Book*, 1979

# Motorcycling
*See also Driving.*

**1** Motorcyclists who don't wear helmets should have their heads examined. And usually do!

**Jerry Dennis**

**2** A cousin of mine who was a casualty surgeon in Manhattan tells me that he and his colleagues had a one-word nickname for bikers: Donors.

**Stephen Fry**, *Paperweight*, 1992

# Murder
*See also Assassination; Capital Punishment; Crime; Guns; The Law; Police.*

**1** From Number Nine, Penwiper Mews,
There is really abominable news:
They've discovered a head
In the box for the bread
But nobody seems to know whose.

**Edward Gorey**

**2** ERIC: It was the corpse. He had a gun in his hand and a knife in his back. Who d'you think poisoned him?
ERNIE: Who?
ERIC: Nobody. He'd been strangled.

**Eric Morecambe and Ernie Wise**, *The Morecambe and Wise Joke Book*, 1979

**3** If the desire to kill and the opportunity to kill came always together, who would escape hanging?

**Mark Twain**

**4** Murder is always a mistake . . . One should never do anything that one cannot talk about after dinner.

**Oscar Wilde**, *The Picture of Dorian Gray*, 1891

**5** It's the old problem, of course – the one that makes life so tough for murderers – what to do with the body.

**P. G. Wodehouse**, *The Code of the Woosters*, 1938

# Music and Musicians
*See also Composers; Folk Music; Jazz; Opera; Rock 'n' Roll; Songs and Singers.*

**1** Q: What do you get when you play New Age music backwards?
A: New Age music.

**Anon.**

**2** Q: What happens when you play country music backwards?
A: You sober up, your wife comes home and your dog comes back to life.

**Anon.**

**3** Country song titles:
'I've Got Tears in My Ears From Lyin' On My Back in Bed While I Cry Over You'

**Harold Barlow**, 1949

'If the Phone Doesn't Ring, It's Me'

**Jimmy Buffett, Wyland Arnold Jennings and Michael E. Utley**, 1985

'If I Said You Had a Beautiful Body, Would You Hold It Against Me?'

**David M. Bellamy**, 1979

'Did I Shave My Legs for This?'

**Deana Carter and Rhonda Hart**, 1995

'Get Your Biscuits in the Oven and Your Buns in the Bed'

**Kinky Friedman**, 1979

'I'd Rather Have a Bottle in Front of Me Than a Frontal Lobotomy'

**Randy Hanzlick**

'If Loving You Is Wrong, I Don't Want To Be Right'

**Raymond Jackson, Carl Hampton and Homer Banks**, 1972

**4** More country song titles
'I Gave Her a Ring, She Gave Me the Finger'
'Don't the Girls All Get Prettier at Closing Time?'

'You Done Stompt on My Heart, an
Squished That Sucker Flat' ('Sweetheart, you
just sorta, Stomped on my aorta')
'Her Teeth Was Stained But Her Heart Was
Pure' (written by Robin Dorsey)
'I Don't Know Whether to Commit Suicide
Tonight or Go Bowlin'' (written by Robin
Dorsey)
'We Used to Kiss Each Other on the Lips,
But Now It's All Over'
'She Used My Tears to Wash Her Socks'
**Quoted in 'Honky Tonking' by Molly Ivins,** *Ms*, 1988

**5** Q: What's the world's greatest optimist?
A: A banjo player with a pager.
**Anon.**

**6** There was an Old Person of Tring
  Who, when somebody asked her to sing,
  Replied, 'Aren't it odd?
  I can never tell "God
  Save the Weasel" from "Pop Goes the
    King."'
**Anon.,** *The New York Times Magazine*, 1946

**7** The music teacher came twice a week to
bridge the awful gap between Dorothy and
Chopin.
**George Ade,** 1866–1944, American playwright

**8** CUSTOMER: What kind of music do you
usually have here?
BARMAN: Oh, we've got both kinds. We've
got country AND western.
**Dan Aykroyd and John Landis,** *The Blues Brothers*,
screenplay, 1980

**9** The English may not like music but they
absolutely love the noise it makes.
**Sir Thomas Beecham,** *A Mingled Chime*, 1944

**10** Madam, you have between your legs an
instrument capable of giving pleasure to
thousands – and all you can do is scratch it.
**Sir Thomas Beecham,** to lady cellist (Attrib.)

**11** We cannot expect you to be with us all
the time, but perhaps you could be good
enough to keep in touch now and again.
**Sir Thomas Beecham,** to musician at rehearsal
(Attrib.)

**12** Why do we have all these third-rate
foreign conductors around when we have so
many second-rate ones of our own?
**Sir Thomas Beecham**

**13** If it isn't a Stradivarius, I've been robbed
of 110 dollars.
**Jack Benny** (Attrib.)

**14** The Steinway people have asked me to
announce that this is a Baldwin piano.
**Victor Borge,** Danish pianist

**15** Music with dinner is an insult both to
the cook and violinist.
**G. K. Chesterton,** 1874–1936, English essayist and poet
(Attrib.)

**16** Extraordinary how potent cheap music
is.
**Noel Coward,** *Private Lives*, 1930

**17** I hate music, especially when it's played.
**Jimmy Durante**

**18** Away with the music of Broadway,
  Be off with your Irving Berlin,
  Oh, I give no quarter
  To Kern or Cole Porter,
  And Gershwin keeps pounding on tin.
  How can I be civil
  While hearing this drivil,
  It's strictly for night-clubbing souses.
  Oh, give me the free 'n' easy
  Waltz that is Viennesy
  And,
  Go tell the band
  If they want a hand,
  The waltz must be Strauss's.
**George and Ira Gershwin,** 'By Strauss', song from *The
Show is On*, 1936

**19** I only know two tunes. One of them is
'Yankee Doodle' and the other isn't.
**Ulysses S. Grant**

**20** Classical music is the kind we keep
thinking will turn into a tune.
**Kin Hubbard,** *Abe Martin's Sayings*, 1915

**21** Of all the noises, I think music the least
disagreeable.
**Samuel Johnson,** quoted in *Morning Chronicle*, 1816

**22** This world is a difficult world, indeed,
  And people are hard to suit,
  And the man who plays on the violin,
  Is a bore to the man with the flute.
**Walter Learned,** *Consolation*

**23** There was a time when music knew its
place. No longer. Possibly this is not music's
fault. It may be that music fell in with a bad

crowd and lost its sense of common decency . . . The first thing that music must understand is that there are two kinds of music – good music and bad music. Good music is music that I want to hear. Bad music is music that I don't want to hear.
**Fran Lebowitz,** *Metropolitan Life,* 1978

**24** The kids today are quite right about the music their parents listened to: most of it was trash. The parents are quite right about what their young listen to: most of it is trash too.
**Gene Lees,** 'Rock', *High Fidelity,* 1967

**25** Music-hall songs provide the dull with wit, just as proverbs provide them with wisdom.
**W. Somerset Maugham,** *A Writer's Notebook,* 1949

**26** I don't like country music, but I don't mean to denigrate those who do. And for the people who like country music, denigrate means 'put down'.
**Bob Newhart**

**27** Without music, life would be a mistake.
**Friedrich Wilhelm Nietzsche,** *The Twilight of the Idols,* 1889

**28** When you are about thirty-five years old, something terrible always happens to music.
**Steve Race,** BBC Radio, 1982

**29** Music is essentially useless, as life is.
**George Santayana,** *Little Essays,* 1920

**30** Artists who say they practise eight hours a day are liars or asses.
**Andres Segovia,** Spanish guitar-player, 1980

**31** . . . music is the brandy of the damned.
**George Bernard Shaw,** *Man and Superman,* 1903

**32** I wish the Government would put a tax on pianos for the incompetent.
**Edith Sitwell,** *Edith Sitwell: Selected Letters 1916–1964,* 1970

**33** And I've often wondered how did it all start?
    Who found out that nothing can
       capture a heart
    Like a melody can?
    Well, whoever it was, I'm a fan.
**Bjorn Ulvaeus and Benny Andersson,** 'Thank You For the Music', 1977

**34** I like Wagner's music better than anybody's. It is so loud that one can talk the whole time without people hearing what one says.
**Oscar Wilde,** *The Picture of Dorian Gray,* 1891

**35** Musical people are so absurdly unreasonable. They always want one to be perfectly dumb at the very moment when one is longing to be absolutely deaf.
**Oscar Wilde,** *An Ideal Husband,* 1895

**36** Music makes one feel so romantic – at least it always got on one's nerves – which is the same thing nowadays.
**Oscar Wilde,** *A Woman of No Importance,* 1893

**37** It was loud in spots and less loud in other spots, and it had that quality which I have noticed in all violin solos of seeming to last much longer than it actually did.
**P. G. Wodehouse,** *The Mating Season,* 1949

# Names

*See also Rock 'n' Roll – Band Names.*

**1** Said Jerome K. Jerome to Ford Madox Ford,
'There's something, old boy, that I've always abhorred:
When people address me and call me "Jerome",
Are they being standoffish, or too much at home?'
Said Ford, 'I agree;
It's the same thing with me.'
**William Cole**, 'Mutual Problem', *The Oxford Book of American Light Verse*, 1979

**2** Marie-Joseph? It's a *lovely* name! It just sounds silly, that's all.
**Dame Edna Everage (Barry Humphries)**, *Housewife Superstar*, one-man show, 1976

**3** Now why did you name your baby 'John'? Every Tom, Dick and Harry is named 'John'.
**Samuel Goldwyn**, 1882–1974, American film producer (Attrib.)

**4** 'Yossarian? Is that his name? Yossarian? What the hell kind of a name is Yossarian?'
Lieutenant Scheisskopf had the facts at his finger tips. 'It's Yossarian's name, sir,' he explained.
**Joseph Heller**, *Catch-22*, 1961

**5** The name of a man is a numbing blow from which he never recovers.
**Marshall McLuhan**, *Understanding Media*, 1964

**6** No good can come of association with anything labelled Gwladys or Ysobel or Ethyl or Mabelle or Kathryn. But particularly Gwladys.
**P. G. Wodehouse**, *Very Good, Jeeves*, 1930

# Narcissism

*See also Egotism; Vanity.*

**1** He fell in love with himself at first sight and it is a passion to which he has always remained faithful. Self-love seems so often unrequited.
**Anthony Powell**, *The Acceptance World*, 1955

**2** A narcissist is someone better looking than you are.
**Gore Vidal**

# Nature

*See also The Country.*

**1** ROSIE: Nature, Mr Allnutt, is what we are put into this world to rise above.
**James Agee**, *The African Queen*, screenplay, 1951

**2** BORIS: To me, nature is . . . I don't know, spiders and bugs and then big fish eating little fish and the plants eating plants, and animals eating . . . It's like an enormous restaurant in the way I see it.
**Woody Allen**, *Love and Death*, screenplay, 1975

**3** Who can ignore a fresh-fallen conker, not pick it up, stare at it, fondle it? From the glorious colour, the rich patina, the silken texture, conkers might not be new-born veg at all, but 200-year-old offcuts of mahogany, whittled and buffed in their tea-breaks by Sheraton's more talented apprentices.
**Alan Coren**, *A Bit on the Side*, 1995

**4** What sublime thoughts filled my mind as I bent to the wind, and trudged through the gorse and heather? I will tell you. I was wondering how much money I shall make out of my next book. Thus does nature keep us in touch with the great realities of existence.
**J. B. Morton**, *Morton's Folly*, 1933

**5** Worship of nature may be ancient, but seeing nature as cuddlesome, hug-a-bear and too cute for words is strictly a modern fashion.
**P. J. O'Rourke**, *Parliament of Whores*, 1991

**6** In nature two things do not occur – the wheel and good taste.
**John Steinbeck**, quoted in *Steinbeck: A Life in Letters*, 1975

# Nausea

*See also Drink; Hangovers; Illness.*

**1** *Chuck, Enough to make you*: (see under Chunder, Technicolour Yawn, Hurl, Play the Whale, Park the Tiger, Cry Ruth). *Chunder* to enjoy oneself in reverse. *Technicolour Yawn*: Liquid Laugh.
**Barry Humphries**, glossary from *Bazza Pulls It Off*, 1972

**2** I've had liquid laughs in bars
And I've hurled from moving cars

And I've chuckled when and where it
   suited me
But, if I could choose a spot
To regurgitate me lot
Then I'd chunder in the old Pacific sea.
**Barry Humphries**, 'The Old Pacific Sea', 1964

**3** Don't worry – the white wine came up with the fish.
**Herman J. Mankiewicz**, after being sick at a Hollywood party (Attrib.)

**4** Every authority on etiquette discusses how to put things into your stomach, but very few discuss how to get them back out in a hurry. Actually, there is no way to make vomiting courteous. You have to do the next best thing, which is to vomit in such a way that the story you tell about it later will be amusing.
**P. J. O'Rourke**, *Modern Manners*, 1983

# Navy, The

*See also The Army; The Sea; Ships; War.*

**1** The Navy's a very gentlemanly business. You fire at the horizon to sink a ship and then you pull people out of the water and say, 'Frightfully sorry, old chap.'
**William Golding**, *Sunday Times*, 1984

**2** The trouble with modern navies is that they have to operate in water, which is ridiculous stuff to get around in and offers no decent cover at all, except for Davy Jones's locker.
**Tony Hendra**, 'EEC! It's the US of E!', *National Lampoon*, 1976

# Needs

**1** That I am totally devoid of sympathy for, or interest in, the world of groups is directly attributable to the fact that my two greatest needs and desires – smoking cigarettes and plotting revenge – are basically solitary pursuits.
**Fran Lebowitz**, *Metropolitan Life*, 1978

**2** All I need is room enough to lay a hat and a few friends.
**Dorothy Parker**

# Negotiations

*See also Meetings.*

**1** When a man tells me he's going to put all his cards on the table, I always look up his sleeve.
**Lord Hore-Belisha**, Secretary of State for War, 1937–40

# Neighbours

*See also The Suburbs.*

**1** Give the neighbour's kids an inch and they'll take a yard.
**Helen Castle**

**2** It's easier to love humanity as a whole than to love one's neighbour.
**Eric Hoffer**, American philosopher

**3** Nothing makes you more tolerant of a neighbour's noisy party than being there.
**Franklin P. Jones**, American comic writer

# Nepotism

*See also The Family.*

**1** Nepotism, *n.* appointing your grandmother to office for the good of the party.
**Ambrose Bierce**, *The Devil's Dictionary*, 1911

**2** Nobody talks more of free enterprise and competition and of the best man winning than the man who inherited his father's store or farm.
**C. Wright Mills**, 1916–62, American sociologist

# Neutrality

*See also Moderation.*

**1** Q: Which is the most neutral country in the world?
A: Tibet – it doesn't even interfere in its *own* internal affairs.
**Anon.**

**2** We know what happens to people who stay in the middle of the road. They get run over.
**Aneurin Bevan**, 1897–1960, British Labour politician

**3** The middle of the road is all of the usable surface. The extremes, right and left, are in the gutters.
**Dwight D. Eisenhower**

**4** An independent is a guy who wants to take the politics out of politics.
**Adlai Stevenson**

# New England

*See also America and the Americans; Boston.*

**1** The most serious charge which can be brought against New England is not Puritanism but February.
**Joseph Wood Krutch**, *The Twelve Seasons*, 1949

**2** There is a sumptuous variety about the New England weather . . . In the spring I have counted one hundred and thirty-six different kinds of weather inside of four and twenty hours.
**Mark Twain**, speech, 1876

# News

*See also Journalism; Newspapers.*

**1** It's not the world that's got so much worse but the news coverage that's got so much better.
**G. K. Chesterton**, 1874–1936, English essayist and poet (Attrib.)

**2** No News Is Preferable.
**Fran Lebowitz**, *Metropolitan Life*, 1978

**3** *News*: anything that makes a woman say, 'For heaven's sake!'
**Edgar Watson Howe**, 1853–1937, American writer

# Newspapers

*See also Journalism; News.*

**1** Instead of being arrested, as we stated, for kicking his wife down a flight of stairs and hurling a lighted kerosene lamp after her, the Rev. James P. Wellman died unmarried four years ago.
**Anon.**, from an American newspaper, quoted by Sir Edward Burne-Jones in a letter to Lady Horner

**2** Sex Change Archbishop in Mercy Palace Dash
**Anon.**, perfect tabloid headline

**3** Newspaper headlines:

Kids Make Nutritious Snacks
Juvenile Court to Try Shooting Defendant
Prostitutes Appeal to Pope
Plane Too Close to Ground, Crash Probe Told
Drunk Gets Nine Months in Violin Case
Something Went Wrong in Jet Crash, Expert Says
Miners Refused to Work After Death
War Dims Hope for Peace
**Some, or all, apocryphal**

**4** FREDDIE STARR ATE MY HAMSTER
*Sun*, front page, 1986

**5** *Variety* headlines

Sticks Nix Hick Pix (1935)
Lizards Eat Arnold's Lunch (1993)
Pic Biz Freaked by Cybergeek's Leaks (1997)
*Variety Almanac*, 1999

**6** I keep reading between the lies.
**Goodman Ace**, 1899–1982, American humorist

**7** I read the newspaper avidly. It is my one form of continuous fiction.
**Aneurin Bevan** (Attrib.)

**8** I love the weight of American Sunday newspapers. Pulling them up off the floor is good for the figure.
**Noel Coward** (Attrib.)

**9** I'm the Clergyman who's never been to London,
   I'm the Clergyman who's never been to Town,
   An enterprising journalist approached me
   And every word I said he jotted down,
   I had to face a battery of cameras
   And hold an extra service in the snow
   And all because I've *never* been to London
   And haven't got the *least* desire to go!
**Noel Coward**, 'The Hall of Fame', *Words and Music*, 1932

**10** Wooing the press is an exercise roughly akin to picnicking with a tiger. You might enjoy the meal but the tiger always eats last.
**Maureen Dowd**, columnist, *The New York Times*

**11** It's like opening a piece of used lavatory paper, reading newspapers.
**Stephen Fry**, *Independent on Sunday*, 1995

**12** The man who never looks into a newspaper is better informed than he who reads them . . .
**Thomas Jefferson**, President of the United States, 1801–9, letter to John Norvell, 1807

**13** Power without responsibility: the prerogative of the harlot throughout the ages.
**Rudyard Kipling**, speech, 1923

**14** When I say 'start' let's have five seconds of silence. (*Pause*) That's pretty good. That gives something for the news media to quote with absolute accuracy.
**Bobby Knight**, Indiana basketball coach, 1982

**15** Everything you read in the newspapers is absolutely true except for the rare story of which you happen to have first-hand knowledge.
**Erwin Knoll**, 1931–94, American editor

**16** People everywhere confuse
   What they read in newspapers with news.
**A. J. Liebling**, *New Yorker*, 1956

**17** You should always believe all you read in the newspapers, as this makes them more interesting.
**Rose Macaulay**, *A Casual Commentary*, 1925

**18** I will say about *The Times* that every 25 years it publishes a book to show how wrong it has been over the great problems of the previous quarter of a century.
**Harold Macmillan**, 1966

**19** Once a newspaper touches a story, the facts are lost for ever, even to the protagonists.
**Norman Mailer**, *Esquire*, 1960

**20** All successful newspapers are ceaselessly querulous and bellicose. They never defend anyone or anything if they can help it; if the job is forced upon them, they tackle it by denouncing someone or something else.
**H. L. Mencken**, *Prejudices*, First Series, 1919

**21** Any man with ambition, integrity – and $10,000,000 dollars – can start a daily newspaper.
**Henry Morgan**, 1950

**22** For the press, progress is not news – trouble is news.
**Richard Nixon**

**23** Early in life I had noticed that no event is ever correctly reported in a newspaper.
**George Orwell**, *Collected Essays, Journalism and Letters*, 1968

**24** I hope we never live to see the day when a thing is as bad as some of our newspapers make it.
**Will Rogers**, 1934

**25** No self-respecting fish would be wrapped in a Murdoch newspaper.
**Mike Royko**, *Chicago Tribune*

**26** It's amazing that the amount of news that happens in the world every day just exactly fits the newspaper.
**Jerry Seinfeld**

**27** Newspapers are unable . . . to discriminate between a bicycle accident and the collapse of civilization.
**George Bernard Shaw**, *Too True to Be Good*, 1931

**28** An editor is one who separates the wheat from the chaff and prints the chaff.
**Adlai Stevenson**

**29** MILNE: Junk journalism is the evidence of a society that has got at least one thing right, that there should be nobody with the power to dictate where responsible journalism begins.
**Tom Stoppard**, *Night and Day*, 1978

**30** RUTH: I'm with you on the free press. It's the newspapers I can't stand.
**Tom Stoppard**, *Night and Day*, 1978

**31** All newspapers and journalistic activity is an intellectual brothel from which there is no retreat.
**Leo Tolstoy**, letter, 1871

**32** With regard to Policy, I expect you already have your own views. I never hamper my correspondents in any way. What the British public wants first, last and all the time is News. Remember that the Patriots are in the right and are going to win. *The Beast* stands by them four square. But they must win quickly. The British public has no interest in a war that drags on indecisively. A few sharp victories, some conspicuous acts of personal bravery on the Patriot side and a colourful entry into the capital. That is *The Beast* Policy for the war.
**Evelyn Waugh**, *Scoop*, 1938

**33** In the old days men had the rack, now they have the Press.
**Oscar Wilde**, 'The Soul of Man under Socialism', 1891

**34** It is useless to dangle rich bribes before our eyes. *Cosy Moments* cannot be muzzled. You doubtless mean well, according to your – if I may say so – somewhat murky lights, but we are not for sale, except at ten cents weekly. From the hills of Maine to the Everglades of Florida, from Sandy Hook to San Francisco, from Portland, Oregon, to Melonsquashville, Tennessee, one sentence is in every man's mouth. And what is that sentence? I give you three guesses. You give it up? It is this: '*Cosy Moments* cannot be muzzled!'
**P. G. Wodehouse**, *Psmith, Journalist*, 1915

# New Year

**1** A New Year's resolution is something that goes in one year and out the other.
**Anon.**

**2** May your troubles in the New Year be as short-lived as your resolutions.
**Anon.**

**3** New Year's Resolutions.
I WILL NOT
Drink more than fourteen alcohol units a week.
Smoke.
Waste money on: pasta-makers, ice-cream machines or other culinary devices which will never use; books by unreadable literary authors to put impressively on shelves; exotic underwear, since pointless as have no boyfriend.
. . . Spend more than earn.
. . . Fall for any of following: alcoholics, workaholics, commitment phobics, people with girlfriends or wives, mysogynists, megalomaniacs, chauvinists, emotional fuckwits or freeloaders, perverts.
**Helen Fielding**, *Bridget Jones's Diary*, 1996

**4** New Year's Resolutions
I WILL

. . . Reduce circumference of thighs by 3 inches (i.e. 1¹/₂ inches each), using anti-cellulite diet.

Purge flat of all extraneous matter.

. . . Be more confident.

Be more assertive.

. . . Be kinder and help others more.

Eat more pulses.

Get up straight away when wake up in mornings.

. . . Form functional relationship with responsible adult.

Learn to programme video.

**Helen Fielding,** *Bridget Jones's Diary,* 1996

**5** New Year's Eve – 'where auld acquaintance be forgot' – unless those tests come back positive.

**Jay Leno,** *The Tonight Show*

# New York

*See also American and the Americans.*

**1** I love short trips to New York; to me it is the finest three-day town on earth.

**James Cameron,** *Witness,* 1966

**2** It seemed almost intolerably shining, secure and well dressed, as though it was continually going to gay parties while London had to stay at home and do the housework.

**Noel Coward,** 1943

**3** We'll have Manhattan,
  The Bronx and Staten
  Island too.
  We'll try to cross
  Fifth Avenue.
  As black as onyx
  We'll find the Bronnix
  Park Express.
  Our Flatbush flat, I guess.
  Will be a great success,
  More or less.

**Lorenz Hart,** 'Manhattan', song, 1925

**4** This is New York, a combat zone, and everyone has to have an angle or they're not allowed over the bridges or through the tunnels. Let them have their angles, it's what they live for. You've got better things to worry about, like making sure the people that actually matter don't try any funny stuff.

**Cynthia Heimel,** 'Lower Manhattan Survival Tactics', *Village Voice,* 1983

**5** If there ever was an aviary overstocked with jays it is that Yaptown-on-the-Hudson, called New York.

**O. Henry,** 'A Tempered Wind', *Gentle Grafter,* 1908

**6** Well, little old Noisyville-on-the-Subway is good enough for me.

**O. Henry,** *Strictly Business,* 1910

**7** A city where everyone mutinies but no one deserts.

**Harry Hershfield**

**8** People say New Yorkers can't get along. Not true. I saw two New Yorkers, complete strangers, sharing a cab. One guy took the tires and the radio; the other guy took the engine.

**David Letterman,** *The Late Show,* CBS

**9** A car is useless in New York, essential everywhere else. The same with good manners.

**Mignon McLaughlin,** *The Second Neurotic's Notebook,* 1966

**10** New York, the nation's thyroid gland.

**Christopher Morley,** *Shore Leave*

**11** In New York beautiful girls can become
      more beautiful by going to Elizabeth
      Arden,
    And getting stuff put on their faces and
      waiting for it to harden,
    And poor girls with nothing to their
      names but a letter or two can get rich
      and joyous
    From a brief trip to their loyous.
    So I can say with impunity
    That New York is a city of opportunity.

**Ogden Nash,** 'A Brief Guide to New York', *Many Long Years Ago,* 1945

**12** The Bronx?
   No, thonx!

**Ogden Nash,** 'Geographical Reflection', *New Yorker,* 1931

**13** Vulgar of manner, overfed,
   Overdressed and underbred;
   Heartless, Godless, hell's delight,
   Rude by day and lewd by night . . .
   Crazed with avarice, lust and rum,

New York, thy name's Delirium.
**Byron Rufus Newton**, *Owed to New York*, 1906

**14** . . . I've been a New Yorker for ten years, and the only people who are nice to us turn out to be Moonies.
**P. J. O'Rourke**, *Rolling Stone*, 1982

**15** New York is like living inside Stephen King's brain during an aneurysm.
**Kevin Rooney**

**16** There's no room for amateurs, even in crossing the streets.
**George Segal**, quoted in *Newsweek*, 1972

**17** It's not Mecca, it just smells like it.
**Neil Simon**, *California Suite*, screenplay, 1978

**18** WILLIAMS: Next thing I knew, I was in New York.
INTERVIEWER: Was that a heavy adjustment for you to make?
WILLIAMS: I was the walking epitome of fur*shirr* meets yo'ass. On my first day in New York, I went to school dressed like a typical California kid: I wore tie-up yoga pants and a Hawaiian shirt, and I kept stepping in dog shit with my thongs.
**Robin Williams**, interview in *Playboy*, 1982

**19** The Sheridan Apartment House stands in the heart of New York's Bohemian and artistic quarter. If you threw a brick from any of its windows, you would be certain to brain some rising interior decorator, some Vorticist sculptor or a writer of revolutionary *vers libre*.
**P. G. Wodehouse**, *The Small Bachelor*, 1927

## New Zealand

**1** If an English butler and an English nanny sat down to design a country, they would come up with New Zealand.
**Anon.**

**2** Terrible Tragedy in the South Seas. Three million people trapped alive!
**Tom Scott**, apocryphal headline, *New Zealand Listener*, 1979

## Noise
*See also Ears; Silence.*

**1** Don't get annoyed if your neighbour

plays his hi-fi at two o'clock in the morning. Call him at four and tell him how much you enjoyed it.
**Anon.**

**2** Noise, *n.* a stench in the ear. The chief product and authenticating sign of civilization.
**Ambrose Bierce**, *The Devil's Dictionary*, 1911

## Nonsense
*See also Humour.*

**1** I never saw a Purple Cow,
I never hope to see one;
But I can tell you anyhow,
I'd rather see than be one.
**Gelett Burgess**, 'The Purple Cow', *The Burgess Nonsense Book*, 1901

**2** Ah, yes! I wrote the 'Purple Cow' –
I'm Sorry, now, I Wrote it!
But I can Tell you, Anyhow,
I'll Kill you if you Quote it!
**Gelett Burgess**, 'Cinq Ans Apres', *The Burgess Nonsense Book*, 1901

## Nostalgia
*See also Memory; The Past.*

**1** Nostalgia ain't what it used to be.
**Anon.**

**2** Before the war and especially before the Boer War, it was summer all the year round.
**George Orwell**, *Coming Up for Air*, 1939

## Novels
*See also Books; Literature; Writers; Writing.*

**1** Every novel should have a beginning, a muddle and an end.
**Peter De Vries**, 1910–93, American novelist

**2** WAGNER: One of the things that makes novels less plausible than history, I find, is the way they shrink from coincidence.
**Tom Stoppard**, *Night and Day*, 1978

**3** I quite admit that modern novels have many good points. All I insist on is that, as a class, they are quite unreadable.
**Oscar Wilde**, 'The Decay of Lying', 1889

**4** Every author really wants to have letters printed in the papers. Unable to make the

grade, he drops down a rung of the ladder and writes novels.
**P. G. Wodehouse**

**5** It has been well said that an author who expects results from a first novel is in a position similar to that of a man who drops a rose petal down the Grand Canyon of Arizona and listens for the echo.
**P. G. Wodehouse**, *Cocktail Time*, 1958

**6** I write about stalwart men, strong but oh so gentle, and girls with wide grey eyes and hair the colour of ripe wheat, who are always having misunderstandings and going to Africa. The men, that is. The girls stay at home and marry the wrong bimbos. But there's a happy ending. The bimbos break their necks in the hunting field and the men come back in the last chapter and they and the girls get together in the twilight, and all around is the scent of English flowers and birds singing their evensong in the shrubbery. Makes me shudder to think of it.
**P. G. Wodehouse**, *Ice in the Bedroom*, 1961

**7** Nothing induces me to read a novel except when I have to make money by writing about it. I detest them.
**Virginia Woolf**

# Nuclear Power

*See also Electricity; Energy; Nuclear War.*

**1** What's all this fuss about plutonium? Now can something named after a Disney character be dangerous?
  They say that if there is a leak in a nuclear power plant the radiation can kill you. Nix! Radiation cannot kill you because it contains absolutely no cholesterol. They say atomic radiation can hurt your reproductive organs. My answer is so can a hockey stick. But we don't stop building them.
  I told my wife that there was a chance that radiation might hurt my reproductive organs but she said in her opinion it's a small price to pay.
**Johnny Carson**, *The Tonight Show*, NBC TV

# Nuclear War

*See also The Bomb; Nuclear Power; Pacifism; War.*

**1** No first-class war can now be fought
Till all that can be sold is bought.
So do get going helter-skelter
And sell each citizen a shelter
Wherein, while being bombed and strafed, he
Can reek and retch and rot in perfect safety.
**Kenneth Burke**, 'Civil Defense', *Collected Poems 1915–1967*

**2** Don'tcha worry, honey chile,
Don'tcha cry no more,
It's jest a li'l ole atom bomb
In a li'l ole lim'ted war.
It's jest a bitsy warhead, chile,
On a li'l ole tactical shell,
And all it'll do is blow us-all
To a li'l ole lim'ted hell.
**Marya Mannes**, 'On Limited Warfare', *Subverse*

**3** I had that bomb dispatched to Moscow the moment we got imminent warning red. Ah, those Ruskies didn't think we had the means of delivering the bomb . . . they overlooked the fact that we have the finest postal system in the world.
**Spike Milligan and John Antrobus**, *The Bed-sitting Room*, 1963

**4** On this the first anniversary of the Nuclear Misunderstanding which led to World War III, I'd like to point out that under a Labour Administration, this was the shortest World War on record, two minutes twenty-eight seconds precisely, including the signing of the Peace Treaty . . .
**Spike Milligan and John Antrobus**, *The Bed-sitting Room*, 1963

# Nudity

*See also The Body; Censorship; Pornography; Prudery; Sex.*

**1** Don't miss our show! Six beautiful dancing girls! Five beautiful costumes!
**Poster** outside nightclub, London

**2** If God had wanted us to walk around naked, we would have been born that way.
**Anon.**

**3** If God had meant us to walk around naked, he would never have invented the wicker chair.
**Erma Bombeck**

**4** I didn't pay three pounds fifty just to see half a dozen acorns and a chipolata.
**Noel Coward**, after watching the male nude scenes in David Storey's *The Changing Room*, 1972

**5** The trouble with nude dancing is that not everything stops when the music does.
**Robert Helpmann**, dancer and choreographer

**6** I'm not *against* half-naked girls – not as often as I'd like to be . . .
**Benny Hill**, *The Benny Hill Show*, Thames TV, 1984

**7** Full-frontal nudity . . . has now become accepted by every branch of the theatrical profession with the possible exception of lady accordion-players.
**Denis Norden**, *You Can't Have Your Kayak and Heat It*, 1973

**8** I think onstage nudity is disgusting, shameful and damaging to all things American. But if I were twenty-two with a great body, it would be artistic, tasteful, patriotic and a progressive religious experience.
**Shelley Winters**, American actress

# Obscenity

*See also Censorship; Pornography; Puritanism; Sex; Swearing.*

**1** Obscenity is whatever gives a judge an erection.
**Anon.**

**2** It's a heavy breather wanting to reverse the charges . . .
**Marc**, cartoon in *The Times*, 1977

**3** Obscenity is what happens to shock some elderly and ignorant magistrate.
**Bertrand Russell**, *Look*, 1954

**4** Obscenity can be found in every book except the telephone directory.
**George Bernard Shaw**

**5** Under certain circumstances, profanity provides a relief denied even to prayer.
**Mark Twain**

# Obstinacy

*See also Arguments; Assertiveness.*

**1** Like all weak men, he laid an exaggerated stress on not changing one's mind.
**W. Somerset Maugham**, *Of Human Bondage*, 1915

**2** *I* am firm; *you* are obstinate; *he* is a pig-headed fool.
**Bertrand Russell**, *Brains Trust*, BBC Radio

**3** He has one of those terribly weak natures that are not susceptible to influence.
**Oscar Wilde**, *An Ideal Husband*, 1895

# Occult, The

*See also Astrology; Superstition.*

**1** Some things have got to be believed to be seen.
**Ralph Hodgson**, *The Skylark and Other Poems*, 1958

**2** Two spoons of sherry
Three oz. of yeast,
Half a pound of unicorn,
And God bless the feast.
Shake them in the colander
Bang them to a chop,
Simmer slightly, snip up nicely,
Jump, skip, hop.
Knit one, knot one, purl two together,

Pip one and pop one and pluck the secret feather.

**T. H. White**, 'The Witch's Work Song', *The Sword in the Stone*, 1938

## Office, The

*See also Big Business; Bosses; Business; Expenses; Meetings; Work.*

**1** A memorandum is written not to inform the reader but to protect the writer.
**Dean Acheson**, American Secretary of State, 1949–53

**2** Stress Is Your Body's Way Of Saying You Haven't Worked Enough Unpaid Overtime.
**Scott Adams**, *Dilbert*, 1999

**3** BOSS (*to Departmental Head*): How many people work in your office?
DEPT. HEAD: About half of them, sir.
**Gyles Brandreth**, *1,000 Jokes: The Greatest Joke Book Ever Known*, 1980

**4** PERSONNEL MANAGER: I like your qualifications Gribson – you have the makings of a first-class underling.
**Hector Breeze**, cartoon in *Private Eye*

**5** Meetings are indispensable when you don't want to do anything.
**J. K. Galbraith**, American economist

**6** A secretary is not a thing
Wound by key, pulled by string.
Her pad is to write in,
And not spend the night in,
If that's what you plan to enjoy.
No!
**Frank Loesser**, 'A Secretary is Not a Toy', song from *How to Succeed in Business Without Really Trying*, 1961

**7** Your face is a company face.
*It smiles at executives then goes back in place.*
The company furniture?
*Oh, it suits me fine.*
The company letterhead?
*A valentine.*
Anything you're against?
*Unemployment.*
**Frank Loesser**, 'The Company Way', song from *How to Succeed in Business Without Really Trying*, 1961

**8** BUSINESSMAN ON PHONE: Miss Bremmer, get me whatever coast I'm not on.
**Bob Mankoff**, cartoon, *The Cartoon Bank*, 1997

**9** . . . an office is not a tea-bar, matrimonial bureau, betting shop, reading room, fashion house or smoking lounge, but a place where paperwork necessary to good management is originated and eventually filed.
**Keith Waterhouse**, *The Passing of the Third-floor Buck*, 1974

**10** I yield to no one in my admiration for the office as a social centre, but it's no place actually to get any work done.
**Katharine Whitehorn**, *Sunday Best*, 1976

## Old Age

*See also Age; Middle Age; Young and Old.*

**1** A 95-year-old man checked in to a posh hotel to celebrate his birthday. As a surprise, some friends sent a call girl to his room. When the man opened the door, he saw before him this beautiful young woman.
She said, 'I've got a present for you.'
He said, 'What is it?'
She said, 'I'm here to give you super sex.'
He said, 'In that case, I'll have the soup.'
**Anon.**

**2** DOCTOR: You're going to live to be eighty.
PATIENT: I AM eighty!
DOCTOR: What did I tell you?
**Anon.**

**3** I'm not saying he's old, but he was the DJ at the Boston Tea Party.
**Anon.**

**4** This old guy goes to the doctor's and the doctor says, 'I've got bad news and I've got worse news. The bad news is you've got Alzheimer's. The worse news is you've got inoperable cancer and you'll be dead in two months.'
And the old man says, 'Well, at least I don't have Alzheimer's.'
**Anon.**

**5** We think he's dead, but we're afraid to ask.
**Anonymous Committee Member**, of 79-year-old Chairman of House Committee, Washington, 1984

**6** Your father is so old, he was the promoter of David vs. Goliath.
*Snaps*, 1994

**7** Your mother is so old she still has her ticket stub from Christians vs. the Lions.
*Snaps*, 1994

**8** My dad's pants kept creeping up on him. By sixty-five he was just a pair of pants and a head.
**Jeff Altman**

**9** I used to dread getting older because I thought I would not be able to do all the things I wanted to do, but now that I am older I find that I don't want to do them.
**Nancy Astor**, British politician, on her eightieth birthday, 1959

**10** I will never be an old man. To me, old age is always fifteen years older than I am.
**Bernard Baruch**, 1870–1965, American businessman and statesman

**11** WICKSTEED: No. Not too old at fifty-three.
A worn defeated fool like me.
Still the tickling lust devours
Long stretches of my waking hours.
Busty girls in flowered scanties
Hitching down St Michael panties.
Easing off their wet-look boots,
To step into their birthday suits.
**Alan Bennett**, *Habeas Corpus*, 1973

**12** You only have to survive in England and all is forgiven you . . . if you can eat a boiled egg at ninety in England they think you deserve a Nobel Prize.
**Alan Bennett**, *The South Bank Show*, London Weekend Television, 1984

**13** He's so old his birth certificate is on a rock.
**Jack Benny**

**14** You're getting older when it takes you more time to recover than it did to tire you out.
**Milton Berle**

**15** I have my eighty-seventh birthday coming up and people ask what I'd most appreciate getting. I'll tell you: a paternity suit.
**George Burns**

**16** I'm at that age now where just putting my cigar in its holder is a thrill.
**George Burns**

**17** George Burns is old enough to be his father.
**Red Buttons**

**18** We talked about growing old gracefully
And Elsie who's seventy-four
Said, 'A, it's a question of being sincere,
And B, if you're supple you've nothing to fear.'
Then she swung upside down from a glass chandelier,
I couldn't have liked it more.
**Noel Coward**, 'I've Been to a Marvellous Party', *Set to Music*, 1938

**19** We're a dear old couple and we *hate* one another
And we've hated one another for a long, long time.
Since the day that we were wed, up to the present,
Our lives, we must confess,
Have been progressively more unpleasant.
We're just sweet old darlings who despise one another
With a thoroughness approaching the sublime,
But through all our years
We've been affectionately known
As the Bronxville Darby and Joan.
**Noel Coward**, 'Bronxville Darby and Joan', *Sail Away*, 1962

**20** Old age is life's parody.
**Simone de Beauvoir**, *The Coming of Age*, 1972

**21** Very, very, very few
People die at ninety-two.
I suppose that I shall be
Safer still at ninety-three.
**Willard R. Espy**, 'Actuarial Reflection'

**22** Being an old maid is like death by drowning, a really delightful sensation after you cease to struggle.
**Edna Ferber**, quoted in *The Algonquin Wits*, by Robert E. Drennan, 1968

**23** I've joined the Olde Thyme Dance Club, the trouble is that there
Are too many ladies over, and no gentlemen to spare.
It seems a shame, it's not the same, But still it has to be,
Some ladies have to dance together,

One of them is me.

**Joyce Grenfell**, 'Stately as a Galleon', *Stately as a Galleon*, 1978

**24** Stately as a galleon, I sail across the floor,
Doing the Military Two-step, as in the
    days of yore.
I dance with Mrs Tiverton; she's light on
    her feet, in spite
Of turning the scale at fourteen stone,
    and being of medium height.
So gay the band
So giddy the sight,
Full evening dress is a must,
But the zest goes out of a beautiful waltz
When you dance it bust to bust.

**Joyce Grenfell**, 'Stately as a Galleon', *Stately as a Galleon*, 1978

**25** I don't feel eighty. In fact I don't feel
anything till noon. Then it's time for my
nap.

**Bob Hope**

**26** You know you're getting old when the
candles cost more than the cake.

**Bob Hope**

**27** Seventy is wormwood
Seventy is gall
But it's better to be seventy
Than not alive at all.

**Phyllis McGinley**, American poet

**28** A man's only as old as the woman he
feels.

**Groucho Marx**

**29** Anyone can get old. All you have to do
is live long enough.

**Groucho Marx**

**30** One of the many pleasures of old age is
giving things up.

**Malcolm Muggeridge**

**31** Senescence begins
And middle age ends
The day your descendants
Outnumber your friends.

**Ogden Nash**, 'Crossing the Border', *You Can't Get There from Here*, 1957

**32** Growing old is like being increasingly
penalized for a crime you haven't
committed.

**Anthony Powell**, *Temporary Kings*, 1973

**33** The denunciation of the young is a
necessary part of the hygiene of older
people, and greatly assists the circulation of
the blood.

**Logan Pearsall Smith**, *Afterthoughts*, 1931

**34** The greatest problem about old age is
the fear that it may go on too long.

**A. J. P. Taylor**, *Observer*, 1981

**35** MRS ALLONBY: I delight in men over
seventy, they always offer one the devotion
of a lifetime.

**Oscar Wilde**, *A Woman of No Importance*, 1893

**36** There's one advantage to being 102. No
peer pressure.

**Dennis Wolfberg**

# Opera

*See also Music and Musicians; Songs and Singers;
The Theatre.*

**1** The opera is like a husband with a foreign
title: expensive to support, hard to
understand, and therefore a supreme social
challenge.

**Cleveland Amory**, NBC TV, 1961

**2** I do not mind what language an opera is
sung in so long as it is a language I don't
understand.

**Sir Edward Appleton**, *Observer*, 1955

**3** No good opera plot can be sensible, for
people do not sing when they are feeling
sensible.

**W. H. Auden**, quoted in *Time*, 1961

**4** People are wrong when they say that the
opera isn't what it used to be. It is what it
used to be – that's what's wrong with it.

**Noel Coward**, *Design for Living*, 1933

**5** Opera in English is, in the main, just
about as sensible as baseball in Italian.

**H. L. Mencken**

**6** The genuine music-lover may accept the
carnal husk of opera to get at the kernel of
actual music within, but that is no sign that
he approves the carnal husk or enjoys
gnawing through it.

**H. L. Mencken**, *Prejudices*, Second Series, 1920

**7** Going to the opera, like getting drunk, is

a sin that carries its own punishment with it.

**Hannah More,** letter to her sister, 1755; quoted in *The Letters of Hannah More*, 1925

**8** There was a time when I heard eleven operas in a fortnight . . . which left me bankrupt and half-idiotic for a month.

**J. B. Priestley,** 'All about Ourselves', 1923

**9** *Parsifal* is the kind of opera that starts at six o'clock. After it has been going three hours, you look at your watch and it says 6.20.

**David Randolph**

**10** Wagner's music is better than it sounds.

**Mark Twain**

**11** Tenors are noble, pure and heroic and get the soprano, if she has not tragically expired before the final curtain. But baritones are born villains in opera.

**Leonard Warren,** *New York World-Telegram and Sun*, 1957

**12** Now momma an' poppa they gotta
    ragazzo
So much-a he eat-a they call a-heem
    Fatso
He cry-a so loud-a they theenk eet-a
    propera
Some day he grow up-a an' seeng at
    L'opera
Tenore per'aps or a-basso profondo
For heem-a they spare-a no sforzo or
    fondo
An cart a-heem off to La Scala Milano;
But Fatso he seeng like da clapped-out
    soprano,
La voce don't flow, eet a-got no vibrato
Da notes a-come out-a all corsa an'
    flat-o.

**J. J. Webster,** 'La Forza del Destino', *Everyman's Book of Nonsense*, 1981

**13** An unalterable and unquestioned law of the musical world required that the German text of French operas sung by Swedish artists should be translated into Italian for the clearer understanding of English speaking audiences.

**Edith Wharton,** *The Age of Innocence*, 1920

**14** I go to the opera whether I need the sleep or not.

**Henny Youngman**

# Opinion Polls

*See also Opinions.*

**1** If, when faced with a Gallup Quiz,
    I tell the pollster
    To mind his own biz,
    Do you suppose
    I'm one of the 'Don't Nose'?

**Freddie Oliver,** *Worse Verse*, 1969

**2** Glad you brought that up, Jim. The latest research on polls has turned up some interesting variables. It turns out, for example, that people will tell you any old thing that pops into their heads.

**Charles Saxon,** cartoon in the *New Yorker*, 1984

# Opinions

*See also Advice; Arguments; Opinion Polls.*

**1** If you can't annoy someone, it does take a bit of the zest out of life.

**Kinsley Amis,** 1987

**2** Too bad all the people who know how to run the country are busy driving taxi cabs and cutting hair.

**George Burns**

**3** Steer clear of overviews. Those of us who have the situation in Lebanon in perspective and know exactly how to plot a gay rights campaign are usually morons. We snap at our children when they have innocent homework questions. We don't notice when our lover has a deadline. We forget to call our best friend back when she's just had root canal.

Homework, root canal and deadlines are the important things in life, and only when we have these major dramas taken care of can we presume to look at the larger questions.

**Cynthia Heimel,** 'Lower Manhattan Survival Tactics', *Village Voice*, 1983

**4** If nobody ever said anything unless he knew what he was talking about, a ghastly hush would descend upon the earth.

**A. P. Herbert,** 1890–1971, English writer and humorist

**5** The degree of one's emotion varies inversely with one's knowledge of the facts – the less you know, the hotter you get.

**Bertrand Russell,** 1872–1970, British philosopher

**6** The fact that an opinion has been widely held is no evidence whatever that it is not utterly absurd.
**Bertrand Russell**, *Marriage and Morals*, 1929

**7** ... an unbiased opinion is always absolutely valueless.
**Oscar Wilde**, 'The Critic as Artist', 1890

**8** ERNEST: Simply this: that in the best days of art there were no art-critics.
GILBERT: I seem to have heard that observation before, Ernest. It has all the vitality of error and all the tediousness of an old friend.
**Oscar Wilde**, 'The Critic as Artist', 1890

## Opportunism
*See also Selfishness.*

**1** Dear Prime Minister,
Thank you for your letter. I am delighted to have the opportunism to serve in your Cabinet.
**Anon.**

**2** I would rather be an opportunist and float than go to the bottom with my principles round my neck.
**Stanley Baldwin**, 1867–1947, British Conservative Prime Minister

## Opportunity
*See also Potential.*

**1** Opportunity, *n.* a favorable occasion for grasping a disappointment.
**Ambrose Bierce**, *The Devil's Dictionary*, 1911

**2** I despise making the most of one's time: half the pleasures of life consist of the opportunities one has neglected.
**Oliver Wendell Holmes, Jr.**

## Optimism
*See also Optimism and Pessimism; Pessimism.*

**1** An optimist is a man who starts a crossword puzzle with a fountain pen.
**Anon.**

**2** Optimism is the content of small men in high places.
**F. Scott Fitzgerald**, *The Crack-up*, 1945

**3** an optimist is a guy
that has never had
much experience
**Don Marquis**, 'certain maxims of archy', *archy and mehitabel*, 1927

**4** I'm an optimist, but I'm an optimist who carries a raincoat.
**Harold Wilson**

## Optimism and Pessimism
*See also Optimism; Pessimism.*

**1** The optimist proclaims that we live in the best of all possible worlds; and the pessimist fears this is true.
**James Branch Cabell**, *The Silver Stallion*, 1926

**2** O, merry is the optimist,
With the troops of courage leaguing
But a dour trend
In any friend
Is somehow less fatiguing.
**Phyllis McGinley**, 'Song against Sweetness and Light', *A Pocketful of Wry*, 1940

**3** 'Twixt the optimist and the pessimist
The difference is droll:
The optimist sees the doughnut
But the pessimist sees the hole.
**McLandburgh Wilson**, 'Optimist and Pessimist'

## Orgies
*See also Promiscuity; Sex.*

**1** An orgy looks particularly alluring seen through the mists of righteous indignation.
**Malcolm Muggeridge**, *The Most of Malcolm Muggeridge*, 1966

**2** Home is heaven and orgies are vile
But you *need* an orgy once in a while.
**Ogden Nash**, *Primrose Path*, 1935

**3** You get a better class of person at orgies, because people have to keep in trim more. There is an awful lot of going round holding in your stomach, you know. Everybody is very polite to each other. The conversation isn't very good but you can't have everything.
**Gore Vidal**, interviewed on *Russell Harty Plus*, London Weekend Television, 1972

## Orphans

*See also Children; Parents.*

**1** At six I was left an orphan. What on earth is a six-year-old supposed to do with an orphan?
**Anon.**

**2** Gertrude De-Mongmorenci McFiggin had known neither father nor mother. They had both died years before she was born.
**Stephen Leacock,** 'Gertrude the Governess', *Nonsense - Novels,* 1911

## Oysters

*See also Eating; Fish and Fishing; Food; The Sea.*

**1** An oyster is a fish built like a nut.
**Anon.**

**2** Than an oyster there's nothing moister.
**Anon.**

**3** According to experts, the oyster
In its shell – or crustacean cloister –
May frequently be
Either he or a she
Or both, if it should be its choice ter.
**Berton Braley**

**4** The oyster's a confusing suitor;
Its masc., and fem., and even neuter.
But whether husband, pal or wife
It leads a painless sort of life.
I'd like to be an oyster, say,
In August, June, July or May.
**Ogden Nash,** 'The Oyster', *Free Wheeling,* 1931

## Pacifism

*See also Peace; Protest; War.*

**1** Join the Army, see the world, meet interesting people – and kill them.
**Pacifist badge,** 1978

**2** Sometime they'll give a war and nobody will come.
**Carl Sandburg,** *The People, Yes,* 1936

## Paranoia

*See also Anxiety; Fear; Insanity.*

**1** Just Because You're Paranoid Doesn't Mean They Aren't Out To Get You.
**Badge,** 1970s

**2** PSYCHIATRIST (*to patient*): You're suffering from paranoia. Anyone'll tell you.
**Hector Breeze,** cartoon in *Private Eye*

**3** I told my psychiatrist that everyone hates me. He said I was being ridiculous – everyone hasn't met me yet.
**Rodney Dangerfield**

**4** Even paranoids have enemies.
**Henry Kissinger**

## Parents

*See also Children; The Family; Fathers; Mothers.*

**1** If worse comes to worst, there is no parenting tool more powerful than a good hug. If you sense that your child is getting into trouble, you must give that child a great big fat hug in a public place with other young people around, while saying, in a loud piercing voice, 'You are MY LITTLE BABY and I love you NO MATTER WHAT!' This will embarrass your child so much that he or she may immediately run off and join a strict religious order whose entire diet consists of gravel. If one hug doesn't work, threaten to give your child another.
**Dave Barry,** *Comic Relief,* 2000

**2** I will never understand children. I never pretended to. I meet mothers all the time who make resolutions to themselves. 'I'm going to develop patience with my children and go out of my way to show them I am interested in them and what they do. I am going to understand my children.' These women wind up making rag rugs, using blunt scissors.

**Erma Bombeck**, *If Life is Bowl of Cherries – What am I Doing in the Pits?*, 1978

**3** Once a child knows that a square millimetre is .00155 square inches, will he ever have respect for a mother who once measured the bathroom for carpeting and found out that she had enough left over to slipcover New Jersey?

**Erma Bombeck**, *If Life is a Bowl of Cherries – What am I Doing in the Pits?*, 1978

**4** When I was in college my parents came to stay with me for the weekend. To get even for my childhood I made them sleep in separate bedrooms. My mother said, 'What are you, crazy? I've been sleeping with this man for years.'

I said, 'I don't care what you do on the outside, but when you're in *my* house . . .'

**Elayne Boosler**, *Comic Relief*, HBO, 1986

**5** FATHER (*to son*): Don't forget – I fought at El Alamein so you could be free to worry about the collapse of the ecosystem!

**Hector Breeze**, cartoon in *Private Eye*

**6** Parenthood: that state of being better chaperoned than you were before marriage.

**Marcelene Cox**, *Ladies' Home Journal*, 1944

**7** I don't think my parents liked me. My bathtub toys were a toaster and a blender!

**Rodney Dangerfield**

**8** The first half of our lives is ruined by our parents, and the second half by our children.

**Clarence Darrow**, 1857–1938, American lawyer

**9** Why do parents always take their children to supermarkets to smack them?

**Jack Dee**, *Just For Laughs*, 1992

**10** Parents – people who use the rhythm method of birth control.

**May Flink**

**11** The real menace in dealing with a five-year-old is that in no time at all you begin to sound like a five-year-old.

**Jean Kerr**, *Please Don't Eat the Daisies*, 1957

**12** They fuck you up, your mum and dad.
They may not mean to, but they do.

They fill you with the faults they had
And add some extra, just for you.

**Philip Larkin**, 'This be the Verse', *High Windows*, 1974

**13 Parental expressions every child should know:**

Some day you'll thank me.
(Statement made by parent who has successfully asserted authority, in order to soften the victory.)
I don't want to hear any more about it.
(Assertion of parental authority after parent has lost argument with child.)

**Judith Martin**, *Miss Manners' Guide to Rearing Perfect Children*, 1984

**14** My father only hit me once – but he used a Volvo.

**Bob Monkhouse**, English comedian

**15** He is too experienced a parent ever to make positive promises.

**Christopher Morley**, *Thunder on the Left*, 1936

**16** Children aren't happy with nothing to ignore
And that's what parents were created for.

**Ogden Nash**, 'The Parent', *Happy Days*, 1933

**17** . . . parents . . . are sometimes a bit of a disappointment to their children. They don't fulfil the promise of their early years.

**Anthony Powell**, *A Buyer's Market*, 1952

**18** I'm trying to decide whether or not to have children. My time is running out. I know I want to have children while my parents are still young enough to take care of them.

**Rita Rudner**, *Comic Relief*, HBO, 1991

**19** You don't ever really want to visualize your parents having sex. It's very uncomfortable. You know in your mind that they had to have sex at least once to have you, but you still kind of maintain the image in your head, 'Well, I don't know. I'm not positive. I can't prove it. I don't know if that actually happened.'

That's why if I found out that I was adopted, that would really come as great news. 'I'm adopted? That's great.' I'd be happy to hear that. That means technically it's possible that my mother and my father are really just really great friends.

I mean sex is a great thing and all but you

don't want to think that your whole life began because somebody maybe had a little too much wine with dinner.
**Jerry Seinfeld**, *SeinLanguage*, 1993

**20** If parents would only realize how they bore their children.
**George Bernard Shaw**, *Misalliance*, 1910

**21** Parentage is a very important profession; but no test of fitness for it is ever imposed in the interest of the children.
**George Bernard Shaw**, *Everybody's Political What's What?*, 1944

**22** COMEDIENNE: So I'm licking jelly off of my boyfriend, right, and all of a sudden I'm thinking, 'Oh, my God, I'm turning into my mother!'
**Sarah Silverman**, *The Larry Sanders Show*, 1998

**23** I saw my parents today. It's all right – they didn't see me or anything.
**Margaret Smith**

**24** Fortunately, my parents were intelligent, enlightened people. They accepted me exactly for what I was: a punishment from God.
**David Steinberg**, *GQ*, 1999

**25** I have found the best way to give advice to your children is to find out what they want and then advise them to do it.
**Harry S. Truman**, Democratic President, 1945–53, television interview, 1955

**26** ELLEN: There's something I gotta tell you about my parents. They're insane.
LAURIE: Well, everyone thinks their parents are insane.
ELLEN: Yeah, but everyone doesn't have a certificate signed by a judge! Believe me, they're the real deal. They bought night-vision goggles to save on light bulbs!
**David Walpert**, *Ellen*, ABC TV, 1998

**27** All women become like their mothers. That is their tragedy. No man does. That is his.
**Oscar Wilde**, *The Importance of Being Earnest*, 1895

**28** Few parents nowadays pay any regard to what their children say to them. The old-fashioned respect for the young is fast dying.
**Oscar Wilde**, *The Importance of Being Earnest*, 1895

**29** The longer I live the more keenly I feel that whatever was good enough for our fathers is not good enough for us.
**Oscar Wilde**, *The Picture of Dorian Gray*, 1891

**30** To lose one parent . . . may be regarded as a misfortune; to lose both looks like carelessness.
**Oscar Wilde**, *The Importance of Being Earnest*, 1895

# Parking

*See also Cars; Driving.*

**1** To my wife, double parking means on top of another car.
**Dave Barry**

**2** Parking is such sweet sorrow.
**Herb Caen**, *San Francisco Chronicle*

**3** I just solved the parking problem. I bought a parked car.
**Henny Youngman**

# Parliament

*See also Government; House of Commons; House of Lords; Politics and Politicians.*

**1** Westminster is the power house transmitting socially sanctioned aggression. It inevitably becomes the Mecca for all those who wish, even as they did in their nurseries, but now without fear of disapproval, to scream with anger, spit at their enemies, bitingly attack opponents, boldly hit out at wrongs, real and imagined. Like moths around a flame, the aggressive flutter around Westminster. Outside Dartmoor and the armed forces, there are no more aggressive men than those sitting in our Parliament.
**Leo Abse**, *Private Member*, 1973

**2** I had better recall before someone else does, that I said on one occasion that all was fair in love, war and parliamentary procedure.
**Michael Foot**, British Labour politician

**3** An angry Parliamentary debate has the same effect upon national events as a slammed door has upon domestic arguments. It is emphatic; it is deeply, though momentarily, satisfying; and it settles nothing at all.

**David Frost and Antony Jay**, *To England with Love*, 1967

**4** There are three golden rules for Parliamentary speakers: 'Stand up. Speak up. Shut up.'

**J. W. Lowther**, Speaker of the House of Commons, 1919

**5** . . . like playing squash with a dish of scrambled eggs.

**Harold Nicolson**, on debating with Nancy Astor in the House of Commons, 1943

**6** The essentially feminine role of Parliament in the constitutional process does indeed put one in mind of the traditional wife in a male (or government) dominated national household. What the master says goes. Parliament may advise, complain, criticize, protest, delay, nag, scream its head off but it does what it's told in the end.

**Norman Shrapnel**, quoted in *Westminster Man* by Austin Mitchell, 1982

# Parties

*See also Champagne; Dance; Drink; Society; Wine.*

**1** I don't go to parties. Well, what are they for,
   If you don't need to find a new lover?
   You drink and you listen and you drink a
      bit more
   And you take the next day to recover.
**Wendy Cope**, 'Being Boring'

**2** . . . one must never go to a party without a clear objective: whether it be to 'network', thereby adding to your spread of contacts to improve your career; to make friends with someone specific; or simply 'clinch' a top deal. Understand where we have been going wrong by going to parties armed only with objective of not getting too pissed.

**Helen Fielding**, *Bridget Jones's Diary*, 1996

**3** It is not done to let anybody be too happy. The moment two people seem to be enjoying one another's company, a good hostess introduces a third element or removes the first.

**Virginia Graham**, American author

**4** The cocktail party is easily the worst invention since castor oil.

**Elsa Maxwell**, 1883–1963, American actress and socialite

**5** ERIC: It was a Gay Nineties Party. It was terrible.
ERNIE: Why was that?
ERIC: All the men were gay and all the women were ninety.

**Eric Morecambe and Ernie Wise**, *The Morecambe and Wise Joke Book*, 1979

**6** A cocktail party is what you call it when you invite everyone you know to come over to your house at six p.m., put cigarettes out on your rug, and leave at eight to go somewhere more interesting for dinner without inviting you. Cocktail parties are very much on their way out among rug-owning, hungry, snubbed people.

**P. J. O'Rourke**, *Modern Manners*, 1983

**7** A small boy, who was a stickler for the literal truth, once said to me that it was wrong to say 'Good-bye' when you had not enjoyed yourself at a party. I enquired what should be substituted for it. He suggested 'Bad-bye'. I have never tried this.

**Arthur Ponsonby**, *Casual Observations*

**8** I delight in the idea of a party but find no pleasure in the reality. The result is that I can neither keep away from parties nor enjoy them.

**J. B. Priestley**, *All about Ourselves and Other Essays*, 1956

**9** The cocktail party – a device for paying off obligations to people you don't want to invite to dinner.

**Charles Merrill Smith**, *Instant Status*, 1972

**10** Nothing is more irritating than not being invited to a party you wouldn't be seen dead at.

**Bill Vaughan**, *Reader's Digest*, 1959

**11** I go to parties, sometimes until four,
   It's hard to leave when you can't find
      the door.
**Joe Walsh**, 'Life's Been Good to Me', song, from *But Seriously Folks*, 1978

**12** Lord Copper quite often gave banquets; it would be an understatement to say that no one enjoyed them more than the host, for no one else enjoyed them at all, while

Lord Copper positively exulted in every minute.
**Evelyn Waugh**, *Scoop*, 1938

**13** There must be some good in the cocktail party to account for its immense vogue among otherwise sane people.
**Evelyn Waugh**, 'Wine in Peace and War'

# Past, The

*See also Ancestors; Antiques; Archaeology; History; Memory; Nostalgia.*

**1** Nothing is more responsible for the good old days than a bad memory.
**Franklin P. Adams**, 1881–1960, American journalist

**2** Mind you, six bob was six bob in them days. You could buy three penny worth of chips and still have change from sixpence.
**Alan Bennett**, 'The Lonely Pursuit', *On the Margin*, BBC TV, 1966

**3** ED: The instant past is as past as slightly pregnant is pregnant!
**Michael Frayn**, *Clouds*, 1976

# Patience

**1** Prayer of the modern American: 'Dear God, I pray for patience. And I want it *right now*!'
**Oren Arnold**, American humorist

**2** Patience, *n.* A minor form of despair, disguised as a virtue.
**Ambrose Bierce**, *The Devil's Dictionary*, 1911

**3** Everything comes to him who hustles while he waits.
**Thomas Alva Edison**, 1847–1931, American inventor

**4** Patience is sometimes considered a virtue when it is actually a case of not knowing what to do.
**Sally Poplin**

# Patriotism

*See also Jingoism; Xenophobia.*

**1** An author's first duty is to let down his country.
**Brendan Behan**, *Guardian*, 1960

**2** 'My country, right or wrong' is a thing no patriot would think of saying except in a desperate case. It is like saying, 'My mother, drunk or sober'.
**G. K. Chesterton**, *Defendant*, 1901

**3** The English, the English, the English are best
   I wouldn't give tuppence for all of the rest.
**Michael Flanders and Donald Swann**, 'Song of Patriotic Prejudice', song from *At the Drop of Another Hat*, 1964

**4** The less a statesman amounts to, the more he loves the flag.
**Kin Hubbard**, 1868–1930, American humorist

**5** Patriotism is the last refuge of a scoundrel.
**Samuel Johnson**, quoted in *Life of Samuel Johnson*, by James Boswell, 1791

**6** Whenever you hear a man speak of his love for his country, it is a sign that he expects to be paid for it.
**H. L. Mencken**

**7** Patriotism is often an arbitrary veneration of real estate above principles.
**George Jean Nathan**, *Testament of a Critic*, 1882–1958

**8** At a sporting event, both men and women should stand during the national anthem . . . Black people should remain seated for a couple of bars and then stand up very slowly to show that, even though they got a raw deal and never asked to come here in the first place, they're still patriotic deep down inside. Aging hippies, members of the Socialist Workers' Party, Vietnam combat veterans, and other nut cases should be sure to stand up because that's what Robert De Niro would do if he were playing them in a movie. He would stand up for the national anthem to show that although he's crazy, it's an American kind of craziness. This makes everyone feel better.
**P. J. O'Rourke**, *Modern Manners*, 1983

**9** Patriotism is the willingness to kill and be killed for trivial reasons.
**Bertrand Russell**, 1872–1970, British philosopher

**10** Patriotism is the virtue of the vicious.
**Oscar Wilde** (Attrib.)

# Peace

*See also Conciliation; Fighting. Pacifism; War.*

**1** George's plans for peace: My first is worldwide, year-round, non-stop folk dancing. In short, everyone in the world would be required to dance all the time. It leaves very little time for fighting, and what combat does occur is inefficient, because the combatants are constantly in motion.

. . . Another plan I have is World Peace Through Formal Introductions. The idea is that everyone in the world would be required to meet everyone else in the world, formally, at least once. You'd have to look the person in the eye, shake hands, repeat their name, and try to remember one outstanding physical characteristic. My theory is, if you knew everyone in the world personally, you'd be less inclined to fight them in a war: 'Who? The Malaysians? Are you kidding? I know those people!'

**George Carlin**, *Brain Droppings*, 1997

**2** It's coexistence
Or no existence.

**Bertrand Russell**, 1872–1970, British philosopher (Attrib.)

**3** Gone are those pleasant nineteenth-century days when a country could remain neutral and at peace just by saying it wanted to.

**William Shirer**, 1904–93, American reporter and foreign correspondent

**4** I'd kill for a Nobel Peace Prize.

**Steven Wright**, American comic

# Perfume

*See also Cosmetics; Smells.*

**1** Perfume is a subject dear to my heart. I have so many favourites: Arome de Grenouille, Okéfénôkée, Eau Contraire, Fume de Ma Tante, Blast du Past, Kèrmes, Je Suis Swell, and Attention S'il Vous Plaît, to name but a few.

**Miss Piggy**, *Miss Piggy's Guide to Life (As Told to Henry Beard)*, 1981

# Pessimism

*See also Optimism; Optimism and Pessimism.*

**1** Life is divided into the horrible and the miserable.

**Woody Allen and Marshall Brickman**, *Annie Hall*, screenplay, 1977

**2** There are bad times just around the corner,
There are dark clouds hurtling through the sky
And it's no good whining
About a silver lining
For we know from experience that they won't roll by,
With a scowl and a frown
We'll keep our peckers down
And prepare for depression and doom and dread,
We're going to unpack our troubles from our old kit bag
And wait until we drop down dead.

**Noel Coward**, 'There are Bad Times Just Around the Corner', song from *Globe Revue*, 1952

**3** A pessimist is a man who has been compelled to live with an optimist.

**Elbert Hubbard**, *The Notebook*, 1927

**4** Things are going to get a lot worse before they get worse.

**Lily Tomlin**

**5** The nice part about being a pessimist is that you are constantly being proven right or pleasantly surprised.

**George Will**, American political columnist

# Pests

*See also Insects.*

**1** What makes
common house flies
trying
is
that they keep
multiflieing.

**Niels Mogens Bodecker**, 'House Flies', *Hurry, Hurry Mary Dear*

# Pets

*See also Cats; Dogs; Vets.*

**1** Springfield Pet Shop: All Our Pets Are Flushable
All Creatures Great and Cheap
You Pet It, You Bought It
**Pet shop signs**, *The Simpsons*, Fox TV

**2** . . . when I was young, I wanted a dog and we had no money . . . I couldn't get a dog because it was too much and they finally opened up in my neighborhood in Flatbush, a damaged pet shop. They sold damaged pets at discount, you know, you could get a bent pussy cat if you wanted; a straight camel, you know. I got a dog that stuttered. Like, cats would give him a hard time and he would go b-b-b-b-bow wow!
**Woody Allen**, recorded live at Mr Kelly's, Chicago, 1964

**3** You will find that the woman who is really kind to dogs is always one who has failed to inspire sympathy in men.
**Max Beerbohm**, *Zuleika Dobson*, 1911

**4** No animal will more repay
   A treatment kind and fair;
   At least so lonely people say
   Who keep a frog (and, by the way,
   They are extremely rare).
**Hilaire Belloc**, 'The Frog', *The Bad Child's Book of Beasts*, 1896

**5** *Meow* means 'woof' in cat.
**George Carlin**, *Brain Droppings*, 1997

**6** But don't you see darling? Giving him an unaffected name like 'Spot' would really be the most affected thing of all.
**William Hamilton**, *William Hamilton's Anti-Social Register*, cartoon, 1974

**7** 8:11 A.M.: I am awakened by the feeling of many tongues on my face. Some tongues snake into my nostrils, some vigorously clean my ears. I feel a large paw on my head. I open my eyes warily. It is only the dogs. 'Wake up, wake up!' they all cry. 'Wake up and let's go to the cupboard of the kitchen where you keep the chopped dead animal!'
   . . . I sit up in bed. Pandemonium ensues. 'Yes, yes!' they all cry. 'You are awake! This is the most fabulous thing that has ever happened in the history of time!'
**Cynthia Heimel**, *If You Leave Me, Can I Come Too?*, 1995

**8** If you [a pet] have been named after a human being of artistic note, run away from home. It is unthinkable that even an animal should be obliged to share quarters with anyone who calls a cat Ford Madox Ford.
**Fran Lebowitz**, *Social Studies*, 1981

**9** No animal should ever jump up on the dining-room furniture unless absolutely certain that he can hold his own in the conversation.
**Fran Lebowitz**, *Social Studies*, 1981

**10** The black dog was the only intelligent member of the family. He died a few years later. He was poisoned, and no one will convince me it wasn't suicide.
**Hugh Leonard**, *Da*, 1973

**11** From **Top ten signs you have a dumb dog**
Lengthy pause after 'bow' as he tries to
   remember 'wow.'
Buries tail, wags bone.
On long car trips, likes to stick his head in
   the glove compartment.
Despite overwhelming evidence, still
   smokes three packs a day.
Constantly chasing people named 'Katz.'
**David Letterman**, *The Late Show*, CBS

**12** ERNIE: What's that you've got there?
ERIC: A lobster.
ERNIE: A lobster? Are you taking it home for tea?
ERIC: No, it's had its tea – now I'm taking it to the pictures.
**Eric Morecambe and Ernie Wise**, *The Morecambe and Wise Joke Book*, 1979

**13** And now a word for dog lovers. Kinky.
**Bill Oddie and Graeme Gardon**, *I'm Sorry I'll Read That Again*, BBC Radio

# Petting

*See also Courtship; Kissing; Sex.*

**1** . . . [he] twisted my nipples as though tuning a radio.
**Lisa Alther**, *Kinflicks*, 1976

**2** The requirements of romantic love are

difficult to satisfy in the trunk of a Dodge Dart.
**Lisa Alther,** *Kinflicks,* 1976

**3** Between the ages of fourteen and twenty-four, foreplay changes from being something that boys want to do and girls don't, to something that women want and men can't be bothered with . . . The perfect match, if you ask me, is between the *Cosmo* woman and the fourteen-year-old boy.
**Nick Hornby,** *High Fidelity,* 1995

**4** Sometimes I got so bored of trying to touch her breasts that I would try to touch her between the legs, a gesture that had a sort of self-parodying wit about it: it was like trying to borrow a fiver, getting turned down, and asking to borrow fifty quid instead.
**Nick Hornby,** *High Fidelity,* 1995

**5** Whoever called it necking was a poor judge of anatomy.
**Groucho Marx**

**6** Half the time, if you really want to know the truth, when I'm horsing around with a girl I have a helluva lot of trouble just finding what I'm looking for, for God's sake, if you know what I mean. Take this girl that I just missed having sexual intercourse with, that I told you about. It took me about an hour just to get her goddam brassiere off. By the time I did get it off, she was about ready to spit in my eye.
**J. D. Salinger,** *The Catcher in the Rye,* 1951

# Philanthropy

*See also Gifts; Wealth.*

**1** Giving away a fortune is taking Christianity too far.
**Charlotte Bingham,** English novelist

**2** No people do so much harm as those who go about doing good.
**Mandell Creighton,** *The Life and Letters of Mandell Creighton,* 1904

**3** A large part of altruism, even when it is perfectly honest, is grounded upon the fact that it is uncomfortable to have unhappy people about one.
**H. L. Mencken,** *Prejudices,* Fourth Series, 1924

**4** A show of altruism is respected in the world chiefly for selfish motives . . . Everyone figures himself profiting by it tomorrow.
**H. L. Mencken**

**5** High-toned humanitarians constantly overestimate the sufferings of those they sympathize with.
**H. L. Mencken,** *Minority Report,* 1956

**6** In the United States doing good has come to be, like patriotism, a favorite device of persons with something to sell.
**H. L. Mencken**

**7** A good deed never goes unpunished.
**Gore Vidal,** (Attrib.)

**8** Philanthropy seems to have become simply the refuge of people who wish to annoy their fellow creatures.
**Oscar Wilde,** *An Ideal Husband,* 1895

**9** 'I have got to take a few pints of soup to the deserving poor,' said Myrtle. 'I'd better set about it. Amazing the way these bimbos absorb soup. Like sponges.'
**P. G. Wodehouse,** *Eggs, Beans and Crumpets,* 1940

# Philosophy

*See also Knowledge.*

**1** I think, therefore I am. I think.
**Anon.,** T-shirt slogan, Bruton, Somerset, 2000

**2** What if everything is an illusion and nothing exists? In that case, I definitely overpaid for my carpet.
**Woody Allen,** *Without Feathers,* 1976

**3** I vastly prefer Sartre's plays to his philosophy. Existentialism works much better in the theatre than in theory.
**A. J. Ayer,** quoted in Kenneth Tynan's *Show People,* 1980

**4** Relaxed Empiricism – I only believe something to be true if someone I know quite well tells me it happened.
**Bill Bailey,** English comedian, Edinburgh, 2000

**5** Philosophy is common sense in a dress suit.
**Oliver S. Braston,** *Philosophy*

**6** . . . philosophy professors are weird guys. You can really freak them out easy. 'Hey, prof, you know how to give yourself déjà

vu? Ask yourself this question: Hey, prof, you know how to give yourself déjà vu?'
**Bob Dubac**, quoted in *GQ*, 1984

**7** Sir,
My husband, T. S. Eliot, loved to recount how late one evening he stopped a taxi. As he got in, the driver said, 'You're T. S. Eliot.' When asked how he knew, he replied: 'Ah, I've got an eye for a celebrity. Only the other evening I picked up Bertrand Russell, and I said to him: "Well, Lord Russell, what's it all about," and, do you know, he couldn't tell me.'
**Valerie Eliot**, letter to *The Times*, 1970

**8** There once was a man who said: 'God
Must think it exceedingly odd
If he finds that this tree
Continues to be
When there's no one about in the Quad.'
**Monsignor Ronald Knox**, 1888–1957, British scholar and poet

**9** Dear Sir,
Your astonishment's odd:
I am always about in the Quad.
And that's why the tree
Will continue to be,
Since observed by
Yours Faithfully,
God.
**Anonymous reply to Monsignor Ronald Knox** (*see above*)

**10** Most philosophical treatises show the human cerebrum loaded far beyond its Plimsoll Mark.
**H. L. Mencken**, *Prejudices*, Fourth Series, 1924

**11** There is no record in human history of a happy philosopher.
**H. L. Mencken**, *Prejudices*, Fourth Series, 1924

**12** People become who they are. Even Beethoven became Beethoven.
**Randy Newman**

**13** . . . as I grew up I became increasingly interested in philosophy, of which they [his family] profoundly disapproved. Every time the subject came up they repeated with unfailing regularity, 'What is mind? No matter. What is matter? Never mind.' After some fifty or sixty repetitions, this remark ceased to amuse me.
**Bertrand Russell**, *Portraits from Memory*, 1956

**14** I think that bad philosophers may have a certain influence, good philosophers, never.
**Bertrand Russell**

**15** The point of philosophers is to start with something so simple as to seem not worth stating, and to end with something so paradoxical that no one will believe it.
**Bertrand Russell**, *Logic and Knowledge*, 1956

**16** Philosophers are as jealous as women; each wants a monopoly of praise.
**George Santayana**, *Dialogues in Limbo*, 1925

**17** A Chinaman of the T'ang Dynasty – and, by which definition, a philosopher – dreamed he was a butterfly, and from that moment he was never quite sure that he was not a butterfly dreaming it was a Chinese philosopher.
**Tom Stoppard**, *Rosencrantz and Guildenstern are Dead*, 1966

**18** . . . if rationality were the criterion for things being allowed to exist, the world would be one gigantic field of soya beans!
**Tom Stoppard**, *Jumpers*, 1972

**19** I'll have to get myself articled to a philosopher . . . Start at the bottom. Of course, a philosopher's clerk wouldn't get the really interesting work straight off. I know that. It'd be a matter of filing the generalizations, tidying up the paradoxes, laying out the premises before the boss gets in – that kind of thing; but after I've learned the ropes I might get a half-share in a dialectic, perhaps, and work up towards a treatise . . .
**Tom Stoppard**, *Albert's Bridge*, BBC Radio, 1967

**20** . . . since an arrow shot towards a target first had to cover half the distance, and then half the remainder, and then half the remainder after that, and so on *ad infinitum*, the result was . . . that though the arrow is always approaching its target, it never quite gets there, and San Sebastian died of fright.
**Tom Stoppard**, *Jumpers*, 1972

**21** Philosophy teaches us to bear with equanimity the misfortunes of others.
**Oscar Wilde** (Attrib.)

**22** It's a small world, but I wouldn't want to paint it.
**Steven Wright**, American comic

# Photography

**1** A: Do you know it's costing me more than two thousand pounds to have my house painted?
B: Wouldn't it be cheaper just to have it photographed?
**Anon.**

**2** My photographs do me an injustice. They look just like me.
**Phyllis Diller**

**3** Some hate broccoli, some hate bacon
I hate having my picture taken.
How can your family claim to love you
And then demand a picture of you?
**Ogden Nash**, 'Waiting for the Birdie', *I'm a Stranger Here Myself*, 1938

**4** *Aperture.* A little hole in the camera through which a wife, child, dog, cat pawing a ball of wool, wedding, swan, Norman church, father up to his neck in sand, interesting old alley, sailor sticking his head out of a porthole, or Midlands couple who were the life and soul of the party that last night in Ibiza, may be observed by the photographer.
**Keith Waterhouse**, 'A–Z of Photography', *The Passing of the Third-floor Buck*, 1974

# Picnics

*See also Eating; Food.*

**1** Upon this theme
I'll briefly touch:
Too far
To go
To eat
Too much.
**A. A. Lattimer**, 'Picnic', *Liberty*

# Plagiarism

*See also Creativity; Literature.*

**1** All work and no plagiarism makes a dull speech.
**Anon.**

**2** Immature poets imitate; mature poets steal.
**T. S. Eliot**, *The Sacred Wood*, 1920

**3** Plagiarize! Let no one else's work evade your eyes,

Remember why the good Lord made your eyes.
**Tom Lehrer**, 'Lobachevski', song, 1953

**4** If you steal from one author, it's plagiarism; if you steal from many, it's research.
**Wilson Mizner**, 1876–1933, American playwright

**5** The only 'ism she believes in is plagiarism.
**Dorothy Parker**, of a woman writer (Attrib.)

# Poets and Poetry

*See also Limericks; Literature; Writers; Writing.*

**1** Anon., Idem, Ibid. and Trad.
Wrote much that is morally bad:
Some ballads, some chanties,
*All* poems on panties –
And limericks, too, one must add.
**Anon.**

**2** The American constitution protects free speech, but only the American sense of humour protects free verse.
**Anon.**

**3** Little Mary from Boston, Mass.
Stepped into water up to her ankles.
It doesn't rhyme now,
But wait till the tide comes in.
**Graffito**, New Haven, 1976

**4** Elegy, *n.* A composition in verse, in which without employing any of the methods of humor, the writer aims to produce in the reader's mind the dampest kind of dejection. The most famous English example begins somewhat like this:

The cur foretells the knell of parting day;
The loafing herd winds slowly o'er the lea
The wise man homeward plods; I only stay
To fiddle-faddle in a minor key.
**Ambrose Bierce**, *The Devil's Dictionary*, 1911

**5** I know that poetry is indispensable, but to what I couldn't say.
**Jean Cocteau**, quoted in the *Observer*, 1955

**6** The only really difficult thing about a poem is the critic's explanation of it.
**Frank Moore Colby**, 1865–1925, American writer and editor

**7** I don't like to boast, but I have probably

skipped more poetry than any other person of my age and weight in this country.

**Will Cuppy**, 1884–1949, American humorist

**8** He tells you, in the sombrest notes,
　If poets want to get their oats,
　The first step is to slit their throats.
　The way to divide
　The sheep of poetry from the goats
　Is suicide.

**James Fenton**, 'Letter to John Fuller', *Children in Exile*, 1984

**9** A true sonnet goes eight lines and then takes a turn for the better or worse and goes six or eight lines more.

**Robert Frost**, 1874–1963, American poet

**10** Writing free verse is like playing tennis with the net down.

**Robert Frost**, speech at Milton Academy, Massachusetts, 1935

**11** . . . I found a simple plan
　Which makes the lamest lyrics scan!
　When I've a syllable de trop,
　I cut it off, with apol.:
　This verbal sacrifice, I know,
　May irritate the schol.:
　But all must praise my dev'lish cunn.
　Who realize that Time is Mon.

**Harry Graham**, 'Poetical Economy', *Deportmental Ditties*, 1909

**12** There is no money in poetry; but then there is no poetry in money, either.

**Robert Graves**

**13** Why be a poet? As a full-time job it's the closest thing there is to goofing off. Just being alive is part of your research, man. So you can act any way you want. Whether you're surly and brooding or jumpy and loony, when people find out you're a poet, it explains everything and they leave you alone. Besides, poets get to wear cool hats and play the bongos.

**Matt Groening**, *Bart Simpson's Guide to Life*, 1996

**14** It's hard to say why writing verse
　Should terminate in drink or worse.

**A. P. Herbert**, *Punch*

**15** I can't understand these chaps who go round American universities explaining how they write poems. It's like going round explaining how you sleep with your wife.

**Philip Larkin**, quoted by John Updike in *The New York Times*, 1986

**16** Show me a poet and I'll show you a shit.

**A. J. Liebling**, 1904–63, American journalist and satirist

**17** Publishing a volume of verse is like dropping a rose petal down the Grand Canyon and waiting for the echo.

**Don Marquis**, quoted in *O Rare Don Marquis*, by E. Anthony, 1962

**18** The crown of literature is poetry. It is its end and aim. It is the sublimest activity of the human mind. It is the achievement of beauty and delicacy. The writer of prose can only step aside when the poet passes.

**W. Somerset Maugham**, *Saturday Review*, 1957

**19** *Vers libre*: a device for making poetry easier to read and harder to write.

**H. L. Mencken**, *A Book of Burlesques*, 1916

**20** Having considered the matter in – of course – all its aspects, I have decided that there is no excuse for poetry. Poetry gives no adequate return in money, is expensive to print by reason of the waste of space occasioned by its form, and nearly always promulgates illusory concepts of life. But a better case for the banning of all poetry is the simple fact that most of it is bad. Nobody is going to manufacture a thousand tons of jam in the expectation that five tons may be eatable. Furthermore, poetry has the effect on the negligible handful who read it of stimulating them to write poetry themselves. One poem, if widely disseminated, will breed perhaps a thousand inferior copies.

**Myles na Gopaleen**, *The Best of Myles*, 1968

**21** I'd rather be a great bad poet than a bad good poet.

**Ogden Nash**

**22** Poets aren't very useful.
　Because they aren't consumeful or very
　produceful.

**Ogden Nash**

**23** A poem is a form of refrigeration that stops language going bad.

**Peter Porter**

**24** The writing of more than seventy-five

poems in any fiscal year should be punishable by a fine of $500.
**Ed Sanders**, 'Codex White Blizzard', *Montemora*, 1980

**25** All poets' wives have rotten lives
Their husbands look at them like knives.
**Delmore Schwartz** (Attrib.)

**26** Poetry is like fish: if it's fresh, it's good; if it's stale, it's bad; and if you're not certain, try it on the cat.
**Osbert Sitwell**

**27** A publisher of today would as soon see a burglar in his office as a poet.
**Henry de Vere Stacpoole**

**28** Poetry is trouble dunked in tears.
**Gwyn Thomas**, Welsh writer

**29** Poetry is to prose as dancing is to walking.
**John Wain**, talk on BBC Radio, 1976

**30** . . . a form of poetry which cannot possibly hurt anybody, even if translated into French.
**Oscar Wilde**, review in the *Pall Mall Gazette*

**31** All bad poetry springs from genuine feeling. To be natural is to be obvious, and to be obvious is to be inartistic.
**Oscar Wilde**, 'The Critic as Artist', 1890

**32** We have been able to have fine poetry in England because the public do not read it, and consequently do not influence it. The public like to insult poets because they are individual, but once they have insulted them, they leave them alone.
**Oscar Wilde**, 'The Soul of Man under Socialism', 1891

**33** Peotry is sissy stuff that rhymes. Weedy people say la and fie and swoon when they see a bunch of daffodils. Aktually there is only one piece of peotry in the english language.

*The Brook*
i come from haunts of coot and hern
i make a sudden sally
and-er-hem-er-hem-the fern
to bicker down a valley.
**Geoffrey Willans and Ronald Searle**, 'Down With Skool', *The Compleet Molesworth*, 1958

**34** I may as well tell you that if you are going about the place thinking things

pretty, you will never make a modern poet. Be poignant, man, be poignant!
**P. G. Wodehouse**, *The Small Bachelor*, 1927

**35** She could never forget that the man she loved was a man with a past. He had been a poet. Deep down in her soul there was always the corroding fear lest at any moment a particularly fine sunset or the sight of a rose in bud might undo all the work she had done, sending Rodney hotfoot once more to his Thesaurus and rhyming dictionary. It was for this reason that she always hurried him indoors when the sun began to go down and refused to have rose trees in her garden.
**P. G. Wodehouse**, *Nothing Serious*, 1950

# Poland and the Poles

**1** There are few virtues that the Poles do not possess – and there are few mistakes they have ever avoided.
**Winston Churchill**, speech, House of Commons, 1945

# Police

*See also Crime; The Law; Law and Order; Prison.*

**1 Five things not to say to a traffic cop**
Hey officer, that's terrific! The police officer who pulled me over yesterday only gave me a warning too!
Hey, you must have been doing at least 130 miles per hour to keep up with me. Great job!
You're not going to check the trunk, are you?
I thought you had to be in relatively good physical condition to be a police officer.
Do you mind holding my beer while I find my driver's license?
**Anon.**

**2** I have never seen a situation so dismal that a policeman couldn't make it worse.
**Brendan Behan**, Irish writer (Attrib.)

**3** When a felon's not engaged in his
employment
Or maturing his felonius little plans
His capacity for innocent enjoyment
Is just as great as any honest man's
Our feelings we with difficulty smother
When constabulary duty's to be done

Ah, take one consideration with another
A policeman's lot is not a happy one.
**W. S. Gilbert,** 'A Policeman's Lot is Not a Happy One',
song from *The Pirates of Penzance*, 1880

**4** Please, if you ever see me getting beaten
up by the police, please put your video
camera down and help me.
**Bobcat Goldthwait,** *Comic Relief*, HBO, 1992

**5** Are you going to come quietly or do I
have to use ear-plugs?
**Spike Milligan,** *The Goon Show*, BBC Radio

**6** Reading isn't an occupation we
encourage among police officers. We try to
keep the paper work down to a minimum.
**Joe Orton,** *Loot*, 1967

**7** FRANK: When I see five weirdos stabbing a
guy in broad daylight, I shoot the bastards.
That's my policy.
MAYOR: That was a Shakespeare in the Park
production, you moron. You killed five
actors. Good ones!
**Jerry Zucker, Jim Abrahams, David Zucker and Pat
Profit,** *The Naked Gun*, screenplay, 1988

# Political Correctness

*See also Sexism.*

**1** Dean Kagan, distinguished faculty,
parents, friends, graduating seniors, Secret
Service Agents, class agents, people of class,
people of color, colorful people, people of
height, the vertically constrained, people of
hair, the differently coiffed, the optically
challenged, the temporarily sighted, the
insightful, the out of sight, the out-of-
towners, the Eurocentrics, the Afrocentrics,
the Afrocentrics with Eurailpasses, the
eccentrically inclined, the sexually
disinclined, people of sex, sexy people,
sexist pigs, animal companions, friends of
the earth, friends of the boss, the
temporarily employed, the differently
employed, the differently optioned, people
with options, people with stock options, the
divestiturists, the deconstructionists, the
home constructionists, the home boys, the
homeless, the temporarily housed at home,
and, God save us, the permanently housed
at home.
**Garry Trudeau,** opening of speech at Yale University
Class Day

# Political Parties

*See also The Conservative Party; The Democratic
Party; Democrats and Republicans; The Labour
Party; Liberals and Conservatives; The Republican
Party.*

**1** There's no way in the world you're going
to make a political party respectable unless
you keep it out of office.
**Will Rogers**

**2** Liberals feel unworthy of their
possessions. Conservatives feel they deserve
everything they've stolen.
**Mort Sahl,** American comedian

# Politics – The American Presidency

*See also Politics – The American Vice-Presidency;
Washington.*

**1** Anybody that wants the presidency so
much that he'll spend two years organising
and campaigning for it is not to be trusted
with the office.
**David Broder,** *Washington Post*, 1973

**2** If Presidents don't do it to their wives,
they do it to the country.
**Mel Brooks**

**3** Now that I am no longer President, I find
that I do not win every game of golf I play.
**George Bush**

**4** In reverse order, our last eight presidents:
A hillbilly with a permanent hard-on; an
upper-class bureaucrat-twit; an actor-
imbecile; a born-again Christian peanut
farmer; an unelected college football
lineman; a paranoid moral dwarf; a vulgar
cowboy criminal; and a mediocre playboy
sex fiend.
**George Carlin,** *Brain Droppings*, 1997

**5** When I was a boy I was told that anybody
could become President; I'm beginning to
believe it.
**Clarence Darrow,** quoted in *Clarence Darrow for the
Defence*, 1941

**6** Higgledy-piggledy,
Benjamin Harrison,
Twenty-third President,
Was, and, as such,
Served between Clevelands, and

Save for this trivial
Idiosyncrasy,
Didn't do much.

**John Hollander,** 'Historical Reflections', *Jiggery-pokery: A Compendium of Double Dactyls,* 1966

**7** Being President is like being a jackass in a hailstorm. There's nothing to do but stand there and take it.

**Lyndon B. Johnson** (Attrib.)

**8** You're asking the leader of the Western world a chickenshit question like that?

**Lyndon Baines Johnson,** to reporter (Attrib.)

**9** . . . the pay is good and I can walk to work.

**John F. Kennedy,** quoted in *A Hero for Our Time,* 1983

**10** When we got into office, the thing that surprised me most was to find that things were just as bad as we'd been saying they were.

**John F. Kennedy,** speech in Washington, 1961

**11** Hillary [Clinton] and Nancy [Reagan] have a lot in common – they're both smarter than their husbands and both consulted the stars for guidance, Nancy with astrology and Hillary with Barbra Streisand.

**Bill Maher,** *Politically Incorrect,* ABC, 1995

**12** Washington couldn't tell a lie, Nixon couldn't tell the truth and Reagan couldn't tell the difference.

**Mort Sahl,** American comedian

**13** In America any boy may become President and I suppose it's just one of the risks he takes.

**Adlai Stevenson,** speech in Indianapolis, 1952

**14** The best reason I can think of for not running for President of the United States is that you have to shave twice a day.

**Adlai Stevenson**

**15** Nobody ever drops in for the evening.

**William H. Taft,** US President 1909–13

**16** All the President is, is a glorified public relations man who spends his time flattering, kissing, and kicking people to get them to do what they are supposed to do anyway.

**Harry S. Truman,** letter to his sister, 1947

**17** Any man who has had the job I've had and didn't have a sense of humor wouldn't still be here.

**Harry S. Truman** (Attrib.), 1955

**18** As to the presidency, the two happiest days of my life were those of my entrance upon the office and my surrender of it.

**Martin Van Buren,** President of the United States, 1837–41

**19** Any American who is prepared to run for President should automatically, by definition, be disqualified from ever doing so.

**Gore Vidal** (Attrib.)

**20** The presidential system just won't work any more. Anyone who gets in under it ought not to be allowed to serve.

**Gore Vidal,** 1980

# Politics – American Presidents

*See also Washington.*

*Listed chronologically:*

### Abraham Lincoln (Republican, 1860–1865)

**1** . . . is a filthy story-teller, despot, liar, thief, braggart, buffoon, usurper, monster, ignoramus, old scoundrel, perjurer, robber, swindler, tyrant, field-butcher, land-pirate.

*Harper's Weekly,* 1860

**2** Abe – have you got a pencil and paper there? Would you take this down? 'You can fool all of the people some of the time and some of the people all of the time. But you can't fool all of the people all the time.' Well, you keep doing it differently, Abe. The last quote I got was 'You can fool all the people all the time . . .'

**Bob Newhart,** 'Abe Lincoln versus Madison Avenue', *The Button-down Mind of Bob Newhart,* album, 1960

**3** . . . is a first-rate second-rate man . . . a mere convenience waiting like any other broomstick to be used.

**Wendell Phillips,** American orator and social reformer (Attrib.)

---

## Theodore Roosevelt (Republican, 1901–1909)

**1** One always thinks of him as a glorified bouncer engaged eternally in cleaning out bar-rooms – and not too proud to gouge when the inspiration came to him, or to bite in the clinches.
**H. L. Mencken**, *Prejudices*, Second Series, 1920

**2** The great virtue of my radicalism lies in the fact that I am perfectly ready, if necessary, to be radical on the conservative side.
**Theodore Roosevelt**, 1906

## Woodrow Wilson (Democrat, 1913–1921)

**1** Mr Wilson's name among the Allies is like that of the rich uncle, and they have accepted his manners out of respect for his means.
*Morning Post*, London, 1919

**2** The spacious philanthropy which he exhaled upon Europe stopped quite sharply at the coasts of his own country.
**Winston Churchill**, *The World Crisis*, 1929

**3** Mr Wilson's mind, as has been the custom, will be closed all day Sunday.
**George S. Kaufman**, 1889–1961, American writer

**4** I feel certain that he would not recognize a generous impulse if he met it on the street.
**William Howard Taft** (Attrib.)

## Warren G. Harding (Republican, 1921–1923)

**1** His speeches left the impression of an army of pompous phrases moving over the landscape in search of an idea; sometimes these meandering words would actually capture a straggling thought and bear it triumphantly a prisoner in their midst, until it died of servitude and overwork.
**William G. McAdoo**, unsuccessful contender for Democratic nomination for president, 1920 and 1924

**2** A tin-horn politician with the manner of a rural corn doctor and the mien of a ham actor.
**H. L. Mencken**, *Lodge*, 1920

## Calvin Coolidge (Republican, 1923–1929)

**1** ... I do wish he did not look as if he had been weaned on a pickle.
**Anon.**, quoted by Alice Roosevelt Longworth

**2** He's the greatest man who ever came out of Plymouth, Vermont.
**Clarence Darrow**, 1857–1938, American lawyer (Attrib.)

**3** Mr Coolidge's genius for inactivity is developed to a very high point. It is far from being an indolent activity. It is a grim, determined, alert inactivity which keeps Mr Coolidge occupied constantly ... Inactivity is a political philosophy and a party program with Mr Coolidge.
**Walter Lippmann**, *Men of Destiny*, 1927

**4** ... simply a cheap and trashy fellow, deficient in sense and almost devoid of any notion of honor – in brief, a dreadful little cad.
**H. L. Mencken**, *Baltimore Evening Sun*, 1924

**5** How can they tell?
**Dorothy Parker**, on being told that Coolidge was dead, 1933 (Attrib.)

**6** He is the first president to discover that what the American people want is to be left alone.
**Will Rogers**, newspaper column, 1924

## Herbert Hoover (Republican, 1929–1933)

**1** I was just standing out in front watching the other acts when a lady walked up to me in the lobby and said, 'Pardon me, young man, could you tell me where I could find the rest room?' and I said, 'It's just around the corner.' 'Don't give me that Hoover talk,' she said. 'I'm serious.'
**Al Boasberg**, for Bob Hope, 1930

**2** In 1932, lame duck President Herbert Hoover was so desperate to remain in the White House that he dressed up as Eleanor Roosevelt. When FDR discovered the hoax in 1936, the two men decided to stay together for the sake of the children.
**Johnny Carson**, *The Tonight Show*, NBC TV

## Franklin D. Roosevelt (Democrat, 1933–1945)

**1** Meeting Franklin Roosevelt was like opening the finest bottle of champagne; knowing him was like drinking it.
**Winston Churchill**

**2** . . . the man who started more creations than were ever begun since Genesis – and finished none.
**Hugh Johnson**, Director, National Recovery Administration, 1933–4, 1937

**3** If he became convinced tomorrow that coming out for cannibalism would get him the votes he so sorely needs, he would begin fattening a missionary in the White House backyard come Wednesday.
**H. L. Mencken** (Attrib.)

## Harry S. Truman (Democrat, 1945–1953)

**1** To err is Truman.
**Republican Party slogan**, 1948

**2** Truman . . . seemed to stand for nothing more spectacular than honesty in war contracting, which was like standing for virtue in Hollywood or adequate rainfall in the Middle West.
**George E. Allen**, *Presidents Who Have Known Me*

**3** Mr Truman believes other people should be 'free to govern themselves as they see fit' – so long as they see fit to see as we see fit.
**I. F. Stone**, 1907–89, American journalist

**4** My choice early in life was either to be a piano-player in a whorehouse or a politician. And to tell the truth, there's hardly any difference.
**Harry S. Truman**, 1962

## Dwight D. Eisenhower (Republican, 1953–1961)

**1** I doubt very much if a man whose main literary interests were in works by Mr Zane Grey, admirable as they may be, is particularly well equipped to be chief executive of this country, particularly where Indian affairs are concerned.
**Dean Acheson**, American Secretary of State, 1953 (Attrib.)

**2** I haven't checked these figures but eighty-seven years ago, I think it was, a number of individuals organized a governmental set-up here in this country, I believe it covered certain eastern areas, with this idea they were following up based on a sort of national-independence arrangement and the program that every individual is just as good as every other individual . . .
**Oliver Jensen**, 'The Gettysburg Address in Eisenhowerese', *New York Herald Tribune*, 1957

**3** Eisenhower is the only living Unknown Soldier.
**Robert S. Kerr**, Oklahoma Senator

**4** If I talk over people's heads, Ike must talk under their feet.
**Adlai Stevenson**, Democratic presidential candidate defeated by Eisenhower in 1952 and 1956

**5** The General has dedicated himself so many times, he must feel like the cornerstone of a public building.
**Adlai Stevenson**

## John F. Kennedy (Democrat, 1961–1963)

**1** He taught us the courage of action in West Berlin, the wisdom of patience in South-East Asia, the action of wisdom in our space race, the patience of courage in our desegregated schools and the active patient wisdom of wise courageous action at the Guantanamo Naval Base.
*National Lampoon*

**2** Knock, knock.
Who's there?
Astronaut.
Astronaut Who?
Astronaut what your country can do for you – ask what you can do for your country.
**Anon.**

**3** . . . the report is that Old Joe Kennedy told Young Jack: 'Don't worry, son. If you lose the election, I'll buy you a country.'
*Time*, 1960

**4** His speaking style is pseudo-Roman: 'Ask not what your country can do for you . . .' Why not say, 'Don't ask . . .'? 'Ask not . . .' is the style of a man playing the role of being President, not of a man being President.
**Herb Gold**, *New York Post*, 1962

**5** Everyone's talking about how young the candidates are. And it's true. A few months

ago Kennedy's mother said, 'You have a choice . . . do you want to go to camp this year or run for President?'
**Bob Hope**, during Kennedy/Nixon presidential campaign, 1960

**6** When we got into office, the one thing that surprised me most was to find that things were just as bad as we'd been saying they were.
**John F. Kennedy**, at his birthday party at the White House, 1961

## Lyndon B. Johnson (Democrat, 1963–1969)

**1** I seldom think of politics more than 18 hours a day.
**Lyndon Johnson**

**2** Hyperbole was to Lyndon Johnson what oxygen is to life.
**Bill Moyers**, American journalist and White House aide

## Richard Nixon (Republican, 1969–1974)
*See also The Vietnam War; Watergate.*

**1** A new book has been released entitled *Friends of Richard Nixon*. It is only one page longer than the work, *Famous Antarctic Television Personalities of the Eighteenth Century*. President Ford said, 'I've spent most of this week reading it, finding it challenging in its scope.'
**'Weekend Update'**, *Saturday Night Live*, NBC TV

**2** In Washington, so the story goes, Republican top strategists huddled, and all were glum indeed – except one. 'I'm sure we'll win, there's no doubt about it,' he enthused. Everyone wanted to know the reason for his confidence. Answer: 'I have a deep and abiding faith in the fundamental bigotry of the American people.'
*Time*, 1960 (the Republican Presidential candidate was Nixon)

**3** There's a theory that provides an answer to the question of President Nixon's attitude to gambling. There was once a small boy in California who had a pony he was very fond of. One day a gambler came to town and, engaging the boy in a game of cards, won the pony. The boy swore never to gamble again . . .
 The reader will have guessed by now that

I am telling Richard Nixon's story. He was that gambler.
**Anon.**

**4** He told us he was going to take crime out of the streets. He did. He took it into the damn White House.
**Revd Ralph D. Abernathy**, 1926–90, American civil rights leader

**5** . . . a Main Street Machiavelli.
**Patrick Anderson**, 1915–79, American political commentator

**6** Look, Nixon's no dope. If the people really wanted moral leadership, he'd give them moral leadership.
**Charles Barsotti**, cartoon, *New Yorker*

**7** Nixon is a purposeless man, but I have great faith in his cowardice.
**Jimmy Breslin**, columnist

**8** . . . a naïve, inept, maladjusted Throttlebottom.
**Emmanuel Celler**, 1888–1981, Democratic Congressman

**9** Nixon just isn't half the man Hitler was.
**Richard Dudman**, *St Louis Post Dispatch*

**10** Do you realize the responsibility I carry? I'm the only person standing between Richard Nixon and the White House.
**John F. Kennedy**

**11** The only problem with drawing Nixon is restraint. Your tendency is to let your feelings come out. He's such a loathsome son of a bitch, and he looks so loathsome.
**Bill Mauldin**, political cartoonist

**12** Ever since Nixon, nobody has asked me why I am teaching a course like Policy Choice as Value conflict.
**Professor Bruce Payne**, Duke University, North Carolina

**13** Richard Nixon means never having to say you're sorry.
**Wilfred Sheed**, *GQ*, 1984

**14** Let's face it, there's something perversely endearing about a man so totally his own worst enemy that even achieving the presidency was merely something he had to do in order to be able to lose it.
**Paul Slansky**, American screenwriter

**15** He is the kind of politician who would cut down a redwood tree and then mount the stump to make a speech for conservation.
**Adlai Stevenson**, 1956

**16** . . . McCarthyism in a white collar.
**Adlai Stevenson**

**17** . . . a little man in a big hurry.
**Robert A. Taft**, Republican Senator

**18** . . . the integrity of a hyena and the style of a poison toad.
**Hunter S. Thompson**

**19** When the cold light of history looks back on Richard Nixon's five years of unrestrained power in the White House, it will show that he had the same effect on conservative/Republican politics as Charles Manson and the Hell's Angels had on hippies and flower people.
**Hunter S. Thompson**

**20** Richard Nixon is a no-good lying bastard. He can lie out of both sides of his mouth at the same time, and even if he caught himself telling the truth, he'd lie just to keep his hand in.
**Harry S. Truman**

**21** . . . it is quite extraordinary! He will even tell a lie when it is not convenient to. That is the sign of a great artist . . .
**Gore Vidal**, interviewed on *Russell Harty Plus*, London Weekend Television, 1972

## Gerald Ford (Republican, 1974–1977)

**1** A year ago Gerald Ford was unknown throughout America. Now he's unknown throughout the world.
**Anon.**, quoted in the *Guardian*, 1974

**2** Richard Nixon impeached himself. He gave us Gerald Ford as his revenge.
**Bella Abzug**, Democratic Congresswoman and feminist

**3** He looks like the guy in the science fiction movie who is the first to see 'The Creature'.
**David Frye**

**4** He's a very nice fellow, but that's not enough, gentlemen. So's my Uncle Fred.
**Hubert Humphrey** (Attrib.)

**5** Gerry Ford is a nice guy, but he played too much football with his helmet off.
**Lyndon B. Johnson**

**6** Gerry Ford is so dumb that he can't fart and chew gum at the same time.
**Lyndon B. Johnson** (Attrib.)

**7** If Ford can get away with this list of issues . . . and be elected on it, then I'm going to call the dictator of Uganda, Mr Amin, and tell him to start giving speeches on airport safety.
**Walter Mondale**, American Vice-President, 1977–81

**8** It troubles me that he played center on the football team. That means he can only consider options for the twenty yards in either direction and that he has spent a good deal of his life looking at the world upside down through his legs.
**Martin Peretz**, Editorial Director, *New Republic*

## Jimmy Carter (Democrat, 1977–1981)

**1** Everybody seems to be disappointed in Jimmy Carter. The other day Miz Lillian was heard muttering, 'To think I voted for him.'
**Joey Adams**, *New York Post*, 1978

**2** Jimmy's basic problem is that he's super cautious. He looks before and after he leaps.
**Joey Adams**, *New York Post*, 1978

**3** Jimmy needs Billy like Van Gogh needs stereo.
**Johnny Carson**, *The Tonight Show*, NBC TV, 1977, of the President's wayward brother, Billy

**4** That suave former farmer of peanuts
Changes views twice a day, driving me
     nuts
What he says in the morning
By night-time he's scorning
Vote Carter? You'd just have to be nuts!
**Stanley K. Fisher**, competition, *New York Magazine*, 1976

**5** I don't know what people have against Jimmy Carter. He's done nothing.
**Bob Hope**, campaigning for Ronald Reagan against Carter, 1980

**6** We're realists. It doesn't make much difference between Ford and Carter. Carter is your typical smiling, brilliant, back-stabbing, bull-shitting Southern nut-cutter.
**Lane Kirkland**, US trades union leader, 1976

**7** I think Jimmy Carter as President is like Truman Capote marrying Dolly Parton. The job is just too big for him.
**Rich Little** (Attrib.)

**8** I would not want Jimmy Carter and his men put in charge of snake control in Ireland.
**Eugene McCarthy**, 1976

## Ronald Reagan (Republican, 1981–1989)

**1** National Security Advisor [William P.] Clark arrived in Lebanon but thought he was in Israel. He wasn't disturbed by the logistical error. 'I'm not sure who's the President of which,' he remarked. Clark said he planned to use his ignorance as a way to mediate tense relations between the two countries by 'avoiding name calling'.
*Off The Wall Street Journal*, 1982

**2** [Secretary of State, Alexander] Haig found a Nicaraguan insurgent under his desk. Haig said this proves 'beyond an irrefutable iota of a doubt' there are communist influences in El Salvador and the State Department. Haig said the Nicaraguan 'was so small I almost missed him', and that he couldn't produce the Nicaraguan rebel for reporters because, 'just as I was bringing him on over here, he slipped through my fingers and disappeared under my rug'.
*Off The Wall Street Journal*, 1982

**3** He has not the remotest idea of what he is about to say, and having said it he has not the remotest recollection of what it was. One can pray only that the Russians are alive to this fact, since if they are not, then none of us will be alive to anything else.
**Alan Coren**, *Punch*, 1984

**4** Ronald Reagan doesn't dye his hair – he's just prematurely orange.
**Gerald Ford** (Attrib.)

**5** People here may be sharply divided over the Reagan administration's policies – but they admire Ronald Reagan for not getting involved in them.
**Edward Kennedy**, Democratic Senator

**6** I read that Nancy Reagan was at the Beverly Hills Hotel to accept her Humanitarian of the Year Award.

I'm glad she beat out that conniving bitch Mother Teresa.
**Jay Leno**, *The Tonight Show*, NBC TV

**7** I believe that Ronald Reagan can make this country what it once was – an arctic region covered with ice.
**Steve Martin** (Attrib.)

**8** Since I came to the White House I got two hearing aids, a colon operation, skin cancer, a prostate operation and I was shot. The damn thing is, I've never felt better in my life.
**Ronald Reagan**, speech to the Washington Gridiron Club, 1987

**9** Sometimes our right hand doesn't know what our far-right hand is doing.
**Ronald Reagan**, on differences between his staff during his first term in office

**10** Reaganomics, that makes sense to me. It means if you don't have enough money, it's because poor people are hoarding it.
**Kevin Rooney**, quoted in *GQ*, 1984

**11** It was the result of many years spent as a mediocre showbiz figure listening to rich, crotchety Republicans yearning for a return to the good old days.
**Mike Royko**, on the roots of Reaganomics, *Chicago Tribune*

**12** . . . a triumph of the embalmer's art.
**Gore Vidal**

**13** There's a lot to be said for being *nouveau riche* and the Reagans mean to say it all.
**Gore Vidal**, 1981

**14** I still think Nancy does most of his talking; you'll notice that she *never* drinks water when Ronnie speaks.
**Robin Williams**, interview in *Playboy*, 1982

## George Bush (Republican, 1989–1993)

**1** Anyone who eats pork rinds, can't be all good.
**Barbara Bush**, on husband George

**2** He can't help it. He was born with a silver foot in his mouth.
**Ann Richards**, Governor of Texas, speech, 1988

## Bill Clinton (Democrat, 1993–2001)

**1** When asked in a poll whether they would sleep with President Clinton, 65% of American women replied, 'Not again.'
**Anon.**, 1998

**2** The President bought six books at a local bookstore. I guess he didn't want to be seen at the checkout counter with just the Cindy Crawford calendar.
**Jay Leno**, on the President's vacation, *The Tonight Show*

**3** The Secret Service has signs all over the island saying, 'Please Do Not Feed the President.'
**David Letterman**, during Bill Clinton's vacation on Martha's Vineyard, *The Late Show*, CBS

**4** President Clinton says he wants $30 million from Congress for contraception and family planning. Thirty million dollars from Congress for contraception? It sound to me like somebody's going to go dating again.
**David Letterman**, *The Late Show*, CBS, 2000

**5** Hillary is really sucking up to the Israelis. She keeps saying, 'You know, my husband's last girlfriend was Jewish.'
**David Letterman**, *The Late Show*, CBS, 1999

**6** A lot of people have warned President Clinton that Bosnia will turn into another Vietnam, which would be embarrassing for him because he'll have to go back to college.
**Bill Maher**, *Politically Incorrect*, ABC, 1993

**7** If Bill Clinton was Moses, he would have come down with the Ten Suggestions.
**Bill Maher**, *Politically Incorrect*, ABC, 1993

**8** I think most of us learned a long time ago that if you don't like the President's position on a particular issue, you simply need to wait a few weeks.
**David Obey**

**9** I think President Clinton misunderstood the role of the president, which is to screw the country as a whole, not individually.
**Betsy Salkind**, American comedy writer

**10** We elected him president, not pope.
**Barbra Streisand**, defending Clinton's lifestyle

## George W. Bush (Republican, 2001–)

**1** George W. Bush released his medical records today. It seems during the Vietnam War he suffered memory loss when he crushed a beer can against his forehead at a fraternity party.
**Jay Leno**, *The Tonight Show*, NBC, 2000

**2** George W. Bush has a new campaign slogan: 'A reformer with results.' I don't know what it means, [but] I think it's better than his old campaign slogan: 'A dumb guy with connections.'
**David Letterman**, *The Late Show*, CBS TV, 2000

# Politics – The American Vice-Presidency

*See also Politics – American Presidents; Politics and Politicians.*

**1** You really do get a chance to meet dead leaders . . . it's known as quiet diplomacy.
**George Bush**, on the number of state funerals he'd attended in four years as Vice-President, speech in Washington, 1985

**2** . . . inside work with no heavy lifting.
**Bob Dole**, quoted on *This Week*, ABC, 1988

**3** The vice presidency ain't worth a pitcher of warm spit.
**John Nance Garner**, Vice-President under Franklin Roosevelt, 1933–40 (Attrib.)

**4** Worst damnfool mistake I ever made was letting myself be elected Vice President of the United States . . . I spent eight long years as Mr Roosevelt's spare tire.
**John Nance Garner**, Vice-President under Franklin Roosevelt, 1933–40, quoted in *Saturday Evening Post*, 1963

**5** Once there were two brothers; one ran away to sea, the other was elected Vice-President – and nothing was ever heard of them again.
**Thomas R. Marshall**, Vice-President under Woodrow Wilson, 1913–21

**6** The man with the best job in the country is the Vice President. All he has to do is get up every morning and say, 'How's the President?'
**Will Rogers**, speech, 1934

**7** The Vice-Presidency is sort of like the last

cookie on the plate. Everybody insists he won't take it, but somebody always does.
**Bill Vaughan**

### Humphrey, Hubert,

*Vice-President of the United States, 1965–1969 (Democrat)*

**1** Hubert Humphrey talks so fast that listening to him is like trying to read *Playboy* magazine with your wife turning over the pages.
**Barry Goldwater**, Republican Senator

## Politics – Axioms

*See also Politics and Politicians.*

**1** It is a good thing to follow the First Law of Holes; if you are in one, stop digging.
**Denis Healey**, British Labour minister, 1983

**2** If it walks like a duck, and quacks like a duck, then it just may be a duck.
**Walter Reuther**, trade union leader, on how to tell a communist

**3** He who slings mud, usually loses ground.
**Adlai Stevenson** (Attrib.), 1954

**4** If you can't stand the heat, get out of the kitchen.
**Harry S. Truman**

## Politics – British Prime Ministers

*See also House of Commons; Parliament; Politics and Politicians.*

*Listed chronologically:*

### William Ewart Gladstone (Liberal, 1868–1874, 1880–1885, 1886, 1892–1894)

**1** They told me how Mr Gladstone read Homer for fun, which I thought served him right.
**Winston Churchill**, *My Early Life*, 1930

**2** He has not a single redeeming defect.
**Benjamin Disraeli** (Attrib.)

**3** . . . honest in the most odious sense of the word.
**Benjamin Disraeli** (Attrib.)

**4** Mr Gladstone speaks to me as if I were a public meeting.
**Queen Victoria** (Attrib.)

### David Lloyd George (Liberal, 1916–1922)

**1** He couldn't see a belt without hitting below it.
**Margot Asquith** (Attrib.)

**2** He did not seem to care which way he travelled, providing he was in the driver's seat.
**Lord Beaverbrook**, *The Decline and Fall of Lloyd George*, 1963

**3** The Happy Warrior of Squandermania.
**Winston Churchill**, debate in House of Commons on 1929 Budget

### James Ramsay Macdonald (Labour, 1924, 1929–1931, 1931–1935)

**1** I have waited fifty years to see the Boneless Wonder sitting on the Treasury bench.
**Winston Churchill**, speech, House of Commons, 1933

**2** We know that he has, more than any other man, the gift of compressing the largest amount of words into the smallest amount of thought.
**Winston Churchill**, speech, House of Commons, 1933

**3** He had sufficient conscience to bother him, but not sufficient to keep him straight.
**David Lloyd George** (Attrib.)

### Stanley Baldwin (Conservative, 1923–1924, 1924–1929, 1935–1937)

**1** I think Baldwin has gone mad. He simply takes one jump in the dark; looks round; and then takes another.
**Lord Birkenhead**, letter to Austen Chamberlain, 1923

**2** He occasionally stumbled over the truth, but hastily picked himself up and hurried on as if nothing had happened.
**Winston Churchill** (Attrib.)

**3** One could not even dignify him with the name of stuffed shirt. He was simply a hole in the air.
**George Orwell**, *The Lion and the Unicorn*, 1941

## Neville Chamberlain (Conservative, 1937–1940)

**1** Listening to a speech by Chamberlain is like paying a visit to Woolworth's. Everything is in its place and nothing above sixpence.
**Aneurin Bevan**, speech, House of Commons, 1937

**2** He saw foreign policy through the wrong end of a municipal drainpipe.
**David Lloyd George** (Attrib.)

**3** . . . the mind and manner of a clothesbrush.
**Harold Nicolson**, 1938

## Winston Churchill (Conservative, 1940–1945, 1951–1955)

**1** I thought he was a young man of promise; but it appears he was a young man of promises.
**A. J. Balfour**, 1899

**2** He is a man suffering from petrified adolescence.
**Aneurin Bevan**

**3** He mistakes verbal felicities for mental inspiration.
**Aneurin Bevan** (Attrib.)

**4** He refers to a defeat as a disaster as though it came from God, but to a victory as though it came from himself.
**Aneurin Bevan**, speech in the House of Commons, 1942

**5** The mediocrity of his thinking is concealed by the majesty of his language.
**Aneurin Bevan** (Attrib.)

**6** At intervals he turned a somersault, exactly like a porpoise; and when his head reappeared at the other end of the bath, he continued precisely where he left off.
**Robert Boothby**, *Recollections of a Rebel*, 1975

**7** Churchill was fundamentally what the English call unstable – by which they mean anybody who has that touch of genius which is inconvenient in normal times.
**Harold Macmillan**, 1975

**8** Winston has devoted the best years of his life to preparing his impromptu speeches.
**F. E. Smith** (Attrib.)

## Clement Attlee (Labour, 1945–1951)
*See also Winston Churchill; The Labour Party.*

**1** He seems determined to make a trumpet sound like a tin whistle . . . He brings to the fierce struggle of politics the tepid enthusiasm of a lazy summer afternoon at a cricket match.
**Aneurin Bevan**, *Tribune*, 1945

**2** Absolutely true – but then he [Clement Attlee] does have a lot to be modest about.
**Winston Churchill**, agreeing with a colleague that Attlee was modest (possibly apocryphal)

**3** . . . a sheep in sheep's clothing.
**Winston Churchill** (Attrib.)

**4** Charisma? He did not recognize the word except as a clue in his beloved *Times* crossword.
**James Margach**, *The Abuse of Power*, 1981

**5** . . . reminds me of nothing so much as a dead fish before it has had time to stiffen.
**George Orwell** (Attrib.)

## Harold Wilson (Labour, 1964–1970, 1974–1976)

**1** The only reason Harold Wilson as a child had to go to school without boots on, was that his boots were probably too small for him.
**Harold Macmillan** (Attrib.)

## Margaret Thatcher (Conservative, 1979–1990)
*See also The Falklands.*

**1** She sounded like the Book of Revelations read out over a railway station public address system by a headmistress of a certain age wearing calico knickers.
**Clive James**, of Margaret Thatcher on television, *Observer*, 1979

**2** I am a great admirer of Mrs Thatcher. She's one of the most splendid headmistresses there has ever been.
**Arthur Marshall**, *Any Questions*, BBC Radio, 1982

**3** Margaret Thatcher had a terrible dream last night. She was caught in a lift with General Galtieri, Arthur Scargill and Jacques Delors. And she only had one handbag.
**Fred Metcalf**, for David Frost, 2001

**4** . . . she is democratic enough to talk down to anyone.
**Austin Mitchell**, *Westminster Man*, 1982

**5** She has Marilyn Monroe's mouth and Caligula's eyes.
**François Mitterrand**

**6** Margaret Thatcher will never speak well on television. Her impulse to tell the microphone to pull itself together is too great.
**Edward Pearce**, *The Senate of Lilliput*, 1983

**7** How can I put this delicately? Let me tell you the rude way. Yours was more like suburban prejudice than real Conservatism.
**Brian Redhead**, interviewing Margaret Thatcher, *Today*, BBC Radio 4, 1993

**8** If I were married to her, I'd be sure to have dinner ready when she got home.
**George Shultz**, American Secretary of State (Attrib.)

**9** I am extraordinarily patient, provided I get my own way in the end.
**Margaret Thatcher**, 1989

**10** I cannot bring myself to vote for a woman who has been voice-trained to speak to me as though my dog had just died.
**Keith Waterhouse**, English humorist

# Politics – Insults

*See also Abuse; Insults; Politics – American President; Politics – British Prime Ministers; Politics and Politicians.*

**1** [Benjamin Franklin] is one continued insult to good manners and decency.
**John Adams**, American President, 1797–1801 (Attrib.)

**2** It is fitting that we should have buried the Unknown Prime Minister by the side of the Unknown Soldier.
**Lord Asquith**, of Bonar Law, British Prime Minister, 1922

**3** I wouldn't piss down Jerry Brown's throat if his heart was on fire.
**James Carville**

**4** Sometimes I think we're the only two lawyers in Washington who trust each other.
**Bob Dole**, US Republican Senator, on himself and his wife Elizabeth

**5** It's Dole's misfortune that when he does smile, he looks as if he's just evicted a widow.
**Mike Royko**, columnist, *Chicago Tribune*, 1988

**6** [US Secretary of State, John Foster Dulles] is the only case I know of a bull who carries his own china shop with him.
**Winston Churchill** (Attrib.)

**7** Everyone enjoys inventing lines about how dull they are: Mike Dukakis's idea of a hot night is rearranging his sock drawer; after he won the New York primary, he went out and painted the town beige. The Republicans have put up a man whose most memorable contribution to political rhetoric is 'deep doo-doo.' Bush thinks 'gosh darn' are fighting words.
**Molly Ivins**, on the Presidential campaign, *Ms.*, 1988

**8** They couldn't pour piss out of a shoe if the instructions were written on the heel.
**Lyndon B. Johnson**

**9** Dan Quayle taught the kids a valuable lesson: if you don't study you could wind up as Vice President.
**Jay Leno**

**10** When they circumcised Herbert Samuel, they threw away the wrong bit.
**David Lloyd George**, on his fellow Liberal, 1930s

**11** Al Gore turned down a chance to be on *The Simpsons*. He explained, 'I've never been animated and I'm not going to start now.'
**Conan O'Brien**, *Late Night with Conan O'Brien*, NBC TV

**12** He has been called a mediocre man; but this is unwarranted flattery. He was a politician of monumental littleness.
**Theodore Roosevelt**, of John Tyler (President, 1841–5)

**13** Sir Alec Douglas-Home, when he was British Foreign Secretary, said he received the following telegram from an irate citizen: 'To hell with you. Offensive letter follows.'
**William Safire**, *The New Language of Politics*, 1968

**14** . . . when political ammunition runs low, inevitably the rusty artillery of abuse is always wheeled into action.
**Adlai Stevenson**, speech, 1952

# Politics and Politicians

*See also Winston Churchill; Congress;
Conservatism; The Conservative Party; Democrats
and Republicans; Elections; Government; House of
Commons; House of Lords; Liberals and
Conservatives; Parliament; Politics – The American
Presidency; Politics – American Presidents; Politics –
The American Vice-Presidency; Politics – Axioms;
Politics – Insults; Political Parties; Power.*

**1** A politician will always be there when he
needs you.
**Anon.**

**2** Politicians are like diapers – they should
be changed regularly and for the same
reason.
**Anon.**

**3** Politics makes estranged bedfellows.
**Goodman Ace**

**4** The first requirement of a statesman is
that he be dull. This is not always easy to
achieve.
**Dean Acheson,** American statesman, 1970

**5** A: Have you ever taken a serious political
stand on anything?
B: Yes, for twenty-four hours I refused to eat
grapes.
**Woody Allen,** *Sleeper,* screenplay, 1973

**6** Politics – the gentle art of getting votes
from the poor and campaign funds from the
rich, by promising to protect each from the
other.
**Oscar Ameringer,** 1870–1943, American Socialist leader
and author

**7** There are three groups that no British
Prime Minister should provoke: the Vatican,
the Treasury and the miners.
**Stanley Baldwin,** 1867–1947, British Conservative
Prime Minister (Attrib.)

**8** The politician is an acrobat. He keeps his
balance by saying the opposite of what he
does.
**Maurice Barrès,** *Mes cahiers,* 1896–1923

**9** Taking into consideration all the
circumstances likely to obtain in the future
and making every allowance for
developments which something, perhaps,
could be done to anticipate, it is perhaps
not too much to say that, in the actual state
of affairs produced by certain events, the
safest course to follow would be to make an
overall study of possible measures to be
taken, with a view to any decision which
might or might not be arrived at in the
search for a basic policy of one kind or
another.
**Beachcomber ( J. B. Morton),** *Daily Express*

**10** The connection between humbug and
politics is too long-established to be
challenged.
**Ronald Bell,** MP, House of Commons, 1979

**11** Here richly, with ridiculous display,
   The Politician's corpse was laid away.
   While all of his acquaintances sneered
      and slanged,
   I wept: for I had longed to see him
      hanged.
**Hilaire Belloc,** 1870–1953, French-born English poet,
essayist and politician

**12** When the audience is a mixed group,
the speaker finds a quick kinship in
geography. He will always have a soft spot
for Devil's Gulch, Arizona, because his
mother was born eighteen miles from there.
Or for East Overshoe, Illinois, because his
Uncle Henry ran a poolroom there in 1912.
At worst, he can always call a town his
'second home' on the ground that he once
stayed overnight at the local hotel and had
his laundry done.
**Robert Bendiner,** 'How to Listen to Campaign
Oratory if You Have to', *Look,* 1960

**13** Politics is the art of looking for trouble,
finding it whether it exists or not,
diagnosing it incorrectly, and applying the
wrong remedy.
**Sir Ernest Benn,** quoted in the *Observer,* 1930

**14** Politics, *n.* A strife of interests
masquerading as a contest of principles.
**Ambrose Bierce,** *The Devil's Dictionary,* 1911

**15** *I* am up-and-coming.
*You* are ambitious.
*He* is on the make.

*I* am a bit of a dandy.
*You* aren't married.
*He* is a security risk.

*I* make a brave stand.
*You* are not afraid to rock the boat.
*He* is a trouble maker.

*I* communicate.
*You* spin.
*He* leaks.
**Craig Brown**, cut-out-and-keep guide to political conjugation, *Daily Telegraph*, 1999

**16** I always wanted to get into politics but I was never light enough to get in the team.
**Art Buchwald**

**17** If you take yourself seriously in politics, you've had it.
**Lord Carrington**, British Foreign Secretary, 1979–82

**18** Every politician is emphatically a promising politician.
**G. K. Chesterton**, *The Red Moon of Meru*

**19** Political ability is the ability to foretell what is going to happen tomorrow, next week, next month and next year. And to have the ability afterward to explain why it didn't happen.
**Winston Churchill**

**20** Politics are almost as exciting as war and quite as dangerous. In war you can only be killed once, but in politics many times.
**Winston Churchill**

**21** A majority is always the best repartee.
**Benjamin Disraeli**, *Tancred*, 1847

**22** Politics is not the art of the possible. It consists in choosing between the disastrous and the unpalatable.
**J. K. Galbraith**, *Ambassador's Journal*, responding to R. A. Buder's 'Politics is the Art of the Possible', 1969

**23** Since a politician never believes what he says, he is surprised when others believe him.
**Charles de Gaulle**, quoted in *Newsweek*, 1962

**24** You know, it's easy to be politically correct and a liberal when you live in a gated community.
**Bobcat Goldthwait**

**25** Every time I make one appointment, I make nine *dis*appointments.
**Bibb Graves**, former governor of Alabama

**26** Probably the most distinctive characteristic of the successful politician is selective cowardice.
**Richard Harris**, 'Annals of Legislation', *New Yorker*, 1968

**27** A politician will do anything to keep his job – even become a patriot.
**William Randolph Hearst**, editorial, 1933

**28** 'What a lovely, lovely moon
And it's in the constituency too.'
**Alan Jackson**, 'The Young Politician'

**29** Son, in politics you've got to learn that overnight chicken shit can turn to chicken salad.
**Lyndon B. Johnson**, to a reporter, 1958

**30** I've just looked up the word 'politics' in the dictionary and it says it's a combination of two words: 'poli' which means many. And 'tics' which means bloodsuckers.
**Max Kauffmann**

**31** The *press conference* is a politician's way of being informative without saying anything. Should he accidentally say something, he has at his side a *press officer* who immediately explains it away by 'clarifying' it.
**Emery Kelen**, *Platypus at Large*, 1960

**32** Mothers all want their sons to grow up to be President but they don't want them to become politicians in the process.
**John F. Kennedy** (Attrib.)

**33** One fifth of the people are against everything all the time.
**Robert Kennedy**, 1964

**34** Politicians are the same all over. They promise to build a bridge even when there's no river.
**Nikita Khrushchev**, remark at Glen Cove, New York, 1960

**35** Politicians say they're beefing up our economy. Most don't know beef from pork.
**Harold Lowman**

**36** The PM – whose motto is . . . 'In Defeat, Malice. In Victory, Revenge!'
**Jonathan Lynn and Antony Jay**, *Yes, Minister*, BBC TV

**37** Being in politics is like being a football coach. You have to be smart enough to understand the game and stupid enough to think it's important.
**Eugene McCarthy**, American Democratic Senator

**38** I have never found, in a long experience

of politics, that criticism is ever inhibited by ignorance.
**Harold Macmillan,** after his son Maurice had written to *The Times* criticizing the Conservative Government, 1963

**39** When you're abroad, you're a statesman; when you're at home, you're just a politician.
**Harold Macmillan**

**40** A politician is an animal that can sit on a fence and keep both ears to the ground.
**H. L. Mencken**

**41** If experience teaches us anything at all, it teaches us this: that a good politician, under democracy, is quite as unthinkable as an honest burglar.
**H. L. Mencken,** *Prejudices, Fourth Series,* 1924

**42** I have spent much of my life fighting the Germans and fighting the politicians. It is much easier to fight the Germans.
**Field Marshal Lord Montgomery,** *Observer,* 1967

**43** Politics is the diversion of trivial men who, when they succeed at it, become important in the eyes of more trivial men.
**George Jean Nathan,** 1882–1958, critic

**44** Political language – and with variations this is true of all political parties, from Conservatives to Anarchists – is designed to make lies sound truthful and murder respectable, and to give an appearance of solidity to pure wind.
**George Orwell,** 'Politics and the English Language', *Shooting an Elephant,* 1950

**45** It is now known that men enter local politics solely as a result of being unhappily married.
**G. Northcote Parkinson,** *Parkinson's Law,* 1957

**46** Public office is the last refuge of a scoundrel.
Alternatively: Public office is the last refuge of the incompetent.
**Boies Penrose,** Senator, Pennsylvania (Attrib.)

**47** The mistake a lot of politicians make is in forgetting they've been appointed and thinking they've been anointed.
**Claude Pepper,** Senator and Congressman, Florida, on the occasion of his 80th birthday, 1981

**48** Politicians who complain about the

media are like ships' captains who complain about the sea.
**Enoch Powell** (Attrib.)

**49** Politics is not a bad profession. If you succeed, there are many rewards; if you disgrace yourself, you can always write a book.
**Ronald Reagan,** American President, 1981–9

**50** All politics are based on the indifference of the majority.
**James Reston,** American journalist

**51** Ask not what you can do for your country. Ask what you can do for yourself.
**Tim Robbins,** *Bob Roberts,* screenplay, 1992

**52** Once a man holds public office he is absolutely no good for honest work.
**Will Rogers**

**53** There is no more independence in politics than there is in jail.
**Will Rogers**

**54** A conservative is a man with two perfectly good legs who, however, has never learned to walk forwards . . . A reactionary is a somnambulist walking backwards . . . A radical is a man with both feet firmly planted – in the air.
**Franklin D. Roosevelt,** 'Fireside Chat', 1939

**55** The most successful politician is he who says what everybody is thinking most often and in the loudest voice.
**Theodore Roosevelt,** American President, 1901–9

**56** Our great democracies still tend to think that a stupid man is more likely to be honest than a clever man, and our politicians take advantage of this prejudice by pretending to be even more stupid than nature made them.
**Bertrand Russell,** *New Hopes for a Changing World,* 1951

**57** A government which robs Peter to pay Paul can always depend on the support of Paul.
**George Bernard Shaw,** *Everybody's Political What's What?,* 1944

**58** He knows nothing and he thinks he knows everything. That points clearly to a political career.
**George Bernard Shaw,** *Major Barbara,* 1905

**59** No matter how thin you slice it, it's still baloney.
**Alfred E. Smith**, Governor of New York, 1919–20, 1923–8

**60** An independent is the guy who wants to take the politics out of politics.
**Adlai Stevenson**, quoted in *The Stevenson Wit*, 1966

**61** They forget if it weren't for graft, you'd get a very low type of people in politics. Men with no ambition.
**Preston Sturges**, *The Great McGinty*, screenplay, 1940

**62** Greater love hath no man than this, that he lay down his friends for his political life.
**Jeremy Thorpe**, on Harold Macmillan's drastic Cabinet reshuffle, 1962

**63** You can fool too many of the people too much of the time.
**James Thurber**

**64** Ninety-eight per cent of the adults in this country are decent, hard-working, honest Americans. It's the other lousy two per cent that get all the publicity. But then – we elected them.
**Lily Tomlin**

**65** A statesman is a politician who's been dead ten or fifteen years.
**Harry S. Truman**, quoted in *New York World-Telegram and Sun*, 1958

**66** Politicians are always deeply shocked to see anything in the newspapers which is not about themselves or their piffling preoccupations, but very few people, in fact, are remotely interested in either.
**Auberon Waugh**, *Spectator*, 1984

**67** When we have finally stirred ourselves to hang them all, I hope our next step will be to outlaw political parties outside Parliament on the grounds that, like amusement arcades, they attract all the least desirable members of society.
**Auberon Waugh**, *Spectator*, 1984

## Pollution
*See also Ecology; The Environment.*

**1** Fight air pollution – inhale.
**Red Buttons**

**2** I simply can't believe nice communities release effluents.
**William Hamilton**, *William Hamilton's Anti-Social Register*, cartoon, 1974

**3** Little Bo-Peep
Has lost her sheep
And thinks they may be roaming;
They haven't fled;
They've all dropped dead
From nerve gas in Wyoming.
**Frank Jacobs**, 'Little Bo-Peep', *Mad Magazine*, 1972

**4** Fall is my favorite season in Los Angeles, watching the birds change color and fall from the trees.
**David Letterman**, *The Late Show*, NBC

## Popularity
*See also Celebrities; Fame; Friends.*

**1** The Texan turned out to be good-natured, generous and likeable. In three days no one could stand him.
**Joseph Heller**, *Catch-22*, 1961

**2** Being popular is important. Otherwise, people might not like you.
**Mimi Pond**, *The Valley Girl's Guide To Life*, 1982

**3** Every effect that one produces gives one an enemy. To be popular one must be a mediocrity.
**Oscar Wilde**, *The Picture of Dorian Gray*, 1891

## Pornography
*See also Censorship; Nudity; Puritanism; Sex; Sexual Perversions.*

**1** Pornography is in the groin of the beholder.
**Anon.**

**2** The Citizens' Committee to Clean Up New York's Porn-Infested Areas continued its series of rallies today, as a huge, throbbing, pulsating crowd sprang erect from nowhere and forced its way into the steaming nether region surrounding the glistening, sweaty intersection of Eighth Avenue and Forty-Second Street. Thrusting, driving, pushing its way into the usually receptive neighborhood, the excited throng, now grown to five times its original size, rammed itself again and again and again into the quivering, perspiring, musty

dankness, fluctuating between eager anticipation and trembling revulsion. Now, suddenly, the tumescent crowd and the irresistible area were one heaving, alternately melting and thawing turgid entity, ascending to heights heretofore unexperienced. Then, with a gigantic, soul-searching, heart-stopping series of eruptions, it was over. Afterwards, the crowd had a cigarette and went home.
**'Weekend Update'**, *Saturday Night Live*, NBC TV

**3** . . . it is written in the stickily overwrought language of the ageing prep-school house-master who had sex once in 1987 and still can't quite believe his luck . . .
**John Diamond**, of *The Erotic Review*, *The Times*, 2000

**4 A word about pornography**
You'll need it. Lots of it. The dirty, filthy, degrading kind. But keep it *well hidden*! Don't discount secret wall panels, trick drawers, holes in the yard, etc., especially if you have teenage boys or a Baptist wife with a housecleaning obsession. Also keep in mind that you could die at any moment, and nothing puts a crimp in a funeral worse than having the bereaved family wonder what kind of sick, perverted beast you were under that kind and genteel exterior.
**John Hughes**, 'Very Married Sex', *National Lampoon*, 1979

**5** At last, an unprintable book that is readable.
**Ezra Pound**, of Henry Miller's *Tropic of Cancer*, 1934

**6 Fill in the blank with the best word or phrase:**
He awoke with a start when two —— slipped naked into his bed.
A: Federal judges B: Militant feminists C: Burglars D: Teenaged girls

Seeing her 42-inch ——, I grew excited.
A: Husband B: Bowling trophy C: Bust D: Heels
**Alphonse Simonaitis**, 'Porno Writer's Aptitude Test', *Playboy*

**7** Perhaps it would help . . . to compose a letter . . . to *The Times*:
Dear Sir,
I hope I am not a prude, but I feel compelled to lodge a protest against the ever-increasing flood of obscenity in dreams. Many of my friends have been as shocked and sickened as myself by the filth that is poured out nightly as soon as our eyes are closed. It is certainly not my idea of 'home entertainment'. Night after night, the most disgraceful scenes of perversion and bestiality are perpetrated behind my eyelids . . . It is imperative that official action should be taken . . .
**Kenneth Tynan**, *The Sound of Two Hands Clapping*, 1975

**8** Western man, especially the Western critic, still finds it very hard to go into print and say: 'I recommend you to go and see this because it gave me an erection.'
**Kenneth Tynan**, *Playboy*, 1977

**9** The worst that can be said about pornography is that it leads not to 'anti-social' acts but to the reading of more pornography.
**Gore Vidal**, *Reflections upon a Sinking Ship*, 1969

# Potential
*See also Opportunity.*

**1** Whom the Gods wish to destroy they first call promising.
**Cyril Connolly**, *Enemies of Promise*, 1938

# Poverty
*See also Begging; Debt; Rich and Poor; Wealth.*

**1** Our family is so poor, Africans send them money.
**Anon.**

**2** Your parents are so poor, they got married for the rice.
*Snaps*, 1994

**3** The trouble with being poor is that it takes up all your time.
**Willem de Kooning**, Dutch-born American artist

**4** I used to think I was poor. Then they told me I wasn't poor, I was needy. Then they told me it was self-defeating to think of myself as needy. I was deprived. Then they told me that underprivileged was overused. I was disadvantaged. I still don't have a dime. But I have a great vocabulary.
**Jules Feiffer**, cartoon in the *Village Voice*, 1965

**5** When I was a kid, my family was so poor I had to wear my brother's hand-me-downs – at the same time he was wearing them.
**Redd Foxx**, *Esquire*, 1972

**6** He couldn't even afford to buy his little boy a yo-yo for Christmas. He just managed to get him a yo.
**Max Kauffmann**

**7** We're really all of us bottomly broke. I haven't had time to work in weeks.
**Jack Kerouac**, *On the Road*, 1957

**8** The furnace tolls the nell of falling steam,
The coal supply is virtually done,
And at this price, indeed it does not seem
As though we could afford another ton.

Now fades the glossy, cherished
      anthracite;
The radiators lose their temperature:
How ill avail, on such a frosty night,
The 'short and simple flannels of the
      poor'.
**Christopher Morley**, 'Elegy Written in a Country Coal-bin', 1921

**9** MENDOZA: I am a brigand: I live by robbing the rich.
TANNER: I am a gentleman: I live by robbing the poor.
**George Bernard Shaw**, *Man and Superman*, 1903

**10** What is the matter with the poor is Poverty: what is the matter with the rich is Uselessness.
**George Bernard Shaw**, *Maxims for Revolutionists*, 1903

**11** Who made your millions for you? Me and my like. What's kep' us poor? Keepin' you rich.
**George Bernard Shaw**, *Major Barbara*, 1907

**12** Poverty is no disgrace to a man, but it is confoundedly inconvenient.
**Sydney Smith**, *His Wit and Wisdom*, 1900

**13** We who are liberal and progressive know that the poor are our equals in every sense except that of being equal to us.
**Lionel Trilling**, *The Liberal Imagination*, 1950

**14** . . . a poor man who is ungrateful, unthrifty, discontented, and rebellious, is probably a real personality, and has much in him. He is at any rate a healthy protest. As for the virtuous poor, one can pity them, of course, but one cannot possibly admire them. They have made private terms with the enemy, and sold their birthright for very bad pottage.
**Oscar Wilde**, 'The Soul of Man under Socialism', 1891

**15** I should fancy that the real tragedy of the poor is that they can afford nothing but self-denial.
**Oscar Wilde**, *The Picture of Dorian Gray*, 1891

**16** There is only one class in the community that thinks more about money than the rich, and that is the poor. The poor can think of nothing else.
**Oscar Wilde**, 'The Soul of Man under Socialism', 1891

# Power

*See also Government; Politics and Politicians; The Ruling Class.*

**1** A friend in power is a friend lost.
**Henry Adams**, *The Education of Henry Adams*, 1907

**2** It is certainly more agreeable to have power to give than to receive.
**Winston Churchill**

**3** Power is the ultimate aphrodisiac.
**Henry Kissinger**, quoted in the *Guardian*, 1976

**4** How a minority
Reaching a majority
Seizing authority
Hates a minority!
**Leonard Harman Robbins**, 1877–1947, American author

**5** Power corrupts, but lack of power corrupts absolutely.
**Adlai Stevenson**, 1963

**6** Nothing but the most acute discomfort in the personal circumstances of my life would ever persuade me to assume power, and my purpose in doing so would be not so much to restructure society as to remove myself from those elements in it which were causing me distress.
**Auberon Waugh**, 'Me and My Junta', *Punch*, 1974

# Praise

*See also Boasts; Compliments; Flattery.*

**1** I never knew a man so *blasé* that his face did not change when he heard that some

action or creation of his had been praised; yes, even when that praise came from men most insignificant.
**Hilaire Belloc**, 'The Silence of the Sea'

**2** The advantage of doing one's praising for oneself is that one can lay it on so thick and exactly in the right places.
**Samuel Butler**, *The Way of All Flesh*, 1903

**3** Some people pay a compliment as if they expected a receipt.
**Kin Hubbard**, 1868–1930, American humorist

**4** I have always said that if I were a rich man, I would employ a professional praiser.
**Sir Osbert Sitwell**, 1892–1969, English writer

**5** Among the smaller duties of life I hardly know any one more important than that of not praising where praise is not due.
**Sydney Smith**, *Lectures on Moral Philosophy*, 1804

**6** I can live for two months on a good compliment.
**Mark Twain**

**7** LADY WINDERMERE: . . . I don't like compliments, and I don't see why a man should think he is pleasing a woman enormously when he says to her a whole heap of things that he doesn't mean.
**Oscar Wilde**, *Lady Windermere's Fan*, 1892

**8** I'm sick of praise. I want money.
**Thomas Wolfe**, *Thomas Wolfe's Letters to his Mother*, 1943

# Prayer
*See also The Church; God; Heaven; Religion.*

**1** God Answers Prayers of Paralysed Little Boy
'No,' Says God.
*the Onion*

**2** Pray, *v.* To ask that the laws of the universe be annulled in behalf of a single petitioner confessedly unworthy.
**Ambrose Bierce**, *The Devil's Dictionary*, 1911

**3** Forgive, O Lord, my little jokes on Thee
And I'll forgive Thy great big one on me.
**Robert Frost**, 'Cluster of Faith', *In the Clearing*, 1962

**4** Prayer gives a man the opportunity of getting to know a gentleman he hardly ever meets. I do not mean his maker, but himself.
**William Inge**, Dean of St Paul's Cathedral, 1911–34

**5** Prayer must never be answered: if it is, it ceases to be prayer and becomes correspondence.
**Oscar Wilde** (Attrib.)

**6** . . . when the Gods wish to punish us they answer our prayers.
**Oscar Wilde**, *An Ideal Husband*, 1895

**7** MARGE: Dear God, this is Marge Simpson. If you stop this hurricane and save our family, we will be forever grateful and recommend you to all our friends.
**Steve Young**, 'Hurricane Neddy', *The Simpsons*, Fox TV, 1996

# Pregnancy
*See also Babies; Birth; Birth Control; Gynaecology; Mothers; Sex; Twins.*

**1** A woman who took the pill with a glass of pond water has been diagnosed three months stagnant.
*The Two Ronnies*, BBC TV

**2** GIRL: Mother, I'm afraid I'm pregnant.
MOTHER: Are you sure it's yours?
**Anon.**

**3** Someone's gonna have to explain it to me,
I'm not sure what it means,
My baby's feeling funny in the mornings,
She's having trouble getting into her jeans.
Her waistline seems to be expanding
Although she never feels like eating a thing,
I guess we'll reach some understanding
When we see what the future will bring.
**Jackson Browne**, 'Ready or Not', song, 1974

# Pride
*See also Boasts; Egotism; Humility; Vanity.*

**1** Godolphin Horne was Nobly Born;
He held the Human Race in Scorn,
And lived with all his Sisters where
His father lived, in Berkeley Square.
And oh! the Lad was Deathly Proud!
He never shook your Hand or Bowed,
But merely smirked and nodded thus:

How perfectly ridiculous!
Alas! That such Affected Tricks
Should flourish in a Child of six!
**Hilaire Belloc**, 'Godolphin Horne', *Cautionary Tales for Children*, 1907

**2** Pride, the never failing vice of fools.
**Alexander Pope**, *An Essay on Criticism*, 1711

# Principles
*See also Morality; Standards.*

**1** You can't learn too soon that the most useful thing about a principle is that it can always be sacrificed to expediency.
**W. Somerset Maugham**, *The Circle*, 1921

**2** I don't like principles . . . I prefer prejudices.
**Oscar Wilde**, *An Ideal Husband*, 1895

**3** The Rev. 'Stinker' Pinker was dripping with high principles . . .
**P. G. Wodehouse**, *The Code of the Woosters*, 1938

# Prison
*See also Crime; The Law; Law and Order.*

**1** It was my belief that they bought the books for the prison by weight. I once got a *Chums* annual for 1917 and a Selfridge's furniture catalogue for my non-fiction or education book.
**Brendan Behan**, *Borstal Boy*, 1958

**2** OFFICER: And the next time you try to escape, you'll be shot at dawn.
ERIC: I'm not worried – I don't get up till nine o'clock.
**Eddie Braben**, *The Best of Morecambe and Wise*, 1974

**3** GOVERNOR: I have always found Christmas to be a very difficult time.
WARDER: Yes, sir. So open to abuse. Contraband, bartering, smuggling. There isn't a Christmas cake comes inside that isn't laced with marijuana.
GOVERNOR: What are we doing about that?
WARDER: I've taken precautions, sir. I've put Mr Barrowclough on to sampling all the food parcels.
GOVERNOR: Has he anything to report?
WARDER: He's still too stoned to tell me, sir.
**Dick Clement and Ian La Frenais**, *Porridge*, BBC TV, 1976

**4** LENNIE: . . . human weakness takes many forms. Desire, greed, lust – we're all here for different reasons aren't we?
FLETCHER: With respect, Godber, we're all here for the same reason – we got caught.
**Dick Clement and Ian La Frenais**, 'Poetic Justice', *Porridge*, BBC TV

**5** PRISONER: . . . I'm going out soon, like.
GOVERNOR: Good, good. Well, don't fall back into your old ways.
PRISONER: No chance of that, sir. Not since t'wife passed away.
GOVERNOR: Oh, I'm sorry. When was this?
PRISONER: A few weeks before I came inside.
GOVERNOR: Poor woman, what happened?
PRISONER: I murdered her.
GOVERNOR (*taken aback*): Well, see that it doesn't happen again.
**Dick Clement and Ian La Frenais**, *Porridge*, BBC TV, 1976

**6** Prison is a Socialist's Paradise, where equality prevails, everything is supplied and competition is eliminated.
**Elbert Hubbard**

**7** That is the whole beauty of prisons – the benefit is not to the prisoner, of being reformed or rehabilitated, but to the public. Prisons give those outside a resting period from town bullies and horrible characters, and for this we should be very grateful.
**Roy Kerridge**, *The Lone Conformist*, 1984

**8** ERIC: I'll never forget my mother's words to me when I first went to jail.
ERNIE: What did she say?
ERIC: Hello, son.
**Eric Morecambe and Ernie Wise**, *The Morecambe and Wise Joke Book*, 1979

**9** Anyone who has been to an English public school will always feel comparatively at home in prison. It is the people brought up in the gay intimacy of the slums who find prison so soul destroying.
**Evelyn Waugh**, *Decline and Fall*, 1928

# Problems
*See also Questions.*

**1** There's no problem so big or complicated that it can't be run away from.
**Graffito**, London, 1979

**2** In my experience, the worst thing you can do to an important problem is discuss it. You know – I really do think this whole business of non-communication is one of the more poignant fallacies of our zestfully over-explanatory age. Most of us understand as much as we need to without having to be told.

**Simon Gray**, *Otherwise Engaged*, 1975

**3** Of life's many troubles, I've known quite
   a few:
  Bad plumbing and earaches and troubles
   with you,
  But the saddest of all, when it's all said
   and done,
  Is to look for your socks and find only
   one.

**Garrison Keillor**, 'The Solo Sock', *We Are Still Married*, 1989

**4** She probably laboured under the common delusion that you made things better by talking about them.

**Rose Macaulay**, *Crewe Train*, 1926

**5** When a man laughs at his troubles he loses a great many friends. They never forgive the loss of their prerogative.

**H. L. Mencken**

**6** The chief cause of problems is solutions.

**Eric Sevareid**, 1913–92, American broadcaster

## Procrastination

*See also Punctuality.*

**1** If it wasn't for the last minute, nothing would ever get done.

**Anon.**

**2** If a thing's worth doing, it's worth doing late.

**Freddie Oliver**, English writer

**3** Things have got so bad, I'm going to join Procrastinators Anonymous.
  Soon.

**Sally Poplin**

**4** My mother always told me that I would never amount to anything because I procrastinate. I told her, 'Just wait!'

**Judy Tenuta**

## Professions

*See also Accountancy; Banking; Insurance; Work.*

**1** Incomprehensible jargon is the hallmark of a profession.

**Kingman Brewster**, American Ambassador to Britain, speech, 1977

**2** All professions are conspiracies against the laity.

**George Bernard Shaw**, *The Doctor's Dilemma*, 1906

## Progress

*See also Change; Evolution; The Future; Inventions; Modern Life.*

**1** Everyone's in favour of progress. It's just change they don't like.

**Anon.**

**2** Carnation Milk is the best in the land;
  Here I sit with a can in my hand –
  No tits to pull, no hay to pitch,
  You just punch a hole in the son of a
   bitch.

**Anon.**, 'The Virtues of Carnation Milk', quoted in *Confessions of an Advertising Man* by David Ogilvy, 1963

**3** My father worked for the same firm for twelve years. They fired him. They replaced him with a tiny gadget this big. It does everything that my father does, only it does it much better. The depressing thing is my mother ran out and bought one.

**Woody Allen**, *The Nightclub Years, 1964–1968*, album, 1972

**4** GEORGE: Books are on their way out, nowadays, didn't you know that. Words are on their last legs. Words, print and also thought. That's also for the high jump. The sentence, that dignified entity with subject and predicate, is shortly to be made illegal. Wherever two or three words are gathered together, you see, there is a grave danger that thought might be present. All assemblies of words will be forbidden, in favour of patterns of light, videotape, every man his own telecine.

**Alan Bennett**, *Getting On*, 1971

**5** All progress is based upon a universal innate desire of every organism to live beyond its income.

**Samuel Butler**, *The Notebooks of Samuel Butler*, 1912

**6** The reason that men oppose progress is not that they hate progress but that they love inertia.
**Elbert Hubbard**, *The Notebook*, 1927

**7** Progress might have been all right once but it has gone on far too long.
**Ogden Nash**

# Prohibition

*See also Abstinence; Drink.*

**1** Once, during Prohibition, I was forced to live for days on nothing but food and water.
**W. C. Fields**

**2** I am certain that the good Lord never intended grapes to be made into jelly.
**Fiorello La Guardia**, 1882–1947, American politician

**3** prohibition makes you
   want to cry
   into your beer and
   denies you the beer
   to cry into
**Don Marquis**, 'certain maxims of archy', *archy and mehitabel*, 1927

**4** The South is dry and will vote dry. That is, everybody sober enough to stagger to the polls will.
**Will Rogers**, 'Oklahoma City', 1926

# Promiscuity

*See also Infidelity; Orgies; Prostitution; Sex.*

**1** She's the original good time that was had by all.
**Bette Davis**, of another actress (Attrib.)

**2** 'Has it ever occurred to you that in your promiscuous pursuit of women you are merely trying to assuage your subconscious fears of sexual impotence?'
   'Yes, sir, it has.'
   'Then why do you do it?'
   'To assuage my fears of sexual impotence.'
**Joseph Heller**, *Catch-22*, 1961

**3** Lady Capricorn, he understood, was still keeping open bed.
**Aldous Huxley**, *Antic Hay*, 1923

**4** What is a promiscuous person? It's usually someone who is getting more sex than you are.
**Victor Lownes**, *Playboy*, 1985

**5** You were born with your legs apart. They'll send you to your grave in a Y-shaped coffin.
**Joe Orton**, *What the Butler Saw*, 1969

**6** The girl speaks eighteen languages and can't say no in any of them.
**Dorothy Parker**, of a famous actress (Attrib.)

**7** I used to be Snow White, but I drifted.
**Mae West** (Attrib.)

# Promises

**1** A politician is known by the promises he doesn't keep.
**Anon.**

**2** The rule is, jam to-morrow and jam yesterday – but never jam to-day.
**Lewis Carroll**, *Through the Looking-Glass*, 1872

**3** Half the promises people say were never kept, were never made.
**Edgar Watson Howe**, 1853–1937, American writer

# Pronunciation

*See also The English Language; Language; Words.*

**1** Q: What word is always pronounced wrong?
A: 'Wrong'.
*The Big Book of Jokes and Riddles*, 1978

**2** Whose cruel idea was it for the word 'lisp' to have an 's' in it?
**George Carlin**

**3** Aitches don't make artists – there ain't no 'H' in 'Art'.
**Albert Chevalier**, 'The Cockney Trajedian', music-hall song

**4** You can't be happy with a woman who pronounces both *d*'s in Wednesday.
**Peter De Vries**, *Sauce for the Goose*, 1981

**5** Dear Miss Manners,
When is a *vase* a *vahz*?

Gentle Reader,
When it is filled with *dah-zies*.
**Judith Martin**, *Miss Manners' Guide to Excruciatingly Correct Behaviour*, 1982

# Proposals

*See also Couples; Courtship; Engagements;*
*Weddings.*

**1** BOY: Don't you understand? I want to marry you. I want you to be the mother of my children.
GIRL: But how many do you have?
**Anon.**

**2** HE: I'd like to marry your daughter.
FATHER: Have you seen my wife yet?
HE: Yes, I have. But I prefer your daughter.
**Anon.**

**3** FATHER: The man who marries my daughter will get a prize.
CLAUD: Can I see the prize first?
**Gyles Brandreth**, *1,000 Jokes: The Greatest Joke Book Ever Known*, 1980

**4** This is an honourable proposal of marriage, made at what I consider a most opportune moment. I can't go through all my life waiting to catch you between husbands.
**Sidney Howard**, etc., *Gone With the Wind*, screenplay, 1939, Clark Gable to Vivien Leigh

**5** Before I was married I was courting my wife ten years. Before I was married. Then I went round to see her father. And I looked straight at him. He said, 'Hello.' I said, 'Hello.' He said, 'What do you want?' I said, 'I've been courting your daughter for ten years.' He said, 'So what?' I said, 'I want to marry her.' He said, 'I thought you wanted a pension.' He said, 'If you marry my daughter, I'll give you three acres and a cow.'
You're quite right – you're quite right. I'm still waiting for the three acres.
**Max Miller**, *The Max Miller Blue Book*, 1975

**6** ERIC: Would you like to hear how I asked her father for his daughter's hand in marriage? I said, 'Sir, the bright sunshine of your daughter's smile has dispelled the dark clouds of my depression!' He said, 'Are you proposing or is this the weather forecast?' . . . I said, 'I would like your daughter for my wife.' He said, 'But I've never even seen your wife. Bring her round and we'll talk about it.'

**7** Once a week is enough to propose to anyone, and it should always be done in a manner that attracts some attention.
**Oscar Wilde**, *An Ideal Husband*, 1895

**8** He had been building one of those piles of thought, as ramshackle and fantastic as a Chinese pagoda, half from words let fall by gentlemen in gaiters, half from the litter in his own mind, about duck shooting and legal history, about the Roman occupation of Lincoln and the relations of country gentlemen with their wives, when, from all this disconnected rambling, there suddenly formed itself in his mind the idea that he would ask Mary to marry him.
**Virginia Woolf**, *Night and Day*, 1919

# Prostitution

*See also Promiscuity; Sex; Vice and Virtue.*

**1** The big difference between sex for money and sex for free is that sex for money usually costs less.
**Brendan Francis**, quoted in *Playboy*, 1985

**2** Prostitution gives her an opportunity to meet people. It provides fresh air and wholesome exercise, and it keeps her out of trouble.
**Joseph Heller**, *Catch-22*, 1961

**3** If a woman hasn't a tiny streak of a harlot in her, she's a dry stick as a rule.
**D. H. Lawrence**, *Pornography and Obscenity*, 1930

# Protest

*See also Reformers; Revolution; Terrorism.*

**1** Gay Whales Against the Bomb!
**Badge**, London, 1982

**2** IGNORE THIS BUTTON.
**Badge**, London, 1978

**3** HELP STAMP OUT FOOTPRINTS!
**T-shirt**, Boston, 1996

**4** Non-violence is a flop. The only bigger flop is violence.
**Joan Baez**, *Observer*, 1967

**5** In the whole range of human occupations is it possible to imagine a poorer thing to be than an iconoclast? It is the lowest of all the unskilled trades.
**G. K. Chesterton**, *Daily News*, 1905

**6** In all life one should comfort the afflicted but verily, also, one should afflict the comfortable, especially when they are comfortably, contentedly, even happily wrong.
**J. K. Galbraith**, American economist, 1989

**7** Light your faith and you can light the world – set fire to the church of your choice.
**Tony Hendra and Michael O'Donoghue**, *National Lampoon's Radio Dinner*, 1972

**8** One fifth of the people are against everything all the time.
**Robert Kennedy**, speech, University of Pennsylvania, 1964

**9** FOLK SINGER: Next I want to sing a song about the House Rules Committee and how the legislative functions of Congress are tyrannized over by its procedural calendar, dominated in turn by an all-powerful chairman hamstringing the processes of democracy.
**Edward Koren**, cartoon in the *New Yorker*

**10** It is not difficult to be unconventional in the eyes of the world when your unconventionality is but the convention of your set.
**W. Somerset Maugham**, *The Moon and Sixpence*, 1919

**11** MILNE: I never got used to the way the house Trots fell into the jargon back in Grimsby – I mean, on any other subject, like the death of the novel, or the sex life of the editor's secretary, they spoke ordinary English, but as soon as they started trying to get me to join the strike it was as if their brains had been taken out and replaced by one of those little golfball things you get in electric typewriters . . . 'Betrayal' . . . 'Confrontation' . . . 'Management' . . . My God, you'd need a more supple language than that to describe an argument between two amoebas.
**Tom Stoppard**, *Night and Day*, 1978

**12** Agitators are a set of interfering meddling people, who come down to some perfectly contented class of the community and sow the seeds of discontent among them. That is the reason why agitators are so absolutely necessary.
**Oscar Wilde**, 'The Soul of Man under Socialism', 1891

# Protestantism
*See also Catholicism; Christianity; The Church; God; Jesus Christ; Prayer; Religion.*

**1** The chief contribution of Protestantism to human thought is its massive proof that God is a bore.
**H. L. Mencken**, *Minority Report*, 1956

# Proverbs
*See also Epigrams; Maxims; Politics – Axioms; Sayings.*

**1** Sick yaks leave light tracks.
**P. Clifton**, 'Meaningless Proverbs', *New Statesman*, 1967

**2** One does not moisten a stamp with the Niagara Falls.
**P. W. R. Foot**, 'Meaningless Proverbs', *New Statesman*, 1969

**3** No leg's too short to reach the ground.
**Lyndon Irving**, 'Meaningless Proverbs', *New Statesman*, 1967

**4** She that knows why knows wherefore.
**Jim Snell**, 'Meaningless Proverbs', *New Statesman*, 1983

**5** He digs deepest who deepest digs.
**Roger Woddis**, 'Meaningless Proverbs', *New Statesman*, 1969

# Prudery
*See also Censorship; Chastity; Morality; Nudity; Pornography; Puritanism.*

**1** MOTHER: Any road, you seem to know a lot about it.
SON: Lesbianism? Yes, well I come across it in literature.
MOTHER: Well, I hope it *is* in literature and not in Halifax.
**Alan Bennett**, *Me! I'm Afraid of Virginia Woolf*, London Weekend Television, 1978

**2** I'm an intensely shy and vulnerable woman. My husband has never seen me naked. Nor has he expressed the least desire to do so.
**Dame Edna Everage (Barry Humphries)**, *Housewife Superstar*, one-man show, 1976

# Psychiatry

*See also Anxiety; Depression and Despair; Insanity; Paranoia; Psychoanalysis; Psychology; Schizophrenia.*

**1** Does the name Pavlov ring a bell?
**Anon.**

**2** Hello, welcome to the Psychiatric Hotline.
If you are an obsessive-compulsive, please press 1 repeatedly.
If you are co-dependent, please ask someone to press 2.
If you have multiple personalities, please press 3, 4, 5 and 6.
If you are paranoid-delusional, we know who you are and what you want. Just stay on the line until we trace the call.
If you are schizophrenic, listen carefully and a little voice will tell you which number to press.
If you are a manic-depressive, it doesn't matter which number you press because nobody's going to answer.
**Anon.**

**3** Psychiatry – the care of the id by the odd.
**Anon.**

**4** There was a young man from Toledo
Who traveled around incognito,
The reason he did
Was to bolster his id
While appeasing his savage libido.
**Anon.**

**5** You go to a psychiatrist when you're slightly cracked and keep going until you're completely broke.
**Anon.**

**6** A psychiatrist is the next man you start talking to after you start talking to yourself.
**Fred Allen**

**7** PSYCHIATRIST (*to patient*): You're lucky Mrs Pindleby – most shoplifters aren't rich enough to be kleptomaniacs.
**Hector Breeze**, cartoon in *Private Eye*

**8** The truth is, Pavlov's dog trained Pavlov to ring his bell just before the dog salivated.
**George Carlin**, *Brain Droppings*, 1997

**9** I'm getting fed up with my psychiatrist. I told him I had suicidal tendencies. From now on I have to pay in advance.
**Rodney Dangerfield**

**10** Anybody who goes to see a psychiatrist ought to have his head examined.
**Samuel Goldwyn**, 1882–1974, American film producer (Attrib.)

**11** NILES: Oh, er, Frasier, I'm sorry to trouble you about this, but could you recommend another couples therapist?
FRASIER: Good Lord, not again! What happened to Dr Prescott?
NILES: Oh, please! Maris had me can Dr Prescott *weeks* ago. Now she wants me to fire Dr Wilfong.
FRASIER: What's her problem with *him*?
NILES: She says his criticism of her is too harsh.
FRASIER: Well, some therapists can be rather blunt and hard-hitting. What did he say?
NILES: He asked her to refrain from catalog shopping during our sessions.
**Joe Keenan**, *Frasier*, NBC

**12** A neurotic is a person who builds a castle in the air. A psychotic is the person who lives in it. A psychiatrist is the one who collects the rent.
**Jerome Lawrence**

**13** DR SCHACHTER: In thirty years as a couples therapist I have never said what I'm about to say. Give up. It's hopeless. You're pathologically mistrustful, competitive to the point of sickness . . . Just see each other at weddings and funerals and the rest of the time, stay as far the hell away from each other as you possibly can.
**Christopher Lloyd**, 'Shrink Rap', *Frasier*, NBC, 1995

**14** LISA SIMPSON WATCHING HER FATHER MOWING THE LAWN IN A DRESS: Why do I get the feeling that someday I'll be describing this to a psychiatrist?
**Jeff Martin**, 'Dead Putting Society', *The Simpsons*, Fox TV, 1990

**15** If you're deep enough in denial to actually think that you did have a happy childhood, then your shrink will tell you that you must be forgetting something.
**Dennis Miller**

**16** My psychiatrist and I have decided that when we both think I'm ready, I'm going to get in my car and drive off the Verrazano Bridge.

**Neil Simon**, *The Last of the Red Hot Lovers*, screenplay, 1969

**17** One should only see a psychiatrist out of boredom.

**Muriel Spark**, British novelist

**18** A psychiatrist is a man who goes to the Folies Bergère and looks at the audience.

**Dr Mervyn Stockwood**, Anglican bishop quoted in the *Observer*, 1961

**19** Sir Roderick Glossop . . . is always called a nerve specialist, because it sounds better, but everybody knows that he's really a sort of janitor to the looney-bin.

**P. G. Wodehouse**, *The Inimitable Jeeves*, 1923

# Psychoanalysis

*See also Depression and Despair; Psychiatry; Psychology.*

**1** *Psychoanalyst*: A Jewish boy who can't stand the sight of blood.

**Anon.**

**2** ANNIE: Oh, you see an analyst?
ALVY: Y-y-yeah, just for fifteen years?
ANNIE: Fifteen years?
ALVY: Yeah, uh, I'm going to give him one more year and then I'm going to Lourdes.

**Woody Allen and Marshall Brickman**, *Annie Hall*, screenplay, 1977

**3** I was in group analysis when I was younger 'cause I couldn't afford private. I was captain of the Latent Paranoid Softball Team. We played all the neurotics on a Sunday morning. The Nail-Biters against the Bed-Wetters.

**Woody Allen**, *The Nightclub Years, 1964–1968*, album, 1972

**4** After a year of therapy, my psychiatrist said to me, 'Maybe life isn't for everyone.'

**Larry Brown**

**5** My analyst doesn't understand me . . .

**Mel Calman**, *Dr Calman's Dictionary of Psychoanalysis*, cartoon, 1979

**6** Psychoanalysis is confession without absolution.

**G. K. Chesterton**, 1874–1936, English essayist and poet

**7** I refuse to endure months of expensive

humiliation only to be told that at the age of four I was in love with my rocking-horse.

**Noel Coward**

## 8 The Benefits of Therapy

If you happen to have experience with Freudian analysis, group psychotherapy, est or some other form of training, your communications to your mate during marital squabbles will be considerably enhanced. For example, if you happen to be in therapy, here are some phrases you might use:
1. 'My psychiatrist says you're inhibiting me.'
2. 'My shrink says I'm not supposed to let you talk to me like that.'
3. 'Nobody in my group has these kinds of problems with *their* husbands.'

**Dan Greenburg and Suzanne O'Malley**, *How to Avoid Love and Marriage*, 1983

**9** You will . . . be able to utilize the special words and phrases you have learned in therapy. Your mate will find these particularly grating. For example:
1. 'Will you stop ACTING OUT and start RELATING?'
2. 'You know what this is about? TRANSFERENCE.'
3. 'What's the psychological PAYOFF in all this for you?'
4. 'Boy, do you have a lot of REPRESSED RAGE.'
5. 'You're a classic example of ANAL-RETENTIVE behavior.'

**Dan Greenburg and Suzanne O'Malley**, *How to Avoid Love and Marriage*, 1983

**10** 'You seem to be reacting to your boyfriend as if he were your father,' your shrink may say stonily (unless she is a strict Freudian, in which case she'll shut up and wait until you think of it yourself, a process that usually takes ten years. This is why strict Freudians have such lovely summer houses).

**Cynthia Heimel**, *Sex Tips for Girls*, 1983

**11** There were 117 psychoanalysts on the Pan Am flight to Vienna and I'd been treated by at least six of them. And married a seventh.

**Erica Jong**, *Fear of Flying*, 1973

**12** Psychoanalysis is the disease it purports to cure.
**Karl Kraus**, 1874–1936, Austrian satirist

**13** After twelve years of therapy, my psychiatrist said something that brought tears to my eyes. He said, 'No hablo ingles.'
**Ronnie Shakes**

# Psychology

*See also The Brain; Psychiatry; Psychoanalysis.*

**1** The difference between a conjuror and a psychologist is that one pulls rabbits out of a hat while the other pulls habits out of a rat.
**Anon.**

**2** Was it nature or nurture which made you a nurturer by nature?
**Chris Allen**, English actor, playwright and humorist, Ealing, 1990

**3** Did you hear what the white rat said to the other white rat? . . . I've got that psychologist so well trained that every time I ring the bell he brings me something to eat.
**David Mercer**, *A Suitable Case for Treatment*, BBC TV, 1962

**4** The object of all psychology is to give us a totally different idea of the things we know best.
**Paul Valéry**, *Tel Quel*, 1943

# Public, The

*See also Mankind.*

**1** The public have an insatiable curiosity to know everything, except what is worth knowing.
**Oscar Wilde**, 'The Soul of Man under Socialism', 1891

# Publishing

*See also Best-sellers; Books; Literature; Novels; Poets and Poetry; Writers; Writing.*

**1** As repressed sadists are said to become policemen or butchers, so those with an irrational fear of life become publishers.
**Cyril Connolly**, *Enemies of Promise*, 1938

**2** Never buy an editor or publisher a lunch or a drink until he has bought an article, story or book from you. This rule is absolute and may be broken only at your peril.
**John Creasey**, 1908–73, British crime writer

**3** It is with publishers as with wives: one always wants somebody else's.
**Norman Douglas**, 1868–1952, British author

**4** Great editors do not discover nor produce great authors; great authors create and produce great publishers.
**John Farrar**, *What Happens in Book Publishing*, 1957

**5** I don't believe in publishers who wish to butter their bannocks on both sides while they'll hardly allow an author to smell treacle. I consider they are too grabby altogether and like Methodists they love to keep the Sabbath and everything else they can lay their hands on.
**Amanda Ros**, 1860–1939, American romantic novelist

**6** I object to publishers: the one service they have done me is to teach me to do without them. They combine commercial rascality with artistic touchiness and pettiness, without being either good business men or fine judges of literature. All that is necessary in the production of a book is an author and a bookseller, without any intermediate parasite.
**George Bernard Shaw**, letter, 1895

# Punctuality

*See also Procrastination.*

**1** Punctuality is something that, if you have it, there's often no one around to share it with you.
**Anon.**

**2** Punctuality: the art of guessing correctly how late the other party is going to be.
**P.C.F.**, *Saturday Evening Post*

**3** The only way of catching a train I ever discovered is to miss the train before.
**G. K. Chesterton**, 1874–1936, English essayist and poet (Attrib.)

**4** I have noticed that the people who are late are often so much jollier than the people who have to wait for them.
**E. V. Lucas**, *Reading, Writing and Remembering*, 1932

**5** I've been on a calendar, but never on time.
**Marilyn Monroe**, *Look*, 1962

**6** Being early is an unpardonable sin. If you are early, you'll witness the last-minute confusion and panic that always attend making anything seem effortlessly gracious. Looking in on this scene is almost as rude as asking someone where he got his face-lift.
**P. J. O'Rourke**, *Modern Manners*, 1983

**7** Punctuality is the virtue of the bored.
**Evelyn Waugh**, *Diaries*, 1976

**8** He was always late on principle, his principle being that punctuality is the thief of time.
**Oscar Wilde**, *The Picture of Dorian Gray*, 1891

## Puns
*See also Comedy; Humour; Laughter; Wit.*

**1** A pun is a short quip followed by a long groan.
**Anon.**

**2** The inveterate punster follows a conversation as a shark follows a ship.
**Stephen Leacock**, 1869–1944, Canadian humorist (Attrib.)

**3** A pun is the lowest form of humor – when you don't think of it first.
**Oscar Levant**, 1906–72, American composer and wit

## Puritanism
*See also Censorship; Morality; Prudery.*

**1** A puritan's a person who pours righteous indignation into the wrong things.
**G. K. Chesterton**, quoted in *The New York Times*, 1930

**2** We have long passed the Victorian era, when asterisks were followed after a certain interval by a baby.
**W. Somerset Maugham**, *The Constant Wife*, 1926

**3** Puritanism: the haunting fear that someone, somewhere, may be happy.
**H. L. Mencken**, *Sententiae*, 1920

**4** Everyone knows about those archaic 'blue laws' – but here are some we *guarantee* you've never heard of.
In Connecticut, it is a felony to exhibit a vasectomy scar while jaywalking with a nun.
In New York it is illegal to wear a blue suit with brown shoes while seducing a haberdasher's daughter.
In Maine it is against the law for an unmarried woman to have a checking account at a sperm bank.
**Larry Tritton**, *Playboy*

**5** The prig is a very interesting psychological study, and though of all poses a moral pose is the most offensive, still to have a pose at all is something.
**Oscar Wilde**, 'The Critic as Artist', 1890

# Questions

*See also Problems; Questions and Answers.*

### 1 Nine points to ponder

Why did kamikaze pilots wear helmets?

When sign makers go on strike, is anything written on their signs?

Why is there only one Monopolies Commission?

When the police arrest a mime, do they tell him he has the right to remain silent?

Why don't sheep shrink when it rains?

Is there another word for synonym?

Why is 'abbreviation' such a long word?

When a deaf kid swears, does his mother wash his hands with soap?

That little indestructible black box they use on planes – why can't they make the whole plane out of the same stuff?

**Anon.**

### 2 Six killer questions

1. Who is buried in Lenin's Tomb?
2. In which city was the Berlin Wall located?
3. Spell 'BBC.'
4. What is the last name of William Shakespeare?
5. Mexico City is the capital of which country?
6. The Australians are natives of which country?

**Anon.**

**3** No question is so difficult to answer as that to which the answer is obvious.

**George Bernard Shaw**

**4** The 'silly question' is the first intimation of some totally new development.

**Alfred North Whitehead**, 1861–1947, British mathematician and philosopher

# Questions and Answers

*See also Questions.*

**1** Of what question is the following the answer: 'Coal Mine'?

The question: What should you say when asked to identify your lump of coal?

**Anon.**

**2** Of what question is the following the answer: '9W'?

The question: Tell me, is that Richard
Wagner with a 'V'?
**Anon.**

**3** Of what question is the following the
answer: 'Washington Irving'?
The question: Who was the first President of
the United States, Max?
**Anon.**

# Quotations

*See also Literature.*

**1** Hush little bright line,
Don't you cry,
You'll be a cliché
By and by.
**Fred Allen**

**2** Quotation: something that somebody
said that seemed to make sense at the time.
**Egon J. Beaudoin**

**3** The surest way to make a monkey out of a
man is to quote him.
**Robert Benchley**, *My Ten Years in a Quandary*, 1936

**4** Quoting, *n.* the act of repeating
erroneously the words of another.
**Ambrose Bierce**, *The Devil's Dictionary*, 1911

**5** Next to being witty yourself, the best
thing is to quote another's wit.
**Christian N. Bovee**, 1820–1904, American lawyer and
author

**6** I might repeat to myself, slowly and
soothingly, a list of quotations beautiful
from minds profound; if I can remember
any of the damn things.
**Dorothy Parker**, 'The Little Hours', *The Portable
Dorothy Parker*, 1944

**7** If, with the literate, I am
Impelled to try an epigram,
I never seek to take the credit;
We all assume that Oscar said it.
**Dorothy Parker**, 'Oscar Wilde', *Sunset Gun*, 1928

**8** I often quote myself. It adds spice to my
conversation.
**George Bernard Shaw**

**9** To be occasionally quoted is the only
fame I care for.
**Alexander Smith**, *Dreamthorp*, 1863

**10** In the dying world I come from,
quotation is a national vice.
**Evelyn Waugh**

**11** I don't know if you happen to be
familiar with a poem called 'The Charge of
the Light Brigade' by the bird Tennyson
whom Jeeves had mentioned when
speaking of the fellow whose strength was
as the strength of ten . . . the thing goes, as
you probably know,

Tum tiddle umpty-pum
Tum tiddle umpty-pum
Tum tiddle umpty-pum

and this brought you to the snapperoo or
pay-off which was 'someone had
blundered'.
**P. G. Wodehouse**, *Jeeves and the Feudal Spirit*, 1954

# Race

**1** Racial prejudice is a pigment of the imagination.
Graffito, Greenwich, 1980

**2** . . . let's look at this pussified, trendy bullshit phrase, Native Americans. First of all, they're not natives. They came over the Bering land bridge from Asia, so they're not natives. There are no natives anywhere in the world. Everyone is from somewhere else. All people are refugees, immigrants or aliens. If there were natives anywhere, they would be people who still live in the Great Rift Valley in Africa where the human species arose. Everyone else is just visiting.
George Carlin, *Brain Droppings*, 1997

**3** BLACK MAN: As a matter of racial pride we want to be called 'Blacks'.
Which has replaced the term 'Afro-American' –
Which replaced 'Negroes' –
Which replaced 'Colored People' –
Which replaced 'Darkies' –
Which replaced 'Blacks'.
Jules Feiffer, cartoon in the *Village Voice*, 1967

**4** The Ku Klux Klan. They wear white sheets and their hats have a point – which is more than can be said for their beliefs.
David Frost and Michael Shea, *A Mid-Atlantic Companion*, 1986

**5** I'll say this about one of us living in an all-white suburb. Crabgrass isn't our biggest problem.
Dick Gregory, black comedian

**6** I waited five days at a white lunch counter but when they finally served me, they didn't have what I wanted anyway.
Dick Gregory, 1960

**7** I was so excited when I came North and sat in the front of the bus, that I missed my stop.
Dick Gregory, 1957

**8** We should be thankful to lynch mobs. I've got a brother who can run a half-mile faster than any white boy in the world.
Dick Gregory

**9** Wouldn't it be a hell of a thing if all this

was burnt cork and you people were being tolerant for nothing?
**Dick Gregory**

**10** Whereas black people can call each other 'nigger' with impunity, a white person may not presume to do so unless he doesn't mind dying.
**Cynthia Heimel**, *Sex Tips for Girls*, 1983

**11** I want to be the white man's brother, not his brother-in-law.
**Martin Luther King** (Attrib.)

**12** I think racism is a terrible thing. I think we should all learn to hate each other on an individual basis.
**Cathy Ladman**

**13** Absolute equality, that's the thing; and throughout the ages we have always defended to the death the sacred right of every Black man, no matter how lowly, to be equal to every other Black man.
**Hugh Leonard**, *Time Was*, 1976

**14** He's really awfully fond of colored people. Well, he says himself, he wouldn't have white servants.
**Dorothy Parker**, 'Arrangement in Black and White', *The Portable Dorothy Parker*, 1944

**15** Beware of Greeks bearing gifts, colored men looking for loans and whites who understand the Negro.
**Adam Clayton Powell**, black Congressman

**16** You ever notice how *nice* white people get when there's a bunch of niggers around? Why, they talk to everybody – 'Hi! How ya doin'? I don't know ya, but here's my wife. Hello!'
**Richard Pryor**, comedy routine quoted in *Playboy*, 1979

**17** If you're born a suspect, everybody is scared of you. I can walk down the street anywhere in America and women will clutch their purses, hold on to their Mace, lock their car doors. If I look up into the windows of the apartments, I can see old ladies on the phone. They've already dialled 9 . . 1 . . . and are just waiting for me to do something wrong.
**Chris Rock**, American comedian

**18** Black names sound more like products you'd find in the drugstore. 'My name is

Advil, this is my wife Cloret. Tylenol, you wanna turn the TV down, it's givin' me a headache! And the twins, Murine and Visine . . .
**Daryl Sivad**

# Railways
*See also Travel.*

**1** STATION ANNOUNCER: The train now arriving on Platforms 6, 7, 8 and 9 . . . is coming in sideways.
**Anon.**

**2** My heart is warm with the friends I make,
And better friends I'll not be knowing;
Yet there isn't a train I wouldn't take
No matter where it's going.
**Edna St Vincent Millay**, 'Travel', *Collected Poems*, 1956

**3** STATION ANNOUNCER: . . . the train now standing on Platform 3 will, we hope, in due course be moved back on to the lines . . . will the passengers who have taken the 4.15 train from Platform 8 to Ponders End, please bring it back again at once . . .
**Richard Murdoch and Kenneth Horne**, *Much Binding in the Marsh*, BBC Radio, 1947

**4** Oh, some like trips in luxury ships,
And some in gasoline wagons,
And others swear by the upper air
And the wings of flying dragons.
Let each make haste to indulge his taste,
Be it beer, champagne or cider;
My private joy, both man and boy,
Is being a railroad rider.
**Ogden Nash**, 'Riding on a Railroad Train', *I'm a Stranger Here Myself*, 1938

**5** Your train leaves at eleven forty-five and it is now but eleven thirty-nine and a half,
And there is only one man ahead of you at the ticket window so you have plenty of time, haven't you, well I hope you enjoy a hearty laugh,
Because he is Dr Fell, and he is engaged in an intricate maneuver
He wants to go to Sioux City with stopovers at Plymouth Rock, Stone Mountain, Yellowstone Park, Lake Louise and Vancouver . . .
**Ogden Nash**, 'Dr Fell and Points West', *Good Intentions*, 1942

# Reading

*See also Books; Dyslexia; Literature; Newspapers; Novels; Poets and Poetry; William Shakespeare; Writers; Writing.*

**1** There are times when I think that the reading I have done in the past has had no effect except to cloud my mind and make me indecisive.
**Robertson Davies**, Canadian journalist and novelist

**2** I honestly believe there is absolutely nothing like going to bed with a good book. Or a friend who's read one.
**Phyllis Diller**

**3** When I want to read a book, I write one.
**Benjamin Disraeli**

**4** HOMER: Marge, I'm bored!
MARGE: Why don't you read something?
HOMER: 'Cos I'm trying to *reduce* my boredom!
**Ken Keeler**, 'Two Bad Neighbours', *The Simpsons*, Fox TV, 1996

**5** . . . magazines all too frequently lead to books and should be regarded by the prudent as the heavy petting of literature.
**Fran Lebowitz**, *Metropolitan Life*, 1978

**6** A bookworm in bed with a new novel and a good reading lamp is as much prepared for pleasure as a pretty girl at a college dance.
**Phyllis McGinley**, 'You Take the High Road', *The Province of the Heart*, 1959

**7** Oh! DO you remember Paper Books
 When paper books were thrilling,
 When something to read
 Was seldom Gide
 Or Proust or Peacock
 Or Margaret Mead
 And seldom Lionel Trilling?
**Phyllis McGinley**, *Times Three: 1932–1960*, 1960

**8** The chief knowledge that a man gets from reading books is the knowledge that very few of them are worth reading.
**H. L. Mencken** (Attrib.)

**9** Don't read science fiction books. It'll look bad if you die in bed with one on the nightstand. Always read stuff that will make you look good if you die in the middle of it.
**P. J. O'Rourke**, *National Lampoon*, 1979

**10** When you come to the end of a crime novel, something at least in this huge, chaotic world has been settled.
**J. B. Priestley**, quoted in the *Manchester Guardian Weekly*

**11** There are two motives for reading a book; one, that you enjoy it; the other, that you can boast about it.
**Bertrand Russell**, 1872–1970, British philosopher

**12** People say that life is the thing, but I prefer reading.
**Logan Pearsall Smith**, *Trivia*, 1917

**13** I just got out of the hospital. I was in a speed-reading accident. I hit a bookmark.
**Steven Wright**, American comic

# Real Estate

*See also Home.*

**1** The best investment on earth is earth.
**Louis S. Glickman**, real estate expert, quoted in the *New York Post*, 1957

**2** GROUCHO MARX: This is the heart of the residential district. Every lot is a stone's throw from the station. As soon as they throw enough stones, we're going to build a station.
**George S. Kaufman and Morrie Ryskind**, *The Cocoanuts*, screenplay, 1929

# Records

*See also Achievement.*

**1** The World Record holder for blowing a bugle whilst riding a bike uphill dragging four hundredweight of pig iron and holding his breath is buried at . . .
**Spike Milligan**

**2** Clufton Bay Bridge is the fourth biggest single-span double-track shore-to-shore railway bridge in the world bar none.
**Tom Stoppard**, *Albert's Bridge*, BBC Radio, 1967

# Reformers

*See also Censorship; Morality; Protest.*

**1** The urge to save humanity is almost always only a false-face for the urge to rule it.
**H. L. Mencken**, *Minority Report*, 1956

# Regrets

**1** My one regret in life is that I am not someone else.
**Woody Allen**

**2** The only thing I regret about my life is the length of it. If I had to live my life again, I'd make all the same mistakes only sooner.
**Tallulah Bankhead**, 1903–68, American actress

**3** The follies which a man regrets most in his life are those which he didn't commit when he had the opportunity.
**Helen Rowland**, *A Guide to Men*, 1922

**4** OLD-AGE PENSIONER (*to his wife*): My only regret is I did it my way.
**James Stevenson**, cartoon in the *New Yorker*, 1974

# Reincarnation

*See also Belief; Death; Heaven.*

**1** If I believed in reincarnation, I'd come back as a sponge.
**Woody Allen**, *Seventeen*, 1972

# Rejection

*See also Courtship; Divorce; Love – Breaking up*

**1** HE: In the barrel you're a pickle
In the gold mine you're a nickel,
You're the tack inside my shoe.
Yeah! I can do without you!
SHE: In the bosom you're a dagger
You're a mangy carpetbagger.
In the theater you're the boo!
I can do without you!
**Sammy Fain and Paul Francis Webster**, 'I Can Do Without You', song from *Calamity Jane*, 1953

**2** ERIC: See that terrific blonde over there?
ERNIE: Yes?
ERIC: She's been annoying me all evening!
ERNIE: I bet she hasn't even *looked* at you!
ERIC: Right – that's what's annoying me!
**Eric Morecambe and Ernie Wise**, *The Morecambe and Wise Joke Book*, 1979

**3** . . . his efforts at conversation were returned unopened.
**Sally Poplin**

# Relationships

*See also Couples; Courtship; Friends; Marriage; Romance.*

**1** Relations between the sexes are so complicated that the only way you can tell if two members of the set are 'going together' is if they are married. Then, almost certainly, they are not.
**Cleveland Amory**, *Who Killed Society?*, 1960

**2** The only way to get rid of cockroaches is to tell them you want a long term relationship.
**Jasmine Birtles**

**3** GEORGE: . . . she calls me up at my office and says, 'We have to talk.'
JERRY: Uh, the four worst words in the English language.
**Larry David and Jerry Seinfeld**, 'Male Unbonding', *Seinfeld*, NBC TV, 1990

**4** Do I believe in commitment? I'm so distressed you even dared to ask me that question that I'll have to start behaving erratically, not call you for days at a time and suddenly change the subject. What's on TV?
**Matt Groening**, *Life in Hell*, 1992

**5** *Relationship*: The civilized conversationalist uses this word in public only to describe a seafaring vessel carrying members of his family.
**Fran Lebowitz**, *Metropolitan Life*, 1978

**6** I should've known my last relationship was going down. I was getting cranky. I said, 'Will you keep the knitting down?' And sexually it was a nightmare. We got into bed and she said, 'I'll race you to sleep.'
**Richard Lewis**, *Comic Relief*, HBO, 1994

# Relatives

*See also Ancestors; Aunts; The Family.*

**1** You see this watch? This is an absolutely fantastic, very fine, elegant gold watch which speaks of breeding and was sold to me by my grandfather on his deathbed.
**Woody Allen**

**2** We must all be very kind to Auntie Jessie,
For she's never been a Mother or a Wife,
You mustn't throw your toys at her

Or make a vulgar noise at her,
She hasn't led a very happy life.
You must never lock her playfully in the
bathroom
Or play tunes on her enamelled Spanish
comb.
Though unpleasant to behold
She's a heart of purest gold
And Charity you know begins at home.
**Noel Coward,** 'We Must All be Very Kind to Auntie Jessie', song, 1920s

**3** Extraordinary thing about the lower classes in England – they are always losing their relations. They are extremely fortunate in that respect.
**Oscar Wilde,** *An Ideal Husband,* 1895

**4** I can't help detesting my relations. I suppose it comes from the fact that none of us can stand other people having the same faults as ourselves.
**Oscar Wilde,** *The Picture of Dorian Gray,* 1891

**5** Relations are simply a tedious pack of people, who haven't got the remotest knowledge of how to live, nor the smallest instinct about when to die.
**Oscar Wilde,** *The Importance of Being Earnest,* 1895

**6** A strange, almost unearthly light comes into the eyes of wronged uncles when they see a chance of getting a bit of their own back from erring nephews.
**P. G. Wodehouse,** *Uncle Dynamite,* 1948

**7** Aunts as a class are like Napoleon. They expect their orders to be carried out without a hitch and don't listen to excuses.
**P. G. Wodehouse,** *Much Obliged, Jeeves,* 1971

**8** Many a fellow who looks like the dominant male and has himself photographed smoking a pipe curls up like carbon paper when confronted by an aunt.
**P. G. Wodehouse,** *The Mating Season,* 1949

# Relativity

*See also Science and Scientists.*

**1** It is impossible to travel faster than light, and certainly not desirable, as one's hat keeps blowing off.
**Woody Allen,** *Side Effects,* 1980

**2** It is said that there are, besides Dr

Einstein himself, only two men who can claim to have grasped the Theory in full. I cannot claim to be either of these . . . The attempt to conceive infinity had always been quite arduous enough for me. But to imagine the absence of it; to feel that perhaps we and all the stars beyond our ken are somehow cosily (though awfully) closed in by curtain curves beyond which is nothing; and to convince myself, by the way, that this exterior is not (in virtue of *being* nothing) something and therefore . . . but I lose the thread.
**Max Beerbohm,** 'A Note on the Einstein Theory', *Mainly on the Air,* 1947

**3** Albert Einstein got prepared,
Took a $c$ and had it $^2$,
Multiplied by $m$ – that's right!
$e$, by gum! – the speed of light.
**Will Bellenger,** *New Statesman,* 1984

**4** There was a young lady named Bright
Whose speed was far faster than light;
She went out one day
In a relative way,
And returned the previous night.
**Professor A. H. Reginald Buller,** *Punch*

**5** I simply ignored an axiom.
**Albert Einstein,** on relativity (Attrib.)

**6** When a man sits with a pretty girl for an hour, it seems like a minute. But let him sit on a hot stove for a minute – and it's longer than any hour. That's relativity.
**Albert Einstein**

# Religion

*See also Belief; The Bible; Catholicism; The Church; Cults; God; Jesus Christ; Missionaries; Prayer; Protestantism.*

**1** HILARY: I imagine when it comes to the next prayer book they won't write He, meaning Him with a capital *h*. God will be written in the lower case to banish any lurking sense of inferiority his worshippers might feel.
**Alan Bennett,** *The Old Country,* 1978

**2** SCHOOLMASTER: Now you're sure you've got the Catechism all buttoned up, Foster?
FOSTER: I'm still a bit hazy about the Trinity, sir.
SCHOOLMASTER: Three in one, one in three,

perfectly straightforward. Any doubts about that see your maths master.
**Alan Bennett**, *Forty Years On*, 1968

**3** Every day people are straying away from the church and going back to God.
**Lenny Bruce**, *The Essential Lenny Bruce*, 1972

**4** There is something wrong with a man if he does not want to break the Ten Commandments.
**G. K. Chesterton**, quoted in the *Observer*, 1925

**5** Drop kick me, Jesus, through the goalposts of life.
**Paul Craft**, 'Drop Kick Me, Jesus', song, 1976

**6** He represented what any minister will tell you is the bane of parish work: somebody who has got religion. It's as embarrassing to a cleric of sensibility as 'poetry lovers' are to a poet.
**Peter De Vries**, *The Mackerel Plaza*, 1958

**7** I do benefits for all religions – I'd hate to blow the hereafter on a technicality.
**Bob Hope**

**8** Perhaps the most lasting pleasure in life is the pleasure of *not* going to church.
**William Inge**, Dean of St Paul's Cathedral, 1911–34 (Attrib.)

**9** All religions are the same: basically guilt, with different holidays.
**Cathy Ladman**

**10** Everybody says they have rights. But you also have responsibilities. You have the right to choose any religion, but you also have the responsibility to pick one that doesn't wake me up on Sunday morning by knocking on my door.
**Bill Maher**

**11** We must respect the other fellow's religion, but only in the sense and to the extent that we respect his theory that his wife is beautiful and his children smart.
**H. L. Mencken**, *Minority Report*, 1956

**12** After coming in contact with a religious man, I always feel that I must wash my hands.
**Friedrich Wilhelm Nietzsche**, *The Antichrist*, 1888

**13** LISA: Prayer – the last refuge of the scoundrel.
**David M. Stern**, 'Bart Gets an F', *The Simpsons*, Fox TV, 1990

**14** The easy confidence with which I know another man's religion is folly, teaches me to expect that my own is also.
**Mark Twain**

**15** Religions die when they are proved to be true. Science is the record of dead religions.
**Oscar Wilde**, 'Phrases and Philosophies for the Use of the Young', 1894

**16** To all things clergic
I am allergic.
**Alexander Woollcott**, 1887–1943, American columnist and critic (Attrib.)

# Republican Party, The
*See also Congress; Conservatism; Democrats and Republicans; The Senate; Washington.*

**1** Why do Republicans fear debate? For the same reason baloney fears the slicer.
**Lloyd Bentsen**, US Congressman and Senator, quoted on *The McLaughlin Group*, NBC TV, 1988

**2** Lincoln was right about not fooling all the people all of the time. But the Republicans haven't given up trying.
**Lyndon B. Johnson**, 1966

**3** Even though they're in a hurry, the Republicans have not forgotten their manners. When it comes to cutting benefits, it's still women and children first.
**Bill Maher**

**4** The Republican Convention opened with a prayer. If the Lord can see his way to bless the Republican Party the way it's been carrying on, then the rest of us ought to get it without even asking.
**Will Rogers**, 1928

**5** The Republicans have a habit of having three bad years and one good one, and the good one always happens to be election year.
**Will Rogers** (Attrib.)

**6** The Republicans have their splits after the election and the Democrats have theirs just before the election.
**Will Rogers** (Attrib.)

**7** A conservative Republican is one who doesn't believe anything new should ever be tried for the first time. A liberal Republican is one who *does* believe something should be tried for the first time – but not now.
**Mort Sahl**, American comedian

**8** I like Republicans, have grown up with them, worked with them and would trust them with anything in the world, except public office.
**Adlai Stevenson**

**9** When Republican speech-makers think they are thinking, they are only rearranging their prejudices.
**Adlai Stevenson**

# Reputation
*See also Celebrities; Fame.*

**1** I'm the girl who lost her reputation and never missed it.
**Mae West** (Attrib.)

**2** One can survive everything nowadays, except death, and live down anything except a good reputation.
**Oscar Wilde**, *A Woman of No Importance*, 1893

# Resignations
*See also Unemployment; Work.*

**1** Galbraith's law states that anyone who says he won't resign four times, will.
**J. K. Galbraith**, American economist, 1973

**2** It seems that nothing ever gets to going good till there's a few resignations.
**Kin Hubbard**, 1868–1930, American humorist

# Respectability
*See also Reputation.*

**1** The more things a man is ashamed of, the more respectable he is.
**George Bernard Shaw**, *Man and Superman*, 1903

**2** He must be quite respectable. One has never heard his name before in the whole course of one's life, which speaks volumes for a man, nowadays.
**Oscar Wilde**, *A Woman of No Importance*, 1893

# Restaurants
*See also Eating; Food; Hotels; Tipping; Waiters; Wine.*

**1** We're Now Rat-Free!
**Sign at Ye Olde Off-Ramp Inn**, *The Simpsons*, Fox TV

**2** GEORGE: I ate on the Motorway. At the Grill n'Griddle. I had Ham n'Eggs. And now I've got 'ndigestion.
**Alan Bennett**, *Getting On*, 1971

**3** NILES: I'd like a petite filet mignon, very lean, not so lean that it lacks flavor, but not so fat that it leaves drippings on the plate, and I don't want it cooked, just lightly seared on either side, pink in the middle, not a true pink but not a mauve either, something in between, bearing in mind the slightest error either way and it's ruined.
**Anne Flett & Chuck Ranberg**, 'Dinner at Eight', *Frasier*, NBC, 1993

**4** WAITER (*to customer*): That fine line between gracious attendance and fawning obsequiousness – tell me, sir, how close did I come?
**William Hamilton**, *William Hamilton's Anti-Social Register*, cartoon, 1974

**5** He ordered as one to the menu born.
**O. Henry**, 1862–1910, American short-story writer

**6** ERIC: Just outside town there was this little place with a sign that said, 'Topless Bar'. So we went in there.
ERNIE: You took your wife into a topless bar?
ERIC: Yes . . . anyway, it turned out to be a bit of a disappointment.
ERNIE: How come?
ERIC: Turned out to be a cafe with no roof on. Still, we decided to eat there. But just as they brought the food, it started to rain.
ERNIE: Oh, no!
ERIC: Oh, yes – it took us an hour and a half to finish the soup!
**Eric Morecambe and Ernie Wise**, *The Morecambe and Wise Joke Book*, 1979

**7** ERIC: We went out for a special meal one night. It was a very posh restaurant. Just to impress the wife, I ordered the whole meal in French. Even the waiter was surprised.
ERIC: Really?
ERNIE: Yes – it was a Chinese restaurant.

ERIC: Was it good value?

ERNIE: Terrific value! For a pound each they serve you all the food you can eat.

ERIC: Fantastic!

ERNIE: The trouble is, they only give you one chopstick.

**Eric Morecambe and Ernie Wise**, *The Morecambe and Wise Joke Book*, 1979

**8** ERNIE: Waiter – there's a fly in my soup!

ERIC: They don't care what they eat, do they, sir?

ERNIE: But what's it doing there?

ERIC: It looks like the breaststroke to me, sir.

ERNIE: I can't believe it! A fly in my soup!

ERIC: Don't make a fuss, sir, they'll all want one.

ERNIE: But it looks like it's dead!

ERIC: Yes, it's the heat that kills them.

**Eric Morecambe and Ernie Wise**, *The Morecambe and Wise Joke Book*, 1979

**9** Our order is taken . . . by a waitress wearing a cowboy hat, a miniskirt, a fringed vest, boots and red garters. 'The key to a successful restaurant,' O'Donoghue says, 'is dressing girls in degrading clothes.'

**Michael O'Donoghue**, quoted by Paul Slansky in *Playboy*, 1983

**10** *Chinese Food*: You do not sew with a fork, and I see no reason why you should eat with knitting needles.

**Miss Piggy**, *Miss Piggy's Guide to Life (As Told to Henry Beard)*, 1981

**11** During dinner, it may be necessary to excuse yourself for a telephone call. However, it is far preferable to have a phone brought to the table . . . as a general rule, white telephones go with fish and poultry, and black ones with anything else. If you are calling during dessert, a small after-dinner phone should be used . . . if you are satisfied, say something like, 'Yes, it is a very nice, light telephone, with a good, clear tone and a smooth, almost velvety action.'

**Miss Piggy**, *Miss Piggy's Guide to Life (As Told to Henry Beard)*, 1981

**12** Eating places with live plants in their windows are always good. Restaurants with peppermills the size of fire extinguishers and big red menus with the entrees spelled with *f*'s instead of *s*'s are always expensive. Italian restaurants with more than 120 entrees are always disappointing. There are no good French restaurants in states which have a *K* in their names. (New Yorque is the exception that proves the rule, whatever that means.)

**Miss Piggy**, *Miss Piggy's Guide to Life (As Told to Henry Beard)*, 1981

# Retirement

*See also Old Age.*

**1** Retirement means twice as much husband on half as much money.

**Anon.**

**2** You're 65 today – and it's the first day of the rest of your life savings!

**Anon.**

**3** Your mother is so dumb, when her boss told her to retire, she went out and bought four Michelins.

*Snaps 4*, 1998

**4** Retirement at sixty-five is ridiculous. When I was sixty-five, I still had pimples.

**George Burns**

**5** . . . one sure way of shortening life.

**Frank Conklin**

**6** Six months ago 541,000 people obeyed a single command I gave. Today it's even difficult to get a plumber to do what I want.

**General Norman Schwarzkopf**, *Observer*, 1991

**7** I married him for better or worse, but not for lunch.

**Hazel Weiss**, after her husband, George Weiss, retired as general manager of the New York Yankees, 1960

# Retractions

**1** *I* have reconsidered it; *you* have changed your mind; *he* has gone back on his word.

**Competition**, *New Statesman*

**2** Man does not live by words alone, despite the fact that sometimes he has to eat them.

**Adlai Stevenson**

# Revenge

*See also Enemies.*

**1** You'll never get ahead of anyone as long as you try to get even with him.
**Lou Holtz**, Arkansas football coach

**2** . . . she got even in a way that was almost cruel. She forgave them.
**Ralph McGill**, on Eleanor Roosevelt

**3** It's far easier to forgive an enemy after you've got even with him.
**Olin Miller**, American writer

# Revolution

*See also Protest; Terrorism; War.*

**1** Insurrection, *n.* an unsuccessful revolution.
**Ambrose Bierce**, *The Devil's Dictionary*, 1911

**2** BALDRICK: . . . I have been supping the milk of freedom. Already our Russian comrades are poised on the brink of revolution and here too, sir, the huddled wossnames, such as myself, sir, are ready to throw off the hated oppressors like you and the lieutenant . . . present company excepted, sir.
BLACKADDER: Go and clean out the latrines.
BALDRICK: Yes, sir, right away, sir.
**Richard Curtis and Ben Elton**, 'Major Star', *Blackadder Goes Forth*, BBC TV, 1989

**3** The successful revolutionary is a statesman, the unsuccessful one a criminal.
**Erich Fromm**, *Escape from Freedom*, 1941

**4** Steal This Book.
**Abbie Hoffman**, title of revolutionary manual, 1971

**5** The first duty of a revolutionary is to get away with it.
**Abbie Hoffman**, 1970

**6** A revolution requires of its leaders a record of unbroken fallibility. If they do not possess it, they are expected to invent it.
**Murray Kempton**, *Part of Our Time*, 1955

**7** Women hate revolutions and revolutionists. They like men who are docile, and well-regarded at the bank, and never late at meals.
**H. L. Mencken**, *Prejudices*, Fourth Series, 1924

**8** Revolutions have never lightened the burden of tyranny: they have only shifted it to another shoulder.
**George Bernard Shaw**, *Man and Superman*, 1903

# Rich and Poor

*See also Begging; Debt; Extravagance; Greed; Money; Poverty; Wealth.*

**1** The poor have more children, but the rich have more relatives.
**Anon.**

**2** Q: Why did Robin Hood only rob the rich?
A: Because the poor had no money.
*The Big Book of Jokes and Riddles*, 1978

**3** ROBIN HOOD: Here is the way it works: we take from the rich and give to the poor – keeping only enough for salaries, travel, equipment, depreciation, and so on, and so on.
**Al Ross**, cartoon in the *New Yorker*

**4** I've been rich and I've been poor; rich is better.
**Sophie Tucker**

# Riddles

*See also Comedy; Humour; Wit.*

**1** Q: What has four wheels and flies?
A: A garbage truck.
**Anon.**

**2** Q: What has sixteen legs, fourteen testicles and two tiny breasts?
A: Snow White and the Seven Dwarfs.
**Anon.**

**3** Q: What's grey, has four legs and a trunk?
A: A mouse going on holiday.
**Anon.**

**4** Q: What happens when the human body is completely submerged in water?
A: The telephone rings.
*The Big Book of Jokes and Riddles*, 1978

**5** Q: What's green and pecks on trees?
A: Woody Wood Pickle.
*The Big Book of Jokes and Riddles*, 1978

**6** Q: What's worse than an octopus with tennis-elbow?

A: A centipede with athlete's foot.
*The Big Book of Jokes and Riddles*, 1978

**7** GEORGE: What is it that sings and has four legs?
GRACIE: Two canaries.
**George Burns and Gracie Allen**, *The Robert Burns Panatela Program*, CBS Radio, 1932

# Rights

**1** The right to be heard does not include the right to be taken seriously.
**Hubert Humphrey**, 1911–1978, Democratic Vice-President

**2** What men value in this world is not rights but privileges.
**H. L. Mencken**, *Minority Report*, 1956

**3** There is only one basic human right, the right to do as you damn well please. And with it comes the only basic duty, the duty to take the consequences.
**P. J. O'Rourke**, speech to the Cato Institute, 1963

# Rock 'n' Roll

*See also The Beatles; Jazz; Music and Musicians; Rock 'n' Roll – Band Names; Rock 'n' Roll – Critics; The Rolling Stones; Songs and Singers.*

**1** Q: What's the difference between a drummer and a drum machine?
A: You only have to punch the instructions into the drum machine once.
**Anon.**

**2** Q: What's the difference between a chiropodist and Ginger Baker?
A: A chiropodist bucks up your feet.
**Anon.**

**3** Q: Why are drummer jokes all one-liners?
A: So that bass players can understand them.
**Anon.**

**4** Q: How many A&R men does it take to change a lightbulb?
A: I'll have to get back to you on that one . . .
**Anon.**

**5** Q: What do you call someone who hangs around with musicians?
A: A bass player.
**Anon.**

**6** Q: What do you call a rock 'n' roll musician who knows four chords?
A: Talented.
**Anon.**

**7** Meat Loaf, or, as he is now known, The Artist Formerly known as Mince . . .
**Anon.**

**8** Dicky Hart and the Pacemakers
**Name of band**, London, 1984

**9** Break Like the Wind
**Spinal Tap album title**, RCA, 1992

**10** Once upon a time, rock music was sung by the young to disgust the old. Now, it seems, it is sung by the old to embarrass the young.
**Craig Brown**, *Sunday Times*, 1993

**11** I think that's just another word for a washed-up has-been.
**Bob Dylan**, on being an 'icon'

**12** Rock 'n' roll is trying to convince girls to pay money to be near you.
**Richard Hell**, rock musician

**13** The greatest line in rock 'n' roll is, 'Awopboraloobop Alopbamboom'. Top that if you can!
**Wilko Johnson**, rock musician (Attrib.)

**14** I tried to charm the pants off Bob Dylan but everyone will be disappointed to learn that I was unsuccessful. I got close . . . a couple of fast feels in the front seat of his Cadillac.
**Bette Midler**, *Rolling Stone*, 1982

**15** Good rock stars take drugs, put their penises in plaster of paris, collectivize their sex, molest policemen, promote self-curiosity, unlock myriad spirits, epitomize fun, freedom and bullshit. Can the busiest anarchist on your block match that?
**Richard Neville**, *Playpower*, 1970

**16** I bit the head off a live bat the other night. It was like eating a Crunchie wrapped in chamois leather.
**Ozzy Osborne**, rock musician

**17** I don't know anything about music. In my line you don't have to.
**Elvis Presley** (Attrib.)

**18** The Filthy Swine, with their folk hit 'My Girl's Head Comes to a Point' again head the Top Twenty this week. The Bedbugs' 'Chewing Old Socks With You' goes down to third place and Cliff Alopecea moves up with 'Individual Fruit Pie of Love'.

Wanda Drainstorm's 'My Old Plastic Granny' stays steady at number four and the Cockroaches have rocketed up from eleventh to fifth place with 'Love Crawled Under the Door'.

The Drips, whose 'Softening of the Brain' kept fifth place for three weeks running, suddenly collapsed and fell out of the charts altogether. Their manager has had them destroyed.

**Peter Simple (Michael Wharton)**, ' "Pop Notes" by Jim Droolberg', _Daily Telegraph_

**19** C'mon Jimmy, get a move on! It's studio time! . . . As you may recall, Thudpucker, every nine months, you emerge from your hermitage to provide your legion of admirers with one crisply produced state-of-the-art rock 'n' roll masterpiece!

**Garry Trudeau**, 'The Jimmy Thudpucker Interview', _Rolling Stone_, 1978

**20** For most rockers, the only thing standing between them and total illiteracy is the need to get through their Mercedes-Benz owner's manuals.

**Garry Trudeau**, 'The Jimmy Thudpucker Interview', _Rolling Stone_, 1978

**21** . . . in the music industry a legend is usually no more than someone with two consecutive hit singles.

**Garry Trudeau**, 'The Jimmy Thudpucker Interview', _Rolling Stone_, 1978

**22** The closest Western Civilisation has come to unity since the Congress of Vienna in 1815 was the week the Sgt Pepper album was released . . .

**Langdon Winner**, 1968, quoted in _The Rolling Stone Illustrated History of Rock & Roll_, 1980

# Rock 'n' Roll – Band Names

_See also Rock 'n' Roll_

**1** Are These My Pants?
The Band Formally Known as Sausage
The Dancing French Liberals of 1848
Four Honkies in a Big Black Car
Grandpa's Become a Fungus
Hitler Stole My Potato
Icky Wicky Chocky Bicky
Phone Bill from Hell
**The Canonical List of Weird Band Names**

**2** Ed Banger and the Nosebleeds
**BBC World Service**, 2000

# Rock 'n' Roll – Critics

_See also Critics – The Artist's View; Rock 'n' Roll._

**1** If a horse could sing in a monotone, the horse would sound like Carly Simon, only a horse wouldn't rhyme 'yacht', 'apricot' and 'gavotte'.

**Robert Christgau**, reviewing Carly Simon's 'You're So Vain', _Village Voice_, 1972

**2** Persistence beyond the call of talent.
**Robert Christgau**, on singer Terry Reid, _Village Voice_

**3** This may be catchy but I refuse to get caught; they may be good at what they do but what they do is so disgusting, that only makes it worse.

**Robert Christgau**, reviewing Seals and Crofts, _Unborn Child_, _Village Voice_, 1974

# Rogues

_See also Insults; Morality; Standards._

**1** Time wounds all heels.
**Jane Ace**, quoted in _The Fine Art of Hypochondria_, by Goodman Ace, 1966

**2** His lack of education is more than compensated for by his keenly developed moral bankruptcy.
**Woody Allen**, _Esquire_, 1975

# Rolling Stones, The

_See also The Beatles; Music and Musicians; Rock 'n' Roll; The Sixties; Songs and Singers._

**1** He moves like a parody between a majorette girl and Fred Astaire.
**Truman Capote**, of Mick Jagger (Attrib.)

**2** If the Stones' lyrics made sense, they wouldn't be any good.
**Truman Capote** (Attrib.)

**3** He's stoned on himself. He's always in complete control and the whole thing is

manipulation. It really bothers me that a twerp like that can parade around and convince everybody that he's Satan.
**Ry Cooder,** on Mick Jagger

**4** Somebody asked me if I was going to see the Rolling Stones. If I want to watch an aging queen prance around to oldies for two hours, I'll rent a Richard Simmons video.
**Bobcat Goldthwait**

**5** Nine months of listening to the Rolling Stones is not my idea of heaven.
**Mick Jagger,** after completing the album *Love You Live,* 1977

**6** At the Grammy Awards, Keith Richards became the first performer ever to accept a posthumous award in person.
**Jay Leno,** *The Tonight Show,* NBC

**7** I think we all admire the Rolling Stones for keeping at it in their fifties, but their fans are too old to be buying souvenirs. Even if you did, would you really want to get that colostomy bag with the big red tongue on it?
**Bill Maher,** *Politically Incorrect,* ABC, 1993

**8** Jagger has got this marvelous sense of the day in which a family breaks up. The son throws acid in the mother's face, the mother stomps the son's nuts in and then the fat cousin comes and says, what is everybody fighting for, let's have dinner. And they sit down . . . British family life continues.
**Norman Mailer** (Attrib.)

**9** Mick Jagger has big lips. I saw him suck an egg out of a chicken. He can play a tuba from both ends. This man has got child-bearing lips . . .
**Joan Rivers,** *An Audience with Joan Rivers,* London Weekend Television, 1984

**10** . . . after *Sticky Fingers* Mick [Jagger] became a debutant. Can't open a paper now without seeing a picture of him at some film opening cooing into Baryshnikov's ear . . . The cat's gone high rent. I mean, the First Lady of Canada starts hanging out with him, and *she's* accused of social climbing . . . Maybe he gets off on fashion shows or having Elaine personally come to his table

to make sure all the shrimp on his plate are facing north.
**Garry Trudeau,** 'The Jimmy Thudpucker Interview', *Rolling Stone,* 1978

# Romance

*See also Courtship; Flirtation; Love; Proposals; Seduction; Sex.*

**1** MANJULA: Until last night I never knew Apu could be so romantic!
MARGE: I can't believe it! He covered your whole bed with wildflowers.
MANJULA: Oh, I'm sure Homer has done that for you.
MARGE: Well sometimes I find pickle slices in the sheets.
**Dan Greaney,** 'I'm with Cupid', *The Simpsons,* Fox TV, 1999

**2** Never Let a Fool Kiss You Or a Kiss Fool You.
**Dr Mardy Grothe,** title of book, 1999

**3** In a mountain greenery
Where God paints the scenery
With the world we haven't a quarrel.
Here a girl can map her own
Life without a chaperone.
It's so good it must be immoral.
It's not amiss.
To sit and kiss.
For me and you
There are no blue laws.
Life is more delectable
When it's disrespectable.
Bless our mountain greenery home.
**Lorenz Hart,** 'Mountain Greenery', song, 1926

**4** I found the ideal girl. Her father is a bookmaker and her brother owns a liquor store.
**Joe E. Lewis,** 1902–71, American comedian

**5** ERIC: She's a lovely girl . . . I'd like to marry her, but her family objects.
ERNIE: Her family?
ERIC: Yes, her husband and four kids.
**Eric Morecambe and Ernie Wise,** *The Morecambe and Wise Joke Book,* 1979

**6** CELIA: Oh Charles – a woman needs certain things. She needs to be loved, wanted, cherished, sought after, wooed, flattered, cossetted, pampered. She needs sympathy, affection, devotion,

understanding, tenderness, infatuation, adulation, idolatry – that isn't much to ask, Charles.
**Barry Took and Marty Feldman**, *Round the Horne*, BBC Radio, 1966

**7** The very essence of romance is uncertainty. If ever I get married, I'll certainly try to forget the fact.
**Oscar Wilde**, *The Importance of Being Earnest*, 1895

**8** Where one goes wrong when looking for the ideal girl is in making one's selection before walking the full length of the counter.
**P. G. Wodehouse**, *Much Obliged, Jeeves*, 1971

# Royalty
*See also The Aristocracy; Class; The Ruling Class; Society; Queen Victoria.*

**1** PETE: ... do you know, at this very moment, Her Majesty is probably exercising the royal prerogative.
DUD: What's that then, Pete?
PETE: Don't you know the royal prerogative? It's a wonderful animal, Dud. It's a legendary beast, half bird, half fish, half unicorn, and it's being exercised at this very moment. Do you know that legend has it that e'er so long as the royal prerogative lives, happiness and laughter will reign throughout this green and pleasant land.
DUD: And the yeoman will stand tall upon this sceptred isle, Pete.
**Peter Cook and Dudley Moore**, *The Dagenham Dialogues*, 1971

**2** Part of a royal education is
To be resigned
To your behind
Becoming numb.
The worst of every coronation is
We always wish we hadn't come.
**Noel Coward**, 'Coronation Chorale', song from *The Girl Who Came to Supper*, 1963

**3** Everyone likes flattery; and when you come to Royalty you should lay it on with a trowel.
**Benjamin Disraeli**, to Matthew Arnold (Attrib.)

**4** One day there will only be five kings left: hearts, spades, diamonds, clubs, and England.
**King Farouk of Egypt**, 1953

**5** After you've met one hundred and fifty lord mayors, they all begin to look the same.
**King George V** (Attrib.)

**6** I was taught a kind of theoretic republicanism which was prepared to tolerate a monarch so long as he recognized that he was an employee of the people and subject to dismissal if he proved unsatisfactory. My grandfather, who was no respecter of persons, used to explain this point of view to Queen Victoria, and she was not altogether sympathetic.
**Bertrand Russell**, *Portraits from Memory*, 1956

**7** Prince Charles is planning to record his own version of Frank Sinatra's hit, 'My Way'. He's going to call it 'One Did It One's Way'.
**Neil Shand**, English wit

**8** We're the envy of the world, we are, having a Royal Family. It's the one thing in the world no one else has got. An' don't talk to me about Norway, and Holland, and Sweden and all that rubbish. I'm talking about Royalty. Not bloody cloth-cap kings riding about on bikes. I mean, that's not Royalty. You'll never see our Queen on a bike. She wouldn't demean herself.
**Johnny Speight**, *The Thoughts of Chairman Alf (Alf Garnett's Little Blue Book)*, 1973

**9** Wednesday July 29th
ROYAL WEDDING DAY!!!!!
How proud I am to be English!
Foreigners must be sick as pigs!
We truly lead the world when it comes to pageantry!
... Prince Charles looked quite handsome in spite of his ears. His brother is dead good-looking; it's a shame they couldn't have swapped heads just for the day. Lady Diana melted my heartstrings in her dirty white dress. She even helped an old man up the aisle. I thought it was very kind of her considering it was her wedding day.
**Sue Townsend**, *The Secret Diary of Adrian Mole Aged 13¾*, 1982

**10** The kingly office is entitled to no respect. It was originally procured by highwayman's methods; it remains a perpetuated crime, can never be anything but the symbol of a crime. It is no more

entitled to respect than is the flag of a pirate.
**Mark Twain**, *Notebook*, 1935

**11** Good kings are the only dangerous enemies that modern democracy has.
**Oscar Wilde**, *Vera, or The Nihilists*, 1883

# Rugby
*See also Sport.*

**1** His air was that of a man who has been passed through a wringer, and his eyes, what you could see of them, had a strange, smouldering gleam. He was so encrusted with alluvial deposits that one realized how little a mere bath would ever be able to effect. To fit him to take his place in polite society, he would certainly have to be sent to the cleaner's. Indeed, it was a moot point whether it wouldn't be simpler just to throw him away.
**P. G. Wodehouse**, *Very Good, Jeeves*, 1930

**2** Rugby football is a game I can't claim absolutely to understand in all its niceties, if you know what I mean. I can follow the broad, general principles, of course. I mean to say, I know that the main scheme is to work the ball down the field somehow and deposit it over the line at the other end, and that, in order to squelch this programme, each side is allowed to put in a certain amount of assault and battery and do things to its fellow-man which, if done elsewhere, would result in fourteen days without the option, coupled with some strong remarks from the Bench.
**P. G. Wodehouse**, *Very Good, Jeeves*, 1930

# Russia and the Russians
*See also Communism; Marxism; Socialism.*

**1** HILARY: One of the advantages of living in Russia is that it's one of the few places where smoking doesn't cause cancer. At least the authorities don't say it does, so one must presume it doesn't.
**Alan Bennett**, *The Old Country*, 1978

**2** I cannot forecast to you the action of Russia. It is a riddle wrapped in a mystery inside an enigma.
**Winston Churchill**, BBC Radio, 1939

**3** In Russia they treated me like a Czar and you know how they treated the Czar.
**Bob Hope**

**4** Ideas in modern Russia are machine-cut blocks coming in solid colors; the nuance is outlawed, the interval walled up, the curve grossly stepped.
**Vladimir Nabokov**, *Pale Fire*, 1962

**5** *Racial characteristics*: brutish, dumpy, boorish lard-bags in cardboard double-breasted suits. Lickspittle slaveys to the maniacal schemes of their blood-lusting Red overlords. They make bicycles out of cement and can be sent to Siberia for listening to the wrong radio station.
**P. J. O'Rourke**, 'Foreigners Around the World', *National Lampoon*, 1976

**6** The Soviet Union would remain a one-party nation even if an opposition party were permitted – because everyone would join that party.
**Ronald Reagan**, *Observer*, 1982

**7** In the United States you have freedom of speech. You can go up to Ronald Reagan and say, 'I don't like Ronald Reagan.' In the Soviet Union you have the same thing. You can go up to Chernenko and say, 'I don't like Ronald Reagan.'
**Yakov Smirnoff**, Russian emigré comedian, quoted in *Newsweek*, 1984

**8** The Russian police have a Missing Persons Department. That's where they decide which persons are going to go missing.
**Yakov Smirnoff**

**9** There are no unemployed either in Russia or in Dartmoor jail, and for the same reason.
**Philip Snowden**, Labour politician, 1932

**10** Q: What is a Russian string trio?
A: A Russian string quartet that has returned from the West.
**David Steel**, quoted in the *Observer*, 1984

# Sales and Selling

*See also Advertising; Consumers; Shopping.*

**1** In salesmanship, a foot in the door is worth two on the desk.
**Anon.**

**2** Is he a good salesman? He could sell underarm deodorant to the Venus de Milo.
**Anon.**

**3** FIRST SALESMAN: I made some very valuable contacts today.
SECOND SALESMAN: I didn't get any orders either.
**Anon.**

**4** *January cover*. If You Don't Buy This Magazine, We'll Kill This Dog.

*February editorial page*: Remember it? The dog that was going to be killed if you didn't buy the issue? You people are really incredible. You had us kill that sweet pooch. And don't for a minute go blaming us. We held the gun, but you sure as hell pulled the trigger . . . though there are those among you who did buy three or four issues to take up whatever slack existed. Those people are to be commended. But it wasn't enough. It was for everyone to pull his or her share. And you didn't.
***National Lampoon***, 1973

# San Francisco

*See also America and the Americans; California.*

**1** When you get tired of walking around San Francisco, you can always lean against it.
**'San Francisco'**, *Transworld Getaway Guide*, 1975–6

**2** San Francisco rock, San Francisco writing, it's always real lightweight, ephemeral stuff. Nothing *important* has ever come out of San Francisco, Rice-A-Roni aside.
**Michael O'Donoghue**, quoted in *Playboy*, 1983

**3** My favorite city is San Francisco, because it's gay. They teach the kids in school: AC DC EFG . . .
**Joan Rivers**, *An Audience with Joan Rivers*, London Weekend Television, 1984

**4** . . . the city that never was a town.
**Will Rogers**

**5** The coldest winter I ever spent was a summer in San Francisco.
**Mark Twain** (Attrib.)

## Satire

*See also Comedy; Humour; Laughter; The Sixties; Wit.*

**1** What arouses the indignation of the honest satirist is not, unless the man is a prig, the fact that people in positions of power or influence behave idiotically, or even that they behave wickedly. It is that they conspire successfully to impose upon the public a picture of themselves as so very sagacious, honest and well-intentioned. You cannot satirize a man who says, 'I'm in it for the money and that's all there is to it.'
**Claud Cockburn**, *Cockburn Sums Up*, 1981

**2** FIRST SATIRIST: The kind of satire I prefer to do is the take-off on the little man . . . his troubles, his pet peeves . . . the little unnoticed bedevilments of life that may not give the audience a belly laugh, mind you, but will give them a smile of recognition. 'Yes – I'm like that,' they'll say. 'There I am. There you are. There we all are. Little Man. Peering off into the middle distance . . . there's my wife. There's my next door neighbor . . .'
SECOND SATIRIST: Together?
FIRST SATIRIST: Smut is *not* satire.
SECOND SATIRIST: Smut, dear sir, is our *only* satire.
**Jules Feiffer**, introduction, *Feiffer's Album*, 1963

**3** . . . satire died the day they gave Henry Kissinger the Nobel Peace Prize.
**Tom Lehrer**, quoted in 'How To Survive Reagan' by Molly Ivins, *The Progressive*, 1986

## Saving

*See also Banking; Budgets; Economics; Rich and Poor; Wealth.*

**1** Saving is a very fine thing, especially when your parents have done it for you.
**Winston Churchill**

**2** Save a little money each month, and at the end of the year you'll be surprised at how little you have.
**Ernest Haskins**

## Sayings

*See also Epigrams; Maxims; Proverbs; Quotations.*

**1** . . . if a thing is worth doing, it is worth doing badly.
**G. K. Chesterton**, *What's Wrong With the World*, 1910

**2** A chrysanthemum by any other name would be easier to spell.
**William J. Johnston**, *Reader's Digest*

**3** People who live in glass houses have to answer the bell.
**Bruce Patterson**

## Scandals

*See also Gossip; Sex.*

**1** Scandal is merely the compassionate allowance which the gay make to the humdrum.
**Saki (H. H. Munro)**, *Reginald at the Carlton*, 1904

**2** One should never make one's debut with a scandal. One should reserve that to give an interest to one's old age.
**Oscar Wilde**, *The Picture of Dorian Gray*, 1891

## Schizophrenia

*See also Insanity; Psychiatry; Psychoanalysis; Psychology.*

**1** So I'm cured of schizophrenia – but where am I now that I need me?
**Graffito**, New York, 1981

**2** Two in every one people in this country are schizophrenic.
**Graffito**, Exeter, 1985

**3** You're never alone with schizophrenia.
**Badge**, London, 1983

**4** Roses are red,
Violets are blue.
I'm schizophrenic
And so am I.
**Billy Connolly**, Scottish comedian

## School

*See also Childhood; Children; Examinations; Sex Education; Teachers and Teaching.*

**1** I went to a tough school. The senior prom

queen was selected by an arm wrestling
contest.
**Anon.**

**2** O vain futile frivolous boy. Smirking. I
won't have it. I won't have it. I won't have
it. Go find the headmaster and ask him to
beat you within an inch of your life. And
say please.
**Alan Bennett,** Forty Years On, 1968

**3** Your high school reunion. You get that
letter in the mail. You feel like you only
have six months to make something of
yourself.
**Drew Carey**

**4** Headmasters have powers at their
disposal with which Prime Ministers have
never yet been invested.
**Winston Churchill,** My Early Life, 1930

**5** BOB: The first week I met you, five years
of age, at Bygate Infants, you split my head
open with a brick in the sandpit.
TERRY: You stole my plasticine!
BOB: No excuse for splitting one's head
open with a brick!
TERRY: See? You sulked about that all these
years. Should have picked up the brick and
hit me back. Instead of which you went
home and told your mother.
BOB: Of course I told me mother. What am I
supposed to say when I go home after my
first day at school with blood streaming
down my new Aertex shirt – I cut myself
shaving?
**Dick Clement and Ian La Frenais,** 'Conduct
Unbecoming', The Likely Lads, BBC TV

**6** I will not call my teacher 'Hot Cakes'.
I will not yell 'She's dead' during roll call.
A burp is not an answer.
I will not torment the emotionally frail.
I will not Xerox my butt.
I will not belch the National Anthem.
**Matt Groening,** Bart's blackboard lines, The Simpsons,
Fox TV

**7** Stand firm in your refusal to remain
conscious during algebra. In real life, I
assure you, there is no such thing as algebra.
**Fran Lebowitz,** Social Studies, 1981

**8** School days, I believe, are the unhappiest
in the whole span of human existence. They
are full of dull, unintelligible tasks, new and

unpleasant ordinance, brutal violations of
common sense and common decency.
**H. L. Mencken,** The Baltimore Evening Sun, 1928

**9** ERNIE: They must have thought you were
very clever at school.
ERIC: They did. Every time the teacher asked
a question, I was the first to put up my
hand.
ERNIE: That was clever.
ERIC: You bet – by the time I got back, the
question had been answered.
**Eric Morecambe and Ernie Wise,** The Morecambe and
Wise Joke Book, 1979

**10** Show me the man who has enjoyed his
schooldays and I will show you a bully and
a bore.
**Robert Morley,** Robert Morley: Responsible Gentleman,
1966

**11** No one ever got a word of sense out of
any schoolmaster. You may, at a pinch, take
their word about equilateral hexagons but
life, life's a closed book to them.
**John Mortimer,** A Voyage Round My Father,
screenplay, 1982

**12** I never let my schooling interfere with
my education.
**Mark Twain**

**13** One of my school reports read as
follows: 'This boy shows great originality
which must be crushed at all costs.'
**Peter Ustinov**

**14** TEACHER: Now I don't want you to
worry, class. These tests will have no effect
on your grades. They merely determine
your future social status and financial
success. If any.
**Jon Vitti,** 'Bart the Genius', The Simpsons, Fox TV, 1990

**15 Skool food**
Or the piece of cod which passeth
understanding.
**Geoffrey Willans and Ronald Searle,** 'Down With
Skool!', The Compleet Molesworth, 1958

**16** The job of masters is supposed to be to
teach boys lessons e.g. geog lat fr. div hist
bot. arith algy and geom.
 Actually most of them prefer BEER and
PUBS. They are always late for brekfast not
like keen alert boys who goble force poridge
cereal with grate gusto and look scorn on

masters pale yelow faces when they see a skool sossage. Then is the time to ask Would you like some cream sir? or Gosh look at my egg sir its all runny. (Manners.)
**Geoffrey Willans and Ronald Searle**, 'Down With Skool!', *The Compleet Molesworth*, 1958

**17** The Only good thing about skool are the BOYS wizz who are noble brave fearless etc. although you have various swots, bulies, cissies, milksops greedy guts and oiks with whom I am forced to mingle hem-hem. In fact any skool is a bit of a shambles.
**Geoffrey Willans and Ronald Searle**, 'Down With Skool!', *The Compleet Molesworth*, 1958

**18** My school motto was '*Monsanto incorpori glorius maxima copia*' which in Latin means, 'When the going gets tough, the tough go shopping.'
**Robin Williams**, interview in *Playboy*, October 1982

**19** . . . the bearded bloke stepped to the footlights and started making a speech. From the fact that he spoke as if he had a hot potato in his mouth without getting a raspberry from the lads in the ringside seats, I deduced that he must be the headmaster.
With his arrival in the spotlight, a sort of perspiring resignation seemed to settle on the audience . . . The speech was on the doings of the school during the past term, and this part of a prize-giving is always apt rather to fail to grip the visiting stranger.
**P. G. Wodehouse**, *Right Ho, Jeeves*, 1934

# Science and Scientists
*See also Relativity.*

**1** A drug is a substance that when injected into a guinea pig produces a scientific paper.
**Anon.**

**2** Ever wondered what the speed of lightning would be if it didn't zigzag?
**Anon.**

**3** Two hydrogens walk into a bar. The first one says, 'Oh, no, I've lost an electron!' The other one says, 'Are you sure?' The first one says, 'I'm positive!'
**Anon.**

**4** Irreproducible research too often leads to great discoveries.
*Journal of Irreproducible Results*

**5** The mouse is an animal which, killed in sufficient numbers under carefully controlled conditions, will produce a Ph.D thesis.
*Journal of Irreproducible Results*

**6** Scientists discovered a link between silicon and melba toast. After fifteen years of exposure to air, silicon turns into melba toast, according to a group of University of California researchers. The findings caused panic among computer makers and other businesses that rely on the silicon chip. However, makers of processed-cheese spreads were elated at the news.
*Off The Wall Street Journal*, 1982

**7** My ignorance of science is such that if anyone mentioned copper nitrate, I should think he was talking about policemen's overtime.
**Dr Donald Coggan**, Archbishop of York (Attrib.)

**8** . . . modern science was largely conceived of as an answer to the servant problem and . . . is generally practised by those who lack a flair for conversation.
**Fran Lebowitz**, *Metropolitan Life*, 1978

**9** Scientists – a crowd that when it comes to style and dash makes the general public look like the Bloomsbury Set.
**Fran Lebowitz**, *Metropolitan Life*, 1978

**10** . . . the further back one goes . . . the science one does encounter is of a consistently higher quality. For example, in studying the science of yesteryear one comes upon such interesting notions as gravity, electricity, and the roundness of the earth – while an examination of more recent phenomena shows a strong trend towards spray cheese, stretch denim, and the Moog synthesizer.
**Fran Lebowitz**, *Metropolitan Life*, 1978

**11** If it squirms, it's biology; if it stinks, it's chemistry; if it doesn't work, it's physics and if you can't understand it, it's mathematics.
**Magnus Pyke**, English scientist

**12** Although this may seem a paradox, all exact science is dominated by the idea of approximation. When a man tells you that he knows the exact truth about anything,

you are safe in inferring that he is an inexact man.
**Bertrand Russell**, 1872–1970, British philosopher

**13** The formula for water is $H_2O$. Is the formula for an ice cube $H_2O$ squared?
**Lily Tomlin**

# Scotland and the Scots
*See also Britain and the British.*

**1** Q: How can you tell if your bagpipes are out of tune?
A: You're blowing into them.
**Anon.**

**2** Q: What's the definition of a gentleman?
A: Someone who knows how to play the bagpipes – but doesn't.
**Anon.**

**3** There are few more impressive sights in the world than a Scotsman on the make.
**J. M. Barrie**, *What Every Woman Knows*, 1908

**4** One often yearns
For the land of Burns
The only snag is
The haggis!
**Lils Emslie**, *Other People's Clerihews*, 1983

**5** For the wife she used to ramble through me pooches
When I was fast asleep aneath the quilt,
In the morning when I woke
I was always stoney broke
That's the reason noo I wear a kilt.
**Harry Lauder**, 'That's the Reason Noo I Wear a Kilt', song, 1906

**6** Is anything worn beneath the kilt?
No, it's all in perfect working order!
**Spike Milligan**, *The Great McGonagall Scrapbook*

**7** SEAGOON: Who's this approaching wearing a transparent kilt?
MACGOONIGAL: That is a special kilt designed for patriotic Scottish nudists.
**Spike Milligan**, *The Goon Show*, BBC Radio, 1959

**8** No McTavish
Was ever lavish.
**Ogden Nash**, 'Genealogical Reflection', *Hard Lines*, 1931

**9** *Racial characteristics*: sour, stingy, depressing beggars who parade around in schoolgirls' skirts with nothing on underneath. Their fumbled attempt at speaking the English language has been a source of amusement for five centuries, and their idiot music has been dreaded by those not blessed with deafness for at least as long.
**P. J. O'Rourke**, 'Foreigners Around the World', *National Lampoon*, 1976

**10** It requires a surgical operation to get a joke well into a Scotch understanding. Their only idea of wit . . . is laughing immoderately at stated intervals.
**Sydney Smith**, *Lady Holland's Memoir*, 1855

**11** It is never difficult to distinguish between a Scotsman with a grievance and a ray of sunshine.
**P. G. Wodehouse**, *Blandings Castle and Elsewhere*, 1935

# Sea, The
*See also The Beach; Fish and Fishing; Holidays; The Navy; Ships; Swimming.*

**1** Did you ever wonder how much deeper the ocean would be without sponges?
**Anon.**

**2** HILARY: Quite candidly, I've never seen the point of the sea. Except where it meets the land. The shore has point, the sea none.
**Alan Bennett**, *The Old Country*, 1978

**3** I'm Millie, a messy old mermaid,
Out and about all the day,
Combing my hair – what little is there
And just shouting my voice away.
If I am a bit thin and p'raps minus a fin,
It's a sin to suppose that I show it.
What a failure I've been in the last forty years,
Every sailor I've seen must have wool in his ears,
If a whaler harpooned me I'd give him three cheers,
I'm well on the rocks and I know it.
**Douglas Byng**, 'Millie the Mermaid – A Lament', *Byng Ballads*

# Seasons, The
*See also Weather.*

**1** Winter is what people go south during.
**Anon.**

**2** First a howling blizzard woke us,
Then the rain came down to soak us,
And now before the eye can focus –
Crocus.
**Lilja Rogers**, *Reader's Digest*, 1964

**3** Now is the winter of our discontent made glorious summer by central heating.
**Jack Sharkey**, *Playboy*, 1965

**4** The first day of spring was once the time for taking the young virgins into the fields, there in dalliance to set an example in fertility for Nature to follow. Now we just set the clock an hour ahead and change the oil in the crankcase.
**E. B. White**, *One Man's Meat*, 1944

**5** It's a sure sign of summer if the chair gets up when you do.
**Walter Winchell**, American newspaper columnist

# Seduction
*See also Charm; Courtship; Flirtation; Petting; Romance; Sex; Sin.*

**1** . . . and then I want to end up *NORWICH*. Yes, well it's an epigrammatic way of saying *KNICKERS OFF READY WHEN I COME HOME*. It's the initial letters, you see, of each word. I know 'Knickers' is spelled with a 'K'. I did go to Oxford – that was one of the first things they taught us. Yes. And in a perfect world it would be *KORWICH*. But it doesn't have quite the same idiomatic force I think as *NORWICH* does it?
**Alan Bennett**, 'The Telegram', *On the Margin*, BBC TV, 1966

**2** I'm looking for a perfume to overpower men – I'm sick of karate.
**Phyllis Diller**

**3** I was at a party feeling very shy because there were lots of celebrities around and I was sitting in a corner alone and a very beautiful young man came up to me and offered me peanuts and he said, 'I wish they were emeralds,' as he handed me the peanuts and that was the end of my heart. I never got it back.
**Helen Hayes**, actress

**4** Fortified with Krug, he produced from behind his back a glow-in-the-dark condom in the shape of a Stealth Bomber called 'The Penetrator'. Great. Now I could read during the dull bits.
**Kathy Lette**, *Altar Ego*, 1998

**5** Music helps set a romantic mood. Some men believe the only good music is live music. Imagine her surprise when you say, 'I don't need a stereo – I have an accordion!' Then imagine the sound of a door slamming.
**Martin Mull**, *Playboy*, 1978

**6** BUD: Cheers.
FRAN: Cheers.
BUD: You know what we're going to do after dinner?
FRAN: The dishes?
**Billy Wilder and I. A. L. Diamond**, *The Apartment*, screenplay, 1960

# Self-Defence
*See also Fighting.*

**1** I can take care of myself. In case of danger I have this cutlass that I carry around with me . . . and in case of real emergency, I press the handle and it turns into a cane so I can get sympathy.
**Woody Allen**

**2** I'm not a fighter, I have bad reflexes. I was once run over by a car being pushed by two guys.
**Woody Allen**

# Selfishness
*See also Egotism; Opportunism; Stinginess.*

**1** 'From now on I'm thinking only of me.'
Major Danby replied indulgently with a superior smile: 'But, Yossarian, suppose everyone felt that way.'
'Then,' said Yossarian, 'I'd certainly be a damn fool to feel any other way, wouldn't I?'
**Joseph Heller**, *Catch-22*, 1961

# Senate, The
*See also Congress; Politics – The American Presidency; Politics – The American Vice-Presidency; Politics and Politicians; Washington.*

**1** Draco wrote his laws in blood; the Senate writes its laws in wind.
**Thomas Connally**, 1877–1963, Democratic Congressman, 1957

**2** Office hours are from twelve to one with an hour off for lunch.
**George S. Kaufman**, 1889–1961, American writer

# Servants

*See also Class.*

**1** I know it's draggy having the au-pair feeding with us; but one has to be madly democratic if one wants to keep them.
**Marc**, *The Trendy Ape*, cartoon, 1968

**2** Actually, I vote Labour – but my butler's a Tory.
**Earl Mountbatten of Burma**, to a Tory canvasser, 1945 (Attrib.)

**3** Before the cleaning lady arrives, it is necessary to vacuum the entire house and straighten up all the rooms, because she works for friends of yours the other six days of the week and you don't want her to tell them how you really live . . .
   . . . It is perfectly proper to ask your cleaning lady to iron, wash windows, polish silver, do the grocery shopping, and clean up after the dog. You can also ask her to jump through a flaming hoop with a cold leg of mutton in her mouth for all the good it will do you. She's going to dust a little, and that's it, no matter what.
**P. J. O'Rourke**, *Modern Manners*, 1983

**4** The cook was a good cook, as cooks go; and as cooks go, she went.
**Saki (H. H. Munro)**, *Reginald*, 1904

**5** When domestic servants are treated as human beings, it is not worth while to keep them.
**George Bernard Shaw**, *Maxims for Revolutionists*, 1903

**6** CECILY: I am afraid that I disapprove of servants.
CARR: You are quite right to do so. Most of them are without scruples.
**Tom Stoppard**, *Travesties*, 1974

**7** It has been my experience, sir, that no lady can ever forgive another lady for taking a really good cook away from her.
**P. G. Wodehouse**, *Carry on, Jeeves*, 1925

**8** My experience, sir, is that when the wife comes in at the front door the valet goes out at the back.
**P. G. Wodehouse**, *Carry on, Jeeves*, 1925

# Seventies, The

*See also The Fifties; The Sixties.*

**1** The seventies saw the spread of California culture (or 'life-style' as it came to be called), oozing from the canyons and condos of that state and slopping itself into the brainpans of previously rational and intelligent people.
   Many among us began applying the words 'therapy' and 'training' to every conceivable activity. And in fact much of the weirdness of the seventies was simply ordinary everyday activities raised to the level of great metaphysical significance.
*National Lampoon*, 1980

**2** It amazes me that any of us managed to write a word of sense during the whole decade considering we were all evidently stupid enough to wear flares . . .
**Martin Amis**, *Experience*, 2000

**3** Ten years ago wives were wives, rather than women, and 'affirmative action' was popping them right in the orthodontia when they stopped baking chocolate chip cookies in their spare time and started screwing around.
   Now, however, it wasn't that simple. Wife-beating, in Marin in the seventies, was considered a crime against humanity second only to lighting a cigarette in a crowded elevator. Not only couldn't Harvey shake Kate until she lost her contact lenses; he couldn't even close her charge accounts.
**Cyra McFadden**, *The Serial*, 1977

# Sex

*See also Birth Control; Bisexuality; Courtship; Flirtation; Homosexuality; Kissing; Love; Orgies; Petting; Pregnancy; Promiscuity; Prostitution; Scandals; Seduction; Sex Education; Sexual Attraction; Sexual Perversions; Sin.*

**1** Sex is bad for one. But it's good for two.
**T-shirt**, London, 1978

**2** Don't Worry. It'll Only Seem Kinky the First Time
**T-shirt**, Miami Beach, 1997

**3** I believe that sex is a beautiful thing between two people. Between five, it's fantastic . . .
**Woody Allen**, *The Nightclub Years, 1964–1968*, album, 1972

**4** I finally had an orgasm . . . and my doctor told me it was the wrong kind.
**Woody Allen**, *Manhattan*, screenplay, 1979

**5** Is sex dirty? Only if it's done right.
**Woody Allen**, *Everything You Always Wanted To Know About Sex*, screenplay, 1972

**6** Sex and death. Two things that come once in a lifetime. Only after death, you're not so nauseous.
**Woody Allen and Marshall Brickman**, *Sleeper*, screenplay, 1973

**7** 'Just put it this way, in my time I've been to bed with well over a hundred women.'
Rosenberg had made some notes of the answers to all his questions until this last one, at which to Jake's distinct annoyance he merely nodded.
**Kingsley Amis**, *Jake's Thing*, 1978

**8** I've tried several varieties of sex. The conventional position makes me claustrophobic. And the others either give me a stiff neck or lockjaw.
**Tallulah Bankhead**, 1903–68, American actress (Attrib.)

**9** LADY RUMPERS: And then you took me.
SIR PERCY: I took *you*? You took *me*. Your Land Army breeches came down with a fluency born of long practice.
**Alan Bennett**, *Habeas Corpus*, 1973

**10** WICKSTEED: What did he look like?
LADY RUMPERS: As I say there was a black-out. I saw his face only in the fitful light of a post-coital Craven A.
**Alan Bennett**, *Habeas Corpus*, 1973

**11** There's a sexual revolution going on, and I think that with our current foreign policy, we'll probably be sending troops in there any minute to break it up.
**Mel Brooks** (Attrib.)

**12** We all know girls do it. But if you ask them to do it, they say no. Why? Because they want to be proper. Finally, after thirteen years of courtship and dates and so on, one night they get drunk and they do it. And after they've done it, that's all they want to do. Now they're fallen, now they're disgraced, and all they want is to do it. You say, 'Let's have a cup of tea.' No, let's do it. 'Let's go to the cinema.' No, I'd rather do it.
**Mel Brooks**, quoted in *Time Out*, 1984

**13** It doesn't matter what you do in the bedroom as long as you don't do it in the street and frighten the horses.
**Mrs Patrick Campbell**

**14** The good thing about masturbation is that you don't have to dress up for it.
**Truman Capote** (Attrib.)

**15** I'm not a good lover, but at least I'm fast.
**Drew Carey**

**16** If God had intended us not to masturbate, he would've made our arms shorter.
**George Carlin**

**17** When turkeys mate, they think of swans.
**Johnny Carson**, *The Tonight Show*, NBC TV

**18** Sex is only the liquid centre of the great New Berry Fruit of friendship.
**Jilly Cooper**, *Super-Jilly*, 1977

**19** What men desire is a virgin who is a whore.
**Edward Dahlberg**, *Reasons of the Heart*, 1965

**20** At certain times I like sex – like after a cigarette.
**Rodney Dangerfield**

**21** If it weren't for pickpockets, I'd have no sex life at all.
**Rodney Dangerfield**

**22** My wife said her wildest sexual fantasy would be if I got my own apartment.
**Rodney Dangerfield**

**23** He had ambitions, at one time, to become a sex maniac, but he failed his practical.
**Les Dawson**, *The Les Dawson Joke Book*, 1979

**24** In the case of some women, orgasms take quite a bit of time. Before signing on with such a partner, make sure you are willing to lay aside, say, the month of June, with sandwiches having to be brought in.
**Bruce Jay Friedman**, 'Sex and the Lonely Guy', *Esquire*, 1977

**25** One of the great breakthroughs in sex has been the discovery of all the new erogenous zones. Once it was thought there were only a handful. Now they are all over the place, with new ones being reported every day. Don't try to go at too many at once. If you do, they will cancel one another out, with some of the traditional old-line ones being neutralized. A sensitive partner can help by tapping you on the shoulder and saying, 'You are tackling too many erogenous zones.'
**Bruce Jay Friedman**, 'Sex and the Lonely Guy', *Esquire*, 1977

**26** Seamed stockings aren't subtle but they certainly do the job. You shouldn't wear them when out with someone you're not prepared to sleep with, since their presence is tantamount to saying, 'Hi there, big fellow, please rip my clothes off at your earliest opportunity.' If you really want your escort paralytic with lust, stop frequently to adjust the seams.
**Cynthia Heimel**, *Sex Tips for Girls*, 1983

**27** We, being modern and liberated and fully cognizant of women's sexual, intellectual, emotional and economic oppression, can never for a moment cease our vigilance against the imperialistic male supremacist. We must never relax our guard against his chauvinistic sexual fantasies.

So don't even for an instant consider keeping the following hidden in the back of your closet: a see-through nurse's uniform . . . a cheerleader's costume . . . a little black French maid's outfit . . .

And if you do, don't tell anyone.
**Cynthia Heimel**, *Sex Tips for Girls*, 1983

**28** Woody Allen was right when someone asked him if he thought sex was dirty and he said, 'If you do it right.' Sex is not some sort of pristine, reverent ritual. You want reverent and pristine, go to church.
**Cynthia Heimel**, *Sex Tips for Girls*, 1983

**29** He moved his lips about her ears and neck as though in thirsting search of an erogenous zone. A waste of time, he knew from experience. Erogenous zones were either everywhere or nowhere.
**Joseph Heller**, *Good as Gold*, 1979

**30** There was little she [Dori Duz] hadn't tried and less she wouldn't.
**Joseph Heller**, *Catch-22*, 1961

**31** *Hospitals, to play*: to engage in congress, or to play cars and garages or hide the sausage.
*Hots, to have the H's for*: to be romantically attracted to.
*Qantas hostie*: a desirable sexual partner.
**Barry Humphries**, glossary from *Bazza Pulls it Off*

**32** Sex is the most beautiful thing that can take place between a happily married man and his secretary.
**Barry Humphries**, *Les Patterson Has a Stand Up*, 1996

**33** The zipless fuck is absolutely pure . . . and it is rarer than the unicorn.
**Erica Jong**, *Fear of Flying*, 1973

**34** Everybody does everything in order to get laid.
**Lawrence Kasdan, Barbara Benedek**, *The Big Chill*, screenplay, 1983

**35** My wife insists on turning off the lights when we make love. That doesn't bother me. It's the hiding that seems so cruel.
**Jonathan Katz**, American comic

**36** A woman occasionally is quite a serviceable substitute for masturbation. It takes an abundance of imagination, to be sure.
**Karl Kraus**, 1874–1936, Austrian satirist

**37** If the Nobel Prize was awarded by a woman, it would go to the inventor of the dimmer switch. This is the greatest sex aid known to womankind. Well, to women over a certain age, say *sixteen*.
**Kathy Lette**, *Altar Ego*, 1998

**38** She bad-mouthed me when we broke up. She said I faked foreplay, that I gave her an anticlimax.
**Richard Lewis**, *Comic Relief*, HBO, 1994

**39** 'What, twins again, Mrs Lovejoy! Do you always have twins?'

'Oh no, Vicar! Lots of times we don't have anything at all!'
**Donald McGill**, seaside postcard, 1930s

**40** Sex is one of the most beautiful, wholesome and natural things that money can buy.
**Steve Martin**

**41** My own belief is that there is hardly anyone whose sexual life, if it were broadcast, would not fill the world at large with surprise and horror.
**W. Somerset Maugham**

**42** Sex is one of the nine reasons for reincarnation . . . The other eight are unimportant.
**Henry Miller**, *Big Sur and the Oranges of Hieronymus Bosch*, 1957

**43** I like the girls who do,
I like the girls who don't;
I hate the girl who says she will
And then she says she won't.
But the girl that I like best of all
And I think you'll say I'm right –
Is the one who says she never has
But looks as though she . . .
'Ere, listen . . .
**Max Miller**, *The Max Miller Blue Book*, 1975

**44** . . . she said, 'Do you mind if I sit down, 'cos I'm pregnant?' I said, 'You don't look it. How long have you been pregnant?' She said, 'Only ten minutes – but doesn't it make you feel tired?'
**Max Miller**, *The Max Miller Blue Book*, 1975

**45** There was a little girl
Who had a little curl
Right in the middle of her forehead.
When she was good, she was very, very good
And when she was bad, she was very, very popular.
**Max Miller**, *The Max Miller Blue Book*, 1975

**46** The orgasm has replaced the Cross as the focus of longing and the image of fulfilment.
**Malcolm Muggeridge**, *The Most of Malcolm Muggeridge*

**47** Sex – the poor man's polo.
**Clifford Odets** (Attrib.)

**48** There are a number of mechanical

devices which increase sexual arousal, particularly in women. Chief among these is the Mercedes-Benz 380SL convertible.
**P. J. O'Rourke**, *Modern Manners*, 1983

**49** . . . there is no petting . . . Modern couples just strip their clothes off and go at it . . . blame must . . . be placed on ex-President Nixon's decision to let the US dollar float in relation to other Western currencies. More than a decade of monetary instability has conditioned people to utilize their assets immediately. If the sex urge is not spent forthwith, it might degenerate into something less valuable – affection, for instance.
**P. J. O'Rourke**, *Modern Manners*, 1983

**50** If all the girls attending it were laid end to end, I wouldn't be at all surprised.
**Dorothy Parker**, of the Yale Prom

**51** I knew nothing about sex before I got married. When my mother told me that the man goes on top and the woman on the bottom, I bought bunk beds.
**Joan Rivers**

**52** Seems to me the basic conflict between men and women, sexually, is that men are like firemen. To us, sex is like an emergency, and no matter what we're doing we can be ready in two minutes. Women, on the other hand, are like fire. They're very exciting, but the conditions have to be exactly right for it to occur.
**Jerry Seinfeld**, *SeinLanguage*, 1993

**53** I practice safe sex. I use an airbag.
**Garry Shandling**

**54** Familiarity breeds contempt – and children.
**Mark Twain**, *Notebook*, 1935

**55** All this fuss about sleeping together. For physical pleasure I'd sooner go to my dentist any day.
**Evelyn Waugh**, *Vile Bodies*, 1930

**56** To err is human – but it feels divine.
**Mae West**

**57** 'But what *is* the love-life of newts, if you boil it right down? Didn't you tell me once that they just waggled their tails at each other in the mating-season?'

'Quite correct.'

'Well, all right if they like it. But it's not my idea of molten passion.'

**P. G. Wodehouse**, *The Code of the Woosters*, 1938

**58** Foreplay is like beefburgers – three minutes each side.

**Victoria Wood**, English comedienne

# Sex Education

*See also School; Sex.*

**1** My father told me all about the birds and the bees. The liar – I went steady with a woodpecker till I was twenty-one.

**Bob Hope**

**2** All teaching in all subjects aims to stimulate interest. It would be odd if this were not true of sex lessons.

**Roger Probert**, Birmingham headmaster, 1973

# Sexism

*See also Feminism; Political Correctness.*

**1** Don't be sexist. Broads hate that!

**T-shirt**, Key West, 1997

# Sexual Attraction

*See also Courtship; Flirtation; Infatuation; Kissing; Sex.*

**1** Alcestis had exercised a mysterious attraction and then an unmysterious repulsion on two former husbands, the second of whom had to resort to fatal coronary disease to get away from her.

**Kingsley Amis**, *Jake's Thing*, 1978

**2** Such precepts are arguable, I know, but I've always gone along with the view that, first, the surest guarantee of sexual success is sexual success (you can't have one without the other and you can't have the other without the one), and, second, that the trappings of sexual success are only fleetingly distinguishable from sexual success itself.

**Martin Amis**, *Success*, 1978

**3** I am the world's sexiest man. Mr Burton and Mr Sinatra take second place to me in the sex-appeal stakes.

Sex-appeal isn't just straight teeth, a square jaw and a solid torso. Look at me.

I'm sixty-three and first thing in the morning I have a face like a woollen mat. And yet I am the most desirable man in the world. Indeed, if I put my mind to it I am sure I could pass the supreme test and lure Miss Taylor away from Mr Burton.

**Noel Coward** (Attrib.)

**4** I am going to hire a hit man and have that little wart rubbed out. I will not have him fouling this beautiful earth. Do you know what that little scum has done? He has wormed his way into my affections.

**Cynthia Heimel**, 'LA Blues', *Playboy*, 1984

**5** Those hot pants of hers were so damned tight, I could hardly breathe.

**Benny Hill**, *The Benny Hill Show*, Thames TV, 1984

**6** A girl whose cheeks are covered with
  paint
Has an advantage with me over one
  whose ain't.

**Ogden Nash**, 'Biological Reflection', *Hard Lines*, 1931

**7** I have a big flaw in that I am attracted to thin, tall, good-looking men who have one common denominator. They must be lurking bastards.

**Edna O'Brien**, 1979

**8** Like most men, I am consumed with desire whenever a lesbian gets within twenty feet.

**Taki**, Greek-born columnist

**9** Outside every thin girl is a fat man trying to get in.

**Katharine Whitehorn** (Attrib.)

**10** . . . he's got – I don't mean to be – well, he looks like he's got a *cheese danish* stuffed in his *pants*!

**Tom Wolfe**, *The Bonfire of the Vanities*, 1984

# Sexual Equality

*See also Equality; Feminism.*

**1** A woman's place is in the House, and the Senate.

**T-shirt**, San Diego, 1991

**2** LEE-ANN: No, you're wrong. You're emancipated. Not like me.

FLORA: Oh yes. Twenty years of education, moral tuition, perseverance and honest toil, and we're all responsible women. Prepared

to tackle the major problems of the age. Ready to meet our husbands right in the middle of the intellectual arena. So long as the Avon Lady doesn't call, or we aren't too busy selling each other Tupperware for five per cent commission.
**Malcolm Bradbury and Christopher Bigsby**, *The After Dinner Game*, BBC TV, 1975

**3** A country that can put men on the moon can put women in the Constitution.
**Margaret Heckler**, Republican Secretary of Health, 1983–5

**4** Women who insist on having the same options as men would do well to consider the option of being the strong, silent type.
**Fran Lebowitz**, *Metropolitan Life*, 1978

# Sexual Perversions

*See also Sex.*

**1** An Argentine gaucho named Bruno
Once said, 'There is something I do know:
A woman is fine
And a sheep is divine,
But a llama is Numero Uno!'
**Anon.**

**2** The Marquis de Sade and Genet
Are most highly thought of today,
But torture and treachery
Are not my sort of lechery,
So I've given my copies away.
**W. H. Auden**, *New York Review of Books*, 1966

**3** I had to give up masochism – I was enjoying it too much . . .
**Mel Calman**, *Dr Calman's Dictionary of Psychoanalysis*, 1979

**4** I ache for the touch of your lips, Dear,
But much more for the touch of your whips, Dear,
You can raise welts
Like nobody else
As we dance to the Masochism Tango.
**Tom Lehrer**, 'The Masochism Tango', song from *An Evening Wasted with Tom Lehrer*, 1959

**5** The uncertain and frenetic nature of modern life has led to the increasing popularity of mild bondage. When you're tied to the bed, at least you know where you're going to be for the next few minutes. And dominant partners enjoy the sense of

having control over a situation, something they never get in real life. The dominant partner should show courtesy, however, and not abuse that position of control. It would be rude to get your sexual satisfaction by tying someone to the bed and then leaving him or her there and going out with someone more attractive.
**P. J. O'Rourke**, *Modern Manners*, 1983

# Shakespeare, William

*See also Acting; Actors and Actresses; Books; The English Language; Language; Literature; The Theatre; Writers; Writing.*

**1** I know not, sir, whether Bacon wrote the words of Shakespeare, but if he did not it seems to me he missed the opportunity of his life.
**J.M. Barrie**, 1860–1937 (British playwright) speech, 1925

**2** The remarkable thing about Shakespeare is that he really is very good, in spite of all the people who say he is very good.
**Robert Graves**, 1964

**3** Brush up your Shakespeare,
Start quoting him now,
Brush up your Shakespeare
And the women you will wow.
With the wife of the British embessida
Try a crack out of *Troilus and Cressida*,
If she says she won't buy it or tike it
Make her tike it, what's more, *As You Like It*.
If she says your behavior is heinous
Kick her right in the *Coriolanus*,
Brush up your Shakespeare
And they'll all kowtow.
**Cole Porter**, 'Brush Up Your Shakespeare', song, from *Kiss Me Kate*, 1948

**4 Hamlet**
Prince Hamlet thought Uncle a traitor
For having it off with his Mater;
Revenge Dad or not?
That's the gist of the plot,
And he did – nine soliloquies later.
**Stanley J. Sharpless**, *New Statesman*

**5** I don't know if you ever came across a play of Shakespeare called *Macbeth*? If you did, you may remember this bird Macbeth bumps off another bird named Banquo and gives a big dinner to celebrate, and picture

his embarrassment when about the first of
the gay throng to turn up is Banquo's ghost,
all merry and bright, covered in blood. It
gave him a pretty nasty start, Shakespeare
does not attempt to conceal.
**P. G. Wodehouse**, *Nothing Serious*, 1950

# Ships

*See also The Navy; The Sea; Travel.*

**1** The new nuclear submarine we have now
is the best. It stays under water for two years
and only comes up to the surface so the
crew can re-enlist.
**Dick Gregory**, black comedian, 1960

**2** . . . a luxury liner is really just a bad play
surrounded by water.
**Clive James**, *Unreliable Memoirs*, 1980

**3** A ship is always referred to as 'she'
because it costs so much to keep one in
paint and powder.
**Chester Nimitz**, American admiral, speech, 1940

**4** The Captain was on the bridge, pretty
sure that he knew the way to New York but,
just to be on the safe side, murmuring to
himself, 'Turn right at Cherbourg, and then
straight on.'
**P. G. Wodehouse**, *Plum Pie*, 1966

# Shopping

*See also Consumerism; Consumers; Credit; Credit
Cards; Selling.*

**1** A Woman's Place Is In the Mall
**Bumper sticker**, New York, 1999

**2** An extravagance is anything you buy that
is of no earthly use to your wife.
**Franklin P. Adams**, 1881–1960, American journalist

**3** A safety check would reveal that there
isn't a shopping cart that does not have all
four wheels working. Unfortunately, all four
are locked in stable directions. Three wheels
want to shop and the fourth wants to go to
the parking lot.
**Erma Bombeck**, *If Life is a Bowl of Cherries – What am I
Doing in the Pits?*, 1978

**4** For women shopping is a sport, much like
deer hunting is to men. They are building a
new mall in my town. Last week, women

were hanging on the fence yelling at the
workmen for taking a lunch break.
**Jeff Foxworthy**

**5** One of the most difficult things in this
world is to convince a woman that even a
bargain costs money.
**Edgar Watson Howe**, 1853–1937, American writer

**6** It makes no difference what it is, a
woman will buy anything she thinks the
store is losing money on.
**Kin Hubbard**, 1868–1930, American humorist

**7** I went into a general store. They wouldn't
let me buy anything specific.
**Steven Wright**, *Just for Laughs*, 1987

# Show Business

*See also Acting; Actors and Actresses; Ballet; Circus;
Dance; Film; Music and Musicians; Songs and
Singers; Television; The Theatre.*

**1** BLACKADDER: The only decent
impression he can do is of a man with no
talent.
**Richard Curtis and Ben Elton**, 'Captain Cook',
*Blackadder Goes Forth*, BBC TV, 1989

**2** PERFORMING SEAL (*to another performing
seal*): Of course, what I'd really like to do is
direct.
**Mort Gerberg**, cartoon in the *New Yorker*

**3** I do twenty minutes every time the
refrigerator door opens and the light comes
on.
**Debbie Reynolds** American actress (Attrib.)

# Silence

*See also Deafness; Ears; Noise.*

**1** Silence is the best substitute for brains
ever invented.
**Henry Fountain Ashurst**, Arizona Senator

**2** Drawing on my fine command of
language, I said nothing.
**Robert Benchley** (Attrib.)

**3** Silence is one of the hardest arguments to
refute.
**Josh Billings**, *The Complete Work of Josh Billings*, 1919

**4** I don't have to tell you it goes without
saying there are some things better left

unsaid. I think that speaks for itself. The less said about it the better.
**George Carlin**, *Brain Droppings*, 1997

**5** Silence – that unbearable repartee.
**G. K. Chesterton**, 1874–1936, English essayist and poet (Attrib.)

**6** 'No comment' is a splendid expression. I'm using it again and again.
**Winston Churchill**

**7** A man is known by the silence he keeps.
**Oliver Herford**, 1864–1935, English-born American writer

**8** Never assume that habitual silence means ability in reserve.
**Geoffrey Madan**, *Twelve Reflections*, 1934

**9** Silence – the most perfect expression of scorn.
**George Bernard Shaw**, *Back to Methuselah*, 1921

# Sin

*See also Evil; Religion; Sex; Temptation; Vice and Virtue.*

**1** Christ died for our sins. Dare we make his martyrdom meaningless by not committing them?
**Jules Feiffer**, American cartoonist

**2** Sin is a dangerous toy in the hands of the virtuous. It should be left to the congenitally sinful, who know when to play with it and when to let it alone.
**H. L. Mencken**, *The American Mercury*, 1929

**3** Pleasure is something that you feel that you should really enjoy, which is really virtuous, but you don't; and sin's something that you're quite sure you shouldn't enjoy but do.
**Ralph Wightman**, *Any Questions*, BBC Radio, 1961

# Sincerity

*See also Honesty; Truth.*

**1** It is dangerous to be sincere unless you are also stupid.
**George Bernard Shaw**, *Man and Superman*, 1903

**2** A little sincerity is a dangerous thing, and a great deal of it is absolutely fatal.
**Oscar Wilde**, 'The Critic as Artist', 1890

# Single Life, The

*See also Bachelors; Courtship; Marriage; Romance.*

**1** 11.45 p.m. Ugh. First day of New Year has been day of horror.

Cannot quite believe I am once again starting the year in a single bed in my parents' house. It is too humiliating at my age.
**Helen Fielding**, *Bridget Jones's Diary*, 1996

**2** '. . . How's your love life, anyway?'

Oh *God*. Why can't married people understand that it is no longer a polite question to ask? We wouldn't rush up to *them* and roar, 'How's your marriage going? Still having sex?'

Everyone knows that dating in your thirties is not the happy-go-lucky free-for-all it was when you were twenty-two . . .

Not being a natural liar, I ended up mumbling shamefacedly to Geoffrey, 'Fine,' at which point he boomed, 'So you *still* haven't got a feller!'
**Helen Fielding**, *Bridget Jones's Diary*, 1996

**3 Questions for the single man**

What if I never find the right person for me?
Would it help if I stuck my head out of my apartment window and screamed 'I'm desperate!'?
Why are women so impressed with guys who are gainfully employed?
What if I get rejected and I die from the humiliation?
What if I meet a woman who doesn't understand my deep need to watch hour after hour of professional sport on TV?
How come I can't have exactly what I want with no obligations?
What if the right person for me turns out to be someone I don't want?
**Matt Groening**, *Life in Hell*, 1992

**4 Questions for the single woman**

Does wondering if you're desperate mean you're desperate?
Could my answering machine be broken?
How could he back out when I had our whole lives planned out down to the last detail?
Even though he was negative, controlling, unsupportive, and abusive, why do I miss that darling man so much?

Can you ever feel enough self-doubt?
Why did that last stupid jerk I didn't really
like stop calling me?
**Matt Groening,** *Life in Hell,* 1992

**5** It's slim pickings out there. When you're
first single, you're so optimistic. At the
beginning you're like: I want to meet a guy
who's really smart, really sweet, really good-
looking, has a really great career . . .

Six months later, you're like: Lord – any
mammal with a day job!
**Carol Leifer**

# Sixties, The
*See also The Beatles; The Fifties; The Rolling Stones;
Satire.*

**1** If you can remember the Sixties, you
probably weren't there.
**Anon.**

**2** The hippies have usurped the
prerogatives of children – to dress up and be
irresponsible.
**Anon.,** quoted in *Atlantic Monthly,* 1967

**3** Sexual intercourse began
  In nineteen sixty-three
  (Which was rather late for me) –
  Between the end of the *Chatterley* ban
  And the Beatles' first LP.
**Philip Larkin,** 'Annus Mirabilis', *High Windows,* 1974

**4** Fashions changed, changed again,
changed faster and still faster: fashions in
politics, in political style, in causes, in
music, in popular culture, in myths, in
education, in beauty, in heroes and idols, in
attitudes, in responses, in work, in love and
friendship, in food, in newspapers, in
entertainment, in fashion. What had once
lasted a generation now lasted a year, what
had lasted a year lasted a month, a week, a
day.
**Bernard Levin,** *The Pendulum Years,* 1970

**5** It was a credulous age, perhaps the most
credulous ever, and the more rational, the
less gullible, the decade claimed to be, the
less rational, the more gullible, it showed
itself. Never was it easier to gain a
reputation as a seer, never was a following
so rapidly and readily acquired. Teachers,
prophets, sibyls, oracles, mystagogues,
avatars, haruspices and mullahs roamed the
land, gathering flocks about them as easily
as holy men in nineteenth-century Russia,
and any philosophy, from Zen Buddhism to
macrobiotics and from violence as an end in
itself to total inactivity as an end in itself,
could be sure of a respectful hearing and a
group of adherents, however temporary
their adherence might prove.
**Bernard Levin,** *The Pendulum Years,* 1970

**6** We began to realize that behind every
hip-head record company there lurks a
giant oil concern. You can't avoid it. Every
time you buy a record, you're offing a
whale.
**Michael O'Donoghue,** *Rolling Stone,* 1972

**7** They'd go up to a table and tell people,
'Hello, I'm your waitress. How's your energy
today? Our lunch special is the Gestalt Sushi
– we give you a live fish, and you take the
responsibility for killing it.'
**Robin Williams,** interview in *Playboy,* 1982

# Skiing
*See also Sport; Travel.*

**1** I went skiing last week and broke a leg.
Fortunately, it wasn't mine.
**Anon.**

**2** There are two main forms of this sport:
Alpine skiing and Nordic skiing. Alpine
skiing involves a mountain and a $5,000 to
$10,000 minimum investment, plus
$300,000 for the condo in Aspen and
however much you spend on drugs. It is a
sport only a handful of people ever master,
and those who do, do so at the expense of
other skills like talking and writing their
own name.
*National Lampoon,* 1979

**3** The sport of skiing consists of wearing
three thousand dollars' worth of clothes
and equipment and driving two hundred
miles in the snow in order to stand around
at a bar and get drunk.
**P. J. O'Rourke,** *Modern Manners,* 1983

# Sleep

*See also Bed; Dreams; Insomnia.*

**1** There's only one sure cure for snoring – insomnia.
**Anon.**

**2** Laugh and the world laughs with you, snore and you sleep alone.
**Anthony Burgess,** *Inside Mr Enderby*, 1968

**3** JERRY: You still using that old alarm clock?
ELAINE: Oh, no, no. I bought a new one today. It's got everything. If you oversleep more than ten minutes a hand comes out and slaps you in the face.
**Larry David and Jerry Seinfeld,** 'The Busboy', *Seinfeld*, NBC TV, 1991

**4** No civilized person goes to bed the same day he gets up.
**Richard Harding Davis,** 1864–1916, American war correspondent

**5** Late last night I slew my wife,
Stretched her on the parquet flooring;
I was loth to take her life,
But I *had* to stop her snoring!
**Harry Graham,** 'Necessity', *Ruthless Rhymes*, 1899

**6** The amount of sleep required by the average person is about five minutes more.
**Max Kauffmann**

**7** You can't sleep until noon with the proper élan unless you have some legitimate reason for staying up until three (parties don't count).
**Jean Kerr,** *Please Don't Eat the Daisies*, 1957

**8** I love sleep because it is both pleasant and safe to use. Pleasant because one is in the best possible company and safe because sleep is the consummate protection against the unseemliness that is the invariable consequence of being awake. What you don't know won't hurt you. Sleep is death without the responsibility.
**Fran Lebowitz,** *Metropolitan Life*, 1978

**9** 12.35 p.m. – The phone rings. I am not amused. This is not my favorite way to wake up. My favorite way to wake up is to have a certain French movie star whisper to me softly at two thirty in the afternoon that if I want to get to Sweden in time to pick up my Nobel Prize for Literature I had better ring for breakfast. This occurs rather less often than one might wish.
**Fran Lebowitz,** *Metropolitan Life*, 1978

**10** ERIC: You know, I heard something this morning that really opened my eyes.
ERNIE: What was it?  ·
ERIC: An alarm clock!
**Eric Morecambe and Ernie Wise,** *The Morecambe and Wise Joke Book*, 1979

**11** I did not sleep. I never do when I am over-happy, over-unhappy, or in bed with a strange man.
**Edna O'Brien,** *The Love Nest*, 1963

**12** You can hit my father over the head with a chair and he won't wake up, but my mother, all you have to do to my mother is cough somewhere in Siberia and she'll hear you.
**J. D. Salinger,** *The Catcher in the Rye*, 1951

**13** Early to rise, early to bed, makes a man healthy, wealthy and dead.
**James Thurber,** 'The Shrike and the Chipmunks', *Fables for Our Time*, 1951

**14** There ain't no way to find out why a snorer can't hear himself snore.
**Mark Twain,** *Tom Sawyer Abroad*, 1894

**15** My wife missed her nap today. Slept right through it.
**Henny Youngman**

# Small Towns

**1** His hometown is so small, the road map is actual size.
**Milton Berle**

**2** I did the traffic at a very, very small-town radio station. The whole report was one sentence: 'The light is green.'
**Jim Patterson**

**3** The town was so small, the all-night drugstore closed at noon.
**Jackie Vernon**

# Smells

*See also Perfume.*

**1** I did not realize what it had done to my breath – one doesn't with garlic – until this afternoon when I stood waiting for somebody to open a door for me and suddenly noticed that the varnish on the door was bubbling.

**Frank Muir**, *You Can't Have Your Kayak and Heat It*, 1973

# Smiles

*See also Happiness; Laughter; Teeth.*

**1** She gave me a smile I could feel in my hip pocket.

**Raymond Chandler**, *Farewell, My Lovely*, 1940

**2** 'But I should like to come,' Miss Spence protested, throwing a rapid Gioconda at him.

**Aldous Huxley**, *Mortal Coils*, 1922

**3** He smiled, bunching his fat cheeks like twin rolls of smooth pink toilet paper.

**Nathaniel West**, *Miss Lonelyhearts*, 1933

**4** What magic there is in a girl's smile. It is the raisin which, dropped in the yeast of male complacency, induces fermentation.

**P. G. Wodehouse**, *The Girl on the Boat*, 1922

# Smoking

*See also Drugs.*

**1** As ye smoke, so shall ye reek.

**Anon.**, *Reader's Digest*, 1949

**2** I read in the *Reader's Digest* that cigarettes are bad for you. So I had to give up reading the *Reader's Digest*.

**Anon.**

**3** Misery is being a smoker and being chased by a mugger who isn't.

**Anon.**

**4** Thank You For Holding Your Breath While I Smoke

**T-shirt**, Miami

**5** I quit smoking. I feel better, I smell better and it's safer to drink from old beer cans around the house.

**Roseanne Barr**

**6** People are so rude to smokers. You'd think they'd try to be nicer to people who are dying.

**Roseanne Barr**

**7** They smoke cigarettes professionally. The smoke is inhaled very sharply and the teeth are bared. Then the head turns to give you a profile and the smoke is exhaled slowly and deliberately and the grey jet stream becomes a beautiful blue cloud of smoke. What are they trying to tell us?

**Jeffrey Bernard**, *Spectator*, 1982

**8** I never smoked a cigarette until I was nine.

**W. C. Fields** (Attrib.)

**9** CHANDLER: This is just like my parents' divorce when I started smoking in the first place.
MONICA: Weren't you *nine*?
CHANDLER: I'm telling you something, you can't beat that first smoke after nap time.

**Shana Goldberg-Meehan & Scott Silveri**, 'The One with the Ski Trip', *Friends*, NBC, 1996

**10** Tobacco is a dirty weed. I like it,
It satisfies no normal need. I like it,
It makes you thin, it makes you lean,
It takes the hair right off your bean
It's the worst darn stuff I've ever seen.
I like it.

**Graham Lee Hemminger**, 'Tobacco', Penn State Froth, 1915

**11** I'm not really a heavy smoker any more. I get through only two lighters a day now.

**Bill Hicks**, American comedian

**12** Smoking is, if not my life, then at least my hobby. I love to smoke. Smoking is fun. Smoking is cool. Smoking is, as far as I am concerned, the entire point of being an adult.

**Fran Lebowitz**, *Social Studies*, 1981

**13** They say if you smoke you knock off ten years. But it's the last ten. What do you miss? The drooling years?

**John Mendoza**

**14** Smoking is very bad for you and should only be done because it looks so good. People who don't smoke have a terrible time finding something polite to do with their lips.

**P. J. O'Rourke**, *Modern Manners*, 1983

**15** I've been smoking for thirty years now and there's nothing wrong with my lung.

**Freddie Starr**, English comedian

**16** Usually we trust that nature has a master plan. But what was it she expected us to do with tobacco?
**Bill Vaughan**

**17** A cigarette is the perfect type of a perfect pleasure. It is exquisite and it leaves one unsatisfied.
**Oscar Wilde**, *The Picture of Dorian Gray*, 1891

**18** LADY BRACKNELL: . . . Do you smoke?
JACK: Well, yes, I must admit I smoke.
LADY BRACKNELL: I am glad to hear it. A man should always have an occupation of some kind. There are far too many idle men in London as it is.
**Oscar Wilde**, *The Importance of Being Earnest*, 1895

**19** Mr Howard Saxby, literary agent, was knitting a sock. He knitted a good deal, he would tell you if you asked him, to keep himself from smoking, adding that he also smoked a good deal to keep himself from knitting.
**P. G. Wodehouse**, *Cocktail Time*, 1958

# Sneezing

**1** Florence felt the swift on-coming of a sneeze. She fumbled in her bag for a handkerchief, and rattled richly among the nine coppers. Several violent explosions followed, and when the spasm subsided, she found her father spraying the air round him with his flask of disinfectant. 'Perhaps it would be wiser if you sat a little further off,' he said.
**E. F. Benson**, *Paying Guests*, 1929

# Snobbery

*See also Ancestors; Haughtiness; Inferiority; Society; Status.*

**1** FIRST LADY: Breeding isn't everything, is it?
SECOND LADY: No, but it's lots of fun.
**Joey Adams**

**2** Auntie Muriel is unambiguous about most things. Her few moments of hesitation have to do with the members of her own family. She isn't sure where they fit into the Great Chain of Being. She's quite certain of her own place, however. First comes God.
Then comes Auntie Muriel and the Queen, with Auntie Muriel having a slight edge.
**Margaret Atwood**, *Life Before Man*, 1979

**3** She [his aunt] was a bit of a social climber – although very much on the lower slopes. I was once on a tram with her going past the gas works in Wellington Road and she said, 'Alan, this is the biggest gas works in England. And I know the manager.'
**Alan Bennett**, *The South Bank Show*, London Weekend Television, 1984

**4** And there is . . . that rich man in Chelsea who is so snobbish that he will not even drive in the same car as his chauffeur.
**David Frost and Antony Jay**, *To England with Love*, 1967

**5** A certain amount of judicious snobbery is quite a good thing, besides being amusing.
**A. L. Rowse**, English historian

**6** He found it very difficult to admit that there were any Royalties whom he did not know personally. The nearest he ever came to it was in saying of the King of Saxony: 'I knew him very well – by sight.'
**Bertrand Russell**, *Portraits from Memory*, 1956

**7** I mustn't go on singling out names. One must not be a name dropper, as Her Majesty remarked to me yesterday.
**Norman St John-Stevas**, British politician, speech, 1979

**8** Laughter would be bereaved if snobbery died.
**Peter Ustinov**, 1955

# Soccer

*See also Sport.*

**1** They beat us five-nil – and we were lucky to score nil.
**Anon.**

**2** . . . he became, if not a master, then an aspiring student of the synonym. On his great days he could avoid using the precise word throughout the duration of a report. He was a man of his time: he never in his life referred to a match as a 'clash'; and only rarely as a 'match'; it was a 'derby', 'duel', 'contest', 'tourney', 'battle', 'renewal of hostilities', 'struggle' ('epic', or, at best, 'titanic'). It was almost unknown for one of his players to shoot or head a goal. They 'drove home', 'converted', 'nodded', 'equalized', 'netted', 'notched', 'reduced the leeway', 'increased their advantage', 'applied the finishing touch' or 'left the custodian helpless'.

**John Arlott**, 'Football Phrases from Regnar's Thesaurus', *Guardian*, 1972

**3** He had a special set of phrases for Christmas Day matches. 'The opposing leader set the sphere a-rolling (it was simply rolling in non-holiday matches) in a seasonable snowstorm.' Occasionally he would note that 'the holiday spirit was much in evidence', or in more extreme circumstances that 'a few spectators, alas, had celebrated not widely, but too well'.

If the referee seemed harsh on Rangers, 'the arbiter showed little seasonal good will towards the homesters': if he gave a penalty to the other side, 'the official proved a veritable Father Christmas to the visitors'. The scorer of a goal had 'earned his slice of chicken'.

**John Arlott**, 'Football Phrases from Regnar's Thesaurus', *Guardian*, 1972

**4** I went down to pass on some technical information to the team – like the fact that the game had started.

**Ron Atkinson**, Aston Villa's manager explaining why he had taken his seat at the touchline earlier than usual during a home defeat against Sheffield United

**5** When Charlie Cooke sold you a dummy, you had to pay to get back into the ground.

**Jim Baxter**, Scottish international on his team mate

**6** A million quid for Mark Hateley? But he can't even trap a dead rat!

**Stan Bowles**, fellow player

**7** Dutch goalkeepers are protected to a ridiculous extent. The only time they are in danger of physical contact is when they go into a red-light district.

**Brian Clough**, Nottingham Forest Manager, 1985

**8** Football hooligans? Well, there are the 92 club chairmen, for a start.

**Brian Clough**

**9** Who wants to be a football manager? Well, people like me who are too old to play, too poor to be a director and too much in love with the game to be an agent.

**Steve Coppell**, Crystal Palace Manager

**10** Last Saturday I watched a really cracking football match. One of those matches you walk home from thinking, 'Yes, that is what soccer is all about.' Fourteen fouls in the first ten minutes, fists flung, throats elbowed, eyes poked, shins hacked, shirts ripped, hair pulled, enough ballistic saliva to fill a trainer's bucket, and a richer variety of air-blueing oaths, I'll wager, than Mary Whitehouse has been able to net in a lifetime's trawling.

Utterly professional. Totally committed. Prodigiously physical. Impressively cynical. Above all, unstintingly competitive, and not a player on the field over twelve years old.

**Alan Coren**, *The Times*, 1995

**11** The centre forward said, 'It was an open goal – but I put it straight over the crossbar! I could kick myself!' And the manager said, 'I wouldn't bother, you'd probably miss!'

**David Frost**, TVam, 1984

**12** [Italian defender] Tardelli's been responsible for more scar tissue than the surgeons of Harefield hospital.

**Jimmy Greaves**, ITV World Cup Panel, 1982

**13** Football is an art more central to our culture than anything the Arts Council deigns to recognise.

**Germaine Greer**, *Independent*, 1996

**14** If soccer was an American soft-drink, it would be Diet Pepsi.

**Lewis Grizzard**

**15** I never went in for aerial challenges at Liverpool. You lose 150 brain cells every time you head a ball. I used to make Mark Lawrenson do all the heading. You have to delegate. It's a captain's prerogative.

**Alan Hansen**

**16** The natural state of the football fan is bitter disappointment, no matter what the score.

**Nick Hornby**, *Fever Pitch*, 1992

**17** The first half was the sort of thing you'd rather watch on Ceefax.

**Gary Lineker**, after watching Wimbledon play in 1993

**18** To say that these men paid their shillings to watch twenty-two hirelings kick a ball is merely to say that a violin is wood and catgut, that *Hamlet* is so much paper and ink. For a shilling the Bruddersford United AFC offered you Conflict and Art.
**J. B. Priestley**, *Good Companions*, 1929

**19** Ossie Ardiles was the difference. It was like trying to tackle dust.
**Joe Royle**, after his Oldham side was knocked out of the FA Cup by Tottenham in January 1988

**20** Look, if you're in the penalty area and aren't quite sure what to do with the ball, just stick it in the net and we'll discuss all your options afterwards.
**Bill Shankly**, soccer manager, to player (Attrib.)

**21** Some people think football is a matter of life and death . . . I can assure you it is much more serious than that.
**Bill Shankly**, Liverpool manager, 1973

**22** Maybe Napoleon was wrong when he said we were a nation of shopkeepers . . . Today England looked like a nation of goalkeepers . . .
**Tom Stoppard**, *Professional Foul*, BBC TV, 1977

**23** Football is all very well as a game for rough girls, but it is hardly suitable for delicate boys.
**Oscar Wilde** (Attrib.)

**24** I said, 'What is the matter with you Tom, what's the trouble?' He said, 'I've got a bad back,' so I told him, I said, 'There's no need to worry about that – our team's got two.'
**Robb Wilton**, BBC Light Programme, 1952

**25** The rules of soccer are simple. Basically it is this: if it moves, kick it. If it doesn't move, kick it until it does.
**Phil Woosnam**, on forming the North American Soccer League, 1974

## Socialism

*See also Communism; Equality; The Labour Party; Marxism; Trade Unions.*

**1** 'Rabbi, can one build socialism in one country?'
'Yes, my son, but one must live in another.'
**Anon.**, quoted in the *Spectator*, 1984

**2** HECKLER: What about the workers' wages?
CANDIDATE: When my party comes to power, workers' wages will be doubled!
HECKLER: And what about the whores and tarts who defile our streets?
CANDIDATE: My friend, when my party comes to power they will be driven underground.
HECKLER: There you go again. Favouring the bloody miners!
**Ian Aitken**, *Guardian*

**3** GEORGE: Fabled names in the annals of the New Left. All with monosyllabic names . . . Stan, Mike, Les, Norm. As if to have two syllables in one's name were an indication of social pretension.
**Alan Bennett**, *Getting On*, 1971

**4** The function of socialism is to raise suffering to a higher level.
**Norman Mailer**

**5** As far as Socialism means anything, it must be about the wider distribution of smoked salmon and caviar.
**Sir Richard Marsh**, former Labour Cabinet Minister, quoted in the *Observer*, 1976

**6** As with the Christian religion, the worst advertisement for Socialism is its adherents.
**George Orwell**, *The Road to Wigan Pier*, 1937

**7** The typical Socialist . . . a prim little man with a white-collar job, usually a secret teetotaller and often with vegetarian leanings.
**George Orwell**, *The Road to Wigan Pier*, 1937

**8** Once the government has embarked upon a course of making all things fair, where is it to stop? Will tall people have to walk around on their knees? Will fat people be strapped to helium balloons? Will attractive people be made to wear ridiculous haircuts?
**P. J. O'Rourke**, *The Enemies List*, 1996

**9** This list has been limited to members and cohorts of the Clinton administration, those simps and ninnies, lava-lamp liberals and condo pinks, spoiled twerps, wiffenpoofs, ratchet-jawed purveyors of monkey doodle and baked wind, piddlers upon merit, beggars at the door of accomplishment, thieves of livelihood,

envy-coddling tax lice applauding themselves for their magnanimity with the money of others, their nose in virtue's bum.
**P. J. O'Rourke**, *The Enemies List*, 1996

**10** We should have had socialism already, but for the socialists.
**George Bernard Shaw** (Attrib.)

**11** Many people consider the things which government does for them as social progress, but they consider the things government does for others as socialism.
**Earl Warren**, 1891–1974, American Chief Justice

**12** At one time Socialism might have been a good idea. Its inspiration, in those days, was generous and humane. Nowadays, it can appeal only to those whose social maladjustment might otherwise push them into the criminal classes, or whose intellectual inadequacies make them hungry for a dogmatic system in which they can hide their inability to think for themselves.
**Auberon Waugh**, *Spectator*, 1984

**13** We'll find it very difficult to explain to the voters that simply by taking over Marks & Spencer we can make it as efficient as the Co-op.
**Harold Wilson**, British Labour Prime Minister, 1973

# Society
*See also The Aristocracy; Parties.*

**1** High society is for those who have stopped working and no longer have anything important to do.
**Anon.**

**2** I sat next to the Duchess at tea;
   It was just as I feared it would be:
      Her rumblings abdominal
      Were truly phenomenal,
   And everyone thought it was me!
**Anon.**

**3** So You Want to Be a Social Climber?
Of all the occupations dealt with here, this is undoubtedly the easiest to crack. It is also, alas, the hardest to stomach – a fact that seems to have had surprisingly little effect upon the hordes that crowd the field.
**Fran Lebowitz**, *Metropolitan Life*, 1978

**4** Dear Miss Manners,
If you had a single piece of advice to offer a couple who want to break into society, what would it be?

Gentle Reader,
Don't bother.
**Judith Martin**, *Miss Manners' Guide to Excruciatingly Correct Behaviour*, 1982

**5** I love London Society! I think it has immensely improved. It is entirely composed now of beautiful idiots and brilliant lunatics. Just what Society should be.
**Oscar Wilde**, *An Ideal Husband*, 1895

# Sociology

**1 The Good Samaritan for Sociologists**
A man was attacked and left bleeding in a ditch. Two sociologists passed by and one said to the other, 'We must find the man who did this – he needs help.'
**Anon.**

**2** . . . the science with the greatest number of methods and the least results.
**J. H. Poincaré**, French scientist and mathematician

# Songs and Singers
*See also Folk Music; Jazz; Music and Musicians; Opera; Rock 'n' Roll; The Theatre.*

**1** Have you heard her sing? If it was a fight, they'd stop it!
**Jerry Dennis**

**2** Q: How many singers does it take to sing 'My Way'?
A: Apparently all of them.
**Jerry Dennis**

**3** I studied all the rhymes that all the lovers sing;
   Then just for you I wrote this little thing.
   Blah, blah, blah, blah moon,
   Blah, blah, blah above;
   Blah, blah, blah, blah croon,
   Blah, blah, blah, blah, love.
   Tra la la la, tra la la la la, merry month of May;
   Tra la la la, tra la la la la, 'neath the clouds of gray.
   Blah, blah, blah your hair,
   Blah, blah, blah your eyes;

Blah, blah, blah, blah care,
Blah, blah, blah, blah skies.
Tra la la, tra la la la, cottage for two,
Blah, blah, blah, blah, blah, darling with
    you.

**Ira Gershwin**, 'Blah, Blah, Blah', song from *Delicious*,
1931

**4** I can hold a note as long as the Chase
National Bank.

**Ethel Merman**, 1909–84, Broadway performer

**5** HOMER: Singing is the lowest form of
communication.

**Steve O'Donnell**, 'All Singing, All Dancing', *The
Simpsons*, Fox TV, 1998

**6** Once in every lifetime a really beautiful
song comes along . . . Until it does, I'd like
to do this one.

**Cliff Richard**, stage act, 1983

## Space

*See also The Future, Travel; The Universe.*

**1** A pair of Martians landed on a country
road in the middle of the night.
    'Where are we?' said one.
    'I think we're in a cemetery,' his
companion answered. 'Look at that
gravestone over there – that man lived to be
109.'
    'What was his name?'
    'Miles to Plymouth.'

**Anon.**

**2** Space . . . is big. Really big. You just won't
believe how vastly hugely mind-bogglingly
big it is. I mean, you may think it's a long
way down the road to the chemist, but
that's just peanuts to space.

**Douglas Adams**, *The Hitch Hiker's Guide to the Galaxy*,
1979

**3** You know something I could really do
without? The Space Shuttle. Why don't
those people go out and get real jobs? It's
the same shit over and over. They get
delayed, they blast off, they get in orbit,
something breaks, they fix it, the President
says hello, Mission Control wakes them up
with a song no one has listened to in twenty
years, the science experiment placed on
board by the third-graders of Frog Balls,
Tennessee, is a big success, and bla, bla, bla.

**George Carlin**, *Brain Droppings*, 1997

**4** Space isn't remote at all. It's only an
hour's drive away if your car could go
straight upwards.

**Sir Fred Hoyle**, *Observer*, 1979

**5** HOMER: Oh, my God! Space aliens! Don't
eat me, I have a wife and kids! Eat them!

**Ken Keeler, Dan Greaney and David S. Cohen**,
'Treehouse of Horror VII', *The Simpsons*, Fox TV, 1996

## Spain and the Spaniards

**1** ERNIE: Didn't you know any Spanish?
ERIC: I knew two words and they reckon
that's all you need to know for
honeymooning in Spain.
ERNIE: And what are they?
ERIC: 'Manana' – that means 'Tomorrow'.
And 'Pyjama' – that means 'Tonight'.

**Eric Morecambe and Ernie Wise**, *The Morecambe and
Wise Joke Book*, 1979

## Speakers and Speeches

*See also Audiences; Hecklers; Pronunciation; Voices.*

**1** Advice for speakers: if you don't know
what to talk about, talk about three
minutes.

**Anon.**

**2** He's a man who is never lost for a few
appropriated words.

**Anon.**

**3** Speeches are like steer horns – a point
here, a point there and a lot of bull in
between.

*Liberty*

**4** The whole art of a political speech is to
put *nothing* into it. It is much more difficult
than it sounds.

**Hilaire Belloc**, *A Conversation with an Angel and Other
Essays*, 1928

**5** I stand up when he nudges me. I sit down
when they pull my coat.

**Ernest Bevin**, Labour politician

**6** I do not object to people looking at their
watches when I am speaking – but I strongly
object when they start shaking them to
make certain they are still going.

**Lord Birkett**, MP and lawyer (Attrib.)

**7** Some microphones work great as long as
you blow into them. So you stand there like

an idiot blowing and saying, 'Are we on? Can you hear me?' Everyone admits they can hear you blowing. It's only when you speak the microphone goes dead.

**Erma Bombeck**, *If Life is a Bowl of Cherries – What am I Doing in the Pits?*, 1978

**8** A heavy and cautious responsibility of speech is the easiest thing in the world: anybody can do it. That is why so many tired, elderly and wealthy men go in for politics.

**G. K. Chesterton**, 1874–1936, English essayist and poet (Attrib.)

**9** Desperately accustomed as I am to public speaking . . .

**Noel Coward**, opening charity bazaar at Oxford (Attrib.)

**10** CHAIRMAN: Chauncey Depew can always produce a speech. All you have to do is give him his dinner and up comes his speech.
CHAUNCEY DEPEW: I only hope that it isn't true that if I give you my speech, up will come your dinner.

**Chauncey Depew**, nineteenth-century railroad executive and US Senator

**11** Spontaneous speeches are seldom worth the paper they are written on.

**Leslie Henson**, quoted in the *Observer*, 1943

**12** The toastmaster introduced the speaker with great fervor, stressing her years of faithful service to the club and eulogizing her ability and charm. Somewhat overwhelmed, the speaker faced the audience. 'After such an introduction,' she said disarmingly, 'I can hardly wait to hear what I've got to say.'

**Adnelle H. Heskett**, *Reader's Digest*

**13** I wasn't allowed to speak while my husband was alive, and since he's gone no one has been able to shut me up.

**Hedda Hopper**, *From Under Your Hat*, 1952

**14** Why don't th' feller who says, 'I'm not a speechmaker,' let it go at that instead o' givin' a demonstration.

**Kin Hubbard**, 1868–1930, American humorist

**15** Hubert, a speech does not need to be eternal to be immortal.

**Muriel Humphrey**, reminder to her husband, American Vice-President Hubert H. Humphrey (Attrib.)

**16** A toastmaster is a man who eats a meal he doesn't want so he can get up and tell a lot of stories he doesn't remember to people who've already heard them.

**George Jessel**, American comedian

**17** The human brain starts working the moment you are born and never stops until you stand up to speak in public.

**Sir George Jessel**, industrialist and Justice of the Peace

**18** When audiences come to see us authors lecture, it is largely in the hope that we'll be funnier to look at than to read.

**Sinclair Lewis**, 1885–1951, American novelist

**19** A speech is like a love affair. Any fool can start it, but to end it requires considerable skill.

**Lord Mancroft**, 1914–87, British politician

**20** A good off-the-cuff informal speech takes more preparation than a formal speech.

**Richard M. Nixon**, speech, New York City, 1955

**21** A speaker who does not strike oil in ten minutes should stop boring.

**Louis B. Nizer**, 1902–94, British-born American lawyer and author

**22** Speeches are like babies – easy to conceive but hard to deliver.

**Pat O'Malley**, actor

**23** A political speech should be like a woman's skirt – long enough to be respectable and short enough to be interesting.

**Adam Clayton Powell**, US Congressman

**24** He can take a batch of words and scramble them together and leaven them properly with a hunk of oratory and knock the White House doorknob right out of a candidate's hand.

**Will Rogers**, on William Jennings Bryan, American lawyer and politician

**25** I am the most spontaneous speaker in the world because every word, every gesture, and every retort has been carefully rehearsed.

**George Bernard Shaw**

**26** The last time I was in this hall was when my late beloved boss, Frank Knox, the Secretary of the Navy, spoke here, and it was

a better speech he gave than the one I'll be giving tonight. I know. I wrote them both.
**Adlai Stevenson**

**27** You spoke so flatteringly about me that for a moment I thought I was dead.
**Harry S. Truman**, reacting to praise from Israeli Ambassador Abba Eban

**28** It usually takes me more than three weeks to prepare a good impromptu speech.
**Mark Twain**

**29** I like the way you always manage to state the obvious with a sense of real discovery.
**Gore Vidal**, The Best Man, 1960

**30** I always said Little Truman [Capote] had a voice so high it could only be detected by a bat.
**Tennessee Williams** (Attrib.)

**31** It just shows, what any member of Parliament will tell you, that if you want real oratory, the preliminary noggin is essential. Unless pie-eyed, you cannot hope to grip.
**P. G. Wodehouse**, Right Ho, Jeeves, 1934

## Spectacles
*See also Eyes.*

**1** Glasses can alter your personality completely – if you empty them often enough.
**Jerry Dennis**

**2** Men seldom make passes
  At girls who wear glasses.
**Dorothy Parker**, 'News Item', 1927

## Spiritualism
*See also Belief; The Occult.*

**1** My grandmother was a medium. At least that's what it said on her knickers.
**Anon.**

**2** It's not hard contacting the dead. The problem is getting through to the living!
**Sally Poplin**

## Spoonerisms

**1** Kinquering Congs their titles take.

You have deliberately tasted two worms and you can leave Oxford by the town drain.

Yes, indeed; the Lord is a shoving leopard.

We all know what it is to have a half-warmed fish within us.
**Revd W. A. Spooner**, Warden of New College, Oxford (mostly apocryphal)

## Sport
*See also Cricket; Soccer; Tennis.*

**1** If at first you don't succeed, then maybe skydiving isn't for you.
**Anon.**

**2** . . . we've just heard that Belgium's tug of war team have been disqualified for pushing.
**Stuart Hall**, BBC Radio 5 Live, 2000

**3** In his quieter moments, he sounds as if his trousers are on fire.
**Clive James**, on motor racing commentator Murray Walker

**4** When it comes to sports I am not particularly interested. Generally speaking, I look upon them as dangerous and tiring activities performed by people with whom I share nothing except the right to trial by jury.
**Fran Lebowitz**, Metropolitan Life, 1978

**5** I hate sports as rabidly as a person who likes sports hates common sense.
**H. L. Mencken**

**6** ERNIE: Excuse me, won't you – I'm a little stiff from badminton.
ERIC: It doesn't matter where you're from.
**Eric Morecambe and Ernie Wise**, The Morecambe and Wise Joke Book, 1979

**7** Serious sport has nothing to do with fair play. It is bound up with hatred, jealousy, boastfulness, disregard of all rules and sadistic pleasure in witnessing violence: in other words it is war minus the shooting.
**George Orwell**, 'The Sporting Spirit', 1945

**8** My question about women's gymnastics is simple. Are we not supposed to be looking at their little rear ends while they're jumping around all over the place? Because I think that's pretty much all I've been doing, and I don't know if it's wrong. I mean, if it's wrong, I'll stop, but no one's ever said anything about it. The announcer never goes, 'In judging this event they throw out the high score, the low score, and stop staring at their little rear ends.'

**Jerry Seinfeld**, *SeinLanguage*, 1993

**9** They thought lacrosse was what you find in la church.

**Robin Williams**, interview in *Playboy*, 1982

# Squalor

*See also Cleanliness; Fastidiousness.*

**1** BLACKADDER: . . . I want you to give the palace a good clean. It's so dirty, it would be unacceptable to a dungbeetle that had lost interest in its career and really let itself go.

**Richard Curtis and Ben Elton**, 'Sense and Senility', *Blackadder the Third*, BBC TV, 1987

**2** There's a HAIR in My Dirt!

**Gary Larson**, title of story about a worm, 1998

# Statistics

*See also Mathematics.*

**1** There are roughly three million people in Wales. It may be estimated that 100 of them have no legs, and another 1,000 of them have only one leg. The remaining 2,998,900 persons have two legs. This makes a total in Wales of 5,998,800 legs shared among all the inhabitants – an average of 1.9996 legs each. Thus, nearly everyone in Wales (99.96%) has more than the average number of legs.

**Robert Adams**, Fellow, Royal Statistical Society, *Daily Telegraph*, 1991

**2** Say you were standing with one foot in the oven and one foot in an ice bucket. According to the percentage people, you should be perfectly comfortable.

**Bobby Bragan**, manager of the Milwaukee Braves

**3** There are three kinds of lies: lies, damned lies and statistics.

**Benjamin Disraeli**, quoted in Mark Twain's *Autobiography*, 1924

**4** 42.7% of all statistics are made up on the spot.

**Steven Wright**

# Status

*See also Class; Snobbery.*

**1** This is my executive suite and this is my executive vice-president, Ralph Anderson, and my executive secretary, Adele Eades, and my executive desk and my executive carpet and my executive wastebasket, and my executive ashtray and my executive pen set and my . . .

**Henry Martin**, cartoon in the *New Yorker*

# Stinginess

*See also Budgets; Economy; Selfishness.*

**1** When it comes to paying, he's the first to put his hand in his pocket. And leave it there.

**Anon.**

**2** ROBBER: Don't make a move, this is a stick-up!
BENNY: What?
ROBBER: You heard me.
BENNY: Mister . . . Mister, put down that gun.
ROBBER: Shut up . . . now, come on . . . your money or your life . . . [*Long pause*] . . . Look bud, I said, 'Your money or your life.'
BENNY: I'm thinking it over!

**Jack Benny**, *The Jack Benny Show*, NBC Radio, 1948

**3** LENNIE: Oh, come on, Fletch. You are mean.
FLETCHER: No, I'm not. Thrifty, perhaps. Frugal.
LENNIE: He unwraps Bounty bars under water so I can't hear he's got one.

**Dick Clement and Ian La Frenais**, 'Poetic Justice', *Porridge*, BBC TV

**4** They asked Jack Benny if he would do something for the Actor's Orphanage – so he shot both his parents and moved in.

**Bob Hope**

**5** My father refused to spend money on me as a kid. One time I broke my arm playing football and my father tried to get a free X-

ray by taking me down to the airport and making me lie down with the luggage.
**Glenn Super**

**6** My Uncle Tom has a peculiarity I've noticed in other very oofy men. Nick him for the paltriest sum, and he lets out a squawk you can hear at Land's End. He has the stuff in gobs, but he hates giving it up.
**P. G. Wodehouse**, *Right Ho, Jeeves*, 1934

## Stock Market
*See also Economics; Money; Wealth.*

**1** A stockbroker is a man who is smart enough to tell you what stocks to buy, and too smart to buy them himself.
**Max Kauffmann**

**2** Rule 1: Don't panic
Rule 2: Panic first.
**Walter Russell Mead**, economist, *Esquire Magazine*, October 1988

**3** Chief executives, who themselves own few shares of their companies, have no more feeling for the average stockholder than they do for baboons in Africa.
**T. Boone Pickens**, *Harvard Business Review*, 1986

## Strength
*See also The Body; Exercise.*

**1** I can lick my weight in wildflowers.
**W. C. Fields** (Attrib.)

## Stupidity
*See also Ignorance; Insults.*

**1** I Put the 'M' in 'Stupid.'
**Sign at WWF event**, 2000

**2** GEORGE: Gracie, let me ask you something. Did the nurse ever happen to drop you on your head when you were a baby?
GRACIE: Oh, no, we couldn't afford a nurse, my mother had to do it.
GEORGE: You had a smart mother.
GRACIE: Smartness runs in my family. When I went to school I was so smart my teacher was in my class for five years.
**George Burns and Gracie Allen**, stage routine, 1920s

**3** FAITH: Lisa, I'm Faith Crowley, Patriotism Editor of Reading Digest.
HOMER: Oh, I love your magazine. My favorite section is 'How to Increase Your Word Power.' That thing is really, really, really . . . good.
**George Meyer**, 'Mr Lisa Goes to Washington', *The Simpsons*, Fox TV, 1991

**4** GROUCHO MARX: . . . you've got the brain of a four-year-old boy, and I bet he was glad to get rid of it.
**S. J. Perelman and others**, *Horsefeathers*, screenplay, 1932

**5** . . . she does not understand the concept of Roman numerals. She thought we just fought World War Eleven.
**Joan Rivers**, *An Audience with Joan Rivers*, London Weekend Television, 1984

**6** James's uncle had just about enough brain to make a jay-bird fly crooked.
**P. G. Wodehouse**, 'The Man Upstairs', 1914

**7** Veronica Wedge was a girl of a radiant blonde loveliness. Nature had not given her more than about as much brain as would fit comfortably into an aspirin bottle, feeling no doubt that it was better not to overdo the thing, but apart from that she had everything.
**P. G. Wodehouse**, *Galahad at Blandings*, 1965

**8** Our village idiot bought himself a pet zebra. Named it 'Spot.'
**Henny Youngman**

## Style
*See also Clothes; Fashion; Looks; Taste.*

**1** Style is knowing who you are, what you want to say, and not giving a damn.
**Gore Vidal**, *Daily Express*, 1973

**2** In matters of grave importance, style, not sincerity, is the vital thing.
**Oscar Wilde**, *The Importance of Being Earnest*, 1895

## Suburbs, The
*See also Neighbours.*

**1** With four walk-in closets to walk in,
Three bushes, two shrubs, and one tree,
The suburbs are good for the children,

But no place for grown-ups to be.
**Judith Viorst**, *It's Hard to be Hip over Thirty . . .* , 1968

# Success

*See also Achievement; Failure.*

**1** Behind every successful man there stands an amazed woman.
**Anon.**

**2** If at first you don't succeed, destroy all the evidence that you tried.
**Anon.**

**3** Success is all a matter of luck. Ask any failure.
**Anon.**

**4** The penalty of success is to be bored by the people who used to snub you.
**Nancy Astor**, 1879–1964, British politician

**5** I don't think the state does enough for artists and writers generally in the way of subsidy and tax relief and so on. I mean, as an artist and a writer, I have to be surrounded by beautiful things and beautiful people. And beautiful people cost money.
**Alan Bennett**, 'The Lonely Pursuit', *On the Margin*, BBC TV, 1966

**6** It is difficult to make a reputation, but it is even more difficult seriously to mar a reputation once properly made – so faithful is the public.
**Arnold Bennett**, 1867–1931, English novelist

**7** Success is the one unpardonable sin against our fellows.
**Ambrose Bierce**

**8** If at first you don't succeed, try, try again. Then quit. No use being a damn fool about it.
**W. C. Fields** (Attrib.)

**9** Gold no longer pretended to understand the nature of success. Instead, he pretended not to. He knew the components that were necessary: none.
  Or maybe one: dumb luck.
**Joseph Heller**, *Good as Gold*, 1979

**10** There's no secret about success. Did you ever know a successful man that didn't tell you all about it.
**Kin Hubbard**, *Abe Martin's Primer*, 1914

**11** Nothing succeeds like reputation.
**John Huston**, 1906–87, American film director

**12** Success didn't spoil me; I've always been insufferable.
**Fran Lebowitz**

**13** The worst part of having success is to try finding someone who is happy for you.
**Bette Midler** (Attrib.)

**14** You wonder how they do it and you
    look to see the knack,
  You watch the foot in action, or the
    shoulder, or the back,
  But when you spot the answer where the
    higher glamours lurk,
  You'll find in moving higher up the
    laurel covered spire,
  That the most of it is practice and the
    rest of it is work.
**Grantland Rice**, American sportswriter, *How To Be a Champion*

**15** The secret of success is to offend the greatest number of people.
**George Bernard Shaw** (Attrib.)

**16** It is fatal to be appreciated in one's own time.
**Osbert Sitwell**, quoted in the *Observer*, 1924

**17** All you need in this life is ignorance and confidence, and then success is sure.
**Mark Twain**, letter, 1887

**18** Failure is very difficult for a writer to bear, but very few can manage the shock of early success.
**Maurice Valency**, 1903–96, playwright and translator

**19** I couldn't wait for success – so I went ahead without it.
**Jonathan Winters**

**20** The usual drawback to success is that it annoys one's friends so.
**P. G. Wodehouse**, 'The Man Upstairs', 1914

# Suicide

*See also Death; Depression and Despair.*

**1** I was suicidal as a matter of fact and would have killed myself. But I was in

analysis with a strict Freudian, and if you kill yourself, they make you pay for the sessions you miss.
**Woody Allen**, *Annie Hall*, screenplay, 1977

**2** Without the possibility of suicide, I would have killed myself long ago.
**F. M. Cioran**, philosopher, 1989

**3** There are many who dare not kill themselves for fear of what the neighbours will say.
**Cyril Connolly**, *The Unquiet Grave*, 1944

**4** Cliffy the Clown says: You can help solve the OVERPOPULATION PROBLEM this quick, easy way! THIS YEAR, WHY NOT COMMIT SUICIDE!? . . . just leave a note telling your loved ones that you did it to help stave off worldwide famine and they will respect and admire you for your courage . . .
**Robert Crumb**, *Zap: The Original Zap Comix*, No. 6, 1973

**5** The great thing about suicide is that it's not one of those things you have to do now or you lose your chance. I mean, you can always do it *later*.
**Harvey Fierstein**, quoted in *New York* magazine, 1983

**6** . . . suicide is our way of saying to God, 'You can't fire me. I quit.'
**Bill Maher**

**7** Suicide is belated acquiescence in the opinion of one's wife's relatives.
**H. L. Mencken**, *A Mencken Chrestomathy*, 1949

**8** I know a hundred ways to die.
I've often thought I'd try one:
Lie down beneath a motor truck
Some day when standing by one.
Or throw myself from off a bridge
Except such things must be
So hard upon the scavengers
And men that clean the sea.
I know some poison I could drink,
I've often thought I'd taste it.
But mother bought it for the sink,
And drinking it would waste it.
**Edna St Vincent Millay**, *From a Very Little Sphinx*, 1929

**9** The thought of suicide is a great consolation: by means of it one gets successfully through many a bad night.
**Friedrich Wilhelm Nietzsche**, *Beyond Good and Evil*, 1886

**10** Guns are always the best method for a private suicide. They are more stylish looking than single-edged razor blades and natural gas has gotten so expensive. Drugs are too chancy. You might miscalculate the dosage and just have a good time.
**P. J. O'Rourke**, *Modern Manners*, 1983

**11** Razors pain you;
Rivers are damp;
Acids stain you;
And drugs cause cramp.
Guns aren't lawful;
Nooses give;
Gas smells awful;
You might as well live.
**Dorothy Parker**, 'Resumé', *Enough Rope*, 1926

# Superstition

*See also Astrology; The Occult.*

**1** DUD: It's very unlucky to put the sugar in before the milk, didn't you know that? . . . it has terrible effects on your life . . . My Aunt Dolly put the sugar in before the milk one day and over the next forty years she lost all her teeth.
**Peter Cook and Dudley Moore**, *The Dagenham Dialogues*, 1971

# Surprise

**1** . . . Aunt Agatha, whose demeanour was now rather like that of one who, picking daisies on the railway, has just caught the down express in the small of the back.
**P. G. Wodehouse**, 'Aunt Agatha Takes the Count', *The Inimitable Jeeves*, 1923

**2** I don't know if you have ever leaped between the sheets, all ready for a spot of sleep, and received an unforeseen lizard up the left pyjama leg? It's an experience which puts its stamp on a man.
**P. G. Wodehouse**, *Thank You, Jeeves*, 1934

# Survival

**1** He had decided to live forever or die in the attempt, and his only mission each time he went up was to come down alive.
**Joseph Heller**, *Catch-22*, 1961

# Swearing

*See also The English Language; Language; Obscenity.*

**1** INTERVIEWER: You've been accused of vulgarity.
BROOKS: Bullshit!
**Mel Brooks**, interview in *Playboy*, 1975

**2** *Madame Bovary* is the sexiest book imaginable. The woman's virtually a nymphomaniac but you won't find a vulgar word in the entire thing.
**Noel Coward** (Attrib.)

**3** Swearing was invented as a compromise between running away and fighting.
**Finley Peter Dunne**, American journalist

**4** *Heck on Earth.* Heck is a place where God sends people when they say things like 'Aw, shoot' instead of 'shit'. Visionaries see it as a warm cloakroom, or perhaps a bus terminal at 3:00 a.m. in August.
**Michael McCormick, P. J. O'Rourke and Michael Civitello**, 'Sin Sundries', *National Lampoon*, 1981

# Sweden and the Swedes

*See also Europe and the EEC.*

**1** *Racial characteristics*: tedious, clean-living boy scout types, strangers to graffiti and littering but who are possessed of an odd suicidal mania. Speculation is that they're slowly boring themselves to death. This is certainly the case if their cars and movies are any indication.
**P. J. O'Rourke**, 'Foreigners Around the World', *National Lampoon*, 1976

**2** First impressions of Stockholm Paradise, second Limbo. Girls very pretty and not disfigured by paint and hairdressing. All look sexually and socially satisfied.
**Evelyn Waugh**, *Diary*, 1947

# Swimming

*See also The Sea; Sport.*

**1** They say that swimming is great exercise. Have you ever seen a whale?
**Milton Berle**

**2** GREENSLADE: Ten miles he swam – the last three were agony.

SEAGOON: They were over land. Finally I fell in a heap on the ground. I've no idea who left it there.
**Spike Milligan**, *The Goon Show*, 1954

# Switzerland and the Swiss

*See also Europe and the EEC.*

**1** The Swiss are not a people so much as a neat clean quite solvent business.
**William Faulkner**, *Intruder in the Dust*, 1948

**2** In Switzerland they had brotherly love, five hundred years of democracy and peace, and what did they produce? The cuckoo clock.
**Graham Greene and Orson Welles**, *The Third Man*, screenplay, 1949

**3** *Racial characteristics*: mountain Jews in whose icy clutches lay the fruits of grave misdeeds committed in every clime.
**P. J. O'Rourke**, 'Foreigners Around the World', *National Lampoon*, 1976

**4** The only nation I've ever been tempted to feel really racist about are the Swiss – a whole country of phobic handwashers living in a giant Barclays Bank.
**Jonathan Raban**, *Arabia through the Looking Glass*, 1979

**5** . . . the train passed fruit farms and clean villages and Swiss cycling in kerchiefs, calendar scenes that you admire for a moment before feeling an urge to move on to a new month.
**Paul Theroux**, *The Great Railway Bazaar*, 1975

**6** Switzerland is simply a large, humpy, solid rock, with a thin skin of grass stretched over it.
**Mark Twain**, 'A Tramp Abroad', 1880

**7** I don't like Switzerland; it has produced nothing but theologians and waiters.
**Oscar Wilde**, during his exile in Europe (Attrib.)

# Sympathy

*See also Adversity.*

**1** Sympathy is a virtue unknown in nature.
**Paul Eipper**, 1891–1964, German photographer and zoologist

**2** To be sympathetic without discrimination is so very debilitating.
**Ronald Firbank**, *Vainglory*, 1915

**3** When you are in trouble people who call to sympathize are really looking for the particulars.
**Edgar Watson Howe**, *Country Town Sayings*, 1911

# Talent

*See also Genius.*

**1** I think this is the most extraordinary collection of talent, of human knowledge, that has ever been gathered together at the White House – with the possible exception of when Thomas Jefferson dined alone.
**John F. Kennedy,** at White House dinner honouring Nobel Prize winners, 1962

# Taste

*See also Appearance; Fashion; Looks; Style.*

**1** Good taste is better than bad taste, but bad taste is better than no taste.
**Arnold Bennett,** quoted in the *Observer*, 1930

**2** Your right to wear a mint-green polyester leisure suit ends where it meets my eye.
**Fran Lebowitz,** *Metropolitan Life,* 1978

**3** MRS ALLONBY: The Ideal Man . . . should never run down other pretty women. That would show he had no taste or make one suspect that he had too much.
**Oscar Wilde,** *A Woman of No Importance,* 1893

# Tattoos

*See also The Body.*

**1** On the chest of a barmaid in Sale
  Were tattooed the prices of ale,
  And on her behind,
  For the sake of the blind,
  Was the same information in Braille.
**Anon.**

**2** I attribute my whole success in life to a rigid observance of the fundamental rule – never have yourself tattooed with any woman's name, not even her initials.
**P. G. Wodehouse,** *French Leave,* 1956

# Taxation

*See also Government; Money.*

**1** Ask not what your country can do for you, but how much it's going to cost you for them to do it.
**Anon.**

**2** I believe we should all pay our tax bill with a smile. I tried – but they wanted cash.
**Anon.**

**3** TAXMAN: The position is that if I don't have one thousand pounds from you soon, you're going to jail.
BUSINESSMAN: Now you're talking. Here's one thousand pounds in used notes.
TAXMAN: Let me give you a receipt.
BUSINESSMAN: What, a thousand nicker in cash and you're going to put it through the books?
*Guardian*

**4** Why does a slight tax increase cost you two hundred dollars and a substantial tax cut save you thirty cents?
**Peg Bracken**, *I Didn't Come Here to Argue*

**5** Any reasonable system of taxation should be based on the slogan of 'Soak the Rich'.
**Heywood Broun**, 1888–1939, American journalist

**6** I have always paid income tax. I object only when it reaches a stage when I am threatened with having nothing left for my old age – which is due to start next Tuesday or Wednesday.
**Noel Coward** (Attrib.)

**7** The rich aren't like us; they pay less taxes.
**Peter De Vries**, 1910–93, American novelist

**8** I used to say I was making a speech on the Senate floor and I said, 'Now, gentlemen, let me tax your memories,' and Kennedy jumped up and said, 'Why haven't we thought of that before.'
**Bob Dole**, quoted in *GQ*, 1999

**9** It's true that nothing is certain except death and taxes. Sometimes I wish they came in that order.
**Sam Levenson**, American humorous writer

**10** The taxpayer – that's someone who works for the federal government but doesn't have to take the civil servant examination.
**Ronald Reagan**, Republican President, 1981–9

**11** The income tax has made more liars out of the American people than golf has.
**Will Rogers** (Attrib.)

**12** Taxes, after all, are the dues that we pay for the privileges of membership in an organized society.
**Franklin D. Roosevelt**, speech, Worcester, Massachusetts, 1936

**13** Income tax returns are the most imaginative fiction being written today.
**Herman Wouk**, American novelist

**14** The income tax people are very nice. They're letting me keep my own mother.
**Henny Youngman**

# Teachers and Teaching

*See also Education; School; Sex Education; University.*

**1** For every person wishing to teach, there are thirty not wanting to be taught.
**Anon.**

**2** A teacher affects eternity; he can never tell where his influence stops.
**Henry Adams**, *The Education of Henry Adams*, 1907

**3** Teachers are overworked and underpaid. True, it is an exacting and exhausting business, this damming up the flood of human potentialities.
**George B. Leonard**, *Education and Ecstasy*, 1969

**4** The decent docent doesn't doze:
 He teaches standing on his toes.
 His student dassn't doze – and does,
 And that's what teaching is and was.
**David McCord**, 'History of Education'

**5** The teacher should never lose his temper in the presence of the class. If a man, he may take refuge in profane soliloquies; if a woman, she may follow the example of one sweet-faced and apparently tranquil girl – go out in the yard and gnaw a post.
**William Lyon Phelps**, 1865–1943, educator and journalist, *Teaching in School and College*

**6** He who can, does. He who cannot, teaches.
**George Bernard Shaw**, *Maxims for Revolutionists*, 1903

**7** . . . everybody who is incapable of learning has taken to teaching – that is really what our enthusiasm for education has come to.
**Oscar Wilde**, 'The Decay of Lying', 1889

# Technology

*See also Computers; Electricity; Inventions; Modern Life; Video Games.*

**1** Sattinger's Law: It works better if you plug it in.

**Arthur Bloch,** *Murphy's Law and Other Reasons Why Things Go Wrong,* 1977

**2** Technology has brought meaning to the lives of many technicians.

**Ed Bluestone,** 'Maxims', *The National Lampoon Encyclopedia of Humor,* 1973

**3** Modern technology
owes ecology
an apology.

**Alan M. Eddison,** *Worse Verse,* 1969

**4** Our toaster works on either AC or DC, but not on bread. It has two settings – too soon or too late.

**Sam Levenson,** *In One Era and Out the Other*

**5** If I had a vibrating pager, I would get a mobile phone and call myself. Stand around hitting redial all day.

**Dan Wilson**

# Teenagers

*See also Adolescence; Childhood; Children; Parents; Youth.*

**1** Akbar and Jeff's Piercing Hut
Where Yesterday's Psychopathology Becomes Today's Middle-Class Youth-Culture Affectation
It's Paintastic! It's Disfigure-iffic!
You must be at least 18 years old, not exactly bright, sexually alienated, tormented by unconscious guilt feelings, reconciled to diminished employment opportunities, have little or no sense of the future, and bring cash in hand.

**Matt Groening,** *Life in Hell,* 1992

**2** Cute teenagers exist only on television, I suspect. I know there are none in my neighborhood.

**Robert MacKenzie,** *TV Guide,* 1979

**3** Teenagers are God's punishment for having sex.

**Patrick Murray**

**4** The best way to keep children home is to

make the home atmosphere pleasant and let the air out of the tires.

**Dorothy Parker** (Attrib.)

# Teeth

*See also Smiles.*

**1** POLLY: Why is it only teeth that decay . . . You don't always have to go to the doctor's to have holes in your arms stopped up, do you? It's a flaw in the design.

**Alan Bennett,** *Getting On,* 1971

**2** . . . that dear little baby tooth, with a small tag attached, reading: 'The first bicuspid that little Willie lost. Extracted from Daddy's wrist on April 5, 1887.'

**W. C. Fields,** *Let's Look at the Record,* 1939

**3** I taste the flavor of your thumbs
While you massage my flabby gums.

**Ernest A. Hooton,** 'Ode to a Dental Hygienist'

**4** I've got a tooth that's driving me to extraction.

**Charlie McCarthy (Edgar Bergen),** *The Chase and Sanborn Hour,* NBC Radio, 1937

**5** All joys I bless, but I confess
There is one greatest thrill:
What the dentist does when he stops the buzz
And puts away the drill.

**Christopher Morley,** 'Song in a Dentist's Chair'

**6** He had one particular weakness: he had faced death in many forms but he had never faced a dentist. The thought of dentists gave him just the same sick horror as the thought of Socialism.

**H. G. Wells,** *Bealby,* 1915

# Telephones

*See also Communication.*

**1** A man telephoned a friend at two o'clock in the morning. 'I do hope I haven't disturbed you,' he said cheerily.
  'Oh, no,' the friend replied, 'that's quite all right. I had to get up to answer the telephone anyway.'

**Anon.**

**2** Incontinence Hotline! Can you hold, please!

**Anon.**

**3** I rang up my local swimming pool and I said, 'Is that the local swimming pool?' And they said, 'It depends where you're calling from.'
**Anon.**

**4** You have reached the —— family. What you hear is the barking of our killer Doberman pinscher, Wolf. Please leave a message after the tone.
**Answering machine message in California,** quoted in *Life,* January 1984

**5** I answer the phone 'Dickerson here' because I'm Dickerson and I'm here. Now what the hell do you want, Martha?
**Charles Barsotti,** *Kings Don't Carry Money,* cartoon, 1981

**6** The marvellous thing about mobile phones is that, wherever you are, whatever you are doing, you can keep them switched off so no one will bother you.
**Guy Browning,** *Guardian Weekend,* 1995

**7** Hello, is this someone with good news or money? No? Goodbye!
**Herb Gardner,** *A Thousand Clowns,* 1965

**8** They [wives] are people who think when the telephone bell rings, it is against the law not to answer it.
**Ring Lardner,** *Say It with Oil,* 1923

**9** There's a new telephone service that lets you test your IQ over the phone. It costs $3.95 a minute. If you make the call at all, you're a moron. If you're on the line for three minutes, you're a complete idiot.
**Jay Leno,** *The Tonight Show*

**10** ERIC: Hey, answer the phone! Answer the phone!
ERNIE: But it's not ringing!
ERIC: Why leave everything till the last minute?
**Eric Morecambe and Ernie Wise,** *The Morecambe and Wise Joke Book,* 1979

**11** Public telephones in Europe are like our pinball machines. They are primarily a form of entertainment and a test of skill rather than a means of communication.
**Miss Piggy,** *Miss Piggy's Guide to Life (As Told to Henry Beard),* 1981

**12** Well, if I called the wrong number, why did you answer the phone?
**James Thurber,** cartoon in the *New Yorker*

**13** I read that 28 per cent of Americans think they can communicate with the dead. The other 72 per cent switched back to AT&T.
**Bob Zany**

# Television

*See also Show Business; Television – Commercials; Television – Game Shows; Television – Shows.*

**1** Dear Ann,
I have a problem. I have two brothers. One brother is in television. The other was put to death in the electric chair for murder. My mother died from insanity when I was three years old. My sisters are prostitutes and my father sells drugs to high school students. Recently I met a girl who was just released from a reformatory where she had served time for smothering her illegitimate child to death. I want to marry her.
My problem is this: If I marry this girl, should I tell her about my brother who works in television?
**Anon.**

**2** 'Guests Who Kill Talk Show Hosts' – on the last Geraldo.
**Anon.**

**3** Television: an electric device which, when turned off, stimulates conversation.
**Anon.**

**4** Photography is going to marry Miss Wireless, and heaven help everybody when they get married. Life will be very complicated.
**Marcus Adams,** Society photographer, quoted in the *Observer,* 1925

**5** Television is the first truly democratic culture – the first culture available to everybody and entirely governed by what the people want. The most terrifying thing is what the people do want.
**Clive Barnes,** *The New York Times,* 1969

**6** . . . I found myself caught up in a fascinating installment of Leeza Gibbons' talk show, *Leeza.* The theme of the show

was: 'Women Who Cannot Correctly Spell Their Own Names.'
**Dave Barry**, *Comic Relief*, 2000

**7** I've been in this business a long time. I was on television when it was radio. When I started people thought television was impossible, and a lot of them still do.
**Milton Berle**, *Variety*, 1978

**8** This guy just invented a microwave television set. He can watch Sixty Minutes in twelve seconds.
**Milton Berle**

**9** It occurs to me that it takes a rather special sort of person to follow soaps. You have to be highly intelligent (to understand them) and as thick as a brick (to want to).
**Alan Coren**, *Mail on Sunday*, 1986

**10** Television is more interesting than people. If it were not, we should have people standing in the corners of our rooms.
**Alan Coren**, *The Times*

**11** Time has convinced me of one thing. Television is for appearing on, not looking at.
**Noel Coward** (Attrib.)

**12** It is a medium of entertainment which permits millions of people to listen to the same joke at the same time, and yet remain lonesome.
**T. S. Eliot**, quoted in the *New York Post*, 1963

**13** It's amazing how many people see you on TV. I did my first television show a month ago, and the next day five million television sets were sold. The people who couldn't sell theirs threw them away.
**Bob Hope**, 1950

**14** All you have to do on television is be yourself, provided, that is, that you have a self to be.
**Clive James**, *Observer*, 1981

**15** If God had not meant everyone to be in bed by ten-thirty, He would never have provided the ten o'clock newscast.
**Garrison Keillor**, *Lake Wobegon Days*, 1984

**16** My favourite (show) title of all time is,

'You Have Naked Pictures of Me and I Want Them Back Now.'
**Ricki Lake**, *Independent on Sunday*, 1996

**17** There you have it, ladies and gentlemen: television – the next best thing to real entertainment.
**David Letterman**, quoted in *M Magazine*, 1992

**18** BART: Dad, when did you record an album?
HOMER: I'm surprised you don't remember, son. It was only eight years ago.
BART: Dad, thanks to television, I can't remember what happened eight minutes ago.
**Jeff Martin**, 'Homer's Barbershop Quartet', *The Simpsons*, Fox TV, 1993

**19** De Gaulle is one of the few politicians who has grasped the point that the balance of advantage is always with the man being interviewed if he cares to seize it. I saw him on French television being asked why he had delayed releasing the Ben Barka story till after the presidential election. Instead of getting hot under the collar, sending for the French equivalent of Sir Hugh Greene, transferring his favours to Radio Monte Carlo, or otherwise manifesting his displeasure, he just hung his old, battered head sheepishly, and muttered in a woeful, strangled voice: '*C'était mon inexpérience*!'
**Malcolm Muggeridge**, letter to *The Times*, 1966

**20** I have had my television aerials removed. It's the moral equivalent of a prostate operation.
**Malcolm Muggeridge** (Attrib.)

**21** Television is to news what bumper stickers are to philosophy.
**Richard Nixon**

**22** Television has made dictatorship impossible, but democracy unbearable.
**Shimon Peres**, Israeli Prime Minister 1995–6, quoted in the *Financial Times*, 1995

**23** Radio and television have lifted the manufacture of banality out of the sphere of handicraft and placed it in that of a major industry.
**Nathalie Sarraute**, *Times Literary Supplement*, 1960

**24** Television is now so desperately hungry

for material that they're scraping the top of the barrel.
**Gore Vidal,** 1955

**25** I hate television, I hate it as much as peanuts. But I can't stop eating peanuts.
**Orson Welles,** quoted in the *New York Herald Tribune,* 1956

**26** Television contracts the imagination and radio expands it.
**Terry Wogan,** Irish-born British broadcaster (Attrib.)

**27** MARGE: Homer, sitting that close to the TV can't be good for you.
HOMER: Talking while the TV's on can't be good for you.
**Julie Thacker,** 'Last Tap Dance in Springfield', *The Simpsons,* Fox TV, 2000

# Television – Commercials

*See also Advertising; Television.*

**1** TV personality Speedy Alka-Seltzer came out of the medicine cabinet this week and admitted that he was a Bi-carbonate. Fearful over possible criticism, the beloved Speedy threw himself into a bathtub and effervesced to death.
**'Weekend Update',** *Saturday Night Live,* NBC

**2** Dogs who earn their living by appearing in television commercials in which they constantly and aggressively demand meat should remember that in at least one Far Eastern country they *are* meat.
**Fran Lebowitz,** *Social Studies,* 1981

# Television – Game Shows

*See also Competitions; Television; Television – Shows.*

**1** And those quiz shows! A woman won a vacation and dropped dead from the shock, but the sponsors kept their word. They sent her body to Bermuda for two weeks.
**Milton Berle,** *Variety*

**2** Hello, good evening and welcome to *Blackmail.* And to start tonight's programme, we go north to Preston in Lancashire and Mrs Betty Teal. Hello Mrs Teal! Now Mrs Teal, this is for fifteen pounds and it's to stop us revealing the name of your lover in Bolton. So, Mrs Teal, send us fifteen pounds by return of post

please and your husband Trevor and your lovely children, Diane, Janice and Juliet, need never know the name of your lover in Bolton.
**Graham Chapman, John Cleese, Eric Idle, Terry Jones and Michael Palin,** *And Now for Something Completely Different,* screenplay, 1971

**3** ANNOUNCER: It's time once again to play *Catch It and You Keep It* and here's your host, Bob Benson!
BOB BENSON: Hi, folks! For you newcomers to *Catch It and You Keep It,* here's how we play the game: I'm standing on a balcony on the tenth floor of the CBS Studios. The contestants are gathered below me in the parking lot. My assistants and I will throw prizes down to the crowd and if they catch them, they keep them!
**Tony Hendra and Michael O'Donoghue,** National Lampoon's *Radio Dinner,* album, 1972

**4** *The Napalm Show*: Host Don Rickles welcomes a celebrity panel to view obscure talent. If, after thirty seconds, the contestant is deemed untalented by the panel, he is sprayed with a toxic defoliant. Tonight a man dry-cleans a goat.
**Mario A. J. Mondelli, Jr.,** competition, *New York Magazine,* 1976

**5** *The $25,000 Sky Jump*: Dressed as fowls of their choice, contestants compete for cash prizes while free-falling from a 747.
**Frank Russo,** competition, *New York Magazine,* 1976

# Television – Shows

*See also Television; Television – Game Shows.*

**1** *The Young Podiatrists*: Hard-hitting drama about the new breed of foot doctors who try to live in and yet change a world not of their own making.
**National Lampoon,** 1978

**2** *Closet Queen*: Victoria rearranges her wardrobe again and her clothes are not amused.
**David J. Mackler,** competition, *New York Magazine,* 1976

**3** *Insect Theater*: Common garden spiders are featured this week in an uncommon production of *Death of a Salesman.*
**Jeff Monasch,** competition, *New York Magazine,* 1976

**4** *Georgette*: Hilarious complications

abound at Ted's funeral, with Phyllis arriving from San Francisco, Rhoda from New York, and Mary and Lou from Minneapolis, only to discover that Carlton has drunk all the embalming fluid.
**Edward Pinsky**, competition, *New York Magazine*, 1976

**5** *Snoopy Visits the PLO*: Special. Snoopy and the entire gang put on a special show for PLO rebels, interview their leaders, join in Palestinian folk songs. Narrated by Vanessa Redgrave.
**Gerald Sussman**, *Not Quite TV Guide*, 1983

# Temper

*See also Anger.*

**1** MRS ALLONBY: Nothing is so aggravating as calmness. There is something positively brutal about the good temper of most modern men. I wonder we women stand it as well as we do.
**Oscar Wilde**, *A Woman of No Importance*, 1893

# Temptation

*See also Flirtation; Sin.*

**1** I can resist everything except temptation.
**Oscar Wilde**, *Lady Windermere's Fan*, 1892

**2** . . . there are terrible temptations that it requires strength, strength and courage to yield to.
**Oscar Wilde**, *An Ideal Husband*, 1895

# Tennis

*See also Sport.*

**1** What a polite game tennis is. The chief word in it seems to be 'sorry' and admiration of each other's play crosses the net as frequently as the ball.
**J. M. Barrie**, 1860–1937, British playwright (Attrib.)

**2** Another play is the rearrange the string number. Never take the rap for a bad return or no return. Whenever you hit a ball into the net, or miss it entirely, bring the game to a grinding halt by checking the strings of your racket, spending sometimes as much as five minutes separating them and testing their strength. This absolves you of any of the responsibility for a bad shot.
**Erma Bombeck**, *If Life is a Bowl of Cherries – What am I Doing in the Pits?*, 1978

**3** I have finally mastered what to do with the second tennis ball. Having small hands, I was becoming terribly self-conscious about keeping it in a can in the car while I served the first one. I noted some women tucked the second ball just inside the elastic leg of their tennis panties. I tried, but found the space already occupied by a leg. Now, I simply drop the second ball down my cleavage, giving me a chest that often stuns my opponent throughout an entire set.
**Erma Bombeck**, *If Life is a Bowl of Cherries – What am I Doing in the Pits?*, 1978

**4** No doubt about it . . . every day in every way, my game grows stronger. I saw one enthusiast the other day playing with his racket out of the press. I'll have to try that.
**Erma Bombeck**, *If Life is a Bowl of Cherries – What am I Doing in the Pits?*, 1978

**5** 'If only I could have a transsexual operation,' I told my wife, 'I know I could improve my forehand.'
     She was very sympathetic: 'Do it if you think it will help your game.'
     'But if I had the operation and then women started beating me, instead of men, it would make me sick.'
     'Women beat you now,' she said.
**Art Buchwald**

**6** 'Good shot,' 'bad luck' and 'Hell' are the five basic words to be used in tennis . . .
**Virginia Graham**, *Say Please*, 1949

**7** Ladies, here's a hint; if you're playing against a friend who has big boobs, bring her to the net and make her hit backhand volleys. That's the hardest shot for the well-endowed. 'I've got to hit over them or under them, but I can't hit through,' Annie Jones used to always moan to me. Not having much in my bra, I found it hard to sympathize with her.
**Billie Jean King**, *The Autobiography of Billie Jean King*, 1983

# Terrorism

*See also Protest; Revolution; War.*

**1** Perhaps one of the more noteworthy trends of our time is the occupation of buildings accompanied by the taking of hostages. The perpetrators of these deeds are

generally motivated by political grievance, social injustice, and the deeply felt desire to see how they look on TV.
**Fran Lebowitz**, *Metropolitan Life*, 1978

## Texas

*See also America – The South.*

**1** You shoot off a guy's head with his pants down, believe me, Texas is not the place you want to get caught.
**Callie Khouri**, *Thelma and Louise*, screenplay, 1991

## Thanksgiving

**1** The Puritans celebrated Thanksgiving because they were saved from the Indians. We celebrate Thanksgiving because we were saved from the Puritans.
**Milton Berle**, *Milton Berle's Private Joke File*, 1989

**2** Thanksgiving is an emotional time. People travel thousands of miles to be with people they see only once a year.
And then discover once a year is way too often.
**Johnny Carson**, *The Tonight Show*, NBC TV

**3** I celebrated Thanksgiving in an old-fashioned way. I invited everyone in my neighbourhood to my house, we had an enormous feast and then I killed them and took their land.
**Jon Stewart**, *GQ*, 1999

## Theatre, The

*See also Acting; Actors and Actresses; Audiences; William Shakespeare; Theatre – Critics.*

**1** Long experience has taught me that in England nobody goes to the theatre unless he or she has bronchitis.
**James Agate**, 1877–1947, British theatre critic

**2** He directed rehearsals with all the airy deftness of a rheumatic deacon producing *Macbeth* for a church social.
**Noel Coward**, on producer J. R. Crawford (Attrib.)

**3** I don't like propaganda in the theatre unless it is disguised so brilliantly that the audience mistakes it for entertainment.
**Noel Coward** (Attrib.)

**4** Since the war a terrible pall of significance has fallen over plays.
**Noel Coward** (Attrib.)

**5** It's a most unusual play,
Feel like throwing my tickets away,
'Cos the boy gets the boy
And the girl gets the girl
And it's way too far off Broadway.
. . . There's no lighting
There's no costumes
Oh what art!
If there only
Were no houselights
I would sneak up the aisle and depart!
**Allan Sherman**, 'It's a Most Unusual Play', *My Name is Allan*, album, 1965

**6** Show me a congenital eavesdropper with the instincts of a Peeping Tom and I will show you the makings of a dramatist.
**Kenneth Tynan**, *Pausing on the Stairs*, 1957

## Theatre – Critics

*See also Audiences; Critics – The Artist's View; The Theatre.*

**1** If the writing of *This was a Man* was slow, the production by Basil Dean was practically stationary. The second act dinner scene between Francine Larrimore and Nigel Bruce made *Parsifal* in its entirety seem like a quick-fire vaudeville sketch.
**Noel Coward**, of the Broadway production of his *This was a Man*, 1926

**2** The day I shall begin to worry is when the critics declare: 'This is Noel Coward's greatest play'. But I know they bloody well won't.
**Noel Coward** (Attrib.)

**3** Richard Briers last night played *Hamlet* like a demented typewriter.
**W. A. Darlington**, reviewing *Hamlet*, *Daily Telegraph*

**4** All through the five acts . . . he played the King as though under momentary apprehension that someone else was about to play the Ace.
**Eugene Field**, reviewing Creston Clarke's *King Lear*, *Denver Tribune*, 1880

**5** I have knocked everything except the

knees of the chorus girls, and God anticipated me there.
**Percy Hammond,** *New York Herald Tribune*

**6** *Celebration*: as in 'a joyous celebration', a phrase popularly employed by Australian drama critics to describe plays by heavily-subsidised left-wing authors which invariably unite the whimsical and the incomprehensible.
**Barry Humphries,** glossary from *A Nice Night's Entertainment*, 1981

**7** As swashbuckling Cyrano, Mr Woodward's performance buckles more often than it swashes.
**Kenneth Hurren,** reviewing *Cyrano de Bergerac*, 1970

**8** I think *The Amorous Prawn* is perhaps the most grisly, glassy-eyed thing I have encountered in the theatre for a very long time, and even outside the theatre its like is rarely met with except on a fishmonger's slab, and now I feel very ill indeed, and would like to lie down. Before doing so I should say that *The Amorous Prawn* is a farce made out of cobwebs and mothballs, my old socks, empty beer bottles, copies of the *Strand Magazine*, dust, holes, mildew, and Mr Ben Travers's discarded typewriter ribbons . . . And now I really must go and lie down and hope I shall feel better in the morning.
**Bernard Levin,** reviewing *The Amorous Prawn*, 1959

**9** Miss Moira Lister speaks all her lines as if they are written in very faint ink on a teleprompter slightly too far away to be read with comfort.
**Bernard Levin,** reviewing *The Gazebo*, 1960

**10** I didn't like the play but then I saw it under adverse conditions – the curtain was up.
**Groucho Marx** (Attrib.)

**11** Miss Stapleton played the part as though she had not yet signed the contract with the producer.
**George Jean Nathan,** reviewing *The Emperor's Clothes*, 1953

**12** Go to the Martin Beck Theater and watch Katharine Hepburn run the gamut of emotions from A to B.
**Dorothy Parker,** reviewing *The Lake*, 1933

**13** It isn't what you might call sunny. I went into the Plymouth Theater a comparatively young woman, and I staggered out of it three hours later, twenty years older, haggard and broken with suffering.
**Dorothy Parker,** reviewing Tolstoy's *Redemption*, *Vanity Fair*, 1918

**14** . . . now that you've got me right down to it, the only thing I didn't like about *The Barretts of Wimpole Street* was the play.
**Dorothy Parker,** *New Yorker*, 1931

**15** . . . she had the temerity to wear as truly horrible a gown as I have ever seen on the American stage. There was a flowing skirt of pale chiffon – you men don't have to listen – a bodice of rose-colored taffeta, the sleeves of which ended shortly below her shoulders. Then there was an expanse of naked arms, and then, around the wrists, taffeta frills such as are fastened about the unfortunate necks of beaten white poodle-dogs in animal acts. Had she not luckily been strangled by a member of the cast while disporting this garment, I should have fought my way to the stage and done her in myself.
**Dorothy Parker,** reviewing *The Silent Witness*, *New Yorker*, 1931

**16** *The House Beautiful* is the play lousy.
**Dorothy Parker,** *Life*

**17** Geraldine McEwan, powdered white like a clownish whey-faced doll, simpered, whined and groaned to such effect as the Queen, that Edward's homosexuality became both understandable and forgivable.
**Milton Schulman,** reviewing *Edward II*, 1968

**18** CHAIRMAN: Is this piece the bold experiment some people hold it to be? Is it a shameless plagiarism from the pen of a true primitive of the theatre – as someone has said – or is it neither of these things? Denzil Pepper – what do you make of this?
PEPPER: This is a hotchpotch. I think that emerges quite clearly. The thing has been thrown together – a veritable ragbag of last year's damp fireworks, if a mixed metaphor is in order.
MISS SALT: Yes. I think it *is* what we must call a hotchpotch. I do think, though . . . I

do think, and this is the point I feel we ought to make, it is, surely, isn't it, an *inspired* hotchpotch?

**N. F. Simpson**, *A Resounding Tinkle*, 1958

**19** MISS SALT: I know Mustard Short is more familiar than I am *about* the attitude to this kind of thing in James Joyce – isn't this . . . haven't we got here an actual *repudiation* on the Joycean model *of* orderliness in a way the writers Spenser was attacking had not?

PEPPER: I'm not at all happy about letting him get away with it on his own terms like that. After all, what happens when a boxer gets knocked out in the ring? He's lost the fight. It's as simple as that. He's lost the fight and it makes no difference that his manager or someone announces through the loudspeaker afterwards that lying flat on his back was a deliberate repudiation of the vertical.

**N. F. Simpson**, *A Resounding Tinkle*, 1958

**20** MUSTARD: Could he, I wonder, be satirizing satire?

CHAIRMAN: A skit on satire itself. How does that strike you, Miss Salt?

MISS SALT: Yes. Yes, I think it very likely. I'm wondering whether perhaps rather than 'skit' the word 'parody' would hit off better what it is he's trying for here. Could he be parodying the whole thing? The whole concept? A parody *of* a skit, if that's possible.

PEPPER: If this is a parody of a skit at all, it must be a parody of a skit *on* something.

MUSTARD: A parody of a skit on satire?

**N. F. Simpson**, *A Resounding Tinkle*, 1958

## Thirst

See also Drink.

**1** I feel as if somebody stepped on my tongue with muddy feet.

**W. C. Fields**, *Never Give a Sucker an Even Break*, screenplay, 1941

## Threats

**1** Young man, if there is such a thing as a tartuffe, you are just that thing. One more

peep out of you and I'll give you a sound trundling.

**W. C. Fields**, *You Can't Cheat an Honest Man*, screenplay, 1939

## Thrift

see Stinginess.

## Tipping

See also Restaurants; Waiters.

**1** DRIFTWOOD (GROUCHO MARX): Do they allow tipping on the boat?

STEWARD: Oh, yes, sir!

DRIFTWOOD: Have you got two fives?

STEWARD: Yes, sir!

DRIFTWOOD: Well then, you won't need the ten cents I was going to give you.

**George S. Kaufman and Morrie Ryskind**, *A Night at the Opera*, screenplay, 1935

**2** ERNIE: Is this my bill?

ERIC: Yes, sir.

ERNIE: I'm terribly sorry – it looks as if I've got just enough money to pay for the dinner but I've got nothing to tip you with.

ERIC: Let me add that bill up again, sir.

**Eric Morecambe and Ernie Wise**, *The Morecambe and Wise Joke Book*, 1979

**3** There are several ways of calculating the tip after a meal. I find that the best is to divide the bill by the height of the waiter.

Thus, a bill of $12.00 brought by a six foot waiter calls for a $2.00 tip.

**Miss Piggy**, *Miss Piggy's Guide to Life (As Told to Henry Beard)*, 1981

**4** 'She once tipped me half a crown.'

'You will generally find that women loosen up less lavishly than men. It's something to do with the bone structure of the head.'

**P. G. Wodehouse**, *Uncle Dynamite*, 1948

## Tolerance

See also Goodness; Hate; Xenophobia.

**1** Always tolerate other people's opinions, but don't be too broadminded to take your own side in a quarrel.

**Anon.**

**2** I count myself very fortunate that as a

person and as a writer I've known people of all sizes. I've known some very small people, very small people indeed. I've also known some very tall people. And, of course, I've known quite a few who came somewhere in between. But knowing in this way, people of literally all sizes, I think my attitude is perhaps more liberal and more tolerant than someone who, whether rightly or wrongly, has confined himself to people of his own size.

**Alan Bennett**, 'The Lonely Pursuit', *On the Margin*, BBC TV, 1966

**3** Sometimes with secret pride I sigh
To think how tolerant am I;
Then wonder which is really mine;
Tolerance, or a rubber spine?

**Ogden Nash**, 'Yes and No', *I'm a Stranger Here Myself*, 1938

## Trade Unions

*See also The Labour Party; Socialism; Work.*

**1** SHOP STEWARD: From now on all wages are doubled, holidays are increased to twelve weeks and we shall only work Fridays.
VOICE FROM THE BACK: Not *every* bloody Friday?
*Guardian*

**2** MRS WICKSTEED: I'm going to my cake-decorating class. I don't really want to, but we're electing a new secretary and it's like everything else: if the rank and file don't go, the militants take over.

**Alan Bennett**, *Habeas Corpus*, 1973

**3** Unions run by workers are like alcoholic homes run by alcoholics, a sure recipe for tyranny.

**Roy Kerridge**, *The Lone Conformist*, 1984

**4** Unionism seldom, if ever, uses such power as it has to insure better work; almost always it devotes a large part of that power to safeguarding bad work.

**H. L. Mencken**, *Prejudices*, Third Series, 1922

**5** MINISTER OF LABOR: . . . the workers of Freedonia are demanding shorter hours.
FIREFLY (GROUCHO MARX): Very well, we'll give them shorter hours. We'll start by

cutting their lunch hour to twenty minutes.

**Arthur Sheekman and Nat Perrin**, *Duck Soup*, screenplay, 1933

## Tramps

*See also Begging; Poverty.*

**1** To listen to tramps talking about 'the road' you would imagine they were perpetually on the move from Plymouth to Dover, Scapa Flow to Beachy Head. Actually, this fabled 'road' was usually the highway between the seafront and Manor House toilets, the convent and off-licence.

**Roy Kerridge**, *The Lone Conformist*, 1984

**2** Trailer for sale or rent,
Rooms to let fifty cents,
No phone, no pool, no pets
I ain't got no cigarettes.
Ah, but two hours of pushing broom buys a
Eight-by-twelve four-bit room
I'm a man of means by no means
King of the Road

**Roger Miller**, 'King of the Road', song, 1964

## Travel

*See also Africa; Expeditions; Flying; Holidays; Hotels; The Mediterranean; Railways; Ships; Xenophobia.*

**1** **Unhelpful Advice For Foreign Tourists:**

When travelling by train, remember that it is considered impolite not to help anyone who is doing *The Times* crossword puzzle.

Comments from the public are always welcome in courts of law. When you start speaking, an usher will call 'Silence in court' to ensure that you are heard without interruption.

London barbers are delighted to shave patrons' armpits.

**V. F. Corleone**

Most foreign tourists know that in London they are encouraged to take a piece of fruit, free of charge, from any open-air stall or display.

**Michael Lipton**
**Competition**, *New Statesman*, 1967

**2** Unhelpful Advice for Foreign Tourists:

Women are not allowed upstairs on buses; if you see a woman there ask her politely to descend.
**David Gordon**

Try the famous echo in the British Museum Reading Room.
**Gerard Hoffnung**

On first entering an Underground train, it is customary to shake hands with every passenger.
**R. J. Phillips**
Competition, *New Statesman*, 1967

**3** There are two classes of travel – first class, and with children.
**Robert Benchley**, *Pluck and Luck*, 1925

**4** It is easier to find a traveling companion than to get rid of one.
**Art Buchwald**, *Vogue*, 1954

**5** . . . polar exploration is at once the cleanest and most isolated way of having a bad time that has yet been devised.
**Apsley Cherry-Garrard**, *The Worst Journey in the World*, 1922

**6** The whole object of travel is not to set foot on foreign land. It is at last to set foot on one's own country as a foreign land.
**G. K. Chesterton**, *Tremendous Trifles*, 1909

**7** The passenger's always right, my boys,
    The passenger's always right.
    Although he's a drip
    He's paid for his trip,
    So greet him with delight.
    Agree to his suggestions,
    However coarse or crude,
    Reply to all his questions,
    Ply him with drink – stuff him with food.
**Noel Coward**, 'The Passenger's Always Right', song from *Sail Away*, 1962

**8** The Taj Mahal
    And the Grand Canal
    And the sunny French Riviera
    Would be less oppressed
    If the Middle West
    Would settle for somewhere rather nearer.
    Please do not think that I criticize or cavil
    At a genuine urge to roam,
    But why oh why do the wrong people travel

When the right people stay back home?
**Noel Coward**, 'Why Do the Wrong People Travel?', song from *Sail Away*, 1962

**9** When one realizes that his life is worthless he either commits suicide or travels.
**Edward Dahlberg**, *Reasons of the Heart*, 1965

**10** To give you an idea how fast we traveled: we left Spokane with two rabbits and when we got to Topeka, we still had only two.
**Bob Hope**

**11** I suggested that she take a trip round the world.
    'Oh, I know,' returned the lady, yawning with ennui, 'but there's so many other places I want to see first.'
**S. J. Perelman**, *Westward Ha!*, 1948

**12** And there's no cure like travel
    To help you unravel
    The worries of living today.
    When the poor brain is cracking
    There's nothing like packing a suitcase
        and sailing away.
    Take a run 'round
    Vienna,
    Granada, Ravenna,
    Siena and then a'
    'Round Rome.
    Have a high time, a low time,
    And in no time
    You'll be singing 'Home, Sweet Home.'
**Cole Porter**, 'There's No Cure like Travel', song, 1934

**13** Like Webster's Dictionary,
    We're Morocco bound.
**Jimmy Van Heusen and Johnny Burke**, title song, *Road to Morocco*, 1942

**14** Everywhere is within walking distance if you have the time.
**Steven Wright**, American comic

# Trust

*See also Belief; Faith.*

**1** I never trust a man until I've got his pecker in my pocket.
**Lyndon B. Johnson** (Attrib.)

**2** He never goes back on his word – without consulting his lawyer.
**Max Kauffmann**

# Truth

*See also Belief; Credulity; Facts; Lies; Sincerity.*

**1** It has always been desirable to tell the truth, but seldom if ever necessary.
**A. J. Balfour**, 1848–1930, British Conservative Prime Minister

**2** I welcome the opportunity of pricking the bloated bladder of lies with the poniard of truth.
**Aneurin Bevan**, replying to a House of Commons speech by Winston Churchill

**3** I should think it hardly possible to state the opposite of the truth with more precision.
**Winston Churchill**, replying to a House of Commons speech by Aneurin Bevan

**4** Pressed for rules and verities,
All I recollect are these:
Feed a cold to starve a fever.
Argue with no true believer.
Think too-long is never-act.
Scratch a myth and find a fact.
**Phyllis McGinley**, *Times Three: 1932–1960*, 1960

**5** I never know how much of what I say is true.
**Bette Midler**, *A View from A Broad*, 1980

**6** Truth is a rare and precious commodity. We must be sparing in its use.
**C. P. Scott**, *Spectator*, 1982

**7** I never give them hell. I just tell the truth and they think it's hell.
**Harry S. Truman**, quoted in *Look*, 1956

**8** If one tells the truth, one is sure, sooner or later, to be found out.
**Oscar Wilde**, 'Phrases and Philosophies for the Use of the Young', 1894

**9** . . . the truth is a thing I get rid of as soon as possible! Bad habit, by the way. Makes one very unpopular at the club . . . with the older members. They call it being conceited.
**Oscar Wilde**, *An Ideal Husband*, 1895

**10** The truth is rarely pure and never simple. Modern life would be very tedious if it were either, and modern literature a complete impossibility.
**Oscar Wilde**, *The Importance of Being Earnest*, 1895

# Twins

*See also Babies; Birth; Pregnancy.*

**1** No wonder I'm unhappy – my twin forgot my birthday.
**Jerry Dennis**

**2** If ever I had twins, I'd use one for parts.
**Steven Wright**, American comic

# Unemployment

*See also Resignations; Retirement; Work.*

**1** 'I quit because the boss used repulsive language.'

'What did he say?'

'He said, "You're fired!"'

**Anon.**

**2** You know you're out of power when your limousine is yellow and your driver speaks Farsi.

**James Baker**, US Secretary of State under President George Bush

**3** Despite all the suggestions I've made over the years, Dobkins, I've never been able to fire you with enthusiasm. Until now.

**David Frost**, 'The Sack and How to Give It', *We British*, BBC TV, 1975

**4** Dobkins, I just don't know what we'd do without you. But we're going to try.

**David Frost**, 'The Sack and How to Give It', *We British*, BBC TV, 1975

**5** Tell me, Dobkins: how long have you been with us – not counting today?

**David Frost**, 'The Sack and How to Give It', *We British*, BBC TV, 1975

**6** I lost my job. No, I didn't really *lose* my job. I know where my job is, still. It's just when I go there, there's this new guy doing it.

**Bobcat Goldthwait**

**7** It's no use saying the Labour Government works if one and a half million do not.

**Joe Haines**, *Daily Mirror*, 1977

**8** There comes a time in every man's life when he must make way for an older man.

**Reginald Maudling**, on being dropped from Mrs Thatcher's Shadow Cabinet, 1976

**9** Nothing is so abject and so pathetic as a politician who has lost his job, save only a retired stud horse.

**H. L. Mencken**

**10** My brother-in-law . . . I wish he would learn a trade, so we'd know what kind of work he was out of.

**Henny Youngman**

# Unhappiness

*See also Depression and Despair; Happiness.*

**1** I have always disliked myself at any given moment; the total of such moments is my life.
**Cyril Connolly**, *Enemies of Promise*, 1938

**2** Men who are unhappy, like men who sleep badly, are always proud of the fact.
**Bertrand Russell**, *The Conquest of Happiness*, 1930

**3** The secret of being miserable is to have leisure to bother about whether you are happy or not.
**George Bernard Shaw**, *Misalliance*, 1914

**4** Noble deeds and hot baths are the best cures for depression.
**Dodie Smith**, *I Capture the Castle*, 1948

**5** Those who are unhappy have no need for anything in this world but people capable of giving them their attention.
**Simone Weil**, *L'Attente de Dieu*, 1949

# Universe, The

*See also Space.*

**1** In the beginning the Universe was created. This has made a lot of people very angry and been widely regarded as a bad move.
**Douglas Adams**, *The Restaurant at the End of the Universe*, 1980

**2** There is no reason why the universe should be designed for our convenience.
**John D. Barrow**, *The Origin of the Universe*, 1994

**3** A universe that came from nothing in the big bang will disappear into nothing at the big crunch. Its glorious few million years of existence not even a memory.
**Paul Davies**, *The Last Three Minutes*, 1994

# University

*See also Education; Teachers and Teaching.*

**1** I was a modest, good-humoured boy. It is Oxford that has made me insufferable.
**Max Beerbohm**, 'Going Back to School', *More*, 1899

**2** PATTERSON: Doesn't he have a gown?
FLORA: Battersea Tech. They just award them clean overalls on graduation.
**Malcolm Bradbury and Christopher Bigsby**, *The After Dinner Game*, BBC TV, 1975

**3** Oxford was like a chat show but with more people.
**Alan Coren**, *The Late Clive James*, Channel Four, 1984

**4** University politics are vicious precisely because the stakes are so small.
**Henry Kissinger**

**5** Like so many ageing college people, Pnin had long ceased to notice the existence of students on the campus.
**Vladimir Nabokov**, *Paris*, 1957

# Vanity

*See also Actors and Actresses; Boasts; Egotism;
Narcissism; Pride.*

**1** The last time I saw him he was walking
down Lover's Lane holding his own hand.
**Fred Allen**

**2** Colonel Chase openly used spectacles for
reading when he was alone, and furtively in
company, slipping them off if he thought
they would be noticed, for they were a little
out of keeping with that standard of perfect
health and vigour of which he was so
striking an example.
**E. F. Benson**, *Paying Guests*, 1929

**3** There but for the grace of God, goes God.
**Winston Churchill**, on Sir Stafford Cripps, Labour
Minister (Attrib.), 1943

**4** I am bursting with pride, which is why I
have absolutely no vanity.
**Noel Coward**, quoted by Kenneth Tynan in *The Sound
of Two Hands Clapping*, 1975

**5** He was like a cock who thought the sun
had risen to hear him crow.
**George Eliot**, *Adam Bede*, 1859

**6** I think a lot of Bernstein – but not as
much as he does.
**Oscar Levant**, 1906–72, American composer and wit,
of Leonard Bernstein

**7** What the world needs is more geniuses
with humility. There are so few of us left.
**Oscar Levant**

**8** My father always wanted to be the corpse
at every funeral, the bride at every wedding
and the baby at every christening.
**Alice Roosevelt Longworth**, on President Theodore
Roosevelt, quoted in *Celebrity Register*, 1963

**9** I have little patience with anyone who is
not self-satisfied. I am always pleased to see
my friends, happy to be with my wife and
family, but the high spot of every day is
when I first catch a glimpse of myself in the
shaving mirror.
**Robert Morley**, *Playboy*, 1979

**10** The affair between Margot Asquith and
Margot Asquith will live as one of the
prettiest love stories in all literature.
**Dorothy Parker**, *New Yorker*, review of *Lay Sermons* by
Margot Asquith, 1927

**11** Never underestimate a man who overestimates himself.
**Franklin D. Roosevelt**, on General Douglas MacArthur

**12** You're so vain.
You prob'ly think this song is about you.
**Carly Simon**, 'You're So Vain', song, 1972

**13** There is no human problem which could not be solved if people would simply do as I advise.
**Gore Vidal** (Attrib.)

**14** To love oneself is the beginning of a life-long romance.
**Oscar Wilde**, 'Phrases and Philosophies for the Use of the Young', 1984

# Vegetables
*See also Eating; Food; Fruit; Vegetarianism.*

**1** The local groceries are all out of broccoli, Loccoli.
**Roy Blount, Jr.**, 'Against Broccoli', *Atlantic Monthly*

**2** Vegetables are interesting but lack a sense of purpose when unaccompanied by a good cut of meat.
**Fran Lebowitz**, *Metropolitan Life*, 1978

**3** I have no religious or moral objection to vegetables but they are, as it were, dull. They are the also-rans of the plate. One takes an egg, or a piece of meat, or fish, with pleasure but then one has, as a kind of penance, to dilute one's pleasure with a damp lump of boskage.
**Frank Muir**, *You Can't Have Your Kayak and Heat It*, 1973

**4** Cauliflower is nothing but cabbage with a college education.
**Mark Twain**, *Pudd'nhead Wilson*, 1894

# Vegetarianism
*See also Cults; Eating; Food; Fruit; Vegetables.*

**1** I didn't fight my way to the top of the food chain to be a vegetarian.
**Bumper sticker**, Boston, 1999

**2** Vegetarians have wicked, shifty eyes and laugh in a cold, calculating manner. They pinch little children, steal stamps, drink water, favour beards.
**Beachcomber ( J. B. Morton)**, 'By the Way', *Daily Express*

**3** . . . life without veal stock, pork fat, sausage, organ meat, demi-glace, or even stinky cheese is a life not worth living.
**Anthony Bourdain**, *Kitchen Confidential*, 2000

**4** A vegetarian is a person who won't eat anything that can have children.
**David Brenner**

**5** No more the milk of cows
Shall pollute my private house
Than the milk of the wild mares of the Barbarian;
I will stick to port and sherry,
For they are so very, very,
So very, very, very Vegetarian.
**G. K. Chesterton**, 'The Logical Vegetarian', 1914

**6** Most vigitaryans I iver see looked enough like their food to be classed as cannybals.
**Finley Peter Dunne**, *Mr Dooley's Philosophy*, 1900

**7** Cookery without meat is *Macbeth* without murder.
**A. A. Gill**, *Le Caprice*, 2000

**8** Vegetarianism is harmless enough, though it is apt to fill a man with wind and self-righteousness.
**Sir Robert Hutchinson**, President, Royal College of Physicians, 1938–41

**9** I'm very fond of pigs; but I don't find it difficult to eat them.
**Robert Runcie (Archbishop of Canterbury)**, 1980

**10** I did not become a vegetarian for my health. I did it for the health of the chickens.
**Isaac Bashevis Singer**, 1904–91, American novelist

**11** I'm a Volvo-vegetarian. I'll eat an animal only if it was accidentally killed by a speeding car.
**Ron Smith**

**12** We were meant to eat meat. We have fangs in our mouth. Everything with fangs eats meat. When was the last time you saw a lion stalking rhubarb?
**Harland Williams**

**13** The first time I tried organic wheat bread, I thought I was chewing on roofing material.
**Robin Williams**, interview in *Playboy*, 1982

# Venice

*See also Italy and the Italians.*

**1** Streets flooded. Please advise.
**Robert Benchley,** telegram to home on arriving in Venice (Attrib.)

**2** Venice is like eating an entire box of chocolate liqueurs in one go.
**Truman Capote** (Attrib.)

# Vets

*See also Animals; Cats; Dogs; Pets.*

**1** The best doctor in the world is a veterinarian. He can't ask his patients what is the matter – he's got to just know.
**Will Rogers,** *The Autobiography of Will Rogers,* 1949

# Vice and Virtue

*See also Evil; Prostitution; Sex; Sin.*

**1** Righteous people terrify me . . . virtue is its own punishment.
**Aneurin Bevan** (Attrib.)

**2** He has all of the virtues I dislike and none of the vices I admire.
**Winston Churchill,** of Sir Stafford Cripps, Labour minister

**3** Vice is its own reward.
**Quentin Crisp,** *The Naked Civil Servant,* 1968

**4** What, after all, is a halo? It's only one more thing to keep clean.
**Christopher Fry,** *The Lady's Not for Burning,* 1948

**5** Vice
  Is Nice
  But a little virtue
  Won't hurt you.
**Felicia Lamport,** 'Axiom to Grind', *Scrap Irony,* 1961

**6** It's been my experience that folks who have no vices have very few virtues.
**Abraham Lincoln**

**7** He hasn't a single redeeming vice.
**Oscar Wilde** (Attrib.)

# Victoria, Queen

**1** LADY D: Is there anything in the newspaper this morning, Withers?
WITHERS: They have named another battleship after Queen Victoria, ma'am.
LADY D: Another? She must be beginning to think there is some resemblance.
**Alan Bennett,** *Forty Years On,* 1968

# Victory and Defeat

*See also Achievement; Competitions; Leadership; Records; Success; Television – Game Shows; War.*

**1** We came; we saw; we kicked ass!
**Dan Aykroyd and Harold Ramis,** *Ghostbusters,* screenplay, 1984

**2** In defeat unbeatable; in victory unbearable.
**Winston Churchill,** of Field Marshal Montgomery of Alamein

**3** The problems of victory are more agreeable than those of defeat, but they are no less difficult.
**Winston Churchill,** speech, House of Commons, 1942

**4** As always, victory finds a hundred fathers, but defeat is an orphan.
**Count Galeazzo Ciano,** Italian fascist politician, diary entry, 1942

**5** Truth is with the victor, who, as you know, also controls the historians.
**Rolf Hochhuth,** German playwright

**6** Winning is like shaving – you do it every day or you wind up looking like a bum.
**Jack F. Kemp,** Republican Congressman

**7** Winning isn't everything – it's the only thing.
**Vince Lombardi,** 1913–70, American football coach

**8** We count on winning. And if we lose, don't beef. And the best way to prevent beefing is – don't lose.
**Knute Rockne,** football coach

**9** It matters not whether you win or lose; what matters is whether *I* win or lose.
**Darrin Weinberg**

# Vietnam War, The

*See also Politics – American Presidents: Richard
Nixon; Protest; The Sixties; War.*

**1** Bombing can end the war – bomb the
Pentagon now!
**Graffito, New York, 1970**

**2** DICK: We've come a long way since that
first Thanksgiving dinner in Plymouth,
when the Pilgrims sat down at the table
with the Indians to eat turkey.
TOM: Boy, I'll say we've come a long way.
Now we're in Paris, sitting down at a table
with the Viet Cong eating crow.
*The Smothers Brothers Comedy Hour*, CBS, 1968

**3** Draft Beer, Not Students.
**Slogan on badge**

**4** End the Vietnam War and bring our kids
home. From Canada.
**Graffito**

**5** Hey, all you kids of draft age – you can
count on Agnew to lay down your life for
his country.
**Anon.**

**6** Napalm is a figment of the collective
imagination of the commie pinko hippie
yippie leftist queers – Agnew.
**Graffito, Vietnam, 1971**

**7** The Cave at the End of the Tunnel.
Humiliating Defeat with Honor.
*National Lampoon*, 1975

**8** Victory in Vietnam will not determine
who is right, only who is left.
**Graffito**

**9** We are the unwilling, led by the
unqualified, doing the unnecessary for the
ungrateful.
**Graffito, American air base, Vietnam, 1970**

**10** Kissinger brought peace to Vietnam the
same way Napoleon brought peace to
Europe: by losing.
**Joseph Heller, *Good as Gold*, 1979**

**11** What do you get when you cross
polystyrene with benzene and flammable
liquid hydrocarbons?

An armed guard for your campus recruiters!
**P. J. O'Rourke, 'Lab Riot', *The National Lampoon
Encyclopedia of Humor*, 1973**

**12** Lyndon Johnson told the Nation
   Have no fear of escalation,
   I am trying everyone to please.
   And though it isn't really war,
   We're sending 50,000 more
   To help save Vietnam from Vietnamese.
**Tom Paxton, 'Lyndon Johnson Told the Nation', song,
1965**

**13** The draft is white people sending black
people to fight yellow people to protect the
country they stole from red people.
**Gerome Ragni and James Rado, *Hair*, 1967**

**14** We met the enemy and he was us.
**General William C. Westmoreland (Attrib.)**

# Violence

*See also Fighting; War.*

**1** I got into a fight one time with a really
big guy and he said, 'I'm going to wipe the
floor with your face!' I said, 'You'll be sorry!'
He said, 'Oh Yeah? Why?' I said, 'Well, you
won't be able to get into the corners very
well.'
**Emo Philips**

# Virginity

*See also Abstinence; Celibacy; Chastity.*

**1** There was a young lady called Wylde,
   Who kept herself quite undefiled
   By thinking of Jesus
   Contagious diseases,
   And the bother of having a child.
**Anon., in *Some Limericks* by Norman Douglas, 1917**

**2** Nature abhors a virgin – a frozen asset.
**Clare Boothe Luce, 1903–87, American
Congresswoman and ambassador**

**3** I've been around so long, I knew Doris
Day before she was a virgin.
**Groucho Marx (Attrib.)**

# Voices

*See also Speakers and Speeches.*

**1** When a woman lowers her voice, it's a

sign she wants something; when she raises
it, it's a sign she didn't get it.
**Sally Poplin**

**2** Her voice trailed away in a sigh that was
like the wind blowing through the cracks in
a broken heart.
**P. G. Wodehouse**, *Full Moon*, 1947

**3** My Aunt Dahlia has a carrying voice . . . If
all other sources of income failed, she could
make a good living calling the cattle home
across the Sands of Dee.
**P. G. Wodehouse**, 'Jeeves and the Song of Songs',
*Very Good, Jeeves*, 1930

## Waiters

*See also Food; Hotels; Restaurants; Tipping.*

**1** WAITER RESPONDING TO WHISTLE FROM DINER WANTING ATTENTION: Good idea! Irritate the person who'll be alone with your food!
**Alan Ball**, *Cybill*, CBS TV

**2** DINER: I'd complain about the service if I could find a waiter to complain to.
**Mel Calman**, *How to Survive Abroad*, cartoon, 1971

**3** By and by
God caught his eye.
**David McCord**, 'Epitaph on a Waiter', *Odds without Ends*, 1945

## Wales and the Welsh

*See also Britain and the British.*

**1** A Welshman is a man who prays on his knees on Sundays and preys on his neighbours all the rest of the week.
**Anon.**

**2** When all else fails
try Wales.
**Christopher Logue**, 'To a Friend in Search of Rural Seclusion'

**3** The land of my fathers? My fathers can have it.
**Dylan Thomas**, 1914–53, Welsh poet (Attrib.)

**4** There are still parts of Wales where the only concession to gaiety is a striped shroud.
**Gwyn Thomas**, *Punch*, 1958

**5** . . . we can trace almost all the disasters of English history to the influence of Wales.
**Evelyn Waugh**, *Decline and Fall*, 1928

## War

*See also The Army; Courage; Enemies; The Falklands; Fighting; Heroes; The Navy; Terrorism; Victory and Defeat; The Vietnam War; Violence.*

**1** When you've seen one nuclear war, you've seen them all.
**T-shirt**, London, 1986

**2** A general and a bit of shooting makes you

forget your troubles . . . it takes your mind off the cost of living.
**Brendan Behan**, *The Hostage*, 1958

**3** I have never understood this liking for war. It panders to instincts already catered for within the scope of any respectable domestic establishment.
**Alan Bennett**, *Forty Years On*, 1968

**4** WICKSTEED: Oh Mavis and Audrey and
    Lilian and Jean
  Patricia and Pauline and NAAFI Christine
  Maureen and Myrtle I had you and more
  In God's gift to the lecher the Second
    World War.
**Alan Bennett**, *Habeas Corpus*, 1973

**5** I'm sick of war for many reasons,
  Three of them will do:
  It's 1815,
  I am French
  And this is Waterloo.
**Mel Brooks**, 'To be or Not to be', song from *To Be or Not to Be*, 1983

**6** There was very little actual shooting in Belgium, but there was plenty of mortar and artillery fire, and it was very noisy, and I thought I would not want to be in the war very long, because of the noise.
**Mel Brooks**, quoted by Kenneth Tynan in *Show People*, 1980

**7** A prisoner of war is a man who tries to kill you and fails, and then asks you not to kill him.
**Winston Churchill**, quoted in the *Observer*, 1952

**8** Nothing in life is so exhilarating as to be shot at without result.
**Winston Churchill**, *The Malakand Field Force*, 1898

**9** BLACKADDER: A war hasn't been fought this badly since Olaf the Hairy, High Chief of all the Vikings, accidentally ordered 80,000 battle helmets with the horns on the inside.
**Richard Curtis and Ben Elton**, 'Major Star', *Blackadder Goes Forth*, BBC TV, 1989

**10** Men love war because it allows them to look serious. Because it is the one thing that stops women laughing at them.
**John Fowles**, *The Magus*, 1965

**11** But that was war. Just about all he could find in its favor was that it paid well and

liberated children from the pernicious influence of their parents.
**Joseph Heller**, *Catch-22*, 1961

**12** I hated the bangs in the war: I always felt a silent war would have been far more tolerable.
**Pamela Hansford Johnson**, *Observer*, 1967

**13** And while Hitler might chortle that his secret weapon was a mighty *Luftwaffe* designed to obliterate the Royal Air Force, England's leaders knew that their secret weapon was that they didn't *have* a Royal Air Force.
**Bruce McCall**, 'That Fabulous Battle of Britain', *Zany Afternoons*, 1983

**14** So it was that ordinary British housewives bent to the task of knitting sandbags, smiling cheerfully among the ungodly mess, while all British manhood flocked to join the army and don the uniform – for there was only one to go around, and they had to take turns.
**Bruce McCall**, 'That Fabulous Battle of Britain', *Zany Afternoons*, 1983

**15** Uncle Jason, an ace in the Royal Flying
    Corps
  grew up and old into a terrible borps.
  He'd take off from tables to play the
    Great Worps
  stretch out his arms and crash to the
    florps.
  His sister, an exSister (now rich) of the
    Porps,
  would rorps forps morps: 'Encorps!
    Encorps!'
**Roger McGough**, 'Uncle Terry', *Sporting Relations*, 1974

**16** Jaw-jaw is better than war-war.
**Harold Macmillan**, British Conservative Prime Minister, 1957–63, speech, 1958

**17** War may make a fool of man, but it by no means degrades him; on the contrary, it tends to exalt him, and its net effects are much like those of motherhood on women.
**H. L. Mencken**, *Minority Report*, 1956

**18** At Victoria Station the R.T.O. gave me a travel warrant, a white feather and a picture of Hitler marked 'This is your enemy.' I

searched every compartment but he wasn't on the train.
**Spike Milligan**, *Adolf Hitler: My Part in His Downfall*, 1971

**19** ERNIE: Where did you spend your war years?
ERIC: Everywhere. I fought with Mountbatten in Burma, with Alexander in Tunis, with Monty at Alamein . . . I couldn't get on with anyone.
**Eric Morecambe and Ernie Wise**, *The Morecambe and Wise Joke Book*, 1979

**20** If ever there's another war,
I hope it's thermonuclear,
a type of war, from what one's told,
much preferable to the old,
in which few bullets ever hit
the people who had started it.
**Mark Mortimer**, *Mort*, 1997

**21** The quickest way of ending a war is to lose it.
**George Orwell**, 'Shooting an Elephant', 1950

**22** History is littered with wars which everybody knew would never happen.
**Enoch Powell**, British Conservative politician 1967

**23** No battle is worth fighting except the last one.
**Enoch Powell** (Attrib.)

**24** You can't say civilization don't advance . . . for every war they kill you a new way.
**Will Rogers**

**25** All wars are popular for the first thirty days.
**Arthur M. Schlesinger, Jr.**, historian and Presidential adviser

**26** Wars make for better reading than peace does.
**A. J. P. Taylor**, *Observer*, 1981

**27** 'I gather it's between the Reds and the Blacks.'
'Yes, but it's not quite as easy as that. You see, they are all Negroes. And the Fascists won't be called black because of their racial pride so they are called White after the White Russians. And the Bolshevists *want* to be called black because of *their* racial pride. So when you *say* black you mean red, and when you *mean* red you say white and when the party who call themselves blacks say

traitors they mean what *we* call blacks, but what *we* mean when *we* say traitors I really couldn't tell you . . . But, of course, it's really a war between Russia and Germany and Italy and Japan who are all against one another on the patriotic side. I hope I make myself plain?'
**Evelyn Waugh**, *Scoop*, 1938

**28** As long as war is regarded as wicked, it will always have its fascination. When it is looked upon as vulgar it will cease to be popular.
**Oscar Wilde**, 'The Critic as Artist', 1890

# Washington

*See also Congress; Politics – The American Presidency; Politics – American Presidents; Politics – The American Vice-Presidency; Politics and Politicians; The Senate.*

**1** Washington – Hubbub of the Universe.
**Anon.**, *Reader's Digest*

**2** There's nothing so permanent as a temporary job in Washington.
**George Allen**, Republican Senator

**3** Washington is a pool of money surrounded by people who want some.
**David Brinkley**, broadcaster

**4** The farther you get away from Washington, the more you think that things are under control there.
**Art Buchwald**

**5** When I first went to Washington, I thought, what is I'il ole me doing with these ninety-nine great people? Now I ask myself, what am I doing with these ninety-nine jerks?
**S. I. Hayakawa**, 1906–92, Republican Senator

**6** I love to go to Washington – if only to be near my money.
**Bob Hope**

**7** Washington is a city of southern efficiency and northern charm.
**John F. Kennedy**, quoted in Arthur M. Schlesinger, Jr., *A Thousand Days*, 1965

**8** If hypocrisy were gold, the Capitol would be Fort Knox.
**Senator John McCain**, 1994

**9** I find in Washington that when you ask

what time it is you get different answers
from Democrats and Republicans; 435
answers from the House of Representatives;
a 500-page report from some consultants on
how to tell time; no answer from your
lawyer and a bill for $1,000.
**R. Tim McNamar**, Deputy Secretary of the Treasury
under President Reagan

**10** Washington is the only place where
sound travels faster than light.
**C. V. R. Thompson**, *Reader's Digest*, 1949

**11** The District of Columbia is a territory
hounded on all sides by the United States of
America.
**Irving D. Tressler**, *Reader's Digest*, 1949

**12** Things get very lonely in Washington
sometimes. The real voice of the great
people of America sometimes sounds faint
and distant in that strange city. You hear
politics until you wish that both parties
were smothered in their own gas.
**Woodrow Wilson**, speech, St Louis, Missouri, 1919

# Watergate

*See also Politics – American Presidents: Richard
Nixon; Washington.*

**1** Dick Nixon before he dicks you.
**Car sticker**, Washington, 1974

**2** RICHARD NIXON: I admit my men made a
sad mistake – they got caught.
**Anon.**

**3** I suppose we should all sing 'Bail to the
Chief'.
**Howard Baker**, Republican Senator, 1974

**4** A group of politicians deciding to dump a
President because his morals are bad is like
the Mafia getting together to bump off the
Godfather for not going to church on
Sunday.
**Russell Baker**, *The New York Times*, 1974

**5** If [President Nixon's secretary] Rosemary
Woods had been Moses' secretary, there
would be only eight commandments.
**Art Buchwald**, 1974

**6** I'm a fan of President Nixon. I worship
the quicksand he walks on.
**Art Buchwald**, 1974

**7** [Presidential Press Secretary] Ron Ziegler
has done for Government credibility what
the Boston Strangler did for door-to-door
salesmen.
**Art Buchwald**, 1974

**8** . . . we've passed from the age of the
common man to the common crook.
**J. K. Galbraith**, American economist, 1974

**9** This we learn from Watergate,
That almost any creep'll
Be glad to help the Government
Overthrow the people.
**E. Y. Harburg**, *At this Point in Rhyme*, 1976

# Wealth

*See also Extravagance; Greed; Money;
Philanthropy; Rich and Poor; Stock Market.*

**1** The Pluto-American Anti-Defamation
League said it will bring pressure to bear on
media to up-grade the image of incredibly
rich people. The newly-formed group,
which hopes to combat negative portrayals
of incredibly rich people on television and
in print, cited the crucial role that
incredibly rich people have played in
American history, and hopes to restore
incredible richness as a 'positive aspect of
American life'.
*Off The Wall Street Journal*, 1982

**2** The rich man has his motorcar,
His country and his own estate.
He smokes a fifty-cent cigar
And jeers at Fate.
He frivols through the livelong day,
He knows not Poverty her pinch.
His lot seems light, his heart seems gay,
He has a cinch.
Yet though my lamp burns low and dim,
Though I must slave for livelihood –
Think you that I would change with him?
You bet I would!
**Franklin P. Adams**, *By and Large*, 1914

**3** Lord Finchley tried to mend the Electric
Light
Himself. It struck him dead: And serve
him right!
It is the business of the wealthy man
To give employment to the artisan.
**Hilaire Belloc**, 'Lord Finchley', *More Peers*, 1911

**4** The Rich arrived in pairs

And also in Rolls Royces;
They talked of their affairs
In loud and strident voices.
(The Husbands and the Wives
Of this select society
Lead independent lives
Of infinite variety.)

**Hilaire Belloc**, 'The Garden Party', *Ladies and Gentlemen*, 1932

**5** The rich are the scum of the earth in every country.

**G. K. Chesterton**, *The Flying Inn*, 1912

**6** Down with the idle rich!
The bloated upper classes.
They drive to Lord's
In expensive Fords
With their jewelled op'ra glasses.

**Noel Coward**, 'Down with the Whole Damn Lot!', song from *Co-optimists*, 1928

**7** Wealth is not without its advantages, and the case to the contrary, although it has often been made, has never proved widely persuasive.

**J. K. Galbraith**, *The Affluent Society*, 1958

**8** Nouveau is Better than No Riche at All.

**Monsieur Marc**, New York Society hairdresser, title of his autobiography, 1983

**9** God shows his contempt for wealth by the kind of person he selects to receive it.

**Austin O'Malley**, 1858–1932, American writer

**10** A fool and his money are soon married.

**Carolyn Wells**, 1869–1942, American author

**11** No woman can be too rich or too thin.

**Duchess of Windsor** (Attrib.)

## Weather

*See also The Seasons.*

**1** And here is the weather forecast.
Tomorrow will be muggy. Followed by Toogy, Weggy, Thurgy and Frigy.

**Anon.**

**2** It was so cold, the wolves were eating the sheep just for the wool.

**Anon.**

**3** A: It's raining cats and dogs!
B: I know – I've just stepped into a poodle.

**Anon.**

**4** Satellite photography in the 1970s gave rise to the long-range weather forecast, a month at a time. This in turn gave rise to the observation that the long-range weather forecast was wrong most of the time. In turn, this gave rise to the dropping of the long-range weather forecast, and to the admission that really accurate forecasting could only cover the next day or two, and not always then.

**Miles Kington**, *Nature Made Ridiculously Simple*, 1983

## Weddings

*See also Couples; Courtship; Engagements; Flirtation; Honeymoons; Proposals; Romance; Seduction; Sex; Sexual Attraction.*

**1** A delighted incredulous bride
Remarked to the groom at her side:
'I never could quite
Believe it tonight
Our anatomies *would* coincide'.

**Anon.**

**2** If it were not for the presents, an elopement would be preferable.

**George Ade**, *Forty Modern Fables*, 1901

**3** Dear Mrs A.
Hooray Hooray
At last you are deflowered.
On this as every other day
I love you. Noel Coward

**Noel Coward**, wedding telegram to Gertrude Lawrence, 1940

**4** I hate it at weddings when old relatives tell me, 'You'll be next, love.' I get my own back at funerals.

**Mandy Knight**, British comedienne

**5** As soon as our engagement appeared in *The Times* wedding presents poured in . . . the majority were frightful, and they came in cohorts – fifteen lamps of the same design, forty trays, a hundred and more huge glass vases. They were assembled at Grosvenor Place . . . When the presents were all arranged Lady Evelyn looked at them reflectively.

'The glass will be the easiest,' she said. 'It only needs a good kick.' She said silver was more of a problem. 'Walter and I had such

luck, *all* ours was stolen while we were on honeymoon.'
**Diana Mosley**, *A Life of Contrasts*, 1977

**6** We're having a little disagreement. What *I* want is a big church wedding with bridesmaids and flowers and a no-expense-spared reception and what *he* wants is to break off our engagement.
**Sally Poplin**

**7** When two people are under the influence of the most violent, most insane, most delusive, and most transient of passions, they are required to swear that they will remain in that excited, abnormal, and exhausting condition continuously until death do them part.
**George Bernard Shaw**, 'Preface', *Getting Married*, 1908

**8** At a wedding you never hear a man clearly say, 'I do,' because we figure we can get out of it later on a technicality.
**Sinbad**

**9** . . . anyone who has set a date for their wedding suddenly becomes besotted with the size of their bottom.
**Mimi Spencer**, *Evening Standard*, 2000

**10** Nothing so surely introduces a sour note into a wedding ceremony as the abrupt disappearance of the groom in a cloud of dust.
**P. G. Wodehouse**, *A Pelican at Blandings*, 1969

## Weight
*See also Diets and Dieting; Figures; Height.*

**1** I'm not fat at all . . . I'm just short for my weight. I should be 9 ft 7 inches.
**Totie Fields**

**2** Nobody ever knew exactly how much Cordie May weighed, but her daddy used to say, 'If I could get $1.25 a pound for that child, I could pay off my truck.'
**Lewis Grizzard**

## Wine
*See also Champagne; Cheese; Drink; Food.*

**1** The point about white Burgundies is that I hate them myself . . . those glasses of Chablis or Pouilly Fuissé, so closely resembling a blend of cold chalk soup and alum cordial with an additive or two to bring it to the colour of children's pee . . .
**Kingsley Amis**, *The Green Man*, 1969

**2** When it came to writing about wine, I did what almost everybody does – faked it.
**Art Buchwald**

**3** FLETCHER: I'd like to warn you, gentlemen, that this should be sipped delicately like a fine liqueur. It shouldn't be gulped down by the mugful. If you do that you will lose the flavour and the bouquet. You will also lose your power of speech.
**Dick Clement and Ian La Frenais**, *Porridge*, BBC TV, 1976

**4** A good general rule is to state that the bouquet is better than the taste, and vice versa.
**Stephen Potter**, *One-upmanship*, 1952

**5** It's a Naïve Domestic Burgundy, Without Any Breeding, But I think you'll be Amused by its Presumption.
**James Thurber**, *Men, Women and Dogs*, cartoon, 1943

## Wit
*See also Comedy; Humour; Laughter; Satire.*

**1** Wit ought to be a glorious treat, like caviare; never spread it around like marmalade.
**Noel Coward**

**2** Wits have one thing in common with bores: they recognize at sight and avoid one another, fearing competition.
**Hesketh Pearson**, *Lives of the Wits*, 1962

**3** There are men who fear repartee in a wife more keenly than a sword.
**P. G. Wodehouse**, *Jill the Reckless*, 1921

## Women
*See also Housewives; Mothers-in-Law; Women – the Male View.*

**1** Next Mood Swing: 7 Minutes.
**T-shirt**, Pasadena, 1996

**2** My vigor, vitality and cheek repel me. I am the kind of woman I would run away from.
**Nancy Astor**, 1879–1964, British politician

**3** Behind almost every woman you ever heard of stands a man who let her down.
**Naomi Bliven,** American critic

**4** I think women tend to be very hard on themselves and push themselves very hard to get things right. We're bombarded with media images of perfection in every area – thinking we're supposed to be the girl in the 24-hour mascara ad with a bottom like two snooker balls who rushes from the gym to the board meeting and home to a perfect husband and kids, to cook a Michelin star dinner for 12 people. Life isn't like that. I think maybe it's a relief to see Bridget [Jones] trying to do it and ending up in her underwear with wet hair and one foot in a pan of mashed potato wanting to shout 'Oh go f*** yourselves' at her guests.
**Helen Fielding,** *Daily Telegraph*, 1999

**5** There are three things a woman ought to look – straight as a dart, supple as a snake, and proud as a tiger lily.
**Elinor Glyn,** *The Sayings of Grandmama and Others*, 1908

**6** The word LADY: Most Often Used to Describe Someone You Wouldn't Want to Talk to for Even Five Minutes.
**Fran Lebowitz,** *Metropolitan Life*, 1978

**7** There is only one political career for which women are perfectly suitable; diplomacy.
**Clare Boothe Luce,** *Observer*, 1982

**8** A woman will flirt with anyone in the world as long as other people are looking on.
**Oscar Wilde,** *The Picture of Dorian Gray*, 1891

**9** Every woman is a rebel, and usually in wild revolt against herself.
**Oscar Wilde,** *A Woman of No Importance*, 1893

**10** MRS ALLONBY: Man, poor, awkward, reliable, necessary man belongs to a sex that has been rational for millions and millions of years. He can't help himself. It is in his race. The History of Women is very different. We have always been picturesque protests against the mere existence of common sense. We saw its dangers from the first.
**Oscar Wilde,** *A Woman of No Importance*, 1893

# Women – the Male View

*See also Men – the Female View; Women.*

**1** If only women came with pull-down menus and on-line help.
**Anon.**

**2** A man without a woman is like a neck without a pain.
**Graffito,** Los Angeles, 1984

**3** You asked me if I knew women . . . Well, one of the things I do *not* know about them is what they talk about while the men are talking. I must find out some time.
**Edward Albee,** *Who's Afraid of Virginia Woolf ?*, 1962

**4** I remembered Cliff Wainwright saying once that women were like the Russians – if you did exactly what they wanted all the time you were being realistic and constructive and promoting the cause of peace, and if you ever stood up to them you were resorting to cold-war tactics and pursuing imperialistic designs and interfering in their internal affairs. And by the way of course peace was more peaceful, but if you went on promoting its cause long enough you ended up Finlandized at best.
**Kingsley Amis,** *Stanley and the Women*, 1984

**5** . . . this may sound ridiculous, but I've never to this day really known what most women think about anything. Completely closed book to me. I mean, God bless them, what would we do without them? But I've never understood them. I mean, damn it all, one minute you're having a perfectly good time and the next you suddenly see them there like – some old sports jacket or something – literally beginning to come apart at the seams.
**Alan Ayckbourn,** *Absurd Person Singular*, 1974

**6** But no woman, so he often thought, had any head for cards; the finesse and subtlety of the game was beyond them, and Miss Howard was wise in refusing to play at all. He wished her refusal to play had extended to the use of the piano.
**E. F. Benson,** *Paying Guests*, 1929

**7** . . . why haven't women got labels on their foreheads saying, 'Danger: Government Health Warning: women can

seriously damage your brains, genitals, current account, confidence, razor blades and good standing among your friends.'
**Jeffrey Bernard**, *Spectator*, 1984

**8** Certain women should be struck regularly, like gongs.
**Noel Coward**, *Private Lives*, 1930

**9** Men don't know much about women. We do know when they're happy, we know when they're crying and we know when they're pissed off. We just don't know in what order these are going to come at us.
**Evan Davis**, American standup comic

**10** If a man speaks in the forest and there is no woman around to hear him, is he still wrong?
**Jerry Dennis**

**11** Women are like elephants to me; they're nice to look at but I wouldn't want to own one.
**W. C. Fields** (Attrib.)

**12** Women have more imagination than men. They need it to tell us how wonderful we are.
**Arnold H. Glasow**, American comic writer

**13** A: Do you believe in clubs for women?
B: Only if every other form of persuasion fails.
**Max Kauffmann**

**14** In point of morals, the average woman is, even for business, too crooked.
**Stephen Leacock**, *The Woman Question*

**15** Women are irrational, that's all there is to that!
   Their heads are full of cotton, hay and rags!
   They're nothing but exasperating, irritating,
   Vacillating, calculating, agitating,
   Maddening and infuriating hags!
**Alan Jay Lerner and Frederick Loewe**, 'A Hymn to Him', song from *My Fair Lady*, 1956

**16** On one issue at least, men and women agree; they both distrust women.
**H. L. Mencken**

**17** When women kiss, it always reminds one of prize fighters shaking hands.
**H. L. Mencken**, *Sententiae*, 1920

**18** After equality, wage parity, liberation of body and soul, and the extension for the ratification of the ERA, women still can't do the following:
*Start barbecue fires. *Hook up a stereo. *Shine shoes. *Anything on a roof. *Decide where to hang a picture. *Investigate mysterious house noises at night. *Kill and dispose of large insects. *Walk past a mirror without stopping to look.
**P. J. O'Rourke and John Hughes**, 'Planet of the Living Women', *National Lampoon*, 1979

**19** When a man takes an interest in a woman's body she accuses him of only taking an interest in her body, but when he doesn't take an interest in her body she accuses him of taking an interest in someone else's body.
**P. J. O'Rourke and John Hughes**, 'Planet of the Living Women', *National Lampoon*, 1979

**20** *Women Jokes*. It is important to remember when making jokes about women, that they are *not* a minority, they *weren't* captured on another continent and brought here in leg-irons (funny shoes, yes, but not leg-irons) and Hitler *didn't* blame them for Germany's loss in World War I. Therefore you can make any kind of fun of them you want.
**P. J. O'Rourke and John Hughes**, 'Planet of the Living Women', *National Lampoon*, 1979

**21** I used to be in favour of women priests but two years in the Cabinet cured me of them.
**Norman St John-Stevas**, ex-member of Mrs Thatcher's Government, 1981

**22** Women and elephants never forget an injury.
**Saki (H. H. Munro)**, *Reginald*, 1904

**23** Changeable women are more endurable than monotonous ones. They are sometimes murdered but seldom deserted.
**George Bernard Shaw**

**24** A woman's place is in the wrong.
**James Thurber** (Attrib.)

**25** I hate women because they always know where things are.
**James Thurber**

**26** I am afraid that women appreciate cruelty, downright cruelty, more than

anything else. They have wonderfully primitive instincts. We have emancipated them, but they remain slaves looking for their masters all the same.
**Oscar Wilde**, *The Picture of Dorian Gray*, 1891

**27** The history of women is the history of the worst form of tyranny the world has ever known. The tyranny of the weak over the strong. It is the only tyranny that lasts.
**Oscar Wilde**, *A Woman of No Importance*, 1893

**28** The only way to behave to a woman is to make love to her, if she is pretty, and to someone else, if she is plain.
**Oscar Wilde**, *The Importance of Being Earnest*, 1895

**29** Women, as some witty Frenchman once put it, inspire us with the desire to do masterpieces, and always prevent us from carrying them out.
**Oscar Wilde**, *The Picture of Dorian Gray*, 1891

**30** Women have a wonderful instinct about things. They can discover everything except the obvious.
**Oscar Wilde**, *An Ideal Husband*, 1895

**31** Hysteria is a natural phenomenon, the common denominator of the female nature. It's the big female weapon, and the test of a man is his ability to cope with it.
**Tennessee Williams**, *The Night of the Iguana*, 1961

**32** I've said it before and I'll say it again – girls are rummy. Old Pop Kipling never said a truer word than when he made that crack about the f. of the s. being d. than the m.
**P. G. Wodehouse**, *Right Ho, Jeeves*, 1934

**33** You know, the more I see of women, the more I think that there ought to be a law. Something has got to be done about this sex, or the whole fabric of Society will collapse, and then what silly asses we shall all look.
**P. G. Wodehouse**, *The Code of the Woosters*, 1938

# Words

*See also The English Language; Language; Names; Pronunciation.*

**1** If there's one word that sums up everything that's gone wrong since the war, it's 'workshop'.
**Kingsley Amis**, *Jake's Thing*, 1979

**2** I always wanted to write a book that ended with the word 'mayonnaise'.
**Richard Brautigan**, *In Watermelon Sugar*, 1969

# Work

*See also Bosses; Collaboration; Laziness; The Office; Trade Unions; Unemployment.*

**1** Delegating is a sign of weakness; let someone else do it.
**Anon.**

**2 The six stages of production**
1. Wild Enthusiasm
2. Total Confusion
3. Utter Despair
4. Search for the Guilty
5. Persecution of the Innocent
6. Promotion of the Incompetent
**Anon.**

**3** I thought I wanted a career. Turns out I just wanted a paycheck.
**Poster**, office, Los Angeles, 1997

**4 Energetic Self-Starter Instantly Despised by Co-workers**

CHARLOTTE, NC – Timothy Benson, 27, a self-described 'fast-learner and motivated self-starter' showed up for his first day of work at Williams & Broderick Accounting 'bright-eyed and bushy-tailed' Monday, instantly earning him the undying hatred of his new co-workers.
'He walks in here, and the first thing he does is hang this poster above his desk that says, "What Can I Do To Make This Company The Best It Can Be?" ' said actuary Lance Douglas, a 14-year veteran of the firm. 'Then he introduces himself to everybody in the office with a big smile and a hearty handshake, and offers to take his department head out to lunch so "we can get to know each other better". God, I hate him.'
*the Onion*, 1999-2000

**5 Parking-Ramp Attendant Moves Slightly**

HOUSTON – Parking-ramp attendant Bill Butler was detected making a slight movement Monday, sending shockwaves through the paid-parking industry. 'He was sitting in his little booth, inert as usual, when his head turned about two degrees to the right,' witness Lynda Ford said. 'I thought I was seeing things, but then, about 30 seconds later, he shifted a tiny bit in his seat.'

Monday's incident is the first reported case of parking-attendant motion since 1983, when a San Diego ticket collector scratched his cheek.
*the Onion*, 1999

**6** Work was like cats were supposed to be; if you disliked and feared it and tried to keep out of its way, it knew at once and sought you out . . .
**Kingsley Amis**, *Take a Girl Like You*, 1960

**7** Anyone can do any amount of work, provided it isn't the work he is supposed to be doing at that moment.
**Robert Benchley**

**8** Wouldn't this be a great world if insecurity and desperation made us more attractive?
**James L. Brooks**, *Broadcast News*, screenplay, 1987

**9** Most people work just hard enough not to get fired and get paid just enough money not to quit.
**George Carlin**, *Brain Droppings*, 1997

**10** Work is much more fun than fun.
**Noel Coward**

**11** HOMER: Listen to me, Mr Bigshot! If you're looking for the kind of employee who takes abuse and never sticks up for himself, I'm your man! You can treat me like dirt and I'll *still* kiss your butt and call it ice cream. And if *you* don't like it, *I* can change!
MR BURNS: I like your attitude – feisty yet spineless! . . . Welcome aboard, son!
**Jeff Martin**, 'I Married Margie', *The Simpsons*, Fox TV, 1991

**12** The easiest job in the world has to be coroner.
You perform surgery on dead people. What's the worst thing that could happen? If everything went wrong, maybe you'd get a pulse.
**Dennis Miller**, *Comic Relief*, HBO, 1991

**13** People who work sitting down get paid more than people who work standing up.
**Ogden Nash**

**14** Work expands so as to fill the time available for its completion.
**C. Northcote Parkinson**, *Parkinson's Law*, 1957

**15** For this real or imagined overwork there are, broadly speaking, three possible remedies. He (A) may resign; he may ask to halve the work with a colleague called B; he may demand the assistance of two subordinates, to be called C and D. There is probably no instance, however, in history of A choosing any but the third alternative.
**C. Northcote Parkinson**, *Parkinson's Law*, 1957

**16** I used to work at the International House of Pancakes. I know what you're thinking. How's that possible? Why? But you set your goals and go for them. It was a dream. I made it happen. It was the worst job I ever had in my entire life . . . People complained all the time about the service. We weren't slow. The floors were sticky. We were stuck in the back trying to get to the tables.
**Paula Poundstone**, *Comic Relief*, HBO, 1986

**17** One of the symptoms of approaching nervous breakdown is the belief that one's work is terribly important. If I were a medical man, I should prescribe a holiday to any patient who considered his work important.
**Bertrand Russell**, *The Autobiography of Bertrand Russell*, vol. 2, 1968

**18** Work is the curse of the drinking classes.
**Oscar Wilde** (Attrib.)

# Writers

*See also Books; Creativity; Critics – The Artist's View; Literature; Novels; Poets and Poetry; Publishers; Reading; William Shakespeare; Writing.*

**1** After being turned down by numerous publishers, he decided to write for posterity.
**George Ade**, *Fables in Slang*, 1900

**2** T. S. Eliot is quite at a loss
When clubwomen bustle across
At literary teas
Crying: – 'What, if you please,
Did you mean by *The Mill on the Floss*'.
**W. H. Auden**, 'T. S. Eliot', *Collected Poems*, 1977

**3** Of all the honours that fell upon Virginia's [Woolf] head, none, I think, pleased her more than the *Evening Standard* Award for the Tallest Woman Writer of 1927, an award she took by a neck from Elizabeth Bowen. And rightly, I think, for she was in a very real sense the tallest writer I have ever known. Which is not to say that her stories were tall. They were not. They were short. But she did stand head and shoulders above her contemporaries, and sometimes of course, much more so.

**Alan Bennett**, *Forty Years On*, 1968

**4** We're all miners in our family. My father was a miner. My mother *is* a miner. These are miner's hands. We're all artists I suppose, really, only I was the first one who had this urge to express myself on paper rather than at the coal face. But under the skin I think I'm still a miner. I suppose in a very real sense I'm a miner writer.

**Alan Bennett**, 'The Lonely Pursuit', *On the Margin*, BBC TV, 1966

**5** H. L. Mencken suffers from the delusion that he is H. L. Mencken. There is no cure for a disease of that magnitude.

**Maxwell Bodenheim** (Attrib.)

**6** Of course, no writers ever forget their first acceptance . . . One fine day when I was seventeen I had my first, second and third, all in the same morning's mail. Oh, I'm here to tell you, dizzy with excitement is no mere phrase!

**Truman Capote**

**7** That's not writing – that's typing.

**Truman Capote**, of Jack Kerouac (Attrib.)

**8** Writing a book is an adventure: it begins as an amusement, then it becomes a mistress, then a master, and finally a tyrant.

**Sir Winston Churchill**

**9** In America only the successful writer is important, in France all writers are important, in England no writer is important, in Australia you have to explain what a writer is.

**Geoffrey Cotterell**, *New York Journal*, 1961

**10** Some day I hope to write a book where the royalties will pay for the copies I give away.

**Clarence Darrow**, 1857–1938, American lawyer

**11** My aged friend, Mrs Wilkinson,
Whose mother was a Lambe,
Saw Wordsworth once, and Coleridge, too,
One morning in her p'ram
Birdlike the bards stooped over her –
Like fledgling in a nest:
And Wordsworth said, 'Thou harmless babe!'
And Coleridge was impressed.
The pretty thing gazed up and smiled,
And softly murmured, 'Coo!'
William was then aged sixty-four
And Samuel sixty-two.

**Walter de la Mare**, 'The Bards'

**12** Nat Hawthorne concealed his asperity
By a surface of delicate clarity;
He produced ambiguity
In rich superfluity,
And laudably free from vulgarity.
Hawthorne's writing achieved perspicuity
Continuity, beauty, acuity;
He won lasting glory
In romance and story –
Though some have complained of tenuity.

**Richard Harter Fogle**, 'Ambiguity, Perspicuity', *The Laurel Review*, 1910

**13** Higgledy-piggledy
Thomas Stearns Eliot
Wrote dirty limericks
Under the rose,
Using synecdoches,
Paranomasias,
Zeugmas, and rhymes he de-
Plored in his prose.

**Anthony Hecht**, 'Vice', *Jiggery-Pokery: A Compendium of Double Dactyls*, 1966

**14** No author is a man of genius to his publisher.

**Heinrich Heine**, 1797–1856, German poet

**15** They're fancy talkers about themselves, writers. If I had to give young writers advice, I would say don't listen to writers talk about writing or themselves.

**Lillian Hellman**, 1905–84, American playwright

**16** The most essential gift for a good writer is a built-in shock-proof shit-detector.

**Ernest Hemingway**

**17** The novelist, afraid his ideas may be

foolish, slyly puts them in the mouth of some other fool and reserves the right to disavow them.
**Diane Johnson**, *The New York Times Book Review*, 1979

**18** He writes the worst English that I have ever encountered. It reminds me of a string of wet sponges; it reminds me of tattered washing on the line; it reminds me of stale bean soup, of college yells, of dogs barking idiotically through endless nights. It is so bad that a sort of grandeur creeps into it. It drags itself out of the dark abysm of pish, and crawls insanely up to the topmost pinnacle of posh. It is rumble and bumble. It is flap and doodle. It is balder and dash.
**H. L. Mencken**, on Warren G. Harding, *Baltimore Evening Sun*, 1921

**19** Almost anyone can be an author; the business is to collect money and fame from this state of being.
**A. A. Milne**, 1882–1956, English writer

**20** Oscar and George Bernard
Cannot be reconciled.
When I'm Wilde about Shaw
I'm not Shaw about Wilde.
**Freddie Oliver**, *Worse Verse*, 1969

**21** When one says that a writer is fashionable one practically always means that he is admired by people under thirty.
**George Orwell**

**22** Writing is the only profession where no one considers you ridiculous if you earn no money.
**Jules Renard**, 1864–1910, French novelist and playwright

**23** It is part of prudence to thank an author for his book before reading it, so as to avoid the necessity of lying about it afterwards.
**George Santayana**, 1863–1952, Spanish-born philosopher and critic

**24** The profession of book-writing makes horse racing seem like a solid, stable business.
**John Steinbeck**

**25** Some American writers who have known each other for years, have never met in the daytime or when both were sober.
**James Thurber**

**26** With a pig's eyes that never look up, with a pig's snout that loves muck, with a pig's brain that knows only the sty, and with a pig's squeal that cries only when he is hurt, he sometimes opens his pig's mouth, tusked and ugly, and lets out the voice of God, railing at the whitewash that covers the manure about his habitat.
**William Allen White**, on H. L. Mencken, 1928

**27** . . . one of the dullest speeches I ever heard. The Agee woman told us for three quarters of an hour how she came to write her beastly book, when a simple apology was all that was required . . .
**P. G. Wodehouse**, *The Girl in Blue*, 1970

**28** Success comes to a writer, as a rule, so gradually that it is always something of a shock to him to look back and realize the heights to which he has climbed.
**P. G. Wodehouse**

# Writing

*See also Books; Clichés; Creativity; Literature; Novels; Plagiarism; Poets and Poetry; Publishers; Reading; Words; Writers.*

**1** I'm working when I'm fighting with my wife. I constantly ask myself, 'How can I use this stuff to literary advantage?'
**Art Buchwald**

**2** I love being a writer. What I can't stand is the paperwork.
**Peter De Vries**, 1910–93, American novelist

**3** I write when I'm inspired, and I see to it that I'm inspired at nine o'clock every morning.
**Peter De Vries**

**4** . . . the tools I need for my trade are paper, tobacco, food and a little whiskey.
**William Faulkner**

**5** The ideal view for daily writing, hour on hour, is the blank brick wall of a cold storage warehouse. Failing this, a stretch of sky will do, cloudless if possible.
**Edna Ferber**, 1887–1968, American writer

**6** Cut out all those exclamation marks. An exclamation mark is like laughing at your own joke.
**F. Scott Fitzgerald**, quoted in *Beloved Infidel*, 1959

**7** Mostly, we authors must repeat ourselves – that's the truth. We have two or three

great moving experiences in our lives –
experiences so great and moving that it
doesn't seem at the time that anyone else
has been caught up and pounded and
dazzled and astonished and beaten and
broken and rescued and illuminated and
rewarded and humbled in just that way ever
before.

**F. Scott Fitzgerald**

**8** Writing is easy; all you do is sit staring at
a blank sheet of paper until the drops of
blood form on your forehead.

**Gene Fowler**, 1890–1960, American writer and editor

**9** Nothing you write, if you hope to be
any good, will ever come out as you first
hoped.

**Lillian Hellman**, 1905–84, American playwright

**10** No man but a blockhead ever wrote,
except for money.

**Samuel Johnson**, quoted by James Boswell in *Life of
Samuel Johnson*, 1791

**11** For forty-odd years in this noble
    profession
  I've harbored a guilt and my conscience
    is smitten.
  So here is my slightly embarrassed
    confession –
  I don't like to write, but I love to have
    written.

**Michael Kanin**, 'My Sin', *Dramatists Guild Quarterly*

**12** So far as good writing goes, the use of
the exclamation mark is a sign of failure. It
is the literary equivalent of a man holding
up a card reading LAUGHTER to a studio
audience.

**Miles Kington**, *Punch*, 1976

**13** A good many young writers made the
mistake of enclosing a stamped, self-
addressed envelope, big enough for the
manuscript to come back in. This is too
much of a temptation for the editor.

**Ring Lardner**, *How to Write Short Stories*

**14** Contrary to what many of you might
imagine, a career in letters is not without its
drawbacks – chief among them the
unpleasant fact that one is frequently called
upon to sit down and write.

**Fran Lebowitz**, *Metropolitan Life*, 1978

**15** I can write better than anybody who can
write faster, and I can write faster than
anybody who can write better.

**A. J. Liebling**, 1904–63, American journalist and satirist

**16** Oh, shun, lad, the life of an author.
  It's nothing but worry and waste.
  Avoid that utensil,
  The laboring pencil,
  And pick up the scissors and paste.

**Phyllis McGinley**, 'A Ballad of Anthologies', 1941

**17** There are three rules for writing the
novel. Unfortunately, no one knows what
they are.

**W. Somerset Maugham** (Attrib.)

**18** Only ambitious nonentities and hearty
mediocrities exhibit their rough drafts. It's
like passing round samples of one's sputum.

**Vladimir Nabokov**

**19** One thing that literature would be
    greatly the better for
  Would be a more restricted employment
    by authors of simile and metaphor.
  Authors of all races be they Greeks,
    Romans, Teutons or Celts,
  Can't seem just to say that anything is
    the thing it is but have to go out of
    their way to say that it is like
    something else.

**Ogden Nash**, 'Very Like a Whale', *The Primrose Path*,
1935

**20** The secret of popular writing is never to
put more on a given page than the common
reader can lap off it with no strain
whatsoever on his habitually slack
attention.

**Ezra Pound**, 1885–1972, American poet

**21** What no wife of a writer can ever
understand is that a writer is working when
he's staring out of the window.

**Burton Rascoe**, American newspaper editor

**22** If you caricature friends in your first
novel they will be upset, but if you don't,
they will feel betrayed.

**Mordecai Richler**, *GQ*, 1984

**23** My prescription for writer's block?
Alimony – the world's greatest muse.

**Dick Schaap**, American sportswriter

**24** The waste basket is the writer's best friend.
**Isaac Bashevis Singer,** 1904–91, American novelist

**25** Alexander Woollcott says good writers should never use the word 'very'. Nuts to Alexander Woollcott.
**H. Allen Smith,** 1907–76, American journalist and humorist (Attrib.)

**26** There's nothing to writing. All you do is sit down at a typewriter and open a vein.
**Red Smith**

**27** Writing a play is like smashing that [glass] ashtray, filming it in slow motion, and then running the film in reverse, so that the fragments of rubble appear to fly together. You start – or at least I start – with the rubble.
**Tom Stoppard,** quoted in Kenneth Tynan's *Show People*, 1980

**28** 'He's supposed to have a particularly high-class style: "Feather-footed through the splashy fen passes the questing vole" . . . would that be it?'
  'Yes,' said the Managing Editor. 'That must be good style. At least it doesn't sound like anything else to me.'
**Evelyn Waugh,** *Scoop*, 1938

**29** Novel-writing is a highly skilled and laborious trade of which the raw material is every single thing one has ever seen or heard or felt, and one has to go over that vast, smouldering rubbish-heap of experience, half stifled by the fumes and dust, scraping and delving until one finds a few discarded valuables.
**Evelyn Waugh,** *The Essays, Articles and Reviews of Evelyn Waugh*, 1984

**30** No passion in the world is equal to the passion to alter someone else's draft.
**H. G. Wells,** 1866–1946, English novelist

**31** I was working on the proof of one of my poems all the morning, and took out a comma. In the afternoon I put it back again.
**Oscar Wilde** (Attrib.)

**32** Ambrose isn't a frightfully hot writer. I don't suppose he makes enough out of a novel to keep a midget in doughnuts for a week. Not a really healthy midget.
**P. G. Wodehouse,** *The Luck of the Bodkins*, 1935

# Xenophobia

*See also Countries; Foreigners; Hate; Immigration; Jingoism; Patriotism; Travel.*

**1** With its open door immigration policy, the United States is perhaps the only state not afflicted with xenophobia, but the very warp and weave of our national fiber is even now being eaten away by swarms of wops, dps, prs, coons and foreigners generally.
*The National Lampoon Encyclopedia of Humor*, 1968

**2** There have been many definitions of hell, but for the English the best definition is that it is a place where the Germans are the police, the Swedish are the comedians, the Italians are the defence force, Frenchmen dig the roads, the Belgians are the pop singers, the Spanish run the railways, the Turks cook the food, the Irish are the waiters, the Greeks run the government and the common language is Dutch.
**David Frost and Antony Jay**, *To England with Love*, 1967

**3** The great and recurring question about abroad is, is it worth getting there?
**Rose Macaulay**, 1881–1958, English novelist (Attrib.)

**4** I think all nations regard each other as dirty in their personal habits, irreligious and morally lax.
**Nancy Mitford**, *Sunday Times*, 1953

**5** Foreigners may pretend otherwise, but if English is spoken loudly enough, anyone can understand it, the British included. Actually, there's no such thing as a foreign language. The world is just filled with people who grunt and squeak instead of speaking sensibly. French may be an exception. But since it's impossible to figure out what French people are saying, we'll never know for sure.
**P. J. O'Rourke**, *Modern Manners*, 1983

**6** If the French were really intelligent, they'd speak English.
**Wilfrid Sheed**, 'Taking Pride in Prejudice', *GQ*, 1984

**7** The points i wish to make about the world are contained in the molesworth newsletter.
(a) the rusians are roters.
(b) americans are swankpots.
(c) the french are slack.

(d) the germans are unspeakable.

(e) the rest are as bad if not worse than the above.

(f) the british are brave super and noble cheers cheers cheers.

**Geoffrey Willans and Ronald Searle**, 'Down With Skool!', *The Compleet Molesworth*, 1958

**8** '*Faute de* what?'

'*Mieux*, m'lord. A French expression. We should say "For want of anything better." '

'What asses these Frenchmen are. Why can't they talk English?'

'They are possibly more to be pitied than censured, m'lord. Early upbringing no doubt has a lot to do with it.'

**P. G. Wodehouse**, *Ring for Jeeves*, 1953

## Young and Old

*See also Age and Ageing; Childhood; Middle Age; Youth.*

**1** From the earliest times the old have rubbed it into the young that they are wiser than they, and before the young had discovered what nonsense this was they were old too, and it profited them to carry on the imposture.
**W. Somerset Maugham**, *Cakes and Ale*, 1930

**2** It's all that the young can do for the old, to shock them and keep them up to date.
**George Bernard Shaw**, *Fanny's First Play*, 1914

## Youth

*See also Adolescence; Age and Ageing; Childhood; Teenagers; Young and Old.*

**1** Youth would be an ideal state if it came a little later in life.
**Lord Asquith**, 1923

**2** The youth of the present day are quite monstrous. They have absolutely no respect for dyed hair.
**Oscar Wilde**, *Lady Windermere's Fan*, 1892

**3** To win back my youth . . . there is nothing I wouldn't do – except take exercise, get up early, or be a useful member of the community.
**Oscar Wilde**, *A Woman of No Importance*, 1893

## Yugoslavia

**1** Clinton Deploys Vowels To Bosnia: Cities Of Sjlbvdnzv, Grznc To Be First Recipients.
**'Operation Vowel Storm'**, *the Onion*, 1995

**2** It's a very long flight to Yugoslavia and you land in a field of full-grown corn. They figure it cushions the landing . . . Now, at night, you can't do anything, because all of Belgrade is lit by a ten-watt bulb, and you can't go anywhere, because Tito has the car. It was a beauty, a green '38 Dodge. And the food in Yugoslavia is either very good or very bad. One day, we arrived on location late and starving and they served us fried chains. When we got to our hotel rooms, mosquitoes as big as George Foreman were waiting for us. They were sitting in armchairs with their legs crossed.
**Mel Brooks**, interview in *Playboy*, 1975

# Index

*References marked with an asterisk indicate collaboration with other writers or composers.*